How to Find What You Need in *The Canadian Writer's Handbook*

1. **Consult the table of contents.** The table of contents (pages v–xvi) offers a comprehensive list of the *Handbook*'s chapters, sections, and subsections. Chapters are designated with Roman numerals, from I to VIII. Sections, numbered consecutively without regard to chapter, are designated with Arabic numerals, from 1 to 80. Subsections are designated with letters within each section (for example, 1a, 1b, 1c). Appendices are numbered from A1 to A3.

2. **Use the shaded tabs.** Used in conjunction with the chapter index on the next page, the shaded tabs that appear on the outer margins of the pages will help you find the chapter you're looking for. In addition, a quick glance at any shaded tab will tell you what section and subsection are being discussed on that page.

3. **Refer to the list of marking symbols and abbreviations.** The list of marking symbols and abbreviations, located on the inside back cover, will direct you to the sections that discuss specific writing problems, such as *faulty parallelism* or *dangling modifier*.

4. **Check the index.** The detailed index (pages 611–31) will direct you to the pages where you will find information on specific topics (such as *dangling modifiers*) and words and phrases (for example, *advice, advise*).

5. **Look over the list of exercises.** Exercises, with page references, are listed by title on pages 633–36.

Chapter Index

Sixth
Edition

The
Canadian
Writer's
Handbook

William E. Messenger
Jan de Bruyn
Judy Brown
Ramona Montagnes

OXFORD
UNIVERSITY PRESS

OXFORD
UNIVERSITY PRESS

Oxford University Press is a department of the University of Oxford.
It furthers the University's objective of excellence in research, scholarship,
and education by publishing worldwide. Oxford is a registered trade mark
of Oxford University Press in the UK and in certain other countries.

Published in Canada by
Oxford University Press
8 Sampson Mews, Suite 204,
Don Mills, Ontario M3C 0H5 Canada

www.oupcanada.com

First Edition published in 1980 (Prentice-Hall)
Second Edition published in 1986 (Prentice-Hall)
Third Edition published in 1995 (Prentice-Hall)
Fourth Edition published in 2005
Fifth Edition published in 2008
Sixth Edition published in 2015

Library and Archives Canada Cataloguing in Publication

Messenger, William E., 1931-2003, author
The Canadian writer's handbook / by William E. Messenger,
Jan de Bruyn, Judy Brown, and Ramona Montagnes. — Sixth edition.

Includes index.
ISBN 978-0-19-544696-8 (pbk.)

1. English language—Composition and exercises.
2. English language—Grammar. 3. Report writing.
I. De Bruyn, Jan, 1918-, author II. Brown, Judy,
1954-2013, author III. Montagnes, Ramona, author

PE1408.M58 2014   808'.042   C2014-902170-4

Cover image: ©2014 Inkart Productions

Oxford University Press is committed to our environment.
Wherever possible, our books are printed on paper which comes from
responsible sources.

Printed and bound in Canada

1 2 3 4 — 18 17 16 15

Contents

V Punctuation   271

Introduction: The Principles of Good Punctuation   272

How to Use Commas, Semicolons, Colons, and Dashes

VI Mechanics and Spelling 321

Introduction: The Conventions of Mechanics and Spelling 322

56 Formatting an Essay 322

57 Abbreviations 325

58 Capitalization 328

Preface

In preparing the sixth edition of this tried and tested guide to research, writing, and documentation, our goal remains the same as it has always been: to help you in what we see as the lifelong project of improving written communication. We know that the improvement of our own writing is a work in progress, and we believe that the same is true of writers at all levels of experience and expertise. Whether you are a longtime writer of English seeking to refresh and refine your abilities or someone who has recently begun to write in English as an additional language, we believe that the suggestions, examples, exercises, and guidelines in this new edition will provide a trustworthy resource that will enable you to write with greater confidence and skill.

To emphasize the bigger picture of writing as communication, this handbook opens and closes with an emphasis on the larger units of writing. We begin with a chapter on principles of composition, ranging from the design of the whole essay to the design of individual paragraphs; we close with a thoroughly updated and revised chapter on research-based writing. In the middle sections of the book, we explore principles of grammar, syntax, and usage at the word and sentence levels. As in previous editions, we devote considerable space to examination of sentence patterns, parts of speech, and sentence structure and variety; we also include chapters on punctuation, mechanics and spelling, and diction—all accompanied by exercises that allow you to practise what you have learned. The three appendices of this edition provide sample essays, detailed explanations of marking symbols and abbreviations, and checklists designed for use at the revising and editing stages of your writing projects.

Overview

The Canadian Writer's Handbook is intended for you to use as a reference work, to consult on particular issues arising from the everyday writing activities, challenges, and questions you encounter. It may also be used as a class text for discussion and study in writing courses, programs, and workshops. We suggest that you begin by considering the ways in which you will be using this book. Then, start to familiarize yourself with it by seeing what it has to offer you. Browse through the table of contents and the index. Look up some sections that arouse your interest. Flip through the pages, pausing now and then for a closer look. Note the running heads at the tops of the pages and the shaded tabs along the outer edges of the pages; note also the chapter index at the beginning of the book, the list of marking symbols inside the back cover, and the list of exercises at the end of the book: these navigational tools can help you find things in a hurry.

Organization

Notice how the material is arranged. Begin to think about how you can best approach it. You may want to begin at the beginning and proceed carefully through the book. But if you already understand basic grammar—the functions of the parts of speech and the principles governing English sentences—you may need only a quick review of chapters II, III, and IV before moving on to the other chapters. Test yourself by trying some of the exercises in each chapter, and check your answers with your instructor or consult this book's website (www.oupcanada.com/Messenger6e).

For Readers and Writers of English as an Additional Language

Our experience as university instructors has given us the opportunity to work with a number of writers engaged in the challenging project of reading and writing in English as an additional language (EAL). Drawing on this experience, we have identified certain aspects of the English language that are particularly troublesome for EAL learners, and we have added extra direction where we felt it was necessary. The sections in which we have added this direction are designated with the following symbol: **EAL** .

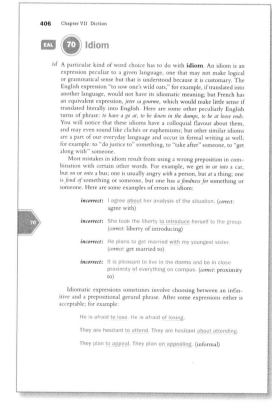

406   Chapter VII Diction

EAL **70** Idiom

id A particular kind of word choice has to do with **idiom**. An idiom is an expression peculiar to a given language, one that may not make logical or grammatical sense but that is understood because it is customary. The English expression "to sow one's wild oats," for example, if translated into another language, would not have its idiomatic meaning; but French has an equivalent expression, *jeter sa gourme*, which would make little sense if translated literally into English. Here are some other peculiarly English turns of phrase: *to have a go at, to be down in the dumps, to be at loose ends*. You will notice that these idioms have a colloquial flavour about them, and may even sound like clichés or euphemisms; but other similar idioms are a part of our everyday language and occur in formal writing as well; for example: to "do justice to" something, to "take after" someone, to "get along with" someone.

Most mistakes in idiom result from using a wrong preposition in combination with certain other words. For example, we get *in* or *into* a car, but *on* or *onto* a bus; one is usually angry *with* a person, but *at* a thing; one is *fond of* something or someone, but one has *a fondness for* something or someone. Here are some examples of errors in idiom:

incorrect: I agree about her analysis of the situation. (*correct:* agree with)

incorrect: She took the liberty to introduce herself to the group. (*correct:* liberty of introducing)

incorrect: He plans to get married with my youngest sister. (*correct:* get married to)

incorrect: It is pleasant to live in the dorms and be in close proximity of everything on campus. (*correct:* proximity to)

Idiomatic expressions sometimes involve choosing between an infinitive and a prepositional gerund phrase. After some expressions either is acceptable; for example:

He is afraid to lose. He is afraid of losing.

They are hesitant to attend. They are hesitant about attending.

They plan to appeal. They plan on appealing. (informal)

Checking Your Work Before Submitting It

When you finish a piece of writing, go through the omnibus checklists in appendix 3. If you find you're not sure about something, follow the cross-references to the sections that will give you the help you need.

Checklists for Use in Revising, Editing, and Proofreading   **605**

Omnibus Checklist for Planning and Revising

As you begin to prepare a piece of your writing for final submission to your reader(s), it is good strategy to ask yourself a series of questions designed to ensure that you have polished your work to the point where you can consider it a finished and appealing discourse. What we have listed here are the kinds of questions we ask ourselves in reading and evaluating students' writing. If you can ask and answer all of the questions we have listed here in the affirmative, your essay should be not just adequate, but very good.

1. **During and after planning the essay, ask yourself these questions:**

   Subject

   ☐ Have I chosen a subject that sustains my interest? (#2a)
   ☐ If I am doing research, have I formulated a researchable question? (#74)
   ☐ Have I sufficiently *limited* my subject? (#2b)

   Audience and Purpose

   ☐ Have I thought about audience and purpose? (#2c)
   ☐ Have I written down a statement of purpose and a profile of my audience?

   Evidence

   ☐ Have I collected or generated more than enough material/evidence to develop and support my topic well? (#2f)

   Organization and Plan

   ☐ Does my *thesis* offer a focused, substantive, [...] the subject (#2h)?
   ☐ Is my *plan* or *outline* for the essay logical in it [...] ment? (#2i)
   ☐ Considering my plan or outline, do I have the [...] *ideas*—neither too few nor too many—for the [...]
   ☐ Are my main ideas reasonably *parallel* in conte [...]
   ☐ Have I chosen the best *arrangement* for the [...] coincide with the arrangement of ideas in the t [...]

2. **During and after your revision of the essa[...] these questions:**

   Title

   ☐ Does the *title* of my essay clearly indicate the [...]
   ☐ Is the title original?
   ☐ Does the title contain something to catch a rea [...]

---

606   Appendix 3

Structure

☐ Does my *beginning* engage a reader's curiosity or interest?
☐ Have I clearly stated my *subject* (and my *thesis*) somewhere near the beginning? (#2j.3)
☐ Have I kept the beginning reasonably short and to the point? (#2j.4)
☐ Does my *ending* bring the essay to a satisfying conclusion? (#1c, #4.9)
☐ Have I used the ending to do something other than re-hash ideas already well presented in the rest of the essay?
☐ Have I kept my ending short enough, without unnecessary repetition and summary?

Unity and Development

☐ Is my essay *unified*? Do all its parts contribute to the whole, and have I avoided digression? (#1a)
☐ Have I been sufficiently *particular* and *specific*, and not left any generalizations unsupported? (#66)

Emphasis

☐ Have I devoted an appropriate amount of space to each part? (#1c)

Paragraphs

☐ Does the *first sentence* of each paragraph (except perhaps the first and last) somehow mention the particular *subject* of the essay? (#1a, #7a.1)
☐ Do the early sentences of each body paragraph clearly state the topic, or part of the topic? Or, is the topic sentence, when it isn't among the first sentences, effective where it is placed? (#7a.1)
☐ Is each body paragraph long enough to develop its topic adequately? (#9b)
☐ Does each paragraph *end* adequately, but not too self-consciously? (#7a.3)

Coherence

☐ Do the sentences in each paragraph have sufficient coherence with each other? (#7)
☐ Does the beginning of each new paragraph provide a clear *transition* from the preceding paragraph? (#7a.1, #1b)
☐ Is the coherence between sentences and between paragraphs smooth? Have I removed all unnecessary or illogical transitional devices? (#7b)

Sentences

☐ Is each sentence (especially if it is compound, complex, or long) internally *coherent*? (#31)
☐ Is each sentence clear and sufficiently *emphatic* in making its point? (#29)

A3

Correcting and Revising Returned Work

When you get a piece of writing back with marks and comments, first look it over alongside appendix 2, "Marking Symbols and Abbreviations Explained." The information there may be enough to help you make the appropriate changes. But if you need more than a reminder about a specific issue or pattern, follow the cross-references and study the sections that discuss and illustrate the relevant principles in detail. You should then be able to edit and revise your work with understanding and confidence.

An important feature of this book is that it discusses and illustrates various issues in several places: in the main discussions and in the exercises that accompany them, in the review exercises at the ends of sections and subsections, in writing and proofreading tips, and in the appendices. If the information you find in one or another of these places isn't enough to clarify a point, remember that you may not yet have exhausted the available resources: try the index to see if it will lead you to still other relevant places.

71  **Wordiness and Concision**

w Generally, the fewer, more precise words you use to make a point, the better. Useless words—often called *deadwood*—clutter up a sentence; they dissipate its force, cloud its meaning, blunt its effectiveness. The writer of the following sentence, for example, used many words where a few would have been clearer:

> ***w:*** What a person should try to do when communicating by writing is to make sure the meaning of wha[t] trying to say is clear.

Notice the gain in clarity and force when the sentence is revised[.]

> ***revised:*** A writer should strive to be clear.

The following sections discuss in greater detail a variety of rela[ted prob]lems that fall into the general category of wordiness. See also[...]

w   **Wordiness**

If you find this mark in the margins of your essays, you may have to take drastic measures. Try thinking of words as costing money, say a loonie apiece; perhaps that will make it easier to avoid a spendthrift style. Mere economy, of course, is not a virtue; don't sacrifice something necessary or useful just to reduce the number of words. But don't use several words where one will not only do the same job but do it better, and don't use words that do no real work at all. Here are some examples of squandered words:

> ***w:*** In today's society, Canada has earned itself a name of respect with many in the world.
>
> ***revised:*** Canada has earned widespread respect. ($11 saved)
>
> ***w:*** His words have a romantic quality to them.

The phrase *to them* does no work. In fact, its effect is negative because it undermines the emphatic crispness of the meaningful part of the sentence. Cut it and save $2.

> ***w:*** Hardy regarded poetry as his serious work; he wrote novels only in order to make enough money to live on.
>
> ***revised:*** Hardy regarded poetry as his serious work; he wrote novels only to make a living. ($5 saved)
>
> ***w:*** Othello's trust in Iago becomes evident during the first encounter that the reader observes between the two characters.
>
> ***revised:*** Othello's trust in Iago becomes evident during their first encounter. ($8 saved)
>
> ***w:*** The flash of lightning is representative of the god's power.
>
> ***revised:*** The flash of lightning represents the god's power. ($2 saved)

See #71, especially #71a; see also *red* (*redundancy*) and #71c, and *rep* (*repetition*) and #71b.

A2

wo   **Word Order**

A misplaced modifier is one kind of faulty word order, but there are other kinds not so easily classified.

> ***wo:*** She was naturally hurt by his indifference.
>
> ***revised:*** Naturally she was hurt by his indifference.

Numbering and Cross-Referencing

This book is divided into sections and subsections that are numbered consecutively throughout, without regard to chapters. Cross-references are to section and subsection numbers, or, occasionally, to chapters. In the index, references are to page numbers. Exercises are numbered according to their sections; note that some sections do not include exercises.

Important Terms

The first one or two times an important term appears, it is in boldface. Pay attention to these terms, for they make up the basic vocabulary necessary for the intelligent discussion of grammar, syntax, style, and the writing process in general.

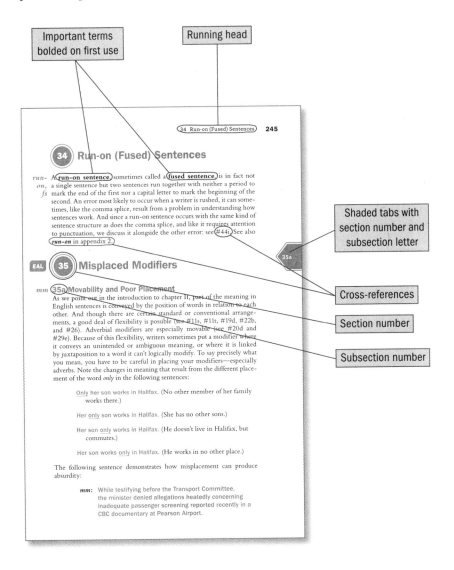

Other Key Features

> **RESEARCH TIP**
> **Expanding or Limiting Search Results**
>
> Most database keyword searches and library catalogue searches allow you to expand or limit your results by using simple words and symbols known as "Boolean operators" to combine search terms. The most common Boolean operators are *AND*, *OR*, and *NOT*. Use *AND* between two terms when you want results that contain both terms; for example, a search for "hunting AND fishing" will return results that mention, to some extent, both hunting and fishing. Use *OR* when you want to find resources that mention one of two (often interchangeable) terms—for example, "caribou OR reindeer." And use *NOT* when you want to exclude a certain term; for example, a search for "hunting NOT fishing" will return results that contain the word *hunting* but not *fishing*. Symbols that commonly function as Boolean operators include the plus sign (+), which generally signifies the same as *AND*, and the minus sign (–), which generally signifies the same as *NOT*. In addition, parentheses can be used to group terms together in complex relationships—for example, "hunting AND (caribou OR reindeer)." Most search systems also recognize the asterisk (*), dollar sign ($), and/or question mark (?) as denoting truncation, meaning that a search for "politic*" might return results that include the words *political, politician, politicize, politico,* and/or *politics*.
>
> Note that most search systems have a "Help" or "About" section that offers advice on how to expand or limit search results. In addition, your school's librarians should be able to answer any questions you have about how to make the most out of database and catalogue searches.

73b

73b The Internet
Internet search engines can provide you with easy access to a vast array of resources related to your topic. Some of these resources—such as government reports and articles in online academic journals—may offer you valuable, trustworthy information. Others—such as independent websites and blogs—are far less reliable. Because most of the information available on the Internet is largely unregulated, you need to evaluate care critically the websites you locate in your research. The followin tions will help you with this task:

1. Look for authoritative information on websites maintained nized and respected researchers, scholars, organizations, o tions. Anonymous and personal websites are not conside

> Numerous boxes to highlight important information

tial, tian; cial, cian, ciate

-tia-		-cia-	
confidential	influential	beneficial	mathematician
dietitian	martial	crucial	mortician
existential	spatial	emaciated	physician
expatiate	substantial	enunciate	politician

ative; itive

-ative		-itive	
affirmative	informative	additive	positive
comparative	negative	competitive	repetitive
imaginative	restorative	genitive	sensitive

ce; se

-ce		-se	
choice	defence	course	expense
evidence	presence	dense	phrase
fence	voice	dispense	sparse

62c

> Canadian advice for Canadian users

> **PROOFREADING TIP**
> *practice, practise; licence, license*
>
> Canadian writers tend to follow the British practice of using the *ce* forms of *practice* and *licence* as nouns and the *se* forms *practise* and *license* as verbs:
>
> > We will practise our fielding at today's slo-pitch practice.
> >
> > Are you licensed to drive?
> >
> > Yes, I've had my driver's licence since I was sixteen.
>
> American writers tend to favour the *ce* spelling of *practice* and the *se* spelling of *license* regardless of whether each is being used as a noun or a verb.
>
> Note also that Canadian as well as British writers generally prefer the *ce* spelling for *offence* and *defence*, while American writers tend to use the *se* spellings of these words.

364   Chapter VI Mechanics and Spelling

62-I Hyphenated Verbs
Verbs, too, are sometimes hyphenated. A dictionary will list most of the ones you might want to use; for example:

double-click	pan-broil	re-educate	sight-read
flip-flop	pole-vault	second-guess	two-time

But be aware that some two-part verbs can never be hyphenated. Resist the temptation to put a hyphen in two-part verbs that consist of a verb followed by a preposition (see #22c–e). Be particularly careful with those word combinations that are hyphenated when they serve as other parts of speech:

I was asked to <u>set up</u> the display. (*but* Many customers admired the <u>set-up</u>.)

<u>Call up</u> the next group of trainees. (*but* The rookie awaited a <u>call-up</u> to the big leagues.)

62-I

Exercise 62i–I Using Hyphens

Insert hyphens wherever they are needed in the following sentences. Consult your dictionary if necessary.

1. The ferry is thirty two and one quarter metres long.
2. The all Canadian team proved too much even for the ex champions.
3. The cold hearted vice president took up motor racing instead of profit sharing.
4. Is that an old fashioned and beautifully made antique salt cellar I see in your china cabinet?
5. The three tough looking youths were set to dish out some abuse.
6. I watched an interesting two hour documentary about an alien smuggling operation.
7. Avoid the scatter shot approach when writing a complaint email to part time employees.
8. The long lived queen has been a full time ruler from an early age.
9. The high school teachers' work to rule action left the basketball players without a coach.
10. Under lock and key, the sporting goods store displayed an array of high powered long range hunting rifles.

> Abundant examples and exercises throughout

Sample Student Essays with Comments and Grades   **551**

> Marked student essays that serve as models for how to edit and format written work

Humans "survived," but they were not all in good health. Also, "generations" is vague. Further development is needed.

Indeed, the body is designed to assimilate what it needs from good food. In this age of technology, people are beginning to forget that the human race survived for generations before nourishment was compressed into little capsules and the entire daily requirement swallowed with a drink of water in one gulp.

I will concede that there are <u>individuals</u> who do need to use these drugs *Be more specific.* or vitamins regularly, and other people who need to use them occasionally. Nevertheless, there is no good reason for the excessive use of medicine found in today's society. People have mistakenly concluded that if a drug can make them "better" when they are sick, then by the same principle, that drug will improve their condition when they are not sick. What could possibly be "better" than good health? Overdosing oneself with medicine is not the way to find out. In fact, *begging the question?* <u>excessive drug use will surely cause more harm than good</u>. Drug companies have had ample time to warn the public about the need to take care when using their *word choice: "controls"?* products. More stringent <u>methods</u> are obviously required.

B– Alec,
This essay is a well-written and thought-provoking argument. Although your introductory paragraph needs to be more focused, your thesis is strong. The body paragraphs are well developed, especially those in which you concede points. But your conclusion should have a stronger call to action. What exactly do you want the reader to do? What are the specific recommendations you want to make? Your argument would also be stronger if you used more specific words, avoided vague generalizations, and gave more examples.

Sample Essay 3
Your title indicates a process essay – is it?
Living with Animals

A1

shift in person   Human beings have always depended on animals to meet <u>our</u> needs. Animals have been used as <u>food, labour, drug testing, and even entertainment</u>. All these *list elements should be parallel* <u>uses</u> for animals are <u>useful</u> even vital for human needs, but management of animal *awk. repetition* <u>uses</u> must be responsible. *thesis: explain how*

Order? Food should be covered first.   Animals can be seen as the first slaves of man. Many pictures <u>can be formed</u> *pas* of oxen plowing fields, of horses pulling carts. I refered to animals as slaves but no *and I sp.* *Can animals – way? Maybe "using animals is one way?"* one opposed it as no one should. <u>Animals</u> were the only <u>way</u> to get things done

80 Methods of Documentation: The Name–Page Method (MLA Style)   **489**

A Book by One Author

```
        1                2
```
MacMillan, Margaret. Paris 1919: Six Months That Changed the World.
    New York: Random, 2001. Print.
```
  3      4       5    6
```

A standard works-cited reference for a book includes

1. the author's name (surname, followed by a comma, and full first name, followed by a period);
2. the full title of the book (italicized), followed by a period;
3. the city of publication, followed by a colon;
4. the name of the publisher (in shortened form), followed by a comma;
5. the year of publication, followed by a period; and
6. the medium of publication, followed by a period.

Note that the medium of publication for an e-book is the type of file you have accessed—for example, "PDF file" or "Kindle file" or, if you cannot identify the type of file, "Digital file."

MLA STYLE

On the Treatment of Publishers' Names

When using MLA style, shorten the name of a work's publisher as much as you can without making it difficult for your reader to identify the publisher. Omit articles (*A, An, The*), generic descriptive words (e.g., *Books, Company, House, Publishers*), and standard business abbreviations (e.g., *Co., Inc., Ltd.*). Use *UP* in place of *University Press* (e.g., *Oxford UP, U of Ottawa P*), and include standard abbreviations wherever you can (see the box on pages 499–500 for a list of abbreviations commonly used in MLA style). Finally, if the publisher's name contains one or more names of individuals, include only the first surname listed (e.g., *McClelland* instead of *McClelland and Stewart*; *Norton* instead of *W.W. Norton and Co.*).

A Book by Two or Three Authors
When you have two or three authors in a works-cited entry, the names following the first name appear in first-name–last-name order:

Somerville, Angus A., and R. Andrew McDonald. The Vikings and
    Their Age. Toronto: U of Toronto P, 2013. Print.

Hoffman-Goetz, Laurie, Lorie Donelle, and Rukhsana Ahmed.
    Health Literacy in Canada: A Primer for Students. Toronto:
    Canadian Scholars', 2014. Print.

80a

Detailed guidelines for
documenting sources
in MLA, APA, Chicago,
and CSE styles

---

80 Methods of Documentation: The Name–Date Method (APA Style)   **513**

Reference List
The reference list appears at the end of your paper and includes the full publication information for all works that you have referenced. It should begin on a new page, with the title "References" centred at the top. Each entry should be formatted with a hanging indent, with the first line beginning flush left and the second and subsequent lines indented.

List entries in alphabetical order, according to the surnames of authors or editors (or titles, when no author or editor is named). List works by the same author(s) or editor(s) chronologically, with the earliest article listed first. Arrange works by the same author published in the same year alphabetically by title, and assign a letter to each entry, following the year:

Darnell, S. (2010a). Power, politics and "sport for development
    and peace": Investigating the utility of sport for international
    development. Sociology of Sport Journal, 27(1), 54–75.

Darnell, S. (2010b). Sport, race, and biopolitics: Encounters with
    difference in "sport for development and peace" internships.
    Journal of Sport & Social Issues, 34(4), 396–417.

Note that in titles of books and articles, only the first letter of the title, the first letter after a colon or a dash, and the first letter of a proper noun are capitalized. In titles of periodicals (and in all titles that appear in the body of the paper), lowercase articles, coordinating conjunctions, and prepositions with fewer than four letters; capitalize all other words.

APA STYLE

On the Treatment of Authors' Names

In an APA-style reference list, use initials in place of authors' full given names. Invert the name of each author, and use commas to separate the names. If a work has been written by seven or fewer authors, include the names of all of the authors in the entry. If the work has eight or more authors, include the first six names followed by three ellipsis points and the final author's name:

Schwartz, S. J., Kim, S. Y., Whitbourne, S. K., Zamboanga,
    B. L., Weisskirch, R. S., Forthun, L. F., . . . Luyckx, K.
    (2013). Converging identities: Dimensions of accultur-
    ation and personal identity status among immigrant
    college students. Culture Diversity and Ethnic Minority
    Psychology, 19(2), 155–165.

80b

Acknowledgements

As with the previous editions of *The Canadian Writer's Handbook*, the sixth edition owes much to the contributions of reviewers, colleagues, friends, fellow writers, and talented and committed editors.

For their determination to strengthen and polish their work and their commitment to grow and change as thinkers and writers, we thank our students. We are especially grateful for their generosity in allowing us to use their questions and insights about writing in this book.

We deeply appreciate the encouragement, advice, and support we receive from the talented and enthusiastic staff of Oxford University Press—especially from David Stover, Phyllis Wilson, Suzanne Clarke, Dave Ward, and Jennifer Weiss. Special appreciation goes to our meticulous, ever-patient, gifted editors, Janice Evans and Peter Chambers.

To all of you, many thanks.

I

Principles of Composition

Introduction: The Writing Process, Essays, and Paragraphs

Writing Essays

Writing Paragraphs

Introduction: The Writing Process, Essays, and Paragraphs

Writing is paradoxical, when you think about it. It is, on the one hand, the most commonplace of activities—something many of us do in one way or another every day of the week, every week of the year. On the other hand, writing is one of the most astonishing and complex acts of communication any of us is asked to undertake in the course of getting an education, doing a job, or living a life.

Writing calls upon us to exercise creativity in generating ideas out of our own experience; it asks us to practise synthesis in entering the world of ideas and in discovering and integrating the ideas of others with insights of our own; it expects us to develop our powers of communication in shaping and presenting our arguments to different audiences of readers; it challenges us to demonstrate our talents for organization, reflection, and revision in working through the writing process from that first idea to the printing of our final draft.

Chapter I investigates the principles of unity, coherence, and emphasis that apply to the larger units of communication, the essay and the paragraph. It provides a guide to the process of composing and writing essays and paragraphs; along the way, it offers advice on writing argument and on composing in-class essays and essay examinations.

1-4 Writing Essays

Writing an essay involves designing the best possible package to contain and convey your ideas. In the early stages, you develop a general sense of your main focus or argument (your thesis), and you have an array of items you want to include (your supporting ideas and preliminary evidence). As you plan and develop your essay, you will work to arrange your ideas and evidence in a logical order. You may end up spending a great deal of time rearranging to make the package look the way you want it to—to give each item the appropriate emphasis. The exact steps you take will depend on the type of essay you are writing, the needs of your audience, and the requirements of your instructor.

1 Unity, Coherence, and Emphasis in Essays

Whatever the details of the assignment, your essay will benefit from your attention to three main principles of composition: **unity**, **coherence**, and **emphasis**. The following three sections offer a brief overview of

1b

these principles as they apply to entire essays; sections #6–8 discuss these principles in greater detail as they apply more specifically to sentences and paragraphs.

1a Unity

To be effective, an essay must be unified. That is, everything in it must be about one topic. In most academic essays, the unifying element is the thesis statement (see #2h), and all points should relate to this statement. As you write your essay, avoid the temptation to insert facts and findings that are interesting but unrelated to your topic or thesis. Take a close look at each paragraph within your essay. If your paragraphs are themselves unified and if you make sure that the opening sentences of each paragraph refer explicitly (or implicitly but unmistakably) to your overall subject or thesis, your essay will be unified. (See #6 for more on paragraph unity and #7a.1 for more on the functions of topic sentences.)

1b Coherence

Coherence, which can be defined as the logical connection of ideas, is important at every level of the writing process. You can achieve coherence by linking your words, sentences, and paragraphs to one another in a way that allows readers to follow your train of thought. This sort of linking requires careful planning and organization.

Transitional words and phrases such as *further, similarly, on the other hand,* and *at the same time* are often useful for establishing structural coherence (see #7b.4). They can provide the necessary connections between paragraphs, but don't overdo it by using them to begin every paragraph. Often you can create the link by repeating a significant word or two from the preceding paragraph, usually from somewhere near its end, and sometimes you can make or strengthen the link with a demonstrative adjective (see #19a), or even a pronoun (see #14). By referring to something

WRITING TIP

On Using Pronouns and Demonstrative Adjectives to Create Coherence

A pronoun or a demonstrative adjective can help to link ideas as long as the antecedent or referent to which it refers is clear. If you are far beyond the antecedent, or if more than one antecedent is possible, you risk confusing your readers rather than building coherence for them. If confusion is possible, repeat the antecedent.

And make it a point to use demonstrative adjectives rather than demonstrative pronouns. Demonstrative adjectives are clear and can add emphasis. Pronouns are not emphatic; rather they can be weak and ambiguous (see #14f, #16c, #19a, #41, and *ref* in appendix 2).

mentioned earlier, a demonstrative adjective or pronoun constructs a bridge between itself and its antecedent or referent. Remember, though, that transitional words and phrases are meant to draw attention to links that exist in the content of consecutive paragraphs. Without an inherent connection between one paragraph and the next, not even explicit transitions will be effective. (See also #7a.1, on topic sentences.)

1c Emphasis

The most emphatic position in an essay is its ending, and the second most emphatic position is its beginning. That is why it is important to be clear and to the point at the beginning of an essay, usually stating the thesis explicitly (see #2j.3), and why the ending of an essay should be forceful. Don't, for example, conclude by repeating your introduction or summarizing your points. And since the last thing readers see is usually what sticks most vividly in their minds, essays often use climactic order, beginning with simple or less elaborate points and ending with more important or complex ones (see #2g.2).

Further, the length of a paragraph within an essay automatically suggests something about the importance of its contents. Although a short, sharp paragraph can be emphatic in its own way, generally a long paragraph will deal with a relatively important aspect of the subject. As you look over your work, check to make sure you haven't skimped on an important point, and also that you haven't gone on for too long about a relatively minor point (see #9).

2 The Process of Planning, Writing, and Revising an Essay

No effective essay can be a mere random assemblage of sentences and paragraphs. It needs a shape, a design, even if only a simple one. How does one get from the blank page to the desired finished product? By taking certain steps, because a piece of writing, like any other product, is the result of a process. The usual steps that a writer takes, whether consciously or not, fall into three major stages:

■ **STAGE I: PLANNING AND PRE-WRITING**
- finding a subject
- limiting the subject
- considering audience and purpose
- choosing methods of development
- developing a preliminary proposal
- gathering evidence
- classifying and organizing the evidence
- formulating a thesis statement
- creating an outline

■ **STAGE II: WRITING**
- writing the first draft
- integrating evidence
- commenting on the significance of the evidence

■ **STAGE III: WRITING**
- revising
- preparing the final draft
- proofreading

Sometimes one or more steps may be taken care of for you; for example, if you are assigned a suitably narrow topic, the first two steps in the first stage will already be taken care of. And often several parts of the process will be going on at the same time; for example, there is often a good deal of overlap among the activities in the planning and pre-writing stage. Sometimes the order of the steps will be different; for example, you may not be clear about your purpose until you have finished gathering and then classifying and organizing evidence. And sometimes in the revising stage, you may want to go back and rethink your purpose, or dig up more material, or even further limit or expand your subject. But all the activities have to happen somehow, somewhere, sometime, for a polished piece of writing to be produced.

WRITING TIP

On Creating a Timeline

As you begin to plan your essay, you should devise a reasonable timeline for gathering evidence, writing, revising, and editing. Be realistic in estimating how much time you will need at each stage, and consider how your assignment will fit in with other projects and commitments you have. If you are unfamiliar with your topic, you should give yourself extra time to do some background reading in the subject area. If you are writing a research paper and you have little experience with the research process, you should also budget extra time for finding, reading, and evaluating sources (see #73–5). In the writing and revising stages, don't assume you will be able to pull everything together in one evening. Many writers like to give themselves at least two weeks between completing their first draft and submitting their final essay. This approach allows them to take a few days away from their work and return to the task of revising and editing with a fresh perspective. If you want a peer to help you edit or proofread your paper—either because you want a second opinion or because you are not confident in your writing skills—make sure to leave extra time to accommodate that person's schedule.

2a Finding a Subject

Your first pre-writing task is to identify the general subject area that you want to explore. In some cases, your instructor may assign a specific subject for you to write about; in such situations, you can move directly to the next step: limiting the subject (see #2b). At other times, the assignment will be more open, and you will have the freedom to choose a subject that interests you.

If you are writing within a specific discipline (for example, history, philosophy, sociology, or political science), you will likely need to choose a subject that relates to your field of study. You might find inspiration by considering one of the following:

- a key term whose meaning has changed over time—for a cultural geography course, you might ask, "What is *gendered space?*";
- a central debate in the discipline—for a Canadian studies course, you might ask, "How do scholars of the 1970s and those of today differ on the evaluation of Pauline Johnson's poetry?";
- a review of the scholarly literature surrounding a particular question in the field—for a children's literature course, you might ask, "How can theories of ecocriticism be applied to the reading of Canadian children's literature set on the Prairies?";
- a question or problem that puzzles you—for a sociology of deviance course, you might ask, "Why do some people reject social norms?";
- a question or issue that crosses disciplinary boundaries—for a human geography course, you might ask, "How will global climate change affect birth rates in Central and South America?"; or
- an idea raised incidentally in lectures or seminars that deserves further investigation—for a film studies course, you might ask, "Do images of children in recent Canadian films provide clues to the way Canadian culture has constructed ideas of childhood?"

Such starting points should make it possible for you to produce a paper distinctive in its approach—something more and better than a cutting and pasting of the views of two or three major sources.

If you are working outside a particular discipline or area of study (for example, if you are enrolled in a general writing course), you may have no limits on the sort of subject matter you can explore in your essay. Some writers find choosing a subject in this sort of situation very challenging, but it needn't be, for subjects are all around us and within us. A few minutes of free-associating in an empty word-processing file or with a pencil and a sheet of paper, jotting down and playing around with questions and any ideas that pop into your head, will usually lead you at least to a subject area if not to a specific subject. Scanning the pages of a magazine, newspaper, or scholarly journal is another way to stimulate a train of thought; editorial and letters pages are usually full of interesting subjects to write about, perhaps to argue about. A conversation or debate with a friend, family member, or classmate might also help you uncover a good subject. The possibilities are almost endless.

Whether your assignment is discipline-specific or more general, you should try to find a subject that interests you. An essay may take weeks or even months to research, write, and polish, so it is a good idea to choose a subject that you will enjoy working with and living with for an extended period of time. Don't, in desperation, pick a subject that bores you, for you may handle it poorly and probably bore your readers as well. If you are assigned a subject that doesn't particularly interest you, try to make it a learning experience: immerse yourself in it; you may be surprised at how interesting it can become.

2b Limiting the Subject

Once you have a subject, you must limit it: narrow it to a topic you can develop adequately within the length of the essay you are writing. More often than not, writers start with subjects that are too big to handle. Seldom do they come up, right away, with a topic like what people's shoes reveal about their characters, or the meaning of water imagery in a particular short story, or the inefficiency of the cafeteria; they're more likely to start with some vague notion about footwear, or about how enjoyable the story was, or about campus architecture. To save both time and energy, to avoid frustration, and to guarantee a better essay, be disciplined at this stage. If anything, overdo the narrowing, for at a later stage it's easier to broaden than it is to cut.

For example, let's say you wanted to write about "travelling"; that's obviously far too broad. "National travel" or "international travel" is narrower, but still too broad. "Travelling in Asia?" Better, but still too large, for where would you begin? How thorough could you be in a mere 500 or even 1500 words? When you find yourself narrowing your subject to something like "How to survive on $25.00 a day in Tokyo" or "What to do if you have only 24 hours in Hong Kong" or "How visiting the Taj Mahal changed my life" or "The day my passport got stolen," then you can confidently look forward to developing your topic with sufficient thoroughness and specificity. (See also #66.)

A good way to limit your subject is to ask questions about it. Formulate a question or series of questions worth investigating and researching. If you start with the broad subject of "air pollution," for example, you might ask yourself, "What type of air pollution do I want to investigate?" You might also ask, "What aspect of air pollution do I want to explore?" If you decide you want to write about the *effects* of *outdoor* air pollution, you might ask, "What *are* the effects of outdoor air pollution?" After identifying several problems associated with this type of pollution—for example, respiratory diseases, acid rain, increased toxins in the food chain—you might decide to focus on respiratory issues. This decision, in turn, will lead to more detailed questions: "What sorts of respiratory diseases are linked to air pollution? How do these diseases impact individuals and communities? Who is most likely to develop these diseases? Is the problem becoming more or less severe?" Eventually, you will arrive at a sufficiently narrow topic such as "The social impact of rising rates of childhood asthma caused by outdoor air pollution."

Exercise 2a–b Finding and Limiting Subjects

List ten broad subject areas that you have some interest in. Then, for each, specify two narrowed topics: (a) one that would be suitable for an essay of about 1500 words (six double-spaced typed pages), and (b) one for an essay of about 500 words.

Examples

1. Broad subject area: Clothing
   a) Narrower topics: Contemporary fashion trends, the significance of clothing styles during the Renaissance
   b) Even narrower topics: Gender differences reflected in contemporary fashion trends, elaborately decorated jackets as status symbols during the Renaissance
2. Broad subject area: Nature
   a) Narrower topics: Canada's most popular trail walks, gardening in the Atlantic provinces
   b) Even narrower topics: The therapeutic effects of walking along Canada's trails, how to grow prize-winning tomato plants in Nova Scotia

---

2c Considering Audience and Purpose

1. Audience

When you write a personal letter, you naturally direct it to a specific reader. If you write a "letter to the editor" of a newspaper, you have only a vague notion of your potential readership, namely anyone who reads that newspaper, but you will know where the majority of them live, and knowing only that much could give you something to aim at in your letter. The sharper the focus you can get on your audience, the better you can control your writing to make it effective for that audience. Try to define or characterize your audience for a given piece of writing as precisely as possible.

Some of the writing you do for school may have only one reader: the instructor. But some assignments may ask you to address a specific audience. For example, your instructor could ask you to address an essay on green roofs to local urban planners. Or she or he might ask you to write a paper on nutrition and pregnancy directed at mothers-to-be. Sometimes an instructor will ask you to write "for an audience of your peers," meaning an audience of individuals whose background knowledge and experiences are similar to your own. In the absence of any other guideline, keep an interested and serious but not fully informed audience in mind.

Identifying your audience will help you decide which words to use and what approach to take to convey your message effectively. If you are writing for readers who are very familiar with the topic, you can feel safe in using discipline-specific terminology without offering a full explanation of what the terms mean. If, on the other hand, you are writing for a more general audience, you may need to include definitions for more specialized terms. In relation to sentences, you may want to use short, direct sentences if you think your audience might have difficulty understanding the issues or ideas you are discussing. If you are writing for an audience that already has a solid understanding of the topic, you will likely want to use longer, more detailed sentences. (See chapter II for more on sentence patterns and conventions.)

Knowing your audience will also help you choose the right tone and approach for your paper. It will let you know whether you should be formal or informal, serious or humorous, detached or personally involved. If you are writing for your instructor and peers (as will most often be the case in an academic setting), you will likely choose a straightforward, matter-of-fact tone and approach. If you are writing a creative or personal essay, however, you may have greater freedom. As you will see in the following section, the tone and approach you choose will also depend on the topic and purpose of your essay.

2. Purpose

All writing has the broad purpose of communicating ideas. In a course, you write for the special purpose of demonstrating your ability to communicate your knowledge to your audience. But you will write more effectively if you think of each essay as having one or more of the following purposes:

1. to inform
2. to convince or persuade
3. to enter into discussion or debate
4. to entertain or impress

Few essays have only one of these purposes. For example, an instructional essay on running a small business may have the primary purpose of informing readers how to run their own businesses, but it may also be trying to convince them that the writer's way is the best way to do it. And to interest readers more, the essay may also be written in an entertaining style. An essay that analyzes a poem may seem to be pure exposition, explaining how the poem works and what it means, but in a sense it will also be trying to persuade readers that the writer's interpretation is a viable one. An

2d

entertaining or even whimsical piece may well have a satiric tone or some kind of implicit "lesson" calculated to spark debate. And so on. Usually one of the four purposes will dominate, but one or more of the others will often be present as well. (And see #3 below, on writing arguments.)

If you are unclear about the purpose of your essay, ask yourself what you hope to accomplish through your writing. Reread the assignment and highlight any guiding words such as *explain, evaluate, analyze,* or *compare and contrast.* If you are still having difficulty identifying the purpose, consult your classmates and discuss the matter with your instructor. The clearer your idea of what you want to do in an essay, and why, and for whom, the better you will be able to make effective rhetorical choices.

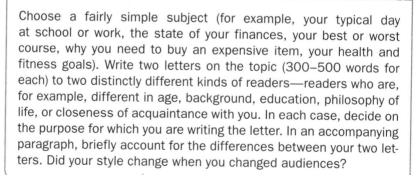

> **WRITING TIP**
> **On Visualizing Your Audience and Purpose**
>
> In the planning stage, write down, as a memo to yourself, a detailed description or profile of your audience and as clear a statement of your purpose as you can formulate. Tape this memo to the wall over your desk. If your ideas become clearer as the work proceeds, you can refine these statements.

> **Exercise 2c** Thinking About Audience and Purpose
>
> Choose a fairly simple subject (for example, your typical day at school or work, the state of your finances, your best or worst course, why you need to buy an expensive item, your health and fitness goals). Write two letters on the topic (300–500 words for each) to two distinctly different kinds of readers—readers who are, for example, different in age, background, education, philosophy of life, or closeness of acquaintance with you. In each case, decide on the purpose for which you are writing the letter. In an accompanying paragraph, briefly account for the differences between your two letters. Did your style change when you changed audiences?

2d Choosing Methods of Development

The **method(s) of development** you use for any given essay will depend on the nature of your topic and on your audience and purpose. Principal methods include *description, narration, definition, classification, analysis into parts, process analysis, comparison and contrast, cause and effect,* and *example and illustration.* The following questions can help you approach essay topics with these methods in mind. In each question, "X" represents the topic being developed.

2d

- *description*: What are the physical features of X?
- *narration*: What is the story/history of X?
- *definition*: What is X?
- *classification*: Into what categories or types can X be divided?
- *analysis*: What are the parts of X and how do they contribute to the whole of X?
- *process analysis*: What are the steps of X, or what are the steps leading to X?
- *comparison and contrast*: How is X similar to Y? How is X different from Y?
- *cause and effect*: What are the causes of or reasons for X? What are the effects or consequences of X?
- *example and illustration*: What are some concrete/specific examples or instances of X?

These methods of development are seldom mutually exclusive. In any paper, one generally dominates, guiding the development of the essay as a whole, while several of the others govern specific sections, paragraphs, or even sentences within the essay (see #5). Some methods naturally overlap—for example, when you are comparing or contrasting you are also necessarily classifying and defining. And almost any method can be thought of as supplying examples to support or clarify an assertion. As long as you maintain the fundamental requirements of unity and coherence, you can mix and combine these methods in any way that serves your purpose.

To demonstrate the ways in which the questions we have listed might operate in the development of a topic, consider the following scenario. Suppose that you have been asked to write a short paper on a personal experience involving air travel across the Canada–United States border. At first, you might draw a blank in thinking about what you want to say about this topic. Applying the questions we have listed would very likely help you to open up the possibilities for development.

The process would look something like this:

TOPIC: a personal experience involving air travel across the Canada–United States border

Definition: What is a personal experience? What constitutes air travel?
- personal experience: something that I have personally experienced
- air travel: someone or something moving from point A to point B via an aircraft

2d

Classification: What types of flights might occur between
major cities?
- commercial passenger flights
- private flights
- cargo flights

Examples: What are my personal experiences with this sort
of travel?
- I've flown to New York City to take in the sights
- I've flown to Albuquerque to visit my aunt

Narration: What is the story I want to tell?
- the story of my recent flight from Vancouver to
New York City

Analysis: What made my flight a positive/negative experience?
- Positive: easy to book online; safe arrival
- Negative: hassle going through security; four-hour
delay; boredom and claustrophobia on the plane

Process Analysis: What steps did my flight involve?
- choosing a destination
- booking a flight
- arriving at the airport in Vancouver
- checking in and going through security
- boarding the plane
- enduring the flight
- disembarking in New York

Effect: What are the consequences of my trip?
- I gained new experiences
- I have greater anxiety about flying in the future

Comparison: What are the essential differences between
travel by air and travel by car, train, or bus?
- air travel is the fastest and safest option
- air travel is more likely to cause anxiety
(common fear of flying)
- air travel generally requires going through
more thorough security checks

Description: What might I describe to enhance my paper?
- the terminal building
- the security gate or customs desk
- the cramped quarters in the airline cabin
- the noise of the aircraft, of fellow passengers

In the early stages of development, you might not find all of the methods of development relevant to your topic. But keep in mind that you may return to them at a later point, for the process of thinking your way through a topic is *recursive*—back and forth—rather than linear.

2e Developing a Preliminary Proposal

Many writers find it helpful to develop a preliminary proposal or statement of purpose once they have a general idea of what they plan to cover in an essay. Writing this sort of brief outline can help you organize your initial ideas on your topic and identify areas in which you will want to gather evidence. In some cases your instructor may ask you to create a proposal as part of the writing assignment (see #76a). Following is a preliminary proposal for a 1000-word paper on immigrant experiences in Canada.

Callie Cheung   History 222/010
10 January 2015

Paper is due: 13 March 2015 (approximately two months)
Target length: 1000 words
Audience: fellow students and instructor, all with an
                 interest in the subject
Subject: nineteenth-century immigrant experiences
                 in Canada
Topic: the responses of Catharine Parr Traill and
                 Susanna Moodie to their first years in
                 Canada (contrast)
Questions: Why did these two individuals—sisters close
                 in age and living close to each other in
                 their first days in Upper Canada—react so
                 differently to their new homeland?
                 How is it that Traill celebrates the land, the
                 people, even the winter weather?
                 How is it that Moodie is so critical of the
                 land, the people (especially her
                 neighbours), and the conditions of life?

Major sources so far:
                 Charlotte Gray's *Sisters in the Wilderness*,
                 Anne Cimon's *Susanna Moodie: Pioneer
                 Author*, Traill's *The Backwoods of Canada*,
                 and Moodie's *Roughing It in the Bush*

2f Gathering Evidence

An essay can't survive on just vague generalizations and unsupported statements and opinions; it must contain specifics: facts, details, data, examples. Whatever your subject, you must gather material by reading and researching, conducting formal interviews, talking to others, or by thinking about your personal experience. And don't stop when you think you have just enough; collect as much information as you can within the time you have allotted for evidence gathering, even two or three times what you can use; you can select the best and bank the rest for future use. In addition, keep in mind that the use of Canadian sources may be important to your objectives and to your readers.

1. Brainstorming

Your first step in gathering evidence will involve brainstorming—thinking about your topic broadly in order to generate as many ideas as you can. Sit down for a few minutes with a pencil and a sheet of paper, write your topic in the centre or at the top, and begin jotting down ideas. Put down everything that comes into your head about your topic. Let your mind run fast and free. Don't bother with sentences; don't worry about spelling; don't even pause to wonder whether the words and phrases are going to be of any use. Just keep scribbling. It shouldn't be long before you've filled the sheet with possible ideas, questions, facts, details, names, and examples. You may even need to use a second sheet. It may help if you also brainstorm your larger subject area, not just the narrowed topic, since some of the broader ideas could prove useful.

2. Asking Questions

Another way to generate material is to ask yourself questions about your subject or topic and write down the answers. Start with the reporter's standard questions: *Who? What? Where? When? Why? How?* and go on from there with more of your own: *What is it? Who is associated with it? In what way? Where and when is it, or was it, or will it be? How does it work? Why is it? What causes it? What does it cause? What are its parts? What is it a part of? Is it part of a process? What does it look like? What is it like or unlike? What is its opposite? What if it didn't exist?* Such questions and the answers you develop will make you think of more questions, and so on; soon you'll have plenty of material that is potentially useful. You may even find yourself writing consecutive sentences, since some questions prompt certain kinds of responses. For example, asking *What is it?* may lead you to begin defining your subject; *What is it like or unlike?* may lead you to begin comparing and contrasting it, classifying it, thinking of analogies and metaphors; *What causes it?* and *What does it cause?* may lead you to begin exploring cause-and-effect relations; *What are its parts?* or *What is it made of?* could lead you to analyze your subject; *How does it work?* or *Is it part of a process?* may prompt you to analyze and explain a process.

3. Consulting Existing Resources

Many academic essays require you to consult a wide variety of reputable books and journal articles, in order to see what scholars and others have said about your topic. Depending on the topic and the assignment, you may also want to review newspaper and magazine articles, websites, videos, sound recordings, and other formally or informally published sources. To find the most reliable, informative, and relevant resources on your topic, you must know where and how to look. (See #73 for detailed information on how to find reliable sources.)

4. Conducting Interviews

In some cases, you may need to speak directly with someone who is knowledgeable about the topic on which you are writing. This interview might occur in person, over the phone, through email, or via teleconferencing software. Whatever the format of the interview, you should follow some basic rules. First, be prepared. Decide in advance on the questions you want to ask during the interview, and do enough background research to allow you to converse knowledgeably about your topic. Second, be professional. Stick to relevant questions, dress appropriately, and be on time. Third, be polite and respectful. If you disagree with something, you can bring up your concerns, but you should avoid attacking or making negative comments about the person's views. Finally, be honest. Don't trick the person you are interviewing into giving you the answer you want to hear. Explain what you are writing about, and make sure the person knows that you may quote her or him in your essay.

Exercise 2f Generating Material

Choose two of your narrowed topics from exercise 2a–b, and brainstorm by peppering them with questions to see how much material you can generate. Then try the same techniques with the larger subjects to see if that will yield any additional useful material. You might also want to try getting together with one or two friends or classmates and bouncing ideas and questions off one another.

2g Classifying and Organizing the Evidence

1. Classifying

As you gather evidence on your topic, you'll begin to see connections between individual ideas. Once you have gathered as much information as you think you might possibly use, you should start putting your material into different categories and deciding how these categories relate to one another. During this part of the process you will also discard the weaker and less relevant details that do not fit into any of the categories, leaving you with only those details that best suit the topic as it is now taking shape. For a tightly limited topic and a short essay, you may have only one group of details, but for an essay of even moderate length, say 750 words or more, you will probably have several groups.

The map that follows was created by a student to classify and organize her ideas for an 800-word paper on the effects of war on the child characters in Joy Kogawa's novel *Obasan*.

Effects of War on Stephen and Naomi Nakane
[Are these effects gendered? Are they the result
of the age difference between Stephen and Naomi?]

Compare & contrast the two
characters according to . . .
① Self-image
② Narrative focus through
language on the children's
status (lack of it)
③ Children's reaction to
internment & relocation

Stephen   **Naomi**

② (self-hatred?)   ① (confused)
                                     +
① (broken . . .)   powerless/feels abandoned

differs from
Stephen in
honouring
traditions

leg (won't heal) ①
violin (target of racial bullying)
records (belonging to his
mother)   evidence

② clings to and ponders stories
 – the Momotaro story/
   a Canadian story
 – the Goldilocks story/is she
   the baby bear or Goldilocks?

①

Stephen compared
to Humpty Dumpty
("all the king's horses and
all the king's men" can't put
him together again: he's a
broken/shattered boy.

①

Naomi identifies with animals—
powerless too.

examples: the baby chicks
the chicken tortured by other children
the kitten trapped in the well

③

(reactions?): he lashes out at
Obsan, he pours himself into
music, excels, becomes an
accomplished musician

he wanders the world: after the
internment, he has no roots, no
home, no sense of belonging

③

(reactions?): silent, unsmiling, timid
speaks through her dolls
stays connected to Obasan & uncle
never marries, always wonders
about her missing mother

WRITING TIP

On Managing Groups of Details in Classifications

Try to classify your material in such a way that you end up with several groups, each of which will correspond to a separate major section of your essay. Remember, though, that an essay with more than seven major sections may be unwieldy for both writer and reader. On the other hand, an organization of only two major sections risks turning into an essay of two large lumps that might be interpreted as two mini essays crammed together; if your material calls for organizing into only two sections, take extra care to ensure that the whole is unified and coherent.

2g

2. Organizing

Once you have classified your material into groups, put the groups into some kind of order. The most common arrangements or **patterns of development** are the following:

- *chronological* (moving through time; used in narration and process analysis);
- *climactic* (moving from the least important to most important point; often used in academic writing);
- *inverse pyramid* (moving from the most important to least important point; often used in journalism);
- *inductive* (moving from data to assertions; often used in writing for sciences and social sciences);
- *deductive* (moving from assertions to supporting data or premises; often used in writing for the humanities);
- *block* (in a comparison of two items, a full discussion of the first item followed by a full discussion of the second item);
- *alternating* (in a comparison of two items, a back-and-forth discussion of the first and second items); and
- *spatial* (moving through space, such as top to bottom or left to right; used in describing physical space).

Don't necessarily accept the first arrangement that comes to mind; consider as many different arrangements as the material will allow, and then select the best one for your purpose and audience. The order should be logical rather than accidental or arbitrary. Ideally, the groups and their details should fall into order naturally, resulting in an arrangement that is the most effective way of presenting the material.

Exercise 2g Classifying and Organizing Evidence

Use the material you generated for the two topics in exercise 2f. Classify each mass into groups of related items and arrange each set of groups into the best order you can think of. In a few sentences, explain why you chose each particular order. Justify your explanation in terms of your audience and purpose.

2h Formulating a Thesis Statement

One of the most crucial parts of the planning or "pre-writing" stage is the formulation of a **thesis statement**. Your thesis statement tells your reader, in one or (less commonly) two concise sentences, what your essay is about; it should highlight the main *purpose* of your paper and reveal your *approach* to your topic. If you are writing an argumentative paper, your thesis will be a concise statement of your main argument—for example, *Children need routine and structure in their lives in order to develop a sense of security and self-discipline.* (See also #3d.2.)

As you plan and develop your essay, your thesis statement will likely go through many changes. During the early stages, as you find and narrow your subject, your thesis may be very broad. As you gather evidence and consider your audience and purpose, you will arrive at a position on your topic, and this position will further shape your thesis. After organizing your evidence and gaining a more thorough understanding of your topic, you might build on your thesis statement to make it more detailed and specific. When it comes time to write your first draft, you will need to take a close look at the wording of your thesis statement and make sure it is both clear and concise. The following examples show how a thesis statement might evolve during the planning stage:

FIRST ATTEMPT: Social media have positive and negative aspects.

GETTING MORE SPECIFIC: Frequent use of social networking sites can lead to negative outcomes.

TAKING A POSITION: We should reduce the amount of time we spend using social networking sites to avoid negative outcomes associated with social media.

AFTER FURTHER RESEARCH AND CONSIDERATION:	Individuals should try to spend no more than 15 minutes a day or 2 hours per week (estimates) using social networking sites because using these sites frequently can lead to feelings of jealousy, increased levels of negative stress, social isolation, depression, anxiety, paranoia, sleep disruptions, difficulty concentrating, headaches, repetitive motion injuries, and eye strain.
REFINED VERSION TO APPEAR IN THE FIRST DRAFT:	People should limit their use of social networking sites because frequent use of these sites can lead to a variety of emotional, psychological, and physical problems.

As you revise and polish your first draft, you will continue to adjust and refine your thesis statement until it says exactly what you want it to say in as few words as possible.

Try to make your thesis as original and intriguing as you can. Avoid overly general statements such as *People need exercise to be healthy* or *Lisa Moore is an excellent novelist.* Instead, say something your potential reader may not have considered: *Because regular exercise helps people maintain a healthy weight and a positive mood, working out every day can help you live life to the fullest* or *In* February, *Lisa Moore uses the literary device of the flashback to reinforce the novel's central theme of the present continually devolving into the past.* Interesting, informative thesis statements draw readers in and make them *want* to read your paper.

WRITING TIP

On Refining Your Thesis Statement

If you suspect that your preliminary thesis statement lacks specificity or significance, try asking yourself "so what?" If your answer to this question is more meaningful or insightful than the statement you started with, incorporate the deeper significance you have uncovered into your thesis.

Exercise 2h Writing Thesis Statements

Formulate a thesis statement for each of the topics you have developed through exercises 2a–b, 2f, and 2g. Make each a single simple or complex sentence (see #12c). Be as detailed, specific, and concise as possible.

2i Creating an Outline

As you work on your thesis, you should also start to develop an **outline**. You can think of the outline as the skeleton of your essay: it provides the structure to which you will attach details and evidence in support of your thesis. And your thesis is the spine that holds everything together.

Your outline should flow naturally from your thesis statement. Ideally, the thesis will contain or at least suggest the main subtopics the essay will cover. Here is an example of a student's outline for a short essay on student happiness:

THESIS STATEMENT: Students who have a social life are happier, smarter, and better prepared for the workforce than students who concentrate only on their studies.

BEGINNING: All work and no play makes a dull student. Although many people, including my parents, believe that students should spend all their time studying, I believe students are better off socializing in moderation at university. Why?

I. They are happier
  A. Friendship
  B. Maturity; balanced perspective toward life

II. They are smarter
  A. Academic support in study groups
  B. Academic support from friends who are strong in certain disciplines

III. They are better prepared for the workforce
  A. Effective network of contacts
  B. Interpersonal skills
  C. Communication skills

ENDING: The next time my parents tell me to get off the phone because I should be studying, I will be ready with my answer. I will tell them I am leading a balanced life, improving academically, and getting ready for my future.

2i

Note in this example the presence of brief beginning and ending statements. Although these sorts of tentative statements aren't essential to an outline, it's usually worth trying to think of something of the sort at this stage. You can easily change what you have written if you think of something better.

Also note the layout of an outline: numerals and letters are followed by periods and a space or two; subheadings are indented at least two spaces past the beginning of the first word of a main heading. Few outlines will need to go beyond one or two levels of subheading, but if further subdivision is necessary, here is the way to indicate successive levels:

I.
II.
    A.
    B.
        1.
        2.
            a.
            b.
                (1.)
                (2.)
                    (a.)
                    (b.)

The Importance of Outlining

An outline drawn up before you write a major essay will usually save you both time and effort at later stages. Writing the draft will be easier and smoother because it follows a plan: you know where you're going. You can avoid such pitfalls as unnecessary repetition, digression, and illogical or otherwise incoherent organization. In other words, a good outline can be like a map that keeps the writer from taking wrong turns, wandering in circles, or getting lost altogether.

Keep in mind, too, that an outline should not be binding. If as you write and revise you think of a better way to organize a part of your essay, or if some part of the outline proves clumsy when you try to set it down in paragraphs, or if you suddenly think of some new material that should be included, by all means go with your instincts and revise accordingly. And as you proceed, you may want to refine your thesis to reflect changes in your ideas. The virtue of using an outline is that rather than drifting about rudderless, you are in control of any changes you make because you make them consciously and carefully, and you will have a record of your changes if you want to rethink them later.

Selecting a Method of Outlining

Outlining of some kind is usually necessary for a good essay. The more complicated the essay, the more important the outline. A short, relatively simple essay can sometimes be outlined in your head or with a few informal jottings, but even a very short essay can be easier to write if you've made a blueprint first.

The method of outlining you use may be your own choice or it may be set by your instructor or by the nature of a project. Some people like the *topic outline* with its brief headings and subheadings, as in the example above. Sometimes a *paragraph outline* will work well, one that simply lists the material you plan to cover in each of the paragraphs that will eventually form the essay. Probably the most useful outline is the *sentence outline*, for it forces you to think about and develop your initial ideas.

Sentence Outlines

A sentence outline resembles a topic outline except that brief headings and subheadings are replaced by complete sentences. The advantage of having to phrase each item as a complete sentence is that you are unlikely to fool yourself into thinking you have something to say when in fact you don't. For example, imagine you are planning an essay on various cuisines and, in a topic outline, you put down the heading "new trends in restaurants." But if you haven't been eating out recently, you might find when you sit down to write your draft that you have little or nothing to say. In a sentence outline, you are compelled to make a statement about the topic, in this case perhaps something like "Although people have their favourite meals at home, when it comes to eating out, they are willing to try different foods." With even such a vague sentence before you, you can more easily begin supplying details to develop your idea; the act of formulating the sentence guarantees that you have at least some ideas about whatever you put down.

As an illustration, here is a student's sentence outline on the topic of the environment:

2i

THESIS STATEMENT: Certain corporations get away with crimes against the environment because profits are all important, our society cannot easily measure the crimes committed, and when the company is prosecuted, the penalties are weak.

BEGINNING: Although corporate crimes against the environment are profound in their impact, corporations are not held accountable or are mildly prosecuted. Three important reasons seem to stand out.

I. There is a conflict between making a profit and protecting the environment.
   A. The strength of economics outweighs ideological or political views.
   B. There is the perception that corporate crime against the environment is not real crime as the people involved are often professional and respectable.

II. It is difficult to determine or measure the extent of crimes against the environment.
   A. Government and regulatory bodies resist releasing facts.
   B. Records and comments from officials that are released are not always consistent.
   C. As corporate crime against the environment is often outside the scope and the know-how of traditional investigative journalism, the media does not always uncover the extent of the activity.

III. Weak penalties and lax enforcement do not deter corporations.
   A. The wording of environmental laws is ambiguous.
   B. Sanctions and penalties are weak.
   C. Prosecution involves expense and political repercussions private citizens' groups may wish to avoid.

ENDING: (Sum up the main points and point to implications for the future or suggest possible solutions.)

2i

The following are some guidelines for putting together a good sentence outline:

1. Make every item from the thesis statement down to the last subheading a single complete major sentence.
2. Use only simple or complex sentences; do not use compound sentences. Since the independent clauses of a compound sentence could themselves be written as separate sentences, having a compound sentence in your outline may mean that two or more headings are masquerading as one; consider making each clause a separate heading.
3. In any kind of outline you need to supply at least two subheadings if you supply any at all. A subheading, by definition, implies division. For this reason, a heading cannot be subdivided into only one part as a subheading. If under "I" you have an "A," then you must also have at least a "B"; if you have a "1," you must also have at least a "2." If you find yourself unable to go beyond one subheading, it probably isn't a subdivision at all but an integral part of the main heading that should be incorporated into it.
4. The headings or subheadings at each level should be reasonably parallel with one another; that is, I, II, III, etc., should have about the same level of importance, as should subheadings A, B, C, and so on. One way to help achieve this balance is to make the sentences at any given level as much as possible grammatically parallel.
5. Few outlines for a typical essay need to go beyond one level of subheading. If an essay is unusually long or complicated, you may find it helpful or necessary to break things down to a second or even third level of subheading. But remember that headings and subheadings should mostly state ideas, propositions, generalizations; the supporting facts can be supplied at the writing stage and don't need to go into the outline. If you find yourself including more than four or five levels of subheading, you may already be itemizing your facts and details.

Exercise 2i (1) Writing Outlines

Return to the two topics you've been working with in exercises 2a–b, 2f, 2g, and 2h. Construct an outline for each one. Make at least one of the outlines a sentence outline. If your thesis statements do not already suggest or contain your major headings, revise them to ensure that they do.

Exercise 2i (2) Revising Weak Outlines

One of the most important functions of an outline is to give you a graphic representation of a projected essay so that before you begin drafting the essay you can catch and correct structural and other flaws (repetition, overlap, illogical organization, introductory material masquerading as part of the body, inadequate thesis statements, subheadings that aren't really subdivisions, and so on). Here are some outlines drafted by students for possible essays. Analyze them critically; pretend that they are your own and that you'll have to try to write essays based on them. Detect their flaws, both major and minor, and then try to revise each so that it could guide you through the first draft of an essay.

1. THESIS STATEMENT: Every Canadian should be fluent in both official languages.
   I. It would be good for the individual.
      A. Improved job opportunities
      B. Increased communication skills
   II. It would be good for the community.
      A. Increased communication and understanding between cultures
      B. Decrease in prejudice and racism
   III. It would be good for the country.
      A. Increased nationalism and patriotism
      B. Establishes a Canadian identity

2. THESIS STATEMENT: Reading is a creative exercise for the imagination.
   I. Reading encourages people to visualize settings of stories.
   II. Reading encourages people to visualize the appearance of characters.
   III. Some plots encourage people to imagine the endings of stories or to fill in missing parts of stories.
   IV. Science-fiction stories provide people with inspiration that allows their imaginations to wander.

3. THESIS STATEMENT: The journal can play an important role in your life.
   I. Motives for keeping a journal
      A. Keeping a record of life
      B. Evaluating and surveying your life
   II. Topics other than the weather to write about in your journal
      A. Personal development
         1. Health, diet, sports

       2. Spirituality, dreams
       3. Books and films, quotes from reviews
   B. Work-related issues
   C. Current events
       1. Celebrities
       2. World events: war
   D. Travel

4. THESIS STATEMENT: The negative effects of television on our lives

   I. It leads to physical decay.
     A. People are less likely to exercise.

   II. It leads to mental decay.
     A. It requires no mental participation.
     B. People are less likely to engage in activities or hobbies that engage the mind or define their personalities.

   III. It leads to social decay.
     A. People do not engage in communal activities together.
     B. People do not eat meals together.
     C. It encourages consumerism over connection with people.

5. THESIS STATEMENT: Stress is a problem in university that must be dealt with.

   I. Different types of stress and what causes them
     A. Unhealthy: stress overload, too much work, not enough rest, bad nutrition
     B. Healthy stress levels: small amounts of pressure, beneficial to some extent, help one learn and grow
     C. Emotional: family problems, love problems, depression, loneliness, inability to concentrate
     D. Physical: work too hard, overdoing it, too much pressure, health problems

   II. Problems that arise with stress
     A. Sustained stress: heart attacks, health problems
     B. Common symptoms: ulcers, insomnia, irritability, sweaty or clammy hands, fidgetiness, higher pulse rate

   II. Treatments: How to cope
     A. Physical: relax, read, take up a hobby, watch TV, do something relaxing
     B. Emotional: relax mind, meditation, exercise
     C. Serious stress: psychotherapy, counselling, get mind away from problems

When you have finished working on these outlines, go back and examine your own two outlines from the preceding exercise. Do you see any possible weak spots in them? If necessary, revise them.

Exercise 2i (3) Constructing and Using Outlines

Construct outlines for proposed essays on three of the following topics:

1. How technology has or has not made our lives more complicated
2. The methods you use to overcome procrastination
3. Whether sixteen is the best age at which to learn to drive
4. The steps to take to ensure a good night's sleep
5. Whether tattoos and piercings make a body beautiful
6. The importance of empathy
7. The reasons dragon myths or legends are universal
8. Why being the only, youngest, middle, or eldest child in the family is the most challenging
9. The meaning of life
10. How to spend a Sunday afternoon

Check your outlines carefully for any weaknesses, and revise them as necessary.

2j Writing the First Draft

Once you have a good outline to follow, the work of writing the first draft becomes smoother and more purposeful. With the shape of the whole essay laid out, you can concentrate on the main tasks of drafting: finding the right words, generating the right kinds of sentences, and constructing good transitions and strong paragraphs. Here are some notes on getting started.

1. Postponing the Beginning

Starting the actual writing can be a challenge: most writers have had the experience of staring at a computer screen or a blank sheet of paper for an uncomfortable length of time while trying to think of a good way to begin. If you have no beginning in mind at this point, don't waste time trying to think of one. Plunge right into the body of the essay, and write it as rapidly as you can. Once you have finished writing the first draft, you'll have a better idea of what it is that needs to be introduced; you can then go back and do the beginning with relative ease. In fact, writers who write a beginning first often discard the original version and write a new one, either because the essay that finally took shape demands a different kind of beginning or because in the midst of composing they thought of a better one.

2. Beginning Directly

Just as it isn't always a good idea to begin a final paragraph with "In conclusion," so it's generally not good practice to open routinely with something mechanical like "In this essay I will discuss" or "This essay is concerned

2j

with." On occasion, such as when your essay is unusually long or complicated or when you are presenting it as part of a seminar, conference, or panel, it may be helpful to explain in advance what your essay is about, to provide readers with what amounts to a brief outline (just as it is then often necessary to provide some summary by way of conclusion). But most essays don't require this kind of beginning and won't engage an audience with such a stiff introduction. As a rule, then, don't talk about yourself and your essay; talk about your topic. Rather than begin by informing readers of what you are going to say (and then at the end reminding them of what you have said), start with something substantial and, if possible, attention-getting. Try to end with something similarly sharp and definitive.

3. Determining Subject and Thesis

However you begin, it is necessary to identify your subject and to state your thesis somewhere near the beginning—usually not later than the first or second paragraph. Even if your title clearly states what your essay is about, you must still identify your topic in the introductory paragraphs. For example, if your title is "Imagery in Shakespeare's Sonnet 65," you should still mention the author, the title of the poem, and the aspect of imagery. The title of your essay is not a part of its content; the essay must be able to stand on its own.

Special circumstances may, on occasion, call for you to delay the full statement of a thesis to near the end—for example, as part of a strategy of building to a climax. Even then, you will probably provide at least some indication of your thesis near the beginning, perhaps in general terms. Or sometimes a thesis can be broken into several parts to be stated at intervals in the course of an essay. On rare occasions, you may want to be mysterious, but readers generally don't like being kept in the dark. (See also #3d.2.)

4. Being Direct, Smooth, and Economical: Some Examples

Begin as directly, smoothly, and economically as you can. Here, for example, are three ways an essay with the title "Imagery in Shakespeare's Sonnet 65" might begin; note how differences in order, punctuation, and wording make each succeeding beginning better and shorter than the one before:

> (1) In Sonnet 65 by William Shakespeare, there is a great deal of imagery.

> (2) William Shakespeare in his Sonnet 65 uses imagery to . . . .

> (3) The imagery in Shakespeare's Sonnet 65 . . . .

Here is the beginning of an essay on one of Shakespeare's sonnets. The writer can't seem to get the engine warmed up:

ineffective: William Shakespeare, famous English poet and writer of plays, has always been known for the way he uses imagery to convey the point he is making in a particular piece of work. Shakespeare's Sonnet 65 is no exception to this, and this is one of the better examples of his work that I have studied, for illustrating his use of imagery.

The best example in the sonnet comes in lines five and six, where Shakespeare compares a "summer's honey breath" and a "wrackful siege of battering days."

Compare this with another student's beginning on the same topic:

effective: In Sonnet 65, Shakespeare appeals to a person's knowledge of visible properties in nature in an attempt to explain invisible properties of love and time.

The second writer has taken control of the material immediately. Even though no particular image has yet been mentioned, the second writer, in one crisp sentence, is far beyond where the first writer, well into a second paragraph, is.

Here is another example of an ineffective beginning. That the writer was in difficulty is shown by the redundancy in the first sentence, the illogicality in the second sentence, and the vague reference and wordy emptiness of the third:

ineffective: Nowadays, in these modern times, different cultures celebrate different holidays in many different ways. Thanksgiving is filled with a seemingly endless variety of memories and emotions. I would imagine this is experienced by almost every family and mine is most certainly not an exception.

The writer's own revision proves that the difficulties were merely the result of floundering, trying too hard to make a beginning; had the beginning been written after the body of the essay was complete, it might have taken this form:

effective: Holidays help define a family. In my family, where expectations are great, Thanksgiving brings out the best and worst of our individual characteristics.

WRITING TIP
On Going from an Outline to a Draft

1. Sometimes a main heading and its subheading from the outline will become a single paragraph in the essay; sometimes each subheading will become a paragraph; and so on. The nature and density of your material will determine its treatment.

2. It may be possible to transfer the thesis statement from your outline to the essay unchanged, but more likely you will want to change it (perhaps several times) to fit the style of the essay. The thesis is the statement of your purpose or of the position you intend to defend in the essay, so it should be as polished as possible. The kind of basic or mechanical statement that is suitable in an outline may be inappropriate in the essay itself.

Exercise 2j Evaluating Beginnings
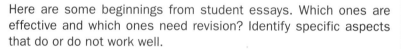

Here are some beginnings from student essays. Which ones are effective and which ones need revision? Identify specific aspects that do or do not work well.

1. Leonardo da Vinci was not concerned so much with explanations of why things worked as he was with how they worked. His scientific interests were as diverse as his other interests; they covered anatomy, geography, geology, mathematics, mechanics, and physics. He dissected several cadavers and developed what are called "transparency drawings"—pictures that show both external and internal features simultaneously. He mapped several cities from an aerial perspective, and there are several entries in his notes concerning the origins of fossils and geological strata. Quite simply, he was a deeply curious man whose life shows what it means to be a true Renaissance man.

2. Problems relating to a society affect all its inhabitants; hence, all its inhabitants must take part in curing society's ills. I find that society is plagued by problems such as degenerating neighbourhoods, growing unemployment, and increasing racism. Cultural conflicts have been the root of most of our problems; thus, if the situation is to improve, some changes must occur.

3. For many people, their first thought after the ring of the alarm clock is of a steaming cup of coffee. Their stumble to the kitchen for this pick-me-up blends with their dreams. The sleepy eyes that measure out the fragrant brown granules flick open after

their owners have savoured that first morning cup of coffee. After a strong cup of coffee, most people perform physical and mental tasks at the peak of their ability. The reason is caffeine.

4. The poem "To an Athlete Dying Young," written by A.E. Housman, structurally contains different periods of time in its stanzas. The different stanzas refer to different times. The rhythm of the poem is not uniform in beat. However, it has a consistent rhyme scheme. This poem is also an example of a dramatic monologue.

5. "Quit while you're ahead" may be an old and worn-out saying, but it aptly applies to A.E. Housman's poem "To an Athlete Dying Young." In this dramatic monologue the speaker seizes upon this idea as a means of consoling the athlete, or those who mourn him. Beauty and victory are fleeting. Not only does the eternal passing of time always bring change, but once our "peak" has been reached, there is no place to go but down. Rather than growing old and watching new athletes break his records, the young athlete in the poem dies at an early age. His victory garland is preserved, "unwithered," by death.

2k Integrating and Commenting on Evidence

As you write your first draft, part of your task will be to integrate the evidence you have collected into your paper. Integrating evidence involves more than simply inserting statements of fact that relate to your arguments and assertions—it requires careful consideration of how the information you have collected fits with your major and minor points and arguments. Your goal should be to ensure that the evidence fits into your essay as logically and seamlessly as possible. The comments you make about your evidence can help you show the reader the relevance and importance of the evidence. Take the time to experiment with what works and what doesn't, and don't be afraid to cut any material that doesn't support the main purpose of your paper.

If your evidence comes from an external source (i.e., if it is not based on your own thoughts or experiences), integration will also involve citing the original source of the information. See #78–80 for more on how to properly incorporate and cite evidence that comes from research.

2-l–n The Final Steps

The product of rapid composition is a first draft. Although some first drafts may come close to being acceptable finished products, don't gamble that your draft can pass for a polished essay. There are three tasks to under-take before you should consider an essay finished: *revising, preparing the final draft,* and *proofreading.*

2-l Revising

Revision (re-vision, literally "scrutinizing again") is an extremely important stage of writing, far too often neglected by less experienced writers. Experienced writers revise a piece of writing at least two or three times. Many writers revise five or even ten or more times before they consider a piece to be finished.

Revise carefully and slowly, looking for any way to improve what you've written. Don't aim just to correct errors made in haste; also aim to remove clutter and improve diction, sentence structure, punctuation, coherence, paragraphing, organization, and so on. Some writers find that going through a draft for one thing at a time is effective—for example, going through it looking only at paragraphing, then going through it again looking only at the structure and variety of sentences, then at punctuation, then at diction, and so on. And you will want to look carefully for those errors you know you tend to make.

Adopt the role of an observant and alert reader looking for strengths, weaknesses, and errors. To do this effectively, try to allow yourself a cooling-off period; wait as long as possible between the drafting and the revising—at least two or three days—so that you can look at your own work with more objectivity, as a dispassionate third-party reader would. If you're having trouble, you may find the checklists in appendix 3 helpful during your revisions.

2m Preparing the Final Draft

When you are through revising a piece of writing, carefully prepare the final draft, the one that will be presented to your reader or readers. Once the work is out of your hands, it's too late to change anything; make sure it's in good shape when it leaves your hands. It should be neat, and it should be in the appropriate format for the kind of writing it is. For most of your academic writing, heed the requirements of your particular audience, and follow carefully the manuscript conventions listed and discussed in #56.

2n Proofreading

Proofreading will have been taking place during revision, of course, and also during drafting, but go over what you consider to be the final copy of your essay when you believe it is ready. This final proofreading will prove worthwhile; despite earlier careful scrutiny, you will probably discover not only typographical errors but also hitherto unnoticed slips in spelling, punctuation, and grammar.

Do your proofreading with exaggerated care. Read each sentence, as a sentence, slowly (and aloud whenever possible); but also read each word as a word; check each punctuation mark, and consider the possibility of adding some or removing some or changing some. Particularly when you proofread for spelling errors, do so as a separate process. You might consider doing this by starting at the end of your work and reading backward, one word at a time, so that you won't get caught up in the flow of a sentence and overlook an error.

Do not put full trust in any of the spelling, grammar, and style checks that are part of word-processing programs. They can't possibly cover all the matters that require attention. And remember that spell checkers can't spot a misspelled word that happens to be the same as some other correctly spelled word—for example, *form* instead of *from*, or *through* instead of *though*; nor can they tell you that you've mistaken, say, *your* for *you're*, or *principal* for *principle*.

3 Argument: Writing to Convince or Persuade

Most of the principles of composition are even more important in argument than in other kinds of writing, though as we have suggested earlier (#2c.2), other kinds of writing, especially exposition, often include an element of argumentation. But when your principal purpose is to convince or persuade, there are several additional points and principles to keep in mind. Here are some brief suggestions and some practical advice to help you write effective arguments.

3a Subject

When you are focusing on your subject for an argumentative essay, keep in mind that there is no point in arguing about easily verifiable facts or generally accepted assumptions (2 + 2 = 4; the sky looks blue; good nutrition promotes good health; oil is a nonrenewable energy source). One cannot argue about facts, only about what the facts mean. Since an argument depends on logical reasoning, when you argue about opinions based on facts you will necessarily use factual data to support your contentions. A collection of unsupported opinions is not an argument but merely a series of assertions.

Similarly, one cannot logically argue about matters of taste. You can't argue that blue is a prettier colour than green; you can only assert that *you* find it prettier, for whatever reason. The subject of an argument should be something that is capable of verification, though the fact that it is being argued about at all indicates that its verification is not automatic or to be taken for granted.

3b Audience

When your *purpose* is to convince or persuade, your knowledge of your *audience* and your constant awareness of that audience are crucial. Consider, for example, how differently you would have to handle your material and your tone depending on whether you were writing to (a) an audience of people basically sympathetic to your position or (b) an audience of people likely to be hostile to your position. Since the effectiveness of an argument depends partly on your gaining or holding the confidence of your readers, or at least getting them to listen to you willingly and with a reasonably open mind, it is important that you avoid presenting anything that might keep them from listening.

Know your audience. Are your readers largely men? women? elderly? young? well-educated? middle-class? business people? students? politically conservative? liberal? wealthy? poor? artistic? athletic? car owners? family oriented? animal lovers? And so on. The more you know about your potential readers and their attitude toward your topic, the better you will know what choices to make so that you can clearly communicate your position and its value as an argument worth thinking about.

3c Evidence

When you are gathering material for an argument, look especially for concrete, specific, precise, factual data that you can use to support your generalizations (see #66b). The effectiveness of your argument will, in part, depend on the quality and the quantity of the evidence you provide both to support your position and to counter your opposition. For example, try to find some statistics you can cite, or some expert you can quote (the appeal to authority), or some common experience or assumption about life that you can remind your readers of (the appeal to common sense). You may be able to make good use of your own experience or that of someone you know well.

But be sure that the evidence you gather and use is both reliable and relevant. Don't cite a rap artist as an authority on a medical question—unless she's also a medical doctor; don't cite as support the results of an experiment that has been superseded by later experiments; don't discuss the style and upholstery of a car if you're arguing about which car provides the most efficient transportation.

3d Organization

Consider audience and purpose when laying out your material. You will find that an outline will often help you. Here are some specific points to keep in mind:

1. Emphasis

Usually, you will want to save your strongest point or points for the end, the most emphatic position of your argument. But since the beginning of your essay is also emphatic, don't open with a weak or minor point. It is usually best to begin with strength and then deal with minor points and proceed to the end in the order of climax. (See also #1c, #9, #29.)

2. Thesis

In an argument, your thesis statement is in effect a proposition that you intend to support; you want to prove it, at least to the satisfaction of your readers. For that reason, it usually appears at the beginning, just as a formal debate begins with a reading of the proposition to be debated. Occasionally, however, you can delay your statement of the thesis until near the end, letting a logical progression of reasoning lead up to it. But don't try for this dramatic effect unless it will work better than stating your proposition up front; for example, consider whether your readers might be put off, rather than drawn in, by being kept in the dark about just what your proposition is. (See also #2j.3.)

3. Methods of Development

Arguments can make use of any of the methods of development: narration (an illustrative anecdote), description (a detailed physical description of something it is important for readers to visualize clearly and perhaps feel emotion toward), comparison and contrast, analysis, and so on (see #2d). But be careful with analogy: using an analogy as the central pillar of an argumentative structure is risky, for opponents can too easily challenge it and pull it apart (see #3h.9); use analogy as an extra illustration or as one of several minor props. Definitions help establish a common ground between you and the reader. And give strong consideration to cause-and-effect analysis (*What caused it? What does it cause? What will it cause?*), often a mainstay of argument: you argue for or against something because of what has happened or is happening or will happen as a result of it.

4. Patterns of Development

Similarly, an argument can use any one or more of the common patterns of development (see #2g.2). An argument is likely, for example, to follow a logical progression, to move from general to specific or from specific to general, and to rise to a climax. But there is one further pattern that often occurs in argument: like a formal debate, many arguments move back and forth between *pro* and *con*, between statements supporting your proposition and statements refuting your opponent's position (see #3f).

3e–h How to Argue: Reasoning Logically

3e Being Reasonable

Appeal to common sense; appeal to authority; above all, appeal to reason. Demonstrate your respect for your reader's intelligence by appealing to it; a reader is then more likely to respect you and your arguments. If you appeal to prejudices and baser instincts you may get through to a few, but thoughtful readers won't respond favourably to such tactics. Appeals to people's emotions (sympathy for the poor or sick, love of children, feelings of patriotism, fear of injury) can be effective additions to an appeal to reason, but they are not a valid substitute for it. Similarly, if you're conducting a reasoned argument you will usually want to adopt a moderate tone. Stridency and sarcasm will only win you points with readers who are already thoroughly in agreement with your position.

3f Including the Opposition

Be fair: bring in and address any major opposing points of view. Your readers are likely to be aware of these and will expect you to address them. If you try to sway your readers by mentioning only what favours your side, you will lose their confidence because they will conclude correctly that you are unfairly suppressing unfavourable evidence. By raising opposing points and doing your best to refute them convincingly, you will not only strengthen the logic of your argument but also present yourself as a reasonable person, willing to concede that there is another side to the issue. Moreover, by taking on the discussion of both sides in a debate, you can often impart a useful back-and-forth movement to your argument, and you can see to it that after refuting the final opposition point, you end on your own strongest points.

3g Using Induction and Deduction

The two principal methods of reasoning, *induction* and *deduction*, occur both separately and in combination in argument. You should know how each works, and it sometimes helps to be aware of which one you are using at any given point so that you can use it effectively.

1. Induction

Inductive reasoning argues from the particular to the general. That is, it uses specific examples to support a general proposition. A team of chemists will argue that their new theory is correct by describing the results of several experiments that point to it. If you want people to vote for mayoral candidate A rather than B, you could point to several instances of A's beneficial actions on behalf of the city while on city council and also perhaps point to several instances of B's harmful decisions. If you wanted to argue against a proposal to cut back on funding for the athletic program at your school, you could cite the major ways in which the program benefits the school and its students; you could also interview other students to show that the majority of your peers agree with you.

Inductive reasoning cannot prove anything; it can only establish degrees of probability. Obviously the number of examples affects the force of such arguments. If the chemists could point to only two successful experiments, the claim for their theory would remain weak; if they could cite a hundred consecutive successes, their argument would be convincing; there would be a strong likelihood that the experiment would work again if tried for the hundred-and-first time.

Be rigorous in presenting your data, but also consider how much detail your audience really needs. If, in a speech or a written argument, you detailed fifty noble acts of candidate A and fifty ignoble acts of candidate B, you would probably lose your audience and turn them against you and your proposition. You would do better to describe a few actions on each side and try to establish that those actions were representative of the two candidates' behaviour.

Similarly, if you interviewed students about the athletic program at your university or college, you would need to talk to enough of them for your sampling to be considered representative; if you polled only elite athletes, you could hardly claim that their opinions were typical. And though the sampling would have to be large for the results to be convincing, it would be the total number that would carry weight, not the detailed opinions of each individual student.

In addition, you must be able to explain any notable exceptions among your examples, for these form the bases of possible opposition arguments. For example, if one of their experiments failed, the chemists would need to show that at that time their equipment was faulty, or that one of their ingredients had accidentally become adulterated. If candidate A had once voted to close a useful facility, you could try to show that financial exigency at that time left no choice, or that the facility, though generally perceived as beneficial, was in fact little used and therefore an unnecessary drain on the city's resources. If you explicitly acknowledge such exceptions and show that they are unimportant or atypical, they can't easily be used against you by a reader who disagrees with you.

2. Deduction

Deductive reasoning argues from the general to the particular. It begins with facts or generally accepted assumptions or principles and applies them to specific instances. For example, we know that oil and other fossil fuels are nonrenewable energy sources that will presumably someday be depleted, and we also know that the world's energy needs are increasing exponentially. Basing their argument on those two facts, energy experts have concluded that it is increasingly important for us to discover or develop alternative sources of energy.

The standard way of representing the process of deductive thinking is the *syllogism*:

MAJOR PREMISE: All mammals are warm-blooded animals.

MINOR PREMISE: Whales are mammals.

CONCLUSION: Therefore, whales are warm-blooded animals.

Syllogistic reasoning is a basic mode of thought, though commonly in everyday thinking and writing one of the premises is omitted as "understood"; for example, if a student says "This term paper is due tomorrow, so I'll have to finish it tonight," the assumed second premise ("I don't want to hand the paper in late") goes without saying.

Deductive reasoning, unlike inductive reasoning, can establish proof, but only if the premises are correct and you follow the rules of logic. For example, if one of the premises is negative, the conclusion must be negative—and two negative premises cannot lead to a conclusion at all.

The term common to both premises—called the "middle" term (in the foregoing example, *mammals*)—cannot appear in the conclusion. Most important, if the conclusion is to be an absolute certainty, this "middle" term must, in at least one of the premises, be all-inclusive, universal, or what is called "distributed"; that is, it must refer to all members of its class, usually with an absolute word like *all, every, no, none, always,* or *never.* If instead it is qualified by a word like *some, most,* or *seldom,* the conclusion can only be a probability, not a certainty (and if both premises include such a qualifier, they cannot lead to a conclusion):

> Most mammals are viviparous.
>
> Whales are mammals.
>
> Therefore, whales are probably viviparous.

Here one could reason further that since whales are not among the oviparous exceptions (platypus, echidna), they are indeed viviparous.

For a conclusion to amount to certainty both premises must be true, or accepted as true:

> No mammals can fly.
>
> Whales are mammals.
>
> Therefore, whales cannot fly.

Here the conclusion is *valid* (the reasoning process follows the rules), but it is not *sound*, since the first premise with its categorical *no* excludes the bat, a flying mammal. Such a conclusion, even if true (as this one is), will be suspect because it is based on a false premise.

If one argues that

> All mammals are four-legged animals.
>
> Whales are mammals.
>
> Therefore, whales are four-legged animals.

The conclusion, however valid, is not only unsound but untrue as well. To be accurate, the first premise would have to refer to *some* or *many*; the conclusion would then have to be something like "whales may be four-legged animals." Here the absurdity is obvious. But it is not uncommon to hear something like "That politician must be anti-business; after all, he is in favour of preserving the environment." In such a case the absurdity may not appear so obvious, but in the syllogism underlying this reasoning the first premise would read something like "Anyone who argues for preserving the environment is against business"; again, changing "Anyone who argues" to the correctly qualified "Some people who argue" renders the conclusion unsound.

Be skeptical whenever you find yourself using—or thinking—absolute terms like *all* and *everyone* and *no one* and *must* ("Everyone benefits from exercise"; "All exams are unfair"; "[All] Lawyers are overpaid"; "No one cares about the elderly"; "Vitamin E must be good for you"): you may be constructing an implicit syllogism that won't stand up, one that an opponent can turn against you. Use such qualifiers as *most* and *some* and *sometimes* when necessary; you won't be able to establish absolute proof or certainty, but you may still have a persuasive argument.

3. Combining Induction and Deduction

Induction and deduction often work together. For example, when you cite instances from candidate A's record, you use induction to establish the general proposition of your candidate's worthiness. But then you implicitly turn to deduction, using that generalization as the basis for a further conclusion: "Candidate A has done all these good things for our city in the past; therefore when elected mayor he or she will do similar good things." (But would the unstated second premise—"A person who behaved in a certain way in the past will continue to behave that way in the future"—require some qualification?)

3h Detecting and Avoiding Fallacies

If you are mounting a counter-argument, it often pays to look for flaws in your opponent's reasoning, such as hidden assumptions and invalid syllogisms. There are several other kinds of recognized, and recognizable, logical fallacies to look for—and, of course, to guard against in your own writing. Most of them amount to either avoiding evidence or distorting evidence, or both, and some are related to or overlap with others. Here are the main ones to watch for:

1. *Argumentum ad Hominem*

Argumentum ad hominem means "argument directed at the person." It refers to an attempt to evade the issue by diverting attention to the person at the centre of the argument: "Mozart lived an amoral life; therefore his music is bound to be bad." Mozart's morality is irrelevant to a discussion of the aesthetic quality of his music. "My opponent is obviously not fit to be mayor; she never goes to church, and her daughter was arrested last year for shoplifting." Neither the candidate's non-attendance at church nor her daughter's arrest—whether or not she was guilty—has any bearing on the candidate's fitness for office. Such tactics, according to their degree of directness or nastiness, are referred to as innuendo or name-calling or mud-slinging.

A similar tactic, known as guilt (or virtue) by association, is an attempt to tarnish (or enhance) someone's or something's reputation through an association with another person or thing. This kind of argument often takes the form of an endorsement: "I always take my car to Caesar's Garage because my friend Manuel says they're great, and he knows a lot about cars." Many instances of this kind of argument turn out to be fallacious because the stated connection between the two things is either not real or irrelevant. A brand of soft drink is not necessarily better because a famous actor is paid to say it is, nor is a politician necessarily evil because he once had his picture taken with someone later convicted of a crime.

2. Argumentum ad Populum

Argumentum ad populum is an "argument directed at the people"—an attempt to evade the issue by appealing to mass emotion. Like *argumentum ad hominem*, this technique uses appeals to prejudices, fears, and other feelings not—or not clearly—relevant to the issue. Often by using what are called "glittering generalities," it calls upon large and usually vague, unexamined popular feelings about religion, patriotism, home and family, tradition, and the like. One version of it, called the "bandwagon" approach, associates mass appeal with virtue: if so many people are doing this or thinking that or drinking this or wearing that, it must be right or good.

3. Red Herring

A red herring is a false or misleading issue dragged across the trail to throw the dogs off the scent. The new matter may be interesting, but if it is fundamentally irrelevant to the question being argued, it is a red herring. For example, *ad hominem* arguments are red herrings, since they divert a reader's or listener's attention from the main question by injecting the issue of personality.

4. Hasty Generalization

A hasty generalization is a generalization for which there is insufficient evidence. It occurs when an arguer jumps to a conclusion that is based on relatively little proof, for example when a team of chemists formulates a theory with only two successful experiments to point to (see #3g.1). Consider another example: just because you and a friend didn't like the food you were served once at a particular restaurant, you aren't justified in asserting that the food is always bad at that restaurant; maybe the regular chef was away that day. But if you've had several such experiences and can find other people who've had similar ones, you'll be closer to establishing that those experiences were typical and therefore sufficient to generalize upon.

5. Begging the Question

Begging the question is assuming as true something that needs to be proved: "The government should be voted out of office because the new tax they've just imposed is unfair to consumers." The arguer here is guilty of begging the question of the tax's unfairness, which needs to be established before it can be used as a premise.

Similar to question-begging is circular reasoning, in which a reason given to support a proposition is little or no more than a disguised restatement of the proposition: "Her consistently good cooking is easy to explain: she's an expert at all things culinary." This is the same as saying she is a good cook because she is a good cook.

6. *Post Hoc Ergo Propter Hoc*

Post hoc ergo propter hoc means "after this, therefore because of this." It refers to oversimplifying the evidence by assuming that merely because B follows A in time, B must be caused by A. It's true that thunder is caused by lightning, but the subsequent power failure may have been caused not by the lightning but by a tree blown down across the power line. Think about common superstitions: if you always wear your green socks during an exam because once when you wore them you wrote a good exam and so you think they bring you good luck, you are succumbing to the *post hoc* fallacy. Consider another example: "As soon as the new government took office, the price of gasoline went up"; the price hike might have nothing to do with the new government, the timing being coincidental.

7. *Either–Or*

The *either–or* fallacy, also called "false dilemma," refers to an oversimplification of an issue by presenting it as consisting of only two choices when in reality it is more complex than that. Some questions do present two clear choices: one either gets up or stays in bed; either one is pregnant or one is not; either one votes in an election or one doesn't. But most arguable issues are not matters simply of black and white; there is often a large area of grey between the extremes. One doesn't have to vote for either A or B; one can perhaps find a third candidate, or one can stay home and not vote for anyone. "If you aren't for us, then you must be against us!" This common cry is false; one could be neutral, impartial, uninterested, or committed to a third option. "The administration at work is either indifferent to employees' needs or against employees in general." Neither unpleasant alternative is likely to be true. This insidious pattern of thinking underlies a good deal of what we think of as prejudice, bigotry, and narrow-mindedness: "If you don't attend a recognized religious institution, then you're not really religious," or "If you don't support the war, you're unpatriotic." Although it is sometimes tempting, don't oversimplify; acknowledge the rich complexity of most issues.

8. Exaggerating the Trivial

When you exaggerate the trivial, you distort the evidence by treating a minor point as if it were a major one. If the point is your own, discerning readers will infer that you lack substantial evidence and have had to fall back on weak arguments. If the point is an opposing one, the audience will infer that you can't refute major points and are trying to make yourself look good by demolishing an easy target. "We should all give more to charity because being generous can give us a warm feeling inside" may be worth mentioning, but not worth dwelling on. On the other hand, don't distort the evidence by trivializing opposition points that are important.

3h

9. False or Weak Analogy

A false or weak analogy occurs when one oversimplifies the evidence by arguing that because two things are alike in some features, they are necessarily alike in one or more others as well. You can say that learning to ride a bicycle is like learning to play the piano: once you learn, you seldom forget; but you would not go on to argue that one should have a bicycle tuned periodically or that one should mount a tail light on the piano for safety while playing at night. Analogies can provide interesting and concrete illustrations; by suggesting similarities they can help define, clarify, explain, or emphasize something. Consider, for example, the following analogy, which we used in #2i: a good outline can be like a map that keeps the writer from taking wrong turns, wandering in circles, or getting lost altogether. We would not expect this analogy to convince you of the importance of an outline, but we hope that, by adding its concrete touch, we help you to understand and perhaps to accept our assertions.

One fairly common argument claims that because city or provincial or other governments are in some ways similar to large business organizations, they need experienced business people to run them. The more similarities you can point to, the stronger the argument. The trouble with this and other arguments from analogy is that no matter how many specific similarities you can come up with, your opponents can usually keep ahead of you by citing an even greater number of specific and significant differences. After all, leading a government may be *like* running a business, but it is not the same thing.

EAL

10. Equivocation

Equivocation involves using a term in more than one sense; being ambiguous, whether accidentally or intentionally: "It is only natural for intelligent people to reject this idea. And as science tells us, natural law is the law of the universe; it is the law of truth and must be obeyed." Aside from the appeal to snobbery and self-esteem (we all like to think we are "intelligent," but just what is "intelligence"?) and the appeal to the prestige of "science" in the modern world (but just how infallible is science?) and the imposing but vague term *universe* and the glittering abstraction *truth*, do the two occurrences of the word *natural* correspond with each other? Don't let the meanings of words shift as you move from one phrase or sentence to the next. Choose and use your words ethically and carefully.

11. Non Sequitur

Non sequitur means "it does not follow." When for whatever reason a general proposition does not follow logically from the particular examples cited to support it, or a conclusion does not logically follow from its premises, it is a non sequitur. The term would apply to any of the fallacies discussed above and also to such leaps of logic as "She can French braid hair; she'd make a good mother" and "I've had singing lessons for five years; I should get the lead role in the opera."

Exercise 3 (1) Detecting Faulty Reasoning

Point out the weak reasoning in each of the following. Identify any particular fallacies you detect.

1. She's a liberal, so she's sure to use the taxpayer's money for all sorts of give-away programs, for that's what "liberal" means: generous.

2. Your advertisement says that you want someone with experience as a computer programmer. I've had a year's experience as a computer programmer, so I'm clearly the person you want for the job.

3. Since peanuts can cause allergic reactions, they should be taken off the market.

4. He's bound to have an inferiority complex. Look at how thin he is!

5. Novels written by women often have women as protagonists. Since this novel has a woman as its protagonist, it was probably written by a woman.

6. In the past, my dishwasher has always been quiet, but now that new people have moved into the apartment next door, the dishwasher is noisy. They must have done something funny to the plumbing.

7. Dogs make better pets than cats because when they wag their tails they're happy; cats flick their tails when they're angry.

8. This critic says Michael Bay's movies are second-rate, but since she's a feminist her judgment won't stand up.

9. If I am not promoted, the company will immediately collapse.

10. Student opinion is overwhelmingly in favour of dropping the first-year science requirement. I took a poll among my fellow English majors, and over 80 per cent of them agreed.

11. The police are supposed to protect society from real criminals. When they give me parking tickets they're not doing their job, for I'm not harming society and I'm certainly not a criminal.

12. We've had an unusually warm winter, no doubt as a result of the meteor shower last year.

13. Fashion models have slim bodies. They must be much healthier than most other people.

14. This party is for lower taxes, and so am I. That's why I am loyal to the party and always vote for its candidates.

15. People who live and work together constitute a social community, and in a democracy social communities should have a measure of self-government. Since the university is such a community, and since the vast majority of those participating in its life are

students, it follows that students should have a major say in the running of the university.

16. Advertising is like fishing. Advertisers use something attractive for bait and cast out their lines to dangle the bait in front of us. They think of consumers as poor dumb fish, suckers who will swallow their stuff hook, line, and sinker. And there's a lesson for us in that: if you bite you'll get hurt, for there's always a nasty hook under the bait. The only way to protect yourself is to make sure you don't fall for any advertiser's pitch.

Exercise 3 (2) Analyzing Arguments and Recognizing Persuasive Techniques

1. In an essay, analyze three or four current magazine advertisements for different kinds of products. Point out all the techniques of persuasion you can find in them. Do they appeal more to emotion than to reason? Are they guilty of any particular fallacies?

2. Look over a week's worth of the editorial and letters pages of a local city or campus newspaper. Select and analyze three or four editorials or letters in order to discover their argumentative techniques.

3. Find a more extended piece of argumentative writing in a magazine with national circulation. Try to find one arguing about some issue of national importance. Analyze it as an argument. Consider its subject, its audience, its structure, its methods of reasoning, its possible weaknesses, and so on. Assign it a grade.

Exercise 3 (3) Including the Opposition

In the following sentence outline for an argumentative essay, the student took little account of points the opposition might raise. Read through it carefully, listing as many opposition arguments as you can think of; then recast the outline so as to include those arguments. You can improve the outline in other ways as well. If you find the counter-arguments compelling, you may want to recast the thesis so that you are arguing for the other side. Include in the revised outline one or more sentences each for both a possible beginning and a possible ending of the essay.

THESIS STATEMENT: In my opinion, it is better to listen to music at home rather than in a concert hall.

3h

I. By staying home instead of going to a concert, people save money on tickets, transportation, and babysitters.
   A. The cost of listening to a recording at home is a fifth of the cost of a ticket to get into a concert.
   B. Any kind of transportation is an additional cost to a music lover who goes to a concert.
      1. Cars require fuel and parking.
      2. Taxis are expensive and hard to get.
      3. Public transit is too slow and full of people who are coughing.
   C. Parents who wish to go to a live concert must hire a babysitter.

II. Music lovers have the comfort and convenience of staying at home.
   A. They have easy access to relatively inexpensive refreshments and to washroom facilities.
   B. They can sit in an open and relaxed manner.
      1. Theatre seats are too compact and uncomfortable.
      2. The cost of refreshments is very expensive.
   C. When one is in a large crowd it is often difficult to concentrate on the music.

III. A digital music file provides perfect sound every time.
   A. You can listen to one piece many times using the repeat function.
   B. You don't have to listen to other people coughing, applauding, or scrunching candy wrappers.

Exercise 3 (4) Writing an Argument

Carefully plan and write an argument of between 1000 and 1250 words (four to five double-spaced typed pages) on some local issue, perhaps something you found while working on part 2 of exercise 3 (2). Take a position you sincerely believe in. Don't pick a topic that you can't deal with fairly thoroughly. Be sure to take into account any major opposition arguments.

4 Writing In-Class Essays and Essay Examinations

Writing an essay in class or during an examination is much like writing an essay in your own room, in the library, or anywhere else—except that you may have to do it faster: you don't have time to think and plan at leisure and at length. Therefore, you need to make the best use of the time you have. All the principles discussed earlier in this chapter still hold, but here is some additional advice to help you work quickly and efficiently:

1. **At the beginning of an examination, read through the whole test right away.** If it has more than one part, budget your time: before you start thinking and writing, decide just how much time you will need or can afford to spend on each part. Make decisions about time allotment based on the mark value of each section of the test.
2. **Read the topics or questions carefully. Don't, in haste, misread or misinterpret**. Don't read wishfully, finding in a question what you want to find instead of what is actually there.
3. **Follow instructions.** If you're asked for an argument, *argue*. If a question asks you to *analyze* a text, don't simply give a summary of it. If it asks you to *justify* or *defend* your opinions or conclusions, don't simply assert them. If it asks for *comparison and contrast*, don't spend too much time on one side of the matter. If it asks you to *define* a term or concept, don't simply describe it or give an example of it, and don't ramble on about your feelings about it or your impressions of it.
4. **Take time to plan.** Don't panic and begin writing immediately. Think for a few minutes. The time you spend planning will ensure that the job of writing is easier and the result clearer. Do a little quick brainstorming. Take the time to make at least a sketch outline, with a thesis or proposition and a list of main points and supporting details; you will then be less likely to wander off the topic or change your thesis as you proceed. It's often a good idea to limit yourself to three or four main points, or parts (in addition, that is, to a beginning and an ending).
5. **Get started.** Once you've drawn up your plan, start writing. If necessary, leave several lines or a page blank at the beginning and plunge right into your first point. Don't waste time trying to think of a beginning if one doesn't occur to you quickly; you can come back and fill it in later. Quite possibly you won't need to supply a separate "beginning" at all. Get to the point quickly and stay with it. Make your thesis clear early on; that may be all you need by way of a beginning. Often you can pick up some key words or phrases from the question or topic and use them to help frame a thesis and get yourself going.
6. **Write carefully.** Whereas in an essay written at home you may write your draft hurriedly and spend most of your time revising and editing, in an exam you have to make most of your changes as you go. (This is

another reason it's important to have a plan: without one, you could, as you pause to tinker with a sentence, lose the thread of your argument.) You won't have time to do much revising; your first efforts at sentences will often have to do. And don't waste time recopying an initial draft, because you are not being tested on your handwriting.

7. **Aim for quality, not quantity.** More is not necessarily better. Your essay should be of reasonable length, and sometimes a required minimum length will be specified. What is most important is that you adequately develop your subject by developing each of your main points. But don't try to impress by going on and on, for then you will likely ramble, lose control of your thesis and your organization, and not give yourself time to edit and proofread.

8. **Be specific.** Provide examples, illustrations, and evidence. By all means generalize, but support your generalizations with specific and concrete details.

9. **Conclude effectively.** Refer to, or restate, your thesis, and if necessary refer again to your three or four main points, but do so in a way that adds something new. Sometimes a single concluding sentence can make a good clincher, especially if it suggests or underscores some result or effect growing out of what your discussion has said. If possible, echo an idea you had in your introduction.

10. **Proofread carefully.** Leave yourself enough time to look for the kinds of mistakes and slips we all make when writing fast. Don't just run your eyes over your sentences, assuming that any errors will leap out at you. Read carefully. If you know that you're prone to certain kinds of errors, look specifically for them.

 ## Writing Paragraphs

Like entire essays, paragraphs require unity, coherence, and well-controlled emphasis in order to be effective. As you might expect, then, they also require a great deal of planning and thought—not only about how ideas will best fit together within the paragraph, but also about how each paragraph will relate to the rest of the written work.

 ## Kinds of Paragraphs

A paragraph can be classified in two ways:

1. according to its function in its larger context or
2. according to the kind of material it contains and the way that material is developed.

Based on function, paragraphs can be classified as *introductory, concluding, transitional*, or *body* paragraphs. Introductory, concluding, and transitional paragraphs are especially designed to begin or end an essay or to provide links between major sections of a longer essay. Body paragraphs fall between the beginning and the end; they offer evidence and elaborate on key points.

Classification based on content and method of development applies mainly to body paragraphs. Under this system, classifications correspond to the principal methods of development—*descriptive, narrative, definitional, classificatory, analytical, comparative, illustrative,* and so on (see #2d). In many cases, however, a single paragraph might fall into multiple categories. Consider the following paragraph, which might appear in the essay on air travel proposed in #2d:

My trip to New York City brought home to me many of the inconveniences of air travel today.	**narrative opening**
When we arrived at the security gates before boarding the plane, we were required to undergo several lengthy and uncomfortable procedures. Passengers were asked to remove coats, belts, and shoes; they were required to dispose of all gels and liquids; and several adult passengers were subjected to invasive full-body computer scans.	**process analysis: the steps in the security process**
These measures put many of us passengers on edge and added a dose of nervousness to the boredom and claustrophobia long associated with cross-border flights.	**effect: immediate effects of security procedures**

 ## Paragraph Unity

An effective body paragraph ordinarily deals with one main idea; its singleness of purpose engages its readers by focusing their attention on that main idea. If a paragraph is disrupted by irrelevant digressions or unnecessary shifts in point of view or focus, readers will lose sight of the main idea. In short, a paragraph has unity when every sentence in it contributes to its purpose and nothing in it is irrelevant to that purpose.

Paragraph Coherence

Though a paragraph is unified because every sentence contributes to the development of its single theme or idea, it could still come apart if it doesn't have coherence. The principle of coherence applies similarly to individual paragraphs as it does to the essay as a whole: it depends on careful organization of ideas and the use of transitional devices that tie the ideas together.

7a Coherence Through Organization: Beginning, Middle, and Ending

A body paragraph has a *beginning*, a *middle*, and an *ending*. Good organization means rational order. Typically, the beginning introduces the main idea; the middle clearly and logically follows from and develops the statement of that idea, and the ending is a natural conclusion that unobtrusively closes the discussion.

1. The Beginning: Topic Sentences

Body paragraphs typically open with a statement of the main idea, called a **topic sentence**. A good topic sentence indicates what the paragraph will be about. It is, in effect, a promise that the rest of the paragraph fulfills. If the paragraph is part of a larger context, such as an essay, the topic sentence will usually perform two other functions:

1. It will refer to the topic of the essay and at least suggest the relation of the paragraph to that topic.
2. It will provide a transition so that the new paragraph flows smoothly from the preceding paragraph.

Since it has so much to do, a good topic sentence, even more than other sentences, should be efficient. Here is one that is not:

> The writer uses a great deal of imagery throughout the story.

The sentence indicates the topic—the story's imagery—but promises nothing more than to show that the story contains a lot of it. But offering a long list of images wouldn't develop an idea; it would merely illustrate what is self-evident. To refine the focus, the writer should say something about the function of the imagery. The following revision is much stronger:

> The story's imagery, most of it drawn from nature, helps to create the story's mood as well as its themes.

The revised topic sentence not only has more substance in itself but also suggests the approach the paragraph will take.

Here is another example of an inefficient topic sentence, taken from the same essay:

> In the second paragraph, the writer continues to use images.

Again, what is needed is something sharper, more specific, such as an assertion that provides a significant idea that can be usefully developed. For example,

> The imagery in the second paragraph contrasts vividly with that of the first.

or

> In the second paragraph, images of death begin the process that leads to the story's ironic conclusion.

A good topic sentence should be more than just a brief indication of what the paragraph will cover; it should be a significant part of the contents of the paragraph.

Note that a paragraph's topic, though single, may consist of more than one part. Further, it does not always need to be stated all in one sentence. In this paragraph, for example, it is not until the end of the second sentence that the topic becomes fully clear. It is not uncommon for a paragraph to have a second topic sentence, one that partly restates the topic and partly leads into the body of the paragraph.

WRITING TIP

On the Placement of Topic Sentences

As you start to develop your essay-writing skills, you should pay extra attention to beginning each body paragraph with a clear, direct topic sentence. When you become more comfortable with the essay-writing process, however, you may want to experiment with the placement of your topic sentences. Sometimes delaying a topic sentence can increase readers' interest by creating a little mystery. And stating a topic (or part of a topic) at the end of a paragraph takes advantage of that most emphatic position (see #8). Note, for example, the first paragraph in #7a.2, in which the first and final sentences work together to capture the main topic of the paragraph. And, rarely, if the focal idea is clear, an author may even choose not to include a topic sentence; this effect is most appropriate in narratives, where each paragraph clearly follows from what has come before it.

See also the notes on beginnings in #2j.

As you polish your essay, pay close attention to the formulation of your topic sentences. Remember that, when used effectively, they can help you achieve both unity and coherence not only in individual paragraphs but also in the essay as a whole (see #1a–b).

2. The Middle

A well-developed body paragraph fulfills the promise of its beginning. If, for example, you were writing a paragraph that began with the last example of a topic sentence above ("In the second paragraph, images of death begin the process that leads to the story's ironic conclusion."), you would have to explain the process and the irony of the story's conclusion, and you would have to show how images of death from the second paragraph set that process in motion. To fulfill your promise effectively, then, you would have to decide how to organize your material. For example, you might first describe the irony of the conclusion and then analyze the images to show how they lead to that conclusion. Or you might start by analyzing the death imagery and then proceed to answer some questions that you could ask yourself: What effect do the images create? How does that effect contribute to the way the story proceeds? How does that process lead to the conclusion? In other words, after considering the different possibilities, you would choose a way of presenting your material, and the order you choose to follow should be one that makes sense; one idea should lead logically to another until you reach your goal. Then your paragraph will be coherent.

Orderly development sometimes occurs automatically as one works through one's ideas in composing paragraphs. But most writers must give some conscious thought to how a particular paragraph can best be shaped. The most common patterns of development writers use to make their paragraphs orderly and coherent are the same as those commonly used to organize entire essays—*chronological, climactic, inverse pyramid, inductive, deductive, block, alternating,* and *spatial* (see #2g.2). Further, some methods of development (see #2d and #5) themselves impose patterns on the arrangement of ideas in a paragraph. Recall that these patterns and methods are not mutually exclusive. In addition to using narration and process analysis, which focus on chronological order, or description, with its focus on spatial order, one can move from cause to effect or from effect to cause, or from a statement about a whole to a division of it into parts (analysis), or from a statement about one thing to a comparison of it with another.

3. The Ending

As you compose and revise your drafts, the endings of your paragraphs will sometimes come naturally. But they are likely to do so only if, when you begin a paragraph, you know just where it is going. The final sentence of a paragraph, like all the others, should be a part of the whole. In other words, the final sentence of a paragraph will most often be a statement growing out of the substance of the paragraph, a sentence that rounds off its paragraph in a satisfying way.

If a paragraph doesn't seem to be ending naturally, you may have to stop and think consciously about it. Here are a few pointers to help you do that:

1. A good ending may point back to the beginning, but it will not merely repeat it; if it repeats something, it will do so in order to put it in the new light made possible by the development of the paragraph.
2. A good ending sentence doesn't usually begin with a stiff "In conclusion" or "To conclude." In fact, sometimes the best way to end a paragraph is simply to let it stop, once its point is made. A too-explicit conclusion might damage the effectiveness of an otherwise good paragraph that has a natural quality of closure at its end.
3. A good ending might have a slight stylistic shift that marks a paragraph's closing, perhaps no more than an unusually short or long sentence. Or an ending might be marked by an allusion or brief quotation, as long as it is relevant and to the point.
4. A good paragraph usually doesn't end with an indented ("block") quotation, or even a shorter full-sentence quotation that isn't set off. Even though you carefully introduce such a quotation, it will almost inevitably leave a feeling that you have abandoned your paragraph to someone else. Complete such a paragraph with at least a brief comment that explains the quotation, justifies it, or re-emphasizes its main thrust.

> **WRITING TIP**
>
> **On Positioning Transitional Material**
>
> It is sometimes possible, but often difficult, to provide forward-looking material at the end of a paragraph. Don't struggle to get something transitional into the last sentence of a paragraph. The work of transition should be done by the first sentence of the next paragraph. In other words, tampering with a paragraph's final sentence merely for transitional purposes may diminish that paragraph's integrity and effectiveness.

7b Structural Coherence

Careful organization and development go a long way toward achieving coherence. But you will sometimes need to use other techniques as well, providing links that ensure a smooth flow of thought from one sentence to another.

The main devices for structural coherence are parallelism, repetition, pronouns and demonstrative adjectives, and transitional words and phrases. Like the methods and patterns of development, these devices are not mutually exclusive: two or more may work together in the same paragraph.

1. Parallelism (see #28c and #40)

Parallel sentence structure is a simple and effective way to bind successive sentences. Similar structural patterns in clauses and phrases work like a call and its echo. But don't try to maintain a series of parallel elements for too long. If the echoes remain obvious, they will be too noticeable and will diminish in power as they get farther from the original. Parallelism, like any other device, should not be overdone.

2. Repetition

Like parallelism, repetition of words and phrases effectively links successive sentences. But the caution against overdoing it is most applicable here. Repetition properly controlled for rhetorical effect can be powerful (as in Martin Luther King's famous "I have a dream" speech), but repetition, especially on paper, can also give the impression of a writer's limited vocabulary or ingenuity. Structure your repetitions carefully; don't put too many too close together. And generally use the device sparingly.

3. Pronouns and Demonstrative Adjectives

As discussed in section #1b, pronouns and demonstrative adjectives contribute to coherence by building bridges between themselves and their antecedents or referents. As long as the antecedent is clear, these bridges provide the reader with a clear path from sentence to sentence within a paragraph.

4. Transitional Terms

Used strategically, transitional words and phrases can create coherence by establishing a logical flow from one sentence to the next. When adding a transitional term, make sure you choose the most suitable one. Here are some of the more common and useful transitional terms:

- terms showing addition of one point to another

also	and	another
besides	further	in addition
moreover		

- terms showing similarity between ideas

again	equally	in other words
in the same way	likewise	similarly

- terms showing difference between ideas

although	but	conversely
despite	even though	however
in contrast	in spite of	nevertheless
on the contrary	on the other hand	otherwise
still	though	whereas
yet		

7b

- terms showing cause and effect or other logical relations

as a result	because	consequently
for	hence	of course
since	then	therefore
thus		

- terms introducing examples or details

for example	for instance	in particular
namely	specifically	that is
to illustrate		

- terms expressing emphasis

chiefly	especially	indeed
mainly	more important	primarily

- terms showing relations in time and space

after	afterward	at the same time
before	behind	beyond
earlier	farther away	here
in the distance	in the meantime	later
meanwhile	nearby	next
simultaneously	subsequently	then
there	to the left	while

These and other such words and phrases, occurring usually at or near the beginnings of sentences, are the glue that helps hold paragraphs together. But if the paragraph isn't unified in its content, and if its parts haven't been arranged to fit with one another, then even these explicit transitional terms won't give much structural coherence to your writing.

WRITING TIP

On Avoiding Overuse of Transitions

Don't overuse transitional terms. If your paragraph already contains structural elements that make it coherent, it won't need any of these. Adding a transitional word or phrase to nearly every sentence will make writing stiff and mechanical sounding.

Exercise 7 Recognizing Coherence

Point out the various means by which coherence is established in the following paragraph, and comment on their effectiveness.

> The Mercers, as David French presents them in his play *Leaving Home*, are much like real families are: essentially good people struggling for understanding and trying not to kill each other. French shows the audience a family much more authentic than the people with pasted-on smiles in those 1950s billboards and magazine advertisements. They have tremendous difficulties at times and tremendous happiness at other times. The cozy walls of their home cannot shut out past history, unhappy memories, miscommunication, and feelings of alienation. Despite, or perhaps because of, their difficulties, they are heartbreakingly recognizable. The Mercer clan is the mid-twentieth-century Canadian family in all its contradictory glory—a force for both good and ill in the lives of its members.

8 Emphasis in Paragraphs

Just as in an entire essay, so in a paragraph the most emphatic position is its ending, and the second most emphatic position is its beginning. That is another reason the opening or topic sentence is such an important part of a paragraph. And an ending, because of its emphatic position, can make or break a paragraph.

But structure and diction are also important. Parallelism and repetition create emphasis. Independent clauses are more emphatic than subordinate clauses and phrases. Precise, concrete, and specific words are more emphatic than vague, abstract, and general ones. A long sentence will stand out among several shorter ones; a short sentence will stand out among longer ones. Keep these points in mind as you compose and revise your paragraphs; let emphasis contribute to the effectiveness of your writing.

9 Length of Paragraphs

There is no optimum length for a paragraph. The length of a paragraph will be determined by its particular function. In narration or dialogue, a single sentence or a single word may constitute a paragraph. In a complex exposition or argumentative essay, a paragraph may go on for a page or more—though such long paragraphs are rare in modern writing. Most body paragraphs consist of at least three or four sentences, and seldom more than nine or ten. Transitional paragraphs are usually short, often two or three sentences in length. Introductory and concluding paragraphs will be of various lengths, depending on the complexity of the material and on the techniques of beginning and ending that the writer is using.

9a Too Many Long Paragraphs

If you find that you are writing many long paragraphs, you may be over-developing, piling more into a paragraph than its topic requires. Or you may not be weeding out irrelevant material. Or you may be dealing in one paragraph with two or more topics that should be dealt with in separate paragraphs. Any of these tendencies can damage the coherence of your writing. Keep in mind that paragraphs are at least as much for readers as they are for writers. Generally, you should give your reader regular breaks to pause and consider your main claims and evidence, which means providing one or two paragraphs per page of your writing.

9b Too Many Short Paragraphs

If you find yourself writing many short paragraphs, you may not be adequately developing your main ideas. The body of a paragraph must be long enough to develop a topic satisfactorily. Merely restating or summarizing the topic is not enough. An excess of short paragraphs can also endanger coherence by splintering your discussion into small parts: when you revise, check to see if two or more related short paragraphs can be integrated to form one substantial paragraph. Generally, a body paragraph in a piece of academic writing should set out a claim and provide well-integrated evidence. It should also comment on and explain the significance of the evidence. This structure calls for several detailed sentences, not just two or three brief statements.

9c Variety

Try to ensure that any extended piece of writing you produce contains a variety of paragraph lengths: long, short, medium. The reader may become unengaged if the essay has a constant similarity of paragraph lengths. (The same is true of sentences of similar length: see #28a). You should also try to provide a variety of patterns and methods of development in your paragraphs. For example, parallelism, however admirable a device, would likely lose its effect if it were the basic pattern in several successive paragraphs.

Normally, then, the paragraphs that make up an extended piece of writing will vary in length. Ensure that each of your paragraphs is as long or as short as it needs to be to achieve its intended purpose. See also #1c.

10 Paragraph Review: A Sample Paragraph with Analysis

The paragraph that follows illustrates principles discussed in the preceding sections of this chapter. The writer has gone on to analyze her handling of the paragraph. Consider analyzing several paragraphs of your own writing in the same way to assess your strengths and weaknesses in this important aspect of writing.

> [1] Can child characters be heroic? [2] Some adult readers might argue that heroism is something beyond the reach of a child. [3] Such readers might add that children lack the experience, the knowledge, and the power required to separate themselves from the adult-dominated communities they know and to embark on the quest into the unsafe, unpredictable world identified with the hero's quest. [4] But consider characters as different as Lewis Carroll's Alice and Philip Pullman's Will Parry. [5] Alice quite happily chooses to enter the bizarre world of Carroll's *Through the Looking Glass*, and she holds her own in encounters with lions, twin boys, bad-tempered eggs, and transmogrifying monarchs. [6] Will Parry, for his part, leaves Oxford to seek his missing father and with Lyra Silvertongue as his companion, leads other children as well as adults through adventure, suffering, and turmoil to establish the Republic of Heaven on Earth.

The writer's analysis of this paragraph follows:

Function
- The paragraph is from the body of the essay.
- It deals with substantial ideas about child heroism in literature.

Methods of Development
- The principal method is argument.
- There is also an element of comparison in sentence 4.
- The writer gives examples to support the argument. See sentences 5 and 6.

Unity
- The paragraph focuses in each of its sentences on how child protagonists can be heroic.

Coherence and Emphasis
- The topic sentence of this paragraph is sentence 1.
- Sentence 1 starts with a question to engage the reader's attention.
- Sentence 2 picks up the key words *child* and *heroism*.

- Sentence 3 picks up the words *readers* and *children*.
- Sentence 4 starts with a strong coordinating conjunction (*but*) that indicates a reversal in thought.
- Sentences 5 and 6 follow parallel structure in content and form.

Length and Development

- With six sentences, the paragraph can be said to be of average length.
- Its development is sufficient for its purpose.

Review Exercises 5–10 Working with Paragraphs

A. Compose topic sentences that will effectively begin paragraphs for *five* of the following:

1. to explain to a ten-year-old how to make a bacon, lettuce, and tomato sandwich
2. to describe an encounter with a panhandler
3. to tell a friend about your experience of seeing an accident happen
4. to introduce an essay on the history of clocks
5. to recount an anecdote about one of your relatives in order to illustrate his or her character
6. to describe your dream house
7. to analyze a particular article you recently read in a newspaper
8. to introduce an essay on the role of fast food in our culture
9. to introduce a short essay about something important you learned when you failed at something
10. to explain what *Canadian* means to you

B. Write separate paragraphs developing two of the topic sentences you composed for part A.

C. Analyze the paragraphs you have written in part B by doing the following exercises:

1. Identify and illustrate the methods of development you used in writing each paragraph.
2. Identify how you ensured that your paragraphs are unified.
3. Identify and illustrate the techniques you used to make your paragraphs coherent.
4. Identify what you intended to achieve with your final sentence for each paragraph.

D. Analyze and evaluate the following body paragraphs. You may also wish to rank them from most to least effective. Consider specifically the principles of unity, coherence, and emphasis, and identify any methods of development at work in the paragraphs.

1. Physical activity is good for people. It contributes greatly to a person's physical and mental well-being. The schedules of varsity teams are very demanding. The swim team has eleven practices a week, of which eight are mandatory—two a day, each an hour and a half in length. The workouts consist of approximately four thousand metres each. The program also consists of running, weight training, and flexibility exercises. Not only does this sort of exercise keep a person in good physical shape, but it also increases mental awareness. Because you are up and active before classes begin, you are more mentally and physically awake than if you had just gotten out of bed.

2. Although some people, like the members of my family, find it a mystery, doing laundry involves only three simple steps. First, different-coloured clothes take different temperatures of water: so put the darks in cold water, the whites in hot water, and the others in warm water. Secondly, you need to tell the machine whether your load is supposed to be cold or hot, so adjust the dial accordingly and put in your detergent. Last but not least, when the cycle is finished, throw your clothes in the dryer, but be careful not to dry them at such a high heat that your favourite cotton sweater becomes your spaniel's favourite jacket.

3. "A home should be a sail not an anchor," so the saying goes. A home should provide inspiration for creativity whether this source for creativity lies in an astounding view or in beautiful and meaningful objects. A home should encourage you to look outward as well as inward.

4. The storyteller makes use of animal metaphors to describe an individual's character by naming him after the animal whose stereotyped personality he possesses. The importance of living creatures in folk tales is twofold. First, the folk tale is used to teach the tribe's children the significance of individual species; and second, the use of animal names suggests a great deal about a character's personality.

5. I am attending university so that I can learn more about myself and the world. So far I have learned that I, like Hamlet, am a procrastinator. And that the world encompasses grades, caffeine, and a few dear kindred spirits.

6. The intertidal fauna in general and specifically tide-pool fauna can act as model systems for population studies (Raffaelli & Hawkins 1996, Johnson 2000). For intertidal organisms, the tidal cycle constitutes a major environmental disturbance, and tidal effects will be especially pronounced for protozoa, which are often abundant in tide pools (Scherren 1900, Fauré-Fremiet 1953). Furthermore, as protozoan generation times are on the order of hours to days, they are useful model-organisms to investigate population dynamics, the effects of disturbance, and cyclic behaviours (e.g., Gause 1934, Holyoak 2000). By recognizing the behaviour and distribution of these organisms, we can provide key information about survival strategies of tide-pool fauna and offer insight into general phenomena concerning the dynamics of populations and metapopulations. This study, thus, focuses on how one protozoan survives in tide pools; in doing so we indicate the occurrence of both general and unique adaptations to a high-disturbance environment.

7. Although the words *ignorance* and *stupidity* are often used interchangeably, there is a difference between them. *Ignorance* is defined as lack of knowledge and *stupidity* is defined as lack of intelligence. To call a person ignorant implies that the person does not know all that is known or can be learned. To call a person stupid implies that the person lacks the ability to learn and know. The words are similar in that they both indicate a deficiency in knowledge or learning, but they differ in that one signifies a permanent condition and the other a condition that may be only temporary. Ignorant people can educate and inform themselves. Stupid people have a dullness of mind that it is difficult or impossible to change.

8. I believe that Jean Piaget's research has clearly shown that games and rule-making contribute to child development. Children learn much about autonomy and democracy while testing the rules of games. In his early research, Piaget chose 1100 children along with the game of marbles to reach his conclusion. The choice of the game of marbles was a good one since it requires no referee and no adult supervision. It is played from early childhood to the pre-teen years. One six-year-old, when asked who he thought had made the rules, replied, "God, my father, and the town council." At about eleven years old, children agree that they can change the rules themselves. Piaget has shown that

the game of marbles provides a way for children to test the quality of rules and the necessity of rules.

9. If beauty is in the eye of the beholder, can the blind experience beauty? Of course. Although, in our ignorance, we sighted people often assume that beauty is purely a visual concept, in truth, beauty can be defined as anything that restores our souls or at least reminds us that we have souls.

10. Everything looks beautiful from the saddle of my horse, especially on a crisp fall day. The autumn sun glints through the fretwork of golden poplar trees that border the road. The track ahead is muddy and well-trampled by many horses' feet. I can hear the clatter of hooves on the concrete, then the soft sucking sound of the mud as we gain momentum and move out to begin our ride. After we gain considerable speed, it happens. That wondrous sensation when horse and rider become one glorious moving body. I feel it now as my horse takes full rein while the blood surges and pounds in my ears and the wind frees my hair as it stings my face. Time ceases to exist here in a world of exhilarating revelation as I become giddy with excitement. Tired, my horse slows down. The spell is broken. The sun has disappeared completely, and the wind is beginning to rise in bone-chilling forecast of the dreary winter days to come. I will be back again, soon.

II

Understanding Sentences

Introduction: The Conventions of Language

Introduction: The Conventions of Language

Words are the building blocks we use to put together language structures that enable us to communicate. Combinations of words produce sentences; combinations of sentences produce paragraphs; combinations of paragraphs can form stories, detailed expositions, descriptions, summaries, and arguments.

When we write, we represent speech sounds with symbols called letters, which combine to form the units called words. Those who share a familiarity with a particular language are able to communicate because each person knows the meaning of the sounds. If you said "Look" when you meant "Listen," you would fail to communicate. The success of the process depends upon the **conventions**, the shared acceptance of what particular words mean.

Putting words together to make sentences is also subject to conventions. We use particular word orders and other standard ways of showing how words are related to each other; and since writing represents speech, we use certain visual devices to help clarify meaning and make communication easier. The conventions governing the arrangement of words and the relations between them constitute the **grammar** of a language. The techniques that help us "hear" writing as something like speaking constitute the conventions of **punctuation**.

The next four chapters of this book describe and illustrate these conventions of language and ways of avoiding errors in their use. Although on occasion we use terms like "rules" and "right" and "wrong," try to think of yourself as studying not the "rules" of grammar and punctuation but their conventions; and think not in terms of what is "right" or "correct" but in terms of what is conventional—that is, mutually agreed upon, and therefore understandable, and therefore effective.

Grammar

The term *grammar* is virtually equivalent to the term *syntax*, which refers to the relations among words and the order of words in individual sentences. Chapters II through V are about sentences, the primary units of communication: how they work, what goes into them, what their varieties are, how their parts are arranged, and how they are punctuated. You may be able to write fairly well without knowing much about these grammatical principles. But if you have any difficulties writing correct and effective sentences, you'll find it much easier to overcome them if you know how sentences work. And you'll find an understanding of sentence grammar especially helpful in improving the effectiveness of your punctuation.

Don't be intimidated by the thought that you're studying "grammar." After all, if you can read and understand these sentences, you already know a great deal of grammar; chances are you absorbed it, unconsciously, as part of everyday life. Now you need only raise some of that understanding into consciousness so that you can use it to help you stick to the conventions and make your writing more effective. You may often be able to trust your intuitive grasp of the way English words and sentences work; but if you find yourself having trouble, especially if you are multilingual and English isn't your first language, you may want to consult the principles more often and apply them more consciously.

We use the vocabulary of traditional grammar both because it has, for many, the virtue of simplicity and familiarity and because it is usually the vocabulary used to study another language. It is also the vocabulary used by dictionaries and other reference books in their definitions and discussions of usage. Learning these terms shouldn't be difficult. If you find the going rough, you may be making it unnecessarily hard for yourself; if you fight the material, it may well fight back. But if you approach it with interest and a desire to learn, you'll find that it will cooperate and that the quality of your writing will improve as you increase your mastery of the conventions. Further, you will not only be learning to follow "rules" in order to produce "correct" sentences but also be learning how to choose one form or usage or order rather than another. Good writing is often a result of being able to make intelligent choices from the alternatives available to you.

This chapter introduces the basic elements and patterns of English sentences and defines and classifies different kinds of sentences. Awareness of these patterns and an ability to recognize phrases and clauses will increase your understanding of sentence grammar.

Sentence Patterns and Conventions

All sentences have a purpose, namely to communicate ideas and/or feelings. And there are conventional ways to convey these ideas and feelings. For example, if your friend tells you,

> I am writing a report on colony collapse disorder.

you know that the sentence is stating a fact, or a supposed fact. If your friend then says,

> Are you familiar with this phenomenon?

you know that you are being asked a question and that you are expected to give an answer. If your friend then says,

> Give me your opinion of my report proposal.

you know you are being asked to do something, being given a mild command. And when your friend says,

> What an ambitious proposal!

you know you are hearing an emphatic expression of strong feeling.

We know how to interpret these different kinds of utterances because we understand and accept the *conventions* of the way sentences communicate. Sentences are classified according to the kind of purpose each has. Sentences that *make statements of fact or supposed fact* are **declarative**:

> Iqaluit is the capital of Nunavut.
>
> This seminar deals with the effects of massive open online courses.
>
> I have heard that *Anne of Green Gables* is tremendously popular in Japan.

Sentences that *ask questions* are **interrogative**; in speech, they often (but not always) end with a rise in the pitch of one's voice; in writing, they end with a **question mark**:

> Do you have that flashlight app on your phone?
>
> Are you going to the concert?
>
> Why? What's the reason?

Sentences that *give commands* or *make requests*, that expect action or compliance, are **imperative**:

> Please print the document.
>
> Don't forget to file your income tax return.
>
> Edit your work carefully before submitting it.

Sentences that *exclaim*, that express strong feeling with vigour or emphasis, are called **exclamatory**; they customarily end with an **exclamation point**:

> That was an unforgettable race!
>
> Not if I can help it!
>
> Amazing!

Like many other traditional categories, however, the ones we've described aren't always so simple or obvious. For example, a sentence may include both *interrogative* and *declarative* elements:

> "What's the speed limit on this street?" the driver asked.

or contain both *imperative* and *declarative* elements:

> Please slow down: You are going too fast.

or be both *imperative* and *exclamatory*:

> Slow down!

And many *imperative* sentences, especially those that make requests, are at least implicitly *interrogative* even though they don't end with a question mark:

> Please forward this message. (Will you please forward
>   this message?)

Sometimes the same basic sense can be expressed in all four ways:

> I need your help.

> Will you help me?

> Help me with this.

> Help!

Nevertheless, you're seldom in doubt about the purpose of sentences you hear, read, speak, or write. Your awareness of the *conventions* guides you. When you try to express your thoughts to others, you know almost instinctively how to frame a sentence to make it do what you want.

But a more conscious grasp of the way sentences work will help you frame them even more effectively. It will help you when you're in doubt. And it will help you not only to avoid weaknesses and errors but also to revise and correct them when they do occur.

Since most sentences in written and academic discourse are *declarative*, their patterns are the ones you need to understand first. Most of the rest of this chapter, then, deals with the basic elements and patterns of declarative sentences. (See #25 and #26 for an expanded discussion of basic sentence elements and their modifiers.)

11a Subject and Predicate, Noun and Verb

A standard declarative sentence consists of two parts: a **subject** and a **predicate**. The subject is what acts or is talked about; the predicate is what the subject does or what is said about it. For example:

Subject	Predicate
Grass	grows.
Birds	fly.
I	disagree.

The essential element of the subject part of a sentence is a **noun** (*grass, birds*) or a **pronoun** (*I*) (see #13 and #14); the essential element of the predicate part of a sentence is a **verb** (*grows, fly, disagree*) (see #17).

11b

Exercise 11a Subject and Predicate

Compose five two-word sentences similar to those in the example above. Each will need a single-word noun or a pronoun as its subject and a single-word verb as its predicate.

11b Articles and Other Modifiers

Few sentences consist of only a one-word subject and a one-word predicate. Frequently, for example, nouns are preceded by articles (*a, an, the*) (see #19c):

Subject	Predicate
The child	smiled.

And both subject and predicate often include **modifiers**, words that change or limit the meaning of nouns and verbs. Nouns are modified by **adjectives** (see #19):

Subject	Predicate
The young child	smiled.
A caged bird	will sing.

Verbs are modified by **adverbs** (see #20):

Subject	Predicate
The young child	smiled triumphantly.
The bird	flew south.

Exercise 11b Articles, Adjectives, and Adverbs in Sentences

Rewrite the sentences you wrote for exercise 11a, adding articles and single-word adjectives and adverbs to them as you think appropriate.

11c–k Basic Sentence Patterns

Such single-word modifiers as those in the example above account for only part of the richness of many sentences, which may feature impressive arrays of modifying phrases and clauses (see, for example, the sentences discussed in #26). Yet complicated as they may seem, almost all English sentences use only a few basic patterns, or combinations of them. If you can recognize and understand the sentence patterns indicated in the chart below and elaborated on in the following pages, you will be well on your way to being able to analyze any sentences you write or read.

Sentence Pattern	Description
1	Subject + Verb
2A	Subject + Verb + Direct Object
2B (Passive Voice)	Subject + Passive Voice Verb
3	Subject + Verb + Indirect Object + Direct Object
4A	Subject + Linking Verb + Subjective Complement (Predicate Adjective)
4B	Subject + Linking Verb + Subjective Complement (Predicate Noun)
5A	Subject + Verb + Direct Object + Objective Complement (Adjective)
5B	Subject + Verb + Direct Object + Objective Complement (Noun)
6 (Expletive)	*There* or *It* + Linking Verb (+ Complement) + Subject

11c Sentence Pattern 1

SUBJECT + VERB

This is the pattern you've already looked at and imitated. The subject, consisting of a noun (with its modifiers) or a pronoun, is followed by the predicate, consisting of a verb (with its modifiers):

Subject	Predicate
Birds	fly.
The yellow birds	flew quickly.
These large, ungainly birds	can fly quite gracefully.
They	soar majestically.

Exercise 11c Sentence Pattern 1

Return to the sentences you wrote for exercise 11b, or compose new ones, this time adding a few more modifiers to some of the nouns and verbs.

11d Sentence Pattern 2A

SUBJECT + VERB + DIRECT OBJECT

In this pattern we expand the basic sentence core by adding a **direct object** to the predicate. A direct object, like a subject, must be either a noun or a pronoun, and the verb must be transitive—that is, it must be able to take a direct object (see #17a):

Subject	Predicate	
Noun or Pronoun	Transitive Verb	Direct Object
I	paint	urban landscapes.
Sandra	enjoys	opera.
It	intrigues	him.
Bahaar	is writing	poems.
Impatient journalists	pursue	tight-lipped celebrities.

In this pattern the subject acts, the verb indicates the action, and the direct object is the product (*landscapes, poems*) or the receiver (*opera, him, celebrities*) of the action. Note that direct objects can, like subject-nouns, be modified by adjectives (*urban, tight-lipped*).

Exercise 11d Sentence Pattern 2A

Compose five sentences following Pattern 2A, some with modifiers and some without.

11e Sentence Pattern 2B (Passive Voice)

SUBJECT (receiver of the action) + PASSIVE VOICE VERB
(+ *by* phrase: agent/performer of the action)

In this pattern the order of the main elements of Pattern 2A is reversed. That is, the former direct object becomes the subject, and the former subject moves to the end of the sentence, after the **preposition** *by* (see #22).

The verb stays in the middle but changes to the passive voice—a form of the verb *be* followed by a **past participle** (see #21d). Use the passive voice strategically—that is, when you want to emphasize the receiver rather than the performer of an action. Make your choice knowing that overuse of the passive can sometimes make writing wordy and unclear. Consider a crime scenario in which a detective might say, using Pattern 2A,

11e

Poison killed him. (active voice)

But in the circumstances it would be more natural to say

He was killed by poison. (passive voice)

Similarly, you can easily transform most sentences in the Pattern 2A category into passive constructions:

Subject	Predicate	
Noun or Pronoun	Verb	Prepositional Phrase
Urban landscapes	are painted	by me.
Opera	is enjoyed	by Sandra.
He	is intrigued	by it.
Poems	are written	by Bahaar.
Tight-lipped celebrities	are pursued	by impatient journalists.

But you can see that such alternatives would be preferable only in unusual circumstances—for example, if you want special emphasis on the product or receiver of the action. Note that in this pattern the *by* phrase is often omitted as unnecessary or unknown:

He has been poisoned (by someone).

See also #17o–p and #29f.

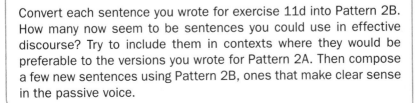

Exercise 11e Sentence Pattern 2B

Convert each sentence you wrote for exercise 11d into Pattern 2B. How many now seem to be sentences you could use in effective discourse? Try to include them in contexts where they would be preferable to the versions you wrote for Pattern 2A. Then compose a few new sentences using Pattern 2B, ones that make clear sense in the passive voice.

11f Sentence Pattern 3

SUBJECT + VERB + INDIRECT OBJECT + DIRECT OBJECT

A sentence with a direct object sometimes also includes an **indirect object**. An indirect object is a noun or pronoun referring to an animate being and identifying the recipient of an action—that is, the person or other living creature to whom or for whom an action occurs.

Subject	Predicate		
Noun or Pronoun	Transitive Verb	Indirect Object	Direct Object
He	sent	his adviser	an email.
Grace	bought	Ari	a new watch.
Rishad	offered	his guests	sushi.

Note that you can usually vary this pattern, and still say essentially the same thing, by changing the indirect object to a prepositional phrase that comes after the direct object:

Subject	Predicate		
Noun or Pronoun	Transitive Verb	Direct Object	Prepositional Phrase
He	sent	an email	to his adviser.
Grace	bought	a new watch	for Ari.
Rishad	offered	sushi	to his guests.

Exercise 11f Sentence Pattern 3

Compose five sentences in Pattern 3. Then rewrite two of them using a prepositional phrase, with *to* or *for*, instead of an indirect object.

11g Sentence Pattern 4A

SUBJECT + LINKING VERB + SUBJECTIVE COMPLEMENT
(predicate adjective)

Some verbs—called **linking verbs** (see #17a)—require something other than an object to complete the idea, something called a **complement**. And since the complement is linked to the subject, it is sometimes called a **subjective complement**. The principal linking verb is *be* in its various forms (see #17f). In Pattern 4A, the verb links the subject with an adjectival modifier in the predicate part of the sentence; the modifier is therefore called a **predicate adjective**:

Subject	Predicate	
Noun or Pronoun	Linking Verb	Subjective Complement (Predicate Adjective)
She	is	curious.
Cellphones	have become	indispensable.
That	smells	awful.

11i

Exercise 11g Sentence Pattern 4A

Compose three sentences following Pattern 4A.

11h Sentence Pattern 4B

SUBJECT + LINKING VERB + SUBJECTIVE COMPLEMENT (predicate noun)

In Pattern 4B, a verb links the subject with a noun or pronoun acting as a subjective complement and called a **predicate noun**:

Subject	Predicate	
Noun or Pronoun	Linking Verb	Subjective Complement (Predicate Noun)
This	is	it.
Annabel Lyon	is	a talented writer.
Raw vegetables	make	healthy snacks.

Exercise 11h Sentence Pattern 4B

Compose three sentences following Pattern 4B.

11i Sentence Pattern 5A

SUBJECT + VERB + DIRECT OBJECT + OBJECTIVE COMPLEMENT (adjective)

Such verbs as *appoint, believe, call, consider, declare, designate, elect, find, judge, make, name, nominate, select,* and *think* are sometimes followed by a direct object and an **objective complement**—a complement describing the object rather than the subject. In Pattern 5A, as in Pattern 4A, the complement is an *adjective*:

Subject	Predicate		
Noun or Pronoun	Transitive Verb	Direct Object	Objective Complement (Adjective)
The committee	declares	the building	unsafe.
The jury	found	them	guilty as charged.
They	made	themselves	comfortable.

Exercise 11i Sentence Pattern 5A

Compose three sentences following Pattern 5A.

11j Sentence Pattern 5B

SUBJECT + VERB + DIRECT OBJECT + OBJECTIVE COMPLEMENT (noun)

In this variation, the objective complement that completes the meaning of the direct object is a *noun*:

Subject	Predicate		
Noun or Pronoun	Transitive Verb	Direct Object	Objective Complement (Noun)
The party	named	her	interim leader.
Jamal	considers	sports	a distraction.
We	judged	the dinner	a success.

Exercise 11j Sentence Pattern 5B

Compose three sentences following Pattern 5B.

11k Sentence Pattern 6 (Expletive)

THERE OR IT + LINKING VERB (+ complement) + SUBJECT

The **expletive** pattern, like Pattern 2B, is something that you should use judiciously. In expletive sentences the word *There* or *It* appears at the beginning, in the place usually occupied by the subject; then comes a linking verb, usually a form of the verb *be*; and then comes the subject. When used strategically, *There* and *It* enable you to make certain kinds of statements in a more natural way or with a different emphasis than you could otherwise. For example, instead of having to say

Subject	Predicate
That life begins at forty	may be true.
No solutions	existed.
No plumbing	was in the cabin.

you can, using Pattern 6, say

Expletive	Linking Verb	Complement	Subject
It	may be	true	that life begins at forty.
There	were		no solutions.
There	was		no plumbing in the cabin.

Here are some further examples of Pattern 6:

There were several protesters waiting to heckle the premier.

It is easy to follow this recipe.

It is challenging to study Sanskrit.

There wasn't a cloud in the sky.

See also #18e, #29f, and #71a.

Exercise 11k (1) Sentence Pattern 6

Try converting the four examples above into a different pattern (e.g., *Several protesters were waiting to heckle the premier*). In what kinds of contexts might the alternative—and more direct—versions be preferable?

Exercise 11k (2) Sentence Pattern 6

Convert the following sentences into Pattern 6:

1. Ten mugs of hot tea are on the table.
2. No way around the obstacle exists.
3. To look directly at a solar eclipse is dangerous.
4. A magnificent celebration occurred.
5. People were everywhere!
6. Waiter, a fly is in my soup.

Do some seem better in the expletive form? Why? How might context determine one's choice?

11m–r

Exercise 11c–k Identifying Sentence
Elements and Patterns

Identify the pattern of each of the following sentences. Label each
subject-noun or subject-pronoun *s* and each predicate-verb *v*. Then
label each direct object *DO*, each indirect object *IO*, each subjective
complement *SC*, and each objective complement *OC*. If you wish,
also label any articles and other modifiers.

1. I love quinoa.
2. Nutritious food nourishes.
3. Some people are superstitious.
4. Bruce finds gardening relaxing.
5. Poor Jo was hit by lightning.
6. There are nine modules in our oceanography course.
7. Jacques brought me luck.
8. The Schmidts are excellent photographers.
9. The authors dedicated their book to their fans.
10. He declared himself fit as a fiddle.
11. Certain music can affect one's emotions.
12. The group elected Wareesha spokesperson.
13. All of these sauces taste too spicy.
14. It is not wise to go hiking alone.
15. The topic of the presentation was identified by the instructor
    and her assistant.

11-l Other Elements: Structure Words

Most declarative sentences use one or more of the above patterns. And
the elements in those patterns—subjects, verbs, modifiers, objects, and
complements—make up the substance of all sentences.

Many sentences also include words like *and*, *but*, *for*, *of*, *under*, and *with*.
Such words are important because they connect other elements in various
ways that establish meaningful relations between them. Such words are
sometimes called **structure words** or **function words**; most of them
belong to two other classes of words, or "parts of speech," **conjunctions**
(see #23) and **prepositions** (see #22). All of these elements are discussed
and illustrated at greater length in chapters III and IV.

11m–r Clauses and Phrases

Before you go on to chapter III, you need to understand the differences
between **clauses** and **phrases** and how they work in sentences. Clauses
and phrases are groups of words that function as grammatical units or

elements *within* sentences but that—except for independent clauses—cannot stand alone *as* sentences.

11m Independent (Main) Clauses

A clause is a group of words containing both a *subject* and a *predicate*. If it is an **independent clause**, it can, as the term indicates, stand by itself as a sentence. Each of the sample sentences in the preceding sections is an independent clause, since each contains the minimum requirement: a noun or pronoun as subject and a verb functioning in the predicate; each is a **simple sentence** (see #12c.1).

But an independent clause can also function as only part of a sentence. For example, if you start with two separate independent clauses—that is, two simple sentences:

> The exam ended.

> The students submitted their papers.

you can combine them to form a **compound sentence** (see #12c.2):

> The exam ended; the students submitted their papers.

> The exam ended, and the students submitted their papers.

> The exam ended; therefore, the students submitted their papers.

Each of the two halves of these sentences is an independent clause; each could stand alone as a sentence.

11n Subordinate (Dependent) Clauses

A **subordinate clause**, unlike an independent clause, usually cannot stand by itself. Even though, as a clause, it contains a subject and a predicate, it is by definition *subordinate, dependent* on another clause—an *independent* one—for its meaning. It therefore must be treated as only part of a sentence, as in the following examples (the subordinate clauses are underlined); these are called **complex sentences** (see #12c.3):

> When the exam ended, the students submitted their papers.

> The students submitted their papers as the exam ended.

> The students submitted the papers that they had written during the exam.

> The exam ended, which meant that the students had to submit their papers.

Note that subordinate clauses often begin with such words as *when, as, that,* and *which,* called **subordinators,** which often clearly signal the presence of a subordinate clause as opposed to an independent clause (see #23c).

Note that subordinate clauses can be used separately, for example in dialogue or as answers to questions, where the context is clear: Why did the students submit their papers? *Because the exam had ended.* Except in such circumstances, a subordinate clause should not stand by itself as if it were a sentence. See #12a and #12b.

11-o Functions of Subordinate Clauses

Like a phrase (see below), a subordinate clause functions as a grammatical unit in its sentence. That is, a subordinate clause can occupy several of the slots in the sentence patterns illustrated just above. For example, a **noun clause** can serve as the subject of a sentence:

> That free speech matters is evident. Pattern 4A

as a direct object:

> Azin knows what she is doing. Pattern 2A

or as a predicate noun:

> The question is what we should do next. Pattern 4B

Adjectival clauses (also called **relative clauses**; see #14d) modify nouns or pronouns, such as a direct object:

> She left her teacher a note that explained her absence. Pattern 3

or a subject:

> The critic who wrote the article confused the facts. Pattern 2A

Adverbial clauses usually modify main verbs:

> We left because we were bored. Pattern 1

11p Phrases

A **phrase** is a group of words lacking a subject and/or predicate but functioning as a grammatical unit within a sentence. For example, a **verb phrase** (see #17e) acts as the verb in this Pattern 1 sentence:

> Most of the wedding guests will be arriving in the morning.

11p

A **prepositional phrase** (see #22) can be an adjectival modifier:

> Most of the wedding guests will be arriving in the morning.

or an adverbial modifier:

> Most of the wedding guests will be arriving in the morning.

11p

The words *Most of the wedding guests* constitute a **noun phrase** functioning as the subject of the sentence. Any noun or pronoun along with its modifiers—so long as the group doesn't contain a subject–predicate combination—can be thought of as a noun phrase. Similarly, a **gerund phrase** (see #21f) can function as a subject:

> Bungee jumping can be risky. | Pattern 4A |

or as a direct object:

> She tried bungee jumping. | Pattern 2A |

A **participial phrase**—always adjectival (see #21d)—can modify a subject:

> Trusting her instincts, Ash gave the candidate her support.
> | Pattern 3 |

or a direct object:

> I am reading an article discussing human cloning. | Pattern 2A |

An **infinitive phrase** (see #21a) can function as a direct object (noun):

> This organization wants to eradicate poverty. | Pattern 2A |

or as a subject (noun):

> It may be impossible to eradicate poverty. | Pattern 6 |

It can also function as an adjective, for example one modifying the subject:

> Their desire to eradicate poverty is idealistic. | Pattern 4A |

or it can function as an adverb, for example one modifying the verb:

> They arranged the agenda to highlight the anti-poverty campaign. | Pattern 2A |

Adverbial infinitive phrases can also act as **sentence modifiers** (see #20a and #20d.4), modifying not the verb or any other single word but rather all the rest of the sentence:

> To be honest, the meeting wasn't very informative.

> To tell the truth, the potatoes were overcooked.

11q

Exercise 11m–p Recognizing Phrases and Clauses

Indicate whether each of the following groups of words is an independent clause, a subordinate clause, or a phrase. Label the subject (*s*) and verb (*v*) of each clause. In the case of a subordinate clause, circle the subordinator.

1. after the conference was over _____
2. his bubble burst _____
3. since no one was paying attention _____
4. down the hall from my office _____
5. but interest rates are rising _____
6. while looking for his cellphone _____
7. not only BC but PEI as well _____
8. rarely have we witnessed such a performance _____
9. for the first time in her life she was speechless _____
10. according to the overly complicated directions in the guidebook _____

11q Appositives

An **appositive** is a word or group of words that renames or restates, in other terms, the meaning of a neighbouring word. For example, if you start with two simple sentences,

> Marc is our lawyer. He looks after our business dealings.

you can turn the first into an appositive by reducing it and combining it with the second:

> Marc, our lawyer, looks after our business dealings.

The noun phrase *our lawyer* is here said to be in apposition to *Marc*.

Most appositives are nouns or noun phrases that redefine, usually in more specific terms, the nouns they follow. But occasionally an appositive precedes the other noun:

> A skilful lawyer, Marc looks after our business dealings.

And occasionally another part of speech can function as an appositive, for example a participial (adjectival) phrase:

> Searching frantically, tossing books and papers everywhere, they failed to find the missing passport.

or a verb phrase:

> Document (provide details of your sources for) this argument.

An appositive can also be a single word, often a name:

> Our lawyer, Marc, looks after our business dealings.

And, rarely, even a subordinate clause can function as an appositive:

> How she travelled—whether she journeyed alone or not— remains a mystery.

Note that an appositive is grammatically equivalent to the term it defines and could replace it in the sentence:

> Our lawyer looks after our business dealings.

> A skilful lawyer looks after our business dealings.

> Tossing books and papers everywhere, they failed to find the missing passport.

> Provide details of your sources for this argument.

> Marc looks after our business dealings.

> Whether she journeyed alone or not remains a mystery.

(For the punctuation of appositives, see #48b and #55g.)

Exercise 11q Using Appositives

Combine each of the following pairs of sentences into a single sentence by reducing one of each pair to an appositive phrase. You may drop some words and rearrange or adjust others, but don't change the basic meaning. For practice, try to write some sentences in more than one way. In each case, identify the appositive phrase you have created by underlining it.

Example: Emily Haines is one of the founding members of the band Metric. She grew up in Peterborough, Ontario.

(a) Emily Haines, <u>one of the founding members of the band Metric</u>, grew up in Peterborough, Ontario.

(b) One of the founding members of the band Metric, <u>Emily Haines</u>, grew up in Peterborough, Ontario.

(c) <u>One of the founding members of the band Metric</u>, Emily Haines grew up in Peterborough, Ontario.

1. Gabrielle is an amateur astronomer. She uses her telescope to scan the skies every night.

2. I always look forward to April. It is the month when the cherry blossoms appear.

3. My grandfather believes in hard work. He tends to his vegetable garden for hours every day.

4. Hong Kong is one of Asia's busiest ports. It is a major commercial centre.

5. The book I read last weekend was *A Dance with Dragons*. It is the fifth volume of George R. R. Martin's *A Song of Ice and Fire* series.

6. Team sports more than occupy her spare time. She plays volleyball, field hockey, and soccer.

7. Tyler was relaxed and confident when he began the competition. He was sure he could win.

8. You can save time by preparing carefully. That is, you can take careful notes and draft a clear plan for your argument.

9. To become a fine architect is not easy. It takes many years of study and apprenticeship.

10. The word *hamburger* is familiar to most Canadians. It comes from the name of a German city.

11r Absolute Phrases

An absolute phrase has no direct grammatical link with what it modifies; it depends simply on juxtaposition, in effect modifying the rest of the sentence by hovering over it like an umbrella. Most absolute phrases amount to a sentence with the verb changed to a participle (see #21d). Instead of using two sentences,

11r

> The website had crashed. She could not access her account.

you can reduce the first to an absolute phrase modifying the second:

> The website having crashed, she could not access her account.

If the original verb is a form of *be*, the participle can sometimes be omitted:

> The thunderstorm (being) over, the tennis match resumed.

Sometimes, especially with certain common expressions, the participle isn't preceded by a noun:

> There were a few rough spots, but generally speaking the rehearsal was a success.

> Judging by the population statistics, we have become a culturally diverse nation.

And sometimes infinitive phrases (see #11p and #21a) function as absolutes:

> To say the least, the campaign was not a success.

You can also think of many absolutes as *with* phrases from which the preposition has been dropped:

> (With) the thunderstorm over, the tennis match resumed.

> Careful measurement is a must, (with) the results dependent on this kind of due attention.

And you can think of most absolute phrases as functioning much like an adverb modifying the rest of the sentence (see #20a and #20d.4):

> *absolute*: All things considered, it was a fair exam.

> *adverb*: Unfortunately, I hadn't studied hard enough.

See also #21i.

Exercise 11r Using Absolute Phrases

Combine each of the following pairs of sentences by reducing one of each pair to an absolute phrase. Remember that if the participle is a form of *be*, it can sometimes be omitted.

> Example: **Everyone present agreed. The motion passed unanimously.**
>
> Everyone present agreeing, the motion passed unanimously.
>
> **Dinner was over and the dishes were washed. The family sat down to watch a movie on television.**
>
> Dinner (being) over and the dishes (being) washed, the family sat down to watch a movie on television.

1. The toddler was very sleepy. Her father carried her upstairs to her bedroom.
2. His nose was running and his eyes were watering. He stopped chopping the onions.
3. The lights flickered, and the computer buzzed. The 100-page report disappeared from the screen.
4. The day was breezy yet warm. They decided to take their golden retriever for a walk in the park.
5. Extra money was hard to come by. He was forced to put aside his plans for a cross-country vacation.

11s Order of Elements in Declarative Sentences

Even if you didn't know the names of some of the bits and pieces, chances are that the samples presented earlier in this section to illustrate the basic sentence patterns felt natural to you; they're the familiar kinds of sentences you use every day without even thinking about their structure. Note that the natural order of the elements in almost all the patterns is the same:

> subject–verb
> subject–transitive verb–object(s)–(objective complement)
> subject–linking verb–subjective complement

The only exception is Pattern 6, the expletive, in which the subject follows the verb (see #11k).

This conventional order of *subject–verb–object or –complement* has proven itself the most direct and forceful pattern of expression:

> War is hell.
> Humpty Dumpty had a great fall.
> We shall defend every village, every town, and every city.

But this order can be altered to create special stylistic effects or special emphasis, and to introduce pleasing variations:

Direct Object	Subject	Transitive Verb
Their generosity	I	have never doubted.

Subjective Complement	Linking Verb	Subject
Long	was	the introduction to this otherwise short speech.

Such inversions aren't wrong, for conventions (or rules) are made to be broken as well as followed; but their very unconventionality demands that they be used judiciously. They are most at home in poetry or highly oratorical prose:

> Thirty days hath September . . .

> And now abideth faith, hope, and charity, these three; but the greatest of these is charity.

> Never in the field of human conflict was so much owed by so many to so few.

Elsewhere such variations are rare, since any unusual pattern almost automatically calls attention to itself, something seldom appropriate in expository prose. But used occasionally, and appropriately, they can be highly effective.

Exercise 11s Using Alternative Word Orders

Try composing four or five declarative sentences that vary the standard order of elements in one way or another. Then choose one of your sentences and use it in a paragraph that you think justifies the unorthodox order.

11t Order of Elements in Interrogative Sentences

The conventional order used in interrogative sentences usually differs from that used in declarative sentences. It is, of course, possible to use the declarative order for a question—for example, in speaking, when one can use stress and end with the rising or falling intonation that usually indicates a question:

> They bought two cars?

thereby conveying a meaning something like

> Do you mean to tell me that they bought two cars?

Unless you're recording or imitating dialogue, you won't use this technique too often in your writing.

Usually, an interrogative sentence, besides ending with the conventional question mark, will take one of the patterns listed below. Note that the first five patterns invite *yes* or *no* answers; the final four, which begin with **question words**, invite more detailed responses.

1. If the verb is a single-word form of *be*, it precedes the subject:

Verb	Subject	Subjective Complement
Is	Nunavut	a province?

2. If the verb is a single word other than some form of *be*, it is necessary to supply a form of the auxiliary verb *do* before the subject; the main part of the verb then follows the subject in the normal way:

Auxiliary Verb	Subject	Main Verb	Direct Object
Does	Nunavut	have	provincial status?

3. If the verb is already a verb phrase (#11p), the first auxiliary comes before the subject:

Auxiliary Verb	Subject	Second Auxiliary	Main Verb
Are	you		daydreaming?
Will	Luis		speak first?
Have	you	been	snowboarding?

If the question includes a negative, the *not* goes before or after the subject, depending on whether one uses the less formal, contracted form:

> Aren't you going?   Are you not going?

4. With questions using expletives (Pattern 6, see #11k), the expletive and the verb are reversed:

    <u>Were there</u> many people at the orientation?

    <u>Was it</u> easy to follow her argument?

11t

5. With so-called "tag" questions, a statement is followed by a verb–pronoun question; in addition, *not* (usually in the contracted form) appears in one or the other of the two parts:

    Shulpa has been hiking, <u>hasn't she</u>?

    Shulpa hasn't been hiking, <u>has she</u>?

6. When a question begins with an interrogative adverb (*where, when, why,* or *how*; see #20a), a form of *do* or another already present auxiliary comes before the subject:

    Why <u>did</u> he say that?

    Where <u>are</u> you going?

7. If an interrogative pronoun (*who, which,* or *what*; see #14c) functions as the subject, the sentence retains standard declarative word order:

    Who will speak first?

    What is your answer?

8. If the opening pronoun is the *object* of the verb or a preposition, it is followed by the added auxiliary *do* or the first part of a verb phrase, the subject, and the rest of the verb:

    Whom did you invite?

    To whom will you give an invitation?

9. A similar reversal occurs when an interrogative pronoun functions as a possessive or other adjective (see #19a):

    Whose (Which, What) political platform do you favour?

    To what (which, whose) problems will the speaker address herself?

See also #22b, on the placement of prepositions in questions.

> ### Exercise 11t Constructing Interrogative Sentences
>
> Select a representative variety of ten sentences from those you've written for earlier exercises in this chapter and rewrite them as questions. Try using two or more different forms of question for some of the sentences.

11u

11u The Structure of Imperative Sentences

It is possible, especially if you want to emphasize the subject, to use the full structure of a declarative sentence when forming an **imperative sentence**:

Subject	Predicate
You	take that back!
You two in the corner	please join the rest of the group.

Still, the conventional form of an imperative sentence uses only the *predicate*, omitting the *subject* (an understood *you*):

> Consider the main argument.
>
> Stretch before you run.
>
> Close the door.
>
> Edit carefully.
>
> Enjoy.
>
> Come into the garden, Maud. (*Maud* is not the subject, but a noun of address; see #13b.)

Sometimes, especially in dialogue or informal contexts, even the verb can be omitted; a complement alone does the job:

> Careful. Easy, now. Steady.

You may think you'll have little use for imperative sentences in your writing. But if you ever want to write a set of instructions, you'll need to use a great many of them. And they can provide useful variety in other contexts as well.

What Is (or Is Not) a Sentence?

Now for a different kind of look at these groups of words called sentences. First, just what is a **sentence**? Most standard definitions are unsatisfactory and unrealistic because they leave out the kinds of sentences we use more often in speech than in formal writing. One common definition, for example, says that a sentence is a group of words with a subject and a verb. But the first sentence of this section, just above, lacks a subject–verb combination. And here are some more sentences that lack one or the other or both:

Yes.	Why?	Go away.	Now or never.
No.	Who, me?	Come here.	Oh my goodness!
Wow!	Never mind.	Sink or swim.	Call me Ishmael.

Out of context, such sentences don't tell us much, but they are clearly acceptable units. Moreover, some groups of words do contain a subject–verb combination but are still not sentences: an opening capital letter and a closing period don't make a subordinate clause a sentence:

I decided to make a list. <u>Before I went shopping.</u>

They bought me the bike. <u>Which I had stared at in the store the week before.</u>

The second clause in each of these is a **fragment** (see #12b).

Another common definition claims that a sentence is a complete thought. But *Yes* and *No* aren't satisfyingly complete without the questions that prompted them, nor are some of the other examples without their respective contexts. Nor is there anything necessarily "incomplete" about such words as *dog, hand, chair, freedom, love*—yet these words are not normally thought of as sentences.

Remember that language is primarily spoken. It is more realistic to define a sentence as *a satisfyingly complete pattern of intonation or expression*: that is, a complete utterance. Your voice and natural tone should tell you whether a certain group of words is or is not a sentence. Make it a practice to read your written work aloud, or at least to sound it out in your mind. Doing so will help you avoid ambiguity.

Keeping in mind our definition of a sentence as a complete utterance, we can identify two *kinds* of sentences: **minor** and **major**. Though this and similar books deal almost exclusively with major sentences, and though you won't have much use for minor sentences in academic writing, you should understand what minor sentences are so that you can use them occasionally for emphasis or other rhetorical effects, or when you are writing a piece of dialogue. And you need to be able to distinguish between the minor sentence, which is acceptable in some academic writing, and the fragmentary expression, which is not.

12a Minor Sentences

A minor sentence is an acceptable pattern of expression that nevertheless lacks either a subject or a finite verb, or both. But it is easy to supply the missing element or elements from context; for whereas major sentences can usually stand by themselves, most minor sentences need a context of one or more nearby sentences in order to make sense—most obviously, for example, as answers to questions. The minor sentence, however, like the major, is grammatically independent.

Minor sentences are usually one of the following four kinds:

1. Exclamations

    Oh!   No problem!
    Wow!   Incredible!

2. Questions or responses to questions

    When? Tomorrow.   How many? Seven.
    Why? What for?   How come? Really?
    Yes. No.   Perhaps. Certainly.

3. Common proverbial or idiomatic expressions

    Down the hatch.   Easy come, easy go.
    Better late than never.   In for a penny, in for a pound.

4. Minor sentences used for rhetorical or stylistic effect: These are more common in narrative and descriptive writing, but they can be effective in other contexts as well. Here is how Charles Dickens begins *Bleak House*:

    London. Michaelmas Term lately over, and the Lord Chancellor sitting in Lincoln's Inn Hall. Implacable November weather. As much mud in the streets, as if the waters had but newly retired from the face of the earth, and it would not be wonderful to meet a Megalosaurus, forty feet long or so, waddling like an elephantine lizard up Holborn Hill.

And so on, for three long paragraphs: not a major sentence in sight.

As the example from Dickens's work suggests, the beginning of a piece of writing is often a good place to try the effects of a minor sentence or two. A writer might begin an essay this way:

> Time, time, time. It is our constant companion and our greatest nemesis.

12b

And here is the beginning from another essay:

> One of the best times of the year in Vancouver is the spring. You know, those weeks in early April brimming with sunshine and new growth. Gardens and parks filled with crocuses, cherry trees in bloom, newly hatched chicks in their nests.

ag 12b Fragments

Don't mistake an unacceptable fragment for an acceptable minor sentence:

> *frag*: I didn't see the film. Because I felt that it would be too violent for my taste.

The *Because* clause is a fragment. The period after *film* should be deleted so that the subordinate clause can take its rightful place in the sentence. (But note that this *Because* clause, like many other fragments, would be acceptable as an answer to a question just before it.)

> *frag*: It was a hilarious moment. One that I'll never forget.

The clause beginning with *One* should be linked to the preceding independent clause with a comma, not separated from it by a period. It can then take its rightful place as a noun clause in apposition to *moment*.

> *frag*: He gave me half his sandwich. Being of a generous nature.

The participial phrase beginning with *Being* is not a separate sentence but an adjective modifying *He*; it should be introduced by a comma, or even moved to the beginning of the sentence:

> *revised*: Being of a generous nature, he gave me half his sandwich.

Note that fragments tend to occur after the independent clauses that they should be attached to.

12c

Indicate whether the italicized group of words in each of the following is a minor sentence or a fragment. (Assume none are being used for rhetorical or stylistic effect.) In examples where the italicized words constitute a fragment, suggest a revision to correct the problem.

1. I don't know who decorated the rainbow cake. *Probably someone very creative.*
2. Just look at the way they play together. *How sweet!*
3. You shouldn't run with scissors. *Even if you are in a hurry.*
4. We chose to eat at this restaurant. *It having a vegan menu, after all.*
5. *Last night, after I went to bed.* I heard a soft scratching on the ceiling above my head.
6. How much wood can a woodchuck chuck? *Plenty.*
7. We stayed at the picnic. *Until the sun went down.*
8. You say you've never seen this man? *Never?*
9. My sister is renovating her condo. *Painting, laying tiles, installing a new stove.*
10. I've decided to invest everything I have in my new business. *Nothing ventured, nothing gained.*

12c Major Sentences

A major sentence is a grammatically independent group of words containing at least two essential structural elements: a subject and a finite verb (see #11a and the note at the end of #17b). Major sentences constitute 99 per cent or more of most college and university writing. They are the sentences whose basic patterns are illustrated in sections #11c to #11k.

Major sentences can be classified grammatically as **simple, compound, complex,** and **compound–complex**.

1. Simple Sentences

A simple sentence has one subject and finite verb unit; it therefore contains only one clause, an independent clause:

s   v
Denis dances.

s   v
The boat leaks.

s   v
The website launched last week.

The subject or the verb, or both, can be compound—that is, consist of more than one part—but the sentence containing them will still be simple:

> <u>Claude and Qian</u> left early. (compound subject)

> She <u>watched and waited</u>. (compound verb)

> <u>The sergeant and his troops</u> <u>moved</u> down the hill <u>and crossed</u> the river. (compound subject, compound verb)

12c

2. Compound Sentences

A compound sentence consists of two or more simple sentences—that is, independent clauses—linked by coordinating conjunctions (see #23a), by punctuation, or by both:

>   s   v   s   v
> <u>The guitarist's amp</u> <u>overheated</u>, and <u>the show</u> <u>ended</u>.

>   s   v   s   v
> <u>The clouds</u> <u>massed</u> thickly against the hills; soon <u>the rain</u> <u>fell</u>
> in torrents.

>   s   v   s   v
> <u>We</u> <u>wanted</u> to hear jazz, but <u>they</u> <u>played</u> bluegrass.

>   s   v   s   v
> <u>Zach's patience and persistence</u> <u>paid</u> off; <u>he</u> not only <u>won</u> the
>   v
> prize but also <u>earned</u> his competitors' respect.

>   s   v   s   v   s   v
> <u>The day</u> <u>was</u> mild, <u>the breeze</u> <u>was</u> warm, and <u>everyone</u> <u>went</u>
> for a swim.

3. Complex Sentences

A complex sentence consists of one independent clause and one or more subordinate clauses; in the following examples, the subordinate clauses are underlined:

> We believe <u>that we have some original plans for the campaign</u>.
>   (noun clause as direct object)

> The strike was averted <u>before we reported for picket duty</u>.
>   (adverbial clause modifying *was averted*)

> This course is the one <u>that calls for the most field research</u>.
>   (adjectival clause modifying *one*)

> Marco Polo, who left his native Venice as a teenager, returned home after twenty-five years of adventure. (adjectival clause modifying *Marco Polo*)

> When the presentation ended, the audience burst into applause which lasted several minutes. (adverbial clause modifying *burst*, adjectival clause modifying *applause*)

> Although it seems premature, the government is proceeding with third reading of the legislation. (adverbial clause of concession, in effect modifying the rest of the sentence)

12c

Note that when the meaning is clear, the conjunction *that* introducing a noun clause, or the relative pronouns *that* and *which* can be omitted:

> She claimed she was innocent.

> He clung to the suitcase he had brought with him.

But see the proofreading tip near the end of #48a.

4. Compound-Complex Sentences

A compound-complex sentence consists of two or more independent clauses and one or more subordinate clauses:

> Because the architect knows that the preservation of heritage buildings is vital, she is consulting widely, but as delays have developed, she has grown impatient, and therefore she is thinking of pulling out of a project that represents everything important to her.

We can analyze this example as follows:

> Because the architect knows (adverbial clause)

> that the preservation of heritage buildings is vital (noun clause)

> she is consulting widely (independent clause)

> but (coordinating conjunction)

> as delays have developed (adverbial clause)

> she has grown impatient (independent clause)

and (coordinating conjunction)

therefore (conjunctive adverb)

she is thinking of pulling out of a project (independent clause)

that represents everything important to her (adjectival clause)

Exercise 12c (1) Recognizing Kinds of Sentences

Label each of the following sentences as simple, compound, complex, or compound-complex.

1. If you read this novel, you will find yourself questioning the narrator's credibility. _____

2. Everybody is going to laugh on cue. _____

3. The trombonist who performed so well at this concert is the same one we saw last summer at the Montreal Jazz Festival. _____

4. The groom mumbled a bit; the bride spoke her vows in a clear, strong voice. _____

5. Grace and Emily love to go running through the forest behind their house, but they never run on the treadmills at their local gym. _____

6. They chose the stocks they judged to be safest, but they lost money in the recession nevertheless. _____

7. Afraid of dark places, the children never venture into their grandparents' shadowy old basement. _____

8. Our classmates concluded a heated debate of the issue, and then we all voted in favour of lowering the voting age to sixteen. _____

9. A philosophy major will learn to think clearly and will acquire a sense of cultural history, and so when she graduates she should probably have the critical-thinking skills and knowledge base to make herself employable. _____

10. Few things are more pleasant than a lovingly prepared and carefully presented elegant meal consisting of several courses, consumed in good company, with soft background music, and accompanied by noble wines. _____

Exercise 12c (2) Constructing Different Kinds of Sentences

First, compose three simple sentences. Next, using as many modifiers as you want, adapt one or more of your three simple sentences to create the following:

1. two compound sentences, each with two independent clauses
2. a compound sentence with three independent clauses
3. two complex sentences, each with one independent and one subordinate clause
4. a complex sentence with one independent and two subordinate clauses
5. three compound-complex sentences

III

Parts of Speech

Introduction: The Parts of Speech and How They Work in Sentences

Introduction: The Parts of Speech and How They Work in Sentences

As you saw in chapter II, *word order* helps determine whether a sentence is asking a question or making a statement. But word order is important in another and even more basic way. The order of elements in Pattern 2A (subject–verb–direct object; see #11d), for example, determines meaning:

> Students need teachers.

Clear enough. We know, from standard English word order, that *Students* is the subject, *need* is the verb, and *teachers* is the direct object. Reversing the order reverses the meaning:

> Teachers need students.

Now we know that *Teachers* are doing the *needing* and that *students* are the objects of the need. If you know a language like German or Latin, you know how different—and in some ways more difficult—such languages can be; for in them it is the *form* of the words, rather than their position, that determines meaning. For example, the following sentence would, in English, not only sound awkward but also be ambiguous:

> Teachers students need.

But the same three words in Latin would be clear because the *forms* of the two nouns would show which was subject and which was object.

The change in a word's form is called **inflection**. Some words in modern English must be inflected in order for sentences to communicate clearly. If, for example, you want the noun *boy* to denote more than one young male, you change it—*inflect* it—by adding an *s* to make it plural: *boys*. If you want to use the verb *see* to denote the act of seeing in some past time, you change its form so that you can say, for example, *I saw* or *I have seen* or *I was seeing*.

English words fall traditionally into eight categories called **parts of speech**. Five of these can be inflected in one or more ways:

- noun
- pronoun
- verb
- adjective
- adverb

The other three are not inflected:

- preposition
- interjection
- conjunction

For example, the preposition *in* is always *in*; the conjunction *but* is always *but*. (The only exceptions occur when words are referred to *as words*, as in "There are too many *and*s in that sentence" and "I don't want to hear any *if*s, *and*s, or *but*s," or in informal or idiomatic usages such as "She knows all the *in*s and *out*s of the process," where such words function as nouns rather than as structure words.)

Note that the term *inflection* applies only to the change of a word's form within its part of speech. That is, when the noun *boy* is inflected to make it plural, the new form, *boys*, is still a noun; when the pronoun *they* is inflected to *them* or *theirs*, the new forms are still pronouns. (Again there is an exception: when you inflect a noun or pronoun for the possessive case before a noun—the *boy's* coat, *their* idea—you turn it into an adjective; some people, however, thinking of *form* rather than *function*, prefer to call these inflected forms "possessive nouns" and "possessive pronouns.")

Many words can be changed so that they function as different parts of speech. For example, the noun *centre* can be made into the adjective *central*, or the noun *meaning* into the adjective *meaningful*, or the verb *vacate* into the noun *vacation*. Such changes, however, are not inflections but **derivations**; a word can be *derived* from a word of a different part of speech, often by the addition of one or more suffixes: *trust, trustful, trust-fully, trustfulness*. And many words, even without being changed, can serve as more than one part of speech; for example:

> She is <u>cool</u> under pressure. (adjective)
>
> He knows how to keep his <u>cool</u> in a crisis. (noun)
>
> Relations between the leaders may <u>cool</u> after the debate. (verb)

The word *word* itself can be a noun ("Use this *word* correctly"), a verb ("How will you *word* your reply?"), or an adjective ("*Word* games are fun"). The word *right* can be a noun (his legal *right*), an adjective (the *right* stuff), an adverb (turn *right*, do it *right*), or a verb (*right* an overturned canoe). Or consider the versatility of the common word *over*:

> The awning hung <u>over</u> the storefront. (preposition)
>
> The game is <u>over</u>. (adjective)
>
> Write that sentence <u>over</u>. (adverb)
>
> "Roger. Message received. <u>Over</u>." (interjection)

The *form* of a word, then, doesn't always determine its *function*. What part of speech a word is depends on its function in a particular sentence.

The rest of this section discusses the eight parts of speech—their inflections (if any) and other grammatical properties; their subcategories; how they work with other words in sentences; and some of their important derivatives (verbals)—and calls attention to some of their potential trouble spots, such as **agreement** and a verb's **tenses**.

 **Nouns**

13a

A **noun** (from the Latin *nomen*, "name") is a word that names or stands for a person, a place, a thing, a class, a concept, a quality, or an action: *queen, country, river, citizen, freedom, silence, investigation*. **Proper nouns** are names of specific persons, places, or things and begin with a capital letter: *Jasmine, Rumpelstiltskin, Winnipeg, England*, the *Titanic*. All the others, called **common nouns**, are capitalized only if they begin a sentence:

> Freedom is a precious commodity.

> Investigation leads to discovery.

or form part of a proper noun:

> Spring Garden Road

> the Peace Arch

> the Ottawa River

or are personified or otherwise emphasized, for example in poetry:

> Our noisy years seem moments in the being
> Of the eternal Silence. . . .
> > (Wordsworth)

(See #58, on capitalization.)

One can also classify nouns as either **concrete**, for names of tangible objects (*doctor, elephant, utensil, barn*), or **abstract**, for names of intangible things or ideas (*freedom, honour, happiness, history*). (See #66.)

Collective nouns are names of collections or groups often considered as units: *army, committee, family, herd, flock*. (See #15e and #18f.)

EAL ### 13a Inflection of Nouns
Nouns can be inflected in only two ways: for **number** and for **possessive case**.

1. For Number

Most common concrete nouns that stand for *countable* things are either
singular (naming a single thing) or **plural** (naming more than one
thing). And though proper nouns generally name specific persons, places,
or things, they too can sometimes logically be inflected for the plural; for
example, there are many *Lams* in the telephone directory, there are several
Londons (e.g., the one in England and the one in Ontario), and since 1948
there have been two *Koreas*. Most singular nouns are inflected to indicate
the plural by the addition of *s* or *es*: *girl, girls; box, boxes*. But some are made
plural in other ways: *child, children; stimulus, stimuli*. (For more on the formation of plurals, see #62m.)

Some concrete nouns, however, called **mass** nouns, name materials that are measured, weighed, or divided, rather than items that are
counted—for example, *silver, oxygen, rice, sand,* and *pasta*. As **uncountable** or noncountable nouns, these are not inflected for the plural.
Also uncountable are abstract nouns and nouns that stand for ideas,
activities, and states of mind or being; for example, *honour, journalism,
skiing, happiness*.

Some nouns, however, can be either countable or uncountable, depending on the context in which they are used. For example:

> Plants need <u>soil</u> to grow. (uncountable)

> Experienced gardeners know the properties of various <u>soils</u>.
> (countable, equivalent to *kinds of soil*)

> They insisted on telling the truth as a matter of <u>honour</u>.
> (uncountable)

> Many <u>honours</u> were heaped upon the returning hero. (countable,
> since *honours* designates specific things like medals, citations,
> or comments of praise)

(See also #15c, #18g, and #19c.5.)

2. For Possessive Case

As we saw in the introduction to this chapter, in English, whether a noun
is a *subject* (**subjective** case) or an *object* (**objective** case) is shown by word
order rather than by inflection. But nouns are inflected for **possessive**
case. By adding an apostrophe and an *s*, or sometimes only an apostrophe,
you inflect a noun so that it shows possession or ownership: *my mother's
job, the children's toys, the students' grades*. (For more on inflecting nouns for
possessive case, see #62n.)

13a

13b Grammatical Function of Nouns

Nouns function in sentences in the following ways:

- as the subject of a verb (see #11a):

  Students work hard.

- as the direct object of a verb (see #11d):

  The chef roasted the vegetables.

- as the indirect object of a verb (see #11f):

  We awarded Yoko the prize.

- as the object of a preposition (see #11f and #22):

  Giselle had to write a personal essay about hobbies.

- as a predicate noun after a linking verb (see #11h):

  Quartz is a mineral.

- as an objective complement (see #11j):

  The judges declared Aiden the winner.

- as an appositive to any other noun (see #11q):

  Andre, the writer, spoke to Roger, the director.

  My brother, Masoud, won the prize, a book about entrepreneurship.

Nouns in the *possessive case* function as adjectives (see #19a):

Mackenzie's project is impressive. (Which project? Mackenzie's.)

I did a day's work. (How much work? A day's.)

or as predicate nouns, after a linking verb:

The expensive-looking coat is Maria's.

Even without being inflected for possessive case, many nouns can also function as adjectives within noun phrases: the *school* mascot, an *evening* gown, the *automobile* industry, the *dessert* course, and so on (see #71g).

A noun (or pronoun) referring to someone being directly addressed, as in dialogue or in a letter, is called a *noun of address*. Such nouns, usually proper names, are not directly related to the syntax of the rest of the sentence and are set off with punctuation:

Yuki, are you feeling well?

Soon, Lea, you'll see what I mean.

Exercise 13b Recognizing Nouns

Underline each noun (including nouns functioning as adjectives) in the following sentences. Determine whether each one is functioning as a subject, a direct object, an indirect object, an object of a preposition, a subjective complement (predicate noun), an objective complement, an appositive, a possessive adjective, an adjective, or a noun of address.

1. The instructor gave her class the afternoon off.
2. My uncle, the famous poet, recently edited another anthology.
3. The list of new college courses was posted outside the admissions office today.
4. Canada's tenth province, Newfoundland, joined Confederation in 1949.
5. Are you comfortable, Sydney?
6. We often think back with pleasure on our childhood.
7. Halifax's mayor presented the speed skater the gold medal.
8. The queen was given a Canadian encyclopedia edited by a distinguished professor.
9. Alex's roommates declared the party over at midnight, and that was the end of our fun.
10. Shakespeare wrote many plays, but *Hamlet*, a tragedy, is his best-known work.

14 Pronouns

A pronoun, as its name indicates, is a word that stands for (*pro*) or *in place of* a noun, or functions like a noun in a sentence. Most pronouns refer to nouns that come earlier, their **antecedents** (from Latin for *coming before*):

Joshua offered an opinion, but he didn't feel confident about it.

Here, *Joshua* is the antecedent of the pronoun *he*, and *opinion* is the antecedent of the pronoun *it*. Occasionally an antecedent can come after the pronoun that refers to it, especially if the pronoun is in a subordinate clause and if the context is clear—that is, if the pronoun couldn't refer to some other noun (see also #16d):

> Although <u>he</u> offered an opinion, <u>Joshua</u> didn't feel confident about it.

14a

There are eight different pronoun types:

- personal
- impersonal
- interrogative
- relative

- demonstrative
- indefinite
- reflexive (or intensive)
- reciprocal

Generally, pronouns perform the same functions as nouns: they are most often subjects of verbs, direct and indirect objects, and objects of prepositions; some can also function as appositives and predicate nouns. Some pronouns are inflected much more than nouns, and some require closer proofreading for case, reference, and agreement than you might think.

The following sections discuss the different kinds of pronoun; their inflections; their grammatical functions in phrases, clauses, and sentences; and the special problems of **case** (#14e), **agreement** (#15), and **reference** (#16).

14a Personal Pronouns

Personal pronouns refer to specific persons or things. They are inflected in four ways:

1. For Person

- **First-person** pronouns (*I*, *we*, etc.) refer to the person or persons doing the speaking or writing.
- **Second-person** pronouns (*you*, *yours*) refer to the person or persons being spoken or written to.
- **Third-person** pronouns (*he*, *she*, *it*, *they*, etc.) refer to the person(s) or thing(s) being spoken or written about.

2. For Number

- **Singular** pronouns (*I*, *she*, etc.) refer to individuals.

> <u>I</u> am writing. <u>She</u> is writing.

- **Plural** pronouns (*we*, *they*, etc.) refer to groups.

> <u>We</u> are writing. <u>They</u> are writing.

(Note that the second-person pronoun *you* can be either singular or plural.)

3. For Gender (second- and third-person pronouns)
- **Masculine** pronouns (*he, him, his*) refer to males.
- **Feminine** pronouns (*she, her, hers*) refer to females.
- The **neuter** pronoun (*it*) refers to ideas or things, and sometimes to animals.

(Note that in the plural forms—*we, you, they*, etc.—there is no indication of gender.)

14a

4. For Case (see also #14e)
- Pronouns that function as **subjects** must be in the **subjective** case:

  I paint. She paints. They are painting.

- Pronouns that function as **objects**—whether direct or indirect—must be in the **objective** case:

  The idea hit them. Give her the book. Give it to me.

- Pronouns that indicate possession or ownership must be in the **possessive** case:

  That turtle is his. This turtle is mine. Where is yours?

(Note that pronouns in the possessive case—*yours, theirs, its, hers*, etc.—do not take an apostrophe before the *s* to indicate possession.)

The following chart shows all the inflections of personal pronouns:

		Subject	Object	Possessive Pronoun	Possessive Adjective
singular	1st person	I	me	mine	my
	2nd person	you	you	yours	your
	3rd person	he	him	his	his
		she	her	hers	her
		it	it		its
plural	1st person	we	us	ours	our
	2nd person	you	you	yours	your
	3rd person	they	them	theirs	their

Possessive (or pronominal) **adjectives** always precede nouns (*My* car is in the shop); **possessive pronouns** may function as subjects, objects, and predicate nouns (Let's take *yours*).

Note that *you* and *it* are inflected only for possessive case, that *his* serves as both possessive pronoun and possessive adjective, and that *her* serves as both objective case and possessive adjective.

14b Impersonal Pronouns

Especially in formal contexts, the **impersonal pronoun** *one*, meaning essentially "a person," serves in place of a first-, second-, or third-person pronoun:

> One must be careful when choosing course electives.

> One must keep one's priorities straight.

The pronoun *it* is also used as an impersonal pronoun in such sentences as the following; note that the impersonal *it* is usually the subject of some form of *be* (see #17f) and that it usually refers to time, weather, distance, and the like:

> It is getting late. It's almost four o'clock.

> It's warm. It feels warmer than it did yesterday.

> It was just one of those things.

> It is two kilometres from here to the station.

✓ PROOFREADING TIP

On Using the Impersonal Pronoun *It*

You may want to edit your work to avoid overuse of the impersonal pronoun *it*. The sentences that are formed using this pattern are known as weak expletives and sometimes delay unnecessarily the true subject of the sentence. The last example could easily be revised to read *The last station is two kilometres from here.*

14c Interrogative Pronouns

Interrogative pronouns are *question words* used usually at or near the beginning of *interrogative sentences* (see #11t). *Who* is inflected for objective and possessive case, *which* for possessive case only:

Subjective	Objective	Possessive
who	whom	whose
which	which	whose
what	what	

Who refers to persons, *which* and *what* to things; *which* sometimes also refers to persons, as in *Which of you is going?* The compound forms *whoever* and *whatever*, and sometimes even *whichever* and *whomever*, can also function as interrogative pronouns. Here are some examples showing interrogative pronouns functioning in different ways:

14c

- as a subject:

  Who said that?

  Which of these books is best?

  What is the baby's name?

- as the direct object of a verb:

  Whom do you suggest for the position?

  What did you give Marcus for his birthday?

- as the object of a preposition (see also #22):

  To whom did you recommend the film?

  To what do I owe this honour?

- as an objective complement:

  What did you call me?

  You've named the baby what?

In front of a noun, an interrogative word functions as an **interrogative adjective**:

Whose bag is this?

Which car shall we take?

For more on *who* and *whom*, see #14e.

14d Relative Pronouns

A **relative pronoun** usually introduces an *adjectival clause*—called a **relative clause**—in which it functions as subject, object, or object of a preposition. The pronoun links, or *relates*, the clause to an antecedent in the same sentence, a noun or pronoun that the whole clause modifies.

The principal relative pronouns are *who, which,* and *that. Who* and *which* are inflected for case:

Subjective	Objective	Possessive
who	whom	whose
which	which	whose
that	that	

Who refers to persons (and sometimes to animals thought of as persons), *which* to things, and *that* to either persons or things. Consider some examples of how relative pronouns function:

Taylor, who is leaving in the morning, will call us later tonight. (*who* as subject of verb *is*; clause modifies *Taylor*)

Joel contacted the reporter whom he had met at the crime scene. (*whom* as direct object; clause modifies *reporter*)

At midnight Sula began to revise her descriptive essay, which was due in the morning. (*which* as subject of verb *was*; clause modifies *essay*)

She avoided working on the report that she was having trouble with. (*that* as object of preposition *with*; clause modifies *report*)

A relative clause is either **restrictive** and unpunctuated, or **nonrestrictive** and set off with punctuation. It is restrictive if it gives us information that is essential to identifying the antecedent (e.g., *whom he had met at the crime scene*); it is nonrestrictive if the information it gives us is not essential to identifying the antecedent and could be left out of the sentence (e.g., *which was due in the morning*). (See also #48.) If the relative pronoun in a restrictive clause is the object of a verb or a preposition, it can usually be omitted:

Joel contacted the reporter [whom or that] he had met.

She avoided working on the report [that or which] she was having trouble with.

But if the preposition is placed before the pronoun (e.g., *with which*), the pronoun cannot be omitted:

> She avoided working on the report with <u>which</u> she was having trouble.

Sometimes the pronoun is necessary to prevent misreading:

> ***confusing***: Different varieties of tea shops sell are medicinal.

A *that* after *tea* prevents misreading the subject of the verb as *different varieties of tea shops*:

> ***clear***: Different varieties of tea <u>that</u> shops sell are medicinal.

When *whose* precedes and modifies a noun in a relative clause, it functions as what is called a **relative adjective**:

> Jana was the one <u>whose</u> advice he most valued.

And sometimes a **relative adverb**, often *when* or *where*, introduces a relative clause (see also #20a):

> Here's an aerial photo of the town <u>where</u> I live. (The clause where *I live* modifies the noun *town*.)

> My parents told me about the time <u>when</u> I ate a crayon. (The *when* clause modifies the noun *time*.)

Sometimes *what* and the *ever* compounds (*whatever, whoever, whomever, whichever*) are also considered relative pronouns, even though they introduce noun clauses (e.g., "Remember *what I said*." "*Take whichever one you want*."). *Who, whom,* and *which* may also introduce such noun clauses.

   For more on *who* and *whom*, see #14e. For more on adjectival clauses, see #19 and #26a.

ca **14e Case** (see also #14a.4)
Determining the correct case of personal, interrogative, and relative pronouns is sometimes challenging. In writing particular sentences and in formal writing generally, the challenge may be to determine whether a pronoun should be in the subjective or objective case. In everyday speech and informal writing, things like "*Who* did you lend the book to?" and "It's *me*" and "That's *her*" upset few people. But in formal writing and strictly formal speech, you should use the correct forms: To w*hom* did you lend the book? It is *I*. That is *she*. If you know how a pronoun is functioning

grammatically, you will know which form to use. Here are some guidelines to help you with the kinds of sentences that sometimes cause problems:

1. A pronoun functioning as the *subject* should be in the *subjective* case. Be particularly careful whenever you use a pronoun as part of a *compound subject* (see #12c.1). Someone who wouldn't say "*Me* am going to the store" could slip and say something like "Susan and *me* studied hard for the exam" instead of the correct

   Susan and I studied hard for the exam.

   If you're not sure, remove the other part of the subject; then you'll know which pronoun sounds right:

   ~~Susan and~~ I studied hard for the exam.

   But even a one-part subject can lead someone astray:

   > *ca:* Us students should stand up for our rights.
   > *revised:* We students should stand up for our rights.

   The pronoun *We* is the subject; the word *students* is an appositive (see #11q) further identifying it, as if saying "We, the students, should . . . ."

2. A pronoun functioning as a direct or indirect *object* should be in the *objective* case. Again, errors most often result from the use of a two-part structure—here, a *compound object*. Someone who would not say "The club asked *I* for my opinion" could slip and say "They asked Ingrid and *I* to take part in the play." When you use a pronoun as part of a compound object, make sure it's in the *objective* case. Again, test by removing the other part:

   They asked ~~Ingrid and~~ me to take part in the play.

PROOFREADING TIP

On Hypercorrection of Pronouns

Don't slip into what is called "hypercorrection." Since many people say things like "Jake and me went camping," others—not understanding the grammar but wishing to seem correct—use the "and I" form even for an object, when it should be "and me." For example, you would say *The new tent was for Jake and me*, not *The new tent was for Jake and I*.

14e

3. A pronoun functioning as the *object* of a preposition should be in the *objective* case:

> *ca:* This secret is between you and I.
>
> *revised:* This secret is between you and me.

Speakers and writers who have learned not to use *me* as part of a compound subject sometimes overcorrect in cases such as this and use *I*; but the objective *me* is correct in this instance, for it is the object of the preposition *between*.

14e

4. A pronoun functioning as a *predicate noun* (see #11h and #25d) after a linking verb should be in the *subjective* case. In other words, if the pronoun follows the verb *be*, it takes the subjective form:

> It is they who must decide, not we.

> The swimmer who won the prize is she, over there by the pool.

> It is I who will be carrying the greater burden.

If such usages sound stuffy and artificial to you—as they do to many people—find another way to phrase your sentences; for example:

> They, not we, must decide.

> The swimmer over by the pool is the one who won the prize.

> I will be the one carrying the greater burden.

Again, watch out for compound structures:

> *ca:* The nominees are Yashmin and me.
>
> *revised:* The nominees are Yashmin and I.

5. Pronouns following the conjunctions *as* and *than* in comparisons should be in the *subjective* case if they are functioning as subjects, even if their verbs are not expressed but left "understood":

> Hiroshi is as tall as I [am].

> Roberta is brighter than they [are].

> Aaron has learned less than I [have].

If, however, the pronouns are functioning as objects, they should be in the *objective* case:

I trust her more than [I trust] him.

See also **so . . . as** in the usage checklist, #72.

6. Use the appropriate case of the interrogative and relative pronouns *who* and *whom*, *whoever* and *whomever*. Although *who* is often used instead of *whom* in speech and informal writing, you should know how to use the two correctly when you want to write or speak more formally.

14e

a. Use the *subjective* case for the *subject* of a verb in a question or a relative clause:

Who is your favourite writer?

Dickens was a novelist who was extremely popular in his own time.

b. Use the *objective* case for the *object* of a verb or preposition:

Whom do you prefer in that role?

He is the candidate whom I most admire.

She is the manager for whom the employees have the most respect.

If such usages with *whom* seem to you unnatural and stuffy, avoid them by rephrasing:

She is the manager that the employees respect most.

c. In noun clauses, the case of the pronoun is determined by its function in its clause, not by other words:

How can you tell who won? (subjective case)

I'll give the trophy to whomever the judges declare the winner. (objective case, object of preposition)

For the possessive case of pronouns with *gerunds*, see #21h.

Exercise 14e (1) Using Correct Pronouns

Underline the correct pronoun in each of the pairs in parentheses.

1. (She, her) and (I, me) will work on the project tonight.
2. There stood Eva, (who, whom) (we, us) had just said goodbye to.
3. Is Tomi the person (who, whom) you think will do the best job?
4. It is to (they, them) that the grant will be awarded.
5. The coach advised Anwar and (I, me) not to miss any more practices.
6. (Who, Whom) do you wish to see?
7. The story was similar to the one (we, us) children had told.
8. This gift will please (whoever, whomever) receives it.
9. The contract outlines the agreement between you and (he, him).
10. Natasha is a better dancer than (I, me), but (I, me) can play the guitar better than (she, her).

Exercise 14e (2) Problem Pronouns

Make up five sentences that use a personal pronoun in the subjective case (*I, he, she, they*) after a form of the verb *be*, and five sentences that use the pronoun *whom* or *whomever* in a correct formal way. Then rewrite each sentence, keeping each one formal but avoiding the possible stuffiness of these usages.

14f Demonstrative Pronouns

Demonstrative pronouns, which can be thought of as pointing to the nouns they refer to, are inflected for *number*:

Singular	Plural
this	these
that	those

This and *these* usually refer to something nearby or something just said or about to be said; *that* and *those* usually refer to something farther away or more remote in time or longer in duration; but there are no precise rules:

Try some of this.

The clerk was helpful; this was what pleased her the most.

These are the main points I will cover in today's lecture.

That looks appetizing.

That was the story he told us the next morning.

Those were his exact words.

Those are the cities you should visit on your holiday.

14g

These pronouns also often occur in prepositional phrases with *like* and *such as*:

Someone who wears a shirt like that has no fashion sense.

I need more close friends like those.

A cute house such as this will sell immediately.

 PROOFREADING TIP

Avoiding Vagueness in Using Demonstrative Pronouns

Useful as demonstrative pronouns can be, employ them sparingly in writing, for they are often vague in their reference. If you think a demonstrative pronoun is too vague, follow it with a noun to turn it into a *demonstrative adjective*: *this* belief, *that* statement, *these* buildings, *those* arguments. See #16c, #41, and **ref** in appendix 2.

EAL ## 14g Indefinite Pronouns

Indefinite pronouns refer to *indefinite* or unknown persons or things, or to indefinite or unknown quantities of persons or things. The only major issue with these words is whether they are *singular* or *plural*. Think of indefinite pronouns as falling into four groups:

- **Group 1**: compounds ending with *body*, *one*, and *thing*. These words function like nouns—that is, they need no antecedents— and they are almost always considered *singular*:

anybody	everybody	nobody	somebody
anyone	everyone	no one	someone
anything	everything	nothing	something

- **Group 2**: a few other indefinite pronouns that are almost always *singular*:

another	each	either	much
neither	one	other	

- **Group 3**: a few that are always *plural*:

both	few	many	several

- **Group 4**: a few that can be either *singular* or *plural*, depending on context and intended meaning:

all	any	more	most
none	some		

For discussions of the important matter of grammatical **agreement** with indefinite pronouns, and examples of their use in sentences, see #15c and #18d.

Only *one* and *other* can be inflected for number, by adding *s* to make them plural: *ones*, *others*. Several indefinite pronouns can be inflected for possessive case; unlike personal pronouns, they take *'s*, just as nouns do (or, with *others'*, just an apostrophe):

anybody's	anyone's	everybody's	everyone's
nobody's	no one's	somebody's	someone's
one's	other's	another's	others'

The remaining indefinite pronouns must use *of* to show possession; for example:

That was the belief <u>of many</u> who were present.

When in the possessive case, indefinite pronouns function as adjectives. In addition, all the words in groups 2, 3, and 4, except *none*, can also function as adjectives (see #19a):

<u>any</u> boat	<u>some</u> people	<u>few</u> people
<u>more</u> money	<u>each</u> day	<u>either</u> direction

The adjective expressing the meaning of *none* is *no*:

Send <u>no</u> attachments.

Sometimes the cardinal numbers (*one*, *two*, *three*, etc.) and the ordinal numbers (*first*, *second*, *third*, etc.) are also classed as indefinite pronouns, for they often function similarly, both as pronouns and as adjectives:

> How many ducks are on the pond? I see <u>several</u>. I see <u>seven</u>. I see <u>ten</u>.

> Do you like these stories? I like <u>some</u>, but not <u>others</u>. I like the <u>first</u> and <u>second</u>, but not the <u>third</u> or <u>fourth</u>.

> He owns <u>two</u> boats.

> Stay tuned for the <u>second</u> thrilling episode.

14h Reflexive and Intensive Pronouns

Reflexive and intensive pronouns are formed by adding *self* or *selves* to the possessive form of the first- and second-person personal pronouns, to the objective form of third-person personal pronouns, and to the impersonal pronoun *one* (see #14a–b).

Singular	Plural
myself	ourselves
yourself	yourselves
himself	themselves
herself	themselves
itself	
oneself	

A **reflexive pronoun** is used as an object when that object is the same person or thing as the subject:

> He treated <u>himself</u> to bubble tea. (direct object)

> One should pamper <u>oneself</u> a little. (direct object)

> She gave <u>herself</u> a break. (indirect object)

> We kept the idea to <u>ourselves</u>. (object of preposition)

These pronouns are also used as **intensive pronouns** to emphasize a subject or an object. An intensive pronoun comes either right after the noun it emphasizes or at the end of the sentence:

Although he let the others leave, Angelo <u>himself</u> will stay.

The professor told us to count up our scores <u>ourselves</u>.

They are also used in prepositional phrases with *by* to mean *alone* or *without help*:

I can solve this problem by <u>myself</u>.

PROOFREADING TIP

On the Use of Intensive and Reflexive Pronouns

Do not use this form of pronoun as a substitute for a personal pronoun:

The team and <u>I</u> [not *myself*] played a great game tonight.

Especially don't use *myself* simply to avoid having to decide whether *I* or *me* is correct in a compound subject or object (see #14e).

14i Reciprocal Pronouns

Like a reflexive pronoun, a **reciprocal pronoun** refers to the subject of a sentence, but this time the subject is always plural. The two reciprocal pronouns themselves are singular and consist of two words each:

each other (referring to a subject involving two)

one another (referring to a subject involving three or more)

They can be inflected for possessive case by adding *'s*:

each other's   one another's

These pronouns express some kind of mutual interaction between or among the parts of a plural subject:

The president and the prime minister praised <u>each other's</u> policies.

The computers in this office in effect speak to <u>one another</u>, even though the employees never do.

Agreement of Pronouns with Their Antecedents

agr Any pronoun that refers to or stands for an *antecedent* (see #14) must **agree** with—i.e., be the same as—that antecedent in **person** (first, second, or third), **number** (singular or plural), and **gender** (masculine, feminine, or neuter). For example:

> Olivia is learning about social networking so that she will be prepared to make her mark in the world of online marketing.

Since the proper noun *Olivia*, the antecedent, is in the third person, singular, and feminine, any pronouns that refer to it must also be in the third person, singular, and feminine: *she* and *her* thus "agree" grammatically with their antecedent.

The following sections (#15a–f) point out the most common sources of trouble with pronoun agreement. Note that these circumstances are similar to those affecting subject–verb agreement (see #18). Note also that these errors all have to do with *number*—whether a pronoun should be *singular* or *plural*. Mistakes in gender and person also occur, but not as frequently (but see #39d, on shifts in person).

15a Antecedents Joined by *and*
When two or more singular antecedents are joined by *and*, use a *plural* pronoun:

> Farah and Chloe launched their new magazine.

If such a compound is preceded by *each* or *every*, however, the pronoun should be *singular*:

> Each article and editorial has its own title.

15b Antecedents Joined by *or* or *nor*
When two or more antecedents are joined by *or* or *nor*, use a *singular* pronoun if the antecedents are singular:

> The dog or the cat is sure to make itself heard.

> Either David or Jonathan will bring his notes.

> Neither Maylin nor her mother gave her consent.

If one antecedent is masculine and the other feminine, rephrase the sentence (see #15d).

Use a *plural* pronoun if the antecedents are plural:

> Neither the players nor the coaches did their jobs properly.

If the antecedents are mixed singular and plural, a pronoun should agree with the nearest one. But if you move from a plural to a singular antecedent, the sentence will almost inevitably sound awkward; try to construct such sentences so that the last antecedent is plural:

> *awkward:*   Neither the actors nor the director could control his temper.
>
> *revised:*   Neither the director nor the actors could control their tempers.

15c

Note that the awkwardness of the first example extends to gender: if the actors included both men and women, neither *his* nor *her* would be appropriate; see #15d. For more information on agreement of verbs with compound subjects joined by *or* or *nor*, see #18c.

15c Indefinite Pronoun as Antecedent

If the antecedent is an *indefinite pronoun* (see #14g), you'll usually use a *singular* pronoun to refer to it. The indefinite pronouns in Group 1 (the compounds with *body*, *one*, and *thing*) are singular, as are those in Group 2 (*another, each, either, much, neither, one, other*):

> Each of the men worked on his own project.
>
> Either of these women is likely to buy that sports car for herself.
>
> Everything has its proper place.

Indefinite pronouns from Group 3 (*both, few, many, several*) are always plural:

> Only a few returned their ballots.

The indefinite pronouns in Group 4 (*all, any, more, most, none, some*) can be either singular or plural, depending on the intended meaning:

> Some of the food on the menu could be criticized for its lack of nutrients.
>
> Some of the ships in the fleet had been restored to their original beauty.

Here the mass noun *food* demands the singular sense for *some*, and the countable noun *ships*, in the plural, demands the plural sense. But confusion sometimes arises with the indefinite pronoun *none*. (See also #18d.) Although *none* began by meaning *no one* or *not one*, it now commonly has the plural sense:

> None of the boys knew how to fix their bicycles.

15d With a mass noun, or if your intended meaning is *not a single one*, treat *none* as singular:

> None of the food could be praised for its quality.

> None of the boys knew how to fix his bicycle. (Here, you could perhaps even change *None* to *Not one*.)

When any of these words function as *adjectives*, the same principles apply:

> Each man worked on his own project.

> Either woman may buy the car for herself.

> Only a few people returned their ballots.

> Some food can be praised for its nutritional value.

> Some ships had been restored to their original beauty.

Note: The word *every* used as an adjective requires a *singular* pronoun:

> Every man has his own project.

15d Pronouns and Inclusive Language: Avoiding Gender Bias

Several indefinite pronouns and indefinite nouns like *person*, as well as many other nouns used in a generalizing way, present an additional challenge: avoiding gender bias.

In centuries past, if a *singular antecedent* had no grammatical gender but could refer to either male or female, it was conventional to use the masculine pronoun *he* (*him, his, himself*) in a generic sense, meaning any person, male or female:

> *biased:* Everyone present at the lecture raised his hand.

> *biased:* A writer should be careful about his diction.

Today this practice is regarded as inappropriate and inaccurate, since it implies, for example, that no women were present at the lecture and that there are no women writers. Such usages reveal the unconsidered assumption that males are the norm. And merely substituting *she* or *her* in all such instances is no solution, since it represents gender bias as well.

You can and should avoid biased language. Colloquially and informally, many writers simply use a plural pronoun:

> *agr*: Anyone who doesn't pay their taxes is asking for trouble.

15d

But this practice is grammatically incorrect. (Note in the example above the clash between the plural pronoun *their* and the singular verb *is*.)

There are better solutions:

1. If you are referring to a group or class consisting entirely of either men or women, it is only logical to use the appropriate pronoun, whether masculine or feminine:

    > Everyone in the room raised his hand.

    > Everyone in the room raised her hand.

    If the group is mixed, try to avoid the problem, for example by using the indefinite article:

    > Everyone in the room raised a hand.

2. Often the simplest technique is to make the antecedent itself plural: then the plural pronoun referring to it is grammatically appropriate, and no problem of gender arises:

    > All those in the room raised their hands.

    > Writers should be careful about their diction.

3. If your purpose and the formality of the context permit, you can use the impersonal pronoun *one*:

    > One should be careful about one's diction.

    If this sounds too formal, consider using the less formal second-person pronoun *you* (but see #16e; you need to be careful when you address the audience directly):

    > You should be careful about your diction.

4. Another option is to revise a sentence so that no gendered pronoun is necessary:

> Everyone's hand went up.

Sometimes the pronoun can simply be omitted:

> A writer should be careful about diction.

15f

5. But if a sentence doesn't lend itself to such changes, or if you want to keep its original structure for some other reason, you can still manage. Don't resort to strings of unsightly devices such as *he/she, him/her, her/ his, him/herself*, or *s/he*. But an occasional *he or she* or *she or he* and the like is acceptable:

> If anyone texts during class, he or she will be asked to leave.

> A writer should be careful about her or his diction.

But don't do this too often, as such repetitions can become tedious and cluttering.

See also **man, woman, etc.** in the usage checklist, #72.

15e Collective Noun as Antecedent

If the antecedent is a *collective noun* (see #13), use either a singular or a plural pronoun to refer to it, depending on context and desired meaning. If the collective noun stands for the group seen as a unit, use a *singular* pronoun:

> The team worked on its power play during the practice.

> The committee announced its decision.

If the collective noun stands for the members of the group seen as individuals, use a *plural* pronoun:

> The team took up their starting positions.

> The committee had no sooner taken their seats than they began chatting among themselves.

15f Agreement with Demonstrative Adjectives

Demonstrative adjectives must agree in number with the nouns they modify (usually *kind* or *kinds* or similar words):

agr: These kind of snakes are very rare.

revised: This kind of snake is very rare.

revised: These kinds of snakes are very rare.

Exercise 15 Correcting Agreement Errors

16a

In each of the following, correct any lack of agreement between pronouns and their antecedents. Revise sentences as necessary to avoid gender bias.

1. Everybody is free to express their own opinion.
2. Una or Gwendolyn will lend you their textbook.
3. Each of the children are going to have to wait to take his own turn.
4. Anyone who thinks for themselves will not be deceived by advertising.
5. After studying his statements for over an hour, I still couldn't understand it.
6. It is usually a good sign when a person starts caring about his appearance.
7. Everyone who wants to play the game will be provided with a pencil to write their answers with.
8. In order to make sure each sentence is correct, check them carefully during revision and proofreading.
9. Dylan and Rohan, who were both very hungry, gave himself permission to indulge in the buffet.
10. One should always study for an exam, even if you think you already know the answers.

 16 **Reference of Pronouns**

ref A pronoun's **reference** to an antecedent must be clear. The pronoun or the sentence will not be clear if the antecedent is remote, ambiguous, vague, or missing.

16a Remote Antecedent
An antecedent should be close enough to the pronoun to be unmistakable; your reader shouldn't have to pause and search for it. An antecedent

should seldom appear more than one sentence before its pronoun within a paragraph. For example:

> *ref*: People who expect to find happiness in material things alone may well discover that the life of the mind is more important than the life filled with possessions. Material prosperity may seem fine at a given moment, but in the long run its delights have a way of fading into inconsequential boredom and emptiness. They then realize, too late, where true happiness lies.

The word *People* is too far back to be a clear antecedent for the pronoun *They*. If the second sentence had also begun with *They*, the connection would be clearer. Or the third sentence might begin with a more particularizing phrase, like "Such people . . . ."

16b Ambiguous Reference
A pronoun should refer clearly to only one antecedent:

> *ref*: When Lea's sister told her that she had won a trip to France, she was very excited.

Each *she* could refer either to Lea (*her*) or to Lea's sister. When revising such a sentence, don't just insert explanatory parentheses; rephrase the sentence:

> *weak*: When Lea's sister told her that she (her sister) had won a trip to France, she (Lea) was very excited.

> *clear*: Lea was very excited when her sister told her about winning a trip to France.

> *clear*: Lea's sister had won a trip to France, and she was very excited when she told Lea about it.

> *clear*: Lea was very excited when her sister said, "I won a trip to France!"

Another example:

> *ref*: His second film was far different from his first. It was an adventure story set in Australia.

A pronoun like *it* often refers to the subject of the preceding independent clause, here *second film*, but *it* is also pulled toward the closest noun or pronoun, here *first*. The problem is easily solved by *combining* the two sentences, reducing the second to a subordinate element:

> *clear*: His second film, an adventure story set in Australia, was far different from his first.

> *clear*: His second film was far different from his first, which was an adventure story set in Australia.

16c Vague Reference

Vague reference is usually caused by the demonstrative pronouns *this* and *that* and the relative pronoun *which*:

> *ref*: The doctors are overworked, and there are no beds available. This is an intolerable situation for the hospital.

Another way of writing this would be to change *This*, after a comma, to *which*:

> *ref*: The doctors are overworked, and there are no beds available, which is an intolerable situation for the hospital.

In both sentences there is a problem with vague reference. *This* in the first example and *which* in the second seem to refer to the entire content of the preceding sentence, but they also seem to refer specifically to the fact that there are no beds available in the hospital. Revision is necessary:

> *clear*: The overworked doctors and the lack of available beds make for an intolerable situation for the hospital.

> *clear*: The doctors are overworked, and there are no beds available. These two circumstances make for an intolerable situation for the hospital.

A *this* or *which* can be adequate if the phrasing and meaning are appropriate:

> *clear*: It is not only the overworked doctors but also the lack of beds which makes the situation intolerable for the hospital.

Another example:

> *ref*: Othello states many times that he loves Iago and that he thinks he is a very honest man; Iago uses this to his advantage.

The third *he* is possibly ambiguous, but more problematic is the vague reference of *this*. Changing *this* to *this opinion, these feelings, this attitude, these mistakes, this blindness of Othello's,* or even *Othello's blindness* makes the reference clearer. Even the *his* is slightly ambiguous: *Iago takes advantage of* would be better.

And don't catch the "this" virus; sufferers of it are driven to begin a large proportion of their sentences and other independent clauses with a *this*. Whenever you catch yourself beginning with a *this*, look carefully to see

16d

- if the reference to the preceding clause or sentence or paragraph is as clear on paper as it may be in your mind;
- if the *this* could be replaced by a specific noun or noun phrase, or otherwise avoided (for example, by rephrasing or subordinating);
- whether, if you decide to keep *this*, it is an ambiguous demonstrative pronoun; if so, try to make it a **demonstrative adjective**, giving it a noun to modify—even if the result is no more specific than "This *idea*," "This *fact*," or "This *argument*" (see #14f and #41).

And always check if an opening *This* looks back to a noun that is in fact singular; it may be that "*These* ideas," "*These* facts," or "*These* arguments" would be more appropriate.

16d Missing Antecedent

Sometimes a writer may have an antecedent in mind but fail to write it down:

> *ref*:   In the early seventeenth century, the Renaissance attitude was concentrated mainly on the arts rather than on developing the scientific part of their minds.

The writer was probably thinking of "the people of the Renaissance." Simply changing *their* to *people's* would clear up the difficulty.

> *ref*:   After the mayor's speech he agreed to answer questions from the audience.

The implied antecedent of *he* is *mayor*, but it isn't there, for the possessive *mayor's* functions as an adjective rather than a noun. Revise the sentence to include a clear antecedent:

> *clear*:   When the mayor finished his speech, he agreed to answer questions from the audience.

clear: After speaking, the mayor agreed to answer questions from the audience.

clear: At the end of his speech, the mayor agreed to answer questions from the audience.

Note that in this last version, *his* comes before its supposed "antecedent," *mayor*—an unusual pattern, but one that is acceptable if the context is clear (for example, if no other possible antecedent for *his* occurred in the preceding sentence) and if the two are close together.

ref: Whenever a student assembly is called, they are required to attend.

Since *student* here functions as an adjective, it cannot serve as an antecedent for *they*. It is necessary to replace *they* with *students*—and then one would probably want to omit the original *student*. Or one could change "student assembly" to "an assembly of students" and retain *they*.

ref: Over half the guests left the party, but it did not stop the band from playing.

Again, there is no antecedent. Change *it* to *their departure*.

16e Indefinite *you*, *they*, and *it*

In formal writing, avoid the pronouns *you*, *they*, and *it* when they are indefinite:

informal: In order to graduate, you must have at least 120 course credits.

formal: In order to graduate, a student must have at least 120 course credits.

(The impersonal *one* would be all right, but perhaps not as effective because it is less specific and more formal.)

informal: In some cities they do not have enough recycling facilities.

formal: Some cities do not have enough recycling facilities.

formal: Some cities' recycling facilities are inadequate.

16e

Although it is correct to use the expletive or impersonal *it* (see #11k and #29f) and say "*It* is raining," "*It* is hard to get up in the morning," "*It* is seven o'clock," and so on, avoid such indefinite uses of *it* as the following:

> *informal*:   It states in our textbook that we should be careful how we use the pronoun *it*.

> *formal*:   Our textbook states that we should be careful how we use the pronoun *it*.

17

Exercise 16 Correcting Faulty Pronoun Reference

Correct any faulty pronoun reference in the following:

1. Summer homes make good retreats—for those who can afford it.
2. You cannot suppress truth, for it is morally wrong.
3. The deadline was a month away, but I failed to meet it, for something happened that prevented it.
4. The tone of the poem is such that it creates an atmosphere of romance.
5. Television usually shows regular commercials, but this is more and more being supplanted by product placement in movies.
6. Sean weeded and planted and watered his flower garden for hours, and his efforts paid off when they bloomed through the summer.
7. I didn't take notes while I sat through the lecture, which I later regretted.
8. According to the news, they say we're not doing enough to combat climate change.
9. It is a good idea to have a hobby, but this shouldn't take over your life.
10. Madison couldn't wait to tell her sister that she had found the ring she thought she had lost.

17 Verbs

Verbs are core parts of speech. A verb is the focal point of a clause or a sentence. As you saw in chapter II, standard sentences consist of subjects and predicates: every subject has a predicate, and the heart of every predicate is its verb.

Verbs are often called "action" words; yet some verbs express little or no action. Think of verbs as expressing not only *action* but also *occurrence*, *process*, and *condition* or *state of being*. All verbs *assert* or *ask* something about their subjects, sometimes by *linking* a subject with a complement. Some verbs are single words; others are phrases consisting of two or more words. Here are some sentences with the verbs underlined:

> He throws curves.

> I thought for a while.

> Zarmina is a lawyer.

> Something happened last night.

> I am running a marathon.

> The CN Tower was completed in 1976.

> By the end of the year, I will have written more than thirty essays.

> Are you listening?

> Will you be needing this file later?

> The fresh bread smells delicious.

> The two columns of figures came out even.

> They will set out for Egypt in June.

(For a discussion of such two-part verbs as *come out* and *set out*, see #22d–e.)

17a Kinds of Verbs: Transitive, Intransitive, and Linking

Verbs are classified according to the way they function in sentences.

A verb normally taking a *direct object* is considered a **transitive verb**. A transitive verb makes a transition, or conveys a movement, from its subject to its object:

> She has good taste.

> He introduced me to his uncle.

> Noam never neglects his lab work.

> She expresses her ideas eloquently.

> He stuffed himself with pizza.

> Where did you put that book?

A direct object answers the question consisting of the verb and *what* or *whom*: Has *what*? Taste. Introduced *whom*? Me. Never neglects *what*? Lab work. Expresses *what*? Ideas. Stuffed *whom*? Himself. Did put *what* where? Book. (See also #11d, #11f, #11i, and #11j.)

17a

A verb that normally occurs without a direct object is considered **intransitive** (see also #11c):

> What has happened to the aquarium's whale?

> The earthquake occurred during the night.

> You should rest for a while.

> He gossiped with his roommate.

> Please stay.

> When will you arrive?

Many verbs, however, can be either transitive or intransitive, depending on how they function in particular sentences:

> I ran my school's newspaper. (transitive)
> I ran to the store. (intransitive)

> I can see the parade better from the balcony. (transitive)
> I can see well enough from here. (intransitive)

> He wished that he were home in bed. (transitive)
> She wished upon a star. (intransitive)

In fact, few verbs are exclusively either transitive or intransitive, as a good dictionary will show you. Verbs felt to be clearly intransitive can often also be used transitively, and vice versa:

> She slept the sleep of the just. (In this sentence, *slept* takes the object *sleep* and therefore is transitive.)

> He leaned back in the chair and remembered. (In this sentence, *remembered* takes no object and therefore is intransitive.)

A third kind of verb is called a **linking** (or copulative) verb. The main one is *be* in its various forms. Some other common linking verbs are *become, seem, remain, act, get, feel, look, appear, smell, sound,* and *taste.* Linking verbs don't have objects, but they are yet incomplete; they need a **subjective complement**. A linking verb is like an equal sign in an equation: something at the right-hand (predicate) end is needed to balance what is at the left-hand (subject) end. The complement will be either a *predicate adjective* or a *predicate noun* (see also #11g and #11h). Here are some examples:

> Angela is not well. (predicate adjective: *well*)
>
> Angela is a lawyer. (predicate noun: *lawyer*)
>
> Mikhail became uneasy. (predicate adjective: *uneasy*)
>
> Mikhail became a pilot. (predicate noun: *pilot*)
>
> The winner is Nathan. (predicate noun: *Nathan*)
>
> The band sounds good. (predicate adjective: *good*)
>
> The surface felt sticky. (predicate adjective: *sticky*)

17a

Occasionally a complement precedes the verb, for example in a question or in a sentence or clause inverted for emphasis:

> How sick are you?
>
> However happy he may have been, he did not let his feelings show to the other contestants.

Like an object, a subjective complement answers the question consisting of the verb and *what* or *whom* (or *who*), or perhaps *how*: Is *what*? A lawyer. Became *what*? Uneasy. Is *who*? Nathan. Sounds *how*? Good. It differs from an object in that it is the equivalent of the subject or says something about the subject.

Such verbs as *act, sound, taste, smell,* and *feel* can of course also function as transitive verbs: She *acted* the part. He *sounded* his horn. I *tasted* the soup. He *smelled* the hydrogen sulphide. He *felt* the bump on his head.

Similarly, many of the verbs that function as linking verbs can also function as regular intransitive verbs, sometimes accompanied by *adverbial* modifiers (see #20): We *looked* at the painting. Santa *is* on the roof. Teresa *is* at home. We *are* here. But whenever one of these verbs is accompanied by a predicate adjective or a predicate noun, it is functioning as a linking verb.

Exercise 17a (1) Using Transitive and Intransitive Verbs

After each transitive verb in the following, supply an object; after each intransitive verb, supply an adverb (or adverbial phrase) or a period. If a particular verb can be either transitive or intransitive, do both.

Examples: Bela *wants* happiness. (tr.)

Aidan *waited* patiently. (intr.)

Moira *speaks* loudly. (intr.)

her mind. (tr.)

1. Xian *expects* _____
2. Yvonne *breathed* _____
3. Jenna *talks* _____
4. Spencer *believed* _____
5. Ricardo *bought* _____
6. They *ordered* _____
7. Yukio *learned* _____
8. Olivier *performed* _____

9. Bri *responded* _____
10. Sonny *teaches* _____
11. Adriana *sings* _____
12. Pierre *repairs* _____
13. Council *vetoed* _____
14. Ela *compromised* _____
15. Soolin *flew* _____
16. Ahmed *left* _____

Exercise 17a (2) Recognizing Subjective Complements

In the following, first identify the complement of each italicized linking verb, and then indicate whether it is a predicate noun or a predicate adjective.

1. She *was* sorry that he *felt* so ill.

Complement of *was*: _____

Complement of *felt*: _____

2. Because he *was* a computer expert, he *was* confident that he could write a software program for the system.

Complement of the first *was*: _____

Complement of the second *was*: _____

3. The book *became* a bestseller even though it *was* scholarly in its examination of black holes.

Complement of *became*: _____

Complement of *was*: _____

4. Since the house *was* well insulated, it *stayed* warm throughout the severe winter.

Complement of *was*: _____

Complement of *stayed*: _____

5. Incredible as it *seems*, the casserole *tasted* as good as it *looked* odd.

Complement of *seems*: _____

Complement of *tasted*: _____

Complement of *looked*: _____

17a

Exercise 17a (3) Using Subjective Complements

After each linking verb, supply (a) a predicate noun and (b) a predicate adjective.

> **Examples:** Kevin *was* (a) an engineer.
>
>   (b) energized.

1. Erika *is* (a) _____.

    (b) _____.

2. Priscilla *became* (a) _____.

    (b) _____.

3. Luigi *remained* (a) _____.

    (b) _____.

4. The government *had been* (a) _____.

    (b) _____.

Exercise 17a (4) Using Verbs

Compose sentences using some common linking verbs other than *be*, *become*, *seem*, and *remain*. Then compose other sentences using the same verbs as either transitive or intransitive verbs, without complements. Can any of the verbs you have chosen function as all three kinds? Try *smell*, for example, or *act*.

17b Inflection of Verbs: Principal Parts

As well as being important in spoken and written communication, verbs are also the most complex, the most highly inflected, of the eight parts of speech. Verbs are inflected

- for **person** and **number**, in order to agree with a subject (#17d);
- for **tense**, in order to show an action's time—present, past, or future—and aspect—simple, perfect, or progressive (#17g);
- for **mood**, in order to show the kind of sentence a verb is in—indicative, imperative, or subjunctive (#17-l and #17m); and
- for **voice**, in order to show whether a subject is active (performing an action) or passive (being acted upon) (#17-o and #17p).

Every verb (except some auxiliaries; see #17e) has what are called its **principal parts**:

1. its **basic** form (the form a dictionary uses in headwords, see #63c)
2. its **past-tense** form
3. its **past participle**
4. its **present participle**

Verbs regularly form both the *past tense* and the *past participle* simply by adding *ed* to the basic form:

Basic Form	Past-Tense Form	Past Participle
push	pushed	pushed
cook	cooked	cooked

If the basic form already ends in *e*, however, only *d* is added:

move	moved	moved
agree	agreed	agreed

Present participles are regularly formed by adding *ing* to the basic form:

Basic Form	Present Participle
push	pushing
cook	cooking
agree	agreeing

But verbs ending in an unpronounced *e* usually drop it before adding *ing*:

move	moving
skate	skating

And some verbs double a final consonant before adding *ed* or *ing*:

grin	grinned	grinning
stop	stopped	stopping

For more on these and other irregularities, see #62c. Further, good dictionaries list any irregular principal parts, ones not formed by simply adding *ed* or *ing* (and see #17c).

It is from these four parts—the basic form and the three principal inflections of it—that all other inflected forms of a verb are made.

Note: The basic form of a verb is sometimes called the **infinitive** form, meaning that it can be preceded by *to* to form an infinitive: *to be, to push, to agree*. Infinitives, participles, and gerunds are called **non-finite verbs**, or **verbals**; they function not as verbs but as other parts of speech (see #21). **Finite verbs**, unlike non-finite forms, are restricted or limited by person, number, tense, mood, and voice; they function as the main verbs in sentences.

17c

17c Irregular Verbs

Some of the most common English verbs are **irregular** in the way they make their past-tense forms and their past participles. Whenever you aren't certain about the principal parts of a verb, check your dictionary, or use the following list, which contains most of the common irregular verbs with their past-tense forms and their past participles (where two are given, the first is the more common). If you need to, memorize these forms; practise by composing sentences using each form (for example: *Choose* the one you want. I *chose* mine yesterday. Have you *chosen* your topic yet?). If you're looking for a verb that is a compound or that has a prefix, look for the main verb: for *misread, proofread*, or *reread*, look under *read*.

Basic or Present Form	Past-Tense Form	Past Participle
arise	arose	arisen
awake	awoke	awoken
bear	bore	borne (born for "given birth to")
beat	beat	beaten
become	became	become
begin	began	begun
bend	bent	bent
bet	bet	bet
bid	bid	bid
bind	bound	bound
bite	bit	bitten
bleed	bled	bled
blow	blew	blown
break	broke	broken
breed	bred	bred

Basic or Present Form	Past-Tense Form	Past Participle
bring	brought	brought
broadcast	broadcast, broadcasted	broadcast, broadcasted
build	built	built
burn	burned, burnt	burned, burnt
burst	burst	burst
buy	bought	bought
cast	cast	cast
catch	caught	caught
choose	chose	chosen
cling	clung	clung
come	came	come
cost	cost	cost
creep	crept	crept
cut	cut	cut
deal	dealt	dealt
dig	dug	dug
dive	dived, dove	dived
draw	drew	drawn
dream	dreamed, dreamt	dreamed, dreamt
drink	drank	drunk
drive	drove	driven
eat	ate	eaten
fall	fell	fallen
feed	fed	fed
feel	felt	felt
fight	fought	fought
find	found	found
fit	fit, fitted	fit, fitted
flee	fled	fled
fling	flung	flung
fly	flew	flown
forbid	forbade	forbidden
forget	forgot	forgotten
forgive	forgave	forgiven
forgo	forwent	forgone
freeze	froze	frozen

Basic or Present Form	Past-Tense Form	Past Participle
get	got	got, gotten
give	gave	given
go	went	gone
grind	ground	ground
grow	grew	grown
hang	hung (hanged for "executed")	hung (hanged for "executed")
hear	heard	heard
hide	hid	hidden
hit	hit	hit
hold	held	held
hurt	hurt	hurt
input	input, inputted	input, inputted
keep	kept	kept
kneel	knelt, kneeled	knelt, kneeled
knit	knitted, knit	knitted, knit
know	knew	known
lay	laid	laid
lead	led	led
leap	leaped, leapt	leaped, leapt
leave	left	left
lend	lent	lent
let	let	let
lie ("recline")	lay	lain
light	lit, lighted	lit, lighted
lose	lost	lost
make	made	made
mean	meant	meant
meet	met	met
mimic	mimicked	mimicked
mow	mowed	mowed, mown
panic	panicked	panicked
pay	paid	paid
prove	proved	proven, proved
put	put	put
quit	quit	quit
read	read (changes pronunciation)	read (changes pronunciation)

17c

Basic or Present Form	Past-Tense Form	Past Participle
rid	rid	rid
ride	rode	ridden
ring	rang	rung
rise	rose	risen
run	ran	run
say	said	said
see	saw	seen
seek	sought	sought
sell	sold	sold
send	sent	sent
set	set	set
sew	sewed	sewn, sewed
shake	shook	shaken
shed	shed	shed
shine	shone (shined for "polished")	shone (shined for "polished")
shoot	shot	shot
show	showed	shown, showed
shrink	shrank, shrunk	shrunk
shut	shut	shut
sing	sang	sung
sink	sank, sunk	sunk
sit	sat	sat
slay	slew	slain
sleep	slept	slept
slide	slid	slid
sling	slung	slung
slink	slunk	slunk
slit	slit	slit
sneak	snuck, sneaked	snuck, sneaked
sow	sowed	sown, sowed
speak	spoke	spoken
speed	sped, speeded	sped, speeded
spend	spent	spent
spin	spun	spun
spit	spat, spit	spat, spit
split	split	split

17c

Basic or Present Form	Past-Tense Form	Past Participle
spread	spread	spread
spring	sprang, sprung	sprung
stand	stood	stood
steal	stole	stolen
stick	stuck	stuck
sting	stung	stung
stink	stank, stunk	stunk
stride	strode	stridden
strike	struck	struck
string	strung	strung
strive	strove, strived	striven, strived
swear	swore	sworn
sweep	swept	swept
swell	swelled	swollen, swelled
swim	swam	swum
swing	swung	swung
take	took	taken
teach	taught	taught
tear	tore	torn
tell	told	told
think	thought	thought
thrive	thrived, throve	thrived, thriven
throw	threw	thrown
thrust	thrust	thrust
traffic	trafficked	trafficked
tread	trod	trodden, trod
wake	woke, waked	woken, waked
wear	wore	worn
weave	wove	woven, wove
weep	wept	wept
wet	wet, wetted	wet, wetted
win	won	won
wind	wound	wound
withdraw	withdrew	withdrawn
wring	wrung	wrung
write	wrote	written

17c

See #17f for a discussion of the irregular verbs *do*, *be*, and *have*.

EAL

17d Inflection for Person and Number

In order to agree with its subject (see #18), a verb is inflected for *person* and *number*. To illustrate, here are four verbs inflected for person and number in the *present tense*, using personal pronouns as subjects (see #14a):

Singular				
Ist person	I walk	I move	I push	I fly
2nd person	you walk	you move	you push	you fly
3rd person	he walks	he moves	he pushes	he flies
	she walks	she moves	she pushes	she flies
	it walks	it moves	it pushes	it flies

Plural				
1st person	we walk	we move	we push	we fly
2nd person	you walk	you move	you push	you fly
3rd person	they walk	they move	they push	they fly

Note that the inflection occurs *only in the third-person singular*, and that you add *s* or *es* to the basic form (first changing final *y* to *i* where necessary; see #62c).

EAL

17e Auxiliary Verbs

Auxiliary or helping verbs go with other verbs to form verb phrases indicating tense, voice, and mood. The auxiliary *do* helps in forming questions (see #11t), forming negative sentences, and expressing emphasis:

<u>Did</u> you get the first question right?

I <u>did not</u> arrive on time.

She <u>doesn't</u> care for asparagus.

I <u>did</u> do my homework!

I <u>do</u> admire that woman.

Do works only in the simple present and simple past tenses (see #17g). The principal auxiliary verbs—*be*, *have*, *will*, and *shall*—enable us to form tenses beyond the simple present and the simple past, as illustrated in #17g. *Be* and *have* go with main verbs and with each other to form the perfect tenses and the progressive tenses; *will* and *shall* (see #17h.3) help form the various future tenses. *Be* also combines with main verbs to form the passive voice (see #17-o and #17p).

Modal Auxiliaries

There are also what are called **modal auxiliaries**. The principal ones are *can, could, may, might, must, should,* and *would*. They combine with main verbs and other auxiliaries to express such meanings as ability, possibility, obligation, and necessity.

The following chart illustrates the principal modal verbs currently in use in North American English:

17e

The Modal	Used to Express . . .
can	ability
could	ability, possibility
may might	permission, possibility
must ought to should	obligation
shall will	prediction, intention
should would	condition

Consider the following examples:

I <u>can</u> understand that.

There <u>could</u> be thunderstorms tomorrow.

The instructor <u>may</u> decide to cancel the quiz.

I <u>might</u> attend, but then again I <u>might</u> not.

<u>Must</u> we wear our uniforms?

Parents <u>ought to</u> do what is best for their children.

People <u>should</u> obey the law.

<u>Shall</u> we go to the club?

I think I <u>will</u> pass the final exam.

You <u>should</u> have received the letter by now.

I <u>would</u> tell you the answer if I <u>could</u>.

To express the negative form, add *not* following the modal auxiliary, or join the auxiliary with the contraction *n't* (e.g., *couldn't, shouldn't, mustn't*; see also #17h.3). In the case of *can*, the negative form becomes *cannot* (or *can't*).

Unlike other verbs (see #17d), modal auxiliaries are not inflected for third-person singular:

> I can go.
>
> You can go.
>
> He or she or it can go.

Nor do these verbs have any participial forms, or an infinitive form (one cannot say *to can*; instead, one must use another verb phrase, *to be able*). But modal auxiliaries can work as parts of perfect tenses as well as of simple present and simple past tenses (see #17g). (For more on modal auxiliaries, see #17n.)

Could, might

Could and *might* also serve as the past-tense forms of *can* and *may*, for example if demanded by the sequence of tenses after a verb in the past tense (see #17i):

> He <u>was</u> sure that I <u>could</u> handle the project.
>
> She <u>said</u> that I <u>might</u> watch the rehearsal if I <u>was</u> quiet.

(For the distinction between *can* and *may*, see **can, may** in the usage checklist, #72. For *should* and *would* as past-tense forms, see #17i.2.)

Might, may

Might and *may* are sometimes interchangeable when expressing possibility:

> She <u>may</u> (<u>might</u>) challenge the committee's decision.
>
> He <u>may</u> (<u>might</u>) have finished the job by now.

But usually there is a difference, with *may* indicating a stronger possibility, *might* a somewhat less likely one.

> Since more rain is forecast, the flood waters <u>may</u> rise overnight. (That is, flood waters *may very well* rise.)
>
> The weather report forecasts sunshine, but the river <u>might</u> still rise overnight. (That is, flood waters *could* rise but probably won't.)

To express a condition contrary to fact (see #17m.2), *might* is the right word:

If you had edited your essay, you <u>might</u> [not *may*] have received a higher grade.

That is, you *didn't* edit carefully, and you *didn't* get a higher grade. *Might* is necessary for clear expression of a hypothetical as opposed to a factual circumstance. Consider the difference in meaning between the following two sentences:

Reducing his speed might have prevented the accident.

Reducing his speed may have prevented the accident.

17f

In the first sentence, *might* is used again to express a condition contrary to fact: the driver did not reduce his speed and the accident was not prevented, but the writer suggests the accident could have been prevented had the driver reduced his speed. The substitution of *may* for *might* in the second sentence changes the situation: in this case, the accident was prevented, and the writer is speculating that this fortunate occurrence may be attributable to the driver's having reduced his speed. See also **may, might** in the usage checklist, #72.

17f Inflection of *do, be,* and *have*

Do, *be*, and *have* are different from the other auxiliaries in that they can also function as main verbs. As a main verb, *do* most often has the sense of "perform, accomplish":

I <u>do</u> my job.

He <u>did</u> what I asked.

She <u>does</u> her best.

Have as a main verb most often means "own, possess, contain":

I <u>have</u> enough money.

July <u>has</u> thirty-one days.

And *be* as a main verb can mean "exist" or "live" (a sense seldom used: "I think; therefore, I *am*"), but it most often means "occur, remain, occupy a place":

The exam <u>is</u> today.

I won't <u>be</u> more than an hour.

The car <u>is</u> in the garage.

(See your dictionary for other meanings of these verbs.)

Even when functioning as auxiliaries, these verbs are fully inflected. Here are the inflections for *do* and *have*, which, as you can see, are irregular:

Singular		
1st person	I do	I have
2nd person	you do	you have
3rd person	he does	he has
	she does	she has
	it does	it has
Plural		
1st person	we do	we have
2nd person	you do	you have
3rd person	they do	they have
past-tense form	did	had
past participle	done	had
present participle	doing	having

The most common verb of all, *be*, is also the most irregular:

Singular	Present Tense	Past Tense
1st person	I am	I was
2nd person	you are	you were
3rd person	he / she / it is	he / she / it was
Plural		
1st person	we are	we were
2nd person	you are	you were
3rd person	they are	they were
past participle	been	
present participle	being	

For a fuller discussion of tense, see the next three sections.

EAL

17g Time and the Verb: Inflection for Tense

Even though verbs must agree with their subjects in person and number (see #17d, #18), they are still the strongest elements in sentences because they not only indicate action but also control time. The verb by its inflection indicates the *time* of an action, an event, or a condition. Through its **tense** a verb shows *when* an action occurs:

past tense: Yesterday, I practised.

present tense: Today, I practise.

future tense: Tomorrow, I will practise.

The adverbs *yesterday*, *today*, and *tomorrow* emphasize the *when* of the action, but the senses of past, present, and future are clear without them:

I practised. I practise. I will practise.

17g

The above examples illustrate the most common tenses: the simple tenses. English contains nine additional tenses that indicate different relationships to time. The following table outlines all twelve.

Tense		Verb Form
1. Simple Present	I / you	dance
	he / she / it	dances
	we / you / they	dance
2. Simple Past	I / you / he / she / it / we / you / they	danced
3. Simple Future	I / you / he / she / it / we / you / they	will dance
4. Present Perfect	he / she / it	has danced
	I / you / we / you / they	have danced
5. Past Perfect	I / you / he / she / it / we / you / they	had danced
6. Future Perfect	I / you / he / she / it / we / you / they	will have danced
7. Present Progressive	I	am dancing
	you	are dancing
	he / she / it	is dancing
	we / you / they	are dancing
8. Past Progressive	I	was dancing
	you	were dancing
	he / she / it	was dancing
	we / you / they	were dancing
9. Future Progressive	I / you / he / she / it / we / you / they	will be dancing
10. Present Perfect Progressive	I / you	have been dancing
	he / she / it	has been dancing
	we / you / they	have been dancing
11. Past Perfect Progressive	I / you / he / she / it / we / you / they	had been dancing
12. Future Perfect Progressive	I / you / he / she / it / we / you / they	will have been dancing

17h The Functions of the Different Tenses

Following are brief descriptions and illustrations of the main functions of each tense. Although these points are sometimes oversimplifications of very complex matters, and although there are other exceptions and variations than those listed, these guidelines should help you to use the tenses and to take advantage of the possibilities they offer for clear expression.

1. Simple Present

Generally, use this tense to describe an action or a condition that is happening now, at the time of the utterance:

> The pitcher <u>throws</u>. The batter <u>swings</u>. It <u>is</u> a high fly ball.
>
> The day <u>is</u> very warm. I <u>am</u> uncomfortable. <u>Are</u> you all right? I <u>can</u> manage.

But this tense has several other common uses. It can indicate a general truth or belief:

> Ottawa <u>is</u> one of the coldest capitals in the world.
>
> Cheetahs <u>can</u> outrun any other animal.
>
> The bigger they <u>are</u> the harder they <u>fall</u>.

or describe a customary or habitual or repeated action or condition:

> I <u>plant</u> trees as a hobby.
>
> Anne <u>spells</u> her name with an e.
>
> I always <u>eat</u> breakfast before going to school.
>
> In Yellowknife, snow <u>starts</u> falling before Halloween.

or describe the characters or events in a literary or other work, or what an author does in such a work (see #17k):

> Oedipus <u>searches</u> for the truth almost like a modern detective.
>
> In the novel, owls <u>deliver</u> the mail to the school.
>
> Dante with the help of Virgil <u>ascends</u> to paradise.

or even express future time, especially with the help of an adverbial modifier of time (see also number 7, on the present progressive, below):

He arrives tomorrow. (adverbial modifier: *tomorrow*)

We leave for London next Sunday. (adverbial modifier: *next Sunday*)

2. Simple Past

Use this tense for a single or repeated action or condition that began and ended in the past (compare number 4 on the present perfect below):

She earned a lot of money last summer.

I was happy when I heard the news.

I painted a picture yesterday.

He went to Paris three times last year.

3. Simple Future

Although there are other ways to indicate future time (see, for example, number 1 on the simple present above and number 7 on the present progressive below), the most common and straightforward is to use the simple future, putting *will* or *shall* before the basic form of the verb:

She will arrive tomorrow morning.

I will paint a picture tomorrow.

We'll have a nice picnic if it doesn't rain.

Shall, once considered the correct form to use with a first-person subject (*I, we*), is now, in North American English, restricted largely to expressing emphasis or determination or to first-person questions asking for agreement or permission or advice, where *will* would sound unidiomatic:

Shall we underline{go}?

With negatives, the contracted forms of *will not* and *shall not* are *won't* and *shan't*:

Won't we arrive on time?

No, I shan't be able to attend.

Note, however, that *shan't* is uncommon in Canadian English.

17h

4. Present Perfect

Use this tense for an action or a condition that began in the past and that continues to the present (compare number 2 on the simple past above); though commonly considered "completed" as of the moment, some actions or conditions referred to in this tense could continue after the present:

> I have earned a lot of money this summer.

> James Bond has just entered the casino.

> The weather has been lovely lately.

> The autobiography course has lasted for two months.

You can use this tense for something that occurred entirely in the past if you feel that it somehow impinges on the present—that is, if you intend to imply the sense of "before now" or "so far" or "already":

> I have painted a picture; take a look at it.

> She has told us how she wants our assignments done.

> I have visited Greece three times.

> We have beaten them at tennis seven out of ten times.

5. Past Perfect

Use this tense for an action completed in the past before a specific past time or event. Notice that there are at least two actions taking place in the past:

> I had painted a picture just before they arrived.

> Though I had seen the film twice before, I went again last week.

> They got to the station only a minute late, but the train had already left.

6. Future Perfect

Use this tense for an action or a condition that will be completed before a specific future time or event:

> By this time next week I will have painted a self-portrait.

> I will already have eaten when you arrive.

17h

Sometimes simple future works as well as future perfect:

> Some experts predict that by the year 2020 scientists <u>will have found</u> a cure for diabetes.

7. Present Progressive

Use this tense for an action or a condition that began at some past time and is continuing now, in the present:

> I <u>am writing</u> my rough draft.

> Climate change <u>is causing</u> a significant rise in sea levels.

17h

Sometimes the simple and the progressive forms of a verb say much the same thing:

> We <u>hope</u> for snow.
> We <u>are hoping</u> for snow.

> I <u>feel</u> giddy.
> I <u>am feeling</u> giddy.

But usually the progressive form emphasizes an activity, or the single-ness or continuing nature of an action, rather than a larger condition or general truth:

> A tax hike <u>hurts</u> many people.
> The tax hike <u>is hurting</u> many people.

> I <u>walk</u> to work.
> I <u>am walking</u> to work.

Like the simple present, the present progressive tense can also express future time, especially with adverbial help:

> They <u>are arriving</u> early tomorrow morning.

You can also express future time with a form of *be* and *going* before an infinitive (see #21a):

> They <u>are going</u> to walk around Stanley Park on New Year's day.

Stative verbs—verbs that express sense, cognitive, or emotional states—don't often appear in the progressive form. Because they express a state of being or mental activity, they are usually found describing static or relatively constant situations. Unless the stative verb is expressing an action, do not use it in the progressive tense.

> ***incorrect***: After being sprayed by the skunk, the dog is smelling bad now. (condition)

The odour of the dog is a condition, not an action. Therefore, you should write, "the dog smells bad." However, if you want to imply the dog's ability to smell is not functioning, you could write the following:

> ***correct***: After having its nose injured, the dog is smelling poorly. (activity)

Here is a short list of some common stative verbs:

appear	be	believe	dislike	feel
hate	hear	imagine	know	like
love	prefer	remember	resemble	see
seem	smell	understand	want	wish

8. Past Progressive

Use this tense for an action that was in progress during some past time, especially if you want to emphasize the continuing nature of the action:

> I remember that I was painting a picture that day.

> He was driving very fast.

> They were protesting the city council's decision.

Sometimes the past progressive tense describes an interrupted action or an action during which something else happens:

> When the telephone rang I was making tempura.

> Just as he was stepping off, the bus started moving.

9. Future Progressive

Use this tense for a continuing action in the future or for an action that will be occurring at some specific time in the future:

> I will be painting pictures as long as I can hold a brush.

> You will be learning things for the rest of your life.

> They will be arriving on the midnight plane.

17h

10. Present Perfect Progressive

Use this tense to emphasize the continuing nature of a single or repeated action that began in the past and that has continued at least up to the present. This tense is suitable for showing trends in the sense of showing changes over time.

I have been working on this sketch for an hour.

The profits have been increasing in the last quarter.

Our book club has been meeting once a week since January.

17h

11. Past Perfect Progressive

Use this tense to emphasize the continuing nature of a single or repeated past action that was completed before or interrupted by some other past action:

I had been painting landscapes for three years before I finally sold one.

We had been expecting something quite different.

I had been pondering the problem for an hour when suddenly the solution popped into my head.

12. Future Perfect Progressive

This tense is seldom used in academic writing. Use it to emphasize the continuing nature of a future action before a specific time in the future or before a second future action:

If she continues to dance, by the year 2030 she will have been dancing for over half her life.

You will already have been driving for about nine hours before you even get to the border.

Exercise 17h (1) Using Verb Tenses

Choose a few fairly standard verbs, ones that you find yourself using often—say, three regular verbs and three from the list of irregular verbs (#17c)—and compose substantive sentences using them in all the tenses illustrated in #17g and #17h.

Exercise 17h (2) Using Auxiliary Verbs

Select ten or so of the sentences you wrote for the preceding exercise and try using *do* and some of the *modal auxiliaries* (see #17e) with them to produce different meanings.

Examples: I do paint pictures.

I did paint pictures.

Didn't you paint pictures?

I may have painted pictures.

Can you paint?

I should be painting the garage.

I should have been painting pictures.

I shouldn't have tried painting the ceiling.

Could I have been painting in my sleep?

They must have been painting all night.

EAL

17i Sequence of Tenses

When two or more verbs occur in the same sentence, they will sometimes be of the same tense, but often they will be of different tenses.

1. Compound Sentences

In a compound sentence, made up of two or more independent clauses (see #12c), the verbs can be equally independent; use whatever tenses the sense requires:

> I am leaving [present progressive] now, but she will leave [future] in the morning.

> The polls have closed [present perfect]; the clerks will soon be counting [future progressive] the ballots.

> He had made [past perfect] his promise, and the committee decided [past] to hold him to it; therefore, they will expect [future] his cooperation in drafting a new business plan in the weeks ahead.

2. Past Tense in Independent Clauses

In complex or compound–complex sentences, if the verb in an independent clause is in any of the past tenses, the verbs in any clauses subordinate to it will usually also be in one of the past tenses. For example:

> I told her that I was sorry.

17i

> They hoped that the newly elected treasurer would not be a gambler, and they promised to investigate any expenses that they deemed to be suspicious.

Refer to a time *earlier* than that of the main verb in the past tense by using the *past perfect* tense:

> By Monday, Marla had finished the short story that I sent her on Friday.

17i

But there are exceptions. When the verb in the subordinate clause states a general or timeless truth or belief, or something characteristic or habitual, it stays in the present tense:

> Einstein showed that space, time, and light are linked.

> They discovered the hard way that money doesn't guarantee happiness.

And the context of the sentence sometimes dictates that other kinds of verbs in subordinate clauses should not be changed to a past tense. If you feel that a tense other than the past would be clearer or more accurate, use it; for example:

> I learned yesterday that I will be able to get into the new program in the fall.

The rule calls for *would*, but *will* is logical and clear. Notice that the adverbial marker "in the fall" tells us the action will occur in the future.
Here is another example:

> In an interview yesterday, Silverman said that he is determined to complete the series of concerts.

To use *was* rather than *is* here would be ambiguous, implying that Silverman's determination was a thing of the past; if it definitely *was* past, then *had been* would be clearer.
And here is one more example of a sentence in which the "sequence of tenses" rule is best ignored:

> The secretary told me this morning that Professor Barnes is ill and will not be teaching class this afternoon.

17j Verb Phrases in Compound Predicates

When a compound predicate consists of two verb phrases in different tenses, don't omit part of one of them:

> **t:**   The leader has never and will never practise nepotism.

Rather, include each verb in full or rephrase the sentence:

> ***revised:***   The leader has never practised and will never practise nepotism.

> ***revised:***   The leader has never practised nepotism and will never do so.

17k Tenses in Writing About Literature

When discussing or describing the events in a literary work, it is customary to use the present tense (see also #17h.1):

> While he <u>is</u> away from Denmark, Hamlet <u>arranges</u> to have Rosencrantz and Guildenstern put to death. After he <u>returns</u> he <u>holds</u> Yorick's skull and <u>watches</u> Ophelia being buried. He <u>duels</u> with Laertes and <u>dies</u>. Without a doubt, death <u>is</u> one of the principal themes in the play.

For the tenses of infinitives and participles, see #21b and #21e.

It is also customary to speak of an author in the present tense when one is discussing his or her techniques in a particular work:

> In *Pride and Prejudice,* ane Austen <u>shows</u> the consequences of making hasty judgments of others.

17-l Mood

English verbs are usually considered to have three moods: **indicative**, **imperative**, and **subjunctive**. The mood of a verb has to do with the nature of the expression in which it's being used. The most common mood is the *indicative*, which is used for statements of fact or opinion and for questions:

> The weather forecast for tomorrow <u>sounds</u> promising.

> Shall we <u>proceed</u> with our plans?

The *imperative* mood is used for most commands and instructions (see #11u):

> <u>Put</u> the extra suitcase in the trunk.

> <u>Don't forget</u> the bubbly.

The *subjunctive* mood in English is less common, and it presents some difficulty. It is discussed below.

17m Using the Subjunctive Mood

The subjunctive has almost disappeared from contemporary English. It survives in some standard expressions or idioms such as "*Be* that as it may," "*Come* what may," "Heaven *forbid*," and "Long *live* the Queen." Otherwise, you need consider only two kinds of instances where the subjunctive still functions.

17m

1. Use the subjunctive in a *that* clause after verbs expressing demands, requests, obligations, requirements, recommendations, suggestions, wishes, and the like:

   > Emma asked that the door <u>be</u> left open.

   > The doctor recommended that she <u>take</u> a vacation.

   > I wish [that] I <u>were</u> in Paris.

2. Use the subjunctive to express conditions that are hypothetical or impossible—often in *if* clauses or their equivalents:

   > He looked as if he <u>were</u> going to explode. (But he didn't explode.)

   > If Lise <u>were</u> here she <u>would</u> back me up. (But she isn't here.)

   An *as if* or *as though* clause almost always expresses a condition contrary to fact, but not all *if* clauses do; don't be misled into using a subjunctive where it's not appropriate:

   > ***wrong:*** He said that if there <u>were</u> another complaint he would resign.

   The verb should be *was*, for the condition could turn out to be true: there may be another complaint.

Since only a few subjunctive forms differ from those of the indicative, they are easy to learn and remember. The third-person-singular subjunctive form loses its *s*:

> ***indicative:*** I like the way she <u>paints</u>.
> ***subjunctive:*** I suggested that she <u>paint</u> my portrait.

The subjunctive forms of the verb *be* are *be* and *were*:

> **indicative**: He is friendly. (I am, you / we / they are)
> **subjunctive**: The judge asked that she be excused. (that I / you / we / they be)

> **indicative**: I know that I am in Edmonton.
> **subjunctive**: I wish that I were in Florence.

Note that both *be* and *were* function with either singular or plural subjects. Note also that the past-tense form *were* functions in present-tense expressions of wishes and contrary-to-fact conditions. Other verbs also use their past tense as a subjunctive after a present-tense wish:

> I wish that I shopped less.

After a past-tense wish, use the standard past-perfect form:

> He wished that he had been more attentive.

> She wished that she had played better.

17n Using Modal Auxiliaries and Infinitives Instead of Subjunctives

The *modal auxiliaries* (see #17e) offer common alternatives to many sentences using subjunctives; they express several of the same moods.

> The doctor told her she should [ought to] take a vacation.

> I wish that I could be in Paris.

> He looked as if he might explode.

> If Lise could have been here, she would back me up.

Another alternative uses the *infinitive* (see #21a):

> It is necessary for us to be there before noon.

> The judge ordered Ralph to attend the hearing.

> Emma asked us to leave the door open.

Exercise 17n Using Subjunctives

Suppose that you are giving a friend some advice about how to deal with noisy neighbours. Compose ten sentences using a variety of subjunctive forms. One sentence may start "If I were you, I would . . . ." Then try to revise each so that it uses a modal auxiliary or an infinitive instead of a subjunctive. You should be able to change most if not all of them.

17p

17-o Voice

There are two voices: **active** and **passive**. The *active* voice is direct:

I made this toy boat.

The *passive* voice is less direct, reversing the normal subject–verb–object pattern (see #11e):

This toy boat was made by me.

Passive voice is easy to recognize; the verb uses some form of *be* followed by a past participle (e.g., *was made*). What in active voice would be a direct object (*boat*) in passive voice becomes the subject of the verb. And passive constructions often leave unmentioned the agent of the action or state they describe: *The toy boat was made* (by whom isn't specified). You may sometimes see this referred to as a *truncated passive*.

17p The Passive Voice

as Using the passive voice, some people can promise action without committing themselves to perform it, and they can admit error without accepting responsibility:

> *passive*: Be assured [by whom?] that action will be taken [by whom?].
>
> *active*: I assure you that I will act.

> *passive*: It is to be regretted [by whom?] that an error has been made [by whom?].
>
> *active*: I am sorry our company made an error.

Although the passive voice has its uses, it is not often preferable to the active voice. When possible, use the direct and more vigorous active voice. Here is an example from a student's paper:

> ***pas:***   All of this is communicated by Tolkien by means of a poem rather than prose. The poetry is shown as a tool employed in order to foreshadow events and establish ideas that otherwise could not be easily communicated to us.

The wordiness of this passage results largely from the passive voice. A change to active voice shortens it, clarifies the sense, and produces a crisper style. Begin by making the agent the subject; the rest then follows naturally and logically:

> ***active:***   Tolkien communicates all this in poetry rather than prose because with poetry he can foreshadow events and establish ideas that would otherwise be difficult to convey.

Here is another example:

> ***pas:***   Mixing the chemicals, hydrogen sulphide was formed.

In this sentence, the passive not only is ineffective but also leads to a *dangling modifier* (see #36); there is no subject in the sentence to explain who is doing the mixing. The frequency of such errors is itself a good reason to be sparing with passive voice. The active voice eliminates the grammatical error:

> ***active:***   By mixing the chemicals, the chemist produced hydrogen sulphide.

EAL   ## When to Use the Passive Voice (see also #29f)
Use the passive voice when the active voice is impossible or when the passive is for some other reason clearly preferable or demanded by the context. Generally, use passive voice

- when the agent, or doer of the act, is indefinite or not known;
- when the agent is less important than the act itself;
- when you want to emphasize either the agent or the act by putting it at the beginning or end of the sentence.

For example:

> It was reported that there were two survivors.

Here the writer doesn't know who did the reporting. To avoid the passive by saying "Someone reported that there were two survivors" would oddly stress the mysterious "someone." And the fact that *someone reported* it is less important than the content of the report.

> The accident was witnessed by more than thirty people.

Here the writer emphasizes the large number of witnesses by putting them at the end of the sentence, the most emphatic point in the utterance.

No doubt you'll want to use passive voice on other sorts of occasions as well, but don't use it unwittingly or uncritically. Remember: a verb in the passive consists of some form of *be* followed by a past participle (*is shown, are decided, was accompanied, has been legalized, will be charged, is being removed, to be announced*). Whenever you find yourself using such verbs, stop to consider whether an active structure would be more effective.

Note: Like mood, voice operates regardless of tense. Don't confuse passive constructions with the past tense just because the past participle is used. Passive constructions can appear in any of the tenses.

18a

Exercise 17p Revising Passive Voice

In the following, change passive voice to active voice wherever you think the revision improves the sentence. Retain the passive wherever you think it is preferable.

1. By planning a trip carefully, time-wasting mistakes can be avoided.
2. The car was driven by Denise, while Yves acted as navigator.
3. Another factor that makes the Whistler ski resort so popular is the variety of après-ski entertainment that can be found there.
4. Some went swimming, some went on short hikes, some just lay around, and volleyball was played by others.
5. According to scientists, it is hoped that the oil spill will be cleaned up by the turbulence of the water.

18 Agreement Between Subject and Verb

gr A verb should agree with its subject in number and person. We say *I see*, not *I sees*; *he sees*, not *he see*; and *we see*, not *we sees*. Sometimes people have trouble making verbs agree with subjects in *number*. Here are the main circumstances to watch out for while editing a first or subsequent draft:

18a Words Intervening Between Subject and Verb

When something plural comes between a singular subject and its verb, the verb must still agree with the subject:

> Far below, a landscape of rolling brown hills and small trees lies among the small cottages.

> Each of the plans has certain advantages.

Neither of the parties was willing to compromise.

The whole experience—the decision to go, the planning, the journey, and especially all the places we went and things we saw—was consistently exciting.

Similarly, don't let an intervening singular noun affect the agreement between a plural subject and its verb:

The plans for the unused space have certain advantages.

The contents of the bag—an assortment of spoons—were surprising.

18b Compound Subject: Singular Nouns Joined by *and*

A compound subject made up of two or more singular nouns joined by *and* is usually plural:

Careful thought and attention to detail are essential.

Coffee and tea were served with dessert.

Occasional exceptions occur. If two nouns identify the same person or thing, or if two nouns taken together are thought of as a unit, the verb is singular:

A common-law spouse and father has an obligation to share the domestic responsibilities.

Macaroni and cheese is a student favourite.

PROOFREADING TIP

On Recognizing When a Singular Verb Is Needed

Phrases such as *in addition to*, *as well as*, and *together with* are prepositions, not conjunctions like *and*. A singular subject followed by one of them still takes a singular verb:

The cat as well as the dog comes when I whistle.

Bruno, along with his brothers, is going to Japan for the summer.

Compound subjects preceded by *each* or *every* take a singular verb:

Each dog and cat has its own bed.

But if you feel an urge to use a singular verb after a two-part subject joined by *and*, make sure you haven't used two nouns that mean the same thing; in such cases, one of the two words is almost always *redundant* (see #71c):

> ***red*:** The strength and power of her argument <u>is</u> undeniable.

Remove one or the other, or replace the two nouns with some other single word, such as *force* in this particular example.

18c Compound Subject: Parts Joined by *or* or a Correlative

18d

When the parts of a subject are joined by the coordinating conjunction *or* (see #23a) or by the correlative conjunctions *either . . . or, neither . . . nor, not . . . but, not only . . . but also, whether . . . or* (see #23b), the part nearest the verb determines whether the verb is singular or plural:

> One or the other of you <u>has</u> the winning ticket. (both parts singular: verb singular; note that the subject is *one or the other*, not *you*)

> Neither the artists nor the politicians <u>feel</u> the arts funding is adequate. (both parts plural: verb plural)

> Neither the mainland nor the islands <u>are</u> interested in building the bridge. (first part singular, second part plural: verb plural)

> Neither my parents nor I <u>was</u> to blame. (first part plural, second part singular: verb singular)

Try to avoid the construction in the previous example, since it usually sounds incorrect (see also #15b). It's easy to rephrase:

> Neither I nor my parents <u>were</u> to blame.

> My parents <u>were</u> not to blame, nor <u>was</u> I.

18d Agreement with Indefinite Pronouns (see also #14g, #15c)

Most indefinite pronouns are singular: *another, anybody, anyone, anything, each, either, everybody, everyone, everything, much, neither, nobody, no one, nothing, one, other, somebody, someone, something.* A few—namely, *all, any, more, most, none, some*—can be either singular or plural, depending on whether they refer to a single quantity or to a number of individual units within a group:

> <u>Some</u> of the pasta <u>is</u> eaten. (a single amount; *pasta* is singular, a mass noun)

> <u>Some</u> of the cookies <u>are</u> missing. (a number of cookies; *cookies* is plural)

All of this novel is good. (a whole novel; *novel* is singular)

All of his novels are well written. (a number of novels; *novels* is plural)

Most of the champagne was drunk. (a single mass; *champagne* is singular)

Most of the cases of champagne have been exported. (a number of cases; *cases* is plural)

None of the work is finished. (a single unit; *work* is singular)

None of the reports are ready. (a number of reports; *reports* is plural)

18e Subject Following Verb
When the normal subject–verb order is reversed, the verb still must agree with the real subject, not some word that happens to precede it:

There is only one answer to this question.

There are several possible solutions to the problem.

Here comes the manager.

Here come the clowns.

Thirty days has September.

Sitting in the coffee shop were my archenemy and his pet turtle.

When compounded singular nouns follow an opening *there* or *here*, most writers make the verb agree with the first noun:

There was a computer and a scanner in the next room.

There was still an essay to be revised and a play to be studied before he could think about sleep.

There was still the play to be read and his lines to be memorized.

But others find this kind of syntax awkward sounding. By rephrasing the sentence you can easily avoid the issue and save a few words as well:

A computer and a scanner were in the next room.

> He still had an essay to revise and a play to study before he could think about sleep.

> He still had to read the play and memorize his lines.

In expletive patterns, *it* takes a singular verb—usually a linking verb (see #17a):

> It *is* questions like these that give the most trouble.

For more on the expletives *it* and *there*, see #11k and #71a.

18f

 PROOFREADING TIP

Agreement and Predicate Nouns

Don't let a predicate noun determine a verb's number; the verb must agree with the subject of the sentence, not the complement (see #11h and #17a):

> The last word in style that year was platform shoes and bell-bottom jeans.

18f Agreement with Collective Nouns

Collective nouns (see #13) are collections or groups that are considered as units and therefore usually take singular verbs:

> The government has passed the legislation.

> The company is planning several events to celebrate its centennial.

But when such a noun denotes the individual members of a group, the verb must be plural:

> His family comes from Korea. (singular)
> His family come from Jamaica, India, and Southern Europe. (plural)

> The audience was composed and attentive. (singular)
> The audience were sneezing, coughing, blowing their noses, and chatting with one another. (plural)

Such words as *number, half*, and *majority* can also be considered collective nouns and either singular or plural. In the following examples, notice how the article—*a* or *the*—changes the verb agreement:

> A number of skiers are heading to the slopes. (*A number of*: plural)

> The number of skiers here is quite large. (*The number of*: singular)

(See also **amount, number** in the usage checklist, #72.)

EAL

18g Nouns That Are Always Singular or Always Plural

Some nouns, because of their meanings, cannot be inflected for number and will always be either singular or plural. Do not be fooled by some singular nouns that look plural because they end in *s*. Some examples of uninflectable nouns include:

> The gold comes from the Yukon. (always singular)

> Oxygen is essential to human life. (always singular)

> Economics is difficult for some people. (always singular)

> Good news is always welcome. (always singular)

> The scissors are in the kitchen. (always plural)

> His glasses are fogged up. (always plural)

> Her clothes are very stylish. (always plural)

For more on *mass* and *countable* nouns, see #13a and #19c.6.

18h Plurals: *criteria, data, media*, etc.

Words of Greek and Latin origin ending in *a* look like singular words but are in fact plural. The following words are plural; they can't be used with singular verbs (see #62m.7):

> criteria (singular is *criterion*)

> phenomena (singular is *phenomenon*)

> strata (singular is *stratum*)

While *criteria, phenomena,* and *strata* should always be treated as plural forms, some similar nouns may take either a singular or plural verb depending on the context. For instance, *data* should be treated as a plural noun in scientific contexts (the singular form is *datum*); in non-scientific practice, it may take a singular verb:

> Some meteorological data <u>are</u> collected by satellites. (plural)

> Data from the poll <u>has been</u> tabulated and entered in the system. (singular)

18i

It was once considered incorrect to use *media* as anything but a plural noun. But today few people object to its use as a singular noun when it is being used to refer to the means of mass communication (TV, radio, newspapers, blogs, and so on) collectively:

> Some argue that the media <u>is</u> responsible for making health care the number-one concern among voters.

But be sure to treat *media* as a plural noun when it is being used to refer to these means individually:

> A local newspaper broke the story, but other media <u>were</u> quick to report it.

18i Agreement with Relative Pronouns

Whether a relative pronoun is singular or plural depends on its antecedent (see #15). Therefore when a relative clause has *who, which,* or *that* as its subject, the verb must agree in number with the pronoun's antecedent:

> Her success is due to her intelligence and perseverance, which <u>have</u> overcome all obstacles. (The antecedent of *which* is *intelligence and perseverance.*)

Questions about agreement most often occur with the phrases *one of those . . . who* and *one of the . . . who*:

> He is one of those people who <u>have</u> difficulty reading aloud.

> He is one of the few people I know who <u>have</u> difficulty reading aloud.

Have is correct, since the antecedent of *who* is the plural *people*, not the singular *one*. The only time this construction takes a singular verb is when *one* is preceded by *the only*; *one* is then the antecedent of *who*:

> He is the only one of those attending who <u>has</u> difficulty reading aloud.

You can avoid the problem by simplifying:

> He has difficulty reading aloud.

> Of those attending, he alone has difficulty reading aloud.

18j

18j Titles of Works and Words Referred to as Words

Titles of literary and other works and words referred to as words should be treated as *singular* even if they are plural in themselves:

> *The Two Gentlemen of Verona* <u>is</u> one of Shakespeare's lesser-known comedies.

> Vivaldi's *Four Seasons* <u>is</u> a superb example of Baroque music.

> *Nervous Nellies* <u>is</u> an out-of-date slang term.

> *Criteria* <u>is</u> the plural form of *criterion*.

Exercise 18 (1) Choosing Correct Verbs

Underline the correct form in each pair of verbs:

1. The committee of physicians (intends, intend) to table its report today.
2. Neither Jason nor Melinda (is, are) interested in moving in.
3. Either my brother or my parents (plans, plan) to visit next week.
4. Most of the students (seems, seem) prepared.
5. My teacher and mentor, Ms. Roi, (wants, want) me to succeed.
6. Inside the envelope (was, were) my name tag and my identification card.
7. Bangers and mash (is, are) a traditional British dish.
8. There (is, are) fresh coffee and muffins on the kitchen table.
9. Unexplained natural phenomena (fascinates, fascinate) the scientific community.
10. Most critics agree that Timothy Findley's *The Wars* (is, are) an important Canadian novel.

Exercise 18 (2) Correcting Faulty
Subject–Verb Agreement

Revise the following sentences to correct any lack of agreement between subject and verb.

1. Studies of the earth's atmosphere indicates that there are more than one hole in the ozone layer.
2. Juliet's love and courage is evident in this scene.
3. Postmodern architecture in North America and Europe have been changing urban skylines.
4. In Canada, the media is largely based in Ottawa and Toronto.
5. This economist writes of the virtue of selfishness, but it seems to me that she, along with those who share her view, are forgetting the importance of cooperation.
6. Everything in this speech—the metre, the repetition of vowels, and the vibrant imagery—lead us to believe that this is the high point of Othello's love and, as far as we know from this play, of his life.
7. The migration of whales attract many tourists to this coastal community.
8. Indeed, the exercise of careful thought and careful planning seem to be necessary for the successful completion of the project.
9. But scandal, unfair politics, and the "big business" of politics has led to the corruption of the system.
10. With innovation comes a few risks.

19a

19 Adjectives

ad An **adjective** modifies—limits, qualifies, or particularizes—a noun or pronoun. Adjectives generally answer the questions *Which? What kind of? How many? How much?*

> The black cat was hungry; he ate five sardines and drank some milk.

19a Kinds of Adjectives
Adjectives fall into two major classes: **non-descriptive** and **descriptive**.

1. Non-descriptive Adjectives
The several kinds of non-descriptive adjectives include some that are basically *structure words* (see #11-l):

- **articles** (see #19c):

    <u>a</u> book   <u>an</u> opinion   <u>the</u> problem

- **demonstrative adjectives** (see also #14f):

    <u>this</u> lamp   <u>that</u> problem   <u>these</u> women   <u>those</u> books

- **interrogative and relative adjectives** (see also #14c–d):

    <u>Which</u> book is best?

    <u>What</u> time is it?

    <u>Whose</u> opinion do you trust?

    She is the one <u>whose</u> opinion I trust.

- **possessive adjectives**—the possessive forms of personal and impersonal pronouns (see #14a–b) and of nouns (see #13b):

<u>my</u> book	<u>her</u> car	<u>his</u> watch
<u>our</u> home	<u>its</u> colour	<u>their</u> heritage
<u>one's</u> beliefs	a <u>man's</u> coat	<u>Hamlet's</u> ego
<u>Shirley's</u> job	the <u>car's</u> engine	the <u>river's</u> mouth

- **indefinite and numerical adjectives** (see #14g):

<u>some</u> money	<u>any</u> time	<u>more</u> fuel	<u>several</u> keys
<u>three</u> ducks	<u>thirty</u> ships	the <u>fourth</u> act	<u>much</u> sushi

2. Descriptive Adjectives

Descriptive adjectives give information about such matters as the size, shape, colour, nature, and quality of whatever a noun or pronoun names:

a <u>hybrid</u> car	a <u>delicate</u> balance
an <u>Impressionist</u> painting	a <u>brave</u> woman
a <u>tempting</u> dessert	a <u>well-done</u> steak
a <u>once-in-a-lifetime</u> chance	<u>Canadian</u> literature
an <u>experimental</u> play	<u>composted</u> leaves
a <u>fascinating</u> place <u>to visit</u>	<u>kitchen</u> towels
a <u>dictionary</u> definition	<u>looking refreshed</u>, he . . .
the festival <u>to exceed all others</u>	the man <u>of the hour</u>

19a

> the rabbits who caused all the trouble
>
> a large, impressive, three-storey, grey, Victorian house

As these examples illustrate, adjectival modifiers can be single (*hybrid, delicate, Impressionist*, etc.), in groups or series (*large, impressive, three-storey, grey, Victorian*), or in compounds (*three-storey, well-done, once-in-a-lifetime*); they can be proper adjectives, formed from proper nouns (*Victorian, Canadian, Impressionist*); they can be words that are adjectives only (*delicate, large*) or words that can also function as other parts of speech (*hybrid, brave, tempting,* etc.), including nouns functioning as adjectives (*kitchen, dictionary*); they can be present participles (*tempting, fascinating*), past participles (*composted*), or infinitives (*to visit*); they can be participial phrases (*looking refreshed*), infinitive phrases (*to exceed all others*), or prepositional phrases (*of the hour*); or they can be relative clauses (*who caused all the trouble*). For more examples see #26a. On the punctuation of nouns in series, see #49; on the overuse of nouns as modifiers, see #71g; on infinitives and participles, see #21a and #21d; on prepositions, see #22; on relative clauses, see #14d and #48a.

19b Comparison of Descriptive Adjectives

Most descriptive adjectives can be inflected or supplemented for *degree* in order to make *comparisons*. The basic or dictionary form of an adjective is called its **positive** form: *high, calm, difficult*. Use it to compare two things that are equal or similar, or with qualifiers such as *not* and *almost* to compare two things that are dissimilar:

> This assignment is as difficult as last week's.
>
> It is not nearly so difficult as I expected.

To make the **comparative** form, add *er* or put *more* (or *less*) in front of the positive form: *higher, calmer, more difficult, less difficult*. Use it to compare two unequal things:

> My grades are higher now than they were last year.
>
> Your part is more difficult than mine.

For the **superlative** form, add *est* or put *most* (or *least*) in front of the positive form: *highest, calmest, most difficult, least difficult*. Generally, use it to compare three or more unequal things:

> Whose talent is the greatest?
>
> He is the calmest and least pretentious person I know.

It is difficult to set rules for when to add *er* and *est* and when to use *more* and *most*. Some dictionaries tell you when *er* and *est* may be added to an adjective; if you have such a dictionary, and it doesn't give those forms for a particular adjective, use *more* and *most*. Otherwise, you can follow these general guidelines:

- For adjectives of one syllable, usually add *er* and *est*:

Positive	Comparative	Superlative
short	shorter	shortest
low	lower	lowest
rough	rougher	roughest
dry	drier	driest
grim	grimmer	grimmest
brave	braver	bravest

You can also use *more* and *most, less* and *least* with many of these positive forms. (And note the spelling changes in the last three examples; see #62c.)

- For adjectives of three or more syllables, usually use *more* and *most* (or *less* and *least*):

beautiful	more beautiful	most beautiful
tiresome	more tiresome	most tiresome
sarcastic	more sarcastic	most sarcastic
fabulous	more fabulous	most fabulous

- For adjectives of two syllables ending in *al, ect, ed, ent, ful, ic, id, ing, ish, ive, less,* and *ous* (and any others where an added *er* or *est* would sound wrong), generally use *more* and *most* (or *less* and *least*):

formal	more formal	most formal
direct	more direct	most direct
polished	more polished	most polished
potent	more potent	most potent
tactful	more tactful	most tactful
manic	more manic	most manic
humid	more humid	most humid
soothing	more soothing	most soothing

childish	more childish	most childish
restive	more restive	most restive
reckless	more reckless	most reckless
serious	more serious	most serious

- For other adjectives of two syllables, you usually have a choice; for example:

gentle	gentler, more gentle	gentlest, most gentle
bitter	bitterer, more bitter	bitterest, most bitter
lively	livelier, more lively	liveliest, most lively
silly	sillier, more silly	silliest, most silly

19b

When there is a choice, the forms with *more* and *most* will usually sound more formal and more emphatic than those with *er* and *est*. In fact, you can use *more* and *most* with almost any descriptive adjective, even one-syllable ones, if you want a little extra emphasis or a different rhythm:

Of all my sister's friends, she is by far the most brave.

But the converse isn't true: adjectives of three or more syllables, and even shorter ones ending in *ous* and *ful* and so on, almost always require *more* and *most* unless you want to use very informal dialogue, or to create a humorous effect, as when Alice finds things in Wonderland to be growing "curiouser and curiouser."

Note that because of their meanings, some adjectives should not be compared: see **unique, etc.** in the usage checklist, #72. See also #42 and #38, on faulty comparison, and *comp* in appendix 2.

PROOFREADING TIP

Avoiding "Doubling-Up" Errors in Adjective Forms

Don't double up a comparative or superlative form as in *more better* or *most prettiest*. If you want emphasis, use the adverbial intensifiers *much* or *far* or *by far*:

much livelier	much more lively
far livelier	far more lively
livelier by far	by far the liveliest
much the liveliest	much the livelier of the two

19c

> **PROOFREADING TIP**
>
> **Irregular Comparative and Superlative Adjective Forms**
>
> A few commonly used adjectives form their comparative and superlative degrees irregularly:
>
> | | | |
> |---|---|---|
> | good | better | best |
> | bad | worse | worst |
> | far | farther; further | farthest; furthest |
> | little | littler; less, lesser | littlest; least |
> | much, many | more | most |
>
> (And see **farther**, **further** in the usage checklist, #72.)
>
> Good dictionaries list all irregular forms after the basic entry, including those in which a spelling change occurs.

Exercise 19b Comparing Adjectives

Come up with five adjectives that don't fit neatly into the guidelines given in #19b. For example, would you use *er* and *est* with *prone*, *lost*, *sudden*, or *sanguine*? Do *er* and *est* work with *slippery*? Think of some descriptive adjectives (other than *unique*) that for some reason don't lend themselves to comparisons at all. (For example, try words that function primarily as nouns or other parts of speech.)

EAL

19c Articles: *a, an,* and *the*

Articles—sometimes considered separately from parts of speech—can conveniently be thought of as kinds of adjectives. Like adjectives, they modify nouns. Like demonstrative and possessive adjectives, they are also sometimes called *markers* or *determiners* because an article indicates that a noun will soon follow.

The definite article (*the*) and the indefinite articles (*a* or *an*) are used idiomatically, and therefore they often challenge people whose first language doesn't include articles. If you aren't sure which article, if any, to use, you should consult an advanced learner's dictionary. This sort of dictionary will tell you whether a noun is countable (and would most likely need an article in its singular form) or uncountable (and would probably not take the indefinite article but might take the definite), or whether it has both countable and uncountable forms depending on context. As an illustration, consider the following definition for *democracy*, which comes from the online version of the *Oxford Advanced Learner's Dictionary* (*OALD*).

democracy NOUN

dɪ'mɒkrəsi (BrE);　　dɪ'mɒːkrəsi (NAmE)

plural **democracies**

---

1 [UNCOUNTABLE]

a system of government in which all the people of a country can vote to elect their representatives

- *parliamentary democracy*
- *the principles of democracy*

2 [COUNTABLE]

a country which has this system of government

- *Western democracies*
- *I thought we were supposed to be living in a democracy.*

3 [UNCOUNTABLE]

fair and equal treatment of everyone in an organization, etc., and their right to take part in making decisions

- *the fight for justice and democracy*

Reproduced by permission of Oxford University Press from *Oxford Advanced Learner's Dictionary*, online version, © Oxford University Press 2014.

It is almost impossible to set down all the rules for article use, but here are some guiding principles.

1. Using the Indefinite Article

The form *a* of the indefinite article is used before words beginning with a consonant (*a dog, a building, a computer, a yellow orchid*), including words beginning with a pronounced *h* (*a horse, a historical event, a hotel, a hypothesis*) and a word beginning with a *u* or *o* whose initial sound is that of *y* or *w* (*a useful book, a one-sided contest*).

The form *an* is used before words beginning with a vowel sound (*an elephant, an opinion, an ugly duckling*) as well as words beginning with an unpronounced *h* (*an honour, an hour, an honest person*). Similarly, the pronunciation of *the* changes from "thuh" to "thee" before a word beginning with a vowel sound.

Generally a person or thing designated by the indefinite article is not specific:

This town needs a larger grocery store.

Each class has a projector.

He wants to buy an emu farm.

The indefinite article *a* is like *one*: it is often used before singular countable nouns. Sometimes it even means *one*:

> I lasted only <u>a</u> week at my new job.

> This will take <u>an</u> hour or two.

2. Using the Definite Article

19c

Generally, the definite article designates one or more particular persons or things whose identity is established by context (familiarity) or a modifier (clauses, phrases, superlative adjectives, ordinal numbers). Also, the definite article is used with some proper nouns.

The can occur with names for objects that the reader is familiar with or that you share knowledge about, indicating that the object is something unique for a given situation:

> Go to <u>the</u> bookstore (the one we both know about) and get <u>the</u> required textbook (the one that is unique to the course).

In this example, the definite article is used in both cases because the context is understood or your reader is familiar with the nouns being modified.

> <u>The</u> grocery store is on <u>the</u> corner.

> <u>The</u> projector faces <u>the</u> front of <u>the</u> class.

> <u>The</u> emu farm lies beyond <u>the</u> river.

If the noun is followed by a **modifying clause** or **phrase**, the definite article is often used:

> My parents gave me <u>the</u> scooter I wanted. (*scooter* is particularized by the modifying clause *I wanted*)

Compare to the use of the indefinite article:

> My parents gave me <u>a</u> scooter. (unspecified)

The definite article can also be used to indicate exclusiveness; *the* is then equivalent to *the only* or *the best*. In fact, we often use *the* in front of **superlative adjectives**:

> He is <u>the</u> happiest person I know.

> She is <u>the</u> most diligent student.

We also can indicate exclusiveness with the use of **ordinals**. Ordinals are numerical adjectives such as *first*, *second*, *third*, and so on.

> The first act of the play takes place in Montreal.

> No one enjoyed the third sequel.

3. Using Articles with Proper Nouns

The definite article goes with some **proper nouns** but not with others. *The* often goes with place names that are plural, and it is standard before several that are not:

the Great Lakes	the Dominican Republic
the Rockies	the Middle East
the Thousand Islands	the Atlantic Ocean
the Canaries	the Mediterranean Sea
the Philippines	the Sahara
the Netherlands	the North Pole

Note that *the* does not precede the names of individual lakes, falls, bays, mountains, or islands: *Lake Superior, Niagara Falls, Hudson Bay, Mount Baker, Gabriola Island.*

The definite article also appears before many proper nouns that name groups of people:

> the Beatles   the Calgary Flames   the Wilsons

It appears before the proper names of specific ships, trains, planes, and other vehicles:

> the *Beagle*   the *Discovery*   the *Orient Express*
>
> the *Titanic*   the *Enola Gay*   the *Royal Canadian Pacific*

And it precedes proper nouns that contain a modifying phrase beginning with *of*:

> the University of Saskatchewan
>
> the Dominion of Canada
>
> the United States of America
>
> the United Kingdom of Great Britain

Also note that *the* is retained in the shorter, more commonly used versions *the United States* and *the United Kingdom.*

The indefinite article rarely appears before a proper noun, although it is sometimes used when a proper noun designates a specific group:

> She declared herself to be a Canadian.

> I could tell by his eyes and his smile that he was a Wilson.

See also #19f.

4. Using Articles with Uncountable Nouns or Plural Nouns

Uncountable nouns, whether mass nouns or abstract nouns, take no article if the mass or abstract sense governs.

> *art*: The poem features a simple praise of nature.

Here *a* must be removed because praise in this context is uncountable. But notice the difference if the concrete noun *hymn* is inserted:

> The poem features a simple hymn of praise to nature.

Avoid using *a* with plural countable nouns:

> *art*: She wanted a writing notebooks.

> *revised*: She wanted writing notebooks.

However, you can use *the* with plural nouns if they are particularized by a modifier:

> *revised*: She wanted the writing notebooks that are made in Italy. (Here *notebooks* is particularized by *that are made in Italy*.)

5. Using Articles with Abstract Nouns

If a usually abstract noun is used in a countable but not particularized sense, the indefinite article precedes it; if in a particularized way, the definite article precedes it:

> This is an honour. (countable)

> He did me the honour of inviting me. (uncountable, specific)

6. Using the Definite Article with Nouns That Represent Groups

The definite article usually precedes an adjective functioning as a noun that represents a group (see #19f):

> The young should heed the advice of the elderly.

> The poor will always have an advocate on city council.

This rule can also be applied to species of animals or inventions when emphasizing the class.

> The horse is a beautiful animal.

> The computer facilitates various modes of communication.

7. Using Articles with Titles of Artistic Works

Titles of artistic works are not usually preceded by articles, but usage is inconsistent, and some idiomatically take the definite article. It would be incorrect to say:

> *art*: Donne's poetic power is evident in the Sonnet X.

And one wouldn't say "the *Paradise Lost*" or "the *Alice's Adventures in Wonderland.*" But in most cases it would be natural to refer to "the *Adventures of Huckleberry Finn*" or "the *Nicomachean Ethics*" (Of course, if *A* or *The* is part of the title, it should be included: *A Midsummer Night's Dream, The Voyage Out.*) If a possessive (or pronominal) adjective or possessive form of the author's name precedes the title, no article is needed: "Aristotle in his *Nicomachean Ethics*," "in Aristotle's *Nicomachean Ethics.*"

8. Using Articles with Names of Academic Fields and Courses

With names of academic fields and courses, whether proper nouns or abstract common nouns, no article is used:

> She is enrolled in Psychology 101.

> He reads books on psychology.

> He is majoring in communications.

Exercise 19c Using Articles

In each blank, place *a*, *an*, or *the*; or put *O* if no article is needed. If two articles could be used, put a slash (/) between them. If an article could be used, but need not, put parentheses around it.

1. In _____ Canadian society, everyone is considered _____ equal.

2. After five years in _____ business, she decided to enrol in _____ international relations program.

3. My sister got _____ award for her work in _____ genetics.

4. There was _____ controversial documentary about _____ drug addiction on _____ television last night.

5. I think you should put _____ onion in _____ stew.

6. _____ art books were worth _____ small fortune, but there was no space for them in _____ Centre.

7. At _____ climactic moment of _____ violin solo, _____ man in _____ audience started to have _____ coughing fit.

8. Currently, _____ city council is divided on its decision whether to bid for _____ Olympics or to invest its energies in _____ clean water policy.

9. In his usual exuberant style, _____ scantily clad chef smashed _____ various condiments and spices on _____ counter in front of _____ hungry and curious studio audience.

10. _____ true happiness is found within us and not in _____ external objects, circumstances, or relationships.

EAL

19d Placement of Adjectives

Adjectival modifiers usually come just before or just after what they modify. Articles always, and other determiners almost always, precede the nouns they modify, usually with either no intervening words or only one or two other adjectives:

Trying to save <u>some</u> money, <u>the</u> manager decided to close <u>his</u> store early.

<u>The wise</u> manager decided not to hire <u>his scatterbrained</u> nephew.

Predicate adjectives (see #11g) almost always follow the subject and linking verb:

> The forest is <u>cool</u> and <u>green</u> and <u>full of mushrooms</u>.

> Shortly after his operation he again became <u>healthy</u>.

Adjectives serving as *objective complements* usually follow the subject–verb–direct object (see #11i):

> I thought the suggestion <u>preposterous</u>.

19d

Most other single-word adjectives, and many compound adjectives, precede the nouns they modify:

> The <u>tall</u>, <u>dark</u>, and <u>handsome</u> hero lives on only in romantic fiction.

> The <u>weather</u> map shows a <u>cold</u> front moving into the <u>northern</u> prairies.

Phrases like "the map weather" or "a front cold" or "the prairies northern" are unidiomatic in English. (Note that order can determine meaning; for example, a *cold head* is not the same thing as a *head cold*: here, adjective and noun exchange functions as they exchange positions.)

But deviations are possible. Poetry, for example, often uses inversions for purposes of emphasis and rhyme:

> <u>Red</u> as a rose is she . . . .

> And he called for his fiddlers <u>three</u>.

Such inversions also occur outside of poetry, but don't use them often, for when the unusual ceases to be unusual it loses much of its power. But if you want a certain emphasis or rhythm, you can put a predicate adjective before a noun (see also #17a):

> <u>Frustrated</u> I may have been, but I hadn't lost my wits or my passport.

or a regular adjective after a noun:

> She did the only thing <u>possible</u>.

> There was food <u>enough</u> for everyone.

Compound adjectives and adjectives in phrases are often comfortable after a noun:

His friend, always <u>faithful and kind</u>, came at once.

Elfrida, <u>radiant and delighted</u>, left the room, <u>secure</u> in her victory.

Relative clauses and various kinds of phrases customarily follow the nouns they modify:

19e

He is one detective <u>who believes in being thorough</u>.

The president <u>of the company</u> will retire next month.

The time <u>to vote</u> is now!

The only adjectival modifier not generally restricted in its position is the participial phrase (see #21d):

<u>Having had abundant experience</u>, Kenneth applied for the job.

Kenneth, <u>having had abundant experience</u>, applied for the job.

Kenneth applied for the job, <u>having had abundant experience</u>.

This movability makes the participial phrase a popular way to introduce variety and to control emphasis (see #29e). But be careful: writers sometimes lean too heavily on *ing* phrases to begin sentences; and such phrases can be awkward or ambiguous, especially in the form of a *dangling modifier*:

> ***dm***: Having had abundant experience, the job seemed just right for Kenneth. (This sentence implies it is the job, not Kenneth, that has the abundant experience.)

See #36; see also #35, on misplaced modifiers.

EAL 19e Order of Adjectives

Adjectives usually follow an idiomatic order: a determiner (an article, possessive, or demonstrative) comes first, then numbers, then adjectives that express a general description, followed by physical-state adjectives (including adjectives related to age, size, shape, colour, and temperature), proper adjectives, and then noun adjuncts (including adjectives ending in *ic*, *ical*, or *al*) before the main noun.

The following chart shows the common order of adjectives:

Determiner	Number	General Description	Physical State	Proper Adjectives	Noun Adjuncts	Main Noun
the	one	talented	young	Canadian	movie	star
Alex's	seventh	expensive	orange		desk	lamp
that		tasty	hot	Indian		dish
your	four	new	square		coffee	mugs
their	two	funny, daring		Australian	theatrical	friends

Adjectives expressing an inherent quality (general description) can be reversed in order. For example, you could write: *Their two daring, funny Australian theatrical friends.* Notice that *daring* and *funny* are separated by commas because they are interchangeable in order. See #49e.

19f Adjectives Functioning as Nouns

If preceded by *the* or a possessive, many words normally thought of as adjectives can function as *nouns*, usually referring to people, and usually in a plural sense (see #19c.6); for example:

the Swedish   the British   the Chinese   the Lebanese
(but Canadians, not *the* Canadians)

the free   the brave   the powerful   the sick and dying
the enslaved   the unemployed   the deceased   the badly injured
the poor   the wealthy   the underprivileged the more fortunate

the abstract   the metaphysical the good   the true

20 Adverbs

ad Adverbs are often thought of as especially tricky. This part of speech is sometimes called the "catch-all" category, since any word that doesn't seem to fit elsewhere is usually assumed to be an adverb. Adverbs, therefore, are a little more complicated than adjectives.

20a Kinds and Functions of Adverbs

Whereas adjectives can modify only nouns and pronouns, adverbs can modify *verbs* (and *verbals;* see #21), *adjectives*, other *adverbs*, and *independent clauses* or *whole sentences.* Adverbial modifiers generally answer such questions as *How? When? Where? Why?* and *To what degree?* That is, they indicate such things as *manner* (How?); *time* (When? How often? How long?);

place and *direction* (Where? In what direction?); *cause, result,* and *purpose* (Why? To what effect?); and *degree* (To what degree? To what extent?). They also express affirmation and negation, conditions, concessions, and comparisons. Here are some examples:

> Fully expecting to fail, he slumped disconsolately in his seat and began the examination.

20a

To what degree? *Fully*: the adverb of degree modifies the participial (verbal) phrase *expecting to fail*. How? *Disconsolately*: the adverb of manner modifies the verb *slumped*. Where? *In his seat*: the prepositional phrase functions as an adverb of place modifying the verb *slumped*.

> For many years they lived very happily together in Yellowknife.

How? *Happily* and *together*: the adverbs of manner modify the verb *lived*. To what degree? *Very*: the intensifying adverb modifies the adverb *happily*. Where? *In Yellowknife*: the adverbial prepositional phrase modifies the verb *lived*. How long? *For many years*: the prepositional phrase functions as an adverb of time or duration modifying the verb—or it can be thought of as modifying the whole clause *they lived very happily together in Yellowknife*.

> Fortunately, the cut was not deep.

To what effect? *Fortunately*: a sentence modifier. To what degree? *Not*: the negating adverb modifies the adjective *deep*.

> Because their budget was tight, they eventually decided not to buy a car.

Why? *Because their budget was tight*: the adverbial clause of cause modifies the verb *decided* or, in a way, all the rest of the sentence. When? *Eventually*: the adverb of time modifies the verb *decided*. The negating *not* modifies the infinitive (verbal) *to buy*.

> Last November it seldom snowed.

When? *Last November*: the noun phrase functions as an adverb of time modifying the verb *snowed*. How often? *Seldom*: the adverb of time or frequency modifies the verb *snowed*.

> Driving fast is often dangerous.

How? *Fast*: the adverb of manner modifies the gerund (verbal) *driving*. When? *Often*: the adverb of time or frequency modifies the adjective *dangerous*.

> If you're tired, I will walk the dog.

The conditional clause modifies the verb (*will walk*).

> Although she dislikes the city *intensely*, she agreed to go *there* in order to keep peace *in the family*.

Intensely (degree) modifies the verb *dislikes*. *There* (place) modifies the infinitive *to go*. *Although she dislikes the city intensely* is an adverbial clause of concession. The prepositional phrase *in order to keep peace in the family* is an adverb of purpose modifying the verb *agreed*. The smaller adverbial prepositional phrase *in the family* modifies the infinitive phrase *to keep peace*, answering the question *Where?*

> Meredith was better prepared than I was.

The adverb *better* modifies the adjective *prepared*; the combination of *better* and the clause *than I was* expresses comparison or contrast.

Adverbs as Condensed Clauses

Some single-word adverbs and adverbial phrases, especially sentence modifiers, can be thought of as reduced clauses:

> Fortunately [It is fortunate that], the cut was not deep.

> When possible [When it is possible], let your writing sit before proofreading it [before you proofread it].

Other Kinds of Adverbs: Relative, Interrogative, Conjunctive

1. The **relative adverbs** *where* and *when* are used to introduce relative (adjective) clauses (see #14d):

   > She returned to the town where she had grown up.

   > Adam looked forward to the moment when it would be his turn.

2. The **interrogative adverbs** (*where, when, why,* and *how*) are used in questions:

   > Where are you going? Why? How soon? How will you get there? When will you return?

3. **Conjunctive adverbs** usually join whole clauses or sentences to each other and indicate the nature of the connection:

   > It was an important question; therefore, they took their time over it.

Only fifteen people showed up. <u>Nevertheless</u>, the promoter didn't let his disappointment show.

The man said he felt fine; <u>however</u>, his doctor ordered him to stay in bed.

For more on conjunctive adverbs, see #44g.

PROOFREADING TIP

On the Placement of *however*

However sometimes sounds overly formal at the beginning of a sentence or clause. Unless you want special emphasis on it, put it at some other appropriate place in the clause. Often, delaying it just one or two words works best:

His doctor, however, ordered him to stay in bed.

PROOFREADING TIP

On Differentiating Between Conjunctive Adverbs and Conjunctions

If you aren't sure whether a particular word is a conjunctive adverb or a conjunction (#23), remember that adverbs can move around in the sentence; conjunctions cannot.

Winston was intelligent <u>and</u> creative; <u>moreover</u>, he was driven to succeed.

Winston was intelligent <u>and</u> creative; he was, <u>moreover</u>, driven to succeed.

20b Forms of Adverbs

1. Adverbs Ending in *ly*

Many adverbs are formed by adding *ly* to descriptive adjectives—for example, *roughly, happily, fundamentally, curiously*. Don't use an adjectival form where an adverbial form is needed:

She is a <u>careful</u> driver. (adjective modifying *driver*)

She drives <u>carefully</u>. (adverb modifying *drives*)

Note: Some common adjectives end in *ly*, among them *burly, curly, early, friendly, holy, homely, leisurely, likely, lively, lovely, lowly, orderly, silly, surly,* and *ugly.* Adding another *ly* to these inevitably sounds awkward. And though some dictionaries label such adjectives as adverbs as well (he walked *leisurely* toward the door; she behaved *friendly* toward the strangers), that usage also often sounds awkward. You can avoid the problem by adding a few words or rephrasing:

He walked toward the door in a leisurely (adj.) manner.

She behaved in a friendly (adj.) way toward the strangers.

She was friendly (adj.) toward the strangers.

In a few instances, however, the *ly* adjectives do also serve idiomatically as adverbs; for example:

He spoke <u>kindly</u> of you.

She rises <u>early</u>.

He exercises <u>daily</u>.

The tour leaves <u>hourly</u>.

Most magazines are published <u>weekly</u> or <u>monthly</u>.

PROOFREADING TIP

On Using *real* and *really, sure* and *surely*

In everyday speech, many people use *real* and *sure* as adverbs; in formal writing, you should use the forms *really* and *surely* when you need to use these words as adverbs:

Her suggestion was <u>really</u> [not *real*] different.

He <u>surely</u> [not *sure*] was right about the weather.

In these examples, the adverbial form is grammatically correct. But the second example may sound odd. Most people would stick with *sure* in an informal context and use *certainly* in a formal one. And *really* is seldom needed at all: see **very** in the usage checklist, #72.

2. Adverbs Not Ending in *ly*

Some adverbs don't end in *ly*—for example, *ahead, almost, alone, down, however, long, now, often, quite, since, soon, then, there, therefore, when,* and *where.* Others without the *ly* are identical in form to adjectives—for example, *far, fast, little, low, more, much,* and *well*:

> He owns a <u>fast</u> car. (adjective)
>
> He likes to drive <u>fast</u>. (adverb)

> They have a <u>low</u> opinion of him. (adjective)
>
> They flew <u>low</u> over the coast. (adverb)

20b

Well as an adjective means "healthy" (I am quite *well*, thank you) or sometimes "satisfactory," "right," or "advisable" (all is *well*; it is *well* you came when you did). When someone asks you about your health, don't say you are *good* (unless you want to imply you are the opposite of *bad* or *evil*). You should say "I am well." Otherwise *well* is an adverb and should be used instead of the frequently misused *good*, which is an adjective. Similarly, *bad* is an adjective, *badly* an adverb. Be careful with these often misused forms:

> She did a <u>good</u> coaching job. The team played <u>well</u>.

> They felt <u>bad</u> for the child, who had played <u>badly</u> in the game.
> (*Felt* is a linking verb here and requires a predicate
> adjective—*bad*—as its subjective complement.)

See also **good, bad, badly, well** in the usage checklist, #72.

3. Adverbs with Short and Long Forms

Some common adverbs have two forms, one with *ly* and one without. With some of these pairs, the form without *ly* is identical to the adjective, but the two do not mean the same thing. Check a dictionary if you aren't sure of the meanings of such pairs as these:

even, evenly	fair, fairly	hard, hardly	high, highly
just, justly	late, lately	near, nearly	right, rightly

With some of the others, the shorter form, although informal, is equivalent, sometimes even preferable, to the longer form; for example:

> Don't talk so <u>loud</u>. Don't talk so <u>loudly</u>.

> Look <u>deep</u> into my eyes. Look <u>deeply</u> into my eyes.

> Come <u>straight</u> home. Come <u>straightly</u> home.

In these examples, the shorter forms sound more natural because the longer forms have fallen out of common usage. But with most other pairs, the form without *ly* is considered to be informal. Therefore, while words such as *cheap, clear, close, direct, loose, quick, quiet, sharp, smooth, strong, tight,* and *wrong* are often used as adverbs, in formal contexts you should use the *ly* form.

PROOFREADING TIP

On Using Adverbs and Adjectives in the Imperative Mood

When you're writing in the imperative mood (see #11n and #17-l), be careful not to use an adverbial form where an adjectival form is required. Be especially careful when writing instructions. It's right to tell readers to "stir the sauce *slowly*," but wrong to tell them to "slice the onion *thinly*." The correct instruction would be "slice the onion *thin*," meaning "slice the onion *until it is* thin." Similarly, you wouldn't tell someone to "sand the wood *smoothly*," but *smooth*—that is, until it is smooth. In such phrases, the modifier goes with the noun, not the verb; therefore, an adjective, not an adverb, is required.

20c Comparison of Adverbs

Like descriptive adjectives, most adverbs that are similarly descriptive can be inflected or supplemented for degree (see #19b). The following are some guidelines on how adverbs are inflected:

- Some short adverbs without *ly* form their comparative and superlative degrees with *er* and *est*; for example:

Positive	Comparative	Superlative
fast	faster	fastest
hard	harder	hardest
high	higher	highest
late	later	latest
low	lower	lowest
soon	sooner	soonest

Less and *least* also sometimes go with the positive form of these adverbs; for example:

Students work <u>least hard</u> on the days following an exam.

They still ran fast, but <u>less fast</u> than they had the day before.

(Note, however, that the second example would be more effective if *less fast* were replaced with *slower*.)

- Adverbs of three or more syllables ending in *ly* use *more* and *most*, *less* and *least*; for example:

happily	more happily	most happily
stridently	less stridently	least stridently
disconsolately	more disconsolately	most disconsolately

- Most two-syllable adverbs, whether or not they end in *ly*, also use *more* and *most*, *less* and *least*, though a few can also be inflected with *er* and *est*; for example:

slowly	more slowly	most slowly
grimly	less grimly	least grimly
fully	more fully	most fully
alone	more alone	most alone
kindly	more kindly, kindlier	most kindly, kindliest
often	more often, oftener	most often, oftenest

- Some adverbs form their comparative and superlative degrees irregularly:

badly	worse	worst
well	better	best
much	more	most
little	less	least
far	farther; further	farthest; furthest

- A few adverbs of place use *farther* and *farthest* (or *further* and *furthest*; see **farther, further** in the usage checklist, #72); for example:

  | down | farther down | farthest down |
  | north | farther north | farthest north |

- As with adjectives, the adverbs *much*, *far*, and *by far* serve as intensifiers in comparisons:

  Angelo and Felix live <u>much</u> more comfortably than they used to.

  They flew <u>far</u> lower than they should have.

  He practises harder <u>by far</u> than anyone else in the orchestra.

20d Placement of Adverbs

1. Adverbs Modifying Adjectives or Other Adverbs

An intensifying or qualifying adverb almost always goes just before the adjective or adverb it modifies:

almost always   strongly confident   very hot

only two   less quickly   most surely

2. Modifiers of Verbs

Whether single words, phrases, or clauses, most modifiers of verbs are more flexible in their position than any other part of speech. Often they can go almost anywhere in a sentence and still function clearly:

Proudly, he pointed to his photo in the paper.

He proudly pointed to his photo in the paper.

He pointed proudly to his photo in the paper.

He pointed to his photo in the paper proudly.

But notice that the emphasis (and therefore the overall effect and meaning) changes slightly. Here is another example; note how much you can control the emphasis:

Because she likes live music, Sue often goes to the jazz club.

Sue, because she likes live music, often goes to the jazz club.

Sue often goes to the jazz club because she likes live music.

And in each version, the adverb *often* could come after *goes* or after *jazz club*.

3. Adverbs of Place

The preceding example also illustrates the only major restriction on adverbial modifiers of the verb. A phrase like *to the jazz club*, like a direct object, almost has to follow the verb immediately or with no more than an *often* or other such word intervening. But sometimes an adverb of place or direction can come first if a sentence's usual word order is reversed to emphasize place or direction:

Off to market we shall go.

There she stood, staring out to sea.

Where are you going? (but: Are you going *there*?)

Downward he plummeted, waiting until the last moment to pull the ripcord.

4. Sentence Modifiers

Sentence modifiers usually come at the beginning, but they, too, can be placed elsewhere for purposes of emphasis or rhythm:

20d

Fortunately, the boxer was able to stand.

The boxer, fortunately, was able to stand.

The boxer was, fortunately, able to stand.

The boxer was able to stand, fortunately.

With longer or more involved sentences, however, a sentence modifier at the end loses much of its force and point, obviously; obviously it works better if placed earlier, as this sentence demonstrates.

See also #44g, on the placement and punctuation of conjunctive adverbs, and #35, on misplaced modifiers.

Exercise 19–20 (1) Recognizing Adjectives and Adverbs

Underline all the single-word adverbs and circle all the single-word adjectives (including articles) in the following sentences:

1. It was hard work, so he decided to work hard.
2. Although she felt happy in her job, she decided, reluctantly, to express very forcefully her growing concern about office politics.
3. The fireplace screen was too hot to touch.
4. When the hikers were fully rested, they cheerfully resumed the leisurely pace of their climb.
5. Surely the government can find some way to raise the necessary revenues fairly.

Exercise 19–20 (2) Correcting Misused Adjectives and Adverbs

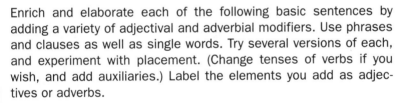

Correct any errors in the use of adjectives and adverbs in the following sentences:

1. Condos are more costlier this year than they were last.
2. She concentrated so hardly that she got a headache.
3. The promotion usually goes to the determinedest and skilfullest employee.
4. The temperature had risen considerable by noon.
5. We enjoyed a real good vacation in the Gatineau Hills.
6. He preferred to wear his denim blue old jacket.
7. Nira isn't writing as good as she usually does.
8. The slowlier you drive, the less fuel you use.
9. He treats his closest friends worstest of all.
10. Which member of the opposition party is the more ambitious politician?

20d

Exercise 19–20 (3) Using Adjectival and Adverbial Modifiers

Enrich and elaborate each of the following basic sentences by adding a variety of adjectival and adverbial modifiers. Use phrases and clauses as well as single words. Try several versions of each, and experiment with placement. (Change tenses of verbs if you wish, and add auxiliaries.) Label the elements you add as adjectives or adverbs.

1. Buskers sing.
2. Smartphones are tools.
3. Politicians lose elections.
4. The goalie was hit by the puck.
5. There are lessons in childhood.

> ### Exercise 19–20 (4) Using Adjectives and Adverbs
>
> Make a list of ten adjectives (other than those listed or discussed above) that can also serve as or be changed into adverbs. Use each adjective in a sentence; then make each an adverb and use it in a sentence. Then choose two of the words and compose sentences using them in their comparative and superlative forms as both adjectives and adverbs.

21 Verbals: Infinitives, Participles, and Gerunds

Infinitives, participles, and gerunds are called **verbals**, forms that are derived from verbs but that cannot function as main or finite verbs. Verbals are **non-finite** forms, not restricted by person and number as finite verbs are (see #17d, and the note at the end of #17b). They function as other parts of speech yet retain some characteristics of verbs: they can have objects, they can be modified by adverbs, and they can express tense and voice. Verbals often introduce *verbal phrases*, groups of words that themselves function as other parts of speech (see #11p). Verbals enable you to inject much of the strength and liveliness of verbs into your writing even though the words are functioning as adjectives, adverbs, and nouns.

21a Infinitives

We sometimes use a form called the **infinitive** to identify particular verbs. We may speak of "the verb *to be*" or "the verb *to live*." (In this book, however, we usually use just the basic or dictionary form: *be, live*; see note in #17b.) An infinitive usually consists of the word *to* (often called "the sign of the infinitive") followed by the basic form: *to be, to live*. Infinitives can function as *nouns*, *adjectives*, and *adverbs*.

1. Infinitives as Nouns

> <u>To save</u> the wolves was Farley Mowat's primary intention.

The infinitive phrase *To save the wolves* is the subject of the verb *was*. The noun *wolves* is the direct object of the infinitive *To save*.

> She wanted <u>to end</u> the game quickly.

The infinitive phrase *to end the game quickly* is the direct object of the verb *wanted*. The infinitive *to end* is modified by the adverb *quickly* and has the noun *game* as its own direct object.

She wanted me <u>to stop</u> the game.

Here *me to stop the game* is the object of the verb *wanted.*

2. Infinitives as Adjectives

His strong desire <u>to be</u> a doctor made him studious.

The infinitive phrase *to be a doctor* modifies the noun *desire*. Since *be* is a linking verb, the infinitive is here followed by the predicate noun *doctor.*

The rarest coins are the ones <u>to collect</u>.

The infinitive *to collect* modifies the pronoun *ones.*

3. Infinitives as Adverbs

She was lucky <u>to have</u> such a friend.

The infinitive phrase *to have such a friend* modifies the predicate adjective *lucky*. The noun phrase *such a friend* is the direct object of the infinitive *to have.*

He went to Niagara-on-the-Lake <u>to experience</u> the Shaw Festival.

The infinitive phrase *to experience the Shaw Festival* is an adverb of purpose modifying the verb *went*; *the Shaw Festival* is the direct object of the infinitive *to experience.*

21b Tense and Voice of Infinitives (see #17g–h, #17-o–p)

Infinitives may be either *present* (to indicate a time the same as or later than that of the main verb):

She wants me <u>to go</u> to St. John's with her.

I was pleased <u>to meet</u> you.

or *present perfect* (to indicate a time before that of the main verb); the *to* then goes with the auxiliary *have*, followed by the verb's past participle:

I was lucky <u>to have met</u> the manager before the interview.

Each of these may also take the *progressive* form, using the auxiliaries *be* and *have*:

I expect <u>to be travelling</u> in Europe this summer.

He was said <u>to have been planning</u> the meeting for months.

Infinitives may also be in the *passive voice*, again putting *to* with the appropriate auxiliaries, then adding a past participle:

> The children wanted <u>to be taken</u> to see Cirque du Soleil.

> He was thought <u>to have been motivated</u> by sheer ambition.

✓ PROOFREADING TIP

Verb Idioms That Omit *to* Before the Infinitive Verb Form

After some verbs, an infinitive can occur without the customary *to*; for example:

> <u>Let</u> sleeping dogs <u>lie</u>.   It <u>made</u> me <u>cry</u>.
>
> We <u>saw</u> the man <u>jump</u>.   He <u>felt</u> the house <u>shake</u>.
>
> I <u>helped</u> her (to) <u>decide</u>.

Make and *let*, verbs used frequently in writing, are of particular note here.

21c Split Infinitives

split Since an infinitive is a unit, separating its parts can weaken it and often results in lack of clarity:

> ***split***: He wanted <u>to</u> quickly <u>conclude</u> the business of the meeting.

> ***split***: She claimed that it was too difficult <u>to</u> very accurately or confidently <u>solve</u> such a problem in the time allowed.

You can usually avoid or repair such splits by rephrasing or rearranging so the adverbs don't interrupt the infinitive:

> He wanted <u>to conclude</u> the business of the meeting quickly.

> She claimed that it was too difficult, in the time allowed, <u>to solve</u> such a problem with any degree of accuracy or confidence.

Occasionally, it is better to split an infinitive than to sound overly formal:

> The space crew vowed <u>to</u> boldly <u>go</u> where no one has gone before.

This split sounds more natural than the formal *boldly to go*, and *boldly* can't be moved to the end of the sentence.

If the infinitive includes a form of *be* or *have* as an auxiliary, an adverb before the last part is less likely to sound out of place:

> The demonstration was thought to have been carefully planned.

> We seem to have finally found the right road.

21d Participles

The **past participle** and **present participle** work with various auxiliaries to form a finite verb's *perfect* and *progressive* tenses (see #17g–h). But without the auxiliaries to indicate *person* and *number*, the participles are non-finite and cannot function as verbs. Instead they function as *adjectives*, modifying nouns and pronouns:

> Beaming happily, Josef examined his freshly sanded bench.

Present participles always end in *ing*, regular past participles in *ed* or *d*. Irregular past participles end variously: *made, mown, broken,* etc. (see #17b–c). A regular past participle is identical to the past-tense form of a verb, but you can easily check a given word's function in a sentence. In the example above, the past-tense form *examined* clearly has *Josef* as its subject; the past participle *sanded*, with no subject, is an adjective modifying *bench*. More examples:

> Painted houses require more care than brick ones.

The past participle *painted* modifies the noun *houses*.

> Impressed, she recounted the film's more thrilling episodes.

The past participle *impressed* modifies the subject, *she*; the present participle *thrilling* modifies the noun *episodes* and is itself modified by the adverb *more*.

> The subject discussed most often was the message behind the song.

The past participle *discussed* modifies the noun *subject* and is itself modified by the adverbial *most often*.

> Suddenly finding himself alone, he became very flustered.

The present participle *finding* introduces the participial phrase *finding himself alone*, which modifies the subject, *he*; *finding*, as a verbal, has *himself* as a direct object and is modified by the adverb *suddenly*. The past participle *flustered* functions as a predicate adjective after the linking verb *became*; it modifies *he* and is itself modified by the adverb *very*.

21e Tense and Voice of Participles (see #17g–h, #17-o–p)

The standard present or past participle indicates a time the same as that of the main verb:

> Being the tallest, Luzia played centre.

Strictly speaking, a past participle by itself amounts to passive voice:

> Worried by what he'd heard, Joe picked up the phone.

With *ing* attached to an auxiliary, participles can also be in the perfect or perfect progressive tense, indicating a time earlier than that of the main verb:

> Having painted himself into a corner, George climbed out the window.

> Having been painting for over two hours, Leah decided to take a break.

Participles in the present progressive and the perfect tenses can also be in the passive voice:

> The subject being discussed was the environment.

> Having been warned, she knew better than to accept the offer.

EAL

PROOFREADING TIP

Present Participles and Sentence Fragments

It is particularly important that you know a present participle when you write one. If you use a present participle and think it's functioning as a finite verb, you may well produce a fragment (see #12b).

> *frag*:   The parking lot being paved.
>
> *frag*:   The meal being prepared for the wedding reception.

Exercise 21d–e Using Participles

Compose sentences using—as single-word adjectives—the present and the past participles of each of the verbs below. Then add auxiliaries and use them as finite verbs.

Example: *stun – stunning – stunned*

She looked *stunning*.   It was a *stunning* blow.
The *stunned* boxer hit the mat.   He lay there, *stunned*.

He *was stunning* us with his revelations.
He *has stunned* others before us.
One *can be stunned* by a jolt of electricity.

1. interest
2. love
3. thrill
4. trouble
5. grow

6. change
7. ride
8. excite
9. dry
10. bake

21g

21f Gerunds

When the *ing* form of a verb functions as a noun, it is called a **gerund**:

Moving offices can be hard work.

André gave himself a good talking to.

Sylvester has a profound fear of flying.

Careful preparation—brainstorming, organizing, and outlining—helps produce good essays.

The gerund *Moving* is the subject of the sentence, and it has *offices* as a direct object. The gerund *talking* is a direct object and is itself modified by the adjective *good*. The gerund *flying* is the object of the preposition *of*. In the final example, the three gerunds constitute an appositive or definition of the subject noun, *preparation* (see #11q).

21g Tense and Voice of Gerunds (see #17g–h and #17-o–p)

As with infinitives and participles, the *perfect* form of a gerund indicates a time earlier than that of the main verb:

My having answered the phone myself may have secured the contract.

And a gerund can be in the passive voice:

> His <u>being praised</u> by the supervisor gave him a big lift.

Be aware, though, that using either the perfect or the passive gerund can produce awkward results:

> The misunderstanding resulted from <u>our not having received</u> the latest information.

> He was proud of <u>her being awarded</u> the gold star for excellence.

Rephrasing such examples to avoid the gerund will produce clearer sentences:

> The misunderstanding resulted because we didn't receive the latest information.

> He was proud of her for receiving the gold star of excellence.

21h Possessives with Gerunds

In formal usage, a noun or a personal pronoun preceding a gerund will usually be in the possessive case:

> <u>His</u> cooking left much to be desired.

> She approved of <u>Bob's</u> cleaning the house.

> Can you explain the <u>engine's</u> not starting?

If the gerund is the subject, as in the first example, the possessive is essential. Otherwise, if you are writing informally, and especially if you want to emphasize the noun or pronoun, you don't need to use the possessive:

> She approved of <u>Bob</u> cleaning the house.

> Can you explain the <u>engine</u> not starting?

Further, in order to avoid awkward-sounding constructions, you usually won't use a possessive form when the noun preceding a gerund is (a) abstract, (b) plural, (c) multiple, or (d) separated from the gerund by modifiers (other than adverbs like *not* or *always* when they sound almost like part of the verbal):

a. He couldn't bear the thought of <u>love striking</u> again.

b. The possibility of the <u>thieves returning</u> to their hideout was slim.

c. There is a good chance of <u>Alberto and Maria agreeing</u> to your proposal.

d. One might well wonder at a <u>man</u> with such expertise <u>claiming</u> to be ignorant.

PROOFREADING TIP

A Gerund Followed Immediately by Another Noun

A gerund followed immediately by another noun will sometimes sound awkward or ambiguous. In such cases, interpose *of* or *the* or some similar term to keep the gerund from sounding like a participle:

his building (of) boats   your organizing (of the) material

my practising (the) piano   his revealing (of, the, of the) sources

---

21i

21i Verbals in Absolute Phrases

Infinitives and participles (but not gerunds) can function in **absolute phrases** (see #11r):

<u>To say the least</u>, the day was memorable.

<u>Strictly speaking</u>, their actions were not legal.

<u>All things considered</u>, the meeting was a success.

Exercise 21 (1) Recognizing Verbals

Identify each verbal in the following sentences as an infinitive, a past or present participle, or a gerund:

1. Coming as he did from the Prairies, he found the coastal scenery to be stunning.
2. She wanted to snowboard, and learning was easier than she had expected.
3. Trying to study hard on an empty stomach is usually not very rewarding.
4. The party was certain to last until midnight, permitting everyone to eat and drink too much.
5. Sent as she had been from one office to another, Cindy was tired of running back and forth and up and down; she was now resolved to go straight to the top.

21i

Exercise 21 (2) Using Verbals

Here are some exercises to help you become familiar with verbals and recognize some of the things you can do with them.

A. In short sentences, use three infinitives as nouns, adjectives, and, if possible, adverbs (they are less common). Then use each in three longer sentences, again as noun, adjective, and adverb, but expanded into infinitive phrases. You needn't simply build on the short sentences, but you may.

Example: *to meditate*

noun:	To meditate is restful. (subject)
	I like to meditate. (object)
	One relaxation technique is to meditate. (predicate noun)
adjective:	I need a place to meditate.
adverb:	She cleared a space in order to meditate.
noun phrase:	To meditate, feet up, before a quietly crackling fire on a cold winter night, staring into the embers, is one of the more relaxing pleasures available to human beings.

B. Compose ten sentences using present and past participles to modify different kinds of nouns—subjects, direct objects, indirect objects, objects of prepositions, predicate nouns, objective complements, appositives.

Exercise 21 (3) Reducing Clauses to Infinitive Phrases

By reducing clauses to phrases, you can often get rid of unnecessary heaviness and wordiness. Practise by reducing each italicized clause in the following sentences to an infinitive phrase that conveys basically the same meaning. Change or rearrange words as necessary.

Example: We wondered *what we should do next.*

We wondered *what to do next.*

1. Remember *that you should be at the computer lab by 3:30.*
2. The quarterback's problem was *that he had to decide* what play *he should use next.*

3. My charismatic cousin gestured to us *that we should follow him into the restaurant.*
4. The time *that you should worry about* is the hour before the race.
5. After her motorbike came to a grinding halt, Abigail pondered *what her next move would be.*

Exercise 21 (4) Reducing Clauses

22

This time reduce each italicized clause to the kind of phrase specified in parentheses after each sentence.

> **Example:** *As she changed her mind,* she suddenly felt much better. **(present participial)**
>
> *Changing her mind,* she suddenly felt much better.

1. Sometimes the best part of a vacation is *when you plan it.* (gerund)
2. Earning the respect of children is something *that you can be proud of.* (infinitive)
3. *Because they felt foolish,* they decided to leave early. (present participial)
4. *The fact that she had won the contest* came as something of a shock to her. (gerund)
5. The bank manager *who wore the colourful wig* started doing the samba. (present participial)

22 Prepositions

Prepositions are structure words or function words (see #11-l); they do not change their form. A preposition is part of a prepositional phrase, and it usually precedes the rest of the phrase, which includes a noun or pronoun as the object of the preposition:

> This is a book <u>about writing</u>.

> She sent an email <u>to her brother</u>.

Make a question of the preposition and ask *what* or *whom* and the answer will always be the object: *About* what? Writing. *To* whom? Her brother.

22a Functions of Prepositions and Prepositional Phrases

A preposition *links* its object to some other word in the sentence; the prepositional phrase then functions as either an *adjectival* or an *adverbial* modifier:

> He laid the camera <u>on the table</u>.

Here, *on* links *table* to the verb *laid*; the phrase *on the table* therefore functions as an adverb describing *where* the camera was laid.

> It was a time <u>for celebration</u>.

Here, *for* links *celebration* to the noun *time*; the phrase therefore functions as an adjective indicating *what kind of* time.

22b Placement of Prepositions

Usually, like articles, prepositions signal that a noun or pronoun soon follows. But prepositions can also come at the ends of clauses or sentences—for example, in a question, for emphasis, or to avoid stiffness:

> Which laptop do you want to look <u>at</u>?

> Which aunt are you buying the card <u>for</u>?

> I want to know what the story is really <u>about</u>.

> They had several issues to contend <u>with</u>.

> The problem he was dealing <u>with</u> seemed insurmountable.

Some would prefer "with which he was dealing," especially in a formal context. But it isn't wrong to end a sentence or a clause with a preposition, in spite of what many people have been taught; just don't do it so often that it calls attention to itself. Remember that Sir Winston Churchill is supposed to have said that repeated use of the preposition in this way was the sort of usage "up with which I will not put."

22c Common Prepositions

Most prepositions indicate a spatial or temporal relation, or such things as purpose, concession, comparison, manner, and agency. Here is a list of common prepositions; note that several consist of more than one word:

about	beneath	including	over
above	beside	in front of	past

according to	besides	in order to	regarding
across	between	in place of	regardless of
across from	beyond	in relation to	round
after	but	inside	since
against	by	in spite of	such as
ahead of	by way of	into	through
along	concerning	like	throughout
alongside	considering	near	till
among	contrary to	next to	to
apart from	despite	notwithstanding	toward(s)
around	down	of	under
as	during	off	underneath
as for	except	on	unlike
at	except for	on account of	until
away from	excepting	onto	up
because of	for	on top of	upon
before	from	opposite	with
behind	in	out	within
below	in addition to	outside	without

22c

A learner's dictionary will be extremely helpful in guiding you in the use of these and other prepositions.

Exercise 22a–c (1) Recognizing Prepositional Phrases

Identify each prepositional phrase in the following sentences and note whether each is adjectival or adverbial.

1. Ricardo went into town to buy some oatmeal for his breakfast.
2. There stood the famous pianist of about thirty, in the hot sunshine, wearing a heavy jacket with the collar turned up.
3. In the morning the president called her assistant on the telephone and told her to come to the office without delay.
4. The bulk of the presents was sent ahead in trunks.
5. The Siamese cat looked under the table for the ball of yarn that had fallen from the chair.

Exercise 22a–c (2) Using Prepositional Phrases

Prepositional phrases are essential components of writing, but they can be overdone. These exercises will give you practice both in using them and in avoiding their overuse.

A. Reducing Clauses to Prepositional Phrases

You'll use prepositional phrases without even thinking about them; but sometimes you should consciously try to tighten and lighten your style by reducing some clauses to prepositional phrases. Reduce the italicized clauses in the following sentences to prepositional phrases. Revise in other ways as well if you wish, but don't change the essential meaning.

22c

Example: The cold front *that is over the coast* will move inland overnight.

The cold front *over the coast* will move inland overnight.

1. *If you have enough stamina*, you can take part in the triathlon.
2. *Because she was so confident*, she entered every race.
3. Students *who have part-time jobs* must budget their time carefully.
4. We need advice *that only a grandmother can give us*.
5. The time *when you should eat dinner* is three hours before you go to sleep.

B. Reducing Clauses to Prepositional Phrases Using Gerunds

Gerunds (see #21f–g) are often used as objects of prepositions. Convert the italicized clauses in the following sentences to prepositional phrases with gerunds.

Example: *Before she submitted the essay*, she proofread it carefully.

Before submitting the essay, she proofread it carefully.

1. *When I had run* only half a block, I felt exhausted.
2. *Although Petra trained rigorously*, she didn't get past the preliminaries.
3. You can't hope to understand *unless you attend all the classes*.
4. *They checked the luggage carefully* and found nothing but clothes and a toothbrush.
5. He deserves some credit *because he tried so hard*.

C. Getting Rid of Excessive Prepositional Phrases

When prepositional phrases come in bunches, they can contribute to wordiness. Practise revising to get rid of clutter: cut the number of prepositional phrases in each of the following sentences (shown in parentheses) at least in half.

Example: Some of the ministers in the Cabinet are in danger of losing their appointments because of the poor quality of their relations with the media and deficits in their department budgets. (8)

Because they have poor media relations and departmental budget deficits, some Cabinet ministers may lose their appointments. (reduced to zero)

1. Sarah got to the top of the mountain first by using several trails unknown to her competitors in the race, which was held during the celebration of the centennial of the province's entry into confederation. (9)
2. The feeling of most of the people at the meeting was that the committee chair spoke in strident tones for too long about things about which he knew little. (7)
3. The irritated ghost at the top of the stairs of the old house shouted at me to get away from his door in a hurry. (6)
4. One of the most respected of modern historians has some odd ideas about the beginning of the war between European nations that broke out, with such devastating consequences, in early August of 1914. (8)
5. Economists' predictions about the rise and fall of interest rates seem to be accurate for the most part, but only within the limits of a period of about three or four weeks, at most, and even at that you have to take them with a grain of salt. (10)

22d

22d Two-Part Verbs; Verb Idioms

English has many two-part and even three-part verbs consisting of a simple verb in combination with another word or words—for example, *act up*, *blow up*, *carry on*, *cool off*, *find out*, *get on with*, *hold up*, *stick up for*. You may think of the added words as prepositions, adverbs, or some sort of "particle." Indeed, sometimes it is difficult to say whether a word like *down* in *sit down* is functioning as part of the verb or as an adverb describing how one can sit; but the *down* and *up* in "sit down to a good meal" and "sit up in your chair" seem more like parts of the verbs than, say, the preposition *at* in "He sat at his desk." Usually you can sense a difference in sound: in "He *took over* the operation" both parts are stressed when said aloud, whereas in "He *took* over three hours to get here" only the *took* is stressed; *over* functions separately. Often, too, the parts of a verb can be separated and still mean the same, whereas the verb and preposition or adverb cannot:

22e

> The children were <u>won over</u> by the actor's exuberance.
>
> The actor's exuberance <u>won</u> the children <u>over</u>.
>
> **Compare:** He <u>won</u> over his nearest opponent by three points.
>
> The construction crew <u>blew up</u> the remains of the old factory.
>
> The construction crew <u>blew</u> the remains of the old factory <u>up</u>.
>
> **Compare:** The wind <u>blew</u> up the chimney.

Some two-part verbs cannot be separated—for example, *look after, run across, see to, sit up, turn in* (as in *go to sleep*). Some simple verbs can take two or more different words to form new verbs; for example:

> think out – think up
>
> try out – try on
>
> fall out – fall in – fall off
>
> fill up – fill in – fill out

Some verbs can use several different words to form idiomatic expressions, as you will discover by looking them up in a learner's dictionary:

> bring about – bring around – bring down – bring forth – bring forward – bring in – bring off – bring on – bring out – bring over – bring to – bring up
>
> let alone – let down – let go – let loose – let off – let on – let up
>
> turn down – turn in – turn loose – turn off – turn on – turn out – turn over – turn to – turn up

See also #62-l, on the spelling of hyphenated verbs.

22e Using Two-Part Verbs: Informality and Formality

By consciously using or avoiding two-part (and three-part) verbs in a piece of writing, you can help control tone. Most of these verbs are standard and idiomatic, but some are informal or colloquial or even slangy—for example, *let up, mess up, shake up, trip up* (and see #64). Even the standard ones are often relatively informal; that is, they have more formal equivalents; for example:

Informal	Formal
give away	bestow; reveal, betray
give back	return
give in	yield, concede
give off	discharge, emit
give out	emit; distribute; become exhausted
give over	relinquish, abandon; cease
give up	despair; stop, renounce; surrender, cede
give way	withdraw, retreat; make room for; collapse

22e

If you choose *buy* as more appropriate to your context than *purchase*, you'll probably also want to use some two-part verbs rather than their more formal, often Latinate, equivalents; for example, you'd probably say *buy up* rather than *acquire*. But if you're writing a strictly formal piece, you may want to avoid the informal terms, or limit yourself to just a couple for contrast or variety.

Exercise 22d–e Using Two-Part Verbs

A. Draw up a list of two-part (and three-part) verbs and their more formal equivalents. Draw on those listed above, but add as many more as you can think of. Take common verbs like *come, go, put, take, get,* and *set,* and try adding on such common prepositions and adverbs as *about, at, away, back, down, in, off, out, over, through, to, up, upon,* and *with.* Consult your dictionary, where multi-part verbs are often treated separately under the entry for the basic verb. If you don't find many listed, look in a bigger dictionary, or a learner's dictionary, such as the *Oxford Advanced Learner's Dictionary.*

B. Compose several sentences—or, better yet, compose two or three separate paragraphs—using as many verbs from your list as you can squeeze in. Read them over, aloud, to see how they sound.

C. Rewrite your sentences (or paragraphs), wherever possible substituting more formal verbs for your originals. Now how do they sound?

Conjunctions

Conjunctions are another kind of structure word or function word (see #11-l). As their name indicates, conjunctions are words that "join together." There are three kinds of conjunctions: *coordinating, correlative,* and *subordinating.*

23a Coordinating Conjunctions

There are only seven **coordinating conjunctions**, so they are easy to remember:

<table>
<tr><td>and</td><td>but</td><td>for</td><td>nor</td><td>or</td><td>so</td><td>yet</td></tr>
</table>

When you use a coordinating conjunction, choose the appropriate one. *And* indicates addition, *nor* indicates negative addition (equivalent to *also not*), *but* and *yet* indicate contrast or opposition, *or* indicates choice, *for* indicates cause or reason, and *so* indicates effect or result. (See also #41, on faulty coordination.)

Some coordinating conjunctions can also be other parts of speech: *yet* can be an adverb (It's not *yet* ten o'clock); *so* can be an adverb (It was *so* dark that . . .), an adjective (Is that *so*?), and a demonstrative pronoun (I liked him, and I told him *so*); *for* is also a common preposition (*for* a while, *for* me); and *but* can be a preposition, meaning *except* (all *but* two).

Coordinating conjunctions have three main functions, which are discussed below.

1. Joining Words, Phrases, and Subordinate Clauses

And, but, or, and *yet* join coordinate elements within sentences. The elements joined are usually of equal importance and of similar grammatical structure and function. When joined, they are sometimes called compounds of various kinds (see #12c.1). Here are examples of how various kinds of sentence elements may be compounded:

I saw <u>Jean</u> and <u>Rohan</u>. (two direct objects)

<u>Jean</u> or <u>Rohan</u> saw me. (two subjects)

They <u>danced</u> and <u>sang</u>. (two verbs)

<u>Tired</u> but <u>determined</u>, the hiker plodded on. (two past participles)

The gnome was <u>short</u>, <u>fat</u>, and <u>melancholic</u>. (three predicate adjectives)

He drove <u>quickly</u> yet <u>carefully</u>. (two adverbs)

The bird flew <u>in the door</u> and <u>out the window</u>.
(two adverbial prepositional phrases)

The children <u>loved the rat</u> but <u>hated the hamster</u>.
(two verbs with direct objects)

People <u>who invest wisely</u> and <u>who spend carefully</u> often have
boring lives. (two adjectival clauses)

I travel <u>when I have the time</u> and <u>when I have money</u>.
(two adverbial clauses)

The career coach told him <u>what he should wear</u> and <u>how he
should speak</u>. (two noun clauses)

Obviously the elements being joined won't always have identical structures, but don't disappoint readers' natural expectations that compound
elements will be parallel. For example, it would be weaker to write the
last example—*The career coach told him what he should wear and how he should
speak*—with one direct object as a clause and the other as an infinitive
phrase (see #40, on faulty parallelism):

> ***weak***: The career coach told him <u>what he should wear</u> and <u>how
> to speak</u>.

When three or more elements are compounded, the conjunction usually appears only between the last two, though *and* and *or* can appear
throughout for purposes of rhythm or emphasis:

> The recipe called for butter, flour, salt, sugar, and eggs.

> There was a tug-of-war <u>and</u> a sack race <u>and</u> an egg race <u>and</u> a
> three-legged race <u>and</u> . . . well, there was just about any kind of
> game anyone could want at a picnic.

And occasionally *and* can be omitted for emphasis (see also #49d):

> There were flowers galore—fuchsias, snap dragons, jonquils,
> dahlias, azaleas, tulips, roses, lilacs, camellias—more kinds of
> flowers than I wanted to see on any one day.

2. Joining Independent Clauses

All seven coordinating conjunctions can join independent clauses to make compound (or compound-complex) sentences (see #12c). The clauses will be grammatically equivalent, since they are independent; but they needn't be grammatically parallel or even of similar length, though they often are both, for parallelism is a strong stylistic force. Here are some examples:

> Jean saw me, <u>but</u> Rohan did not.

23a

> The players fought, the umpires shouted, <u>and</u> the fans booed.

> The kestrel flew higher and higher, in ever-wider circles, <u>and</u> soon it was but a speck in the sky overhead.

> I won't do it, <u>nor</u> will she. (With *nor* there must be some sort of negative in the first clause. Note that after *nor* the normal subject–verb order is reversed.)

> There was no way to avoid going to the presentation, <u>so</u> I decided to get as much out of the experience as I could.

 PROOFREADING TIP

On Using the Conjunction *so*

The conjunction *so* is informal; in formal writing, you can almost always indicate cause–effect relations with a *because* or *since* clause instead:

> <u>Because</u> there was no way to avoid going to the presentation, I decided to get as much out of the experience as I could.

And so, however, is acceptable; but don't overuse it, because it is a weak transition:

> We overslept, <u>and so</u> we missed the keynote address.

---

3. Joining Sentences

In spite of what many of us have been taught, it isn't wrong to begin a sentence with *And* or *But*, or for that matter any of the other coordinating conjunctions. Be advised, however, that *For*, since it is so similar in meaning to *because*, often sounds strange at the start of a sentence, as if introducing a fragmentary subordinate clause (see #23c). In addition, the coordinating conjunction *So* often sounds too colloquial. But the rest, especially *And* and *But*, make good openers—as long as you don't overuse them. An opening *But* or *Yet* can nicely emphasize a contrast or other turn of thought (as in the preceding sentence). An opening *And* can also be emphatic:

> He told the employees of the company he was sorry. And he meant it.

Both *And* and *But* as sentence openers contribute to paragraph coherence (see #7b.4). And, especially in a narrative, a succession of opening *Ands* can impart a feeling of rapid pace, even breathless excitement. Used too often, such openings can become tedious, but used carefully and when they feel natural, they can be effective.

For punctuation with coordinating conjunctions, see chapter V, especially #44a–c and #55d.

23a

Exercise 23a Using Coordinating Conjunctions

Put an appropriate coordinating conjunction in each blank. If more than one is possible, list all options.

1. I'm sure Leo _____ Hazel will win.
2. Exhausted _____ determined, Sasha found the strength to finish the race.
3. Uma was late for the meeting, _____ she had a good excuse.
4. There is only one solution to this problem, _____ I know what it is.
5. No one likes noise pollution, _____ some people insist that we have to live with it.
6. Her brother is not cynical, _____ is he insensitive.
7. We were puzzled by the professor's humorous comments, _____ we had expected her to speak seriously on the subject.
8. The tuba solo came as a surprise, _____ Tomas and Uli were expecting an organ concerto.
9. We could stay up all night studying, _____ we could quickly skim over our notes _____ get a good night's sleep.
10. Michael swore he would never be drawn back into a life of crime. _____ fate had other plans.

23b Correlative Conjunctions

Correlative conjunctions come in pairs. They *correlate* ("relate together") two parallel parts of a sentence. The following are the principal ones:

either . . . or	neither . . . nor
whether . . . or	both . . . and
not . . . but	not only . . . but also

23b

Correlative conjunctions enable you to write sentences containing forcefully balanced elements, but don't overdo them. They are also more at home in formal than in informal writing. Some examples:

Either Rodney or Elliott is going to drive.

She accepted neither the first nor the second job offer.

Whether by accident or by design, the number turned out to be exactly right.

Both the administration and the student body are pleased with the new plan.

She not only plays well but also sings well.

Not only does she play well, but she also sings well.

Notice, in the last two examples, how *also* (or its equivalent) can be moved away from the *but*. And in the last example, note how *does* is needed as an auxiliary because the clause is in the present tense. Except for these variations, make what follows one term exactly parallel to what follows the other: *the first* || *the second*; *by accident* || *by design*; *plays well* || *sings well*. (See also #40, on faulty parallelism.)

Further, with the *not only . . . but also* pair, you should usually make the *also* (or some equivalent) explicit. Its omission results in a feeling of incompleteness:

incomplete: He was not only smart, but charming.

complete: He was not only smart, but also charming.

complete: He was not only smart, but charming as well.

EAL To ensure that you use this correlative pairing effectively, keep in mind the following:

1. For clauses containing *compound verbs* (one or more auxiliary verbs attached to a main verb), place *not only* at the beginning of the clause and then place the first auxiliary verb before the subject. Then, place *but* before the subject of the second clause and *also* after the auxiliary verb.

   > He has been a great star and he has served his fans well.

   > Not only *has* he been a great star, <u>but</u> he has <u>also</u> served his fans well.

2. For sentences in the *simple present* or *simple past* tenses (other than those in which the main verb is *be*), you must add the appropriate form of *do* (*do*, *does*, or *did*) before the subject of the *not only* clause when *not only* appears at the beginning of the clause.

   > She looks rested and she looks happy.

   > Not only *does* she look rested, <u>but</u> she <u>also</u> looks happy.

   > She looked rested and she looked happy.

   > Not only *did* she look rested, <u>but</u> she <u>also</u> looked happy.

   > She is rested and she is happy.

   > Not only *is* she rested, <u>but</u> she is <u>also</u> happy.

3. When *not only* appears inside the clause, you do not have to reverse the order of the auxiliary verb and subject, nor do you have to add *do*, *does*, or *did*.

   > She has worked hard at her job and at her hobbies.

   > She has worked hard <u>not only</u> at her job <u>but also</u> at her hobbies.

See #18c for *agreement* of verbs with subjects joined by some of the correlatives.

23c Subordinating Conjunctions

A **subordinating conjunction** introduces a *subordinate* (or *dependent*) clause and links it to the *independent* (or *main* or *principal*) clause to which it is grammatically related:

> She writes <u>because</u> she has something to say.

23c

The subordinating conjunction *because* introduces the adverbial clause *because she has something to say* and links it to the independent clause whose verb it modifies. The *because* clause is *subordinate* because it cannot stand by itself: by itself it would be a *fragment* (see #12b). Note that a subordinate clause can also come first:

> Because she has something to say, she writes articles for magazines.

23c

Even though *Because* does not occur between the two unequal clauses, it still links them grammatically.

> That Raj will win the prize is a foregone conclusion.

Here *That* introduces the noun clause *That Raj will win the prize*, which functions as the subject of the sentence. Note that whereas a coordinating conjunction is like a spot of glue between two structures and not a part of either, a subordinating conjunction is an integral part of its clause. In the following sentence, for example, the subordinating conjunction *whenever* is a part of the adverbial clause that modifies the imperative verb *Leave*:

> Leave whenever you feel tired.

Here is a list of the principal subordinating conjunctions:

after	if	that	where(ever)
although	if only	though	whereas
as	in case	till	whether
as though	lest	unless	which
because	once	until	while
before	rather than	what	who
even though	since	whatever	why
ever since	than	when(ever)	

There are also many terms consisting of two or more words ending in *as*, *if*, and *that* that serve as subordinating conjunctions, including *inasmuch as*, *insofar as*, *as long as*, *as soon as*, *as far as*, *as if*, *even if*, *only if*, *but that*, *except that*, *now that*, *in that*, *provided that*, *in order that*.

Some subordinating conjunctions can also function as adverbs, prepositions, and relative pronouns. But don't worry about parts of speech at this point. Think of all these terms as *subordinators*, including the relative pronouns and relative adverbs (*who, which, that, when, where*) that introduce adjectival clauses. If you understand their *subordinating* function, you will understand the syntax of complex and compound–complex sentences (see #12c) and will be able to avoid *fragments* (see #12b).

23c

Exercise 23c (1) Recognizing Subordinate Clauses

Identify the subordinate clauses in the following passage and indicate how each is functioning: as adjective, adverb, or noun. (Remember that sometimes relative pronouns are omitted; see #14d and #48a.) What words do the adjectival and adverbial clauses modify? How does each noun clause function? (You might begin by identifying the *independent* clauses.)

Once upon a time, when he was only eight, Selwyn decided he wanted to be a marine biologist. He especially liked to play in the numerous tide pools found outside the Peggys Cove cabin where his family stayed every summer. As he grew older, he discovered that in order to become a marine biologist, one had to study many different and difficult subjects that seemed far removed from ocean life. Whenever he worked on his math, statistics, or computer problems in stuffy rooms, he kept longing to walk on the beach. That he became a successful field scientist and expert on the microorganisms found in tide pools is, therefore, not surprising. What most people don't know is that when Selwyn became a full professor, he didn't need to worry about doing analysis anymore because he had graduate students who enjoyed working with numbers and who derived satisfaction from developing new approaches to data analysis. So while they crunched numbers, Selwyn puttered around happily ever after on shorelines all over the world looking deep into tide pools.

Exercise 23c (2) Writing Subordinate Clauses

Combine each of the following pairs of simple sentences into a single complex sentence by subordinating one clause and attaching it to the other with one of the subordinators listed in #23c. You may want to change, delete, or add some words, reverse the clauses, or otherwise rearrange words. Experiment with different subordinators.

Example: The digital revolution has changed how most businesses operate. Its largest impact has been on how we communicate with friends and family.

(Though, Although) the digital revolution has changed how most businesses operate, its largest impact has been on how we communicate with friends and family.

1. The art gallery won't open until next week. The leak in the roof hasn't been repaired yet.
2. Most Canadians support strict gun laws. They are unwilling to pay higher taxes to see these laws enforced.
3. Some students may not have paid all their fees. They would not yet be considered officially registered.
4. First you should master the simple sentence. Then you can work on rhyming couplets.
5. The children ate most of their Halloween candy. They were completely wired.

24 Interjections

An **interjection** is a word or group of words *interjected* or dropped into a sentence in order to express emotion. Strictly speaking, interjections have no grammatical function; they are simply thrust into sentences and play no part in their syntax, though sometimes they act like sentence modifiers. They are often used in dialogue and are not that common in academic writing.

But—good heavens!—what did you expect?

So, it has come to this!

It was, well, a bit of a disappointment.

A mild interjection is usually set off with commas. A strong interjection is sometimes set off with dashes and is often accompanied by an exclamation point (see #50b and #53c). An interjection may also be a minor sentence by itself (see #12a):

Ouch! That hurt!

Ok. I guess this means that the lesson is over.

Thanks John! Your advice on the project was most helpful.

Review Exercises Chapter III
Recognizing and Using Parts of Speech

24

A. Recognizing Parts of Speech

To test yourself, see if you can identify the part of speech of each word in the following sentences. Can you say how each is functioning grammatically?

1. The skyline of Toronto provides a striking example of what modern architecture can do to distinguish a major city.
2. Waiter, there's a fly doing the back crawl in my soup!
3. Well, to tell the truth, I just did not have the necessary patience.
4. Why should anyone be unhappy about paying a fair tax?
5. Neither the captain nor the crew could be blamed for the terribly costly ferry accident.
6. The elevator business has been said to have its ups and downs.
7. Brandon, please put back the chocolate cake.
8. While abroad, I learned to make do with only three large suitcases and one full-time chauffeur.
9. In a few seconds, *Wikipedia* told us much more than we needed to know.
10. Help!

B. Using Different Parts of Speech

Write some sentences using the following words as different parts of speech—as many different ones as you can. Each is good for at least two different parts of speech.

before	best	cover	cross	down	fine
last	left	near	plant	rose	round
set	shed	still	study	train	wrong

IV

Writing Effective Sentences

Introduction: Examining How Sentences Work

Chapter IV deals with the way the various elements work together in sentences. It is designed to enable you to understand how sentences work and how to avoid common problems. If you have difficulty with the terms and concepts discussed in this chapter, you may need to review previous chapters on sentences and parts of speech.

Basic Sentence Elements and Their Modifiers

Subject, Verb, Object, Complement

Consider again the bare bones of a sentence. The two essential elements are a *subject* and a *verb* (see #11a). Also significant are *objects* and *complements*. The following discussion reveals the ways in which these elements are closely connected to one another, with the verb acting as the focal and uniting element. (For a discussion of the *order* in which these elements occur, see #11s–u.)

25a Subject
The subject is what is talked about. It is the word or phrase answering the question consisting of *who* or *what* and the verb. More precisely, it is the source of the action indicated by the verb, or the person or thing experiencing or possessing the state of being or the condition indicated by the verb and its complement:

> Jessica drove the bulldozer. (*Who* drove? Jessica. Jessica is the source of the action of driving.)

> We are happy about the outcome. (*Who* is happy? We are. We are experiencing the state of being happy.)

> Ravi is a physician. (*Who* is a physician? Ravi. Ravi is the person in the state or condition of being a physician.)

> Recycling is vital. (*What* is vital? Recycling. Recycling possesses the condition of being vital.)

The subject of a sentence will ordinarily be one of the following: a basic noun (see #13), a pronoun (see #14), a gerund or gerund phrase (see #21f), an infinitive or infinitive phrase (see #21a), or a noun clause (see #11-o):

British Columbia joined Confederation on 20 July 1871. (noun)

He is a Manitoba historian. (pronoun)

Staring can be an aggressive act. (gerund)

Checking the website is part of our daily routine. (gerund phrase)

To travel is to enjoy life. (infinitive)

To order broccoli is to make a healthy choice. (infinitive phrase)

Whoever signs the contract is legally responsible. (noun clause)

Rarely, a prepositional phrase serves as the subject; see #22a.

25b Finite Verb

The **finite verb** is the focal point of the clause or the sentence. It indicates both the nature and the time of the action (see #17a):

> The prime minister will respond during question period. (action: responding; time: the future)

> Lewis Carroll invented the adventures of Alice for a child named Alice Liddell. (action: inventing; time: past)

> Edmonton has numerous distinct neighbourhoods. (action: having, possessing; time: present)

> Syntax is word order. (state of being: being something; time: present)

25c Direct Object

If a verb is *transitive* (see #17a), it will have a direct object to complete the pattern (see #11d). Like the subject, the direct object may be a noun, a pronoun, a gerund or gerund phrase, an infinitive or infinitive phrase, or a noun clause:

> The lineup includes Arcade Fire. (noun)

> The increase in gasoline taxes worried us. (pronoun)

> Our economy needs farming. (gerund)

> He enjoys writing reports. (gerund phrase)

> We wanted to participate. (infinitive)

You need to define your terms. (infinitive phrase)

The reporter revealed that his source feared retaliation. (noun clause)

Along with a direct object, there may also be an indirect object or an objective complement (see #11f, #11i, and #11j).

We gave you a blank cheque. [*you*: indirect object; *cheque*: direct object]

She judged the situation untenable. [*situation*: direct object; *untenable*: objective complement]

25d Subjective Complement

Similarly, a *linking verb* (see #17a) typically requires a subjective complement to complete the pattern. This complement will usually be either a *predicate noun* or a *predicate adjective* (see #11g and #11h). A predicate noun may be a noun or a pronoun, or (especially after *be*) a gerund or gerund phrase, an infinitive or infinitive phrase, or a noun clause:

We are friends. (noun)

Was he the one? (pronoun)

His passion is travelling. (gerund)

His passion is travelling the back country. (gerund phrase)

My first impulse was to run. (infinitive)

Our next challenge will be to take action. (infinitive phrase)

She remains what she has long been: a loyal friend. (noun clause)

A predicate adjective will ordinarily be a descriptive adjective, a participle, or an idiomatic prepositional phrase:

The other team's fans are obnoxious. (descriptive adjective)

The novel's plot is intriguing. (present participle)

They seem dedicated. (past participle)

The government is out of ideas. (prepositional phrase)

The linking verb *be* (and sometimes others) can also be followed by an adverbial word or phrase (I am *here*; he is *in his office*).

26 Modifiers

Modifiers add to the core grammatical elements listed above. They limit or describe other elements so as to modify—that is, to change—a listener's or reader's idea of them. The two principal kinds of modifiers are *adjectives* (see #19) and *adverbs* (see #20). Also useful, but less frequent, are *appositives* (see #11q) and *absolute phrases* (see #11r and #21i). An adjectival or adverbial modifier may even be part of the core of a sentence if it completes the predicate after a linking verb (Recycling is *vital*; Ziad is *home*). An adverb may also be essential if it modifies an intransitive verb that would otherwise seem incomplete (Ziad lives *in a condominium*). But generally modifiers do their work by adding to—enriching—a central core of thought.

26a

26a Adjectival Modifiers

Adjectival modifiers modify nouns, pronouns, and phrases or clauses functioning as nouns. They commonly answer the questions *Which? What kind of? How many?* and *How much?* An adjectival modifier may be a single-word adjective, a series of adjectives, a participle or participial phrase, an infinitive or infinitive phrase, a prepositional phrase, or a relative clause:

Early settlers of western Canada encountered sudden floods, prolonged droughts, and early frosts. (single words modifying nouns immediately following)

We are skeptical. (predicate adjective modifying the pronoun *We*)

That the author opposes deregulation is evident in her first paragraph. (predicate adjective modifying the noun clause *That the author opposes deregulation*)

Four ambitious young students are competing for the prestigious internship. (series modifying *students*)

The train station is filled with commuters and tourists. (noun functioning as adjective, modifying *station*)

Grinning, he replied to her text message. (present participle modifying *he*)

Brimming with confidence, they began their performance. (present participial phrase modifying *they*)

They continued the climb toward the summit, <u>undaunted</u>. (past participle modifying *they*)

Lijuan applied for the position, <u>having been encouraged to do so by her adviser</u>. (participial phrase, perfect tense, passive voice, modifying *Lijuan*)

They prepared a meal <u>to remember</u>. (infinitive modifying *meal*)

Our tendency <u>to favour jazz</u> is evident in our playlists. (infinitive phrase modifying *tendency*)

The report <u>on the evening news</u> focused on forest fires in northern British Columbia. (prepositional phrase modifying *report*)

The lacrosse team, <u>which was travelling to a tournament in Winnipeg</u>, filed slowly through airport security. (relative clause modifying *team*)

26b Adverbial Modifiers

Adverbial modifiers modify verbs, adjectives, other adverbs, and whole clauses or sentences. They commonly answer the questions *How? When? Where?* and *To what degree?* An adverbial modifier may be a single word, a series, an infinitive or infinitive phrase, a prepositional phrase, or an adverbial clause:

Mix the chemicals <u>thoroughly</u>. (single word modifying the verb *mix*)

As new parents, we are <u>completely</u> happy. (single word modifying the adjective *happy*)

They planned their future together <u>quite</u> enthusiastically. (single word modifying the adverb *enthusiastically*)

<u>Apparently</u>, the experiment is being delayed. (single word modifying the rest of the sentence)

He loves her <u>truly</u>, <u>madly</u>, <u>deeply</u>. (series modifying the verb *loves*)

<u>To succeed</u>, you must work well with others. (infinitive modifying the verb *must work*)

She was lucky <u>to have been selected</u> for the exchange program. (infinitive phrase modifying the predicate adjective *lucky*)

The passenger ship arrived <u>at the port</u>. (prepositional phrase modifying the verb *arrived*)

We disagreed <u>because we were taking different theoretical approaches</u>. (clause modifying the verb *disagreed*)

The election results trickled in slowly <u>because the ballots were being counted by hand</u>. (clause modifying the adverb *slowly*, or the whole preceding clause, *The election results trickled in slowly*.)

Shut off your computer <u>when you leave on vacation</u>. (clause modifying the preceding independent clause)

26c Overlapping Modifiers

26c

The preceding examples are meant to illustrate each kind of adjectival and adverbial modifier separately. But many sentences are more complicated, largely because modifiers overlap in them. Modifiers occur as parts of other modifiers: single-word modifiers occur as parts of phrases and clauses, phrases occur as parts of other phrases and as parts of clauses, and subordinate clauses occur as parts of phrases and as parts of other clauses. Here are examples illustrating some of the possible structural variety. (You may want to check sections #11c–k in order to match these sentences and their clauses with the various patterns they include.)

They walked briskly toward the waiting car.
> *briskly* – adverb modifying *walked*
> *toward the waiting car* – adverbial prepositional phrase modifying *walked*
> *waiting* – participial adjective modifying *car*

He purchased a few of the off-the-rack suits.
> *of the off-the-rack suits* – adjectival prepositional phrase modifying *few*
> *off-the-rack* – hyphenated prepositional phrase, adjective modifying *suits*

Hoping to learn to perform brilliantly, the cast rehearsed until dawn.
> *Hoping to learn to perform brilliantly* – participial phrase modifying *cast*
> *to learn to perform brilliantly* – infinitive phrase, object of the participle *hoping*
> *to perform brilliantly* – infinitive phrase, object of the infinitive *to learn*
> *brilliantly* – adverb modifying infinitive *to perform*
> *until dawn* – adverbial prepositional phrase modifying *rehearsed*

It was daunting to think of the consequences that might ensue.

> *to think of the consequences that might ensue* – infinitive phrase, delayed subject of sentence
>
> *of the consequences* – adverbial prepositional phrase modifying infinitive *to think*
>
> *that might ensue* – relative clause modifying *consequences*
>
> *daunting* – participle, predicate adjective modifying subject

The students developed the argument, an intriguing one for them, that postmodern architecture might someday become a distant memory.

> *an intriguing one for them* – appositive phrase further defining *argument*
>
> *intriguing* – participle modifying *one*
>
> *for them* – adverbial prepositional phrase modifying *intriguing*
>
> *someday* – adverb modifying *might become*
>
> *that postmodern architecture might someday become a distant memory* – relative clause modifying *argument*

With several generous donations, we purchased what the homeless shelter had needed since October: warm blankets to distribute in cold weather.

> *With several generous donations* – adverbial prepositional phrase modifying *purchased*
>
> *several generous* – adjective series modifying *donations*
>
> *what the homeless shelter had needed since October* – noun clause, direct object of *purchased*
>
> *since October* – adverbial prepositional phrase modifying *had needed*
>
> *warm blankets to distribute in cold weather* – appositive phrase modifying the noun clause *what the homeless shelter had needed since October*
>
> *to distribute* – adjectival infinitive modifying *blankets*
>
> *in cold weather* – adverbial prepositional phrase modifying *distribute*

Because she wanted to become better educated, she enrolled in an online course.

> *Because she wanted to become better educated* – adverbial clause modifying the independent clause *she enrolled in an online course* (or just the verb *enrolled*)
>
> *to become better educated* – infinitive phrase, direct object of *wanted*
>
> *better* – adverb modifying *educated*, the predicate adjective after *become*
>
> *in an online course* – adverbial prepositional phrase modifying *enrolled*
>
> *online* – adjective modifying *course*

He was a child who, being quite introverted in large groups of adults, chose a quiet corner where he could read a book.

who chose a quiet corner where he could read a book – relative clause modifying the predicate noun *child*

where he could read a book – relative clause modifying *corner*

being quite introverted in large groups of adults – participial phrase modifying the relative pronoun *who*

introverted – past participle, predicate adjective after *being*

quite – adverb modifying *introverted*

in large groups of adults – adverbial prepositional phrase modifying *introverted*

of adults – adjectival prepositional phrase modifying *groups*

The book being one of the kind that puts you to sleep, she laid it aside and dozed off.

The book being one of the kind that puts you to sleep – absolute phrase

of the kind that puts you to sleep – adjectival prepositional phrase modifying *one*

that puts you to sleep – relative clause modifying *kind*

to sleep – adverbial prepositional phrase modifying *puts*

I am the only member who knows what must be done when parliament reconvenes.

who knows what must be done when parliament reconvenes – relative clause modifying *member*

what must be done when parliament reconvenes – noun clause, direct object of *knows*

when parliament reconvenes – adverbial clause modifying verb *must be done*

These examples suggest the richness of structure that is possible, the kind you undoubtedly create at times without even thinking about it. But think about it. Try concocting sentences with these sorts of syntactical complexities. Working with sentences in this way can help you to develop greater variety in your writing.

26d Using Modifiers: A Sample Scenario

Suppose you were asked to write a short paper on your reading habits. In getting your ideas together and taking notes, you might draft a bare-bones sentence such as this:

Recently, I've been reading fiction.

It's a start. But you soon realize that it isn't exactly true to your thoughts. It needs qualification. So you begin modifying its elements:

Recently, I've been reading <u>historical</u> fiction.

The adjective specifies the kind of fiction you've been reading—you're focused on novels and short stories written about the past. Then you add an adjectival prepositional phrase to further limit the word *fiction*:

> Recently, I've been reading historical fiction <u>about the First World War</u>.

Then you realize that while the fiction you've been reading has been primarily historical and about World War I, you haven't read it all; therefore you insert another adjective to further qualify the noun *fiction*:

> Recently, I've been reading <u>Canadian</u> historical fiction about the First World War.

Then you realize that *Canadian historical fiction* implies that you are familiar with all such fiction. But you quickly see a way to revise the sentence to convey your thoughts accurately; you put the adjective *much* in front of the verb:

> Recently, I've been reading <u>much</u> Canadian historical fiction about the First World War.

So far, so good. But you're not entirely satisfied with the sentence; you suspect that a reader might want a little more information about your reference to Canadian fiction about the First World War. You could go on to explain in another sentence or two, but you'd like to get a little more substance into this sentence. Then you have this thought: you can help clarify your point and at the same time inject some rhythm by adding a participial phrase modifying *fiction*:

> Recently, I've been reading much Canadian historical fiction <u>representing our longstanding ambivalence</u> about the First World War.

You rather like it. But working on this sentence has got you thinking. Before you leave it you consider your reasons for reading such fiction. You decide that you're doing this reading because this fiction focuses on a major event of the twentieth century, and because it tells stories of a time when Canada is said to have earned its national independence but when it also experienced deep political divisions over conscription. You feel the words beginning to come, and you consider your options: you can put the explanation in a separate sentence; you can join it to your present sentence with a semicolon or a colon or a coordinating conjunction like *for*, creating a compound sentence; or you can integrate it more closely by making it a subordinate clause, turning the whole into a complex sentence. You decide on the third method and put the new material in a *because* clause modifying the verb *have been reading*. And while you're thinking about it, you begin to feel that, given the way your sentence has developed, the word *reading* now sounds rather bland, weak because it doesn't quite reveal your seriousness. So you decide to change it to the more precise verb *studying*. Now your sentence is finished, at least for the time being:

> Recently, I've been studying much Canadian historical fiction about the First World War, because this fiction focuses on a major event of the twentieth century and because it tells stories of a time when Canada is said to have earned its national independence but also to have experienced deep political divisions over conscription.

26c

By adding modifiers, a writer can enlarge the reader's knowledge of the material being presented and impart precision and clarity to a sentence, as well as improve its style. Minimal or bare-bones sentences can themselves be effective and emphatic; use them when they are appropriate. But many of your sentences will be longer. And it is in elaborating and enriching your sentences with modifiers that you as author and stylist can exercise much of your control: you take charge of what your readers will learn and how they will learn it.

Exercise 26 Using Modifiers

Choose five of the following ten bare-bones sentences and flesh them out with various kinds of modifiers. Compose several expanded sentences for each. Use some single-word modifiers, but try to work mainly with phrases and clauses, including some noun clauses. Identify each modifier. Keep the sentences simple or complex, not compound or compound-complex (see #12c).

Air travel can be an ordeal.
Recycling requires planning
   and cooperation.
Canadians puzzle Americans.
Hollywood movies follow trends.
The restaurant was reviewed by
   the journalist.

Stop.
We are investigating.
Time is passing.
Think sustainably.
Punctuation matters.

27-29 Length, Variety, and Emphasis

27 Sentence Length

How long should a sentence be to achieve its purpose? That depends. A sentence may, in rare cases, consist of one word, or it may go on for a hundred words or more. There are no strict guidelines to tell you how long to make your sentences. If you're curious, do some research to determine the average sentence length in several pieces of writing you have handy—for example, this and other textbooks, a recent novel, a collection of essays, newspaper and magazine articles, emails, websites you visit regularly, a piece of your own recent academic writing. You'll probably find that the average is somewhere between 15 and 25 words per sentence, that longer sentences are more common in formal and specialized writing, and that shorter sentences are more at home in informal and popular writing, in email, and in narrative and dialogue. There are, then, some general guidelines, and you'll probably fit your own writing to them. But if you're far off what seems to be the average for the kind of writing you are doing, you may need to make some changes to adapt to the writing situation.

27a Short Sentences

If you receive feedback that you're writing an excessive number of short sentences, try

- building them up by elaborating their elements with modifiers, including various kinds of phrases and clauses (see #26d);
- combining some of them to form compound subjects, predicates, and objects or complements;
- combining two or more of them—especially if they are simple sentences—into complex or compound-complex sentences. (Creating compound sentences will also work, but it isn't always the best solution. Because compound sentences are made up of simple sentences joined by punctuation and coordinating conjunctions, they often read like a series of shorter, simple sentences.)

27b Long Sentences

If you find yourself writing too many long sentences, check them for three possible problems:

1. You may be rambling or trying to pack too much into a single sentence, possibly destroying its unity (see #41) and certainly making it difficult to read. Try breaking it up into more unified or more easily manageable parts.

2. You may be using too many words to make your point. Try cutting out any deadwood (see #71).

3. You may have slipped into what is called "excessive subordination"— too many loosely related details obscuring the main idea, or confusing strings of subordinate clauses modifying each other. Try removing some of the clutter, and try reducing clauses to phrases and phrases to single words (see exercises 21 [3], 21 [4], and 22a–c [2]).

 # Sentence Variety

To create emphasis (see #29) and avoid monotony, vary the lengths and kinds of your sentences. This is a process you should engage in when revising your draft to strengthen its style. Examine some pieces of prose that you particularly enjoy or that you find unusually clear and especially readable: you will likely discover that they contain both a pleasing mixture of short, medium, and long sentences and a similar variety of kinds and structures.

28c

28a Variety of Lengths
A string of short sentences will sound choppy and fragmented; avoid the staccato effect by interweaving some longer ones. On the other hand, a succession of long sentences may make your ideas hard to follow; give your readers a break—and your prose some sparkle—by using a few short, emphatic sentences to change your pace occasionally. Even a string of medium-length sentences can bore readers into inattention. Impart some rhythm, some shape, to your paragraphs by varying sentence length. Especially consider using a short, emphatic sentence to open or close a paragraph, and occasionally an unusually long sentence to end a paragraph.

28b Variety of Kinds
A string of simple and compound sentences risks coming across to a reader as simplistic. In some narratives and in certain technical and business documents, successive simple and compound sentences may be appropriate for recounting a sequence of events, but when you're writing prose in other modes and especially in academic writing, let some of the complexity of your ideas be reflected in complex and compound-complex sentences. Keep in mind, however, that a string of complex and compound-complex sentences may become oppressive. Give your readers a breather now and then by employing a simple or short compound sentence.

28c Variety of Structures
Try to avoid an unduly long string of sentences that use the same syntactical structure. For example, though the standard order of elements in declarative sentences is subject–verb–object or –complement, consider

varying that order occasionally for the purpose of emphasis (see #11s and #29). Perhaps use an occasional interrogative sentence (see #11t), whether a rhetorical question (a question that doesn't expect an answer) or a question that you proceed to answer as you develop a paragraph. An occasional expletive pattern or passive voice can be refreshing—if you can justify it on other grounds as well (see #11e, #11k, #17p, and #29f).

In particular, try not to begin a string of sentences with the same kind of word or phrase or clause—unless you are purposely setting up a controlled succession of parallel structures for emphasis or coherence (see #7b.1). Imagine the effect of several sentences beginning with such words as *Similarly*, *Especially*, *Consequently*, or *Nevertheless*. Whatever else the sentences contained, the sameness would be distracting. Or imagine a series of sentences all starting with a subject-noun, or with a present-participial phrase. To avoid such undesirable sameness, take advantage of the way modifiers of various kinds can be moved around in sentences (see #11q, #11r, #19d, #20d, and #29e).

29 Emphasis in Sentences

emph To communicate effectively, make sure your readers perceive the relative importance of your ideas the same way you do. Learn to control emphasis so that what you want emphasized is what gets emphasized.

You can emphasize whole sentences in several ways:

- Set a sentence off by itself, as a short paragraph. (Use this strategy judiciously.)
- Put an important sentence at the beginning of a paragraph or, even better, at the end.
- Put an important point in a short sentence among several long ones, or in a long sentence among several short ones.
- Shift the style or structure of a sentence to make it stand out from those around it (see #8).

In similar ways, you can emphasize important parts of individual sentences. The principal devices for achieving emphasis *within* sentences are position and word order, repetition, stylistic contrast, syntax, and punctuation.

29a Endings and Beginnings
The most emphatic position in a sentence is its ending; the second most emphatic position is its beginning. Consider these two sentences:

Kerr's new play features seven young actors.

Seven young actors appear in Kerr's new play.

Each sentence emphasizes both *Kerr's new play* and the *seven young actors*, but the first emphasizes the *seven young actors* a little more, whereas the second emphasizes *Kerr's new play* a little more. Further, the longer the sentence, the stronger the effect of emphasis by position. Consider the following:

a. The best teacher I've ever had was my high-school chemistry teacher, a brilliant woman in her early fifties.

b. A brilliant woman in her early fifties, my high-school chemistry teacher was the best teacher I've ever had.

c. My high-school chemistry teacher, a brilliant woman in her early fifties, was the best teacher I've ever had.

d. The best teacher I've ever had was a brilliant woman in her early fifties who taught me chemistry in high school.

29b

Each sentence contains the same three ideas, but each distributes the emphasis differently. In each the last part is the most emphatic, the first part next, and the middle part least. Think of them as topic sentences (see #7a.1): sentence *a* could introduce a paragraph focusing on the quality of the teacher but emphasizing her intelligence, her age, and her gender; sentence *b* could introduce a paragraph focusing more on the quality of her teaching; sentence *c* could open a paragraph stressing the quality of the teaching and the nature and level of the subject; details of age, gender, and intelligence would be incidental; sentence *d* may seem the flattest, the least emphatic and least likely of the four, but it could effectively introduce a mainly narrative paragraph focusing on the writer's good experience in the class.

Note that in all four versions the part referring to "the best teacher I've ever had" comes either first or last, since the superlative *best* would sound unnatural in the unemphatic middle position—unless the writer acknowledged its inherent emphasis in some other way, for example by setting off the appositive with a pair of dashes (see #50b):

My high-school chemistry teacher—the best teacher I've ever had—was a brilliant woman in her early fifties.

29b Loose Sentences and Periodic Sentences

A *loose, cumulative,* or *"right-branching"* sentence makes its main point in an early independent clause and then adds modifying subordinate elements:

The concert began modestly, minus special effects and fanfare, with the performers sitting casually onstage and taking up their instruments to play their first song.

Such sentences are common, for they are "loose" and comfortable, easygoing, natural. In contrast to the loose sentence is the *periodic* (or "*left-branching*") sentence, which wholly or partly delays its main point, the independent clause, until the end:

> With the performers sitting casually onstage and taking up their instruments to play their first song, the concert began modestly, minus special effects and fanfare.

Full periodic sentences are usually the result of careful thought and planning. However, they can sometimes sound contrived, less natural, and therefore should not be used without forethought. They can also be dramatic and emphatic, creating suspense as the reader waits for the meaning to fall into place. When you try for such suspense, don't separate subject and predicate too widely, as a writer did in this sentence:

> *ineffective*: The abrupt change from one moment when the air is alive with laughing and shouting, to the next when the atmosphere resembles that of a morgue, is dramatic.

Many sentences delay completion of the main clause only until somewhere in the middle rather than all the way to the end. To the degree that they do delay it, they are partly periodic.

29c The Importance of the Final Position

Because the end of a sentence is naturally so emphatic, readers expect something important there; it is best not to disappoint them by letting something incidental or merely qualifying fall at the end, for then the sentence itself will fall: its energy and momentum will be lost, its essential meaning distorted. For example:

> *emph*: That was the best essay I've written, I think.

The uncertain *I think* should go at the beginning or, even less emphatically, after *That* or *was*.

> *emph*: Cramming for exams can be counterproductive, sometimes.

The qualifying *sometimes* could go at the beginning, but it would be best after *can*, letting the emphasis fall where it belongs, on *cramming* and *counterproductive*.

29d Changing Word Order

Earlier sections point out certain standard patterns: for example, subject–verb–object or –complement (#11c–j); single-word adjectives preceding nouns—or, if predicate adjectives, following them (#19d); and so on. But variations are possible, and because these patterns are recognized as standard, any departures from them stand out (see #11s and #19d for examples). Be careful, for if the inverted order calls attention to itself at the expense of meaning, the attempt may backfire. In the following sentence, for example, the writer strained a little too hard for emphasis. Can you achieve it in some less risky way?

> *wo*: It is from imagination that have come all the world's
> great literature, music, architecture, and works of art.

29e Movable Modifiers

Many modifiers other than single-word adjectives are movable, enabling you to shift them or other words to where you want them. Appositives, for instance, can sometimes be transposed (see #11q). And you can move participial phrases, if you do so carefully (see #19d). Absolute phrases (see #11r), since they function as sentence modifiers, can usually come at the beginning or the end—or, if syntax permits, in the middle.

But adverbial modifiers are the most movable of all (see #20d). As you compose, and especially as you revise your drafts, consider the various possible placements of any adverbial modifiers you've used. Take advantage of their flexibility to exercise maximum control over the rhythms of your sentences and, most important, to get the emphases that will best serve your purposes. Some examples:

> Two patrol cars crept <u>slowly and quietly</u> into the parking lot.

Would the adverbs be more emphatic at the end? Try it:

> Two patrol cars crept into the parking lot <u>slowly and quietly</u>.

A little better, perhaps. Now try them at the beginning, and instead of *and*, use punctuation to emphasize the slowness:

> <u>Slowly, quietly,</u> two patrol cars crept into the parking lot.

Another example, from a rough draft:

> *draft*: When I entered university I naturally expected it to
> be different from high school, but I wasn't prepared
> for the impact it would have on the way I lived my
> day-to-day life.

Clear enough. But the writer decided to try separating the independent clauses and using a conjunctive adverb to get a little more of the emphasis he felt he needed:

> *revised*: When I entered university I naturally expected it to be different from high school. However, I wasn't prepared for the impact it would have on the way I lived my day-to-day life.

But that sounded too stiff (as *However* oftentimes does at the beginning of a sentence). After some further tinkering with the adverbs, he came up with this:

> *revised*: When I entered university I expected it to be different from high school—naturally. I was not, however, prepared for the impact it would have on the way I lived my day-to-day life.

Setting *naturally* off with a dash at the end of the first sentence added a touch of self-mockery. And moving *however* a few words into the second sentence not only got rid of the stiffness but also, because of the pause produced by its commas, added a useful emphasis to *not*, now spelled out in full.

29f Using the Expletive and the Passive Voice for Emphasis

Two of the basic sentence patterns, the *expletive* (#11k) and the *passive voice* (#11e, #17p), can be weak and unemphatic in some contexts. Used strategically, however, they can enable you to achieve a desired emphasis. For example:

> Passive voice can be used to move a certain word or phrase to an emphatic place in a sentence.

Here, putting the verb in the passive voice (*can be used*) makes *Passive voice* the subject of the sentence and enables this important element to come at the beginning; otherwise, the sentence would have to begin less strongly (e.g., with *You can use passive voice*). And consider this next example, which makes strategic use of the expletive pattern:

> There are advantages to using the expletive pattern for a deliberate change of pace in your writing.

In this case, opening the sentence with *There* is preferable to opening with these long and unwieldy alternatives:

> *ineffective*: Advantages to using the expletive pattern for a deliberate change of pace in your writing are significant.

or

> *ineffective*: Using the expletive pattern for a deliberate change
> of pace in your writing can be advantageous.

Use expletives and passive voice when you need to delete or delay mention
of the agent or otherwise shift the subject of a sentence. But use these patterns only when you have good reason to do so.

29g Emphasis by Repetition

You may wish to repeat an important word or idea in order to emphasize
it, to make it stay in your readers' minds. Unintentional repetition can be
wordy and tedious (see #71b); but intentional, controlled repetition—
used sparingly—can be very effective, especially in sentences with balanced or parallel structures:

> We particularly enjoy his lyrics—his witty, poignant, brilliant
> lyrics.

> If you have the courage to face adventure, the adventure can
> sometimes give you courage.

> If it's a challenge they seek, it's a challenge they'll find.

> Many Vancouver shops are filled with souvenirs: souvenir
> key chains, souvenir T-shirts, souvenir postcards, souvenir
> coffee mugs.

29h Emphasis by Stylistic Contrast

A stylistically enhanced sentence—for example, a periodic sentence
(#29b), a sentence with parallel or balanced structure (#40, #29g), or a
richly metaphorical or allusive sentence (#65)—stands out beside plainer
sentences. For that reason, such a sentence may be most effective at the end
of a paragraph (see #7a.3). In the same way, a word or phrase that differs
in style or tone from those that surround it may stand out (and note that
such terms often gravitate toward that position of natural emphasis, the
end of the sentence):

> When the judge chastised the defence attorney for her
> sarcasm, her client went ballistic.

> The chef—conservative as her behaviour sometimes appears—
> dazzles the kitchen staff with her gutsy culinary experiments.

> My grandmother may be almost ninety years old, but she
> approaches each day with a child's *joie de vivre*.

Terms from other languages naturally stand out, but don't make the mistake of using them pretentiously, for some readers are unimpressed by them or even resent them; use one only after due thought, and preferably when there is no satisfactory English equivalent. And be careful not to overshoot: too strong a contrast may jar; the first example above works only because the emphasis deriving from the shift to colloquialism is deliberate.

29i Emphasis by Syntax

Put your most important claims in independent clauses; put lesser claims in subordinate clauses and in phrases. Sometimes you have more than one option, depending on what you want to emphasize:

Avoiding his eyes, she spoke hesitantly.

Speaking hesitantly, she avoided his eyes.

But more often the choice is determined by the content. Consider the way subordination affects emphasis in the following pairs of sentences:

original: I strolled into the laboratory, when my attention was attracted by the pitter-pattering of a little white rat in a cage at the back.

revised: When I strolled into the laboratory, my attention was attracted by the pitter-pattering of a little white rat in a cage at the back.

original: Choosing my courses carefully, I tried to plan my academic schedule around my co-op work placement.

revised: Because I was trying to plan my academic schedule around my co-op work placement, I chose my courses carefully.

original: I had almost finished downloading the file when the power failed and I lost my connection to the network.

revised: When I had almost finished downloading the file, the power failed and I lost my connection to the network.

See also #41 and #23c.

29j Emphasis by Punctuation

An exclamation point (!) denotes emphasis. But using exclamation points is not the only way, and usually not the best way (especially in academic writing), to achieve emphasis with punctuation. Try to make your sentences appropriately emphatic without resorting to this sometimes artificial device. Arrange your words so that commas and other marks fall where you want a pause for emphasis (see #29e). Use dashes, colons, and even parentheses judiciously to set off important ideas. Occasionally use a semicolon instead of a comma in order to get a more emphatic pause (but only in a series or between independent clauses). (See chapter V for detailed information on punctuation.)

PROOFREADING TIP

Avoiding Artificial Emphasis

As much as possible, avoid emphasizing your own words and sentences with such mechanical devices as underlining, italics, quotation marks, and capitalization. See #58r and #60d.

29j

Exercise 27–29 Sentence Length, Variety, and Emphasis

Below are four paragraphs from draft versions of student essays. For practice, revise each one to improve the effectiveness of sentence length, variety, and emphasis. Try not to change the basic sense in any important way, but make whatever changes will make the paragraphs effective.

1. My father drove up to the campsite and chose an empty spot close to the lake, up against the thickly covered mountainside. We had just unpacked our equipment and set up our tent when an elderly man walked up our path. He introduced himself and told us that he was camped farther up the mountain, about a hundred yards away. He told us that only an hour before, as he walked toward his campsite, he saw a huge black bear running away from it. He said he then drew closer and saw that his tent was knocked down and his food scattered all over the ground. He suggested that we might want to move our camp to a safer place, not so close to this bear's haunts.

2. The sky promised hot and sunny weather as we quickly finished closing side-pockets and adjusting straps on our packs in preparation for our hike up Black Tusk, which is in Garibaldi Provincial Park, a hike which was to be on a trail I had never seen before and which I therefore had been looking forward to with great enthusiasm. And that's what I felt as we set off in the early morning light on the first leg of the journey which would take us to the top in a few hours.

3. The way time passes can be odd. The mind's sense of time can be changed. I remember an experience that will illustrate this. It

happened when I was nine. I rode my bike in front of a car and got hit. I don't remember much about this experience. However, a few details do come to mind. These include the way the car's brakes sounded suddenly from my right. I never even saw the car that hit me. And I remember flying through the air. It was a peculiar feeling. The ground seemed to come up slowly as I floated along. Time seemed almost to have stopped. But then I hit the ground. And then time sped up. A neighbour ran up and asked if I was all right. My parents pulled our car up. They carefully put me in it. And all of a sudden I was at the hospital, it seemed. It all must have taken twenty or thirty minutes. To me it seemed that only a minute or two had passed since I had hit the ground.

4. It's not so difficult to repot a houseplant, although many plant-owners procrastinate about doing this because they think it's too messy and time-consuming, when actually repotting takes very little time and effort if you follow a simple set of instructions such as I'm about to give you. And you'll find that when you've done the repotting both you and your plant will benefit from the process because the plant will then be able to receive fresh minerals and oxygen from the new soil which will make it grow into a healthier plant that will give you increased pleasure and enjoyment.

30 Analyzing Sentences

Grammatical analysis is not an end in itself (though some people enjoy it as a kind of game). Its purpose is to give you insight into the accepted structures of the basic unit of communication, the sentence, so that you can construct clear sentences and discover and eliminate weaknesses in your writing.

Practise analyzing your own and others' sentences. The better you understand how sentences work, the better able you will be to write effective and correct sentences. You should be able to account for each word in a sentence: no essential element should be missing, nothing should be left over, and the grammatical relations among all the parts should be clear. If these conditions aren't met, the sentence in question is likely to be misleading or ambiguous. If words, phrases, and clauses fit the roles they are being asked to play, the sentence should work.

The first step in analyzing a sentence is to identify the main parts of its basic structure: the *subject*, the *finite verb*, and the *object* or *complement*, if any. (If the sentence is other than a simple sentence, there will be more than one set of these essential parts.) Then determine the modifiers of these elements, and then the modifiers of modifiers.

30a The Chart Method

Here is a convenient arrangement for analyzing the structure of relatively uncomplicated sentences:

The veteran journalist harshly criticized the young politician.

Subject	Finite Verb	Object or Complement	Adjectival Modifier	Adverbial Modifier
journalist	criticized	politician (direct object of verb *criticized*)	The (modifies *journalist*) veteran (modifies *journalist*) the (modifies *politician*) young (modifies *politician*)	harshly (modifies *criticized*)

This most beautiful summer is now almost gone.

Subject	Finite Verb	Object or Complement	Adjectival Modifier	Adverbial Modifier
summer	is (linking verb)	gone (predicate adj.)	This (demonstrative adj. modifying *summer*) beautiful (modifies *summer*)	most (modifies *beautiful*) now (modifies *is*) almost (modifies *gone*)

The very befuddled Kyle realized that learning Sanskrit was not easy.

Subject	Finite Verb	Object or Complement	Adjectival Modifier	Adverbial Modifier	Other
Kyle	realized	that . . . easy (noun clause as direct object)	The, befuddled (modify *Kyle*)	very (modifies *befuddled*)	
learning (gerund)	was (linking verb)	easy (predicate adj.) Sanskrit (obj. of *learning*)		not (modifies *easy*)	that (sub. conj.)

In the last example, the items below the dotted line belong to the subordinate clause of this complex sentence.

30b The Vertical Method

For more complicated sentences, you may find a different method more convenient, for example one in which the sentence is written out vertically:

When the canoe trip ended, Philip finally realized that the end of his happy summer was almost upon him.

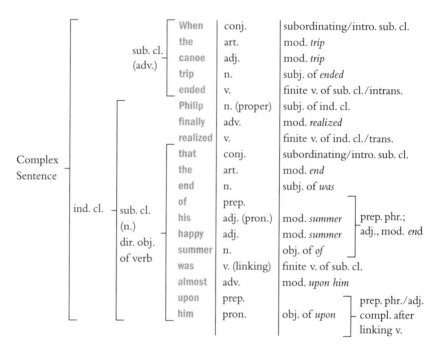

As you can see, this method challenges you to account for the grammatical function of every word in the sentence.

30c The Diagramming Method

The diagramming method involves deconstructing a sentence and transforming it into a pictorial representation. The resulting diagram visually demonstrates the relationships between and among sentence elements. Here are sample diagrams of a few simple sentences:

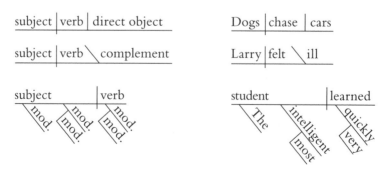

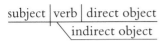

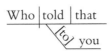

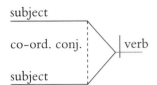

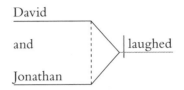

Compound, complex, and compound-complex sentences are diagrammed following similar patterns. If you are interested in learning more about how to diagram sentences, visit the companion website for this book (www.oupcanada.com/Messenger6e).

30c

Exercise 30 Analyzing Sentences

A. Try analyzing the following sentences by using first the chart method and then the vertical method. (If you want an extra challenge, also try a using the diagramming method. See the companion website for additional examples that will help you with this task.) After you've finished, identify the advantages and disadvantages of the different methods. Which method do you prefer?

1. Children danced to the music of the piper.

2. A chinook is a warm wind blowing eastward off the Rocky Mountains.

3. Many potentially good films are spoiled by sensationalism.

4. Both the beaver and the maple leaf are Canadian emblems.

5. Although she was discouraged, Suki persevered, and after a few more tries she succeeded in clearing the two-metre bar.

B. Use the vertical method to analyze this longer, more complicated sentence. You may want to challenge a classmate: see which of you can write down the greatest number of grammatical facts about the sentence.

> Constructed of stone and cedar, the large house that the Smiths built on the brow of Murphy's Bluff—an exposed promontory—was so sturdy that even the icy blasts of the continual north wind in December and January made no impression on it.

Common Sentence Problems

In the remaining sections of this chapter we define some common problems that can affect the clarity of sentences and suggest ways to avoid or correct them.

The three sentence errors that can most impede clear communication in your writing are the *fragment*, the *comma splice*, and the *run-on sentence*. Some readers consider these three errors to be serious signs of flawed writing. Edit closely for them.

 ## Sentence Coherence

coh   Although the word *coherence* usually refers to the connection between sentences and between paragraphs (see #1b, #7), the parts of a sentence must also cohere. Each sentence fault discussed in the next sections (#32–42) is capable of making a sentence incoherent. If a sentence lacks coherence, the fault probably lies in one or more of the following: faulty arrangement (*faulty word order, misplaced modifier*), unclear or missing or illogical connections and relations between parts (*faulty reference, lack of agreement, dangling modifier, faulty coordination, faulty logic, faulty alignment*), syntactic shift from one part to another (*mixed construction, shift in perspective, faulty parallelism*); or the weakness may be due to something that can only be labelled *unclear* (see *cl* in appendix 2). Consult the following sections as necessary to ensure that your sentences are coherent within themselves.

 ## Fragments

frag   A **fragment** is a group of words that is not an acceptable sentence, either major or minor, but that is punctuated as if it were a sentence (that is, started with a capital letter and ended with a period). The fragment is discussed along with the minor sentence, which it sometimes resembles, in #12a and #12b. See also *frag* in appendix 2.

 ## Comma Splices

cs   A **comma splice** occurs when two independent clauses are joined with only a comma, rather than with a semicolon. Although the error usually stems from a misunderstanding of sentence structure, it is discussed under *punctuation*, since it requires attention to punctuation marks: see #44e–g. See also *cs* in appendix 2.

34 Run-on (Fused) Sentences

n-
n,
fs

A **run-on sentence**, sometimes called a **fused sentence**, is in fact not a single sentence but two sentences run together with neither a period to mark the end of the first nor a capital letter to mark the beginning of the second. An error most likely to occur when a writer is rushed, it can sometimes, like the comma splice, result from a problem in understanding how sentences work. And since a run-on sentence occurs with the same kind of sentence structure as does the comma splice, and like it requires attention to punctuation, we discuss it alongside the other error: see #44i. See also *run-on* in appendix 2.

35 Misplaced Modifiers

35a

m ## 35a Movability and Poor Placement

As we point out in the introduction to chapter II, part of the meaning in English sentences is conveyed by the position of words in relation to each other. And though there are certain standard or conventional arrangements, a good deal of flexibility is possible (see #11s, #11t, #19d, #22b, and #26). Adverbial modifiers are especially movable (see #20d and #29e). Because of this flexibility, writers sometimes put a modifier where it conveys an unintended or ambiguous meaning, or where it is linked by juxtaposition to a word it can't logically modify. To say precisely what you mean, you have to be careful in placing your modifiers—especially adverbs. Note the changes in meaning that result from the different placement of the word *only* in the following sentences:

> Only her son works in Halifax. (No other member of her family works there.)
>
> Her only son works in Halifax. (She has no other sons.)
>
> Her son only works in Halifax. (He doesn't live in Halifax, but commutes.)
>
> Her son works only in Halifax. (He works in no other place.)

The following sentence demonstrates how misplacement can produce absurdity:

> **mm:** While testifying before the Transport Committee, the minister denied allegations heatedly concerning inadequate passenger screening reported recently in a CBC documentary at Pearson Airport.

The adverb *heatedly* belongs before *denied*, the verb it modifies. The adjectival phrase *reported in a recent CBC documentary* belongs after *allegations*, the noun it modifies. And the adverbial phrase *at Pearson airport* belongs after the phrase *concerning inadequate passenger screening*.

Usually it is best to keep modifiers and the words they modify as close together as possible. Here is an example of an adjective out of place:

> ***mm:***   Love is a <u>difficult</u> emotion to express in words.

> ***clear:***   Love is an emotion (that is) difficult to express in words.

and an example of a misplaced relative clause:

> ***mm:***   Every year the Royal St. John's Regatta is held on Quidi Vidi Lake, <u>which has been called "the world's largest garden party."</u>

Is it the lake that has been called "the world's largest garden party"? The writer likely meant something else:

> ***clear:***   Every year the Royal St. John's Regatta, which has been called "the world's largest garden party," is held on Quidi Vidi Lake.

✔️ **PROOFREADING TIP**

On the Placement of *only*, *almost*, and Similar Adverbs

Pay particular attention to such adverbs as *only*, *almost*, *just*, *merely*, and *even*. In speech, we often place these words casually, but in writing we should put them where they clearly mean what we want them to:

> ***mm:***   Hardy <u>only</u> wrote novels as a sideline; his main interest was poetry.

> ***clear:***   Hardy wrote novels <u>only</u> as a sideline; his main interest was poetry.

> ***mm:***   His mother built that shed by hand, and it <u>almost</u> stood for thirty years.

> ***clear:***   His mother built that shed by hand, and it stood for <u>almost</u> thirty years.

35b Squinting Modifiers

int A **squinting modifier** is a word or phrase put between two elements either of which it could modify. That is, the modifier "squints" so that a reader can't tell which way it is looking; the result is ambiguity:

> *squint*:   It was so warm <u>for a week</u> we did hardly any skiing at all.

Which clause does the adverbial phrase modify? It is ambiguous, even though the meaning would be about the same either way. A speaking voice could impart clarifying emphasis to such a sentence, but a writer must substitute words or structures for the missing vocal emphasis. Here, adding a simple *that* removes the ambiguity:

> *clear*:   It was so warm that for a week we did hardly any skiing at all.

> *clear*:   It was so warm for a week that we did hardly any skiing at all.

Another example:

> *squint*:   My sister advised me <u>now and then</u> to travel in the Rockies.

This time, rearrangement is necessary:

> *clear*:   My sister now and then advised me to travel in the Rockies.

> *clear*:   My sister advised me to travel now and then in the Rockies.

Even a modifier at the end of a sentence can, in effect, squint. When rearrangement doesn't work, further revision may be necessary:

> *ambig*:   He was overjoyed when she agreed for more reasons than one.

> *clear*:   He was overjoyed for more reasons than one when she agreed.

> *clear*:   He had more than one reason to be overjoyed when she agreed.

> *clear*:   He was overjoyed because she had more than one reason for agreeing.

PROOFREADING TIP

On Split Infinitives

An awkwardly split infinitive—*to* + an adverb + a verb—is also caused by a kind of misplaced modifier; see #21c.

Exercise 35 Correcting Misplaced Modifiers

Revise the following sentences to eliminate awkwardness resulting from misplaced modifiers.

1. Rory claimed he wanted to just belong.
2. It merely seemed a few days before he returned from his journey to Nepal.
3. She decided that on this day she would skip dinner entirely in the morning.
4. I could see my grandmother coming through the window.
5. They discussed booking a trip around the world for two days but decided against it.
6. A piano stood in the centre of the stage with its outline only visible to the audience in the darkness.
7. I pledged to always listen to my children when I became a parent.
8. Our submissions were accepted if they were postmarked only by midnight.
9. The newspaper only published three letters to the editor yesterday.
10. I only was a child, but I could even understand the most complex equations.

 Dangling Modifiers

dm Like a pronoun without an antecedent (#16d), a **dangling modifier** has no word in the rest of the sentence to attach to; instead it is left dangling, grammatically unattached, and so it often tries to attach itself, illogically, to some other word. Most dangling modifiers are *verbal phrases*; be watchful for them in editing drafts of your work.

36a Dangling Participial Phrases (see #21d)

> ***dm***:   Strolling casually beside the lagoon, my eyes fell upon
> two children chasing a pair of geese.

Since the adjectival phrase wants to modify a noun, it tries to link with the
subject of the adjacent clause, *eyes*. One's eyes may be said, figuratively, to
"fall" on something, but they can scarcely be said to "stroll." To avoid the
unintentionally humorous dangler, simply change the participial phrase to
a subordinate clause:

> ***revised***:   As I strolled casually beside the lagoon, my eyes fell
> upon two children chasing a pair of geese.

Or, if you want to keep the effect of the opening participial phrase, rework
the clause so that its subject is the logical word to be modified:

> ***revised***:   Strolling casually beside the lagoon, I let my gaze fall
> upon two children chasing a pair of geese.

Here is another example, one with no built-in absurdity:

> ***dm***:   Living in a small town, there was a strong sense of
> community among us.

To correct the dangling participle, you need to provide something for the
phrase to modify, or revise the sentence in some other way:

> ***revised***:   Living in a small town, we had a strong sense of
> community among us.

> ***revised***:   Since we lived in a small town, there was a strong
> sense of community among us.

In the next example, passive voice causes the trouble (see #17p):

> ***dm***:   Looking up to the open sky, not a cloud could be seen.

> ***revised***:   Looking up to the open sky, I could not see a cloud.

> ***revised***:   There wasn't a cloud to be seen in the open sky.

36b Dangling Gerund Phrases (see #21f)
When a gerund phrase is the object of a preposition, it can dangle much like a participial phrase:

> ***dm:*** After being informed of the correct procedure, our attention was directed to the next steps.

It isn't "our attention" that was "informed." The use of the passive voice contributes to the confusion here.

> ***revised:*** After being informed of the correct procedure, we were directed to attend to the next steps.

But this revision is still passive and somewhat awkward. Such a sentence can be better revised another way:

> ***revised:*** After informing us of the correct procedure, the instructor directed our attention to the next steps.

36c Dangling Infinitive Phrases (see #21a)

> ***dm:*** To follow this complex argument, the speaker's thoughts must be fully explored.

Ineffective passive voice is again the issue, depriving the infinitive phrase of a logical word to modify.

> ***revised:*** To follow this complex argument, one must explore the speaker's thoughts fully.

The next example is more complicated:

> ***dm:*** To make the instructor's lab demonstration successful, it requires the students' cooperation.

Here the infinitive phrase seems to be the antecedent of *it*. Dropping the *it* lets the phrase act as a noun; or the sentence can be revised in some other way:

> ***revised:*** To make the instructor's lab demonstration successful will require the students' cooperation.

> ***revised:*** If the instructor's lab demonstration is to succeed, the students will have to cooperate.

36d Dangling Elliptical Clauses

An **elliptical clause** is an adverbial clause that has been abridged so that its subject and verb are only understood, or implied rather than stated; the subject of the independent clause then automatically serves also as the implied subject of the elliptical clause. If the implied subject is different from the subject of the independent clause, the subordinate element will dangle, sometimes illogically.

> *dm*: Once in disguise, the hero's conflict emerges.

It isn't "the hero's *conflict*" that is in disguise, but the *hero*. Either supply a logical subject and verb for the elliptical clause, or retain the elliptical clause and make the other subject logically agree with it:

> *revised*: Once the hero is in disguise, his conflict emerges.

> *revised*: Once in disguise, the hero begins to reveal his conflicts.

Another example:

> *dm*: When well marinated, put the pieces of tofu on the grill.

Here the understood subject is *the pieces*, but the subject of the independent clause of this imperative sentence is an understood *you*. Give the elliptical clause a subject and verb:

> *revised*: When the pieces of tofu are well marinated, put them on the grill.

36e Dangling Prepositional Phrases and Appositives (see #22 and #11q)

A prepositional phrase can also dangle. In this example, an indefinite *it* (see #16e) is the issue:

> *dm*: Like a child in a toy shop, it is all she can bear not to touch everything.

> *revised*: Like a child in a toy shop, she can hardly bear not to touch everything.

And so can an appositive prove to be problematic:

> *dm*: A superb racing car, a Ferrari's engine is a masterpiece of engineering.

36e

The phrase seems to be in apposition with the noun *engine*, but it is illogical to equate an engine with an entire car (the possessive *Ferrari's* is adjectival). Revise it:

> ***revised***:   A superb racing car, <u>a Ferrari</u> has an engine that is a masterpiece of engineering.

Exercise 36 Correcting Dangling Modifiers

Revise the following to eliminate dangling modifiers.

1. Sitting quiet and fascinated, the busy hummingbird was gazed at by the baby in her playpen.
2. By using first-person narration, readers are led by the author to wonder about the reliability of the story.
3. In order to cook, one must be creative, thereby being adept at substituting one ingredient for another.
4. Looked at in this light, one has to find Hamlet very much like other people.
5. The lead researcher suggested testing small samples and then studying their composition when heated.
6. Being the youngest member of the community, it is harder for me to convince the elders of my experience.
7. When not going to school or working, my activities range from playing tennis to surfing the Internet.
8. By using this style it added more tension to the dialogue.
9. The colonel began to send groups of reinforcements to the weakened position only to be ambushed in the mountain passes.
10. Whispering in the darkened theatre, our popcorn spilled onto the floor.

  Mixed Constructions

mix   Avoiding mixed constructions can be a particular challenge for anyone whose first language has a different sentence structure than English has. To begin a sentence with one construction and then inadvertently shift to another can create confusion for one's readers:

> ***mix***:   Eagle Creek is a small BC community is located near Wells Gray Provincial Park.

The writer here sets up two clauses containing the verb *is* but then fails to include a subject for the second clause. Either drop the first *is* and add commas around the resulting appositive phrase ("a small BC community"), or add *that* or *which* before the second *is*.

> *mix:* Since my credit card payment was late, therefore I have to pay interest.

Here the writer begins with a subordinating *Since* but then uses *therefore* to introduce the second clause, which would be correct only if the first clause were independent. Fix this by dropping either the *Since* or the *therefore* (if you drop *Since*, change the comma to a semicolon to avoid a comma splice: see #44e).

Exercise 37 Correcting Mixed Constructions

Revise the following to eliminate mixed constructions.

1. The reason for the decrease in tourism was due to the fear of terrorism.
2. Soccer happens to be a sport is very popular in Brazil.
3. I found that the children's literature website to be very useful.
4. The new styles were popular with both men or women alike.
5. Since, for most of us, our earliest recollections are mere fragments of things that made up our childhoods, we therefore must rely on the objects or ideas around us to trigger the past.
6. Just because people like to watch reality television programs is not a sign of a decadent society.
7. Even though I hadn't read the novel, yet I could understand the main themes.
8. As I sped too quickly around the corner caused me to spin out of control.
9. I realized I had two options: (1) join my nemesis's volleyball team or (b) recruit enough people to form my own team.
10. By exercising regularly, eating well, and getting enough sleep will improve my health.

---

38 Faulty Alignment

Poor **alignment** results when two or more elements in a sentence are illogically or incongruously aligned with each other. Such errors often take the form of a verb saying something illogical about its subject—an error sometimes called *faulty predication*; that is, what is predicated about the subject is an impossibility. For example:

> ***al, pred***: Many new inventions and techniques occurred during
> this period.

An invention could, with some strain, be said to *occur,* but *techniques* do not *occur.* Revision is necessary; one possibility is to use an expletive and the passive voice:

> ***revised***: During this period there were many new inventions,
> and many new techniques were developed.

In the next example the verb repeats the meaning of the subject:

> ***al, pred***: The setting of the story takes place in Manitoba.
>
> ***revised***: The story takes place in Manitoba.
>
> ***better***: The story is set in Manitoba.

Errors in predication often occur with a form of *be* and a complement:

> ***al, pred***: The amount of gear to take along is the first step to
> consider when planning a long hike.

But an *amount* cannot be a *step*; revision is needed:

> ***revised***: The first step in planning a hike is to decide how
> much gear to take along.

Note that this revision also removes the other illogicality: one does not *consider* a *step*; rather the considering, or deciding, is itself the step. Another example:

> ***al, pred***: The value of good literature is priceless.

It is not the *value* that is priceless, but the *literature* itself. Here is a similar error, of a common kind:

> ***al, pred***: The cost of my used car was relatively inexpensive.
>
> ***revised***: The cost of my used car was relatively low.
>
> ***revised***: My used car was relatively inexpensive.

Other errors in alignment aren't errors in predication, but they are similar to them in using words illogically:

> ***al***: In her opening remarks, the speaker described the
> occurrences, environment, and hopes of her family.

38

It is logical to speak of a family having hopes and an environment, but not *occurrences*; substitute *experiences*.

> **al:** Its fine texture was as smooth and hard as a waterworn rock.

This sentence, which illogically equates *texture* and *rock*, is also a form of incomplete comparison. Insert *that of* after *hard as*. (See ***comp*** in appendix 2.)

> **al:** Professions such as a doctor, a lawyer, and an engineer require extensive post-secondary education.

This sentence is illogical because *being* a doctor, a lawyer, or an engineer is not a *profession*. Change *profession* to *professional*:

> **revised:** Professionals such as doctors, lawyers, and engineers require extensive post-secondary education.

Or recast the sentence completely:

> **revised:** Professions such as medicine, law, and engineering require extensive post-secondary education.

Exercise 38 Improving Alignment

Revise the following sentences to remove illogical or incongruous alignment.

1. I decided not to buy it, for the price was too expensive.
2. Even religious principles were being enlightened during this period.
3. It is clear that this general conception of his ability is greatly underestimated.
4. The only source of light in the house came through the windows.
5. Its shape is a rectangle about three times as long as it is wide.
6. The poem expresses the meaningless and useless achievements of war.
7. The character of the speaker in the poem seems euphoric and energetic.
8. The need for such great effort on the part of the reader represents serious weakness in the writing.
9. Life and death was a constant idea in the back of the pioneers' minds.
10. She started university at a very young age.

39 Shifts in Perspective: Inconsistent Point of View

shift,
pv

Be consistent in your point of view within a sentence and, except in special cases, from one sentence to the next. Avoid illogical shifts in the *tense*, *mood*, and *voice* of verbs, and in the *person* and *number* of pronouns.

39a Shifts in Tense (see #17g–h)

shift: She <u>read</u> the article on the website and then <u>comments</u> on it before logging off.

This sentence begins in the past tense but shifts to the present. However, all of the events described in this sentence occurred at a particular time in the past. So, change *comments* to the past tense to coincide with *read*.

39b Shifts in Mood (see #17-l–m)

shift: If it <u>were</u> Sunday and I <u>was</u> through with my work, I would go skiing with you.

This sentence begins and ends in the subjunctive mood (*were, would go*), but *was* is indicative. Correct this by changing indicative *was* to subjunctive *were*.

shift: First <u>put</u> tab A in slot B; next <u>you will put</u> tab C in slot D.

Omit *you will* to correct the shift from imperative to indicative.

39c Shifts in Voice (see #17-o–p)

shift: Readers should not ordinarily have to read instructions a second time before some sense <u>can be made</u> of the details.

shift: We drove thirty kilometres to the end of the road, after which five more kilometres <u>were covered</u> on foot.

Such shifts from active to passive could also be marked *pas*. In this case, stay with the active voice (and the same subject):

revised: Readers should not ordinarily have to read instructions a second time before they can make sense of the details.

revised: We drove thirty kilometres to the end of the road and then covered another five kilometres on foot.

39c

39d Shifts in Person of Pronoun (see #14a–b)

Shifts in person from words such as *one*, *a person*, *somebody*, or *someone* to the second-person *you*, while common in informal conversation, are likely to be questioned in print, and particularly in the more formal contexts of academic writing. Edit to produce consistency in person.

> *shift*: If one volunteers locally, you will make valuable connections to others in the community.

> *revised*: If you volunteer locally, you will make valuable connections to others in the community.

> *revised*: If one volunteers locally, he or she will make valuable connections to others in the community.

While *you* is an ineffective replacement for *someone*, it can be used effectively in the first revision suggested above. To avoid gender bias in references to *one* of unspecified gender, use *he or she* as in the second revision above.

39e Shifts in Number of Pronoun (see #14a)

> *shift*: If the committee wants its recommendations followed, they should have written their report more carefully.

The committee changed from a collective unit (*it*) to a collection of individuals (*they*, *their*); the committee should be either singular or plural throughout. See also #15e and #18f. (The errors in #39d and #39e could also be marked *agr*: see #15.)

40 Faulty Parallelism

// Parallelism, the balanced and deliberate repetition of identical grammatical structures (words, phrases, clauses) within a single sentence, can be a strong stylistic technique. Not only does it make for vigorous, balanced, and rhythmical sentences, but it can also help develop and tie together paragraphs (see #7b.1). Like any other device, parallelism can be overdone, but more commonly it is underused. Of course, if you're writing an especially serious piece, like a letter of condolence, you probably won't want to use lively devices like parallelism and metaphor. But in most writing, some parallel structure is appropriate. Build parallel elements into your sentences, and now and then try making two or three successive sentences parallel with each other. Here is a sentence from a paper on computer crime. Note how parallelism (along with alliteration) strengthens the first part, thereby helping to set up the second part:

> Although one can distinguish the malicious from the mischievous or the harmless hacker from the more dangerous computer criminal, security officials take a dim view of anyone who romps through company files.

Be careful as you experiment, for it is easy to set up a parallel structure and then lose track of it. Study the following examples of **faulty parallelism**. (See also #23a–b.)

40a With Coordinate Elements

Coordinate elements in a sentence should have the same grammatical form. If they don't, the sentence will lack parallelism and therefore be ineffective.

> *fp*: Reading should be engrossing, active, and a challenge.

The first two complements are predicate adjectives, the third a predicate noun. Change *a challenge* to the adjective *challenging* so that it will be parallel.

The coordinate parts of compound subjects, verbs, objects, and modifiers should be parallel in form.

> *fp*: Eating huge meals, too many sweets, and snacking between meals can lead to obesity.

This sentence can be corrected either by making all three parts of the subject into gerunds:

> *revised*: Eating huge meals, eating too many sweets, and snacking between meals can lead to obesity.

or by using only the first gerund and following it with three parallel objects:

> *revised*: Eating huge meals, too many sweets, and between-meal snacks can lead to obesity.

Another example:

> *fp*: He talks about his computer in terms suggesting a deep affection for it and that also demonstrate a thorough knowledge of it.

Simply change the participial phrase (*suggesting* . . .) to a relative clause (*that suggest* . . .) so that it will be parallel with the second part.

It is particularly easy for a writer to produce faulty parallelism by omitting a second *that*:

> *fp*: Marvin was convinced <u>that the argument was unsound</u> and <u>he could profitably spend some time analyzing it</u>.

A second *that*, before *he*, corrects the error and clarifies the meaning, for this slip is not only a breakdown of parallelism but also an implied shift in point of view (see #39); it could be marked *shift* or *pv* as well as *fp*; it could also be marked *ambig*. The omission of a second *that* invites a reader to take *he could profitably spend some time analyzing it* as an independent clause (expressing the writer's own opinion about what Marvin should do) rather than a second subordinate clause expressing a part of Marvin's opinion, which is what the writer intended. (See also *shift, pv* in appendix 2.)

40b With Correlative Conjunctions (see #23b)
Check for parallel structure when using correlative conjunctions:

> *fp*: Whether <u>for accessing the latest news</u> or <u>in finding the quickest route to the park</u>, the Internet is probably the best source we have.

The constructions following the *whether* and the *or* should be parallel: change *in* to *for*.
The correlative pair *not only . . . but also* can be particularly troublesome:

> *fp*: She not only <u>corrected my grammar</u> but also <u>my spelling</u>.

The error can easily be corrected:

> *revised*: She not only corrected <u>my grammar</u> but also corrected <u>my spelling</u>.

> *revised*: She corrected not only <u>my grammar</u> but also <u>my spelling</u>.

Both of these revisions make what follows *not only* parallel in form to what follows *but also*. The second version, however, is more economical. See also #23b, on *not only . . . but also*.

40c In a Series
In any series of three or more parallel elements, make sure that little beginning words like prepositions, pronouns, and the *to* of infinitives precede either the first element alone or each of the elements. And don't omit needed articles:

> *fp*: The new library is noted for <u>a large auditorium</u>, <u>state-of-the-art computer lab</u>, <u>an impressive collection of journals</u>, and <u>brilliant, hard-working staff</u>.

40c

In this example, the article *a* is missing before the second and fourth items and should be added to make the items parallel. Another way to fix this would be to remove the articles and insert the possessive pronoun *its* before the first item.

> *fp***:** She urged her teammates <u>to obey the rules</u>, <u>to think positively</u>, and <u>ignore criticism</u>.

Since *to* occurs in the first two phrases, it should lead off the third phrase as well—or else be omitted from the second one. If necessary, check your work by jotting down the items in such a series in a vertical list after the word that introduces them: any slips in parallelism should then be clearer to you.

> *correction***:** She urged her teammates   to obey the rules,
>
> to think positively,
>
> **and**   to ignore criticism.

40c

Exercise 40 Correcting Faulty Parallelism

Revise the following sentences in order to repair faulty parallelism.

1. Disagreements over the war were not only apparent between elected officials and voters, but between various elements of the armed forces as well.
2. People adopt roles in life that they are most comfortable with, or will benefit them the most.
3. Not only was our trip like an adventure, but also very much like a marathon.
4. It is significant that the prosecutor ignored the jury and to try to address his comments to the judge.
5. Part of the report is not only concerned with the present situation but also prepares the way for the important reforms that are ahead.
6. We are told that we should eat more fibre, less fat, and exercise regularly.
7. The homeless are a neglected group in our society, and our own lives.
8. Around 1750, it became clear to the French that the arrival of the few English traders was only the beginning and soon masses of settlers would follow and overwhelm the French empire in North America.
9. He says that when he graduates he wants to be a teacher, a home owner, and travel.

10. A pet not only gives an older person something to care for, but also a sense of companionship.
11. Today, even newspapers from across the world can be read on the same day of publication via the Internet rather than a magazine shop.
12. The mountaineers had to cope with obsolete or too few pieces of new equipment.
13. The speaker narrates the poem as if he has walked along the streets at night more than once before and that he is acquainted with what goes on around him during his walks.
14. There are many kinds of smiles. For example, there are smiles of pleasure, winning, idiotic grins, courtesy, shared secrets, embarrassment, surprise, leers, sneers, and hiding anger.
15. Everything the fortuneteller told me was happy and exciting: I would marry an intelligent woman, have two children, one who will become a famous author, and the other will be a doctor, travel all over the world, and live until I'm ninety-five, healthy as a young man.

41

41 Faulty Coordination: Logic, Emphasis, and Unity

fc,
og,
ph,
u
If unrelated or unequal elements—usually clauses—are presented as coordinate, the result is **faulty coordination**.

> *fc:* Watches are usually water-resistant <u>and</u> some have the ability to glow in the dark.

There is no logical connection between the two clauses—other than that they both say something about watches. The ideas would be better expressed in separate sentences. Coordinating two such clauses produces a sentence that also lacks **unity**. Here is another example, from a description of a simple object; the lack of unity is even more glaring:

> *fc:* One might find this kind of a jar in an antiques store <u>and</u> it can be used for anything from cotton balls to rings and things, or just to stand as a decoration.

The suggestion about the antiques store should either be in a separate sentence or be subordinated.

Similarly, if two elements are joined by an inappropriate coordinating conjunction, the result is again faulty coordination—sometimes referred to as "loose" coordination. Here is an example of this more common weakness:

> *fc*: Nationalism can affect the relations between nations by creating a distrustful atmosphere, <u>and</u> an ambassador's innocent remark can be turned into an insult by a suspicious listener.

The *and* misrepresents the relation between the two clauses; the second is not an additional fact but rather an example or result of the fact stated in the first. It would be better either to join the two clauses with a semicolon or colon, or to change *and* to *in which*, and to drop the comma, thereby subordinating the second clause. (The first clause could be made subordinate by adding an opening *Because*, but this would distort **emphasis**, since the first clause appears to be more important; see #29i). Here is another example, from a description of how a particular scene in *Hamlet* should be staged:

> *fc*: In this scene Rosencrantz is the main speaker of the two courtiers; therefore he should stand closer to Hamlet.

This sentence could be sharpened. The first clause would be better subordinated:

> *revised*: Because in this scene Rosencrantz is the main speaker of the two courtiers, he should stand closer to Hamlet.

The original *therefore* does express this relation, but the sentence was nonetheless a compound one, tacitly equating the two clauses. Emphasis and clarity are better served by letting the syntax acknowledge the logically subordinate nature of the first clause.

Sometimes faulty coordination produces a sentence that lacks not just clarity but also **logic** (*log*):

> *fc, log*: Alliteration is a very effective poetic device when used sparingly <u>but</u> appropriately.

The meaning expressed by *but* here is entirely illogical. *But* implies opposition, yet it is likely that a poet who uses alliteration sparingly would also use it appropriately. *And* would be a better coordinator here.

A particularly weak form of loose coordination overlaps with the overuse of *this* (see #16c and *ref* in appendix 2):

> *fc*: The poem's tone is light and cheery, <u>and this</u> is reinforced by the mainly one-syllable words and the regular rhythm and rhyme.

If you ever find such an *and this* in your draft, try to revise it, for not only is the coordination weak, but the demonstrative *this* is weak as well, since it has no antecedent:

> *revised*: The poem's light and cheery tone is reinforced by the mainly one-syllable words and the regular rhythm and rhyme.

Another kind of faulty coordination links several short independent clauses with coordinating conjunctions, mostly *and*'s; the result is a loose string of seemingly unrelated parts. Such sentences tend to ramble on and on, emphasizing very little.

> *fc, rambling*: The ferry rates were increased and the bigger commercial vehicles had to pay more to use the ferry service and so the cost of transporting goods rose and the consumers who bought those goods had to pay more for them but they had to pay higher fares on the ferries as well and naturally most people were unhappy about it.

The information needed to make the point is here, but ineffective syntax leaves the reader floundering, trying to decipher the connections and the thoughts behind the whole utterance. The *but* seems to be used less for logic than for variety, and the vague *it* at the end effectively dissipates any emphasis the sentence might have had. A little tinkering sorts out the facts, shortens the sentence by almost half, reduces the five coordinating conjunctions to a pair of correlative conjunctions, reduces the six independent clauses to two independent and one subordinate, and achieves some emphasis at the end:

> *revised*: Not only did the increased ferry rates cost travellers more, but, since the operators of commercial vehicles also had to pay more, the cost of transported goods rose as well, affecting all consumers.

See also #29i and #27b.

Exercise 41 (1) Using Subordination

Convert each of the following pairs of sentences into a complex sentence by subordinating one or the other.

1. The book was well written. I did not find it rewarding.
2. The wind was very cold. She wore a heavy sweater.
3. It stopped snowing. We shovelled the driveway.
4. She read a good book. He played solitaire.
5. The meeting was contentious. A consensus was reached.

41

Exercise 41 (2) Correcting Faulty Coordination

Revise the following sentences to eliminate faulty or loose coordination; aim for good subordination, unity, emphasis, and logic. You may also find that you can reduce wordiness.

1. There are no windows in the room, and all lighting is from artificial sources.
2. At this point Ophelia becomes confused, and this becomes evident when she speaks her next line.
3. Patrick Lewis is a compelling character, and *In the Skin of a Lion* is a great novel about early twentieth-century Toronto.
4. The last appearance of the ghost is in the "closet" scene and the purpose of its appearance is to prevent Hamlet from diverging from his "blunted purpose."
5. Her experiments with sweet peas were unusual and they were interesting.
6. Older people have already been through what others are experiencing, and this enables them to help.
7. Experts are not always right, and they are seldom wrong.
8. The city's streets are well paved and some of them badly need repair.
9. He is a genius; some people claim that he is an imposter.
10. The stores are usually the first to remind us that Christmas is coming and set the mood with decorations, music, and advertising.

42 Faulty Logic

og Clear and logical thinking is essential to clear and effective writing. For example, avoid sweeping statements: over-generalization is one of the most common weaknesses in writing. Precise claims and statements of fact will make your writing clearer. Make sure that the evidence you use is sound and that the authorities you cite are credible, current, and reliable. Such matters are particularly important in argumentative writing. Weak reasoning will make the point you're trying to argue less convincing. You will want to avoid such logical missteps as begging the question, reasoning in a circle, jumping to conclusions, and leaning on false analogies, which can seriously decrease the effectiveness of an essay. (See #3e–h.)

There are many ways in which logic is important even in something so small as a sentence. The problems discussed in the preceding sections, from #35 on, are in many instances problems in logic. Following are some examples of other ways in which sentences can be illogical. Unsound reasoning leads to sentences like this:

> *log*: You could tell that James's father was proud of him, for he had the boy's picture on his desk.

The conclusion may seem reasonable, but it should at least be qualified with a *probably*, or more evidence should be provided; for there are other possible reasons for the picture's being on the desk. James's mother could have put it there, and the father not bothered to remove it; perhaps he's afraid to. Or he could feel love for his son, but not pride. Or he could be feigning love and pride for appearances' sake, knowing inside that he doesn't feel either. Here's another example:

> *log*: Wordsworth is <u>perhaps</u> the first English Romantic poet, <u>for</u> his major themes—nature and human life—are characteristic of the Romantic style of poetry.

To begin with, the word *perhaps* is ineffective: either the writer is making a point of Wordsworth's primacy and there is no "perhaps" about it, or there is no point to be made and the whole clause is superfluous. Even more serious is the way evidence is given to substantiate the statement: if the mere presence in his poetry of themes common to Romanticism makes him first, then all Romantic poets are first. The writer probably meant something like "Wordsworth is the first English Romantic poet to develop the major themes of the Romantic movement." As for these "major themes," just how valid is the implication that "human life" is especially characteristic of Romantic writers? No amount of revision can repair this muddy thinking.

Even if writers know clearly what they want to say, they have to choose and use words thoughtfully:

> *log*:   The town is <u>surrounded</u> on one side by the ocean.

If the town were indeed *surrounded* by the ocean, it would be an island. The correct word here is *bounded*. This error might equally well be designated an error in diction: see #69 and *ww* (wrong word) in appendix 2.

Faulty logic can also affect the way writers put sentences together:

> *log*:   Having a car with bad spark plugs or points or a dirty carburetor causes it to run poorly and to use too much gas.

This sentence could just as easily be marked *ss* (sentence structure, or sentence sense). The intention is clear, but the verb, *causes*, has as its subject the gerund *having*; consequently the sentence says that the mere possession of the afflicted car is what causes it to run poorly—as if one could borrow a similar car and it would run well. A logical revision:

> *revised*:   Bad spark plugs or bad points or a dirty carburetor cause a car to run poorly and to use too much gas.

Faulty comparisons are another cause of illogicality:

> *log, comp*:   French painting did not follow the wild and exciting forms of Baroque art as closely as most European countries.

Again the meaning is apparent, but the syntax faulty; readers would be annoyed at having to revise the sentence themselves in order to understand it. The sentence says either that "European countries followed the wild and exciting forms of Baroque art" to some degree or that "French painting followed most European countries more closely than it followed the wild and exciting forms of Baroque art," neither of which makes sense. Simply completing the comparison straightens out the syntax and permits the intended meaning to come through unambiguously:

> *revised*:   French painting did not follow the wild and exciting forms of Baroque art as closely as did <u>that</u> of most European countries.

See also *comp* in appendix 2.

Another kind of ambiguity appears in this sentence:

> *log*: Numerous scientific societies were founded in every developed country.

The intended meaning is probably that every developed country had at least one scientific society—but it could just as well mean that there were numerous such societies in each country. See also *ambig* and *cl* (clarity) in appendix 2.

Here's another kind of illogical sentence:

> *log*: His lack of cynicism was visible in every paragraph of his essay.

The meaning is clear, but a reader might find it odd to think of a *lack* being *visible*. Put it more logically:

> *revised*: Every paragraph of his essay revealed his idealism.

Make sure that nouns are inflected to agree logically with the context:

> *log*: All the legislators appeared at the committee to express their view on health care reforms.

Clearly the legislators expressed their *views*, not just one *view*.

Sometimes an extra word creeps in and weakens an otherwise logical sentence:

> *log*: Alexander Graham Bell is known as the modern inventor of the telephone.

The writer was probably thinking subconsciously of the telephone as a *modern* invention, and the word just popped into the sentence. Thinking critically, one sees that the word *modern* implies that there have been one or more earlier, perhaps even ancient, inventors of the telephone.

Finally, make sure your sentences actually say something worth saying. Here's one that doesn't:

> *log*: The mood and theme play a very significant part in this poem.

This could be called an "empty" sentence (the weak intensifier *very* suggests that the writer subconsciously felt the need to prop it up). It would be illogical for the *theme* of a poem to play other than a significant part in it.

Exercise 42 Improving Logic

Revise the following sentences to eliminate errors in logic.

1. As he approached the shore, he felt a challenge between himself and the sea.
2. Milton's influence on other subsequent poets was very great.
3. Some auto accidents are unavoidable but can be prevented by proper maintenance.
4. Shakespeare fashioned *A Midsummer Night's Dream* around the theme of love and created the characters and situations to illustrate it in the best possible way. Thus he freely used a variety of comic devices in developing the theme.
5. By the use of imagery, diction, symbolism, and sound, we may also see the structure of the plot.
6. It employed the technique of using projected images on a screen and a corresponding taped conversation which visually enforced the lesson.
7. Throughout history philosophers have been discussing and proposing theories about our purpose on earth, and thus far they can be divided into three general camps.
8. Through the use of too much abstract language, jargon, and clichés, the clarity and effectiveness of this article have been destroyed.
9. As I think back to the days when we were in our early teens, we had a lot of fun together.
10. After his wife died, his paintings of excited forms changed to quiet ones.

Review Exercise, Chapters II, III, and IV
Sentence Errors and Weaknesses

The following sentences contain various kinds of errors and weaknesses discussed in the preceding chapters. Decide what is wrong with each sentence, label it with the appropriate correction symbol, and then revise the sentence in order to eliminate the problem. Some of the sentences have more than one thing wrong with them.

1. Our coach is overbearing, tall, overpaid, and over forty.
2. One receives this impression when the colour of the picture is considered.

3. Many organic diseases present symptoms that are very similar to autism.

4. Great distances now separate he and his father.

5. The writer's skill was very good.

6. It's true that love and romance come when you least expect it.

7. No one has ever scored as many points as Schmidt has.

8. The poem is separated into two parts. The first being his memories and an account of how he reacted to his father's death.

9. Its shape is rounded somewhat resembling a keyhole.

10. I pulled over to the side of the road in a green truck I had borrowed from my roommate, and because the weather was warm I was dressed only in a bathing suit and a bandana, which I had tied around my head.

11. Borelli supposed that there was a tendency for celestial bodies to attract each other but a fluid pressure prevented this.

12. Shakespeare's *Othello* is a brilliant but tragic story of the betrayal of the Moor of Venice by his most trusted lieutenant, Iago.

13. The whole meaning of Housman's poem is that it is better to die young with honour and glory intact than to have someone take it away from you.

14. The forefinger along with the other digits of the hand have enabled us to evolve to the position of being a creative and destructive species.

15. Since the mayor couldn't run the government right this term, how can anyone think he's about to do it right if he is re-elected?

16. Smitty is so eager about Michael's friendship, and this is easy to understand even the first time one reads the story.

17. Those who are actually involved in this holiday frenzy may find themselves feeling like enjoying each other's company, hang out with good friends, visit family, get in touch with old friends, and give to their loved ones and even to strangers.

18. At present the fees are already very expensive.

19. By creating an atmosphere of concern for the main character we are more open to the message of the story.

20. What a university stands for more than anything else is an institution where one furthers his education.

21. He has an old rundown house, but repairs are something he has neither money for nor feels the need to get done.

22. I feel faint; the reason is because I am hungry.

42

23. Her success is credited to her astute powers of judgment, her cleverness, and her judiciousness.

24. The president beamed as the audience cheered; when the excitement dies down, she collects her notes and leaves the stage.

25. Physical activity of any kind is always beneficial for the individual.

42

Punctuation

Introduction: The Principles of Good Punctuation

p There are two common misconceptions about punctuation: first, punctuation is of no importance—it has little to do with the effectiveness of written English—and second, good punctuation is a mystery whose secrets are available only to those with a special instinct. Those who believe one or both of these misconceptions may punctuate poorly, whether through fear or lack of concern or both.

First, good punctuation is essential to clear and effective writing. It helps writers clarify meaning and tone and, therefore, helps readers understand what writers communicate: try removing the punctuation marks from a piece of prose, and then see how difficult it is to read it. Punctuation points to meaning that in spoken language would be indicated by pauses, pitch, tone, and stress. In effect, punctuation helps readers *hear* a sentence the way a writer intends. Commas, semicolons, colons, and dashes help to clarify the internal structure of sentences; often the very meaning or beauty of a sentence depends on how it is punctuated.

Second, the principles of good punctuation are not mysterious; mastering them shouldn't be difficult. Even the most inexperienced writers depend on punctuation to help them understand what they read; becoming more aware of the way punctuation operates in the writing of others will help writers generally control punctuation in their own writing.

And here yet another misconception needs to be examined: what are often called the "rules" of punctuation aren't rules but conventions. These conventions have come to be agreed upon by writers and readers of English for the purpose of clear and effective communication. Although good writers do sometimes stray from these conventions, they usually do so because they have a sufficient command of them to break a "rule" in order to achieve a desired effect.

A good way to improve your punctuation sense is to become more aware of others' punctuation. Look not only for weaknesses but strengths as well. If you do this consciously as you read, you will soon acquire a better sense of what punctuation does and how it does it.

The following discussions cover the common uses of punctuation and even some relatively uncommon ones. If you find it hard to grasp the principles, you may need to review the appropriate sections on grammar and sentence structure in the preceding chapters. As you will see, many of the principles not only allow but even invite you to exercise a good deal of choice.

Note that *hyphens* and *apostrophes* are dealt with in the discussion of spelling in chapter VI: see #62i–l, #62m.8, and #62n–o.

Internal Punctuation: Comma, Semicolon, Colon, and Dash

43 (in circle)

43a Comma ,

The **comma** is a light separator. It is the most neutral and most used punctuation mark. A comma makes a reader pause slightly. Use it to separate words, phrases, and clauses from each other when no heavier or more expressive mark is required or desired.

Main Functions of Commas

Commas have three main functions; if you know these functions, you should have little trouble with commas:

1. Generally, use a comma between independent clauses joined by a coordinating conjunction (*and, but, or, nor, for, so, yet*; see #23a; see also #44a and #44e–f):

    > We went to the National Gallery, and then we walked to the Parliament Buildings.

    > Most of us went back to college in the fall, but Jade was tempted by an opportunity to travel, so she took off for Italy.

2. Generally, use commas to separate items in a series of three or more (see #49a):

    > It is said that early to bed and early to rise will make one healthy, wealthy, and wise.

    > Robert Bateman, Emily Carr, and Mary Pratt are three Canadian painters.

    See #55c on a common error with such constructions.

3. Generally, use commas to set off parenthetical elements, such as interruptive or introductory words, phrases, and clauses; nonrestrictive appositives; and nonrestrictive relative clauses (see #45–48):

    > There are, however, some exceptions.

    > Grasping her briefcase firmly, she walked away.

43a

E.M. Forster's last novel, *A Passage to India*, is both serious
and humorous.

Poutine, which was first served in Quebec, is now popular
across Canada.

Other Conventional Uses of the Comma

1. Use a comma between elements of an emphatic contrast:

    This is a practical lesson, not a theoretical one.

2. Use a comma to indicate a pause where a word has been acceptably
    omitted:

    Ron is a conservative; Sally, a radical.

    To err is human; to forgive, divine.

3. Use commas to set off a noun of address (see #13b):

    Simon, please pay attention to the speaker.

    Thank you, Ava, for your wonderful speech.

4. Generally, use commas with a verb of speaking before or after a quo-
    tation (see also #54d–e):

    Then Alain remarked, "That movie gave me nightmares."

    "I thought it was a comedy," said Megan laughingly.

5. Use commas after the salutation of informal letters (Dear Gail,) and
    after the complimentary close of all letters (Yours truly,). In formal
    letters, a colon is conventional after the salutation (Dear Mr. Eng:).

6. Use commas with specific dates when the number of the day follows
    the name of the month:

    She left on January 11, 2010, and was gone a month. (Note the
        comma *after* the year.)

    But note that no comma is required for the day-month-year format:

    She left on 11 January 2010 and was gone a month.

    Whichever style you choose, make sure you use it consistently.

When referring only to month and year, you may use a comma or not, but again, be consistent:

The book was published in March, 2014, in Canada.

It was published here in March 2014.

7. Use commas to set off geographical names and addresses:

She left Fredericton, New Brunswick, and moved to Calgary, Alberta, in hopes of finding a better-paying job. (Note the commas *after* the names of the provinces.)

The RCMP Heritage Centre is located at 5907 Dewdney Avenue, Regina, Saskatchewan, Canada.

For some common errors with commas, see #55a–h.

43b

43b Semicolon ;

The **semicolon** is a heavy separator, often almost equivalent to a period or "full stop." It forces a much longer pause than a comma does. Compared with the comma, it is used sparingly. Basically, semicolons have only two functions:

1. Generally, use a semicolon between closely related independent clauses that are not joined by one of the coordinating conjunctions (see #23a.1 and #44d):

Some people like coffee; others prefer tea.

The lab had 20 new tablet computers; however, there were 25 students in the class.

2. Use a semicolon instead of a comma if a comma would not be heavy enough, for example if the clauses or the elements in a series have internal commas of their own (see #44b and #49b):

Their class presentation examined three novels written by Canadian authors and set largely outside Canada: Will Ferguson's *419*, which is set primarily in Nigeria; Esi Edugyan's *Half-Blood Blues*, which takes place in Baltimore, Berlin, and Paris; and Patrick deWitt's *The Sisters Brothers*, which is set in Oregon and California.

See #55j for some common misuses of the semicolon.

43c Colon :

Colons are commonly used to introduce lists, examples, and long or formal quotations, but their possibilities in more everyday sentences are often overlooked. The reason a colon is useful is that it looks forward or anticipates: it gives readers a push toward the next part of the sentence. In the preceding sentence, for example, the colon sets up a sense of expectation about what is coming. It points out, even emphasizes, the relation between the two parts of the sentence (that is, the second part clarifies what the first part says). A semicolon in the same spot would bring readers to an abrupt halt, leaving it up to them to make the necessary connection between the two parts. Here are more examples:

> The simple sculpture evoked complex feelings: loss, isolation, yearning, and hope.

> Let me add just this: anyone who expects to lose weight must be prepared to exercise.

> It was an unexpectedly lovely time of year: trees were in blossom, garden flowers bloomed all around, the sky was clear and bright, and the temperature was just right.

> The rain came down during the race: we soon started slipping on the slick pavement.

Nevertheless, don't get carried away and overuse the colon: its effectiveness would wear off if it appeared more than once or twice a page.

See #55k on how to avoid a common misuse of the colon.

43d Dash —

The **dash** is a popular punctuation mark, especially in email and other informal communications. Hasty writers often use it as a substitute for a comma, or where a colon would be more emphatic. Use a dash only when you have a definite reason for doing so. Like the colon, the dash sets up expectations in a reader's mind. But whereas the colon sets up an expectation that what follows will somehow explain, summarize, define, or otherwise comment on what has gone before, a dash suggests that what follows will be somehow surprising, involving some sort of twist, or at least a contrary idea. Consider the following sentence:

> The teacher praised my wit, my intelligence, my organization, and my research—and penalized the paper for its poor spelling and punctuation.

Here the dash adds to the punch of what follows it. A comma there would deprive the sentence of much of its force; it would even sound odd, since the resulting matter-of-fact tone would not be in harmony with what the sentence was saying. Only a dash can convey the appropriate *tone* (see the introduction to chapter VII). Another example:

> What he wanted—and he wanted it very badly indeed—was the last piece of chocolate cake.

To set off the interrupting clause with commas instead of dashes wouldn't be "incorrect," but the result would be weaker, for the content of the clause is clearly meant to be emphatic. Only dashes have the power to signal that emphasis; commas would diminish the force of the clause (see #50).

The dash is also handy in some long and involved sentences, for example after a long series before a summarizing clause:

> Our longing for the past, our hopes for the future and our neglect of the present moment—all these and more go to shape our everyday lives, often in ways unseen or little understood.

Even here, the emphatic quality of the dash serves the meaning, though its principal function in such a sentence is to mark the abrupt break.

As with colons, don't overuse dashes. They are even stronger marks, but they lose effectiveness if used often.

How to Use Commas, Semicolons, Colons, and Dashes

Between Independent Clauses

44a Comma and Coordinating Conjunction

Generally, use a comma between independent clauses joined by one of the coordinating conjunctions (*and, but, or, nor, for, so, yet*; see #23a.3):

> We could go out for dinner, or we could stay home.

> I wanted to do something I had never done before, and dogsledding sounded fun.

> Fiona knew she shouldn't tell Ivan what she really thought of his plan, yet she couldn't stop herself.

> It was a serious speech, but Kyoko included many jokes along the way, and the audience loved it.

PROOFREADING TIP

On Using Commas Before *but, yet, for,* and *so*

Independent clauses joined by *but* and *yet*, which explicitly mark a contrast, will almost always need a comma, even if they are short or parallel, or have the same subject:

> It was windy, yet it was warm.

And when you join two clauses with the coordinating conjunction *for*, always put a comma in front of it to prevent its being misread as a preposition:

> Anita was eager to leave early, for the restaurant was sure to be crowded.

The conjunction *so* almost always needs a comma, but remember that *so* is considered informal (see the proofreading tip near the end of #23a.2).

44a

If the clauses are short, or if only one of a pair of clauses is short, the comma or commas may be omitted:

> The road was smooth and the car was running well and the weather was perfect.

> We studied for weeks so we were well-prepared to take our final exams in Canadian history and modern politics.

But sometimes even with a short clause, the natural pause of a comma may make the sentence read more smoothly and clearly:

> The building was respectably old, for the ivy had climbed nearly to the top of its three storeys.

When the clauses are parallel in structure, the comma may often be omitted:

> Art is long and life is short.

> He smirked and she simpered.

When two clauses have the same subject, a comma is less likely to be needed between them:

It was windy and it was wet. (A comma here would detract from the effect produced by the parallel structure and alliteration of these two short clauses.)

The play was well produced and it impressed everyone who saw it.

When the subject is omitted from the second clause, a comma should not be used (see #55d):

It was windy and wet.

44b Semicolon and Coordinating Conjunction

You will sometimes want to use a semicolon between independent clauses even though they are joined by a coordinating conjunction. A semicolon is appropriate when at least one of the clauses contains other punctuation:

Distracted as he was, the English professor, Herbert, the best cryptic crossword player in the district, easily won the contest; and no one who knew him—or even had only heard of him— was in the least surprised.

44c

44c Dash and Coordinating Conjunction

When you want a longer pause to create extra emphasis before a coordinating conjunction, use a dash:

Sameer swore that he was sorry for all his mistakes—but he went right on making them.

For a different rhetorical effect, change *but* to the more neutral *and*; a dash then takes over the contrasting function:

Sameer swore that he was sorry for all his mistakes—and he went right on making them.

Similarly, consider the different effects of these two versions of the same basic sentence:

It may not be the easiest way, but it's the only way we know.

It may not be the easiest way—but it's the only way we know.

Even a period could be used between such clauses, since there is nothing inherently wrong with beginning a sentence with *And* or *But*. Even as sentence openers, they are still doing their job of coordinating. See #23a.3.

44d Semicolon Without Coordinating Conjunction

To avoid a *comma splice* (see #44e), generally use a semicolon between independent clauses that are not joined with one of the coordinating conjunctions (*and, but, or, nor, for, yet, so*):

> Winning the award is not important; it is the honour of being nominated that matters.

> Naieli was exhausted and obviously not going to win; nevertheless, she persevered and finished the race.

44e Comma Splice

cs Using only a comma between independent clauses not joined with a coordinating conjunction results in a **comma splice**:

> *cs:* The prime minister is elected, the senate members are not.

> *cs:* I didn't fully understand what I had witnessed, I just knew it was wrong.

> *cs:* He desperately wanted to eat, however he was too weak to get out of bed.

A semicolon signals that an independent clause comes next. But a comma tells readers that something subordinate comes next; an independent clause coming instead would derail their train of thought. A comma with a coordinating conjunction is enough to prevent the derailment of thought:

> The prime minister is elected, but the senate members are not.

With few exceptions (see #44f), a comma *without* a coordinating conjunction is not enough. In most such sentences, then, in order to avoid seriously distracting your readers, use semicolons:

> I didn't fully understand what I had witnessed; I just knew it was wrong.

> Adverbs can usually move around in a sentence; conjunctions are not as flexible.

> Vancouver, the largest city in British Columbia, is not the capital of the province; Victoria has that distinction.

For a discussion of ways to correct comma splices, see *cs* in appendix 2.

44f Commas Alone Between Independent Clauses

There are a few exceptions to the convention that a comma alone is not strong enough to separate independent clauses. For example, a comma rather than a semicolon may be appropriate if the clauses are short enough that a reader can take them both in with a single glance, and especially if they are also parallel in structure:

> He cooked, she ate.

> Lightning flashed, thunder roared.

Relatively short independent clauses in a series of three or more, especially if they are grammatically parallel, may also be separated by commas rather than semicolons:

> I saw, I shopped, I bought.

> He cooked, she ate, they fell in love.

> If you want to do well, you must read carefully, you must write thoughtfully, and you must revise thoroughly.

44g

44g Semicolons with Conjunctive Adverbs and Transitions

Be sure to use a semicolon and not just a comma between independent clauses that you join with a conjunctive adverb, and yes, that includes *however* and *therefore*. Here is a list of most of the common ones:

accordingly	finally	likewise	similarly
afterward	further	meanwhile	still
also	furthermore	moreover	subsequently
anyway	hence	namely	then
besides	however	nevertheless	thereafter
certainly	indeed	next	therefore
consequently	instead	nonetheless	thus
conversely	later	otherwise	undoubtedly

The same caution applies to common transitional phrases such as these:

after this	if not	in the meantime
as a result	in addition	on the contrary
for example	in fact	on the other hand
for this reason	in short	that is

Conjunctive adverbs often have the *feel* of subordinating conjunctions, but they are not true conjunctions. Think of them as adverbs doing a joining or "conjunctive" job:

> The text was convoluted; therefore, Marie got a headache as she read it.

Here *therefore* works very much like *so*; nevertheless, *therefore* is a conjunctive adverb and requires the semicolon.

> The tornado almost flattened the town; however, only Dorothy and her dog were reported missing.

Here *however* works very much like *but*; nevertheless, *however* is a conjunctive adverb and requires the semicolon.

44h

> **PROOFREADING TIP**
>
> **On the Comma Following *however***
>
> Note that whereas other conjunctive adverbs will often, but not always, be followed by commas, *however* as a conjunctive adverb (unless it ends a sentence) is always followed by a comma to prevent its being misread as a regular adverb meaning "in whatever way" or "to whatever degree," as in "However you go, just make sure you get there on time."

44h Dashes and Colons Without Coordinating Conjunctions

Dashes and colons may also be used between independent clauses not joined by coordinating conjunctions. Use a dash when you want stronger emphasis on the second clause; use a colon when the second clause explains or enlarges upon the first (see #43c and #43d). In many sentences, either a dash or a colon would work; the choice depends on the desired tone or emphasis:

> The film was dreadful from beginning to end: a plausible plot must have been the last thing on the director's mind.

> The proposal horrified Jon—it was ludicrous.

> Derek took the evolutionary way out: he turned and ran.

> It was a rare occasion—everyone at the meeting agreed on what should be done.

Note that a comma would not be correct in any of these examples. A semi-colon would work, but it would be weak and inappropriate (except perhaps in the first example). But note that a *period*, especially in the second and third examples, would achieve a crisp and emphatic effect by turning each independent clause into a separate sentence.

44i Run-on (Fused) Sentences

n–
n,
fs

Failure to put any punctuation between independent clauses where there is also no coordinating conjunction results in a **run–on** or **fused** sentence:

> *run-on*: Philosophers' views did not always meet with the approval of the authorities therefore there was constant conflict between writers and the church or state.

A semicolon after *authorities* corrects this serious error.

> *revised*: Philosophers' views did not always meet with the approval of the authorities; therefore, there was constant conflict between writers and the church or state.

44i

See #34; see also **run-on** in appendix 2.

Exercise 44 (1) Punctuating Between Independent Clauses

Insert whatever punctuation mark (other than a period) you think works best between the independent clauses in the following sentences. You may decide that some need no punctuation. Could some be punctuated in more than one way?

1. Everyone thought the digital revolution would reduce our use of paper we were wrong.
2. Jamil needed some help with his lab report so he thought he would make an appointment with a tutor.
3. Cartoons are enjoyed by both children and adults sometimes adults enjoy them more.
4. Some people eat to live others live to eat.
5. It was a fascinating hypothesis but it was greeted with silence.
6. His belly shook he had a red nose he was surrounded by reindeer.
7. The hurricane warning went up and most people sauntered to their shelters others continued to watch TV.
8. Easy come easy go.
9. You live you learn.
10. The strike was over the people were jubilant.

Exercise 44 (2) Correcting Comma Splices and Run-ons

Correct any comma splices and run-on sentences in the following:

1. I had not been back in ages therefore I was surprised to see all the changes.
2. We started to edit the next edition of the newsletter, soon the office was littered with coffee cups and paper.
3. Atwood uses figurative language, however the literal sense is sufficiently clear.
4. But we sat silent the scene before us on the stage had left us stunned.
5. They make faces at each other each time they pass on the street.
6. This press release doesn't acknowledge women exist therefore they will never buy the product.
7. Life in those days was a gruelling chore, but at least life was short.
8. The dictator's statue stood for almost thirty years however it was toppled in less than an hour.
9. We pushed off from the shore the canoes were buffeted by the waves we found ourselves unexpectedly in the water.
10. Things went surprisingly well the first person to look at the house wanted to buy it.

45 To Set Off Adverbial Clauses

45a Commas with Introductory Clauses

Generally, use a comma between an introductory adverbial clause and an independent (main) clause:

> After I had selected all the items I wanted, I discovered that I had left my wallet at home.

> Since she was elected by a large majority, she felt that she had a strong mandate for her policies.

> When the party was over, I went straight home.

When the introductory clause is short and when there would be no pause if the sentence were spoken aloud, you may often omit the comma. But if omitting the comma could cause misreading, retain it:

Whenever I wanted, someone would bring me something to eat.

After the sun had set, high above the mountains came the fighter jets.

45b Commas with Concluding Clauses

A comma may or may not be needed between an independent clause and a following adverbial clause. If the subordinate clause is essential to the meaning of the sentence, it is in effect *restrictive* and should not be set off with a comma; if it is not essential but contains only additional inform-ation or comment, it is *nonrestrictive* and should be set off with a comma (see #48). Consider the following examples:

I went straight home when the party was over.

She did an excellent job on her second essay, although the first one was a disaster.

In most cases, concluding adverbial clauses will be necessary and won't require a comma. When in doubt, try omitting the clause to see if the sentence still says essentially what you want it to.

45b

Exercise 45 Punctuating Adverbial Clauses

Insert commas where you think they are necessary in the following sentences. Indicate where you think a comma would be optional.

1. Although it was almost midnight he knew he had to stay up and finish writing the report.
2. You may begin now if you want to.
3. You may begin whenever you wish.
4. The snowboarding is especially good this year because the snow is plentiful.
5. Because the snow is plentiful this year the snowboarding is especially good.
6. Before you move to Paris you should study French.
7. Sleeping in on the weekend is a fundamental right though my family does not recognize the fact.
8. Some people can tell where commas are required when they read the sentences aloud and listen for the natural pauses.
9. After Anna finished the report which showed marked improvement in profits she seemed less happy than she had before she began the report.
10. However you look at it the solution needs to be simple and practical or the boss will not approve of it.

46 To Set Off Introductory and Concluding Words and Phrases

46a Adverbs and Adverbial Phrases

Generally, set off a long introductory adverbial phrase with a comma:

> After many years as leader of the committee, Jean retired gracefully.

> To get the best results from your ice cream maker, you must follow the instruction manual carefully.

> Just like all the other long-time employees, Radha felt loyal to the company.

Generally, set off a word or short phrase if you want a distinct pause, for example for emphasis or qualification or to prevent misreading:

> Unfortunately, the weather didn't cooperate.

> Generally, follow my advice about punctuation.

> Usually, immature people are difficult to work with.

Of the conjunctive adverbs, *however* is most often set off, though the others frequently are as well (see #44g and #55f).

When such words and phrases follow the independent clause, most will be restrictive and therefore not set off with commas:

> Jean retired gracefully after many years as leader of the committee.

> You must follow the instruction manual carefully to get the best results from your ice cream maker.

> Aarti moved to Calgary in 2011.

If you intend the concluding element to complete the sense of the main clause, don't set it off; if it merely provides additional information or comment, set it off. The presence or absence of punctuation tells your readers how you want the sentence to be read.

46b Participles and Participial Phrases

Always set off an introductory participle or participial phrase with a comma (see #21d):

> Finding golf unexpectedly difficult, Kevin sought extra help.

> Feeling victorious, Shirin left the room.

> Having been in the computer lab so long, Jason scarcely recognized the world when he emerged.

> Puzzled, Haley turned back to the beginning of the chapter.

Closing participles and participial phrases almost always need to be set off as well. Read the sentence aloud; if you feel a distinct pause, use a comma:

> Kevin sought extra help, finding golf unexpectedly difficult.

> Higher prices result in increased wage demands, contributing to inflationary pressures.

Occasionally such a sentence will flow clearly and smoothly without a comma, especially if the modifier is essential to the meaning:

> Shirin left the room feeling victorious.

> Haley sat there looking puzzled.

If the closing participle modifies a predicate noun or a direct object, there usually should not be a comma:

> He was a man lacking in courage.

> I left him feeling bewildered. (He was bewildered.)

But if the participle in such a sentence modifies the subject, if it could also conceivably modify the object, then a comma is necessary:

> I left him, feeling bewildered. (I was bewildered.)

Only the presence or absence of the comma tells a reader how to understand such a sentence.

PROOFREADING TIP

Commas and Gerunds; Commas and Participial Phrases

Don't mistake a gerund for a participle (see #21d and #21f). A gerund or gerund phrase functioning as the subject should not be followed by a comma (see #55a):

> *participle*: Dancing in the street, we celebrated the arrival of summer.
>
> *gerund*: Dancing in the street is a wonderful release of energy.

 PROOFREADING TIP

Commas and Infinitive Phrases

Don't mistake a long infinitive phrase functioning as a subject noun for one functioning as an adverb (see #21a):

> *noun*: To put together a meal for six without help is a remarkable feat.
>
> *adverb*: To put together a meal for six without help, you need to be very organized or a professional chef.

46c Absolute Phrases

Always set off absolute phrases with commas (see #11r and #21i):

> The doors locked and bolted, they went to bed feeling secure.
>
> Arun went on stage, head held high, a grin spreading across his face.

Exercise 46 Punctuating Opening and
Closing Words and Phrases

Insert commas where you think they are necessary in the following
sentences. Indicate any places where you think a comma would be
optional.

1. In December my family always goes skiing.
2. We walked slowly soaking up the sights and sounds along the waterfront.
3. At the end of the lecture I had no clearer understanding of the subject than I had when I came in.
4. The dog walked and fed I decided to relax with a murder mystery.
5. The brain regulates and integrates our senses allowing us to experience our environment.
6. Raising prices results in increased wage demands adding to inflation.
7. Following the instructions I poured the second chemical into the beaker with the first and shook them shutting my eyes in the expectation of something unpleasant.
8. As usual before going to bed I turned on the eleven o'clock news.
9. To make a long story short I found my aunt looking healthier than I'd ever seen her before.
10. Looking pop-eyed and furious the coach stared back at the referee without saying a word.

To Set Off Concluding Summaries and Appositives

Both dashes and colons can set off concluding summaries and appositives. Some writers think dashes are best for short concluding elements and colons for longer ones; but what matters isn't their length but their relation to the rest of the sentence. Use colons for straightforward conclusions, dashes for emphatic or unexpected ones. For example, the following sentences express a conventional idea, with the colon straightforwardly, with the dash somewhat emphatically:

He wanted only one thing from life: happiness.

He wanted only one thing from life—happiness.

But with a less expected final word the tone changes:

> He wanted only one thing from life—everything.

Here a colon would do, since a colon followed by a single word automatically conveys some emphasis, but the strength of the idea would not be as well served by the quietness of a colon as it is by the dash. The same principles apply to setting off longer concluding appositives and summaries, though colons are more common; use a dash only when you want to take advantage of its special emphasis.

48 To Set Off Nonrestrictive Elements

Words, phrases, and clauses are nonrestrictive when they are not essential to the principal meaning of a sentence. Nonrestrictive elements should be set off from the rest of the sentence, usually with commas, though dashes and parentheses can also be used (see #50). A restrictive modifier is essential to the meaning and should not be set off:

> *restrictive*:   Anyone wanting a job at the firm should fill out an application.

> *nonrestrictive*:   Kayla, wanting a job at the firm, filled out an application.

In the second sentence, the participial phrase explains why Kayla filled out an application, but the sentence is clear without it: "Kayla filled out an application"; the phrase *wanting a job at the firm* is therefore not essential and is set off with commas. But without the phrase the first sentence wouldn't make sense: "Anyone should fill out an application"; the phrase *wanting a job at the firm* is essential and is not set off. Questions about restrictive and nonrestrictive elements most often arise with *relative clauses* (see #11-o and #14d); *appositives*, though usually nonrestrictive, can also be restrictive, and some other elements can also be either restrictive or nonrestrictive (see #45b and #46a–b).

48a Restrictive and Nonrestrictive Relative Clauses

Always set off a nonrestrictive relative clause; do not set off restrictive relative clauses:

> She is a woman who likes to travel.

The relative clause is essential and is not set off.

> Alena, who likes to travel, is going to Greece this summer.

Now the relative clause is merely additional—though explanatory—information: it is not essential to the identification of Alena, who has been explicitly named, nor is it essential to the meaning of the main clause. Being nonrestrictive, then, it should be set off. Consider the following pair of sentences:

> *incorrect*: Students, who are hard-working, should expect much from their education.

> *correct*: Students who are hard-working should expect much from their education.

Set off as nonrestrictive, the relative clause applies to all students, which makes the sentence untrue. Left unpunctuated, the relative clause is restrictive, making the sentence correctly apply only to students who are in fact hard-working.

> The book, which I so badly wanted to read, was not available for download.

> The book which I so badly wanted to read was not available for download.

With the clause set off as nonrestrictive, we must assume that the book has been clearly identified in an earlier sentence. Left unpunctuated, the clause identifies "The book" as the particular one the speaker wanted to read but which was not available.

48a

PROOFREADING TIP

Determining Whether a Clause Is Restrictive

If you can use the relative pronoun *that*, you know the clause is restrictive; *that* cannot begin a nonrestrictive clause:

> The book <u>that</u> I wanted to read was not available for download.

Further, if the pronoun can be omitted (see #14d) altogether, the clause is restrictive, as with *that* in the preceding example and *whom* in the following:

> The person [whom] I most admire is the one who works hard and plays hard.

> **PROOFREADING TIP**
>
> **Using *that* and *which* in Relative Clauses**
>
> *That* is much more common than *which* in restrictive clauses. Indeed, some writers prefer to use *which* only in nonrestrictive clauses. But the use of *which* in both nonrestrictive and restrictive clauses is widely accepted across North America.

48b Restrictive and Nonrestrictive Appositives

Always set off a nonrestrictive appositive:

> Maya, <u>our youngest daughter</u>, keeps the lawn mowed all summer.

> Tristan—<u>my current accountant</u>—is very imaginative.

> *King Lear* is a noble work of literature, <u>one that will live in human minds for all time</u>.

> Virginia is going to bring her sister, <u>Vanessa</u>.

In the last example, the comma indicates that Virginia has only the one sister. Left unpunctuated, the appositive would be restrictive, meaning that Virginia has more than one sister and that the particular one she is going to bring is the one named Vanessa.

Don't mistake a restrictive appositive for a nonrestrictive one:

> *incorrect*: The proceedings were opened by union leader, Peter Wong, with remarks attacking the government.

The commas are wrong, since it is only his name, Peter Wong, that clearly identifies the person who opened the proceedings; the appositive is therefore restrictive. But alter the sentence slightly:

> The proceedings were opened by the union's leader, Peter Wong, with remarks attacking the government.

Now the phrase *the union's leader*, with its definite article, identifies the person; the name itself, *Peter Wong*, is only incidental information and is therefore nonrestrictive. This example works only if the union has been introduced in an earlier sentence.

> *incorrect*: According to spokesperson, Janina Fraser, the economy is improving daily.

revised: According to spokesperson Janina Fraser, the
economy is improving daily.

revised: According to the spokesperson, Janina Fraser, the
economy is improving daily.

The definite article makes all the difference. But even the presence or
absence of the definite article is not always a sure test:

incorrect: One of the best-known mysteries of the sea is that of
the ship, *Mary Celeste*, the disappearance of whose
entire crew has never been satisfactorily explained.

correct: One of the best-known mysteries of the sea is that of
the ship *Mary Celeste*, the disappearance of whose
entire crew has never been satisfactorily explained.

The phrase *the ship* is insufficient identification; the proper name is needed
and is therefore restrictive. This error most often occurs when a proper
name follows a defining or characterizing word or phrase. In the reverse
order, such a phrase is set off as a nonrestrictive appositive:

Janina Fraser, the spokesperson, said the economy is
improving daily.

See #55g for more on restrictive appositives.

48c *Because* Clauses and Phrases

Adverbial clauses or phrases beginning with *because* (or otherwise conveying that sense) can be a problem when they follow an explicit negative.
When *because* follows a negative, punctuate the sentence so that it means
what you want it to:

Mary didn't pass the exam, because she had stayed up all night
studying for it: she was so groggy she couldn't even read the
questions correctly. (She didn't pass.)

Mary didn't pass the exam because she had stayed up all night
studying for it. Last-minute review may have helped, but her
thorough grasp of the material would have enabled her to pass
it without the cramming. (She would have passed anyway.)

Often you can best avoid the possible awkwardness or ambiguity by simply
rephrasing a sentence in which *because* follows a negative.

48c

48d Modifiers with *such as*

Nonrestrictive modifiers beginning with *such as* should be set off with commas:

> Robyn played all kinds of sports, such as hockey, baseball, and lacrosse.

But be careful not to mistake a nonrestrictive *such as* modifier for a restrictive one. Consider the following example:

> Antibiotics, such as penicillin, are ineffective against the disease.

Because the modifier *such as penicillin* is set off, the sentence implies that *all* antibiotics (of which penicillin is an example) are ineffective against the disease. If the commas were removed, the modifier would become restrictive, and the meaning would change: the sentence would imply that only those antibiotics that are like penicillin are ineffective, though other antibiotics might not be.

48d

Exercise 48 Punctuating Nonrestrictive Elements

Decide whether the underlined elements in the following sentences are restrictive or nonrestrictive and insert punctuation as required.

1. The student who takes studying seriously is the one who is most likely to succeed.
2. The novels I like best are those page-turners you can buy at the drugstore.
3. This movie which was produced on a very low budget was a popular success.
4. Whitehorse the capital of Yukon has a thriving arts community.
5. Pliny the Elder wrote about some interesting herbal remedies involving bat dung and garlic.
6. Sentence interrupters such as parenthetical definitions can be set off with commas.
7. Michel Tremblay the playwright is a Quebec writer with a national reputation.
8. *The Orenda* written by Joseph Boyden is set in the early seventeenth century.
9. My twin brother Greg is very proud of his partner Martin.
10. In the view of the small-town newspaper editor James Borred the three-metre worm was nothing to get excited about.

Between Items in a Series

49a Commas

Generally, use commas between words, phrases, or clauses in a series of three or more:

> He speaks English, French, Spanish, and Hindi.

> He stirred the sauce frequently, carefully, and hungrily.

> She promised the voters to cut taxes, to limit government spending, and to improve transportation.

> Carmen explained that she had visited the art gallery, that she had walked in the park, and that eventually she had gone to a movie.

Note that some writers prefer to omit the final comma (known as the "Oxford comma" or the "serial comma"), but this common practice can be misleading. The pause created by this comma gives your sentences a better rhythm, and it helps you avoid the kind of possible confusion apparent in sentences like these:

> The manufacturers sent us shirts, wash-and-wear slacks and shoes. (The shoes were wash-and-wear?)

> They prided themselves on having a large and bright kitchen, a productive vegetable garden, a large recreation room with a huge fireplace and a large pond. (The pond was in the recreation room?)

> The Speech from the Throne discussed international trade, improvements in transportation, slowing down inflation and emergency-response measures. (Do we want to slow down emergency-response measures?)

Also see #49e, for information about special cases involving commas between adjectives.

49b Semicolons

If the phrases or clauses in a series are unusually long or contain other internal punctuation, you might want to separate them with semicolons rather than commas:

> How wonderful it is to awaken in the morning when the birds are clamouring in the trees; to see the bright light of a summer

49b

> morning streaming into the room; to realize, with a sudden
> flash of joy, that it is Sunday and that this perfect morning is
> completely yours; and then to loaf in a deck chair without a
> thought of tomorrow.

> Fredericton, New Brunswick; Charlottetown, Prince Edward
> Island; and St. John's, Newfoundland and Labrador are all major
> cities in Atlantic Canada.

49c Dashes

You can also emphasize items in a series by putting dashes between them—but don't do it often. The sharpness of the breaks greatly heightens the effect of a series:

> Rising taxes—rising insurance rates—rising gas costs—
> skyrocketing food prices: it is becoming more and more difficult
> to live decently and still keep within a budget.

Here the omission of *and* before the final item, together with the repetition and parallel structure, heightens the stylistic effect by adding to the stridency; even the colon adds its touch. But dashes can also be effective in a quieter context:

> Upon rounding the bend we were confronted with a
> breathtaking panorama of lush valleys with meandering
> streams—flower-covered slopes—great rocks and trees—and,
> overtopping all, the mighty peaks with their hoods of snow.

49d Colons

Colons, too, can be used in a series but even more rarely than dashes. Colons add emphasis because they are unusual, but mainly their anticipatory nature produces a cumulative effect suitable when successive items in a series build to a climax:

> He held on: he persevered: he fought back: and eventually he
> won out, regardless of the punishing obstacles.

> It blew: it rained: it hailed: it sleeted: it even snowed—it was a
> most unusual June even for Medicine Hat.

(Note how the dash in the last example prepares for the final clause.)

49e Series of Adjectives

Use commas between two or more adjectives preceding a noun if they are parallel, each modifying the noun itself; do not put commas between adjectives that are not parallel:

He is an intelligent, dedicated, ambitious student.

She is a tall young woman.

She wore new black leather boots, a long red coat, and a scarf with blue, white, and grey stripes.

In the first sentence, each adjective modifies *student*. In the second, *tall* mod–ifies *young woman*; it is a *young woman* who is *tall*, not a *woman* who is *tall* and *young*. In the third, *new* modifies *black leather boots*, *black* modifies *leather boots*, and *long* modifies *red coat*; *blue*, *white*, and *grey* all separately modify *stripes*.

PROOFREADING TIP

Deciding When to Separate Adjectives with a Comma

If you're having trouble telling whether or not two or more adjectives are parallel, try inserting *and* between them. If *and* sounds logical there, the adjectives are probably parallel and should be separated by a comma; if *and* doesn't seem to work, a comma won't either. Another test is to change the order of the adjectives. If it sounds odd to say *a felt purple hat* instead of *a purple felt hat*, then the adjectives probably aren't parallel. Finally, remember that no comma is needed after a number (*three blind mice*) or after common adjectives for size or age (*tall young woman*; *long red coat*; *new brick house*). See also #54e.

49e

Exercise 49 Punctuating Series

Punctuate the following sentences as necessary.

1. The things I expected from my education were maturity spiritual growth and a career.
2. Parsnips sardines and peanut butter were the ingredients for my new culinary creation.
3. The cheerful conscientious young man wore a tight purple shirt embossed with a white drawing of a skull and crossbones very long black dirty trousers and a dangling silver necklace consisting of various small sharp household objects.
4. The smiling cherubic baby with the chubby cheeks soon began to crawl fall and squall.
5. The recital was over the audience leapt to their feet they applauded wildly and the pianist pleased with his performance bowed.

Punctuation Marks That Come in Pairs

Punctuating Sentence Interrupters

Sentence interrupters are parenthetical elements—words, phrases, or clauses—that interrupt the syntax of a sentence. Although we discuss some of these under other headings, here we stress two points: (1) interrupters are set off at *both* ends; (2) you can choose from among three kinds of punctuation marks to set them off: a pair of commas, a pair of dashes, or a pair of parentheses.

50a Interrupters Set Off with Commas

Set off light, ordinary interrupters with a pair of commas:

> Thank you, <u>Omar</u>, for this much needed advice and the martini. (noun of address)

> Could you be persuaded to consider this money as, <u>well</u>, a loan? (mild interjection)

> Robert Munsch, <u>a children's book author</u>, is a favourite with the preteen crowd. (nonrestrictive appositive phrase)

> Mr. Hao, <u>feeling elated</u>, left the judge's office. (participial phrase)

> At least one science course, <u>such as botany or astronomy</u>, is required of all students. (prepositional phrase of example)

> You may, <u>on the other hand</u>, find it more convenient to take a Web-based course. (transitional prepositional phrase)

> It was, <u>all things considered</u>, a successful concert. (absolute phrase)

> Grandparents, <u>who are wise and loving</u>, should be allowed to spend a lot of time with their grandchildren. (nonrestrictive relative clause)

> This document, <u>the lawyer says</u>, will complete the contract. (explanatory clause)

> Jet lag, <u>it now occurs to me</u>, may be responsible for our falling asleep at dinner. (clause expressing afterthought)

50b Interrupters Set Off with Dashes

Use a pair of dashes to set off abrupt interrupters or other interrupters that you wish to emphasize. An interrupter that sharply breaks the syntax of a sentence will often be emphatic for that very reason, and dashes will be appropriate to set it off:

> The increase in enrolment—over fifty per cent—demonstrates the success of our program.

> The stockholders who voted for him—quite a sizable group—were obviously dissatisfied with our recent conduct of the business.

> He told me—believe this or not!—that he would never eat fast food again.

> Stephen Jay Gould—the well-known scientist—began his career by studying snails.

In the last example, commas would suffice, but dashes work well because of both the length and the content of the appositive. Wherever you want emphasis or a different tone, you can use dashes where commas would ordinarily serve:

> The employee of the year—Denise Dione—was delighted to receive the prize.

> The modern age—as we all know—is a noisy age.

Dashes are also useful to set off an interrupter consisting of a series with its own internal commas:

> *confusing*: Sentence interrupters are parenthetical elements, words, phrases, or clauses, that interrupt the syntax of a sentence.

> *clear*: Sentence interrupters are parenthetical elements—words, phrases, or clauses—that interrupt the syntax of a sentence.

50c Interrupters Set Off with Parentheses

Use parentheses to set off abrupt interrupters or other interrupters that you wish to de-emphasize; often interrupters that could be emphatic can be played down in order to emphasize the other parts of a sentence:

> The stockholders who voted for him (quite a sizable group) were obviously dissatisfied with our recent conduct of the business.

It is not possible at this time (it is far too early in the growing season) to predict with any confidence just what the crop yield will be.

Speculation (I mean this in its pejorative sense) is not a safe foundation for a business enterprise.

Some extreme sports (hang-gliding, for example) involve unusually high insurance claims.

By de-emphasizing something striking or unexpected, parentheses can also achieve an effect similar to that of dashes, though by an ironic tone rather than an insistent one.

50c

PROOFREADING TIP
Punctuation Marks That Occur in Pairs

Remember, punctuation marks that set off sentence interrupters come in pairs. If you put down an opening parenthesis you shouldn't omit the closing one. But sometimes writers accidentally omit the second dash or—especially—the second comma. Reading aloud, perhaps with exaggerated pauses, can help you spot that a mark is missing.

Exercise 50 Punctuating Sentence Interrupters

Set off the underlined interrupters with commas, dashes, or parentheses. Be prepared to defend your choices.

1. It was seven o'clock in the evening <u>a mild autumn evening</u> and the crickets were beginning to chirp.
2. No one <u>at least no one who was present</u> wanted to disagree with the speaker's position.
3. Early one Sunday morning <u>a morning I will never forget</u> the phone rang unexpectedly.
4. Since it was only a mild interjection <u>no more than a barely audible snort from the back of the room</u> he went on with scarcely a pause and finished his speech.
5. And then suddenly <u>out of the blue and into my head</u> came the only possible answer.

51 Parentheses ( )

Parentheses have three principal functions in non-technical writing: (1) to set off certain kinds of interrupters (see #50c), (2) to enclose cross-reference information within a sentence, as we just did and as we do throughout this book, and (3) to enclose numerals or letters setting up a list or series, as we do in this sentence. Note that if a complete sentence is enclosed in parentheses within another sentence (here is an example of such an insertion), it needs neither an opening capital letter nor a closing period. Note also that if a comma or other mark is called for by the sentence (as in the preceding sentence, and in this one), it comes *after* the closing parenthesis, not before the opening one. Exclamation points and question marks go inside the parenthesis only if they are a part of what is enclosed. (When an entire sentence or more is enclosed, the terminal mark of course comes inside the parenthesis—as does the period at the end of this sentence.)

52 Brackets [ ]

Brackets (often referred to as "square brackets," since some people use the term *brackets* also to refer to parentheses) are used primarily to enclose something inserted in a direct quotation (see #54j). And if you have to put parentheses inside parentheses—as in a footnote or a bibliographical entry—change the inner ones to brackets.

53 End Punctuation: Period, Question Mark, and Exclamation Point

The end of every sentence must be marked with a period, a question mark, or an exclamation point. The period is the most common terminal punctuation; it ends the vast majority of sentences. The question mark is used to end direct questions or statements that are intended as questions. The exclamation point is used to end sentences that express strong emotion, emphatic surprise, or even emphatic query. Sometimes you will need to consider just what effect you want to achieve. Note, for example, the different effects of the following; in each instance, the end punctuation dictates the tone of voice and distribution of emphasis and pitch with which the sentence would be said aloud:

We won. (matter-of-fact)

We won! (surprised or emphatic)

We won? (skeptical or surprised)

53a Period .

Use a **period** to mark the end of statements and neutral commands:

> Some Canadians celebrate New Year's Day by taking a "polar bear" swim in ice-cold bodies of water.

> Roger Ebert, the beloved film reviewer, died in 2013.

> Don't believe everything you read on the Internet.

Use a period after most abbreviations:

abbr.	Mr.	Ms.	Dr.	Jr.
Ph.D.	B.A.	St.	Mt.	etc.

Generally use a period in abbreviated place names:

B.C.	P.E.I.	Nfld.	N.Y.	Mass.

But note that two-letter postal abbreviations do not require periods:

BC	PE	NL	NY	MA

Periods are not used after metric and other symbols (unless these symbols occur at the end of a sentence):

cm	km	kg	mc^2	ml
kJ	C	Hz	Au	Zr

Periods are often omitted with initials, especially of groups or organizations, and especially if the initials are acronyms—that is, a group of initials pronounced as words (AIDS, JPEG, NATO):

UN	WHO	EU	NASA	NHL
RCMP	RAF	CBC	MLA	APA
TV	MP	HTML	FAQ	PTSD

When in doubt, consult a good dictionary. If there is more than one acceptable usage, be consistent: stick with the one you choose.

PROOFREADING TIP

On Abbreviations and Periods

(1) Although *Ms.* is not a true abbreviation, it is usually followed by a period.

(2) Some Canadian writers and publishers follow the British convention of omitting the period after abbreviations that include the first and last letter of the abbreviated word: *Mr, Mrs, Dr, Jr, St,* etc.

(3) If an abbreviation falls at the end of a sentence, as it does in the previous sentence, the period following the abbreviation serves as the sentence's period.

53b Question Mark ?

Use a **question mark** at the end of direct questions:

53b

> Who is the greatest poet of all time?

> When will the lease expire?

Do not use a question mark at the end of an indirect question: see #55i.

Note that a question mark is necessary after questions that aren't phrased in the usual interrogative way (as might occur if you were writing dialogue):

> You're leaving so early? (i.e., "Are you leaving so early?")

> You want him to accompany you? (i.e., "Do you want him to accompany you?")

A question appearing as a sentence interrupter still needs a question mark at its end:

> I went back to the beginning—what else could I do?—and tried to get it right the second time.

> The man in the scuba outfit (what was his name again?) took a rear seat.

Since such interrupters are necessarily abrupt, dashes or parentheses are the appropriate marks to set them off.

See also #11t.

53c Exclamation Point !

Use an **exclamation point** after an emphatic statement or after an expression of emphatic surprise, emphatic query, or strong emotion:

> She came in first, yet it was only her second time in professional competition!

> What a great guy!

> You don't say so!

> Isn't it beautiful today!

> Not again!

> Wow!

Occasionally an exclamation point may be doubled or tripled for emphasis. It may even follow a question mark, to emphasize the writer's or speaker's disbelief:

> She said what?!

> You bought what?! A giraffe?! What were you thinking?!

This device should not be used in formal and academic writing.

PROOFREADING TIP

On Using Exclamation Points

Use exclamation points sparingly, if at all, in formal writing. Achieve your desired emphasis by other means: see #29j.

PROOFREADING TIP

Ending a Sentence with a Dash or an Ellipsis

The dash and the three dots of an ellipsis (see #54i) are sometimes used at the end of a sentence, especially in dialogue or at the end of a paragraph or a chapter in order to indicate a pause, a fading away, or an interruption, or to create mild suspense.

Punctuation with Quotations: Using Quotation Marks " "

There are two kinds of quotation: dialogue or direct speech (such as you might find in a story, novel, or nonfiction narrative or other essay) and verbatim quotation from a published work or other source (as in a research paper). For the use of quotation marks around titles, see #59b–c.

54a Direct Speech
Enclose all direct speech in quotation marks:

> I remember hearing my mother say to my absentminded father, "Henry, why is the newspaper in the fridge?"

In written dialogue, it is conventional to begin a new paragraph each time the speaker changes:

> "Henry," she said, a note of exasperation in her voice, "why is the newspaper in the fridge?"
> "Oh, yes," he replied. "The fish is wrapped in it."
> She examined it. "Well, there may have been a fish in it once, but there is no fish in it now."

54b

Even when passages of direct speech are incomplete, the part that is verbatim should be enclosed in quotation marks:

> After only two weeks, he said he was "fed up" and that he was "going to look for a more interesting job."

54b Direct Quotation from a Source
Enclose in quotation marks any direct quotation from another source that you run into your own text:

> According to Margaret Atwood in *Negotiating with the Dead*, "writing has to do with darkness, and a desire or perhaps a compulsion to enter it, and, with luck, to illuminate it, and to bring something back out to the light."

Even if you choose to use only a few words or phrases from another source, the quoted words must be enclosed in quotation marks:

> According to Margaret Atwood in *Negotiating with the Dead*, "writing has to do with darkness" and the desire to "illuminate" that darkness.

1. Prose

Prose quotations of no more than four lines are normally run into the text. Quotations of more than four lines should be treated as "block" quotations: they should begin on a new line and be indented approximately ten spaces:

> In *A Short History of Progress*, Ronald Wright compares contemporary civilization to a speeding ship:
>
>> Our civilization, which subsumes most of its predecessors, is a great ship steaming at speed into the future. It travels faster, further, and more laden than any before. We may not be able to foresee every reef and hazard, but by reading her compass bearing and headway, by understanding her design, her safety record, and the abilities of her crew, we can, I think, plot a wise course between the narrows and bergs looming ahead.

Do not place quotation marks around a block quotation, but do reproduce any quotation marks that appear in the original:

> Budgets can be important. As Dickens has Mr. Micawber say in *David Copperfield*,
>
>> "Annual income twenty pounds, annual expenditure nineteen nineteen six, result happiness. Annual income twenty pounds, annual expenditure twenty pounds ought and six, result misery."

If you're quoting only a single paragraph or part of a paragraph, do not include the paragraph indentation. If you are quoting a passage that is longer than one paragraph, include the indentations for the second and subsequent paragraphs; use three additional spaces for an indentation.

2. Poetry

A quotation of one, two, or three lines of poetry is generally run into your text. When you run in more than one line of poetry, indicate the line breaks with a slash mark or virgule, with a space on each side:

> Dante's spiritual journey begins in the woods: "Midway this way of life, we're bound upon / I woke to find myself in a dark wood / Where the right road was wholly lost and gone."

54b

Set off quotations of four or more lines of poetry in the same way you would set off a block quotation. If you want to give special emphasis to shorter quotations of two or three lines, you may set them off as well.

54c Single Quotation Marks: Quotation Within Quotation ' '

Put single quotation marks around a quotation that occurs within another quotation; this is the only standard use for single quotation marks in North America:

> In Joseph Conrad's *Heart of Darkness*, after a leisurely setting
>
> of the scene by the unnamed narrator, the drama begins when
>
> the character who is to be the principal narrator first speaks:
>
> "'And this also,' said Marlow suddenly, 'has been one of the
>
> dark places of the earth.'"

(Note, however, that in British usage single quotation marks appear around the main quotation and double quotation marks are used only for quotations within quotations.)

54d With Verbs of Speaking Before Quotations

When verbs of speaking precede a quotation, they are usually followed by commas:

> Helen said, "There is something nasty growing in my fridge."

> Adriana fumbled around in the dark and asked, "Now where are the matches?"

(Note that when a quotation ends a sentence, its own terminal punctuation serves also as that of the sentence.)

With short or emphatic quotations, commas often aren't necessary:

> He said "Hold your horses," so we waited a little longer.

> Someone shouted "Fire!" and we all headed for the exits.

Again, punctuate a sentence the way you want it to be heard; your sense of its rhythm should help you decide.

If a quotation is long, especially if it consists of more than one sentence, or if the context is formal, a colon will probably be more appropriate than a comma to introduce it:

> When the movie was over, Sofia turned to her companion and said: "We have wasted ninety minutes of our lives. The movie

> lacked an intelligent plot, sympathetic characters, and an interesting setting. Even the soundtrack was pathetic."

If the introductory element is itself an independent clause, then a colon or period must be used:

> Sofia turned to her companion and spoke: "What a waste of time."

Spoke, unlike *said*, is here an intransitive verb.

If you work a quotation into your own syntax, don't use even a comma to introduce it:

> It is often said that "[s]ticks and stones may break my bones, but words will never hurt me"—a singularly inaccurate notion.

54e

54e With Verbs of Speaking After Quotations

If a verb of speaking or a subject–verb combination follows a quotation, it is usually set off by a comma placed inside the closing quotation mark:

> "You attract what you manifest in your personality," said the speaker.

> "I think there's a fly in my soup," she muttered.

But if the quotation ends with a question mark or an exclamation point, no other punctuation is added:

> "What time is it?" asked Francis, looking up.

> "I insist that I be heard!" he shouted.

If the clause containing the verb of speaking interrupts the quotation, it should be preceded by a comma and followed by whatever mark is called for by the syntax and the sense. For example,

> "Since it's such a long drive," he said, "we'd better get an early start."

> "It's a long drive," he argued; "therefore I think we should start early."

> "It's a very long way," he insisted. "We should start as early as possible."

54f With Quotations Set Off by Indention

Colons are conventionally used to introduce "block" quotations:

> Jane Austen begins her novel *Pride and Prejudice* with the
> following observation:
>
>> It is a truth universally acknowledged, that a single man
>> in possession of a good fortune must be in want of a wife.
>> However little known the feelings or views of such a man
>> may be on his first entering a neighbourhood, this truth is so
>> well fixed in the minds of the surrounding families, that he is
>> considered as the rightful property of some one or other of
>> their daughters.

54g Words Used in a Special Sense

As we do with the word *block* in #54f above, put quotation marks around
words used in a special sense or words for which you wish to indicate some
qualification:

> What she calls a "ramble" I would call a thirty-kilometre hike.
>
> He had been up in the woods so long he was "bushed," as some
> Canadians might put it.

 PROOFREADING TIP

On the Use of Quotation Marks to Call Attention to Words

Some writers put quotation marks around words referred to as
words, but it is generally better practice to italicize them (see #60c):

> The word *toboggan* comes from a Mi'kmaq word for sled.

Don't put quotation marks around slang terms, clichés, and the
like. If a word or phrase is so weak or inappropriate that you have
to apologize for it, you shouldn't be using it in the first place. And
the last thing such a term needs is to have attention called to it.
Even if a slang term is appropriate, putting quotation marks around
it implicitly insults readers by presuming that they won't recognize slang when they see it. And avoid using quotation marks for
emphasis; they don't work that way.

54h Other Marks with Quotation Marks

Put periods and commas inside closing quotation marks; put semicolons and colons outside them:

> "Knowing how to write well," he said, "can be a source of great pleasure"; and then he added that it had "one other important quality": he identified it simply as "hard work."

(Note, however, that in British usage periods and commas, as well as question marks and exclamation points, also are placed outside quotation marks unless they are part of what is being quoted.)

54i Ellipses for Omissions . . .

If when quoting from a written source you decide to omit one or more words from the middle of the passage you are quoting, indicate the omission with the three spaced periods of an **ellipsis**. For example, if you wanted to quote only part of the passage from Austen quoted in #54f, you might do it like this:

> As Jane Austen wryly observes, "a single man in possession of a . . . fortune must be in want of a wife."

Note that you do not need to indicate an ellipsis at the beginning of a quotation unless the quotation begins with a capital letter and could be mistaken for a complete sentence.

When the ellipsis is preceded by a complete sentence, include the period (or other terminal punctuation) of the original before the ellipsis points. Similarly, if when you omit something from the end of a sentence, what remains is grammatically complete, a period (or question mark or exclamation point, if either of these is more appropriate) goes before the ellipsis. In either case, the terminal punctuation marking the end of the sentence is closed up:

> As Jane Austen wryly observes, "a single man in possession of a good fortune must be in want of a wife. . . . this truth is so well fixed in the minds of the surrounding families, that he is considered as the rightful property of some one or other. . . ."

Other punctuation may also be included before or after the ellipsis if it makes the quoted material clearer:

> However little known the feelings or views of such a man may be . . . , this truth is so well fixed in the minds of the surrounding families.

54i

Three periods can also indicate the omission of one or more entire sentences, or even whole paragraphs. Again, if the sentence preceding the omitted material is grammatically complete, it should end with a period preceding the ellipsis.

An ellipsis should also be used to indicate that material from a quoted line of poetry has been omitted. When quoting four or more lines of poetry, use a row of spaced dots to indicate that one or more entire lines have been omitted:

> E.J. Pratt's epic "Towards the Last Spike" begins:
>
> It was the same world then as now—the same,
>
> Except for little differences of speed
>
> And power, and means to treat myopia.
>
> . . . .
>
> The same, but for new particles of speech. . . .

54j

Note that some instructors may ask that all ellipses added to quotations be enclosed in square brackets. Check with the reader of your work for his or her preference.

PROOFREADING TIP

On Ineffective Omission of Material from a Quotation

Don't omit material from a quotation in such a way that you distort what the author is saying or destroy the integrity of the syntax. Similarly, don't quote unfairly "out of context"; for example, if an author qualifies a statement in some way, don't quote the statement as if it were unqualified.

54j Brackets for Additions, Changes, and Comments [ ]

Keep such changes to a minimum, but enclose in square brackets any editorial addition or change you find it necessary to make within a quotation—for example, a clarifying fact or a change in tense to make the quoted material fit the syntax of your sentence:

> The author states that "the following year [2010] marked a turning point in [his] life."
>
> One of my friends wrote me that her "feelings about the subject [were] similar to" mine.

Use the word *sic* (Latin for *thus*) in brackets to indicate that an error in the quotation occurs in the original:

> One of my friends wrote me: "My feelings about the subject are similiar [*sic*] to yours."

See also #78. For further information on quotations, see the most recent edition of the *MLA Handbook for Writers of Research Papers*.

55 Avoiding Common Errors in Punctuation

55a Unwanted Comma Between Subject and Verb

Generally, do not put a comma between a subject and its verb unless some intervening element calls for punctuation:

> ***no p*:** His enthusiasm for the project and his desire to be of help, led him to add his name to the list of volunteers.

Don't be misled by the length of a compound subject. The comma after *help* in the last example is just as wrong as the comma in the following sentence:

> ***no p*:** Kiera, addressed the class.

But if some intervening element, for example an appositive or a participial phrase, requires setting off, use a *pair* of punctuation marks (see #50):

> His enthusiasm for the project and his desire to be of help, both strongly felt, led him to add his name to the list of volunteers.

> Kiera—the first presenter—addressed the class.

55b Unwanted Comma Between Verb and Object or Complement

Although in Jane Austen's time it was conventional to place a comma before a clause beginning with *that*, today this practice is considered an error. Do not put a comma between a verb and its object or complement unless some intervening element calls for punctuation. Especially, don't mistakenly assume that a clause opening with *that* always needs a comma before it:

> ***no p*:** Hafiz realized, that he could no longer keep his eyes open.

The noun clause beginning with *that* is the direct object of the verb *realized* and should not be separated from it. Only if an interrupter requires setting

55b

off should there be any punctuation:

> Hafiz realized, moreover, that he could no longer keep his
> eyes open.

> Hafiz realized, as he tried once again to read the paragraph,
> that he could no longer keep his eyes open.

Another example:

> *no p*: Ottawa's principal claim to fame is, that it has the
> world's longest skating rink.

Here the comma intrudes between the linking verb *is* and its complement, the predicate noun consisting of a *that* clause.

55c Unwanted Comma After Last Adjective of a Series
Do not put a comma between the last adjective of a series and the noun it modifies:

> *p*: How could anyone fail to be impressed by such an
> intelligent, outspoken, resourceful, fellow as Jonathan is?

The comma after *resourceful* is wrong, though it may briefly feel right because a certain rhythm has been established and because there is no *and* before the last of the three adjectives.

55d Unwanted Comma Between Coordinated Words and Phrases
Generally, don't put a comma between words and phrases joined by a coordinating conjunction; use a comma only when the coordinate elements are clauses (see #44a):

> *no p*: The dog and cat circled each other warily, and then went
> off in opposite directions.

> *no p*: I was a long way from home, and didn't know how to get
> there.

> *no p*: She was not only intelligent, but also very kind.

The commas in these three sentences are all unnecessary. Sometimes a writer uses such a comma for a mild emphasis, but if you want an emphatic pause a dash will probably work better:

> The dog and cat circled each other warily—and then went off in

opposite directions.

Or the sentence can be slightly revised in order to gain the emphasis:

I was a long way from home, and I had no idea how to
get there.

She was not only intelligent; she was also very kind.

55e Commas with Emphatic Repetition

If the two elements joined by a conjunction constitute an emphatic repetition, a comma is sometimes optional:

I wanted not only to win, but to win overwhelmingly.

This sentence would be equally correct and effective without the comma. But in the following sentence the comma is necessary:

It was an object of beauty, and of beauty most spectacular.

Again, sounding a sentence over to yourself will sometimes help you decide.

55f Unwanted Comma with Short Introductory or Parenthetical Element

Generally, do not set off introductory elements or interrupters that are very short, that are not really parenthetical, or that are so slightly parenthetical that you feel no pause when reading them:

no p: Perhaps, she was trying to tell us something.

no p: But, it was not a case of mistaken identity.

no p: Therefore, he put on his mukluks.

no p: We asked if we could try it out, for a week, to see if we
really liked it.

When the pause is strong, however, be sure to set the element off:

It was only then, after the very formal dinner, that we were all
able to relax.

Often such commas are optional, depending on the pattern of intonation the writer wants:

In Canada(,) the change of the seasons is sharply evident.

In Canada(,) as elsewhere, money talks.

Last year(,) we went to Quebec City.

The committee(,) therefore(,) decided to table the motion.

After dinner(,) we all went for a walk.

As she walked(,) she thought of her childhood in Dartmouth.

Sometimes such a comma is necessary to prevent misreading:

incorrect: After eating the cat Irene gave me jumped out the window.

revised: After eating, the cat Irene gave me jumped out the window.

See also #46a.

55g Unwanted Comma with Restrictive Appositive

Don't incorrectly set off proper nouns and titles of literary works as nonrestrictive appositives (see #48b). For instance, it's "Mordecai Richler's novel *Barney's Version*," not "Mordecai Richler's novel, *Barney's Version*." Richler, after all, wrote more than one novel.

p: In her poem, "Daddy," Sylvia Plath explores her complicated relationship with her father.

p: The home port of the Canadian Coast Guard icebreaker, *Terry Fox*, is St. John's, Newfoundland.

The punctuation makes it sound as though Plath wrote only this one poem and that the *Terry Fox* is the only icebreaker in the Canadian Coast Guard's fleet. The titles are restrictive: if they were removed, the sentences would not be clear. If the context is clear, the explanatory words often aren't needed at all:

In "Daddy" Plath explores . . .

The home port of the *Terry Fox* is . . .

If Sylvia Plath had in fact written only one poem, or if the Canadian Coast Guard had only one icebreaker, it would be correct to set off the title. Similarly, it would be correct to set off a title after referring to an author's "first novel" or the like, since an author, regardless of how many novels she or he has written, can have only one *first* novel. The urge to punctuate before titles of literary works sometimes leads to the error of putting a comma between a possessive and the title.

> ***p*:**   I remember enjoying Elise Partridge's, "To a Flicker Nesting in a Telephone Pole."

55h Unwanted Comma with Indirect Quotation

Do not set off indirect quotations as if they were direct quotations:

> ***no p*:**   The author says, that civilization as we have come to know it is in jeopardy.

> ***no p*:**   If you ask Tomiko she's sure to say, she doesn't want to go.

In an indirect quotation, what was said is being reported, not quoted. If Tomiko is quoted directly, a comma is correct:

> If you ask Tomiko she's sure to say, "I don't want to go."

See also #54a and #54d.

55i Unwanted Question Mark After Indirect Question

Don't put a question mark at the end of indirect questions—questions that are only being reported, not asked directly:

> ***p*:**   I asked what we were doing here?

> ***p*:**   She wanted to find out what had happened in the parking lot?

> ***p*:**   What he asked himself then was how he was going to explain it to the shareholders?

Each of these sentences should end with a period rather than a question mark.

55j Unwanted Semicolon with Subordinate Element

Do not put a semicolon in front of a mere phrase or subordinate clause:

> ***p*:**   They cancelled the meeting; being disappointed at the low turnout.

> ***p*:**   Only about a dozen people showed up; partly because there had been too little publicity and no free muffins.

Those semicolons should be commas. Since a semicolon signals that an *independent* clause is coming, readers are distracted when only a phrase or subordinate clause arrives. If you find yourself trying to avoid comma splices and overshooting in this way, devote some further study to the comma splice (#44e) and to learning how to recognize an independent clause (see #11m–n and p). Similarly, don't put a semicolon between a subordinate clause and an independent clause:

> *p*: After the show, when they got home, tired and with their eardrums ringing; Sheila said she was never going to another musical again.

> *revised*: After the show, when they got home, tired and with their eardrums ringing, Sheila said she was never going to another musical again.

Change the semicolon to a comma. The presence of earlier commas in the sentence doesn't mean that the later one needs promoting to semicolon; there is no danger here of confusing the reader as there sometimes is when a coordinating conjunction is used to join two independent clauses that contain internal punctuation (see #44b).

55k

55k Unwanted Colon After Incomplete Construction

Do not use a colon after an incomplete construction; a colon is appropriate only after an independent clause:

> *p*: She preferred gluten-free foods such as: quinoa, rice, and beans.

The prepositional *such as* needs an object to be complete. Had the phrase been extended to "She preferred such foods as these" or ". . . as the following," it would have been complete, an independent clause, and a colon would have been correct.

> *revised*: She preferred gluten-free foods such as the following: quinoa, rice, and beans.

Here is another example of this common error:

> *p*: His favourite pastimes are: swimming, hiking, and sipping hot chocolate by the fire.

> *revised*: His favourite pastimes are swimming, hiking, and sipping hot chocolate by the fire.

Since the linking verb *are* is incomplete without a complement, the colon is incorrect. Remember in academic writing not to use a colon after a preposition or after a form of the verb *be*. Scientific and business writing does allow for the use of a colon after the verb *be* or a preposition if the colon introduces a list that begins on a separate line.

55-I Unwanted Double Punctuation: Comma or Semicolon with a Dash

Avoid putting a comma or a semicolon together with a dash. Use whichever mark is appropriate.

Review Exercises, Chapter V Punctuation

A. Correcting Punctuation

Correct any errors in punctuation in the following sentences—many of which come from students' papers. You may also want to make other improvements: practise your revising techniques.

1. Oscar Wilde who was known for his wit once famously wrote I can resist anything but temptation.
2. I believe, that for a number of reasons, genetically modified food should be carefully regulated.
3. He was not a frightening poltergeist but an irritating one he hid the remote control and moved the coffee table.
4. Many of Shakespeare's plays are about royalty, as in the Lancastrian tetralogy *Richard II Henry IV (1) Henry IV (2)* and *Henry V.*
5. His childlike features were deceptive as we discovered when the alien from the planet Zotar began to give us detailed instructions on how to build a time machine.
6. When you spend time with close friends you get a different perspective life seems less narrow and serious.
7. With him too, she felt comfortable.
8. I would like to wake up in the morning especially a beautiful morning such as this and not feel the burden of work.
9. The encounter that deepened his feelings, occurred at age nine.
10. Therefore one must always remember to be polite when encountering a ghostly stranger in a train station.
11. This then, was the plan. Return to our campsite for the night, and tackle Black Tusk the next morning.
12. I joined in; dancing haltingly at first and then more confidently.
13. As a person exercises the muscle of the heart becomes stronger therefore, it can pump more blood while beating less.

55-I

14. However I always wake up the next day with the worst sort of headache the emotional headache.

15. The meal started with grilled artichokes followed by mushroom ravioli and finished with a lemon tart.

16. It was after all, exactly what he had asked for.

17. Crisp memories of laughing eyes, loving smiles and peaceful easy feelings still linger.

18. A computer hard drive is easy to install just remember to ground yourself before you touch the hard drive.

19. Did Sheila Watson write *The Double Hook*.

20. Eighteenth-century mathematicians unlike their counterparts in the seventeenth century, were able to develop both pure and applied mathematics. Leonhard Euler, a notable genius in both these fields contributed invaluably to every branch of mathematics.

21. Another classic film, that explores the effects of war on individual lives, is *Casablanca*.

22. It began to rain, nevertheless, since they were on the sixteenth fairway they went ahead and finished the round.

23. When the tyrant stood up and said you rascals you will get what you deserve a brick fell on his head.

24. To me this indicates, that although he remembers the details of the events he describes, there is an enormous space of time, between the events and the present, that makes the details intangible.

25. The sounds of the sonata are soft and never harsh which helps create the melancholy mood.

B. Using Punctuation

Punctuate the following sentences as you think best, indicating possible alternatives and places where you think punctuation is optional. Be prepared to defend your choices. Some sentences may not need punctuating.

1. When the meeting ended he went to a pub for a drink.

2. Doggedly Peyvand finished his essay.

3. Soon those parts became unappealing and she decided to fire her current agent.

4. In 2010 he moved to Halifax Nova Scotia and bought a small reputable art gallery specializing in expensive striking white minimalist sculpture.

55-1

5. She felt uneasy about the trip yet she knew she had to go and meet her sister flying in from Hong Kong.

6. I took the book that I didn't like back to the library but I still had to pay a fine.

7. Mary Winnie and Cora came to the party together but left separately.

8. He had a broad engaging smile even though he had three teeth missing.

9. Having heard all she wanted Bridget walked out of the meeting.

10. But once you've taken the first few steps the rest will naturally be easy.

11. The poem was short the novel long the poem was good the novel better.

12. Perhaps we can still think of some way out of this mess.

13. But Canadians don't think that way they prefer to sit back and wait.

55-1

14. Last summer we visited Hastings the site of the battle won by William the Conqueror in 1066.

15. A warm bath a good book and freshly laundered sheets were all she wanted.

16. There are only three vegetables I can't tolerate turnips turnips and turnips.

17. In the good old days the doctor a specialist in family practice made house calls all morning.

18. August 16 1977 is when Elvis Presley died.

19. He had to finish the novel quickly or he wouldn't get his advance.

20. We arrived we ate we partook in boring conversation we departed and that's all there was to the evening.

21. You must plan your budget carefully in times of inflation so remember to buy lottery tickets.

22. She is the only woman I know who wears pantyhose every day whatever the season.

23. His several hobbies were stamp collecting woodworking chess and fishing.

24. The two opponents settled the question amicably at the meeting and then went home to write nasty letters to each other and to the editor of the local newspaper.

25. He would rather make up a lie than stick to the boring truth that was his downfall

VI

Mechanics and Spelling

Introduction: The Conventions of Mechanics and Spelling

To communicate clearly, you must follow not only the conventions of grammar and punctuation but also the conventions of spelling and mechanics. Why? Consider, for example, what might happen if you were to break from spelling conventions and spell the word *cat* as *kat*. Your readers would probably understand you, but they would wonder why you had strayed from the conventional spelling, and to that extent you would have lost touch with them. Mechanical issues such as poor formatting or awkward use of italics can be equally distracting. In either case, by deviating from the standard conventions, you would be defeating your purpose: clear and effective communication.

This chapter offers some practical advice on how to follow standard conventions of mechanics and spelling. By following these conventions, you will add consistency, clarity, and a sense of professionalism to your writing. If you have trouble with spelling, you will find the advice on spelling rules—in section #62—particularly valuable.

(56) Formatting an Essay

In most cases, you will be required to prepare your essay using word-processing software. Make sure to save your work frequently, and always create backup files. As you format your essay, keep in mind that your aim is to produce a document with a professional appearance. Unless directed otherwise, follow these conventions:

1. Use a plain, readable font (12-point Times New Roman or 10-point Arial). Do not try to spruce up your essay with fancy fonts: these will only detract from the professional appearance of your work.

2. Double-space your essay throughout and leave margins of about 1 inch (2.5 cm) on all four sides of the page. Set the margins either fully justified or justified flush left with a ragged (i.e., unjustified) right-hand margin. Many writers prefer the left-align option because full justification may cause inconsistent spacing.

3. Label all pages after a title page in the top right-hand corner. Include your surname before the page number, as a precaution against misplaced pages. Most word-processing software will enable you to generate these "headers" automatically. Page numbers should be set as Arabic numerals, without periods, dashes, slashes, circles, or other decorations.

4. For a long essay or research paper, begin about 1 inch (2.5 cm) from the top of the page, at the left margin, and on separate double-spaced lines put your name, your instructor's name, the course number, and the date of submission; then double-space again and put the title, centred. (For an illustration, see the sample research paper at the end of #80a.) If you wish or are instructed to use a separate title page, centre the title about 1 inch (2.5 cm) from the top of the first page following the title page. (For the format of a title page, see the sample research paper at the end of #80b.)

5. Set the title in standard font size and in upper- and lowercase roman letters, making sure to capitalize the title correctly (see #58m). Do not put the whole title in capital letters or in boldface type, and do not underline it or put a period after it. Do not put your title in quotation marks (unless it is in fact a quotation); if it includes the title of a poem, story, book, etc., or a ship's name, use italics or quotation marks appropriately (see #59). Do not use the title of a published work by itself as your own title. Here are some examples of effective titles:

> The Structure of Dennis Lee's "Civil Elegies"
>
> Altered States: Addiction and Perception in Boyden's "Painted Tongue"
>
> Of Pigoons and Wolvogs: Wildlife in *Oryx and Crake*
>
> "How Are the Mighty Fallen": The Sinking of the *Titanic*

6. Indent the first line of each paragraph one tab length (approximately five spaces). Do not leave extra space between paragraphs. Indent long block quotations two tab lengths (approximately ten spaces). Do not leave any additional space before or after a double-spaced block quotation.

7. Leave only one space after any terminal punctuation, and remember to leave spaces before and after each of the three dots of an ellipsis (see #54i). Use two unspaced hyphens to make a dash, with no space before or after them; most word-processing software will automatically convert two hyphens to a dash.

8. Generally, do not divide words at the end of a line. The word-wrap feature of your word-processing software should automatically move a word that might otherwise be divided to the beginning of the next line. If, for some reason, you do need to divide a word, make sure you do so between syllables. (If you are uncertain, check your dictionary for the word's syllabication.)

56

9. Print your document on plain white recycled paper of good quality, 8.5 by 11 inches (21 by 28 cm). Use only one side of each page. Make sure there is plenty of ink in the cartridge before you press "print."

10. If after proofreading your hard copy you decide that you have to make changes, open the file, make the appropriate emendations, save the changes, and reprint the page or pages you have revised.

11. Fasten the pages of your essay together with a paper clip. Do not use a staple. If your essay is quite long, you may want to enclose it in a folder.

If you are preparing a handwritten document, as may be the case for an in-class essay or an examination, use a format similar to what you would create using word-processing software. Write on every other line, using blue or black ink, and write as legibly as possible. Use lined paper with clean edges. To change or delete a word or short phrase, draw a single horizontal line through it and write the new word or phrase, if any, above it. If you wish to insert a word or short phrase, place a caret (‸) *below* the line at the point of insertion and write the addition *above* the line. If you wish to start a new paragraph where you haven't indented, put the paragraph symbol (¶) in the left margin and insert a caret where you want the new paragraph to begin. If you wish to cancel a paragraph indentation, write "No ¶" in the left margin. (See the list of proofreading and marking symbols in appendix 3 for more marks you might want to use to indicate changes to a handwritten essay.)

56

PROOFREADING TIP

On Breaking a Web Address at the End of a Line

If a web address (also known as a *URL*, or *uniform resource locator*) needs to be spread over two lines, you may need to manually insert a break so that the division does not interrupt an important component of the address. When this is the case, the break should appear *after* one of the slashes in the web address:

> Nick Walker's article "Crowdsourcing Bird Science" is available online at http://www.canadiangeographic.ca/ magazine/oct13/citizen_scientist_birder.asp.

Do not introduce a hyphen to indicate the break, for it may appear as though the hyphen is part of the address.

(57) Abbreviations

br Abbreviations are expected in technical and scientific writing, legal writing, business writing, memos, reports, reference works, bibliographies and works cited lists, footnotes, tables and charts, and sometimes in journalism. The following relatively few kinds are in common use. (See also the box that lists some common scholarly abbreviations on pages 499–500.)

57a Titles Before Proper Names

The following abbreviations can be used with or without initials or given names: *Mr., Mrs., Ms., M., Mme., Mlle., Dr.,* and *St.*:

Mr. Eng	Mr. Marc Ramsay
Mrs. Sharma	Mrs. L.W. Smith
Ms. Bostan	Ms. Tazim Khan
M. Joubert	M. Stéphane Dion
Mme. Girard	Mme. Nathalie Gagnon
Mlle. Sevigny	Mlle. R. Pelletier
Dr. Grewal	Dr. P. Francis Fairchild
St. Beatrice	St. Francis Xavier

In informal writing, abbreviations of professional or honorific titles can also be used, but only before proper names with initials or given names:

Prof. Hana Jamalali (*but* Professor Jamalali)

Sen. H.C. Tsui (*but* Senator Tsui)

Gov. Gen. David Johnston (*but* Governor General Johnston)

Rev. Lois Wilson (*more formally*, the Reverend Lois Wilson)

Hon. Ujjal Dosanjh (*more formally*, the Honourable Ujjal Dosanjh, the Honourable Mr. Dosanjh)

In formal writing, always spell out these and similar titles.

57b Titles and Degrees After Proper Names

David Adams, M.D. (*but not* Dr. David Adams, M.D.)

Claire T. McFadden, D.D.S.

Martin Luther King, Jr.

Eva-Marie Kröller, Ph.D., F.R.S.C.

Academic degrees not following a name may also be abbreviated:

Shirley is working toward her B.A.

Amir is working on his M.A. thesis.

57c Standard Words and Abbreviations Used with Dates and Numerals

720 B.C.E. (*or* 720 B.C., *or* 720 B.P.)

231 C.E. (*or* A.D. 231), the second century C.E. (*or* the second century A.D.)

7 a.m. (*or* 7 A.M.), 8:30 p.m. (*or* 8:30 P.M.)

no. 17 (*or* No. 17)

Note that the abbreviations *B.C.E.* ("before the common era") and *C.E.* ("common era") are more common than their alternatives. Also note that A.D. (*Anno Domini*) precedes the date when numerals are used.

57d Agencies and Organizations Known by Their Initials

Capitalize names of agencies and organizations commonly known by their initials:

UNICEF   CAW   CBC   CNN   RCMP   NATO   WHO

(See also #53a.)

57e Scientific and Technical Terms Known by Their Initials

Some scientific, technical, or other terms (usually of considerable length) are commonly known by their initials:

DNA   DDT   SARS   BTU   URL   HTML
ISP   FM   WMD   GST   ISBN   MP

(See also #53a.)

57f Latin Expressions Commonly Used in English

i.e. (that is)	etc. (and so forth)
e.g. (for example)	vs. (versus)
cf. (compare)	et al. (and others)

Note that in formal writing, it is better to spell out the English equivalent.

57f

PROOFREADING TIP

On Using Latin Expressions and Abbreviations

1. If you use *e.g.*, use it only to introduce an example or list of examples; following the example or list, write out *for example*:

   > Deciduous trees—e.g., oaks, maples, and birches—lose their leaves in the fall.

   > Deciduous trees—oaks, maples, and birches, for example—lose their leaves in the fall.

   Note also that if you introduce a list with *e.g.* or *for example* or even *such as*, it is illogical to follow it with *etc.* or *and so forth*.

2. Generally, use a comma after *i.e.* or *e.g.*, just as you would if you wrote out *that is* or *for example*. Test for the pause by reading the abbreviation aloud as either *that is* or *for example*.

3. The abbreviation *cf.* stands for the Latin *confer*, meaning "compare." Do not use it to mean "see"; for that, the Latin *vide* (*v.*) would be correct.

4. Use *etc.* sparingly. Use it only when there are at least several more items to follow and when they are reasonably obvious:

   > ***correct:*** Learning the Greek alphabet—alpha, beta, gamma, delta, etc.—isn't really difficult.

   > ***incorrect:*** He considered several possible occupations: accounting, teaching, nursing, etc.

   In the case of the last example, a reader can have no idea of what the other possible occupations might be. Further, don't write *and etc.: and* is redundant, since *etc.* (*et cetera*) means "and so forth."

57g

57g Terms in Official Titles

Capitalize abbreviated terms used in official titles being copied exactly:

Johnson Bros., Ltd.   Enbridge Inc.

Ibbetson & Co.   *Quill & Quire*

PROOFREADING TIP

On the Use of the Ampersand (&)

Don't use the ampersand (&) as a substitute for *and*; use it only when presenting the title of a company or a publication exactly, as shown in #57g.

58 Capitalization

cap,   Generally, capitalize proper nouns, abbreviations of proper nouns, and
uc   words derived from proper nouns, as discussed below.

58a Names and Nicknames

Capitalize names and nicknames of real and fictional people and individual animals:

Frederick Banting	Ann-Marie MacDonald
Maurice "Rocket" Richard	Clarissa Dalloway
King Kong	Rumpelstiltskin

58b Professional and Honorific Titles

Capitalize professional and honorific titles when they directly precede and thus are parts of names:

Professor Tamara Jones (*but* Tamara Jones, professor at Mount Allison)

Captain Janna Ting (*but* Janna Ting is a captain in the police force.)

Rabbi Samuel Singer (*but* Mr. Singer was rabbi of our synagogue.)

In the past, it was customary to capitalize the titles of certain rulers and religious figures in all contexts—for example, *the Queen of England*; *the Pope*; *the Dalai Lama*. Today, these terms tend to be lowercased unless they precede the title holder's name. Yet some writers and publishers—particularly journalists and newspapers—make it a policy to always capitalize these titles. Many also capitalize the terms *prime minister* and *president* when referring to a particular leader. In your own writing, you should aim for consistency in whatever practice you adopt.

58b

PROOFREADING TIP

On Capitalizing Titles After Names

Normally titles that follow names aren't capitalized unless they have become part of the name:

> Stephen Harper, prime minister of Canada
>
> Beverley McLachlin, justice of the Supreme Court
>
> Roméo Dallaire, the senator

but

> Catherine the Great
>
> Ivan the Terrible
>
> Smokey the Bear

58c Words Designating Family Relationships

Capitalize words designating family relationships when they are used as parts of proper names and also when they are used in place of proper names, except following a possessive:

> Uncle Peter (*but* I have an uncle named Peter.)
>
> There's my uncle, Peter. (*but* There's my Uncle Peter.)
>
> I told Father about it. (*but* I told my father about it.)
>
> I have always respected Grandmother. (*but* Diana's grandmother is a splendid woman.)

58d Names of Places and Nationalities

Capitalize place names—including common nouns (*river*, *street*, *park*, etc.) when they are parts of proper nouns (see #13):

North America	Canada	Northwest Territories
Moose Jaw	Hudson Bay	Vancouver Island
Lake Superior	Mount Etna	the Miramichi River
Yonge Street	Trafalgar Square	Kootenay National Park
the Amazon	the Rockies	the Gobi Desert

58d

Also capitalize the names of nationalities and terms used for the populations of regions or cities:

Canadian	Iraqi	North American
Manitoban	Haligonian	Vancouverite

 PROOFREADING TIP

On Capitalizing *North*, *South*, *East*, *West*

As a rule, don't capitalize *north*, *south*, *east*, and *west* unless they are part of specific place names (North Battleford, West Vancouver, the South Shore) or designate specific geographical areas (the frozen North, the East Coast, the Deep South, the Northwest, the Wild West, the Far East).

Since writers in Canada usually capitalize *East*, *West*, and *North* (and sometimes South) to refer to parts of the country (the peoples of the North, the settlement of the West), it makes sense to capitalize *Eastern*, *Western*, *Northern*, and *Southern* when they refer to ideas attached to parts of the country (Northern peoples, Western settlement). Otherwise, except for cases when they appear as parts of specific place names (the Eastern Townships), these adjectives should not be capitalized. This practice applies even to cases such as *northern Canada*, *eastern Canada*, and *western Canada*, which are not specific place names but descriptions of geographic regions.

58e Months, Days, and Holidays

Capitalize the names of the months, days of the week, holidays, holy days, and festivals:

January	Monday	Canada Day	Labour Day
Christmas	Hanukkah	Ramadan	Diwali

Do not capitalize the names of the seasons: spring, summer, autumn, fall, winter.

58f Religious Names

Capitalize names of deities and other religious names and terms:

Allah	Apollo	God	the Holy Ghost
Buddha	the Prophet	the Virgin Mary	Vishnu
the Bible	the Talmud	the Torah	the Qur'an
Buddhism	Hinduism	Islam	Taoism

58g Names of Organizations and Their Members
Capitalize the names of organizations and other groups and of their members;

>the New Democratic Party, New Democrats
>
>the Bloc Québécois, the Bloc, Bloquistes
>
>the Roman Catholic Church, Roman Catholics
>
>Scouts Canada, Scouts
>
>the Royal Canadian Air Cadets, Cadets
>
>International Brotherhood of Teamsters, Teamsters
>
>the Vancouver Canucks, the Toronto Blue Jays

58h Names of Institutions, Sections of Government, Historical Events, and Buildings
Capitalize names of institutions; sections of government; historical events, periods, and documents; and specific buildings:

>McGill University, The Hospital for Sick Children
>
>the Ministry of Health, Parliament, the Senate, the Cabinet, the Opposition
>
>the French Revolution, the Great War, World War I, the Gulf War
>
>the Middle Ages, the Renaissance; the Enlightenment
>
>the Magna Carta, the Treaty of Versailles, the Charter of Rights and Freedoms
>
>Canada Place, the CN Tower, the British Museum, the Museum of Civilization, Westminster Abbey

58i

58i Academic Courses and Languages
Capitalize specific academic courses, but not the subjects themselves, except for languages:

>Philosophy 101, Fine Arts 300, Mathematics 204, English 112, Food Writing, Humanities 101
>
>an English course, a major in French (*but* a history course, an economics major, a degree in psychology)

58j Derivatives of Proper Nouns

Capitalize derivatives of proper nouns:

Celtic	Christian	Shakespearean
Miltonic	Keynesian	Edwardian

PROOFREADING TIP

On Words Once but No Longer Capitalized

Some words derived from proper nouns—and some proper nouns themselves—are so much a part of everyday usage or refer to such common things that they were never or are no longer capitalized; some examples:

bible (in secular contexts), biblical

herculean, raglan, martial, quixotic, erotic, jeremiad, bloomers, gerrymander, malapropism

hamburger, frankfurter, french fries, champagne, burgundy, roman and italic, denim, china, japanned, venetian blinds

vulcanize, macadamize, galvanize, pasteurize, ampere, volt, watt

---

58k Abbreviations of Proper Nouns

Capitalize abbreviations of proper nouns:

PMO   TVA   CUPE   CUSO   P.E.I   B.C.   the BNA Act

Note that abbreviations of agencies and organizations commonly known by their initials do not need periods (see #57d), but that non-postal abbreviations of geographical entities such as provinces usually do. When in doubt, consult your dictionary. See also #53a.

58-l *I* and *O*

Capitalize the pronoun *I* and the vocative interjection *O*:

O my people, what have I done unto thee? (Micah 6:3)

Do not capitalize the interjection *oh* unless it begins a sentence.

58m Titles of Written and Other Works

In the titles of written and other works, including student essays, use a capital letter to begin the first word, the last word, and all other important words; leave uncapitalized only articles (*a*, *an*, *the*) and conjunctions and prepositions less than five letters long (unless one of these is the first or last word):

The Hunger Games	"The Metamorphosis"
Man of Steel	"The Fall of the House of Usher"
A River Runs Through It	"Open Secrets"
As for Me and My House	"O Canada"
Roughing It in the Bush	"Go Tell It on the Mountain"
In the Skin of a Lion	"In Flanders Fields"

But there can be exceptions; for example, the conjunctions *Nor* and *So* are usually capitalized, the relative pronoun *that* is sometimes not capitalized (*All's Well that Ends Well*), and in Ralph Ellison's "Tell It Like It Is, Baby" the preposition-cum-conjunction *like* demands capitalization.

If a title includes a hyphenated word, capitalize the part after the hyphen only if it is a noun or adjective or is otherwise an important word:

Self-Portrait

The Scorched-Wood People

Murder Among the Well-to-do

Capitalize the first word of a subtitle, even if it is an article:

Beyond Remembering: The Collected Poems of Al Purdy

See #59 for more on titles.

58n First Words of Sentences

Capitalize the first word of a major or minor sentence—of anything, that is, that concludes with terminal punctuation:

Racial profiling. Now that's a controversial topic. Right?

58-o First Words of Quotations That Are Sentences

Capitalize the first word of a quotation that is intended as a sentence or that is capitalized in the source, but not fragments from other than the beginning of such a sentence:

When he said "Let me take the wheel for a while," I shuddered at the memory of what had happened the last time I had let him "take the wheel."

If something interrupts a single quoted sentence, do not begin its second part with a capital:

> "It was all I could do," she said, "to keep from laughing out loud."

58p First Words of Sentences Within Parentheses
Capitalize the first word of an independent sentence in parentheses only if it stands by itself, apart from other sentences. If it is incorporated within another sentence, it is neither capitalized nor ended with a period (though it could end with a question mark or exclamation point: see #51 and #53).

> She did as she was told (there was really nothing else for her to do), and the tension was relieved. (But of course she would never admit to herself that she had been manipulated.)

58q First Words of Sentences Following Colons
An incorporated sentence following a colon *may* be capitalized if it seems to stand as a separate statement or requires emphasis:

> There was one thing, she said, that we must never forget: No one has the right to the kind of happiness that deprives someone else of deserved happiness.

The current trend, however, is away from capitalization:

> It was a splendid night: the sky was clear except for a few picturesque clouds, the moon was full, and even a few stars shone through.

> It was no time for petty quarrels: everything depended on unanimity.

58r With Personification and for Emphasis
Although it is risky and should not be done often, writers who have good control of tone can occasionally capitalize a personified abstraction or a word or phrase to which they want to impart a special importance of some kind:

> In Gavin's quest to succeed, Greed and Power came to dominate his every waking thought.

> Only when it begins to fade does Youth appear so valuable.

Sometimes the slight emphasis of capitalization can be used for a humorous or ironic effect:

> He insisted on driving His Beautiful Car: everyone else preferred to walk the two blocks without benefit of jerks and jolts and carbon monoxide fumes.

And occasionally, but rarely, you can capitalize whole words and phrases or even sentences for a special sort of graphic emphasis:

> When we reached the excavation site, however, we were confronted by a sign warning us in no uncertain terms to KEEP OUT—TRESPASSERS WILL BE PROSECUTED.

> When she made the suggestion to the group, she was answered with a resounding YES.

Clearly in such instances there is no need for further indications of emphasis, such as quotation marks or underlining, though the last example could end with an exclamation point.

59 Titles (see also #58m)

59a

59a Italics for Whole or Major Works

 Use italics (see #60) for titles of written works published as units, such as books, book-length poems, magazines, journals, newspapers, and plays; for films and television programs; for entire websites; for paintings and sculptures; and for full musical compositions (other than single songs), such as operas and ballets:

> Have you read Michael Crummey's *The Wreckage*?

> *Paradise Lost* is Milton's greatest work.

> *The New Yorker* is a weekly magazine.

> The scholarly journal *Canadian Literature* is published quarterly.

> I prefer *The Globe and Mail* to the *National Post*.

> I recommend that you see the Shaw Festival's production of *Arms and the Man*.

> *Maps to the Stars* is a satirical film directed by David Cronenberg.

> *The Passionate Eye* is a CBC program featuring the best in current documentaries.

> *Urban Dictionary* is an evolving website that informally chronicles regional slang terms not found in most dictionaries.
>
> Picasso's *Guernica* is a disturbing representation of the Spanish Civil War.
>
> Michelangelo's *David* is worth a trip to Florence.
>
> We saw a fine production of Puccini's *La Bohème*.
>
> One tires of hearing Ravel's *Bolero* played so often.

Note that instrumental compositions may be known by name or by technical detail, or both. A title name is italicized (Beethoven's *Pastoral Symphony*); technical identification is usually not (Beethoven's Sixth Symphony, or Symphony no. 6, op. 68, in F major).

59b Quotation Marks for Short Works and Parts of Longer Works

Put quotation marks around the titles of short works and of parts of longer works, such as short stories, articles, essays, short poems, chapters of books, songs, individual episodes of television programs, and sections of websites:

> "A Wilderness Station" is a story by Alice Munro that begins in Ontario in the 1850s.
>
> Journalist Alison Motluk won an award for her article "Is Egg Donation Dangerous?"
>
> "Her Gates Both East and West" is the final poem in Al Purdy's last collection of poems.
>
> The final chapter of Carol Shields' last novel is called "Not Yet."
>
> Leonard Cohen's "Joan of Arc" and "Democracy" are songs featured in this documentary about the music of Canada.
>
> Of the ten episodes in the CBC documentary *Hockey: A People's History,* I enjoyed the first one, "A Simple Game," the best.
>
> "The History of English," a section within the website *Oxford Dictionaries Online,* provides a very brief overview of historical influences on the English language.

There can be exceptions, however. Some works, for example Coleridge's *The Rime of the Ancient Mariner*, E.J. Pratt's *Towards the Last Spike*, and Conrad's *Heart of Darkness*, although originally parts of larger collections, are fairly long and have attained a reputation and importance as individual works; most writers feel justified in italicizing their titles.

59c Titles Within Titles

If an essay title includes a book title, the book title is italicized:

> "Things Botanical in *The Lost Garden* and *A Student of Weather*"

If a book title includes something requiring quotation marks, retain the quotation marks and italicize the whole thing:

> *From Fiction to Film: James Joyce's "The Dead"*

If a book title includes something that itself would be italicized, such as the name of a ship or the title of another book, either put the secondary item in quotation marks or leave it in roman type (i.e., not italicized):

> *The Cruise of the "Nona"*

> *D.H. Lawrence and* Sons and Lovers: *Sources and Criticism*

✓ PROOFREADING TIP

On *the* as Part of a Title

Double-check in the titles you cite for the role of the definite article, *the*: italicize and capitalize it only when it is actually a part of the title: Margaret Laurence's *The Stone Angel*; Yann Martel's *Life of Pi*; Roman Polanski's *The Pianist*; the *Partisan Review*; *The Canadian Encyclopedia*; the *Atlas of Ancient Archaeology*.

Practice varies with the definite article as part of the name of a newspaper. Unless you are following a style that recommends a different approach, try to refer to a newspaper the way it refers to itself—on its front page or masthead: the Victoria *Times Colonist*; the Regina *Leader-Post*; *The Vancouver Sun*; the *Calgary Herald*; *The Globe and Mail*.

60 Italics

ital **Italics** are a special kind of slanting type that contrasts with the surrounding type to draw attention to a word or phrase, such as a title (see #59a). The other main uses of italics are discussed below. In handwritten work, such as an exam, represent italic type by underlining.

60a Names of Ships, Trains, and Planes

Italicize names of individual ships, trains, planes, and other vehicles:

the *Golden Hind*	the *Argo*
the *Orient Express*	the *20th Century Limited*
the *Spirit of St. Louis*	the *Bonaventure*
the *Discovery*	*Mariner IX*

60b Non-English Words and Phrases

Italicize non-English words and phrases that are not yet sufficiently common to be entirely at home in English. English contains many terms that have come from other languages but that are no longer thought of as non-English and are therefore not italicized; for example:

arroyo	bamboo	chutzpah
eureka	genre	jihad
moccasin	prairie	spaghetti
sushi	tableau	vacuum

There are also words that are sufficiently Anglicized not to require italicizing but that usually retain their original accents and diacritical marks; for example:

cliché	façade	fête	Götterdämmerung	naïf

But English also makes use of many terms still felt by many writers to be sufficiently non-English to need italicizing, for example:

au courant	*au fait*	*Bildungsroman*
carpe diem	*coup d'état*	*je ne sais quoi*
mise en scène	*outré*	*savoir faire*
schadenfreude	*Weltanschauung*	*zakat*

Many such expressions are on their way to full acceptance in English. If you are unsure, consult a good, up-to-date dictionary.

60c Words Referred to as Words

Italicize words, letters, numerals, and the like when you refer to them as such:

The word *helicopter* is formed from Greek roots.

There are two *r*'s in *embarrass*. (Note that only the *r* is italicized; the *s* making it plural stays roman.)

The number *13* is considered unlucky by many otherwise rational people.

Don't use *&* as a substitute for *and*.

See also #54g. For the matter of apostrophes for plurals of such elements, see #62m.8.

60d For Emphasis

On rare occasions, italicize words or phrases—or even whole sentences—that you want to emphasize, for example, as they might be stressed if spoken aloud:

One thing he was now sure of: *that* was no way to go about the task.

Careful thought should lead one to the conclusion that *character*, not wealth or connections, will be most important in the long run.

Remember that *Fredericton*, not Saint John, is the capital of New Brunswick.

If people try to tell you otherwise, *don't listen to them*.

He gave up his ideas of fun and decided instead to finish his education. *It was the most important decision of his life.*

Like other typographical devices for achieving emphasis (boldface, capitalization, underlining), this method is worth avoiding, or at least minimizing, in academic and other forms of writing. No merely mechanical means of emphasis is, ultimately, as effective as punctuation, word order, and syntax. Easy methods often produce only a transitory effect, and repeated use soon saps what effectiveness they have. Consider the following sentences and decide which of them you find most emphatic:

Well, I felt just *terrible* when he told me that!

I felt terrible, just terrible, when he told me that.

I can think of only one way to describe how I felt when he told me that: I felt terrible.

 **Numerals**

num Numerals are appropriate in technical and scientific writing, and newspapers sometimes use them to save space. But in ordinary writing certain conventions limit their use. The following sections discuss the situations in which numerals are most widely used.

61a Time of Day
Use numerals for the time of day with *a.m.* or *p.m.* and *midnight* or *noon*, or when minutes are included:

> 3 p.m. (*but* three o'clock, three in the afternoon)

> 12 noon, 12 midnight (these are often better than the equivalents, *12 p.m.* and *12 a.m.*, which may not be understood)

> 4:15, 4:30 (*but* a quarter past four; half past four)

61b Dates
Use numerals for dates:

> September 11, 2001, *or* 11 September 2001

The year is almost always represented by numerals, and centuries are written out:

> Was 2000 the last year of the twentieth century or the first year of the twenty-first century?

 PROOFREADING TIP

Adding Suffixes to Numerals in Dates

The suffixes *st, nd, rd,* and *th* go with numerals in dates only if the year is not given; or the number may be written out:

May 12, 2013	May 12th
the twelfth of May	May twelfth

61c Addresses

Use numerals for addresses:

2132 Fourth Avenue	4771 128th Street
P.O. Box 91	Apartment 8

61d Technical and Mathematical Numbers

Use numerals for technical and mathematical numbers, such as percentages and decimals:

31 per cent	31%
37 degrees Celsius	37°C
2.54 centimetres	2.54 cm

61e Parts of a Written Work

Use numerals for page numbers, chapters, and other divisions of a written work, especially in documentation (see #80a–d):

page 27, p. 27, pp. 33–38	line 13, lines 3 and 5, ll. 7–9
Chapter 4, Ch. 4, chapter IV	Section 3, section III
Part 2, part II	Book IX, canto 120 (IX, 120)
Act 4, Scene 2; act IV, scene ii	2 Samuel 22: 3, II Samuel 19: 1

61f

61f Statistics and Numbers of More Than Two Words

Generally, spell out numbers that can be expressed in one or two words; use numerals for numbers that would take more than two words:

four; thirty; eighty-three; two hundred; seven thousand; 115; 385; 2120

one-third; one-half; five thirty-seconds

three dollars; five hundred dollars; $2.48; $717

If you are writing about more than one number, say for purposes of comparison or giving statistics, numerals are usually preferable:

Enrolment dropped from 250 two years ago, to 200 last year, to only 90 this year.

Don't mix numerals and words in such a context. On the other hand, if in your writing you refer alternately to two sets of figures, it may be better to use numerals for one and words for the other:

> We're building a 60-foot border; we can use either five 12-foot timbers or six 10-foot timbers.

61g Avoiding Numerals at the Beginning of a Sentence

Don't begin a sentence with a numeral. Either spell out the number or rewrite the sentence so that the number doesn't come first:

> *num:* 30–40% goes for taxes.
>
> *revised:* Thirty to forty per cent goes for taxes.
>
> *revised:* Taxes consume from 30 to 40 per cent.

> *num:* 750 people showed up to watch the chess tournament.
>
> *revised:* As many as 750 people came to watch the chess tournament.
>
> *revised:* The chess tournament drew 750 interested spectators.

61h Commas with Numerals

Commas have long been conventional to separate groups of three figures in long numbers:

> 3,172,450   17,920

In the International System of Units (abbreviated SI, for Système International), however, groups of three digits on either side of a decimal point are separated by spaces; with four-digit numbers a space is optional:

> 7723   *or*   7 723
>
> 3 172 450
>
> 3.1416   *or*   3.141 6 (*but* 3.141 59)

Note, however, that monetary figures of more than three digits are always separated with commas:

> $3,500   £27,998.06   ¥30,000

Also note that street addresses are usually not separated by commas or spaces:

> 18885 Bay Mills Avenue

61i Hyphens to Indicate Ranges

Use a hyphen between a pair of numbers indicating a range:

pages 73-78   June 20-26   1999-2005   3 p.m.-5 p.m.

In these examples, the hyphen is equivalent to the word *to*. If you introduce the range with *from*, however, you must write out the word *to*: *from June 20 to June 26*. And if you use *between*, you must write out the word *and*: *between June 20 and June 26*.

Note: Most professional publications (including this book) use a punctuation mark called an *en dash* (–) rather than a hyphen to indicate a range between numbers. An en dash is longer than a hyphen but shorter than a full dash; typically, it is the same width as a capital *N*. Many people consider the en dash to be the more proper mark to use to indicate a range, but the hyphen is generally an acceptable substitution in unpublished documents, including student essays.

61j Apostrophes to Indicate Omissions

Although the practice is rare in formal writing, apostrophes can be used to indicate that obvious numbers have been omitted, especially in dates:

back in '83   the summer of '09

the roaring '20s   the '90s

Note: If an apostrophe is already present to indicate a plural (see #62m.8), you may omit the apostrophe that indicates omission: the *20's*, the *90's*.

62 Spelling Rules and Common Causes of Error

sp Some writers have little trouble with spelling; others have a lot—or is that "alot"? Even confident writers must consult a dictionary occasionally; poor spellers need to do this all the time. The good news is that good spelling comes with practice; taking the time to look up a word now will help you remember its proper spelling the next time you need to use it.

English spelling isn't as bizarre as some people think, but there are oddities. Sometimes the same sound can be spelled in several ways (<u>f</u>ine, o<u>ff</u>er, <u>ph</u>one, cou<u>gh</u>; or s<u>o</u>, s<u>oa</u>p, s<u>ow</u>, s<u>ew</u>, b<u>eau</u>, d<u>ough</u>), or a single element can be pronounced in several ways (c<u>ough</u>, t<u>ough</u>, d<u>ough</u>, thr<u>ough</u>, b<u>ough</u>, f<u>ough</u>t). When such inconsistencies occur in longer and less familiar words, sometimes only a dictionary can help us. And remember, a dictionary isn't *pre*scribing but *de*scribing: it isn't commanding us to be *correct* but simply recording the currently accepted *conventions*.

English has changed a great deal over the centuries, and it is still changing. Old words pass out of use, new words are added, conventions of grammar evolve, pronunciations and spellings change. Words in transition may have more than one acceptable meaning or pronunciation or spelling. The past tense of *dream* can be either *dreamed* or *dreamt*. The past tense of *slide* changed from *slided* to *slid* a century or so ago; will the past tense of *glide* someday be *glid*? Just a few decades ago *dove* was considered unacceptable as the past tense of *dive*; now, it is at least as acceptable as *dived*. And so on. Dictionaries can tell you what is preferred or accepted right now—just make sure you're using a dictionary that is up to date.

In Canada, we also have to contend with the influence of British and American spelling. Broadly speaking, Canadian conventions—whether of spelling, punctuation, usage, or pronunciation—are closer to American than to British, and where they are changing, they are changing in the direction of American conventions. Most Canadians say "zed" rather than "zee" when referring to the final letter of the alphabet, but we say and spell *aluminum* rather than *aluminium*. The pronunciation of the word *lieutenant* continues to shift away from the British "leftenant" and toward the American "lootenant." Most Canadians write *centre* and *theatre* rather than *center* and *theater*; but we write *curb* rather than *kerb*. Endings in *our* (colour, honour, labour, etc.) are more conventional than those in *or*, but both are widely accepted. The same is true of endings in *ise* or *ize*, though the latter is clearly preferred. We have the useful alternatives *cheque* (bank), *racquet* (tennis), and *storey* (floor); Americans have only *check*, *racket*, and *story* for both meanings. But *draught* is losing ground to *draft*, and *program* and *judgment* are rapidly replacing *programme* and *judgement*.

Where alternatives exist, either is correct. But be consistent. If you choose *analyze*, write *paralyze* and *modernize*; if you choose *centre*, write *lustre* and *fibre*; if you spell *honour*, then write *humour, colour, vapour,* and *labour*. But if you do choose the *our* endings, watch out for the trap: when you add the suffixes *ous, ate* or *ation, ize* (or *ise*), and *ious*, you must drop the *u* and write *humorous, coloration, vaporize, laborious,* and there is no *u* in *honorary*.

But such dilemmas, if they are dilemmas, are infrequent. The real spelling difficulties, those shared by all writers of English, are of a different sort.

Many spelling errors can be prevented only with the help of a good dictionary. Many others, however, fall into clear categories. Familiarizing yourself with the main rules and the main sources of confusion will help you avoid these errors.

62a *ie* or *ei*

The old jingle should help: use *i* before *e* except after *c*, or when sounded like *a* as in *neighbour* and *weigh*.

ie:	achieve, believe, chief, field, fiend, shriek, siege, wield
***ei* after *c*:**	ceiling, conceive, deceive, perceive, receive
***ei* sounded like *a*:**	eight, neighbour, sleigh, veil, weigh

62a

When the sound is neither long *e* nor long *a*, the spelling *ei* is usually right:

counterfeit, foreign, forfeit, height, heir, their

But there are several exceptions; for example:

ei: either, neither; leisure; seize; weird

ie: financier; friend; mischief; sieve

When in doubt, consult your dictionary.

62b–c Prefixes and Suffixes

The more you know about how words are put together, the less trouble you will have spelling them. Many of the words that give writers difficulty are those with prefixes and suffixes. Understanding how these elements operate will help you avoid errors.

62b Prefixes

A **prefix** is one or more syllables added to the beginning of a root word to form a new word. Many common spelling mistakes could be avoided by recognizing that a word consists of a prefix joined to a root word. For example, consider the word *prefix*: *pre* is a prefix that comes from a Latin word meaning "before"; *fix* is a root that means "fasten" or "place." Combined, these elements literally mean "something fastened before." *Prefix* is not a difficult word for most writers to spell, but recognizing its prefix and root will ensure that it is spelled correctly.

One mistake writers often make is omitting the last letter of a prefix when it is the same as the first letter of the root. When a prefix ends with the same letter that the root begins with, the result is a double letter; don't omit one of them:

ad + dress = address   mis + spell = misspell

com + motion = commotion   un + necessary = unnecessary

(Similarly, don't omit one of the doubled letters in compounds such as *beachhead*, *bookkeeping*, and *roommate*.)

In some cases, the first letter of the root is doubled to replace the last letter of a prefix in order to make the resulting word less difficult to pronounce. Writers unaware of the prefix sometimes forget to double the consonant. The Latin prefix *ad*, meaning "to, toward, near," is commonly affected this way. For example, it became *af* in front of *facere* (a Latin verb meaning *to do*); hence our word *affect* has two *f*'s. Here are some other examples:

ad	>	ac	in	access, accept, accommodate
		al	in	alliance, allusion
		an	in	annul, annihilate
		ap	in	apprehend, apparatus, application

(margin tab) 62b

com	>	col	in	*collide, colloquial, collusion*
		con	in	*connect, connote*
		cor	in	*correct, correspond*
ob	>	oc	in	*occasion, occupy, occult*
		of	in	*offend, offer*
		op	in	*oppose, oppress*
sub	>	suc	in	*success, succumb*
		suf	in	*suffer, suffix*
		sug	in	*suggest*
		sup	in	*suppress, supply, support*

Note the structure of the frequently misspelled *accommodate*: both *ac* and *com* are prefixes, so the word must have both a double *c* and a double *m*. It may help to think of the meaning of the word: "to make room for." Be sure to *make room for* the two *c*'s and the two *m*'s.

Errors can also be prevented by correctly identifying a word's prefix. A writer who knows that the prefix of *arouse* is *a* and not *ar* will not be tempted to spell the word with a double *r*. Knowing that the prefix of *apology* is *apo*, not *ap*, will curb the temptation to spell the word with a double *p*. (Knowing that the root is from the Greek *logos* would also help.) Familiarize yourself with prefixes. The following are some of the more common prefixes, along with their meanings:

a	not, without (*amoral*); onward, away, from (*arise, awake*); to, at, or into a particular state (*agree*); utterly (*abash*)
	▶ VARIANT **an** before a vowel (*anaemia*)
ab	off, away, from (*abduct, abnormal, abuse*)
	▶ VARIANT **abs** before *c, t* (*abscess, abstain*)
ad	denoting motion toward (*advance*), change into (*adapt*), or addition (*adjunct*)
	▶ VARIANT **ac** before *c, k, q* (*accept, acknowledge, acquire*)
	af before *f* (*affirm*)
	ag before *g* (*aggravate*)
	al before *l* (*allocate*)
	an before *n* (*annotate*)
	ap before *p* (*apprehend*)
	ar before *r* (*arrive*)
	as before *s* (*assemble*)
	at before *t* (*attend*)

62b

ante   before (*antecedent*)

anti   opposed to, against (*anti-hero*, *antibacterial*)

bi   two, twice (*bicoloured*, *biennial*)
        ▶ VARIANT   **bin**   before a vowel (*binoculars*)

by   subordinate, secondary (*by-election*, *by-product*)

com   with, together (*combine*, *command*)
        ▶ VARIANT   **col**   before *l* (*collocate*, *collude*)
                     con   before *c, d, f, g, j, n, q, s, t, v,* and
                                sometimes before vowels
                                (*concord*, *condescend*, *confide*)
                     cor   before *r* (*correct*)

de   down, away from (*descend*, *de-ice*); completely
        (*denude*)

di   twice, two (*dichromatic*, *dilemma*)

dis   not (*disadvantage*); denoting reversal (*disappear*),
        removal (*dismember*), or separation (*disjoin*,
        dispel, *dissect*)
        ▶ VARIANT   **dif**   before *f* (*diffuse*)

dys   bad, difficult (*dysfunctional*)

e   electronic (*email*, *e-zine*)

en   in, into, inside (*ensnare*, *engulf*; *encrust*, *energy*);
        used in verbs ending in *en* (*enliven*)
        ▶ VARIANT   **em**   before *b, p* (*embed*, *embolden*)

epi   upon, above (*epidemic*, *epicentre*); in addition
        (*epilogue*)

ex   out (*exclude*, *exodus*); upward (*extol*); thoroughly
        (*excruciate*); into the state of (*exasperate*)
        ▶ VARIANT   **e**   (*elect*, *emit*)
                     ef   before *f* (*efface*)

for   denoting prohibition (*forbid*), neglect (*forget*), or
        abstention (*forbear*, *forgo*)

fore   in front, beforehand (*forebear*, *foreshadow*, *forecourt*)

hyper   over, beyond, excessively (*hypersensitive*); relating to
        hypertext (*hyperlink*)

hypo   under, below normal (*hypotension*)

in   not, without (*infertile*); in, toward (*influx*, *inbounds*)
        ▶ VARIANT   **il**   before *l* (*illegal*, *illegible*)
                     im   before *b, m, p* (*immature*, *imbibe*)
                     ir   before *r* (*irrelevant*, *irradiate*)

inter   between, among (*interactive*)

62b

intra	on the inside (*intravenous, intramural*)
intro	in, inward (*introvert*)
mis	wrongly, badly (*misapply, mismanage*); expressing negativity (*misadventure, mischief*)
multi	more than one, many (*multicoloured, multiple*)
ob	blocking, opposing, against (*obstacle, object*); to, toward (*oblige*)

    ▶**VARIANT**   **oc**   before *c* (*occasion*)
                  of   before *f* (*offend*)
                  op   before *p* (*oppose*)

para	beyond or distinct from but analogous to (*paranormal, paramilitary*); protecting from (*parachute*)

    ▶**VARIANT**   **par**   before a vowel (*parody*)

per	through, all over, completely (*pervade, perforate, perfect*)
peri	around, about (*perimeter*)
pre	before (*precaution, precede*)
pro	supporting (*pro-industry*); forward or away (*proceed*); before (*proactive*)

    ▶**VARIANT**   **pur**   (*pursue*)

re	once more, afresh (*reactivate, restore, revert*); mutually (*resemble*); in opposition (*repel*); behind, back (*remain, recluse*)

62b

PROOFREADING TIP
Recognizing Prefixes

The following are some words with their prefixes in capital letters; after each is a common misspelling that knowing the prefix would have prevented:

Right	*Wrong*	*Right*	*Wrong*
AFOREmentioned	aformentioned	MILLImetre	milimetre
BY-product	biproduct	MINIature	minature
CONTROversial	conterversial	PENinsula	penninsula
DEscribe	discribe	PERsuade	pursuade
DIAlogue	diologue	PORtray	protray
DISappoint	dissappoint	PROfessor	proffessor

se	apart, without (*separate, secure*)
sub	denoting subsequent or secondary action (*subdivision*); lower, less, below (*subalpine, subculture*)

> ▶ VARIANT   suc   before *c* (*succeed*)
>   suf   before *f* (*suffix*)
>   sug   before *g* (*suggest*)
>   sup   before *p* (*support*)

syn	united, acting together (*synchronize*)

> ▶ VARIANT   sym   before *b, m, p* (*symbiosis, symmetry*)

un	not (*unhappy*); the opposite of (*unselfish*); a lack of (*unrest*); denoting reversal (*undress*), removal (*unmask*), or release (*unburden*)
uni	one (*unicorn, unicycle*)

62c Suffixes

A **suffix** is one or more syllables added to the end of a root word to form a new word, often changing its part of speech. For example:

Root	Suffix	New Word
appear (v.)	ance	appearance (n.)
content (adj.)	ment	contentment (n.)
occasion (n.)	al	occasional (adj.)
occasional (adj.)	ly	occasionally (adv.)

Suffixes, like prefixes, can give writers difficulty. For example, if you add *ness* to a word ending in *n*, the result is a double *n*: *barrenness, openness, stubbornness*. And remember that the correct suffix is *ful*, not *full*: *spoonful, cupful, shovelful, bucketful, roomful, successful*. The following sections should help you avoid the common spelling mistakes that writers make when adding suffixes.

Final *e* Before a Suffix

When a suffix is added to a root word that ends in a silent *e*, certain rules generally apply. If the suffix begins with a *vowel* (*a, e, i, o, u*), the *e* is usually dropped:

desire + able = desirable	forgive + able = forgivable
sphere + ical = spherical	argue + ing = arguing
come + ing = coming	allure + ing = alluring
continue + ous = continuous	desire + ous = desirous
sense + ual = sensual	rogue + ish = roguish

62c

But note that the word *dyeing* retains the *e* to distinguish it from *dying*. Also note that if a word ends with two *e*'s, both are pronounced and therefore not dropped: *agreeing, fleeing.*

If the suffix begins with *a* or *o*, most words ending in *ce* or *ge* retain the *e* in order to preserve the soft sound of the *c* (like *s* rather than *k*) or the *g* (like *j* rather than hard as in *gum*):

> notice + able = noticeable   outrage + ous = outrageous

(Note that *vengeance* and *gorgeous* also have such a silent *e*.) Similarly, words like *picnic* and *frolic* require an added *k* to preserve the hard sound of the *c* before suffixes beginning with *e* or *i*: *picnicked, picnicking; frolicked, frolicking; politicking.* (An exception to this rule is *arc: arced, arcing.*) When the suffix does not begin with *e* or *i*, these words do not add a *k*: *tactical, frolicsome.*

If the suffix begins with a *consonant*, the silent *e* of the root word is usually not dropped:

> awe + some = awesome   effective + ness = effectiveness
>
> definite + ly = definitely   hoarse + ly = hoarsely
>
> immediate + ly = immediately   mere + ly = merely
>
> immense + ly = immensely   separate + ly = separately
>
> involve + ment = involvement   woe + ful = woeful

But note a common exception: *awe + ful = awful.*

And there is a subgroup of words whose final *e*'s are sometimes wrongly omitted. The *e*, though silent, is essential to keep the sound of the preceding vowel long:

> completely   extremely   hopelessness   livelihood
>
> loneliness   remoteness   severely   tasteless

But such an *e* is sometimes dropped when no consonant intervenes between it and the long vowel:

> due + ly = duly   true + ly = truly   argue + ment = argument

Final *y* After a Consonant and Before a Suffix

When the suffix begins with *i*, keep the *y*:

> baby + ish = babyish   carry + ing = carrying
>
> try + ing = trying   worry + ing = worrying

(Note: Words ending in *ie* change to *y* before adding *ing*: *die + ing = dying; lie + ing = lying.*)

62c

When the suffix begins with something other than *i*, change *y* to *i*:

happy + er = happier	duty + ful = dutiful
happy + ness = happiness	silly + est = silliest
harmony + ous = harmonious	angry + ly = angrily

Some exceptions: *shyly, shyness*; *slyer, slyly*; *flyer* (though *flier* is sometimes used); *dryer* (as a noun—for the comparative adjective use *drier*).

Doubling of a Final Consonant Before a Suffix

When adding a suffix, *double* the final consonant of the root if all three of the following apply:

(a) that consonant is preceded by a single vowel,
(b) the root is a one-syllable word or a word accented on its last syllable, and
(c) the suffix begins with a vowel.

One-syllable words:

bar + ed = barred	bar + ing = barring
fit + ed = fitted	fit + ing = fitting
fit + er = fitter	
hot + er = hotter	hot + est = hottest
shop + ed = shopped	shop + ing = shopping
shop + er = shopper	

Words accented on last syllable:

allot + ed = allotted	allot + ing = allotting
commit + ing = committing	commit + ed = committed
occur + ed = occurred	occur + ing = occurring
occur + ence = occurrence	
propel + ed = propelled	propel + ing = propelling
propel + er = propeller	

But when the addition of the suffix shifts the accent of the root word away from the last syllable, do not double the final consonant:

infer + ed = inferred	infer + ing = inferring	BUT inference
prefer + ed = preferred	prefer + ing = preferring	BUT preference
refer + ed = referred	refer + ing = referring	BUT reference

62c

Do not double the final consonant if it is preceded by a single consonant (*sharp* + *er* = *sharper*) or if the final consonant is preceded by two vowels (*fail* + *ed* = *failed*, *stoop* + *ing* = *stooping*) or if the root word is more than one syllable and *not* accented on its last syllable (*parallel* + *ing* = *paralleling*) or if the suffix begins with a consonant (*commit* + *ment* = *commitment*).

PROOFREADING TIP

On Doubling the Final Consonant *l* or *p*

Unlike *parallel*, other words often double a final *l*, even when they are of two or more syllables and not accented on the final syllable; for example, *labelled* or *labeled*, *traveller* or *traveler*. Either form is correct, though the Canadian preference is for the doubled *l*. (Some even double the *l* at the end of *parallel*, in spite of the present double *l* preceding it.)

The word *kidnap* is a similar exception, for the obvious reason of pronunciation: either *kidnapped* (and *kidnapping*) or *kidnaped* (and *kidnaping*) is correct. Another exception is *worship*: either *worshipped* or *worshiped*, *worshipping* or *worshiping*. In both instances, the double final consonant is preferred in Canada.

62c

The Suffix *ly*

When *ly* is added to an adjective already ending in a single *l*, that final *l* is retained, resulting in an adverb ending in *lly*. If you pronounce such words carefully you will be less likely to misspell them:

accidental + ly = accidentally   cool + ly = coolly

incidental + ly = incidentally   mental + ly = mentally

natural + ly = naturally   political + ly = politically

If the root ends in a double *l*, one *l* is dropped: *full* + *ly* = *fully*, *chill* + *ly* = *chilly*, *droll* + *ly* = *drolly*.

Particularly Troublesome Word Endings

Several groups of suffixes and other word endings consistently plague weak spellers and sometimes trip even good spellers. There are no rules governing them, and pronunciation is seldom any help; one either knows them or does not. Whenever you aren't certain of the correct spelling, check your dictionary. The following examples will at least alert you to the potential trouble spots.

PROOFREADING TIP

On Adding the Suffix *ally*

Many adjectives ending in *ic* have alternative forms ending in *ical*. But even if they don't, nearly all add *ally*, not just *ly*, to become adverbs—as do nouns like *music* and *stoic*. Again, careful pronunciation will help you avoid error:

alphabetic, alphabetical, alphabetically

basic, basically

cyclic, cyclical, cyclically

drastic, drastically

scientific, scientifically

symbolic, symbolical, symbolically

An exception: *publicly*.

able, ably, ability; *ible, ibly, ibility*

It should be helpful to remember that many more words end in *able* than in *ible*; yet it is the *ible* endings that cause the most trouble:

62c

-able		*-ible*	
advisable	inevitable	audible	inexpressible
comparable	laudable	contemptible	irresistible
debatable	noticeable	deductible	negligible
desirable	quotable	eligible	plausible
immeasurable	respectable	flexible	responsible
indispensable	syllable	forcible	tangible
indubitable	veritable	incredible	visible

ent, ently, ence, ency; *ant, antly, ance, ancy*

-en-		*-an-*	
apparent	independent	appearance	flamboyant
confidence	inherent	attendance	hindrance
coherent	permanent	blatant	irrelevant
consistent	persistence	brilliant	maintenance
excellent	resilient	concomitant	resistance
existence	tendency	extravagant	warrant

tial, tian; cial, cian, ciate

-tia-		*-cia-*	
confidential	influential	beneficial	mathematician
dietitian	martial	crucial	mortician
existential	spatial	emaciated	physician
expatiate	substantial	enunciate	politician

ative; itive

-ative		*-itive*	
affirmative	informative	additive	positive
comparative	negative	competitive	repetitive
imaginative	restorative	genitive	sensitive

ce; se

-ce		*-se*	
choice	defence	course	expense
evidence	presence	dense	phrase
fence	voice	dispense	sparse

62c

 PROOFREADING TIP

practice, practise; licence, license

Canadian writers tend to follow the British practice of using the *ce* forms of *practice* and *licence* as nouns and the *se* forms *practise* and *license* as verbs:

> We will <u>practise</u> our fielding at today's slo-pitch <u>practice</u>.

> Are you <u>licensed</u> to drive?

> Yes, I've had my driver's <u>licence</u> since I was sixteen.

American writers tend to favour the *ce* spelling of *practice* and the *se* spelling of *license* regardless of whether each is being used as a noun or a verb.

Note also that Canadian as well as British writers generally prefer the *ce* spelling for *offence* and *defence*, while American writers tend to use the *se* spellings of these words.

cede; ceed; sede

Memorize if necessary: the *sede* ending occurs only in *supersede*. The *ceed* ending occurs only in *exceed*, *proceed*, and *succeed*. All other words ending in this sound use *cede*: *accede*, *concede*, *intercede*, *precede*, *recede*, *secede*.

62d Changes in Spelling of Roots

Be careful with words whose roots change spelling, often because of a change in stress, when they are inflected for a different part of speech, for example:

clear, clarity	maintain, maintenance
curious, curiosity	prevail, prevalent
despair, desperate	pronounce, pronunciation
exclaim, exclamatory	repair, reparable
generous, generosity	repeat, repetition
inherit, heritage, BUT heredity, hereditary	

62e Faulty Pronunciation

Acquire the habit of correct pronunciation; sound words to yourself, exaggeratedly if necessary, even at the expense of temporarily slowing your reading speed. Here is a list of words some of whose common misspellings could be prevented by careful pronunciation:

62e

academic	disgust	insurgence	prevalent
accelerate	disillusioned	interpretation	pronunciation
accidentally	elaborate	intimacy	quantity
amphitheatre	emperor	inviting	repetitive
analogy	environment	irrelevant	reservoir
approximately	epitomize	itinerary	sacrilegious
architectural	escape	larynx	separate
athlete	especially	lightning	significant
authoritative	etcetera	limpidly	similar
biathlon	evident	lustrous	strength
camaraderie	excerpt	mathematics	subsidiary
candidate	February	negative	suffocate
celebration	film	nuclear	surprise
conference	foliage	optimism	temporarily
congratulate	further	original	triathlon

controversial	government	particular	ultimatum
definitely	governor	peculiar	village
deteriorating	gravitation	permanently	villain
detrimental	hereditary	phenomenon	visible
dilapidated	hurriedly	philosophical	vulnerable
disgruntled	immersing	predilection	wondrous

PROOFREADING TIP

Spelling Unpronounced Sounds

Don't omit the *d* or *ed* from such words as *used* and *supposed*, *old-fashioned* and *prejudiced*, which are often pronounced without the *d* sound. And be careful not to omit whole syllables that are near duplications in sound. Here are some examples of words that are frequently "telescoped," or pronounced without key sounds:

Right	*Wrong*	*Right*	*Wrong*
convenience	~~convience~~	institution	~~instution~~
criticize	~~critize~~	politician	~~politian~~
examining	~~examing~~	remembrance	~~rembrance~~
inappropriate	~~inappriate~~	repetition	~~repition~~

62f Confusion with Other Words

Don't let false analogies and similarities of sound lead you astray.

A writer who thinks of a word like:	may spell another word wrong, like this:	instead of right, like this:
air	~~ordinairy~~	ordinary
breeze	~~cheeze~~	cheese
comrade	~~comraderie~~	camaraderie
conform	~~conformation~~	confirmation
democracy	~~hypocracy~~	hypocrisy
desolate	~~desolute~~	dissolute
diet	~~diety~~	deity
exalt	~~exaltant~~	exultant
familiar	~~similiar~~	similar
ideal	~~idealic~~	idyllic
knowledge	~~priviledge~~	privilege

62f

prize	~~surprize~~	surprise
religious	~~sacreligious~~	sacrilegious
restaurant	~~restauranteur~~	restaurateur
sink	~~zink~~	zinc
size	~~rize~~	rise
solid	~~solider~~	soldier
summer	~~grammer~~	grammar
young	~~amoung~~	among

62g Homophones and Other Words Sometimes Confused

1. Be careful to distinguish between **homophones** that are pronounced alike but spelled differently. Here are some that can be troublesome; consult a dictionary for any whose meanings you aren't sure of (and see #69):

aisle, isle
allowed, aloud
alter, altar
assent, ascent
bear, bare
birth, berth
board, bored
boarder, border
born, borne
break, brake
by, buy, bye
capital, capitol
carrot, karat
complement, compliment
council, counsel
course, coarse
desert, dessert
die, dye, dying, dyeing
discreet, discrete
forth, fourth
hail, hale
heal, heel
hear, here
heard, herd

heroin, heroine
hole, whole
its, it's
led, lead
manner, manor
meat, meet
past, passed
patience, patients
piece, peace
plain, plane
pore, pour
pray, prey
presence, presents
principle, principal
rain, rein, reign
right, rite, write
road, rode, rowed
seas, sees, seize
sight, site, cite
stationary, stationery
there, their, they're
to, too, two
whose, who's
your, you're

62g

2. There are also words that are not pronounced exactly alike but that are similar enough to be confused. Again, look up any whose meanings you aren't sure of:

accept, except	diary, dairy
access, excess	emigrate, immigrate
adopt, adapt, adept	eminent, imminent, immanent
adverse, averse	enquire, inquire, acquire
advice, advise	ensure, insure, assure
accept, except	envelop, envelope
affect, effect	evoke, invoke
afflicted, inflicted	illusion, allusion
allude, elude	incident, incidence, instant, instance
angle, angel	incredulous, incredible
appraise, apprise	ingenious, ingenuous
assume, presume	insight, incite
bizarre, bazaar	later, latter
breath, breathe	liqueur, liquor
choose, chose	loose, lose
cloth, clothe	moral, morale
conscious, conscience	quite, quiet
custom, costume	tack, tact
decent, descent, dissent	than, then
decimate, disseminate	whether, weather
device, devise	while, wile

62g

PROOFREADING TIP

On the Limitations of Spell Checking

Your word-processing program's spell-check feature will help you catch spelling mistakes like *grammer* and *surprize*, but it will *not* help you when you've used *principle* when you meant to use *principal*, *birth* instead of *berth*, *forth* instead of *fourth*, *to* or *two* instead of *too*, or *their* instead of *there* or *they're*. You will need to catch such slips in your own close checking of your documents.

3. Be careful also to distinguish between such terms as the following, for although they sound the same, they function differently depending on whether they are spelled as one word or two:

already, all ready	awhile, a while
altogether, all together	everybody, every body
anybody, any body	everyday, every day
anymore, any more	everyone, every one
anyone, any one	maybe, may be
anytime, any time	someday, some day
anyway, any way	sometime, some time

62h One Word or Two?

Do not spell the following words as two or three separate or hyphenated words; each is one unhyphenated word:

alongside	lifetime	outshine	sunrise
background	nevertheless	setback	sunset
countryside	nonetheless	spotlight	throughout
easygoing	nowadays	straightforward	wrongdoing

The following, on the other hand, should always be spelled as two un-hyphenated words:

a bit	at least	in order (to)
a few	close by	in spite (of)
after all	even though	no longer
all right (*alright* is informal)	every time	(on the) other hand
a lot	in between	(in) other words
as though	in fact	up to

✓ **PROOFREADING TIP**

On *Cannot* and *Can Not*

The word *cannot* should usually be written as one word; write *can not* only when the *not* is part of another construction (as in "I can *not only* sing *but also* play guitar") or when you want special emphasis on the *not*.

62i Hyphenation

To hyphenate or not to hyphenate? That is often the question. There are some firm rules; there are some sound guidelines; and there is a large territory where only common sense and a good dictionary can help you find your way. Since the conventions are constantly changing, make a habit of checking your dictionary for current usage. Here are the main points to remember:

1. Use hyphens in compound numbers from *twenty-one* to *ninety-nine*.

2. Use hyphens with fractions used as adjectives:

    A two-thirds majority is required to defeat the amendment.

    When a fraction is used as a noun, you may use a hyphen, though many writers do not:

    One quarter of the members abstained from voting.

3. Use hyphens with compounds indicating time, when these are written out:

62i

    seven-thirty   nine-fifteen   eleven-twenty

4. Use hyphens with prefixes before proper nouns:

    all-Canadian   pan-Asian   pseudo-Modern

    anti-Fascist   post-Victorian   semi-Gothic

    ex-Prime Minister   pre-Babylonian   trans-Siberian

    non-Communist   pro-Liberal   un-American

    But there are well–established exceptions, for example:

    antichrist   postmodern   transpacific

    postcolonial   transatlantic

5. Use hyphens with compounds beginning with the prefix *self*:

    self-assured   self-deluded   self-made

    self-confidence   self-esteem   self-pity

(The words *selfhood*, *selfish*, *selfless*, and *selfsame* are not hyphenated, since *self* is the root, not a prefix.)

Note that hyphens are conventionally used with certain other prefixes: *all-important, ex-premier, quasi-religious*. Hyphens are conventionally used with most, but not all, compounds beginning with *vice* and *by*: *vice-chancellor, vice-consul, vice-president, vice-regent*, etc., BUT *viceregal, viceroy*; *by-election, by-product*, etc., BUT *bygone, bylaw, byroad, bystander, byword*. Check your dictionary.

6. Use a "suspension" hyphen after the first prefix when you use two prefixes with one root, even if the resulting word would not normally be hyphenated:

> The audience was about equally divided between pro- and anti-Liberals.

> You may choose between the three- and the five-day excursions.

> You may either pre- or postdate the cheque.

7. Use hyphens with the suffixes *elect* and *designate*:

> mayor-elect　ambassador-designate　prime minister-designate

8. Use hyphens with *great* and *in-law* in compounds designating family relationships:

> mother-in-law　sister-in-law　son-in-law
>
> great-aunt　great-grandfather　great-great-grandmother

9. Use hyphens to prevent a word's being mistaken for an entirely different word:

> He recounted what had happened after the ballots had been re-counted.

> If you're going to re-strain the juice, I'll restrain myself from drinking it now, seeds and all.

> Once at the resort after the bumpy ride, we sat down to re-sort our jumbled fishing gear.

> Check out the great sale prices of the goods at the check-out counter.

10. Use hyphens to prevent awkward or confusing combinations of letters and sounds:

> anti-intellectual　e-learning　re-echo
>
> doll-like　photo-offset　set-to

62i

11. Hyphens are sometimes necessary to prevent ambiguity:

> *ambig*: The ad offered six week old kittens for sale.
>
> *clear*: The ad offered six week-old kittens for sale.
>
> *clear*: The ad offered six-week-old kittens for sale.

Note the difference a hyphen makes to the meaning of the last two examples.

In the following, hyphenating *levelling out* removes the possibility of misreading the sentence:

> To maintain social equality, we need a levelling-out of benefits.

62j Compound Nouns

Some nouns composed of two or more words are conventionally hyphenated, for example:

free-for-all	jack-o-lantern	merry-go-round	trade-in
half-and-half	runner-up	rabble-rouser	two-timer

But many nouns that one might think should be hyphenated are not, and others that may once have been hyphenated, or even two separate words, have become so familiar that they are now one unhyphenated word. Usage is constantly and rapidly changing, and even dictionaries don't always agree on what is standard at a given time. Some dictionaries still record such old-fashioned forms as *to-night* and *to-morrow* as alternatives; use *tonight* and *tomorrow*. Clearly it is best to consult a dictionary that is both comprehensive and up-to-date and use the form it lists first.

62k Compound Modifiers

When two or more words occur together in such a way that they act as a single adjective before a noun, they are usually hyphenated in order to prevent a momentary misreading of the first part:

a <u>well-dressed</u> man	<u>greenish-grey</u> eyes
<u>middle-class</u> values	<u>voice-activated</u> dialing
a <u>once-in-a-lifetime</u> chance	a <u>three-day-old</u> strike

When the modifying words occur after a noun, misreading is unlikely and no hyphen is needed:

The man was <u>well dressed</u>.

Her eyes are <u>greenish grey</u>.

But many compound modifiers are already listed as hyphenated words; for example, the *Canadian Oxford Dictionary* lists these, among others:

first-class	habit-forming	open-minded	tongue-tied
fly-by-night	matter-of-fact	right-hand	warm-blooded
good-looking	narrow-minded	short-lived	wide-eyed

Such modifiers retain their hyphens even when they follow the nouns they modify:

The tone of the speech was quite matter-of-fact.

PROOFREADING TIP

On Hyphens and Adverbs Ending in *ly*

Since one cannot mistake the first part of a compound modifier when it is an adverb ending in *ly*, even in front of a noun, do not use a hyphen:

She entered the <u>brightly lit</u> room.

The <u>superbly wrought</u> sculpture was the centre of attention.

62k

Exercise 62j–k Checking Hyphenation

What does your dictionary say about the following terms? Should they be two separate words, hyphenated, or one unhyphenated word? (As an experiment, look some of them up in more than one dictionary; you'll likely find differences.)

1. duty free
2. half life
3. half moon
4. home stretch
5. long time
6. red alert
7. time out
8. world war
9. world wide
10. world weary

62-I Hyphenated Verbs

Verbs, too, are sometimes hyphenated. A dictionary will list most of the ones you might want to use; for example:

double-click	pan-broil	re-educate	sight-read
flip-flop	pole-vault	second-guess	two-time

But be aware that some two-part verbs can never be hyphenated. Resist the temptation to put a hyphen in two-part verbs that consist of a verb followed by a preposition (see #22c–e). Be particularly careful with those word combinations that are hyphenated when they serve as other parts of speech:

> I was asked to set up the display. (*but* Many customers admired the set-up.)

> Call up the next group of trainees. (*but* The rookie awaited a call-up to the big leagues.)

62-1

Exercise 62i–I Using Hyphens

Insert hyphens wherever they are needed in the following sentences. Consult your dictionary if necessary.

1. The ferry is thirty two and one quarter metres long.
2. The all Canadian team proved too much even for the ex champions.
3. The cold hearted vice president took up motor racing instead of profit sharing.
4. Is that an old fashioned and beautifully made antique salt cellar I see in your china cabinet?
5. The three tough looking youths were set to dish out some abuse.
6. I watched an interesting two hour documentary about an alien smuggling operation.
7. Avoid the scatter shot approach when writing a complaint email to part time employees.
8. The long lived queen has been a full time ruler from an early age.
9. The high school teachers' work to rule action left the basketball players without a coach.
10. Under lock and key, the sporting goods store displayed an array of high powered long range hunting rifles.

PROOFREADING TIP

Compounds That Change Their Spelling with the Part of Speech

Note that some expressions can be spelled either as two separate words or as compounds, depending on what part of speech they are functioning as; for example:

He works full time. He has a full-time job.

Be sure to back up your files, and store the backup in a safe place.

If you get too dizzy you may black out. You will then suffer a blackout.

62m Plurals

1. Regular Nouns
For most nouns, add *s* or *es* to the singular form to indicate plural number:

62m

one building, two buildings	one box, two boxes
one cat, two cats	one church, two churches
one girl, two girls	one wish, two wishes

Note that the *es* ending is standard when a word ends in *s*, *x*, *ch*, *sh*, or *z*. One notable exception, however, is that *s* is used if the *ch* ending is pronounced as a *k* sound: *stomach, stomachs; epoch, epochs.*

2. Nouns Ending in *o*
Some nouns ending in *o* preceded by a consonant form their plurals with *s*, while some use *es*. For some either form is correct—but use the one listed first in your dictionary. Here are a few examples:

altos	echoes	cargoes *or* cargos
pianos	heroes	mottoes *or* mottos
solos	potatoes	zeros *or* zeroes

If the final *o* is preceded by a vowel, usually only an *s* is added:

arpeggios	cuckoos	ratios
cameos	embryos	studios

3. Nouns Ending in *f* or *fe*

For some nouns ending in a single *f* or an *fe*, change the ending to *ve* before adding *s*, for example:

knife, knives	life, lives	shelf, shelves
leaf, leaves	loaf, loaves	thief, thieves

But for some simply add *s*:

beliefs	gulfs	safes
griefs	proofs	still lifes

Some words ending in *f* have alternative plurals:

dwarfs *or* dwarves	scarves *or* scarfs
hoofs *or* hooves	wharves *or* wharfs

The well-known hockey team called the *Maple Leafs* is a special case, a proper noun that doesn't follow the rules governing common nouns.

4. Nouns Ending in *y*

For nouns ending in *y* preceded by a vowel, add *s*:

bays	guys	toys
buoys	keys	valleys

For nouns ending in *y* preceded by a consonant, change the *y* to *i* and add *es*:

city, cities	cry, cries	kitty, kitties
country, countries	family, families	trophy, trophies

Exception: Most proper nouns ending in *y* simply add *s*:

There are two <u>Lilys</u> and three <u>Zacharys</u> in my class.

From 1949 to 1990 there were two <u>Germanys</u>.

But note that we refer to the Rocky Mountains as the *Rockies* and to the Canary Islands as the *Canaries*.

5. Compounds

Generally, form the plurals of compounds simply by adding *s*:

backbenchers	lieutenant-governors	prizewinners
forget-me-nots	major generals	second cousins
great-grandmothers	merry-go-rounds	webmasters

But if the first part is a noun and the rest is not, or if the first part is the more important of the two nouns, that one is made plural:

daughters-in-law	jacks-of-all-trades	poets laureate
governors general	mayors elect	townspeople
holes-in-one	passersby	

But there are exceptions, and usage is changing. Note, for example, *spoonfuls* (this is the form for all nouns ending in *ful*). And a few compounds conventionally pluralize both nouns, for example: *ups and downs.* And a few are the same in both singular and plural, for example: *crossroads, daddy-long-legs, underpants.*

6. Irregular Plurals

Some nouns are irregular in the way they form their plurals, but these are common and generally well known, for example:

foot, feet	child, children	mouse, mice	woman, women

Some plural forms are the same as the singular, for example:

one deer, two deer	one series, two series
one moose, two moose	one sheep, two sheep

62m

7. Borrowed Words

The plurals of words borrowed from other languages (mostly Latin and Greek) can pose a problem. Words used formally or technically tend to retain their original plurals; words used more commonly tend to form their plurals according to English rules. Since many such words are in transition, you will probably encounter both plural forms. When in doubt, use the preferred form listed in your dictionary. Here are some examples of words that have tended to retain their original plurals:

alumna, alumnae	madame, mesdames
alumnus, alumni	medium, media (*mediums*
analysis, analyses	for people who claim to
bacterium, bacteria	communicate with spirits)
basis, bases	nucleus, nuclei
crisis, crises	parenthesis, parentheses
criterion, criteria	phenomenon, phenomena
datum, data	stimulus, stimuli
hypothesis, hypotheses	stratum, strata
kibbutz, kibbutzim	synthesis, syntheses
larva, larvae	thesis, theses

But note that it has become acceptable in informal and non-scientific contexts to treat *data* and *media* as if they were singular.

Here are some borrowed words that have both forms, the choice often depending on the formality or technicality of the context:

antenna	antennae (insects) *or* antennas (radios, etc.)
apparatus	apparatus *or* apparatuses
appendix	appendices *or* appendixes
beau	beaux *or* beaus
cactus	cacti *or* cactuses
château	châteaux *or* châteaus
curriculum	curricula *or* curriculums
focus	foci *or* focuses (focusses)
formula	formulae *or* formulas
index	indices *or* indexes
lacuna	lacunae *or* lacunas
matrix	matrices *or* matrixes
memorandum	memoranda *or* memorandums
referendum	referenda *or* referendums
stratum	strata *or* stratums
syllabus	syllabi *or* syllabuses
symposium	symposia *or* symposiums
terminus	termini *or* terminuses
ultimatum	ultimatums *or* ultimata

And here are a few that now tend to follow regular English patterns:

bureau, bureaus	sanctum, sanctums
campus, campuses	stadium, stadiums
genius, geniuses (*genii* for mythological creatures)	

Opinion, as well as usage, is divided on the spelling of the plurals of many of the borrowed words listed in this section. Most writers, for example, find *criterions* and *phenomenons* odd, preferring the original *criteria* and *phenomena*. On the other hand, many no longer object to *data* and *media* as singular nouns. And *agenda*, originally the plural of *agendum*, is now simply a singular noun with its own plural, *agendas*. Your dictionary should indicate any irregular plurals; if you aren't sure of a word, look it up.

62m

PROOFREADING TIP

Spelling Accented Words from Other Languages

If you use or quote words from other languages that have such dia-critical marks as the cedilla (¸), the circumflex (ˆ), the tilde (˜), the umlaut (¨), or acute (ˊ) or grave (ˋ) accents, write them accurately. For example:

façade	*cañon*	*passé*
fête	*Götterdämmerung*	*à la mode*

See also #60b.

8. Letters, Numerals, Symbols, and Words Used as Words

An apostrophe and an *s* may be used to form the plural, but only of letters, numerals, symbols, and words referred to as words:

> She knew her *ABC*'s at the age of four.
>
> Study the three *R*'s.
>
> *Accommodate* is spelled with two *c*'s and two *m*'s.
>
> Between them they have three Ph.D.'s.
>
> There are two 7's in my street address.
>
> It happened in the 1870's.
>
> Indent all ¶'s five spaces.
>
> There are too many *and*'s in that sentence.

Note that when a word, letter, or figure is italicized, the apostrophe and the *s* are not.

Many people prefer to form such plurals without the apostrophe: *R*s, 7s, 1870s, *and*s. But this practice can be confusing, especially with lowercase letters and words, which may be misread:

> *confusing*: How many ss are there in *Nipissing*?
>
> *confusing*: Too many *this*s can spoil a good paragraph.

In cases such as these, it is clearer and easier to use the apostrophe. Keep in mind that it is sometimes better to rephrase instances that are potentially awkward:

> *Accommodate* is spelled with a double *c* and a double *m*.
>
> *And* is used too many times in that sentence.

62m

PROOFREADING TIP

Apostrophes Misused with Regular Common and Proper Nouns

Beware of the "grocer's apostrophe," so called because of its frequent appearance on signs in store windows:

incorrect:	Banana's and tomato's are sold here.
correct:	Bananas and tomatoes are sold here.
incorrect:	Escape the winter blah's with one of our romantic weekend getaway's.
correct:	Escape the winter blahs with one of our romantic weekend getaways.

Use *'s* only in cases such as those outlined above; don't use it to form any other kind of plural—that is, of regular common and proper nouns.

62m

Exercise 62m Forming Plurals

Write out what you think is the correct plural form of each of the following nouns. Then check your dictionary to see if you are right.

1. 2000 _____
2. aide-de-camp _____
3. alley _____
4. bonus _____
5. bus _____
6. cloverleaf _____
7. embargo _____
8. fifth _____
9. fish _____
10. fly-by _____
11. gloss _____
12. goose _____
13. handful _____
14. mongoose _____
15. mosquito _____
16. museum _____
17. *n* _____
18. octopus _____
19. ox _____
20. plateau _____
21. radius _____
22. serf _____
23. shoe _____
24. society _____
25. speech _____
26. staff _____
27. territory _____
28. wife _____
29. yellow _____
30. *yes* (used as a word) _____

62n Possessives

1. To form the possessive case of a singular or a plural noun that does not end in *s*, add an apostrophe and *s*:

Emily's briefcase	a day's work	the car's colour
Canada's capital	deer's hide	the girl's teacher
children's books	yesterday's news	the men's jackets

2. To form the possessive of compound nouns, use *'s* after the last noun:

The prime minister's speech   Logan and Mateo's party

If the nouns don't actually form a compound, each will need the *'s*:

Logan's and Mateo's versions of the dinner party were markedly different.

3. You may correctly add an apostrophe and an *s* to form the possessive of singular nouns ending in *s* or an *s* sound:

Keats's poems	a platypus's bill
the class's achievement	the index's usefulness

62n

However, some writers prefer to add only an apostrophe if the pronunciation of an extra syllable would sound awkward:

Achilles' heel	for convenience' sake
Bill Gates' foundation	Moses' sons

But the *'s* is usually acceptable: *Achilles's heel*; *for convenience's sake*; *Moses's sons*; *Bill Gates's Foundation*. In any event, one can usually avoid possible awkwardness by showing possession with an *of* phrase instead of *'s* (see number 5, below):

the poems of Keats	the sons of Moses
the bill of a platypus	for the sake of convenience

4. To indicate the possessive case of plural nouns ending in *s*, add only an apostrophe:

the cannons' roar	the girls' sweaters
the Joneses' garden	the Chans' cottage

> **PROOFREADING TIP**
> **On Forming/Spelling Possessive Pronouns**
>
> Do not use apostrophes in possessive pronouns:
>
> | | |
> |---|---|
> | hers (NOT her's) | its (NOT it's) |
> | ours (NOT our's) | theirs (NOT their's) |
> | yours (NOT your's) | whose (NOT who's) |
>
> (See also #14a.)

5. Possessive with *'s* or with *of*: Especially in formal writing, the *'s* form is more common with the names of living creatures, the *of* form with the names of inanimate things:

the cat's tail	the leg of the chair
the girl's laptop	the contents of the report
Sheldon's home town	the surface of the desk

    But both are acceptable with either category. The *'s* form, for example, is common with nouns that refer to things thought of as made up of people or animals or as extensions of them:

the team's strategy	the committee's decision
the company's representative	the government's policy
the city's bylaws	Canada's climate
the factory's output	the heart's affections

    or things that are "animate" in the sense that they are part of nature:

the dawn's light	the wind's velocity
the comet's tail	the sea's surface
the tree's roots	the sky's colour

    or periods of time:

today's paper	a day's work
a month's wages	winter's storms

    Even beyond such uses the *'s* is not uncommon; sometimes there is a sense of personification, but not always:

beauty's ensign	the razor's edge
freedom's light	the ship's helm
time's fool	at death's door

62n

If it seems natural and appropriate to you, go ahead and speak or write of *a car's engine, a book's contents, a rocket's trajectory, a poem's imagery,* and the like.

Conversely, for the sake of emphasis or rhythm you will occasionally want to use an *of* phrase where *'s* would be normal—for example, *the jury's verdict* lacks the punch of *the verdict of the jury.* You can also use an *of* phrase to avoid awkward pronunciations (see above: those who don't like the sound of *Dickens's novels* can refer to *the novels of Dickens*) and unwieldy constructions (*the opinion of the minister of finance* is preferable to *the minister of finance's opinion*). Further, whether you use *'s* or just *s* to form the plural of letters, numerals, and the like (see #62m.8), it is probably best, in order to avoid ambiguity, to form possessives of abbreviations with *of* rather than with apostrophes: *the opinion of the MP, the opinion of the MP's, the opinion of the MPs.*

6. Double possessives: There is nothing wrong with double possessives, showing possession with both an *of* phrase and a possessive inflection. They are standard with possessive pronouns and can be used similarly with common and proper nouns:

a favourite of mine a friend of the family *or* of the family's

a friend of hers   a contemporary of Shakespeare *or* of Shakespeare's

62-o

And a sentence like "*The story was based on an idea of Shakespeare*" is at least potentially ambiguous, whereas "*The story was based on an idea of Shakespeare's*" is clear. But if you feel that this sort of construction is unpleasant to the ear, you can usually manage to revise it to something like "*based on one of Shakespeare's ideas.*" And avoid such double possessives with a *that* construction: His hat was just like that of Arthur's.

62-o Contractions

Use apostrophes to indicate omitted letters in contractions:

aren't (are not)	it's (it is)
can't (cannot)	she's (she is)
doesn't (does not)	they're (they are)
don't (do not)	won't (will not)
I'm (I am)	wouldn't (would not)
isn't (is not)	you're (you are)

When forming contractions, make sure you place the apostrophe where the letters have been omitted, *not* where the two words have been joined.

Exercise 62m–o (1) Using Apostrophes

Insert apostrophes where necessary in the following:

1. I dont know whether this book is hers, but theres no doubt its value has increased since the 1930s.
2. Clearly he doesnt know whats going on: itll take him a weeks study to catch up.
3. Our end-of-term reports are ready, but well have to revise them.
4. It isnt the resumé that will get the job but whom you know that will count.
5. Bonnies guess is closer than Jesss, but the jars full and accurate count of beans wont be verified till Monday.
6. The professors comments about Richs paper pointed out its errors.
7. I have two years experience in working with apostrophe problems.
8. It doesnt matter whether one wins or loses but how one plays the game.
9. When all the cars alarms started, the Joness neighbours had to shut their windows.
10. The Canadians approach to traffic is to stop for Canada geese and other passersby.

62-o

Exercise 62m–o (2) Using Apostrophes

In the following sentences, supply any missing apostrophes and correct any instances of their misuse, and any associated errors.

1. Childrens toys are often made in country's where the children do not play because theyre working.
2. How many *ss* are in *associates*?
3. The two main characters are each others foils.
4. He acted without a moments hesitation.
5. We will meet again in three weeks time.
6. Have you read Herman Hesss *The Glass Bead Game*?
7. If its to perform it's duties properly, the committees agenda needs to undergo numerous changes.
8. You can buy boys and girls swim suits in many of the local malls shops.
9. The Harriss came to dinner.
10. When someone misuse's apostrophe's's, it shows they dont understand the rules'.

62p Third-Person-Singular Verbs in the Present Tense

The third-person-singular, present-tense inflection of verbs is usually formed by following the same rules that govern the formation of plurals of nouns. For example:

I brief him. She briefs me.	I lurch. It lurches.
I buy. He buys.	I portray. He portrays.
I carry. She carries.	I run. He runs.
I wait. She waits.	I try. She tries.
I lift. It lifts.	I wish. He wishes.

But be careful, for there are exceptions; for example:

He loafs on weekends and wolfs his food.

She hoofs it to work every day.

Exercise 62p Inflecting Verbs

Supply the present-tense, third-person-singular form of each of the following verbs:

1. atrophy _____
2. buy _____
3. chafe _____
4. choose _____
5. comb _____
6. condone _____
7. convey _____
8. echo _____
9. go _____
10. grasp _____
11. leaf _____
12. mouth _____
13. rally _____
14. reach _____
15. relieve _____
16. revoke _____
17. search _____
18. ski _____
19. swing _____
20. tunnel _____

62q

62q Spelling List

In addition to the words listed and discussed in the preceding pages, other words often cause spelling problems. Following is a list of frequently misspelled words. If you are at all weak in spelling, you should test yourself on these words, as well as those discussed earlier. But you should also keep your own spelling list: whenever you misspell a word, add it to your list, and try to decide which rule the error violates or which category of error it falls into. Write only the correct spelling of the word: never write a misspelled word—even deliberately—when making your list, since this may reinforce the incorrect spelling in your mind when your goal should be to forget it. If a word continues to give you trouble, it can help to concentrate not on the rules that govern its spelling but on how the word looks, by taking a mental "photo" of it. Practise spelling the words on your list until you have mastered them.

absorption	accessible	accumulate
acknowledgement	acquaintance	advertise
aesthetic (*or* esthetic)	affection	aging
allege	amateur	analyze (*or* analyse)
anonymous	apartment	appall (*or* appal)
architect	arctic	arithmetic
auxiliary	axe (*or* ax)	beggar
beneficent	buoyant	burglar
buried	cafeteria	calendar
cartilage	catalogue	category
cemetery	chagrin	changeable
clamour (*or* clamor)	coincide	colleague
colossal	column	committee
complexion	conqueror	conscientious
consensus	convenient	courteous
criticism	cylinder	decrepit
defensive	delusion	devastation
diameter	diminution	discipline
dissatisfied	dissipate	drunkenness
eclectic	ecstasy	efficient
elegiac	embarrassment	endeavour (*or* endeavor)
enforce	engrave	enterprise
equipment	erupt	exaggerate
excel	exercise	exhaust
exhilarating	exorbitant	experience
exuberant	fallacy	fascination
feasible	fiery	flourish

62q

fluorescent	foresee	forty
furor	gaiety	gauge
genealogy	gist	glamorous
grateful	grievous	guarantee
guard	happened	harass
heinous	hesitancy	hierarchy
homogeneous	hygiene	hygienist
hypocrite	idiosyncrasy	ignorance
illegitimate	illiterate	imagery
implement	imposter	inadequacy
indispensable	industrialization	initiative
inoculate	interrupt	intriguing
jealousy	jewellery (*or* jewelry)	judgment (*or* judgement)
knowledgeable	laboratory	liaison
library	likelihood	lineage
liquefy	luxury	magnificent
manoeuvre (*or* maneuver)	manufacture	medieval (*or* mediaeval)
melancholy	memento	metaphor
millennium	minuscule	mischievous
monologue	monotonous	naive
naïveté	necessary	numerous
obstacle	omniscient	ostracize (*or* ostracise)
paraphernalia	parliament	pastime
perfectible	perseverance	persistent
personnel	phony (*or* phoney)	plagiarism
playwright	porous	possession
predecessors	prejudice	primitive
propaganda	proscenium	putrefy
quandary	quizzically	rarefied
recognize	reflection	relevant
reminisce	rhythm	ridiculous

62q

shepherd

simultaneous

skiing

species

subconsciously

susceptible

syrup

therefore

tongue

unforeseen

vehicle

whisky (*or* whiskey)

shiny

siphon (*or* syphon)

solely

straddle

subtly

symbolic

temperament

threshold

tyranny

unfortunately

veterinarian

wintry

simile

skeptic (*or* sceptic)

soliloquy

strategy

superintendent

synonymous

temperature

tomorrow

undoubtedly

unmistakable

weary

withdrawal

62q

VII

Diction

Introduction: Style and the Larger Elements of Composition

"Proper words in proper places make the true definition of a style": Jonathan Swift's definition of style may be the best, at least for simplicity and directness. In its broadest sense, style consists of everything that is not the content of what is being expressed. It is the manner more than the matter: everything that is a part of the way something is said constitutes its style.

But though many of us distinguish between style and content to facilitate discussion and analysis, the distinction is in some ways arbitrary, for the two are inseparable. Since the way in which something is expressed inevitably influences the effect, it is necessarily part of what is being expressed. "I have a hangover" may say essentially the same thing as "I'm feeling a bit rough this morning," but the different styles of the statements create different effects, different meanings. The medium is a substantial part of the message.

An important attribute of style is tone, often defined as a writer's attitude toward both subject matter and audience. Tone in writing is analogous to tone in speech. We hear or describe someone as speaking in a sarcastic tone of voice, or as sounding cheerful, or angry, or matter-of-fact. Writing, like speech, can "sound" ironic, conversational, intimate, morbid, tragic, frivolous, cold, impassioned, comic, coy, energetic, phlegmatic, detached, sneering, contemptuous, laudatory, condescending, and so forth. The tone of a piece of writing—whether an essay or only a sentence—largely determines the feeling or impression that writing creates.

The style of a piece of writing, including its tone, arises from such features as syntax, point of view, and even punctuation. But it is largely determined by diction: by choice of words, figurative language, and sounds. Diction, then, is near the heart of effective writing and style. This chapter isolates the principal challenges writers encounter in choosing and using words, and it offers some suggestions for overcoming them.

WRITING TIP

Style and Diction in Electronic Communication

Many of the principles outlined in this chapter apply not only to formal writing assignments but to all written communication that is meant to be professional, including emails to professors and colleagues, school-related blog posts, and comments made on course websites. While you may be accustomed to using slang, imprecise words, and incomplete sentences in the emails and online messages you send to your close friends, you should avoid using informal words and phrases when you are communicating in academic or professional contexts. You should also make an effort to be as concise as possible when communicating electronically—your readers will appreciate not having to skim through a lengthy message to uncover essential information.

VII

(63) About Dictionaries

The first suggestion is the simplest one: when you think "diction," think "dictionary." Make sure you have access to a good dictionary, and use it to full advantage. Become familiar with it: find out how it works, and discover the variety of information it offers. A good dictionary doesn't merely give you the spelling, pronunciation, and meaning of words; it also offers advice on such matters as usage and idioms to help you decide on the best word for a particular context; it lists irregularities in the principal parts of verbs, in the inflection of adjectives and adverbs, and in the formation of plurals; it supplies etymologies (or word histories); it tells you if a word or phrase is considered formal, informal, slang, or archaic. And it usually has an interesting and useful introduction and relevant appendices.

Whether you're browsing through the reference section of your library or its website, or considering the vast selection of dictionaries online or at your local bookstore, you may feel overwhelmed by the number of dictionaries available to you. The following sections offer some advice on how to find the dictionary that's most appropriate for your needs.

63a Kinds of Dictionaries

Dictionaries range in scope and function from extensive works offering detailed word histories to tiny word books designed to fit in your pocket. Most of the information you will require as a student will be contained in one of three kinds of dictionary: an unabridged dictionary, an abridged dictionary, or a learner's dictionary.

1. Unabridged Dictionaries

Unabridged dictionaries offer the most comprehensive view of English as it is now and has been used. The *Oxford English Dictionary* (*OED*), the most famous of unabridged dictionaries, is based on historical principles, which means that it presents definitions for each word, accompanied by historical quotations, in the order of their first recorded use. The *OED* is most useful when you want to see how the meaning of a word has changed over time. For example, a look at the *OED*'s entry for *silly* will enable you to trace the word to its Old English roots, when it meant "happy, fortunate, prosperous," to Middle English, when its meanings included "spiritually blessed" and "deserving of pity or sympathy," to the sixteenth century, when it came to be used to mean "lacking in judgment or common sense." Most libraries subscribe to the *OED Online*, which is updated quarterly and offers a convenient way to search for the information you might need.

Not all unabridged dictionaries are based on historical principles. *Webster's Third New International Dictionary, Unabridged* (1961) and the *Random House Webster's Unabridged Dictionary* (second edition, 2005) are excellent unabridged dictionaries that offer extensive information on the modern meanings of words. Though the former is rather out of date, an

63a

updated version is available online for a monthly or annual fee. The latter is available on CD-ROM. (Be aware that there is no copyright on the name *Webster's*, so many American dictionary publishers use the name in their titles hoping that the good reputation of the famous American lexicographer Noah Webster will rub off on their own products.)

2. Abridged Dictionaries

Although some questions will require you to consult an unabridged dictionary, an abridged dictionary is the most useful for the everyday needs of most students and writers. Abridged dictionaries range in length and level of detail, but the most practical are "college" or "desk" dictionaries that include words and senses in current use, along with some historical senses, pronunciations, illustrative examples, etymologies, usage notes, and "encyclopedic" entries that provide information on people and places.

There are some very good desk dictionaries produced in Canada, including the *Canadian Oxford Dictionary* (second edition, 2004; available online) and the *Collins Canadian Dictionary* (2010). Although high-quality British and American dictionaries can also be useful, we recommend using Canadian dictionaries because they offer a more accurate reflection of the language as it is spoken, written, and used by Canadians.

Some students find it useful to keep an abridged dictionary on hand during lectures or research sessions. Dictionaries available online, on CD-ROM, or for download are particularly convenient for students who take notes using a laptop computer or another electronic device. Because they are not restricted to a set word count, electronic dictionaries tend to contain more entries and more extensive definitions and examples than do their printed counterparts. Most online dictionaries also offer more current information, because they are updated several times per year.

63a

EAL

3. Learner's Dictionaries

Although learner's dictionaries are designed especially for people whose first language is not English, the advice on usage and grammar and the defining style of several excellent learner's dictionaries make them enormously helpful even to native speakers of English. Some learner's dictionaries use a limited defining vocabulary of a few thousand words likely to be understood, or at least recognized, by readers of English as an additional language. This reduces the chances that a definition will contain words the user will have to look up.

A good learner's dictionary features numerous notes and examples to illustrate the idiomatic use of words. It may also contain information on such matters as understanding English grammar and spelling, and writing tests, essays, and letters. Some excellent learner's dictionaries include the *Oxford ESL Dictionary for Learners of English* (new edition, 2012), the *Oxford Advanced Learner's Dictionary* (eighth edition, 2010), the *Collins Cobuild Advanced Learner's English Dictionary* (fifth edition, 2006), and the *Longman Dictionary of Contemporary English* (fifth edition, 2009).

63b Features of Dictionaries

Most people who consult a dictionary are looking for one of two things: the meaning of a word, or the spelling of a word. When assessing a dictionary, it is helpful to know how its editors made their decisions about meaning and spelling. Was their research based on analysis of a large corpus of English texts? Did they consult recent sources to capture new words and usages? If it is a Canadian dictionary, what kind of research was used to determine preferred Canadian spellings? All of this sort of information can usually be found in the preface or introduction of a printed dictionary; online dictionaries generally offer this sort of information on a web page that links to their home page.

You will also want to make sure that the dictionary you're using is up to date and not just a recent reissue of an older work. When comparing dictionaries, have a list of newer words and see how many of them are included in each of the dictionaries you're considering. This should give you a good indication of whether or not a dictionary is sufficiently up to date.

Beyond meaning and spelling, a dictionary entry includes several features that may be useful. Deciding how important each of the following is to you will help you decide which dictionary is most appropriate for your needs.

1. Syllable Breaks

Most North American dictionaries indicate syllable breaks in headwords and other bold forms by means of points (·), pipes (|), or other symbols.

fan·tas·tic   im|pres|sion   won◊der◊ful

Knowing an unfamiliar word's syllabication can make the word easier to pronounce.

2. Pronunciations

All dictionaries contain pronunciations, though some may not provide pronunciations for all words. A dictionary may transcribe a word's pronunciation using the International Phonetic Alphabet, or IPA, so that various sounds are represented by specific symbols that are usually displayed across the bottom of the page. Or it may "respell" the word using a combination of letters and diacritical marks to indicate long and short vowels.

	IPA	Respelling
curtains	ˈkɜrtənz	kûr′tnz
eavestroughing	ˈiːvzˌtrɒfiŋ	ēvz′trôfiŋ
shrivel	ˈʃrɪvəl	shriv′əl
cookie	ˈkʊki	kook̄′ē

The IPA transcriptions, though they may appear at first confusing, produce the most accurate representations of a word's pronunciation. The respelling method offers an easier way to convey a reasonably accurate pronunciation without the user's having to learn a complicated set of symbols. Many electronic dictionaries further simplify the process of interpretation by offering sound recordings that allow users to hear how a word is pronounced. Some even offer multiple recordings to illustrate, for example, standard North American as well as British pronunciations.

3. Examples and Illustrations

Definitions for technical words can often be enhanced with illustrations. Consider the following definition for *helicopter*, from the *Canadian Oxford Dictionary*: "a type of aircraft without wings, obtaining lift and propulsion from horizontally revolving overhead blades or rotors, and capable of moving vertically and horizontally." This definition, though accurate, likely will not produce for the reader a perfect idea of a helicopter the way an accompanying illustration would.

In a similar but often more practical way, a definition may be greatly enhanced by a written example that shows the way a word is used in a sentence. This is an important feature of learner's dictionaries, which strive to show their users not just what words mean but how they should be used in speech.

4. Usage Information

An important thing to remember about dictionaries is that they are descriptive, not prescriptive. They record the language as it is actually used, not as some people think it should be used. As a result, most dictionaries include words or senses that may meet with the disapproval of some users. For example, most dictionaries include two nearly opposite definitions for the word *peruse*: "to read thoroughly or carefully" (the original sense), and "to read in a casual manner" (the more common sense). Many critics object to the second use, yet it would be inappropriate for a dictionary to exclude this sense, since it is the one most people have in mind when they use the word. A good dictionary will point out the usage issue in a brief note in the entry.

Most dictionaries also include register labels to indicate whether a word is formal, informal, slang, archaic, and so on.

5. Idioms and Phrasal Verbs

An idiom is an expression whose meaning is not easily deduced from the meanings of the words it comprises—for example, *off the top of my head*, *out on a limb*, *be run off one's feet* (see #70). Idioms and phrasal, or two-part, verbs (see #22d) are often defined toward the end of a word's entry. Bear in mind that an idiom such as *off the top of my head* could be defined at the entry for *top* or the entry for *head*.

6. Derivatives

A derivative is a word derived from another, such as *quickness* or *quickly* from *quick*. It is common for dictionaries to "nest" undefined derivatives

63b

at the main entry for a word if the derivatives' meanings can be easily deduced. For example, a word like *logically* does not require a separate definition as long as *logical* is well defined; the reader can safely assume that *logically* means "in a logical manner." But the word *practically* should not be nested in the entry for *practical*, since it has a sense beyond "in a practical manner." Be aware that some shorter dictionaries nest derivatives that should be defined separately; this is something you should keep in mind when evaluating the usefulness of a dictionary.

7. Etymologies

Knowing a word's etymology, its original form and meaning, can sometimes help you remember or get a clearer idea of its meaning. For example, knowing that the word *recalcitrant* comes from a Latin word meaning "kicking back," from *calx*, "heel," may help you remember that it means "stubborn, uncooperative." And knowing that *peruse* comes from the prefix *per*, meaning "thoroughly," plus *use* will help you understand why some critics object to its use to mean "read in a casual manner." A word's etymology can be fascinating as well as helpful: *climax* comes from a Greek word for ladder, *vegetable* comes from a Latin verb meaning "to be healthy," *pyjamas* comes from a Persian word meaning "leg clothing." If you find this kind of information interesting, make sure your dictionary goes into detail in its etymologies. Reading that *berserk* comes from an Old Norse compound meaning "bear coat" or that *amethyst* comes from a Greek word meaning "not drunk" without any accompanying explanation can be unsatisfying.

8. Canadian Content

Because Canada has its own political, cultural, historical, and geographical realities, it has its own words to describe these realities. As a result of Canada's unique history and settlement patterns, Canadian English also includes words borrowed from languages that do not appear in other varieties of English. Since dictionaries inevitably describe and reflect the language and culture of the country in which they are edited, American dictionaries and British dictionaries overlook some words, senses, spellings, and pronunciations that are unique to Canadian English. Good Canadian dictionaries, such as the *Canadian Oxford Dictionary* and the *Gage Canadian Dictionary*, which are not merely Canadian adaptations produced in other countries, offer a more accurate view of Canadian English than do either American or British dictionaries.

9. Encyclopedic Entries

Some abridged dictionaries include entries for important people, places, and events. These entries may be quite short, consisting of little more than a person's years of birth and death or a city's population, or they may provide more information about a person's life and work or a city's importance. If you are considering dictionaries with encyclopedic entries, pick a couple of people or places and see how various dictionaries treat them.

63b

63c Three Sample Dictionary Entries

The following three entries, from an abridged, a compact, and a learner's dictionary, illustrate some of the features just described. Dictionaries follow certain conventions, but each features a unique design. A final consideration when judging the suitability of a dictionary is how easy it is for you to navigate through it.

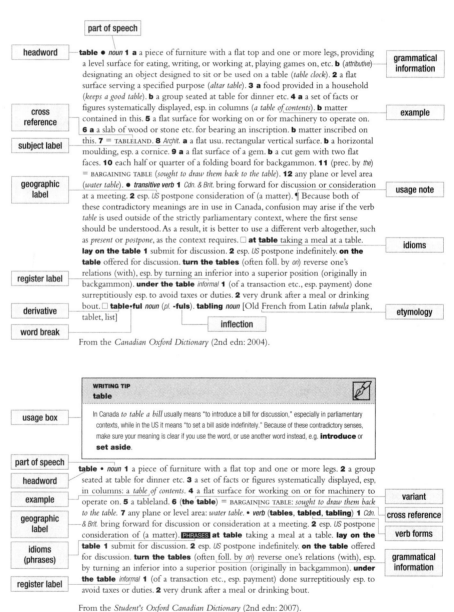

From the *Canadian Oxford Dictionary* (2nd edn: 2004).

From the *Student's Oxford Canadian Dictionary* (2nd edn: 2007).

63c

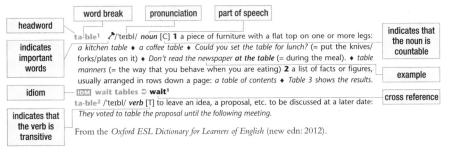

word break	pronunciation	part of speech

headword

indicates important words

ta·ble¹ /'teɪbl/ *noun* [C] **1** a piece of furniture with a flat top on one or more legs: *a kitchen table* ♦ *a coffee table* ♦ *Could you set the table for lunch?* (= put the knives/forks/plates on it) ♦ *Don't read the newspaper **at the table*** (= during the meal). ♦ *table manners* (= the way that you behave when you are eating) **2** a list of facts or figures, usually arranged in rows down a page: *a table of contents* ♦ *Table 3 shows the results.*

indicates that the noun is countable

example

idiom

IDM **wait tables** ⊃ **wait¹**

cross reference

indicates that the verb is transitive

ta·ble² /'teɪbl/ *verb* [T] to leave an idea, a proposal, etc. to be discussed at a later date: *They voted to table the proposal until the following meeting.*

From the *Oxford ESL Dictionary for Learners of English* (new edn: 2012).

64 Level

ev In any piece of writing, use words that are appropriate to you, to your topic, and to the circumstances in which you are writing. That is, consider the *occasion*, the *purpose*, and the *audience*. Avoid words and phrases that call attention to themselves rather than to the meaning you want to convey. In writing a formal academic essay, adopt diction appropriate to the discipline in which and the audience for which you are writing. In other writing for your courses or for the workplace, avoid slang and colloquial or informal terms at one extreme, and pretentious language at the other. Of course there will be times when one or the other, or both, will be useful—for example, to make a point in a particularly telling way, to achieve a humorous effect, or to make dialogue sound realistic. But it is usually preferable to adopt a straightforward, moderate style, a level of diction that both respects the intelligence of the reader and strives to communicate with the reader as effectively as possible. (See also #22e.)

64

 PROOFREADING TIP

Checking on the Sound of Your Prose

Reading your work aloud can help you identify whether the level of your writing is either too high or too low. You'll likely find that you will stumble over or overemphasize words that are too formal, and you will likely read informal words and phrases in a casual or offhand manner. Reading aloud can also help you find and adjust unpleasant patterns of sound and rhythm, such as excessive alliteration or too regular a metrical pattern (e.g., "at the top of the tree sat a bird on a branch"), jarring repetitions of sound (e.g., "they put strict restrictions on lending, which constricted the flow of funds"), or accidental rhyme (e.g., "at that time he was in his prime; the way he later let himself go was a crime").

64a Slang

Since **slang** is diction opposite to **formal diction**, it is seldom appropriate in a formal context. There is nothing inherently wrong with slang; it is undeniably a colourful part of the language and can help you express complicated ideas with clarity and force. But its very liveliness and vigour make it short-lived: some slang terms remain in vogue only for a few weeks, some linger on for a few years, and new ones are constantly popping up to replace those going out of fashion. Some slang terms eventually become part of the standard written language, but most slang is so ephemeral that dictionaries cannot keep up with it.

It is principally slang's transitoriness that makes it ineffective to use in the kind of writing you may be doing for your courses. A word or phrase that is *hot* (or *cool*) when you write it may sound stale and dated soon after. Much slang is also limited to particular social groups, classes, or professions, and it is often regional as well. Hence terms that may be vivid to you and your friends may be unintelligible to an outsider, such as someone older or from a different place. Or, given the nature of some slang words, a reader who finds them intelligible may also find them offensive.

If you are considering using slang in your writing, consult not only one or more good dictionaries but also members of your audience: trust your ear, your common sense, and your good taste.

64a

Exercise 64a Thinking About Slang

List as many slang terms as you can think of for each of the following. Which are current in your vocabulary? Which, if any, would you consider using in an academic essay? In a letter to a friend? In a letter to a parent or an uncle or an aunt?

1. angry
2. mad (adj.)
3. intoxicated
4. very good
5. cheat (v.)
6. court (v.)
7. beautiful
8. talk (v.)
9. bore (n.)
10. stupid person
11. criminal (n.)
12. police officer
13. man
14. woman
15. child
16. friend
17. sweetheart
18. food
19. eat
20. inspiring

PROOFREADING TIP

On Slang and the Use of Quotation Marks

If you do use a slang term, do not use quotation marks to call attention to it (see #54g).

64b Informal or Colloquial Usage

f,
•q
Even dictionaries can't agree on what constitutes slang versus **informal** or **colloquial** usage. Slang terms are in one sense simply extreme examples of the colloquial or informal. Nevertheless, there are many words and phrases that may be labelled *inf* or *colloq* in a dictionary, and although not slang, they do not ordinarily belong in formal writing. For example, unless you are aiming for a somewhat informal level, you should avoid such abbreviations as *esp., etc., no., orig.,* and *OK*; and you may wish to avoid contractions (*can't, don't,* etc.), though they are common in many books and in everyday speech.

Here are more examples of informal or colloquial usages that would be out of place in strictly formal writing:

Informal or Colloquial	Acceptable Equivalents
absolutely	very, thoroughly
a lot of, lots of, lots	much, many, a great deal of
anyplace, everyplace, noplace, someplace	anywhere, everywhere, nowhere, somewhere
around	approximately
awful	bad, ill, ugly, unpleasant, etc.
back of, in back of	behind
be sure and	be sure to
chance of + gerund (e.g., chance of getting)	chance + infinitive (chance to get)
expect (as in "I expect you want me here")	suppose, suspect, imagine
figure	think, believe, etc.
fix (n.)	predicament
fix (v.)	prepare (food or drink); manipulate fraudulently (an election, a contract, a competition)

64b

funny	odd, peculiar, strange, unusual
guess (as in "I guess that . . .")	believe, suppose, think
how come	why
mean	cruel, evil, deceitful, etc.
most (as in "most everyone")	almost, nearly
nice	agreeable, attractive, pleasant, etc.
nowhere near	not nearly, not at all, not anywhere near
out loud	aloud
over with	ended, finished, done
photo	photograph
plan on + gerund (e.g., plan on going)	plan + infinitive (plan to go)
quite, quite a bit, quite a few, quite a lot	somewhat, rather, many, a large amount, much
real, really (as intensive adverb)	very, greatly, surely
right away, right now	immediately, at once
shape (good, bad, etc.)	condition
show up	appear, arrive; prove better than, best
size up	judge, assess
sure and (as in "be sure and call")	sure to
terrible, terribly (also as vague modifiers)	unpleasant, uncomfortable, very, extremely
try and	try to
wait on (as in "I'm waiting on a delivery")	await, wait for

In addition, many words have been so overused for gushy and exaggerated effect, especially in advertising, that they can now seldom be used with precision in formal writing. For example:

awesome	epic	fantastic	incredible	legendary
lifestyle	marvellous	stupendous	terrific	tremendous

If you find yourself using any of these words in an essay, take a moment to consider whether you are using the word in a formal sense; if necessary, consult your dictionary.

Exercise 64a–b Using Formal Diction

Provide formal substitutes for each of the slang or informal terms and phrases below. Use your dictionary or thesaurus as necessary. Then compose sentences for at least ten of the listed terms, using them in ways that you think would be acceptable in relatively formal writing.

1. shocker
2. humongous
3. just saying
4. chump
5. kid (n. referring to humans)
6. con (n. and v.)
7. ditzy
8. cook up
9. crackdown
10. crummy
11. jock
12. cute
13. bawl out
14. down the tube
15. face the music
16. hanging out with
17. high and mighty
18. ditch (v.)
19. hunch
20. jerk (n.)
21. miss out
22. fall guy
23. on the spot
24. scrounge
25. bellyache (n. and v.)
26. slouch (n.)
27. baby bump
28. conniption
29. buddy
30. up the creek

64c

64c "Fine Writing"

Unnecessarily formal or pretentious diction is called "fine writing"—an ironic term of disapproval. Efforts to impress with such writing almost always backfire. For example, imagine yourself trying to take seriously someone who wrote "It was felicitous that the canine in question was demonstrably more exuberant in emitting threatening sounds than in attempting to implement said threats by engaging in actual physical assault," instead of simply saying "Luckily, the dog's bark was worse than its bite." This is an exaggerated example, but it illustrates how important it is to be natural (within reason) and straightforward. Writers who overreach themselves often use supposedly elegant terms incorrectly. The individual who wrote "Riding majestically down the street on a magnificent float was the festival queen surrounded by all her courtesans" was striving for sophistication, but succeeded only in getting an undesired laugh from the reader who knew the correct meaning of *courtesans*.

Exercise 64c Thinking About Highly
Formal Words

For each of the following words, provide one or more equivalents that
are less formal and more natural. Use your dictionary or thesaurus
as necessary. Which of these words do you recognize but not use
yourself? Which do you consider to be in your working vocabulary?
Mark any that you think should not necessarily be avoided as pretentious or overly formal in a non-academic context.

64c

1. assiduity
2. bellicose
3. cachinnation
4. circumambient
5. collation
6. colloquy
7. comminatory
8. compotation
9. concatenation
10. confabulate
11. conflagration
12. crepuscular
13. defenestration
14. divagation
15. doff
16. egress
17. eleemosynary
18. equitation
19. erstwhile
20. frangible
21. gustatory
22. hebdomadal
23. impudicity
24. ineluctable
25. jejune

26. lubricity
27. lucubrations
28. matutinal
29. mentation
30. objurgation
31. obloquy
32. orthography
33. otiose
34. pellucid
35. penurious
36. peregrinations
37. propinquity
38. raison d'être
39. rebarbative
40. repast
41. rubicund
42. salubrious
43. sartorial
44. *schadenfreude*
45. serendipitous
46. sesquipedalian
47. superincumbent
48. tenebrous
48. veridical
50. visage

65 Figurative Language

ig Strictly speaking, **figurative language** includes mostly "figures of speech," such as personification, synecdoche, metonymy, hyperbole, litotes, and even paradox, irony, and symbolism. Generally, however, the term *figurative language* refers to *metaphoric* language, whose most common devices are the **simile** and the **metaphor**. A simile is an explicit comparison that is usually marked by *like* or *as*:

> The river is like a snake winding across the prairie.

> The Internet is like a highway without speed limits.

A metaphor, on the other hand, is an implicit comparison; the items being compared are assumed to be identical:

> The river is a snake winding its way across the prairie.

> The Internet is a highway without speed limits.

Often a metaphor is condensed into a *verb*:

> The river snakes its way across the prairie.

an adjective:

> The serpentine river meanders across the prairie.

or an adverb:

> The river winds snakily across the prairie.

65

Figurative language is often an important element of good style. Writing that lacks this kind of language will be relatively dry, flat, and dull. But remember that a good metaphor doesn't merely enhance style: it also sharpens meaning. Use metaphors not only for their own sake, but to convey meaning more effectively. For example, to say that "the hillside was covered with a profusion of colourful flowers" is clear enough; but if one writes instead that "the hillside was a tapestry of spring blossoms," the metaphor not only enriches the style but also provides readers with something *concrete* (see #66a), an *image* (that of the tapestry) that helps them visualize the scene.

65a Inappropriate Metaphors

If you force a metaphor into your writing just to embellish style, it will likely be inappropriate and call attention to itself rather than enhance the desired meaning. It will, to use a tired but still expressive simile, stick out like a sore thumb. For example, "the tide of emotion suddenly stopped" doesn't work, since tides don't start and stop; they ebb and flow. And a phrase like "bomb craters blossoming all over the landscape" works only if one intends the inherent discord between bombs and blossoms. And a simile such as "he ran like an ostrich in heat" may confuse the reader with inappropriate associations.

65b Overextended Metaphors

Extended metaphors can be effective, but don't become so enamoured with a metaphor that you extend it too far, to the point where it takes control of what is being said:

> When she came out of the surf her hair looked like limp spaghetti. A sauce of seaweed and sand, looking like spinach and grated cheese, had been carelessly applied, the red flower fastened in her tresses looked like a wayward piece of tomato, and globs of mud clung like meatballs to the pasty pasta of her face. The fork of my attention hovered hesitatingly over this odd dish. Clearly I would need more than one glass of the red wine of remembered beauty and affection to wash it all down.

65c

This may all be very clever, but after the first sentence—the spaghetti image itself being somewhat questionable—the reader quickly loses sight of the original descriptive intention and becomes mired in all the associated metaphors and similes; in short, a reader is likely to feel fed up, or in this case giddy, and turn to something less overdone.

65c Dead Metaphors

Guard against dead metaphors and clichés (see #71e). English contains many dead metaphors like the "*leg* of a table," "*branching* out," and "*flew* to the rescue," which are acceptable since we no longer think of them as metaphors. But many other metaphors, whether altogether dead or only moribund but with little metaphoric force left, can be ineffective. Such overused phrases as *the ladder to success, making mountains out of molehills, nipped in the bud, flogging a dead horse,* and *time is running out* are usually muddying and soporific instead of enlivening and clarifying.

Occasionally, a dead or trite metaphor can be revivified if consciously used in a fresh way. For example, the hackneyed phrase *bit off more than he could chew* was given new life by the person who, discussing Henry James's writing, said that James "chewed more than he bit off." But take some care, for such attempts can misfire; like an overextended metaphor, they sometimes call attention to their own cleverness at the expense of the intended meaning.

65d Mixed Metaphors

Edit out of your writing incongruously mixed metaphors. The person who wrote, of the Great Depression, that "what began as a zephyr soon blossomed into a giant" had lost control of the metaphor. The following paragraph about Shakespeare's *Othello* was written by one who obviously began with the good intention of using metaphors to describe the evil of Iago, but who became lost in a maze of contradictions and incongruities:

> Iago has spun his web and like a spider he waits. His beautiful web of silk is so fragile and yet it captures the souls of its victims by gently luring them into his womb. Unsuspecting are those unfortunate creatures who sense the poisonous venom oozing through their veins. It has a tranquil effect, for it numbs the mind with its magical potion. The victims are transformed into pawns as they satisfy the queen's appetite and so they serve their purpose.

Here, in contrast, is a paragraph that successfully uses a single extended metaphor to create its effect:

> I remember vividly my first days as a student teacher. They were the closest I have ever come to knowing what it must feel like to be part of a high-wire act. Walking into that high school classroom for the first time was like taking the first tentative steps onto the wire: the eyes of the audience were upon me, my knees were shaking, and I was struggling to keep my balance. But as that first morning went on and as my students and I moved forward into the lesson, I felt the exhilaration of the high-wire performer as she finds her equilibrium and moves with confidence to the middle and then the end of that tightrope. The only thing missing was the cheering.

Certainly, then, use figurative language. It can lend grace and charm and liveliness and clarity to your writing. But be alert to its potential pitfalls: inappropriate, overextended, and mixed metaphors.

66 Concrete and Abstract Diction; Weak Generalizations

66a Concreteness and Specificity

Concrete words denote tangible things, capable of being apprehended by our physical senses (*children, skyscraper, flowers, parks, broccoli, ice, fire, walking*). **Abstract** words denote intangibles, like ideas or qualities (*postmodernism, agriculture, nature, health, creativity, progress*). Much of the writing you do is likely a blend of the abstract and the concrete. The more concrete your writing, the more readily your readers will grasp it, for the concreteness will provide images for their imaginations to respond to. If you write

Transportation is becoming a major problem in our city.

and leave it at that, readers will understand you. But if you write, or add,

In the downtown core of this city, far too many cars and far too few buses travel the streets.

you know that your readers will see exactly what you mean: in their minds they will see the traffic jams and the overloaded buses.

As your writing moves from generalizations to specifics, it will move from the abstract to the concrete. And the more specific your writing is, the clearer and more effective it will often be. *General* and *specific* are relative terms: a general word designates a *class* (e.g., *modes of transportation*); a less general or more specific word designates members of that class (*vehicles, ships, airplanes*); a still more specific word designates members of a still smaller class (*cars, trucks, bicycles, buses*); and so on, getting narrower and narrower, the classes and sub-classes getting smaller and smaller, until—if one wants or needs to go that far—one arrives at a single, unique item, a class of one, such as the particular car sitting in your own parking spot, driveway, or garage.

Of course it is appropriate to write about "plant life," and then to narrow it, say, to "flowers"; and if you can write about "marigolds," "roses," "daffodils," and so on, you'll be more specific. Even the generalization "fire" is unquestionably vivid, but "forest fires" makes it sharper, and mentioning the specific example of "the huge bush fires in Queensland" will likely enable you to make your point even more sharply. Don't vaguely write "We experienced a warm day" when you could write more clearly, "We stayed outdoors all afternoon in the 25-degree weather," or "We basked in the warm spring sunshine all afternoon." Don't write "I found the city interesting" when you could write "I admired the city's architecture and enjoyed its night life," or, better still, "I was fascinated by the well-preserved architecture in the city's French quarter, and I enjoyed the fine cafés, restaurants, and jazz clubs that I found there."

The following passage makes sense, but its abstractness and generality prevent it from being more memorable or effective:

If one makes a purchase that a short time later proves to have been ill-advised due to the rapid deterioration of quality, then it is the opinion of this writer that one has every right to seek redress either by expressing one's displeasure to the individual who conducted the original transaction or, if it should prove necessary, by resorting to litigation.

Writers sometimes assume that this kind of language is good because it sounds formal and sophisticated. But notice how much more vivid a revised version is:

> If you buy a car on Thursday and the engine falls out of it on Saturday, I think you should complain to the dealer who sold it to you, and sue the dealership if necessary to get back the good money you paid for what turned out to be a useless vehicle.

Of course, abstract and general terms are legitimate and often necessary, for one can scarcely present all ideas concretely, and the kind of concrete language illustrated in the above example is hardly appropriate to all situations. Try, though, to be as concrete and specific as your subject and the context will allow.

66b Weak Generalizations

A common weakness of student writing is an overdependence on unsupported generalizations. Consider: "Children today are reluctant readers." Few readers would or should accept such a general assertion, for the statement calls for considerably more illustration, evidence, and qualification. It evokes all kinds of questions: All children? Of all ages? In all countries? What are they reluctant to read? What is the connotation of "reluctant" here? Is such reluctance really something new? Merely stating a generalization or assumption is not enough; to be clear and effective it must be illustrated and supported by specifics.

Here are two essays on the same topic. Read the first one through:

66b

> Travel can be a very broadening experience for people who go with the intention of having their eyes opened, which may often occur by unpleasant means. Culture shock can be a very unpleasant and hurtful experience to people who keep their eyes and minds closed to different attitudes or opinions. This problem of culture shock is an example of why people should prepare for the unexpected and try to learn from difficult experiences, rather than keeping a closed mind which will cause them to come away with a grudge or hurt feelings.
>
> Besides causing negative attitudes, travel can also confirm the prejudices of people with narrow minds. For

example, I once met an older man from England who had travelled around the world visiting the last vestiges of the British empire. He had even travelled to apartheid South Africa, and still come away with his colonialist attitudes.

Even if one goes to a country with an open mind, one may still come away with a superficial perception of that country. It takes time to get to know a country and understand its people. The time one spends in a country will thus greatly affect one's perception of that country.

Time is also needed before travelling begins, for people to read and learn about the area they will be going to. This background will enable them to look for things they might otherwise never see, and they will appreciate more the things they do discover. For example, if one knows something about the architecture of a country before one visits it, one can plan one's trip to include visits to buildings of special interest.

Thus an open, well-prepared mind will benefit from the experiences of travel, but otherwise travel is likely to have a very negative, narrowing effect on people's minds.

66b

Now, without looking back at the essay, ask yourself what it said. You will probably have a vague sense of its thesis, and chances are you will remember something about a well-travelled but still narrow-minded traveller from England, and perhaps something about the advisability of knowing something in advance about foreign architecture—for those are the only two concrete items in the essay. (Think how much more vivid and therefore meaningful and memorable the point about architecture would have been had it included a reference to a specific landmark, such as the Leaning Tower of Pisa or the Taj Mahal or the Parthenon or St. Paul's Cathedral.)

Now read the second essay, noting as you read how much clearer its points are than the relatively unsupported generalizations of the first essay:

Travel can be broadening. The knowledge gained in the areas of historical background, cultural diversity, and the range of personalities encountered in foreign lands gives us a fuller outlook on ourselves, on Canada and Canadian issues, and on our position in the global context.

The impact of history upon visitors to other lands is immense indeed. One cannot help but feel somewhat small when looking across valley upon valley of white crosses in France, coming face to face with the magnitude of death that occurred during the world wars of the last century. Before long, one realizes that many of the events that took place years ago have an effect upon the way in which we live today. In some areas, scars of the relatively recent past remain. The bits of rubble left from the once formidable Berlin Wall, for example, remind visitors that the way they live is not the same way others live, that, indeed, for decades millions lived grim and limited lives, never dreaming that in their lifetimes revolutionary changes would bring freedom, if not immediate comfort and prosperity.

This is not to say that there are not pleasant aspects of history as well. Sixteenth-century cobblestone lanes, usually less than three metres wide, still remain in many old English villages, surrounded by Tudor cottages, complete with thatched roofs, oil lamps, and sculpted wrought-iron fences. Standing in such an environment and thinking about

66b

the writings of masters like Shakespeare brings out a much deeper and richer taste than merely reading about them in a classroom at home. And places like this remind us of how our ancestors lived, making it easier to understand the customs and ideas of the past.

In going through different foreign lands, one cannot ignore the great cultural diversity. This is best illustrated by contrasting fiestas in Spain and Oktoberfest in Munich with Canadian celebrations. Many countries, besides having different languages (and dialects of those languages), also have their own dress, holidays, and religious beliefs. This variety is often startling to the tourist, who often takes it for granted that what is standard for him or her is also the norm throughout much of the rest of the world.

Above all, the differences among people from other countries are what leave a visitor with the most lasting impression. From the street person in the slums of Casablanca, to the well-dressed gentleman walking briskly in the streets of Hanover, to the British executive sipping beer in "the local" on Hyde Street, there are myriad personalities as one travels through other lands. When we look at the world from this perspective, realizing that we are not all the same, we are better equipped to understand many of the problems throughout the globe.

66b

The first essay is not without a message, for unsupported generalizations do have content, do say something; but the message of the second is clearer, more forceful; readers will better understand and remember what it said because their minds have something concrete and specific to hang on to.

Exercise 66 (1) Using Specific Diction

For each of the following words, supply several increasingly specific terms; take at least a few all the way to a single specific item.

1. car
2. art
3. answered
4. said
5. food
6. drink (v.)
7. drink (n.)
8. people
9. mythical thing
10. entertainment
11. creature
12. structure
13. see
14. touch
15. move
16. concept
17. freedom
18. music
19. clothing
20. story
21. work
22. interesting
23. social media
24. emotion
25. dance (n.)
26. performance
27. perform
28. technology
29. plant (n.)
30. exercise (n.)

Next, compose a paragraph in which you use one or two of these general terms in the first sentence and develop your idea by using increasingly specific terms.

66b

Exercise 66 (2) Being Concrete and Specific

Rewrite this vague and abstract paragraph from a letter of application for an entry-level research position at a community newspaper. The ad for the position called for details of the applicant's educational and employment experience, so in your revision, try to make the paragraph sharp and vivid by supplying concrete and specific details wherever suitable.

My education and job experience make me a good person to work in your organization. At university, I have been studying courses in arts and science, and I have done quite a bit of research and writing of various things along the way. I have worked as a volunteer in my community, and over the years, I have been employed in three jobs that have given me good experience working in a busy office setting.

Connotation and Denotation

Keep **connotation** in mind both to convey the meaning you intend and to avoid conveying particular shades of meaning you do not intend. A word may **denote** (literally mean) what you want it to yet **connote** (suggest) something you don't intend. For example, if you describe someone as "brash," your reader will understand the denotative meaning of "confident" but will also understand you to feel at least somewhat negative about the quality you are describing; if you in fact approve of the quality (and the person), you'll use a word like "self-assured," for its connotation is favourable rather than unfavourable.

Exercise 67 Recognizing Connotation

Label each of the following words as having a favourable (f), neutral (n), or unfavourable (u) connotation; it might help if you place the words in each group on a scale running from *most favourable* to *most unfavourable*. Explain cases where you think some could be labelled more than one way, depending on context. Use your dictionary if necessary.

1. artless crass dense dull dumb feeble-minded foolish green ignorant inept ingenuous innocent naive obtuse shallow simple slow stupid thick unsophisticated unthinking vapid

2. bony gangly gaunt lanky lean rawboned scrawny skinny slender slight slim spare spindly svelte thin trim twiggy underweight weedy willowy

3. artful astute calculating clever crafty cunning devious diplomatic foxy greasy guileful insinuating oily scheming shrewd slimy slippery sly smooth suave tricky unctuous wily

4. arrogance assurance audacity boldness brazenness cheek chutzpah confidence daring effrontery gall highhandedness impertinence impudence insolence nerve presumption pride temerity

5. academic bookish bookworm brain brainworker egghead geek genius highbrow intellectual mind nerd pedant pundit sage savant scholar smarty thinker whiz

PROOFREADING TIP

On Using a Thesaurus

It is best not to use an electronic or printed thesaurus without using a standard dictionary in conjunction with it. Words listed together in such books are not necessarily identical in meaning; they can be subtly different not only in denotation but, especially, in connotation as well. A thesaurus is a vocabulary-building tool, but it should be used with care, for it can trap unwary writers into saying things they don't mean. As an example, consider the fact that many of the words in each group in the following exercise were listed in a thesaurus simply as synonyms.

68 Euphemism

ph **Euphemisms** are substitutes for words whose meanings are felt to be unpleasant and therefore, in certain circumstances, undesirable. In social settings we tend to ask for the location not of the toilet, which is what we want, but of the restroom, the bathroom, the washroom, or the powder room. Interestingly, the word *toilet* was itself once a euphemism.

But the euphemism is sometimes abused. Euphemisms used to gloss over some supposed unpleasantness may actually deceive. Innocent civilians killed in bombing raids are referred to as "collateral damage," and assassination squads are termed "special forces." What was once faced squarely as an economic depression is now, in an attempt to mitigate its negative implications, termed a "recession," or an "economic downturn," or even a mere "growth cycle slowdown." Government officials who have patently lied admit only that they "misspoke" themselves.

Such euphemisms commonly imply a degree of dignity and virtue not justified by the facts. Calling genocide "ethnic cleansing" seriously distorts the meanings of both *ethnic* and *cleansing*. Some euphemisms cloud or attempt to hide the facts in other ways. Workers are "laid off" or "declared redundant" or even "downsized" rather than "fired." A man who has died in a hospital is said to have "failed to fulfill his wellness potential" or undergone a "negative patient-care outcome." A spy is directed to "terminate with extreme prejudice" rather than "assassinate," execute," or "murder." An escalation in warfare is described as a "troop surge"; a civil war is referred to as "factional unrest" or "an insurgency." George Orwell, in his 1946 essay "Politics and the English Language," referred to such usages as linguistic dishonesty.

Other euphemisms help people avoid the unpleasant reality of death, which is often called "passing away" or "loss"; the lifeless body, the cadaver or corpse, is deemed "the remains." Such usages may be acceptable, even desirable, in certain circumstances, since they may enable one to avoid aggravating the pain and grief of the bereaved. But in other circumstances, direct, more precise diction is preferable.

Euphemisms that deceive are obviously undesirable. Others may be acceptable if circumstances seem to justify them, but one must exercise taste and judgment.

Exercise 68 Avoiding Euphemisms

Supply more straightforward equivalents for the following terms.

1. untruth _____
2. indisposed _____
3. friendly fire _____
4. in custody _____
5. repeat offender _____
6. between jobs _____
7. weather event _____
8. lady of the night _____
9. freedom fighter _____
10. convenience fee _____
11. tactical withdrawal _____
12. correctional facility _____
13. surveillance satellites _____
14. job action, work stoppage _____
15. negative revenue enhancement _____
16. underprivileged, disadvantaged _____

---

(69) Wrong Word

ww Any error in diction is a "wrong word," but a particular kind of incorrect word choice is customarily marked **wrong word**. The use of *infer* where the correct word is *imply* is an example. Don't write *effect* when you mean *affect*. Don't write *ex-patriot* when you mean *expatriate*. (Such errors are also sometimes marked *spelling* or *usage*: see the lists of often-confused words, #62f and #62g; and see the usage checklist, #72.) But other kinds of wrong word choices occur as well; here are a few examples:

> ***ww*:** She said her sister, <u>which</u> she earlier described as very
> beautiful, would be at the party.

ww: Most men would have remembered spending several days in an open <u>ship</u> with little water and under the tropic sun as a terrible hardship, but Marlow recalls only that he felt he could "last forever, outlast the sea, the earth, and all men."

ww: Many miles of beach on the west coast of Vancouver Island are <u>absent</u> of rocks.

Whom, not *which*, is the correct pronoun for a person (see #14d). The word *ship* won't do for a small open vessel like a rowboat; *boat* is the appropriate word here. The wrong phrase came to the third writer's mind; *devoid of* was the one wanted (and see #70, on idiom). See also **nsw** (no such word) in appendix 2.

Exercise 69 Avoiding Wrong Words

Correct the wrong words in the following sentences.

1. The conference is intended to focus attention on the problems facing our effluent society.
2. We departured for the cabin on a calm, barmy day in July.
3. The company's representatives claimed to be authoritarians on the subject.
4. Politicians try to maintain an impressionable image in the eyes of the public.
5. The author decided to altar the structure of the forward to her latest novel.
6. Some shoppers stopped buying coffee because they found the price so absorbent, if not gastronomical.
7. The premier of Alberta led her party to the best of her possibilities.
8. He was deciduously on the wrong tack with that theory.
9. It was an incredulous display of manual dexterity.
10. The cat was very expansive, weighing over twenty pounds.
11. We tried to convince her that her fear was entirely imaginative.
12. The populous song plummeted to the top of the chart in recorded time.
13. Currant and former students alike claimed that the principle held allusions of grandeur.
14. The politician promised to remain vigilante in overviewing the collection of vital intelligence on weapons of mass production.
15. The officers appraised the community of the elicit activities that had been going on in the locale bowling ally, and they promised to restore disorder as soon as plausible.

 **Idiom**

id A particular kind of word choice has to do with **idiom**. An idiom is an expression peculiar to a given language, one that may not make logical or grammatical sense but that is understood because it is customary. The English expression "to sow one's wild oats," for example, if translated into another language, would not have its idiomatic meaning; but French has an equivalent expression, *jeter sa gourme*, which would make little sense if translated literally into English. Here are some other peculiarly English turns of phrase: *to have a go at, to be down in the dumps, to be at loose ends.* You will notice that these idioms have a colloquial flavour about them, and may even sound like clichés or euphemisms; but other similar idioms are a part of our everyday language and occur in formal writing as well; for example: to "do justice to" something, to "take after" someone, to "get along with" someone.

Most mistakes in idiom result from using a wrong preposition in combination with certain other words. For example, we get *in* or *into* a car, but *on* or *onto* a bus; one is usually angry *with* a person, but *at* a thing; one is *fond of* something or someone, but one has *a fondness for* something or someone. Here are some examples of errors in idiom:

> *incorrect*: I agree <u>about</u> her analysis of the situation. (*correct*: agree with)
>
> *incorrect*: She took the liberty <u>to introduce</u> herself to the group. (*correct*: liberty of introducing)
>
> *incorrect*: He plans to get married <u>with</u> my youngest sister. (*correct*: get married to)
>
> *incorrect*: It is pleasant to live in the dorms and be in close proximity <u>of</u> everything on campus. (*correct*: proximity to)

Idiomatic expressions sometimes involve choosing between an infinitive and a prepositional gerund phrase. After some expressions either is acceptable; for example:

> He is afraid <u>to lose</u>. He is afraid <u>of losing</u>.
>
> They are hesitant <u>to attend</u>. They are hesitant <u>about attending</u>.
>
> They plan <u>to appeal</u>. They plan <u>on appealing</u>. (informal)

But some terms call for one or the other:

> They propose to go. They are prepared to go.
>
> They insist on going. They are insistent on going.

And sometimes when a word changes to a different part of speech, the kind of phrase that follows must also change:

> It was possible to complete the project in three days. We agreed on the possibility of completing the project in three days.
>
> Our tennis coach emphasized basic skills. Our tennis coach puts emphasis on basic skills.
>
> It is pleasant to remember. She spoke of the pleasantness of remembering.

But it isn't always predictable:

> He intended to go. He spoke of his intention to go.
>
> He had every intention of going.

And sometimes a *that* clause is the only idiomatic possibility:

> I asked them to attend. I recommended that they attend.
>
> I requested that they attend.

See also **different from, different than**; **let, make**; **recommend**; and **very** in the usage checklist, #72.

Idiom is a matter of usage. But a good learner's dictionary such as the *Oxford Advanced Learner's Dictionary* (*OALD*) can often help. For example, if you look up *adhere* in the *OALD*, you will find that it is to be used with *to*, so you would know not to write "adhere on" or "adhere with." Or, should you be wondering about using the word *oblivious*, your dictionary will inform you that it can be followed by either *of* or *to*. (And see **agree to, agree with, agree on** and **differ from, differ with** in the usage checklist, #72.)

Other references that help with idiom (and with other matters) are *Fowler's Modern English Usage*, the *Canadian Oxford Dictionary* (and the *Student's Oxford Canadian Dictionary*), and the *Guide to Canadian English Usage*. Students for whom English is an additional language will benefit from using specialized learner's dictionaries, which offer a wealth of information about idiomatic uses of articles and prepositions and examples of idioms used in complete sentences (see #63a.3).

Exercise 70 Correcting Idioms

Correct the unidiomatic usages in the following sentences.

1. We discussed about global warming.
2. He suggested me to use this new product.
3. Last summer I was bestowed with a scrawny, mangy mutt.
4. Desdemona had unquestioning faith of Iago's character.
5. The class emphasized on mathematics skills.
6. Where is the library at?
7. I am amazed with the report's suggestions.
8. Lovers and poets create dream worlds in which only they can inhabit.
9. Ironically, although Huck fails, Tom succeeds to free Jim.
10. My sister is angry at me because I lost her favourite hat.
11. The generation gap between them is evident by their uneasiness of each other's boredom.
12. She has an unusual philosophy toward modern technology.
13. Tanya made us to laugh with stories of her adventures in the Yukon.
14. The analysis is weak because it lacks in specific details.
15. Moments after I got into the bus, I realized I was heading toward the wrong direction.

71

71 Wordiness and Concision

w Generally, the fewer, more precise words you use to make a point, the better. Useless words—often called *deadwood*—clutter up a sentence; they dissipate its force, cloud its meaning, blunt its effectiveness. The writer of the following sentence, for example, used many words where a few would have been clearer:

> *w:* What a person should try to do when communicating by writing is to make sure the meaning of what he is trying to say is clear.

Notice the gain in clarity and force when the sentence is revised:

> *revised:* A writer should strive to be clear.

The following sections discuss in greater detail a variety of related problems that fall into the general category of wordiness. See also exercise

22a–c(2.C), on getting rid of the clutter of excessive prepositional phrases, and #17p and #29f, on the passive voice. For tips on checking your work for conciseness during the proofreading stage, see the proofreading tip on pages 421–22.

71a Excessive Expletive Constructions

When used to excess, expletive constructions can be a source of weakness and wordiness (see #11k and #29f). There is nothing inherently wrong with them (there are many in this book—two already in this sentence), and they can help us to form certain kinds of sentences the way we want to. Nevertheless writers sometimes use them when a tighter and more direct form of expression would be preferable. If you can get rid of an expletive without creating awkwardness or losing desired emphasis, do so. Don't write

> *w*:   There are several reasons that it is important to revise carefully.

when you can easily get rid of the excess caused by the *there are* and *it is* structure:

> *revised*:   Careful revision is important for several reasons.
>
> *revised*:   For several reasons, careful revision is important.

> *w*:   It is one of the rules in this dorm that you make your own bed.
>
> *revised*:   One rule in this dorm requires you to make your own bed.
>
> *revised*:   In this dorm you must make your own bed.

> *w*:   In this small city, there are over a hundred people without housing.
>
> *revised*:   Over a hundred people in this small city are homeless.

Eliminating ineffective expletives from your writing may not save you a great number of words, but it will make what you are saying more powerful. Note that you strengthen your style by using verbs that are stronger than the verb *to be*.

71b Unnecessary Repetition

ep   Repetition can be useful for coherence and emphasis (see #7b.2, #8, and #29g). But unnecessary repetition usually produces wordiness, and often awkwardness as well. Consider this sentence:

> *rep*:   Looking at the general appearance of the garden, you can see that special consideration was given to the choice of plants for the garden.

The sentence is wordy in general, but one could begin by pruning the repetitious phrase *for the garden*. Another example:

> **rep:** She is able to make the decision to leave her job and to abide by her decision.

Here *make the decision* could be shortened to *decide*, or the final *her decision* could be simply *it*.

71c Redundancy

red Redundancy, another cause of wordiness, is repetition of an idea rather than a word. (The term *redundancy* can mean "excess" in general, but it is also used to designate the particular stylistic weakness known technically as "tautology.") Something is redundant if it has already been expressed earlier in a sentence. In the preceding sentence, for example, the word *earlier* is redundant, since the idea of *earlier* is present in the word *already*: repeating it is illogical and wordy. To begin a sentence with "In my opinion, I think . . ." is redundant. To speak of "a new innovation" or "cooperating together" is to be redundant. The blogger who described a movie as having "a stellar all-star cast" evidently didn't consider what *stellar* means. And the person who wrote, in a letter to a prospective employer, that "an interview would be mutually helpful to both of us" might not make a good first impression. Here are some other frequently encountered phrases that are redundant because the idea of one word is present in the other as well:

actual fact	erode away
added bonus	evolve over time
advance planning	few in number
attach together	follow after
basic fundamentals	general consensus
but nevertheless	mental attitude
character trait	more preferable
close scrutiny	mutually interdependent
collaborate together	necessary prerequisite
completely eliminate	new record
consensus of opinion	past history
continue on	protest against
depreciate in value	reduce down
disappear from sight	refer back
enter into	revert back

71c

One common kind of redundancy is called "doubling"—adding an unnecessary second word (usually an adjective) as if to make sure the meaning of the first is clear:

red: The report was brief and concise.

Either *brief* or *concise* alone would convey the meaning. Sometimes an insecure writer goes to even greater lengths:

red: The report was brief, concise, and to the point.

71d Ready-Made Phrases

"Prefabricated" or formulaic phrases that leap to our minds whole are almost always wordy. They are a kind of cliché (see #71e), and many also sound like jargon (see #71h). You can often edit them out of a draft altogether, or at least use shorter equivalents:

a person who, one of those who

at the present time, at this time, at this point in time (use *now*)

at that time, at that point in time (use *then*)

at the same time (use *while*)

by and large

by means of (use *by*)

due to the fact that, because of the fact that, on account of the fact that, in view of the fact that, owing to the fact that
    (use *because*)

during the course of, in the course of (use *during*)

except for the fact that (use *except that*)

for the purpose of (use *for, to*)

for the reason that, for the simple reason that (use *because*)

in all likelihood, in all probability (use *probably*)

in a very real sense

in colour (as in "was blue in colour")

in fact, in point of fact

in height (use *high*)

in length (use *long*)

in nature

in number

71d

in order to (use *to*)

in reality

in shape (as in "was rectangular in shape")

in size

in spite of the fact that (use *although*)

in the case of

in the event that (use *if*)

in the form of

in the light of, in light of (use *considering*)

in the midst of (use *amid*)

in the near future, in the not too distant future (use *soon*)

in the neighbourhood of, in the vicinity of (use *about, near*)

in this day and age (use *now, today*)

manner, in a . . . manner

period of time (use *period, time*)

personal, personally

previous to, prior to (use *before*)

the fact that

up until, up till (use *until, till*)

use of, the use of, by the use of, through the use of

when all is said and done

with the exception of (use *except for*)

with the result that

And the prevalence of certain ready-made phrases can lead writers to insert these phrases where they do not make sense. One student, accustomed to hearing and using the common phrase *point of view*, unthinkingly tacked *of view* onto *point* in the following sentence: "My dentist made the point of view that flossing is good for one's gums." Two-part verbs (see #22d) sometimes trip up writers in the same way: *fill in* is correct for "*Fill in* this form," but not for "The pharmacist *filled in* the prescription."

71e Triteness, Clichés

trite   Trite or hackneyed expressions, clichés, are another form of wordiness:
cliché they are tired, worn out, all too familiar, and therefore generally contribute little to a sentence. Since they are, by definition, prefabricated phrases, they are another kind of deadwood that can be edited out of a draft. Many trite

phrases are metaphors, once clever and fresh, but now so old and weary that the metaphorical sense is weak at best (see #65c); for some, the metaphor is completely dead, which explains errors such as "tow the line" (for "toe the line"), "the dye is cast" (for "the die is cast"), "dead as a doorknob" (for "dead as a doornail"), and "tarnish with the same brush" (for "tar with the same brush"). "To all intents and purposes" now sometimes comes out "to all intensive purposes"; "taken for granted" becomes "taken for granite"; "by a hair's breadth" turns up as "by a hare's breath"; and so on. A writer aiming for "time immemorial" instead wrote "time in memoriam." Another referred to the passage of a lifetime as "from dawn to dust."

Of course clichés can be useful, especially in speech; they can help one fill in pauses and gaps in thinking and get on to the next point. Even in writing they can sometimes—simply because they are so familiar—be an effective way of saying something. And they can be used for a humorous effect. But in writing, in all such instances, they should be used consciously. It isn't so much that clichés are bad in themselves as that the thoughtless use of clichés weakens style. Generally, then, avoid them, especially if you are aiming to communicate with an audience from another culture. No list can be complete, but here are a few more examples to suggest the kinds of expressions to edit from your work:

a bolt from the blue	doomed to disappointment
a far cry	each and every
a heart of gold	easier said than done
a matter of course	fast and furious
all things being equal	few and far between
as a last resort	first and foremost
as a matter of fact	from dawn till dusk
as the crow flies	gentle as a lamb
beat a hasty retreat	give an arm and a leg
bored to tears	go out on a limb
busy as a bee	good as gold
by leaps and bounds	if and when
by no manner of means	in a manner of speaking
by no means	in one ear and out the other
clear as crystal (or mud)	in our world today
conspicuous by its absence	in the long run
cool as a cucumber	in this day and age
corridors of power	it goes without saying

71e

it stands to reason	pride and joy
last but not least	raining cats and dogs
lock, stock, and barrel	rears its ugly head
love at first sight	rude awakening
many and diverse	sadder but wiser
moment of truth	seeing is believing
needless to say	sharp as a tack
nipped in the bud	slowly but surely
no way, shape, or form	smart as a whip
off the beaten path	strike while the iron is hot
on the right track	strong as an ox
one and only	take one for the team
one and the same	the wrong side of the tracks
over and above	to all intents and purposes
par for the course	what goes around comes around
part and parcel	when all is said and done

71f Edit for the almost automatic couplings that occur between some adjectives and nouns. One seldom hears of a circle that isn't a *vicious* circle, or an inferno that isn't a *blazing* inferno, or a tenement that isn't a *run-down* tenement. A few more examples:

acid test	drastic action	penetrating insight
ardent admirers	festive occasion	perfectly clear
budding genius	foreseeable future	proud possessor
bulging biceps	hearty breakfast	sacred duty
blushing bride	heated opposition	serious concern
complete surprise	just desserts	severe stress
final outcome	knee-jerk reaction	tangible proof
devastating effect	pea-soup fog	vital role

71f Overuse of Nouns

The overreliance on nouns is another source of deadwood; it is also a form of jargon. The focus of a sentence or clause is its main verb; the verb activates it, moves it, makes it go. Too many nouns piled on one verb can slow a sentence down, especially if the verb is *be* or some other verb with little or no action in it. Consider the following:

> The opinion of the judge in this case is of great significance to the outcome of the investigation and its effects upon the behaviour of all the members of our society in the future.

The verb in this sentence must struggle to move the great load of nouns and prepositional phrases along to some kind of finish. One could easily improve the sentence by reducing the proportion of nouns to verbs and making the verbs more vigorous:

> The judge's decision will inevitably influence how people act.

The piling up of nouns that end in *tion* can also weaken style and bury meaning:

> The depredations of the conflagration resulted in the destruction of many habitations and also of the sanitation organization of the location; hence the necessity of the introduction of activation procedures in relation to the implementation of emergency preparations for the amelioration of the situation.

Here is a simpler version:

> Since the fire destroyed not only many houses but also the water-treatment plant for the town, emergency procedures had to be set up quickly.

The verbs in this revised sentence have a third as much noun–baggage to carry as the original verb (*resulted*) had. There is nothing inherently wrong with nouns ending in *tion*; the damage is done when they come in clusters.

71g Nouns Used as Adjectives

Another insidious trend is the unnecessary use of nouns as adjectives. Of course, many nouns function adjectivally, and some such nouns have become so idiomatic that they form parts of compounds:

> bathroom, bath towel, bathtub
>
> business school, business card, businessperson
>
> fire alarm, fire engine, firewood
>
> heart attack, heart monitor, heart-smart
>
> lunch hour, lunch box, lunchroom
>
> school board, school book, schoolteacher
>
> web browser, webmaster, website

Such nouns-cum-adjectives are quite acceptable, but the practice can be carried too far. "Lounge chair" is clearly preferable to "chair for lounging," but just as clearly "medicine training" does not conform to the usages of English as well as "medical training" or "training in medicine," nor "poetry skills" as well as "poetic skills" or "skill in poetry." In these last two examples, since there is a standard adjectival form available, the simple nouns need not and should not be so used.

But increasingly in recent years, speakers and writers—especially those in government, business, and the media—have settled for, or even actively chosen, noun combinations that contribute heavily to the jargon cluttering the language, cumbersome phrases such as *learning facilitation, resource person, demonstration organizer, cash flow position, opinion sampling, consumer confidence number.* Newspapers report that "a weapons of mass destruction update is expected next month," where "an update on weapons of mass destruction" would be better. The piling up of several nouns, as in such phrases as *the labour force participation rate, the Resource Management Personnel Training and Development Program,* and *a city park recreation facility area* can confuse or alienate readers.

Resist this tendency. Resist in particular the tendency to use such combinations when a single, more precise word will do—for example, don't write *emergency situation* in place of *emergency* or *crisis situation* in place of *crisis.* (Try to avoid the unnecessary use of the word *situation* altogether.)

71g

Exercise 71g Evaluating Nouns Used as Adjectives

Evaluate the following phrases in which nouns are used as adjectives. Are some unacceptable? If so, what alternatives can you suggest? Would some be acceptable only in certain contexts? Comment on them in other ways if you wish.

1. task fragmentation
2. worker injuries
3. child poverty
4. computer system
5. information technology
6. job description
7. resource planning
8. customer satisfaction
9. customer billing
10. customer complaints
11. staff organization
12. regime change
13. safety aspects
14. department manager
15. fear factor
16. work schedule
17. profit outlook
18. overkill situation
19. clean-up crew
20. face time

PROOFREADING TIP

On Nouns Functioning as Verbs

Many nouns also function quite normally as verbs. But some usages have provoked criticism. For example, though it is now commonly accepted, some people once objected to the use of *chair* as a verb, as in "to chair a meeting"; and *contact*, meaning "get in touch with," was once criticized, although it is widely accepted today.

Certain other nouns have not received such widespread acceptance as verbs, and you may be best to avoid them in formal writing. For instance, some critics accept *critique* as a verb, but some do not; some also continue to object to *parent* as a verb, and to its gerund *parenting*. Many wince when they hear *dialogue* used as a verb, or of something *transitioning*. And many still deplore referring to someone as having *gifted* another with a present, or *impacted* a process, or *authored* a piece of writing, or *Googled* (or *googled*) something online, or *suicided*. And see **-ize** in the usage checklist, #72.

71h Jargon

ʼg The word *jargon*, in a narrow sense, refers to terms peculiar to a specific discipline, such as psychology, chemistry, literary theory, or computer science, terms unlikely to be fully understood by an outsider. Here we use it in a different sense, to refer to all the incoherent, unintelligible phraseology that clutters contemporary expression. The private languages of particular disciplines or special groups are quite legitimately used in writing for members of those communities. Much less legitimate is the confusing, incomprehensible language that so easily finds its way into the speech and writing of most of us. Therefore, we should all be on guard against creeping bureaucratese and the like, baffling terms from other disciplines and from business and government that infiltrate everyday language. Bombarded by such words and phrases, we may uncritically use them in our own speech and writing, often assuming that automatic prestige attaches to such language. Most readers, however, will be bored or frustrated rather than impressed by this sort of language.

The following list is a sampling of words and phrases that are virtually guaranteed to decrease the quality of expression, whether written or spoken. Some of the terms sound pretentious and technical, imported from specialized fields; others are fuzzy, imprecise, unnecessarily abstract; and still others are objectionable mainly because they are overused, whether as true clichés or merely popular jargon. If you are thinking of using these words or phrases in your writing, consider the context in which you are writing. Are you, for example, writing an academic essay in a particular discipline in which such language is appropriate? Are you addressing readers who will be familiar and comfortable with such language? Ask yourself whether another word or words would communicate your thoughts more effectively. If you can't come up with a more suitable alternative, then you are likely choosing well.

access (as a verb)

affirmative, negative

along the lines of, along that line, in the line of

angle

area

aspect

at that point in time (*then*)

at this point in time (*now*)

background (as a verb)

basis, on the basis of, on a . . . basis (see #72)

bottom line

case

concept, conception

concerning, concerned

connection, in connection with, in this (that) connection

considering, consideration, in consideration of

definitely

dialogue (especially as a verb)

escalate

eventuate

evidenced by

expertise

facet

factor

feedback

hopefully (see #72)

identify with

image

impact (especially as a verb)

implemented, implementation

importantly

indicated to (for *told*)

infrastructure

71h

input, output

in regard to, with regard to, regarding, as regards

in relation to

in respect to, with respect to, respecting

interface (especially as a verb)

in terms of (see #72)

in the final analysis

-ize (-ise) verbs (see #72)

lifestyle

marginal

meaningful, meaningful dialogue

mega-

motivation

ongoing

on stream

on the order of

on the part of

parameters

personage

persons

phase

picture, in the picture

posture

profile, low profile

realm

relate to

relevant

replicate

scenario, worst-case scenario

sector

self-identity

situation

standpoint, vantage point, viewpoint

type, -type (see #72)

viable

-wise (see #72)

worthwhile

71h

Of course, many of these words can be used in normal and acceptable ways. But even such acceptable words can be used as jargon, and those in this list are among the most likely offenders. For example, *angle* is a good and useful word, but in such expressions as "looking at the problem from a different angle" it begins to become jargon. *Aspect* has precise meanings, but they are seldom honoured; the writer of the following sentence didn't know them, but just grabbed at an all too familiar word: "Due to money aspects, many high-school graduates would rather work than enter university." Here *aspects* has no real meaning at all (and see **due to** in the usage checklist, #72). A phrase like "For financial reasons" or "Because of a need for money" would be far better. Unless you use *case* to mean a box or container, a medical case, a legal case, or a grammatical case, or in phrases like "in case of fire," you are likely to create wordy jargon with it: "In most cases, students who worked hard got good grades." Why not "Most students who worked hard got good grades"? And why say "He replied in the affirmative" when "He said yes" would do? *Realm* means a kingdom, and it can—or once could—be useful metaphorically in phrases like "the realm of literature" or "the realm of ideas"; but it has long been so loosely and widely applied that most careful writers avoid it except in its meaning of *kingdom*. Only as jargon does the verb *relate to* mean "understand" or "empathize with" or "interact meaningfully with." And so on. If you read and listen carefully you will often find the listed terms, and others like them, being used in ways that impede clear, concise, and precise expression.

71h

✓ **PROOFREADING TIP**

On Using Short Rather Than Long Word Forms

Writers addicted to wordiness and jargon will prefer long words to short ones, and pretentious-sounding words to relatively simple ones. Generally, choose the shorter and simpler form. For example, the shorter word in each of the following pairs is preferable:

analysis, analyzation	(dis/re)orient, (dis/re)orientate
connote, connotate	preventive, preventative
consultative, consultitative	remedy (v.), remediate
courage, courageousness	symbolic, symbolical
existential, existentialistic	use (n. & v.), utilize, utilization

PROOFREADING TIP
Checking for Conciseness

As you proofread your first draft, look closely for unnecessary words and phrases. Read slowly, and stop to revise any sentences that seem too wordy. The following list offers some starting points to help you with this task.

1. If you find an *expletive construction*, remove the opening *there* or *it* and the linking verb, and move the subject to the beginning of the sentence. In many cases, the result will be greater clarity. (See #11k, #29f, and #71a.)

2. If you find *a repeated word, phrase, or idea*, ask yourself whether the repetition serves a definite purpose (e.g., emphasizing an important concept or improving stylistic coherence). If you decide it does not, remove the repetition. Transform any resulting fragments into full sentences, perhaps by adding new information that enhances the discussion, or work them into an existing sentence. (See #71b–c.)

3. If you find r*eady-made phrases or clichés*, cut them. Try to fill in any resulting gaps with a single word or a short, straightforward phrase. (See #71d–e.)

4. If you find *metaphoric language*, ask yourself whether it both enhances your style and sharpens your meaning. If you think your reader might not understand the comparison you are trying to make, either rephrase or remove the comparison. If you find an inappropriate, overextended, dead, or mixed metaphor, remove it. (See #65.)

5. If you find *too many adjectives or adverbs*, cut as many as you can without losing your meaning. If you find a series of adjectives or adverbs, remove all but the most appropriate modifier; or try to replace the series with a single, more precise word (e.g., "frivolous" instead of "foolish, silly, unnecessary"). You may want to use your dictionary to find the most appropriate word or words. (See #19, #20, and #26.)

6. If you find *too many nouns* in the same sentence, recast the sentence. Put the focus on the main verb, take out all vague or redundant nouns, and try to turn some of the nouns into other parts of speech (e.g., "the *poet's* style" instead of "the

71h

style of *the poet*"; "the narrator *focuses* on the prize" instead of "*the focus* of the narrator is on the prize"). Again, you may want to use your dictionary. (See #71f.)

7. If you find *nouns unnecessarily used as adjectives*, try replacing the noun-adjectives with true adjectives (e.g., "*musical* talent" instead of "*music* talent"). Consult your dictionary when necessary. (See #71g.)

8. If you see *a cluster of vague or generic words*, see if you can come up with one or a few specific words that will more precisely convey your meaning. For example, instead of writing "he *had a strong wish for* power," you could write "he *desired* power." You may want to consult your dictionary.

9. If you find *too many short, simple clauses*, try changing some to phrases or even single words (see #11m–o and exercises 21[3], 21[4], 22a–c[2.A], and 22a–c[2.B]). Sometimes you can replace an adjectival (relative) clause with one or a few adjectives (e.g., "the friendly, charming man" instead of "the man who was friendly and charming"). If the relative clause is restrictive, try removing the relative pronoun (e.g., "the woman ~~that~~ she knew"). If the relative clause is nonrestrictive, try turning it into an appositive (e.g., "Ottawa, ~~which is~~ the capital of Canada"). (See #14d, #19, and #26a.).

10. If you find *a cluster of prepositional phrases*, restructure your sentences to remove as many of the phrases as you can. (See #11p, #22a, and exercise 22a–c[2.C].)

11. If you find *a sentence written in the passive voice*, try rewriting it in the active voice. If the resulting sentence doesn't shift the focus away from what is important, keep it. (See #17p and #29f.)

12. If you find *a sentence or a paragraph that is interesting but off topic*, cut it. Pay extra attention to anything you feel tempted to place within parentheses or set as footnote or an endnote; most such information is unnecessary. (See #1a.)

71h

Exercise 71a–h (1) Removing Wordiness

Revise the following sentences to eliminate wordiness.

1. Nature is a very strong, powerful image in this poem.
2. Most people would rather flee away from danger than face it squarely.
3. Another device used by the playwright was one of repetition.
4. There were two hundred people outside the auditorium, pressing against the ropes.
5. These things were the very things that caused him his puzzlement and his bafflement.
6. Since he has both positive and negative qualities of human nature, Othello is far from perfect and his faults are many in number.
7. Advances in developments of modern information technology greatly contribute to making the equipment necessary for computerization of machinery more and more feasible for potential users.
8. Her confidence in expressing her views caused her to develop her faith in herself, which added to her visible strength.
9. By and large, the president and the prime minister both shared the same view of the foreseeable future, and they both predicted that they would soon be facing a crisis situation.
10. In the event that enough food cannot be supplied for all the people in the world, humankind will have to deal with hunger, starvation, and widespread famine.
11. The courses being offered at this point in time require much more research and thought rather than the age-old memory work that used to plague the education system not too long a time ago.
12. In terms of fuel economy and price, this car is better than any other in its class.
13. Golding's *Lord of the Flies* concerns a group of young children, all boys, who revert back to barbaric savagery.
14. He is adventurous in that he likes a challenge and is willing to try new experiences, but he is not adventurous to the point of insanity, though.
15. In the past six months, I have been subjected to moving from two locations to other surroundings.

71h

Exercise 71a–h (2) Reducing Wordiness
by Combining Sentences

Try reducing wordiness and improving clarity by combining two or more sentences in each of the following groups.

1. In my opinion, I do not think I can make a definite determination as to the source of the explosion at this point in time. I am, however, in the process of reviewing the evidence that exists surrounding the explosion.

2. Parents who wish to see a concert live but do not want to be disturbed by their children have no choice except to leave them attended at home. In this case, the parents would have to hire a babysitter. As a result, the parents end up paying the babysitter as well as for the concert.

3. At soccer practice, our coach would single out the players who had the least team spirit. An example of this would be the passing drills in practices. The players who lagged behind on the field would be asked to run laps after practice.

4. There are a surprising number of lawyers and stockbrokers playing this game, which involves being able to participate in strategic planning. This may be because many lawyers and stockbrokers thrive on strategic planning. After all, lawyers and stockbrokers must be good at strategic planning in order to excel in their chosen careers.

5. Looking ahead into the future, the economist sees even less rapid growth in Canada's national economy. The point I am trying to make is that when all is said and done, Canada's citizens will be in for a rude awakening if Canada, as a country, does not strike while the iron is hot and take advantage of every sort of advantage available in relation to boosting international trade agreements with other countries.

EAL **72** # Usage Checklist: Some Troublesome Words and Phrases

us This section features words and phrases that have a history of being especially confusing or otherwise troublesome. Study the whole list carefully, perhaps marking for frequent review any entries you recognize as personal problem spots. Like any such list, this one is selective rather than exhaustive; we have tried to keep it short enough to be manageable. As with the list of frequently misspelled words (#62q), then, you should keep a list of your own for special study. You can often supplement the information and advice provided here by consulting a good dictionary—especially one that includes notes on usage. See also the index and previous discussions of words sometimes confused (#62f–g), slang (#64a), informal or colloquial usage (#64b), triteness and clichés (#71e), overuse of nouns (#71f), nouns used as adjectives (#71g), and jargon (#71h).

absolute (See **unique, etc.**)

actually (See **very.**)

advice, advise
Advice is a noun, usually used in uncountable form. *Advise* is the transitive verb form.

> The travel agent gave me good underline{advice} on finding hotels. (noun)

> Lily advised her sister to consider taking a computer science course. (transitive verb in past tense form; its direct object is *her sister*)

affect, effect
Affect is a transitive verb meaning "to act upon" or "to influence"; *effect* is a noun meaning "result, consequence":

> They tried to affect the outcome, but their efforts had no effect.

Note: *Effect* can also be a verb meaning "to bring about, to cause"; see your dictionary for other meanings of *affect*.

agree to, agree with, agree on
Use the correct preposition with *agree*. One agrees *to* a proposal or a request, or agrees *to* do something; one agrees *with* someone about a question or an opinion, and certain climates or foods agree *with* a person; one agrees *on* (or *about*) the terms or details of something settled after negotiation, or agrees *on* a course of action.

ain't
A nonstandard contraction, *ain't* is primarily equivalent to *aren't* and *isn't*. Avoid it in all writing unless for deliberate colloquial or humorous effect.

along the lines of (See **in terms of.**)

alternate, alternative; alternately, alternatively
Alternate (adjective) means "by turns" or "every other one." *Alternative* (adjective or noun) refers to one of a number of possible choices (usually

two). Don't use *alternate* or *alternately* when the sense has something to do with choice:

> In summer they could water their lawns only on <u>alternate</u> days.
>
> The squares on the board are <u>alternately</u> red and black.
>
> The judge had no <u>alternative</u>: he had to dismiss the charges.
>
> I found the <u>alternative</u> method to be much simpler.
>
> She could resign or, <u>alternatively</u>, she could wait to be fired.

Alternate (adjective or noun) is used legitimately to refer to a substitute or standby: "Each delegate to the convention had a designated *alternate*. She served as an *alternate* delegate."

although, though

These conjunctions introduce adverbial phrases or clauses of concession. They mean the same, but *although* with its two syllables usually sounds smoother, less abrupt, at the beginning of a sentence; *though* is more commonly used to begin a subordinate clause following an independent clause, though it can be slightly emphatic at the start of a sentence. But the two words are not always interchangeable: in *even though* and *as though* one cannot substitute *although*, and *although* cannot serve as an adverb at the end of a sentence or clause. (See also **while**.)

among (See **between, among**.)

amount, number

Use *number* only with countable nouns, *amount* only with mass, uncountable nouns: a *number* of coins, an *amount* of change; a large *number* of factories, a large *amount* of industrialization. *Number* usually takes a singular verb after the definite article, and a plural verb after the indefinite article (see #18f).

> The <u>number</u> of students taking the workshop <u>is</u> encouraging.
>
> A <u>number</u> of students <u>are</u> planning to take the workshop.

(See also **less, fewer**.)

and/or

This is worth avoiding, unless you're writing legal phraseology. Write "We'll get there on foot or horseback, or both," rather than "We'll get there on foot and/or horseback." And with more than two items, *and/or* muddies meaning: "This bread can be made with wheat, barley, *and/or* rye."

angry (See **mad**.)

anyplace, someplace
These colloquial synonyms for *anywhere* and *somewhere* should be avoided in formal writing.

anyways
This is nonstandard; use *anyway*.

as
To avoid ambiguity, don't use *as* in such a way that it can mean either "while" or "because":

> *ambig*: As I was walking after dark I tripped over a tree root.

> *ambig*: The cherries jubilee caught fire as I added the brandy.

Because of such potential ambiguity, some writers have banished *as* in the sense of *because* from their vocabularies. (See also **like, as, as if, as though** and **so . . . as**.)

as . . . as (See **equally as** and **so . . . as**.)

as being
Don't follow with *being* when *as* alone is enough:

> He always thinks of himself as the life of the party.

as if (See **like, as, as if, as though**.)

as regards (See **in terms of**.)

as such
This phrase shouldn't be used as if it were equivalent to *thus* or *therefore*:

> *us*: My uncle wants to be well liked. As such, he always gives
> expensive gifts.

In this phrase, *as* is a preposition and *such* is a pronoun that requires a clear noun antecedent:

> My uncle is a generous man. As such, he always gives me
> expensive gifts.

as though (See **like, as, as if, as though**.)

72

as to
This is a stiff jargon phrase worth avoiding; rephrasing will usually improve expression:

> *ineffective*: He made several recommendations <u>as to</u> the best method of proceeding.

> *better*: He recommended several methods of proceeding.

> *ineffective*: I was in doubt <u>as to</u> which road to take.

> *better*: I was not sure which road to take.

awaiting for
Awaiting is not followed by the preposition *for*; *waiting* is:

> I was <u>awaiting</u> the train's arrival.

> I was <u>waiting for</u> the light to change.

a while, awhile
Most authorities object to the adverb *awhile* instead of the noun phrase *a while* in some positions, for example after a preposition such as *for*, *in*, or *after*: sleep for *a while*, go in *a while*, rose after *a while*. *Awhile* is generally acceptable in places where *for a while* could be substituted: sleep *awhile*.

bad, badly (See **good, bad, badly, well**.)

basis, on the basis of, on a . . . basis
Basis is a perfectly good noun, but some prepositional phrases using it are worth avoiding when possible, for outside of technical contexts they usually amount to wordy jargon.

> She made her decision <u>on the basis of</u> the committee's report.

This can easily be improved:

> She based her decision on the committee's report.

The other phrase—*on a . . . basis*—is sometimes useful, but more often than not it can profitably be edited out: *on a daily basis* is usually jargon for *daily*; *on a temporary basis*, for *temporarily*; *on a regular basis*, for *regularly*; *on a voluntary basis*, for *voluntarily*; and so on. (See also **in terms of**.)

because (See **reason . . . is because**; see also #48c.)

because of (See **due to**.)

beside, besides

Beside, a preposition, means "next to, in comparison with"; *besides* as an adverb means "in addition, also, too, as well"; as a preposition, *besides* means "in addition to, except for, other than":

> She stood beside her brother.

> Her objections were minuscule beside those of her brother.

> She had to pay the cost of repairs and the towing charges besides.

> Besides the cost of repairs, she had to pay towing charges.

> There was no one on the beach besides the three of us.

> Besides this, what am I expected to do?

between, among

Generally, use *between* when there are two persons or things, and *among* when there are more than two:

> There is ill feeling between the two national leaders.

> They divided the cost equally among the three of them.

On occasion *between* is appropriate for groups of three or more, for example if the emphasis is on the individual persons or groups as overlapping pairs, or on the relation of one particular person to each of several others:

> It seems impossible to keep the peace between the nations of the world.

> One expects there to be good relations between a prime minister and the members of the caucus.

bi-

Bimonthly and *biweekly* usually mean "every two months" and "every two weeks," respectively. But since the prefix *bi* is sometimes also used to mean "twice," *bimonthly* and *biweekly* could mean the same as *semimonthly* and *semiweekly*—that is, "twice a month" and "twice a week." In order to be clear, therefore, you may want to avoid these terms and spell out "every two months," "twice a month," or something similar. Note that *biannual* ("twice a year") is distinguished from *biennial* ("every two years"), but you may want to avoid these terms as well if you think your reader might be confused by them.

can, may (could, might)

Opinion and usage are divided, but in formal contexts it is still advisable to use *can* to denote ability, *may* to denote permission:

> He <u>can</u> walk and juggle oranges at the same time.

> <u>May</u> I have your attention, please?

> He knew that he <u>might</u> leave if he wished, but he <u>could</u> not make himself rise from his chair.

But both *may* and *can* are commonly used to denote possibility: "Things *may* (*can*) turn out worse than you expect. Anything *can* (*may*) happen." And *can* is often used in the sense of permission, especially in informal contexts and with questions and negatives ("*Can* I go?" "No, you *cannot*!") or where the distinction between ability (or possibility) and permission is blurred ("Anyone with an invitation *can* get in"). (See also **may, might**.)

can't barely (hardly, never, only, scarcely)

Barely, hardly, never, only, and *scarcely* are regarded as negatives or as having a negative force. Therefore don't use words like *can't, don't, couldn't,* and *without* with them, for the result is an ungrammatical double negative. Use instead the positive forms: I *can* hardly believe it. He *could* scarcely finish on time. She emerged *with* hardly a scratch.

compare to, compare with

In formal contexts, use *compare to* to liken one thing to another, to express similarity:

> Shall I <u>compare</u> thee <u>to</u> a summer's day?

> He <u>compared</u> his thought process <u>to</u> an assembly line.

and *compare with* to measure or evaluate one thing against another:

> She <u>compared</u> the sports car <u>with</u> the SUV to see which would be best for her.

> He <u>compared</u> favourably <u>with</u> the assistant she had had the previous year.

> <u>Compared with</u> a desk job, farm work is more healthful by far.

complementary, complimentary

Complementary is the adjective describing something that adds to or completes something else. *Complimentary* is the adjective describing something free (e.g., *complimentary* tickets) or comments intended to praise or flatter someone.

> Complementary exercises reinforcing the principles covered in this module are available on the course website. (The exercises will complete the module.)

> We won complimentary passes to the film festival. (The passes are free.)

> Audience members' comments on our presentation were complimentary. (The presenters received praise.)

complete (See **unique, etc.**)

comprise, compose
Distinguish carefully between these words. Strictly, *comprise* means "consist of, contain, include":

> The municipal region comprises seven cities and towns.

Compose means "constitute, form, make up":

> The seven cities and towns compose the municipal region.

Don't use *comprise* in the passive voice—saying, for example, that some whole "is comprised of" several parts; use *is composed of*:

> The municipal region is composed of seven cities and towns.

continual, continuous
These words are sometimes considered interchangeable, but *continual* more often refers to something that happens frequently or even regularly but with interruptions, and *continuous* to something that occurs constantly, without interruptions:

> The speaker's voice went on in a continuous drone, in spite of the heckler's continual attempts to interrupt.

For something that continues in space rather than time, *continuous* is the correct adjective:

> The bookshelf was continuous for the entire length of the hallway.

could (See **can, may.**)

different from, different than
In contemporary North American usage, both *from* and *than* are idiomatic after *different*. Some critics, however, still view *different than* as colloquial; as a result, you may want to stick with *different from* in formal writing.

differ from, differ with
To *differ from* something or someone is to be unlike in some way; to *differ with* someone is to disagree, to quarrel:

> She differed from her colleague in that she was less prone than he to differ with everyone on every issue.

disinterested, uninterested
The adjective *disinterested* means "impartial, objective, free from personal bias"; *uninterested* means "not interested":

> We must find a judge who is disinterested in the case, for she will then try it fairly; we assume that she will not also be uninterested in it, for then she would be bored by it, and not pay careful attention.

due to
Use *due to* only as a predicate adjective + preposition after a form of the verb *be*:

> The accident was due to bad weather.

Avoid using it as a preposition to introduce an adverbial phrase, especially at the beginning of a sentence; use *because of* or *on account of* instead:

> Because of the bad weather, we had an accident.

each other, one another (See #14i.)

effect, affect (See **affect, effect.**)

either, neither
As indefinite pronouns or adjectives, these usually refer to one or the other of two things, not more than two; for three or more, use *any, any one*, or *none*:

> Either of these two advisers can answer your questions.

> Neither of the two answers is correct.

> Any (one) of the four proposals is acceptable.

> None of the four of us drove in today.

If *either* or *neither* is part of a correlative conjunction (see #23b), it can refer to more than two:

> Either Carla, Kiu, or Peter will act as referee.

enormity

Many people object to the use of this noun to mean "immensity, great size, enormousness." To avoid possible disputes, use it only in the sense "monstrous wickedness, heinousness" or "immoderateness, immorality."

> The judge emphasized the enormity of the crime.

equal (See **unique, etc.**)

equally as

Avoid this redundancy by dropping one word or the other or by substituting *just as.*

> Her first novel was highly praised, and her second is equally good.

> In a storm, one port is as good as another.

especially, specially

Especially means "particularly, unusually"; *specially* means "specifically, for a certain or special purpose":

> It's especially cold today; I'm going to wear my specially made jacket.

-ess (See **man, woman, etc.**)

essential (See **unique, etc.**)

farther, further

Use *farther* and *farthest* to refer to physical distance; use *further* and *furthest* to refer to time and degree, and to mean something like "more" or "in addition":

> To go any farther down the road is the furthest thing from my mind.

> Rather than delay any further, he reached for the book farthest from him.

> Without further delay, she began her speech.

Further, only *further* can function as a sentence adverb, as in this sentence.

fatal (See **unique, etc.**)

feel(s)
Don't loosely use the word *feel* when what you really mean is *think* or *believe*. *Feel* is more appropriate to emotional or physical attitudes and responses, *think* and *believe* to those dependent on reasoning:

> The defendant <u>felt</u> cheated by the decision; she <u>believed</u> that her case had not been judged impartially.

> I <u>feel</u> hungry; I <u>think</u> I had better have something to eat.

fewer (See **less, fewer.**)

figuratively (See **literally, figuratively.**)

following
If you avoid using *following* as a preposition meaning simply "after," you'll avoid both the criticism of those who object to it as pretentious and the possibility of its being misread as a participle or a gerund:

> *ambig:*   <u>Following</u> the incident, she interviewed those involved to gain further details.

former, latter
Use these only when referring to the first or second of two things, not three or more (when *first* or *last* would be appropriate), and only when the reference is clear and unambiguous—that is, when it is to something immediately preceding.

from the standpoint (viewpoint) of (See **in terms of.**)

fulsome
Although frequently used to mean "full, copious, abundant," the word actually means "excessive" or "too generous and therefore insincere":

> The mayoral candidate offered a <u>fulsome</u> apology to his opponent.

further (See **farther, further.**)

good, bad, badly, well
To avoid confusion and error with these words, remember that *good* and *bad* are adjectives, *badly* and *well* adverbs (except when *well* is an adjective meaning "healthy"). (See also #20b.2.)

The model looks <u>good</u> in that suit. (He is attractive.)

That suit looks <u>bad</u> on you because it fits <u>badly</u>.

Konrad acted <u>bad</u>. (He was naughty.)

Konrad acted <u>badly</u>. (His performance as Hamlet was terrible.)

I feel <u>good</u>. (I am happy, in good spirits.)

I feel <u>bad</u>. (I have a splitting headache.)

She feels <u>bad</u> about what happened. (She broke her mother's laptop.)

Cassie looks <u>well</u>. (She looks healthy, not sick.)

This wine travels <u>well</u>. (It wasn't harmed by the long train journey.)

The infielders played especially <u>well</u> today; they are all <u>good</u> players.

The steak smells <u>good</u>. (It smells delicious.)

Fido doesn't smell <u>well</u>. (He has a poor sense of smell.)

half a(n), a half
Both are correct; use whichever sounds smoother or more logical. But don't use *a half a(n)*; one article is enough.

hanged, hung
Use the past-tense form *hanged* only when referring to a death by hanging. For all other uses of the verb *hang*, the correct past form is *hung*.

happen, occur
These verbs sometimes pose a problem for students with English as an additional language. Both verbs are intransitive and cannot take the passive-voice form in any tense.

> *wrong*: The revolution <u>was happened</u> in 1917.
>
> *right*: The revolution <u>happened</u> in 1917.

> *wrong*: My grandparents' wedding <u>was occurred</u> almost forty years ago.
>
> *right*: My grandparents' wedding <u>occurred</u> almost forty years ago.

he or she, his or her, he/she, s/he (See #15d.)

herself, himself, myself, etc. (See #14h.)

hopefully
In formal writing, use this adverb, meaning "full of hope," only to modify a verb or a verbal adjective:

> "Will you lend me ten dollars?" I asked hopefully.

> Smiling hopefully, she began to untie the package.

To avoid potential ambiguity, don't use it as a sentence adverb (in spite of its similarity to such acceptable sentence adverbs as *happily* and *fortunately*):

> *ambig*:   Hopefully, many people will enter the contest.

Instead use *I hope* or *We hope* or *One hopes*.

hung (See **hanged, hung**.)

imply (See **infer, imply**.)

impossible (See **unique, etc.**)

in, into
These terms are often interchangeable, but usually you will want to use *in* to indicate location inside of, or a state or condition, and *into* to indicate movement toward the inside of, or a change of state or condition; in other words, generally use *into* with verbs of motion and the like:

> We moved into our new home in the suburbs.

> After getting into trouble, he was in a bad temper.

in connection with (See **in terms of**.)

infer, imply
Use *imply* to mean "suggest, hint at, indicate indirectly" and *infer* to mean "conclude by reasoning, deduce." A listener or reader can *infer* from a statement something that its speaker or writer *implies* in it:

> Her speech strongly implied that we could trust her.

> I inferred from her speech that she was trustworthy.

The word *inference*, then, means "something inferred, a conclusion"; it does not mean "implication" or "innuendo."

infinite (See **unique, etc.**)

in relation to (See **in terms of**.)

inside of (See **off of**.)

in terms of
This phrase is contemporary clutter. Note that it is similar, sometimes even equivalent, to other wordy expressions (see **basis** and **-wise**). Although it is common in speech, and though occasionally it is the precisely appropriate phrase, it is more often vague. If you can avoid it, especially in writing, do so; don't write sentences like these:

> ***wordy***: He tried to justify the price increase in terms of [or *on the basis of*] the company's increased operating costs.

> ***wordy***: In terms of experience [or *Experience-wise*], she was as qualified for the post as anyone else applying for it.

Instead use sentences such as these:

> He tried to justify the increase in price by citing the company's increased operating costs.

> She was as experienced as anyone else applying for the post.

And note the further family resemblance of this phrase to *along the lines of, in connection with, in relation to, in (with) regard to, as regards, regarding, in (with) respect to,* and *from the standpoint (viewpoint) of.* (See also #71d and #71h.)

in (with) regard(s) to
Drop the *s*: *in (with) regard to.* *As regards* is acceptable. But see #71h and **in terms of**.

in (with) respect to (See **in terms of**.)

into (See **in, into**.)

irregardless
This is nonstandard, as your dictionary should tell you. The correct word is *regardless*.

is when, is where

Avoid these phrases in statements of definition, where adverbial clauses following linking verbs are considered ungrammatical:

> ***us:*** A double play is when two base runners are put out during one play.

> ***rev:*** In a double play, two base runners are put out during one play.

> ***rev:*** A double play occurs when two base runners are put out during one play.

In the second revision, the adverbial clause beginning with *when* is acceptable because *occurs* is not a linking verb.

its, it's

Its is the possessive form of *it*; *it's* is the contracted form of *it is*, or occasionally of *it has* (as in "It's been a long day"). Proofread carefully for these usages.

-ize

This suffix is often overused in business and other jargon (e.g., *finalize, concretize, prioritize*), sometimes leading to absurdities ("The minister claimed he had been *pressurized* to resign"). The *ize* ending remains acceptable in established words, but avoid using it to make new ones. (See the proofreading tip following #71g.)

72

kind of, sort of

Used adverbially, as in "*kind of* tired" or "*sort of* strange," these terms are colloquial—as they are when followed by an article, as in "I had a bad *kind of an* afternoon" or "She was a peculiar *sort of a* guide." Avoid such usages in formal writing. (See also **type** and #15f.)

lack, lack of, lacking, lacking in

Lack in its various forms and parts of speech can sometimes pose problems for students with English as an additional language. Note the following standard usages:

> This paper lacks a clear argument. (*lack* as a transitive verb)

> A major weakness of his argument was its lack of evidence. (*lack* as a noun followed by the preposition *of*)

> Lacking confidence, she hired a web designer to do the work. (*lacking* as a present participle followed by a direct object)

> Lacking in experience, they had difficulty in job interviews. (*lacking* as a present participle in combination with the preposition *in*)

latter (See **former, latter**.)

lay (See **lie, lay**.)

lend (See **loan**.)

less, fewer
Fewer refers to things that are countable; *less* refers to things that are uncountable, or considered as units:

fewer cars, less traffic   fewer hours, less time

fewer dollars, less money   fewer shouts, less noise

(See also **amount, number**.)

less, least; more, most (See #19b and #20c.)

let, make
The verbs *let* and *make* are parts of an idiom that causes problems, especially for those with English as an additional language. When *let* or *make* is followed by a direct object and an infinitive, the infinitive does not include the customary *to*:

      id: They let me to borrow their new car.

revised: They let me borrow their new car.

      id: Our professor made us to participate in the experiment.

revised: Our professor made us participate in the experiment.

(See also the proofreading tip in #21b.)

lie, lay
Since *lay* is both the past tense of *lie* and the present tense of the verb *lay*, some writers habitually confuse these two verbs. If necessary, memorize their principal parts: *lie, lay, lain; lay, laid, laid*. The verb *lie* means "recline" or "be situated"; *lay* means "put" or "place." *Lie* is intransitive; *lay* is transitive:

I lie down now; I lay down yesterday; I have lain down several times today.

I lay the book on the desk now; I laid the book on the desk yesterday; I have laid the book on the desk every morning for a week.

The book lies on the desk now; the book lay on the desk yesterday; the book has lain on the desk for an hour.

like, as, as if, as though
Like is a preposition:

> Roger is dressed exactly like Kazuhiro.

But if Kazuhiro is given a verb, then he becomes the subject of a clause, forcing *like* to serve incorrectly as a conjunction; use the conjunction *as* when a clause follows:

> ***us***: Roger is dressed exactly like Kazuhiro is.

> ***revised***: Roger is dressed exactly as Kazuhiro is.

In slightly different constructions, use *as if* or *as though* to introduce clauses:

> It looks like rain.
>
> It looks as if [or *as though*] it will rain.

> He stood there like a statue.
>
> He stood there as though [or *as if*] he were a statue.

literally, figuratively
Literally means "actually, really." *Figuratively* means "metaphorically, not literally." Don't use *literally* when the meaning is figurative:

> ***us***: She was literally swept off her feet. (Unless her feet actually left the ground, use *figurative*.)

loan, lend
Although some people restrict *loan* to being a noun, it is generally acceptable as a verb equivalent to *lend*—except in such figurative uses as "Metaphors *lend* colour to one's style" and "*lend* a hand."

mad
Although commonly used in informal contexts to mean "angry," *mad* in formal contexts is usually restricted to the meaning "insane, crazy."

make (See **let, make.**)

man, woman, -ess, Ms., etc.
Like the use of *he* as a generic pronoun (see #15d), the general or generic use of the word *man* causes difficulties. To avoid biased language, you should avoid using the term *man* where it could include the meaning *woman* or *women*. If you're referring to a single individual, often simply substituting *person* or even *human being* will do. In some contexts *one* or *you* may work well. If you're referring to the race, instead of *man* or *mankind*,

use *human beings, humanity, people, humankind,* or *the human race.* Instead of *manmade,* use *synthetic* or *artificial* or *manufactured.* (Note that several words beginning with *man,* such as *manufacture, manuscript,* and *manoeuvre,* come not from the English word *man* but from the Latin *manus,* "hand.") Similarly, in compounds designating various occupations and positions, try to avoid the suffix *man* by using gender-neutral terms such as *firefighter, police officer, letter carrier, worker, spokesperson, chairperson* (or just *chair*), *anchorperson* (or just *anchor*), *businessperson,* or *salesperson.*

Another concern is the suffix *ess.* Usefully gender-specific (and power-designating) terms like *princess, empress, duchess,* and *goddess* are firmly established, but there is seldom if ever any need to refer to an *authoress* or *poetess* when simply *author* or *poet* will serve; many now eschew *actress,* finding *actor* more suitable for both sexes. *Stewardess* has given way to *flight attendant;* and *waitress* and *waiter* have been replaced by *server.* The suffix *ette,* as in *usherette,* is similarly demeaning; use *usher.* In addition, use the title *Ms.* for a woman unless you know that a specific woman prefers *Miss* or *Mrs.*

Further, don't thoughtlessly gender-stereotype occupations and other activities that are engaged in by both men and women. And don't highlight a person's gender unless it is somehow relevant to the context—for example, if a patient has specifically requested to see a male doctor, or if a person is notable as the first female to hold her position. (Note that *female* and *male,* rather than *woman* and *man,* are the appropriate terms to use when referring to gender.)

may (See **can, may.**)

may, might

Don't confuse your reader by using *may* where *might* is required:

1. after another verb in the past tense:

    us: She thought she <u>may</u> get a raise. (use *might*)

    In the present tense, either *may* or *might* would be possible:

    She thinks she <u>may</u> get a raise. (It's quite likely that she will.)

    She thinks she <u>might</u> get a raise. (It's less likely, but possible.)

2. for something hypothetical rather than factual:

    us: This imaginative software program <u>may</u> have helped Beethoven compose.

The word *may* makes it sound as if it is possible that the program *did* help Beethoven, which is of course absurd. Use *might.* (For other examples, see #17e.)

72

media (See #18h and #62m.7.)

might (See **may, might** and **can, may**.)

more, most; less, least (See #19b and #20c.)

Ms. (See **man, woman, etc.** and #53a.)

myself, herself, himself, etc. (See #14h.)

necessary (See **unique, etc.**)

neither (See **either, neither**.)

number (See **amount, number**.)

occur (See **happen, occur**.)

of
Avoid incorrect use of *of* as a result of mispronunciation:

> ***ww*:** We would <u>of</u> stayed for dinner if not for the weather. (use *have*)

Because of the way we sometimes speak, such verb phrases as *would have, could have, should* have, and *might have* are mispronounced (*would've, could've, should've, might've*). Because of the way we hear these words, the *'ve* mistakenly becomes *of*.

off of
Including *of* after the prepositions *off, inside,* and *outside* is usually unnecessary:

> She fell <u>off</u> the fence

> He awoke to find himself <u>inside</u> a large crate

> She remained in the hall <u>outside</u> the room

on account of (See **due to**.)

one another (See #14i.)

oral, verbal (See **verbal, oral**.)

outside of (See **off of**.)

perfect (See **unique, etc.**)

plus (See *d* in appendix 2.)

possible (See **unique, etc.**)

put forth (See **set forth.**)

quote
In formal contexts, use *quote* only as a verb; don't use it as a noun, equivalent to *quotation* or *quotation mark.*

raise, rise
The verb *raise* is transitive, requiring an object: "I *raised* my hand; he *raises* alpacas." *Rise* is intransitive: "The temperature *rose* sharply; I *rise* each morning at dawn." If necessary, memorize their principal parts: *raise, raised, raised; rise, rose, risen.*

rarely ever
The constructions *rarely ever* and *seldom ever* are unnecessarily wordy and should be avoided in formal writing. Omit *ever* and simply use *rarely* or *seldom.*

real, really
Don't use *real* as an adverb. (See the proofreading tip in #20b.) See also **very.**

reason . . . is because
Although this construction has long been common, especially in speech, many people object to it as (a) redundant, since *because* often means simply "for the reason that," and (b) ungrammatical, since adverbial *because* should not introduce noun clauses after a linking verb (critics for the same reason object to *it is because, this is because,* and the like). We suggest that you avoid these phrases in formal writing.

reason why
The *why* in this phrase is often redundant, as in "The reason *why* I'm taking Spanish is that I want to travel in South America." Check to see if you need the *why.*

recommend
When this transitive verb appears in a clause with an indirect object, that object must be expressed as a prepositional phrase with *to* or *for*, and it must follow the direct object:

> *id:* She recommended me this restaurant.

> *id:* She recommended to me this restaurant.

> *revised:* She recommended this restaurant to me.

A number of other verbs fit the same idiomatic pattern as *recommend*. Among the most common are *admit, contribute, dedicate, demonstrate, describe, distribute, explain, introduce, mention, propose, reveal, speak, state*, and *suggest*. Note, however, that with several of these verbs, if the direct object is itself a noun clause, it usually follows the prepositional phrase to avoid confusion:

> He admitted to me that he had been lying.

> She explained to me what she intended to do.

regarding (See **in terms of**.)

replace (See **substitute, replace**.)

rise, raise (See **raise, rise**.)

seldom ever (See **rarely ever**.)

sensual, sensuous
Although the meanings of these words overlap, *sensuous* is traditionally used to refer broadly to intellectual or physical pleasure derived from the senses, while *sensual* usually refers to the gratification of physical—particularly sexual—appetites:

> Some poets, responding to the beauty of their surroundings, write sensuous poetry.

> We are studying the sensual features of contemporary love poetry.

set, sit
Set (principal parts *set, set, set*) means "put, place, cause to sit"; it is transitive, requiring an object: "He *set* the glass on the counter." *Sit* (principal parts *sit, sat, sat)* means "rest, occupy a seat, assume a sitting position"; it is intransitive: "The glass *sits* on the counter. May I *sit* in the easy chair?"— though it can be used transitively in expressions like "I sat myself down to listen."

set forth
As a stiff, unwieldy substitute for *express(ed)* or *present(ed)* or *state(d)*, this phrase is an attempt at sophistication that misfires. *Put forth* is similarly weak.

shall, will; should, would (See #17e, #17h.3, and #17i.2.)

she or he, her or his, she/he, s/he (See #15d.)

simple, simplistic
Don't use *simplistic* when all you want is *simple*. *Simplistic* means "oversimplified, unrealistically simple":

> We admire the book for its simple explanations and straightforward advice.

> The author's assessment of the war's causes was narrow and simplistic.

since
Since can refer both to time ("*Since* April we haven't had any rain") and to cause ("*Since* she wouldn't tell him, he had to figure it out for himself"). Therefore don't use *since* in a sentence where it could refer either to time or to cause:

> *ambig:* Since you went away, I've been sad and lonely.

sit, set (See **set, sit**.)

so, so that, therefore
As a conjunction, *so* is informal but acceptable (see #23a.3); just don't overwork it. To introduce clauses of purpose and to avoid possible ambiguity, you will often want to use *so that* or *therefore* instead:

> He sharpened the saw so that it would cut the boards properly.

> She cleverly changed her story several times, so that we couldn't be sure what actually happened.

> She changed her story several times; therefore we couldn't be sure what actually happened.

so . . . as, as . . . as
In strictly formal contexts, use *so* or *so . . . as* with negative comparisons; use *as* or *as . . . as* only with positive comparisons:

> Jo was almost as tall as he was, but she was not so heavy.

> He was not so quick as he once was, but he was as strong as ever.

someplace (See **anyplace, someplace**.)

sort of (See **kind of, sort of**.)

specially (See **especially, specially**.)

state

State is a stronger verb than *say*; reserve *state* for places where you want the heavier, more forceful meaning of "assert, declare, make a formal statement."

substitute, replace

Don't use the verb *substitute* when you mean *replace*. To keep your meaning straight, avoid using *substitute* with *by* or *with*; use it only with *for*:

> ***us***: The fries were <u>substituted by</u> a tossed salad. (use *replaced by*)

> ***us***: I <u>substituted</u> the term paper <u>with</u> three shorter essays. (use *replaced . . . with*)

> ***revised***: The server kindly <u>substituted</u> a tossed salad <u>for</u> the fries.

> ***revised***: I was permitted to <u>substitute</u> three short essays <u>for</u> the term paper.

sure, surely

Don't use *sure* as an adverb. (See the proofreading tip in #20b.)

72

suspect, suspicious

The adjectives *suspect* and *suspicious* can both mean "arousing suspicion," but confusion may arise in some cases because *suspicious* can also mean "feeling suspicion." Be sure to make your meaning clear.

> ***ambig***: He was a very <u>suspicious</u> man.

> ***clear***: He was <u>suspicious</u> of everyone he met.

> ***clear***: I thought his actions highly <u>suspect</u>.

> ***clear***: All of us were <u>suspect</u> in the eyes of the police.

tend to, tends to

These words are often no more than filler. Don't say "My French teacher *tends to* mark strictly" when what you mean is "My French teacher *marks* strictly."

therefore (See **so, so that, therefore**.)

these (those) kinds (sorts), this (that) kind (sort) (See #15f.)

though, although (See **although, though**.)

till, until, 'til
Till and *until* are both standard and have the same meaning. *Until* is somewhat more formal and is usually preferable at the beginning of a sentence. The contraction *'til* is little used nowadays, except in informal contexts, such as personal letters.

too
Used as an intensifier, *too* is sometimes illogical; if an intensifier is necessary in such sentences as these, use *very*:

> **ww:** I don't like my cocoa <u>too</u> hot.
>
> **revised:** I don't like my cocoa <u>very</u> hot.

> **ww:** She didn't care for the brown suit <u>too</u> much.
>
> **revised:** She didn't care for the brown suit <u>very</u> much.

But often you can omit the intensifier as unnecessary:

> She didn't care much for the brown suit.

(See **very**.)

toward, towards
These are interchangeable, but in North American English, the preposition *toward* is usually preferred to *towards*, just as the adverbs *afterward*, *forward* (meaning *frontward*), and *backward* are to their counterparts ending in *s*.

true facts
The adjective *true* is redundant. Facts are, by definition, true.

type, -type
In general, avoid using *type* other than when referring to printed or typed letters. The phrase *type of* is often unnecessary, mere deadwood: "She is an intelligent [type of] woman." And *type* used as an adjective or part of an adjective (e.g., "a new type of device" or "an intelligent-type person") is not only unnecessary but colloquial as well. (See also **kind of, sort of**.)

uninterested (See **disinterested, uninterested**.)

unique, absolute, necessary, essential, complete, perfect, fatal, equal, (im)possible, infinite, etc.

In writing, especially formal writing, treat these and other such adjectives as absolutes that cannot logically be compared or modified by such adverbs as *very* and *rather*. Since by definition something *unique* is the *only one of its kind* or *without equal*, clearly one thing cannot be "more unique" than another, or even "very unique"; in other words, *unique* is not a synonym for *unusual* or *rare*. Similarly with the others: one thing cannot be "more essential" or "more perfect" than another. And note that you can easily get around this semantic limitation by calling one thing, for example, "more nearly perfect," "more nearly equal," or "closer to complete" than another, or by referring to something as "almost unique" or "nearly unique" (but you could simply call it "very rare" or "highly unusual").

until (See **till, until, 'til**.)

usage, use, utilize, utilization

The noun *usage* is appropriate when you mean customary or habitual use ("British usage"), or when a particular verbal expression being characterized in a particular way ("an ironic usage," "an elegant usage"). Otherwise the shorter noun *use* is preferable. As a verb, *use* should nearly always suffice; *utilize*, often pretentiously employed instead of *use*, should carry the specific meaning "put to use, make use of, turn to practical or profitable account." Similarly, the noun *use* will usually be more appropriate than *utilization*. Phrases like *use of, the use of, by the use of*, and *through the use of* tend toward jargon and are almost always wordy.

verbal, oral

Although these words are commonly used interchangeably, you may want to preserve the still useful distinction between them. *Verbal* means "pertaining to words," which could be either written or spoken; *oral* means "spoken aloud."

very

When revising, you may find that where you have used *very* you could just as well omit it. Often it is a vague substitute for a more precise adverb or adjective:

> It was very sunny today. (magnificently sunny?)

> I was very tired. (exhausted?)

> Her embarrassment was very obvious. (It was either obvious or it wasn't; drop *very*, or change it to something like *painfully*.)

The same goes for *really* and *actually*. Such weak intensifiers sometimes even detract from the force of the words they modify.

Note that before some past participles, it is idiomatic to use another word (e.g., *much* or *well*) along with *very*:

You are very much mistaken!

Sharon is very well prepared for the role.

way, ways
In formal usage, especially in writing, don't use *ways* to refer to distance; *way* is correct:

We were a long way from home.

They had only a little way to go.

well (See **good, bad, badly, well**.)

when, where (See **is when, is where**.)

while
As a subordinating conjunction, *while* is best restricted to meanings having to do with time:

Vijay mowed the lawn while Sam raked the grass.

When it means *although* (*though*) or *whereas*, it can be imprecise, even ambiguous:

While I agree with some of his reasons, I still think my proposal is better. (*Although* would be clearer.)

While she does the cleaning, he cooks the meals. (Fuzzy or ambiguous; *whereas* would make the meaning clear.)

(See also **although, though**.)

will, shall (See #17h.3.)

-wise
This suffix, in its sense of "with reference to" (and equivalent phrases), is so overused in modern jargon (*moneywise, sales-wise, personnel-wise*, etc.) that it is now employed mainly as a source of humour ("And how are you otherwise-wise?"). Therefore avoid the temptation to tack it onto nouns to coin new adverbs. You can easily find a better way to say what you mean (see **in terms of**):

not: Grammarwise, Stephen is doing well.

but: Stephen is doing well with grammar.

> ***not:*** This is the best car I've ever owned, <u>powerwise</u>.
>
> ***but:*** This car has more power than any other I've owned.

woman (See **man, woman, etc**.)

would, should (See #17e and #17i.2.)

Review Exercise, Chapter VII Diction

Revise the following sentences to strengthen the diction and normalize the usage; correct any other errors you find, as well.

1. She was so nervous her legs literally turned to jelly.
2. In the winter even less tourist dollars are spent.
3. The team comprises a close-knit unit that functions on a collective basis.
4. Strategy-wise, we want to position our best speakers in an advantageous situation.
5. Today, environmentalists are trying to substitute the word *buy* with the word *recycle*.
6. I denote a real sense of pride here.
7. Because this particular word occurs frequently throughout the course of the play, it achieves a certain importance.
8. Her striving to be a perfectionist was evident in her business.
9. Hopefully, this weekend's events will turn out to be successful.
10. He was ignorant as to the proper use of the tools.
11. As is so often the case, one type of error leads to another.
12. This passage is a very essential one in the novel.
13. His metaphors really bring out a sinister feeling which one feels while reading it.
14. Eliot sees his poetry as occupying a kind of niche in a long conveyer belt of accumulated knowledge and poetry.
15. Based on what he inferred, I could imply that what was occurred was wrong.
16. He felt himself to be in a powerless situation.
17. I resolved to do my best in terms of making friends and working hard.
18. The hulls of the tankers were ripped open in a majority of cases, dumping countless barrels of oil in the sea.
19. Hamlet spends the whole play trying to reach a situation where he can revenge his father's death.

72

20. This poem is concerned with the fact that one should grasp an opportunity quickly.

21. He is only in town on a once-in-a-while basis.

22. The prime minister is waiting for the premiers to show their bottom lines.

23. As she gave me so much money I thanked her profusely.

24. The deal may not have gone ahead if Anderson hadn't been so tenacious and persistent.

25. People in watching these shows or movies may develop a love for violence as a result of watching this type of program.

26. This man thought it was incumbent upon him to extract revenge.

27. In Olympic sports nationalism is increasingly becoming a more important factor.

28. She saw that this was the last remaining remnant of a very, very important species.

29. For more than a million Canadians, back pain is an incapacitating experience which slows ordinary movements and turns routine tasks into tortuous events.

30. We are all intensely involved in profiting on the expenses of other people.

31. The contribution of the coalition to the passage of the legislation was capitalized on by the opposition.

32. He is as equally at ease hobnobbing with celebrities as he is relaxing in his own home.

33. These instructions are contingent to your acceptance.

34. The prime minister's reply, he complained, was "warm and gratuitous but not very specific."

35. Iago is regarded by all as an honest, truthful man.

36. The character of Nicholas is recognizable to people who really exist in the world.

37. She has him at her beckon call.

38. This book about a politician will have a negative effect in terms of the interests of his opponents.

39. The premier has tried to pressurize the legislature to go along with his proposals.

40. After going only a hundred miles the ship was forced to return to its point of origination.

41. You'll also be amazed, too, at our low prices on basic apparel.

42. The new program will cost in the realm of five million dollars.

43. You can expect similar-type amounts of precipitation over the Canada Day long weekend.

72

44. The minister said that he would not want to be categorized with respect to a reply to that statement.
45. There was a general consensus in the neighbourhood that ambulance service in the area was frequently inadequate regarding response time.
46. One must judge the various proposals on an equal basis.
47. We have to reconsider the proposal in terms of the legal aspects of that sort of solution.
48. It seems like he is rather mad at her for daring to try and deceive him.
49. The road trip took longer than we expected due to our continuously stopping to see the sights.
50. A meteoroid is when a small thing made up of metal and/or rock travels through space.

Omnibus Review Exercise, Chapters II–VII Sentence Errors and Weaknesses

Each of the following sentences contains at least one error or weakness of a kind discussed in this book; many contain more than one. Practise your proofreading and revising. Label the sentences with the appropriate correction symbols.

1. The nature of his errors were not serious.
2. In today's world it is becoming increasingly more difficult to find relatively inexpensive ways to use your leisure time.
3. The room was furnished with the new chrome and plastic furniture but it wasn't very attractive.
4. There was a clear increase in strength of Protestant power, especially in England and Prussia who had benefitted from the treaty of Utrecht.
5. Us producers at CBC want to feature a few more Canadian athletes at a young age.
6. He was charged of embezzling over ten thousand dollars.
7. As for ancient man, being civilized was of no concern to one who was battling the many forces of nature such as hunting wild animals for food and shelter from the weather.
8. The reason why their cars don't live as long is because most people have no idea of how to properly look after their cars.
9. This book provides what I think is indisputedly the best account of those troubled years.

10. Friends say the feisty-type newspaperwoman would have liked to have become an artist.
11. There were artists which continued to study and produce classical works and there were artists which developed new ideas in their fields.
12. As a single parent with two high schoolers, it took two jobs to stay afloat.
13. During that period of time we talked to him on a nightly basis.
14. An old Victorian mansion has a mysterious basement room that, by entering allows members of the household to travel through time.
15. There's no question it was a tragedy, and there's also no question that it may have been prevented.
16. A hobby such as playing music in a band gives more than just enjoyment, it gives relaxation, self satisfaction, it is educational, and it is competitive.
17. During the long drought, many water areas, such as lakes and reservoirs, were drying up.
18. Based on her findings, she concluded that comedy was more healthful than tragedy.
19. The Board of Directors of *Design For Today* wishes to express their appreciation for assistance from many local individuals and businesses.
20. There are many arguments with respect to the importance of a university education in today's society.
21. In this modern day and age it is not unusual to find people who are ignorantly unaware of the technology of how things in our society work.
22. She had so many assignments over the holiday that she felt bogged under.
23. The police acts against violators of this minor law only on a complaint basis.
24. They substituted butter with margarine in the belief that it was healthier.
25. The silver mentioned in the beginning and the end of the story not only symbolize freedom but they foreshadow a better future.
26. As a general observation, my grandfather was a very introspective-type individual.
27. He is one of those people, (and there are many of them) who does not understand economics.
28. Tonight's specialty is a dish that is a feast not only for the eyes but a treat for the palate as well.

72

29. Failure to produce efficiently together with failure to reduce imports have had serious economic consequences.

30. The show employs flashbacks to fill in the protagonists background as a former Vietnam veteran and ex-New Orleans cop.

31. Our opponent merely sights her party's ideology and says things are all right—but ask yourself, can you afford anymore?

32. The government permits the sale of surplus material abroad on an intermittent basis.

33. I hope you will forgive me pointing out certain weaknesses in your argument.

34. Under the Canadian charter for rights and freedoms, every man in Canada has the freedom to believe what he chooses to believe.

35. The laws were made by the parlament and enforced by a police force, which is a similar system to the present.

36. We shouldn't act in terms of a knee-jerk reaction to the present situation what we should do is identify solutions.

37. She concluded from her investigation that under the new policy women employees may in fact receive a smaller increase than they may have otherwise received.

38. The English aristocracy, which was mainly comprised of wealthy landowners, did not however, in spite of their comfortable lifestyle, know the manners and etiquette that seemed to elevate the French aristocracy.

39. He promised he would take me to the movies, in spite of how much work that he hasn't finished yet, but has to do.

40. As a valued Acme Bank customer we are pleased to extend to you the opportunity to apply for a personal loan at exceptional fixed interest rates.

41. The fact that there are many people who I can relate to, adds to a sense of security for me because I feel that I am liked and I have a position with them in society, which enhances my self-identity.

42. Further implications for disaster in postponing the driving experience to an older age could be encountered in those people wishing to use the car as their primary means of transportation to work or a post-secondary institution.

43. The poem mentions statues pictures and stairways, all of these seem to enable the reader to picture Prufrock better and the people he associates with.

44. An older person has already made a lot of mistakes in their life and sharing their mistakes with new generations will keep from every generation having to start from a beginning.

45. I am still not sure whether or not I did the right thing about coming here but everyone thought it was, so here I am.

46. Some people may view Hamlet as a feeble, gutless young man who can't make up his mind about anything and this is what I believed at first but by reading the play carefully and by observing Hamlet's actions this can't be true.

47. A hobby is often a nice way to relax or to just sit down and read a favourite novel or listen to some music, anything, just as long as it is relaxing.

48. I'm lucky to live in a great country, have a family who I love and am loved in return, have caring relations acquaintances, and the opportunity to meet strangers who may someday be friends.

49. With no increase in salaries, increased teaching loads, and cutbacks in research facilities, faculty is starting to slip away that university has already lost at least seven faculty members since January, and there are strong indications of many more to come.

50. By portraying the Queen as being blind to the situation of hate between Hamlet and the King, and the fact that she does not seem to even consider the fact that the King killed her previous husband, the audience's attitude toward the King is made even stronger.

72

VIII

Research, Writing, and Documentation

Introduction: Producing a High-Quality Research Essay

Introduction: Producing a High-Quality Research Essay

Chapter VIII outlines the stages of writing a research essay and the details to keep in mind to do a good job. A paper based on research should conform to the principles governing any good essay. It should represent you as a thinker, and it should contribute your distinctive perspectives on a question of interest to you. Research essays also call upon writers to seek out the findings and the views of others who have investigated a topic and to give full credit to those sources.

The techniques outlined in this chapter are not the only possible approaches to finding sources and writing a research paper, but they have proven useful to many writers. Some of the steps and details may seem mechanical, and some may look like unnecessary fiddling, but all of them will help you produce a high-quality paper. In your own studies, an instructor may ask you to follow a different method—for example, to take notes or compile your bibliography in a different way. After you gain some experience, you may yourself devise or discover a method that works best for you. No one method is sacrosanct: the important thing is to have a method. The alternative is likely to be confusion, error, and wasted effort.

73 Preparing to Find Sources

Before you receive your first research assignment, you should prepare yourself by learning where and how to find reliable sources of information. At this preliminary stage, you will need to learn your way around the various research-related resources offered through your library and its website. You will also need to learn how to distinguish between sources that are academically sound and sources that are not—especially if you are searching for information on the Internet.

73a Libraries and Databases

Most of the research you do for an academic research paper will involve using library resources. This means that you will need to learn your way around your library and its website. The most important resources for you to explore are your library's **catalogue** and its collection of **databases**, both of which you should be able to access through your library's website. Your library's website likely also offers detailed guidelines and advice on using these electronic resources; if you have any questions not answered on the site or in the following discussion, you can always consult a librarian. Reference librarians can provide invaluable assistance as you find your way through the myriad of electronic and non-electronic resources available to you.

RESEARCH TIP

Choosing the Most Reliable Sources

When you are gathering information for an academic research essay, you should look for articles published in academic journals; these articles are peer-reviewed and therefore the most credible sources of information for academic purposes. Most books written by academics and published by university presses are also peer-reviewed and highly reliable. Also reliable are reports published by well-respected governmental and non-governmental agencies and organizations. Books published by commercial presses and aimed at general readers may contain some useful information, but they are also likely to contain opinions and beliefs that are not supported by sound research. Newspapers and magazines can be good sources of information about current or recent events, but use them cautiously; even the most highly respected journalistic sources frequently contain minor or even major errors. Generally, unless you have a strong reason for consulting them, stay away from personal websites, blogs, discussion boards, or other Internet-based sources that present informally published material; most such sources are not considered to be reliable. Finally, while reference works—encyclopedias, dictionaries, guidebooks, and so on—can help you gain a general understanding of your topic, you should not rely on them as sources for your paper; they do not provide the level of analysis necessary for an academic essay.

If your library offers remote access to electronic versions of journal articles, books, and other sources of information, you may be able to do much of your research from home. But you should still take the time to visit and become acquainted with your library's main building or buildings, as there will likely be times when you need to consult a printed book or ask for in-person assistance from a librarian. Note that in many cases you will need to set up an online account or provide proof of your status as a student in order to make full use of all of your library's resources.

73a

A Catalogue Search

A library catalogue contains brief descriptions of all sources available through the library, including books, journals, audio and video recordings, maps, and musical scores. Some electronic catalogue entries may provide a link to the full text of the source, but in many cases you will need to use the **call number** provided in the entry to find the source on the library shelves.

Most catalogues allow you to perform a **simple search** or an **advanced search**. In a simple search, you can look for a resource by typing a specific

title, part of a title, an **author's name**, or **keywords** related to your topic into the catalogue's main search field. Simple searches work best when you are looking for a commonly available book, or when you want to perform a broad search to discover what books and other resources are available on your topic. In contrast, advanced searches—in which you can specify the title, the author, and keywords as well as additional information such as the format, language, publisher, year of publication, and even genre of the resource—work best when you have a more specific idea of what you want to find. For example, an advanced search could help you find the entry for the 1948 film adaptation of *Hamlet* directed by Laurence Olivier without having to sort through all the other versions of *Hamlet* in your library's collection.

As you learn how to use your library's catalogue, practise recording the title, author or creator, and call number of any sources you might want to explore. If you are working on your own computer, an easy way to keep track of this information is to copy and paste it into a separate file, perhaps your working bibliography (#74b). Many library systems also allow you to save a copy of the catalogue entry in your library account or send it to your personal email account for later retrieval.

Note that the catalogue entry for a hard-copy source will tell you whether the item is available to be checked out, checked out, on hold, or available for reference only. This information can help you determine how you will pursue the source. If the item is available or due to be returned shortly, you may want to place a hold on it to ensure that another student doesn't sign it out before you have a chance to retrieve it. If the item has been checked out for an extended period or is already on hold, you will need to decide whether you have time to wait for it to become available; if you do not, you may need to search for the item somewhere else, such as in your local public library or bookstore. If the item is available for reference

73a

RESEARCH TIP

Requesting Material from Another Library

If you are looking for a book or other source that is not available in your library or through online channels, consult your library's website or a librarian about the possibility of requesting the material from another library. (This option is often called an "interlibrary loan.") Be aware, however, that it can take several weeks for an item to arrive, especially if the item must be shipped from a geographically distant location.

only, you will find it in the library, where all students can access it; you will be able to consult the resource while you are in the library, but you will not be able to take it home with you.

A Database Search

Online databases provide information about—and often access to—articles published in newspapers, magazines, and academic journals. Your library likely subscribes to many databases. Some are general and cover many topics; others are tailored to specific subject areas or disciplines. Read the descriptions of the available options, and explore a few that seem relevant to your studies. If none of the discipline-specific options sound right, start with one of the general databases.

Once you have identified a database that you want to explore, you can begin your search. Most databases allow you to search by title, author, subject, or keywords. Searches for specific titles or authors are useful if you already have a good idea of what you want to find—for example, if you have done some preliminary research and identified specific articles you would like to read or specific researchers whose work appears to be relevant to your topic. Subject searches are helpful if you are familiar with your discipline and with the controlled terms that researchers and publishers assign to articles' subject fields. (Most databases offer a summary of acceptable subject terms.) If you are not very familiar with the discipline in which you are writing, if you are still in the process of narrowing your topic, or if you are interested in finding a variety of articles that are broadly related to your topic, your best option is to use keywords.

Keyword searches provide the greatest flexibility because they allow you to search for various combinations of terms that may appear throughout an article. Depending on the terms you use, a keyword search may return no results or it may return hundreds, not all of which will be of interest to you. To get the best results from this sort of search, choose your words carefully. If your search turns up too many articles that are not directly related to your topic, try using more specific terms. Conversely, if your search turns up too few relevant articles, try searching for synonyms, different forms, or variant spellings of the words you've chosen. If you find that you are having little luck even after using different words and spellings, try searching a different database.

When you identify an article you are interested in reading, you may be able to access the electronic version directly through the database you are using. If the article is not available online—for example, if it is an older article that has not yet been digitized—you may need to find the printed version on your library's shelves. To do so, perform a catalogue search to find the call number assigned to the journal in which the article was published, then go to the library to retrieve the issue or volume you need.

73a

RESEARCH TIP
Expanding or Limiting Search Results

Most database keyword searches and library catalogue searches allow you to expand or limit your results by using simple words and symbols known as "Boolean operators" to combine search terms. The most common Boolean operators are *AND, OR,* and *NOT.* Use *AND* between two terms when you want results that contain both terms; for example, a search for "hunting AND fishing" will return results that mention, to some extent, both hunting and fishing. Use *OR* when you want to find resources that mention one of two (often interchangeable) terms—for example, "caribou OR reindeer." And use *NOT* when you want to exclude a certain term; for example, a search for "hunting NOT fishing" will return results that contain the word *hunting* but not *fishing.* Symbols that commonly function as Boolean operators include the plus sign (+), which generally signifies the same as *AND,* and the minus sign (–), which generally signifies the same as *NOT.* In addition, parentheses can be used to group terms together in complex relationships—for example, "hunting AND (caribou OR reindeer)." Most search systems also recognize the asterisk (*), dollar sign ($), and/or question mark (?) as denoting truncation, meaning that a search for "politic*" might return results that include the words *political, politician, politicize, politico,* and/or *politics.*

Note that most search systems have a "Help" or "About" section that offers advice on how to expand or limit search results. In addition, your school's librarians should be able to answer any questions you have about how to make the most out of database and catalogue searches.

73b

73b The Internet

Internet search engines can provide you with easy access to a vast array of resources related to your topic. Some of these resources—such as government reports and articles in online academic journals—may offer you valuable, trustworthy information. Others—such as independent websites and blogs—are far less reliable. Because most of the information available on the Internet is largely unregulated, you need to evaluate carefully and critically the websites you locate in your research. The following suggestions will help you with this task:

1. Look for authoritative information on websites maintained by recognized and respected researchers, scholars, organizations, or institutions. Anonymous and personal websites are not considered to be

authoritative enough for scholarly research. Openly editable resources such as *Wikipedia* are also not suitable sources for an academic paper.

2. Look for the credentials of the identified authors of the article or website and consider these credentials when weighing the research value of the material.

3. Check that the websites you plan to use are current. Most credible websites provide a "last updated" line at the bottom of each page. If a page has not been updated in many months, or if the information seems outdated, don't treat the material as if it were up-to-date.

4. Check that the claims and evidence offered on the site are supported with detailed and accurate documentation.

5. Question the validity of material that displays a strong bias. Signs of bias include an unwillingness to acknowledge and reasonably consider opposing viewpoints, selective omission of key information that does not support the author's view, appeals to emotion rather than reason, and ties to an organization that endorses a particular political or religious view.

6. Be critical of material that contains errors in spelling and grammar. If the authors haven't taken the time to proofread and polish their work, it is likely that they haven't been rigorous in checking their facts.

7. Be cautious about using a website whose links to other sites are broken, as it may not be well maintained or particularly reliable in its content.

8. Avoid using sites that present information you know to be inaccurate or that use faulty logic (see #3h and #42).

Of course, you can also use an open Internet search in conjunction with library resources. For example, your Internet search might lead you to discover the titles of books or articles that you can then access through your library. The search engine *Google Scholar* can be particularly useful for finding the titles of potential sources. This freely available search engine limits its search results to records of articles written by academics, and these records provide all of the details you need to find the article through your library.

 # Creating a Research Plan

Once you have been given a research project, you should begin creating a **research plan**, a strategy that will help you to focus your research and especially to budget the right amount of time to spend on the assignment. Start working on this plan early—that is, no more than a day or two after you first receive the assignment—and revise it as circumstances change.

Your plan should consist first of a **researchable question**. This question should be of sufficient interest and importance to sustain you through the research and writing process. As you move on and gain more insight into the topic, be confident enough to modify the original question.

As important as determining the researchable question is establishing a **realistic timeline** for the stages of your project. Be careful to leave enough time for finding, reading, and evaluating your sources, and for summarizing and synthesizing the information they contain. Try to set a firm date for the end of your research and the beginning of your writing, and give yourself at least a week for the writing and polishing of the drafts of your essay. (For more on creating a timeline for your paper, see the writing tip near the beginning of #2.)

74a Compiling a Preliminary Bibliography

Once you have decided on a researchable question and established a timeline, the next step is to compile a **preliminary bibliography**—a rough list of articles, books, websites, and other resources that may provide useful information about your topic. Begin by searching your library's catalogue, online databases, and the Internet (see #73). When you find a source that looks promising, record its title, its format, the name(s) of its author(s) or creator(s), and any other details that will help you retrieve it at a later date—for example, its call number, the name of its publisher, the date of its publication or creation, the name of the database in which you found it, or the URL (uniform resource locator) or DOI (digital object identifier) assigned to it. You may also want to locate a few of the most recent and relevant sources on your list and consult their reference pages to find additional sources. And if you decide to go to the library to locate a book, take a quick look at books whose call numbers are similar to the one you went there to find; if any of these books appear to be useful, add them to your preliminary bibliography.

74b Developing a Working Bibliography

When you think you have listed enough sources in your preliminary bibliography, the next step is to transform your preliminary list of sources into a **working bibliography**—a more formal list of the sources you plan to consult, along with brief notes on the usefulness of each source. First, you should decide on the format in which you will work. One option is to create a computer file that is dedicated to your working bibliography. If you've already developed your preliminary bibliography in an electronic file, you can use this file as the basis for your working bibliography. Another option is to create bibliography cards using index cards or small pieces of paper (ideally no smaller than 3 by 5 inches, or 8 by 12 centimetres). The choice between these two options depends on whether you prefer to take notes on a computer or by hand.

Whichever method you choose, order the bibliographic entries alphabetically (by the first author's last name), and make sure that you keep the entries separate from one another. If you are working in a computer file, you may want to enclose each entry in a text box, to make sure that you do not accidentally reformat the document and merge separate entries. In addition, try to format the bibliographical information exactly as it will appear in your final bibliography (see the paper at the end of #80a)—this will save you time later on in the process. Record this information accurately and completely: double-check spellings, dates, page numbers, and all other details. If you aren't sure which citation style you should be using, ask you instructor what she or he expects.

As you evaluate each resource to see how useful it looks, record your comments about its likely worth as a source. Such notes are especially important if you are compiling an annotated bibliography (see #76b). You should note, for example, whether the source is scholarly and credible, whether it is promising or appears to be of little or no use, whether it looks good for a particular part of your project, or whether one part of it looks useful and the rest not. Be as specific as you can be, for a glance at such a note may later save you the trouble of having to find and review the source for a second time.

You may also want to include a label, sometimes called a **slug** (see #75c), with each entry, indicating what part of your subject the resource pertains to. You may want to make each slug correspond to your preliminary outline (see #2i); this information too could save you time. You might also want to note just how thorough your examination of the source was; if you just glanced at it, you may want to return to it, but if you found it so interesting that you read it carefully and even took notes (#75), then you will know that you need not return to it later.

Below is an example of an entry in a working bibliography. (The entry goes with the sample MLA research paper that appears later in this chapter, on pages 502–9.) Note the arrangement and completeness of the note: it begins with the slug; it provides full bibliographic information, organized in MLA style; it concisely comments on the usefulness of the resource; and it concludes with the URL of the page from which the article was retrieved.

74b

Imagination and Belief

Cole, Stewart. "Believing in Tigers: Anthropomorphism and Incredulity in Yann Martel's *Life of Pi*." *Studies in Canadian Literature* 29.2 (2004): 22–36. *MLA International Bibliography*. Web. 12 Oct. 2011.

* scholarly article written by a respected academic
* comments on the distinction between subjective and objective truth
* objects to comparison between believing in the story and believing in God
* bibliographical information may be useful

Accessed at http://journals.hil.unb.ca/index.php/scl/article/view/12747/13691 on 12 October 2011.

75 Taking Notes

Once you have a general sense of the usefulness of the resources that you have included in your working bibliography, you will be ready to begin taking more detailed notes. For these notes you will need to create either a new file on your computer or a new stack of index cards. If you are using index cards, choose cards that differ from your bibliography cards in either size or colour (or both), so that you don't mix up the different types of cards. In each new note, you will need to include at least three things:

1. the note itself,
2. the exact source, and
3. a label or slug indicating what part of your subject the note pertains to.

(These elements are discussed in greater depth below, in #75a–c.)

Initially, as you explore and attempt to limit your subject (see #2b), your notes will likely be brief and of a general nature. As you become more familiar with your topic, however, you will start looking for and recording specific details, data, and arguments. And at some point early in the note-taking stage, you should be able to construct a preliminary outline or plan (see #2i), which will help you decide what kinds of notes to take.

At first you may be uncertain about the usefulness or relevance of some of the material you come across. Be generous with yourself: take substantive notes. If you toss aside a source that doesn't look useful now, you may discover later that you need it after all; it is better to spend a few minutes taking some precise notes than to find at a later time that you need to go back and re-read the source or, worse yet, make a return trip to the library only to find that the source has been borrowed by someone else.

Keep in mind that taking notes in your own words is by far preferable to cutting and pasting together materials you have recorded verbatim or copied directly from electronic sources, for it forces you to actively filter the source material and summarize it as much as possible in your own terms. In fact, copying at this stage delays your synthesis of sources and increases your risk of recording someone else's thoughts without any note of the original source. Whether inadvertent or not, the inclusion of such material in finished essays without proper acknowledgement constitutes **plagiarism** (see #78e).

75a The Note Itself

The following tips will help you prepare clear, effective notes that you can rely on when writing your first draft.

1. **Create a new text box or card for each point**. Limiting the content of each note to a single point will give you the freedom to rearrange your notes as you see fit at various stages. If you try to cram more than one point into a single note, you won't be able to rearrange your material as easily.

RESEARCH TIP

Keeping Your Preliminary Notes

Do not delete any of your electronic notes or throw away any of your note cards, even if you think they will be useless, for at a later stage you may decide to use some of them after all. In fact, don't throw anything away: keep all your notes, jottings, scribblings, lists, and drafts, for they may prove useful later when you want to check back on something or, in the light of new discoveries, restore something you earlier discarded. You may even find that something you are unable to use in one essay turns out to be useful in another assignment.

2. **Distinguish carefully between direct quotation and para-phrase or summary** (see #78). Generally, quote only when you feel strongly that the author's own way of putting something will be especially effective in your essay. When you do quote directly, be careful: your quotation must accurately reproduce the original, including its punctuation, spelling, and even any peculiarities that you think might be incorrect (see item 9 below); do not "improve" what you are copying. In fact, it is a good idea to double-check for absolute accuracy immediately after writing a note, and then to mark the note as checked (e.g., by adding a check mark or the word *verified* in red beside the quotation). And when you do quote directly, put large quotation marks around the quotation so that you cannot possibly later mistake it for summary or paraphrase. This safeguard is particularly important when a note is part quotation and part summary or paraphrase: the quotation marks will help keep your work clear.

3. **Enclose your own ideas in square bracket**s. If a note consists of a combination of (a) summary or paraphrase or quotation and (b) your own interjected thoughts or explanations or opinions, enclose your own ideas in square brackets—or, to be even safer, in double square brackets ([[ ]]); you might even want to initial them or to write "MY OWN IDEA" beside the note to reinforce your memory of the material as an insight of your own. This will prevent you from later assuming that the ideas and opinions came from your source rather than from you.

4. **Use your own words**. As much as possible, express the material in your own words when taking notes. The more you can assimilate and summarize information at the note-taking stage, the less interpreting you will need to do later—and it will never be fresher in your mind than at the time when you are taking the note. If you don't assimilate the information then, you may well have to return to the source to find out why you quoted it in the first place. It is all too easy to forget, over a period of days, weeks, or even months, just what the point was.

75a

This is especially true if you are working on two or three different papers at once, as many students often are.

5. **Quote from the original source**. When you quote, or even paraphrase or summarize, do so from the original source if possible. Second-hand quotations may be inaccurate or misleading. Seek out the most authoritative source—the original—whenever possible, rather than accept someone else's reading of it. Similarly, if more than one edition or version of a source exists, use the most authoritative or definitive one—usually the most recent.

6. **Distinguish between facts and opinions**. If you are quoting or paraphrasing a supposed authority on a subject, be careful not to let yourself be unduly swayed. Rather than note that "Aspirin is good for heart and stroke patients," say that "Dr. Jones claims that Aspirin is good for heart and stroke patients." Rather than write that "the province is running out of natural resources," say that "the premier believes, after reading the report given to her by the investigating committee, that the province is running out of natural resources." The credibility of your own presentation may well depend on such matters of attribution.

7. **Be careful with the page numbers**. If a passage that you are quoting, summarizing, or paraphrasing runs over from one page to another in your source, be sure to indicate where the page break occurs, for you may later decide to use only a part of the material, and you must know which page that part came from in order to provide accurate documentation. A simple method is to indicate the end of a page with one or two slashes (/ or //).

8. **Enclose explanatory material in square brackets**. Whenever you insert explanatory material—for example, a noun or noun phrase to explain a pronoun in a quotation—use square brackets (see #54j).

9. **Use [*sic*] to indicate an error**. When there is something in a quotation that is obviously wrong—whether it is a factual mistake or a mistake in the writing, such as a spelling error—insert [*sic*] after it (see #54j).

10. **Indicate ellipses**. Whenever you omit a word or words from a quotation, use three spaced periods to indicate the ellipsis (see #54i).

75b The Source

At the bottom of each text box or note card, identify the **source**. Include the last name of the author or creator, the relevant page numbers, and a shortened version of the title of the work. Double-check these details to ensure you do not credit the note to the wrong source. If the note comes from more than one page, indicate the inclusive page numbers; the note itself will show where the page changes (see #75a.7). If you will be following MLA style in your paper, you must also note the date on which you accessed any electronic sources, for you will need to include this information in the works-cited entry for the source (see #80a).

75b

75c The Slug

At the top of each text box or note card, record a **slug**. The slug should consist of a word or brief phrase identifying the topic of the note, and if possible indicating just what part of your essay the note belongs in. Be as specific as possible: this slug will be helpful when it comes to organizing the notes before writing the essay. If you've prepared a good outline (#2i), a key word or two from its main headings and subheadings with the corresponding numerals will be the logical choice to use as a slug.

75d Recording Your Own Ideas

In addition to taking notes from other sources, preserve your own ideas, insights, and flashes of inspiration as you go along. However fragmentary or tentative they may seem at first, they are likely to be valuable at a later stage. Even if you suddenly have so strong an idea about something that you feel sure you will remember the idea forever, *write it down*; otherwise there is a good chance you will forget it, for another strong idea may dislodge it a few minutes later. It is also a good idea to add your initials or "MY OWN IDEA" beside the note, so that you can easily identify it as your own.

 # Preparing Preliminary Assignments

In some situations, your instructor may ask you to prepare and submit a preliminary assignment before you submit your research essay. The most common types of preliminary assignments related to research papers are **academic proposals, annotated bibliographies**, and **critical summaries**. While the following three sections offer brief overviews to prepare you for what to expect from these sorts of assignments, the descriptions are by no means exhaustive. Different class assignments will have different requirements. In practice, you should always read an assignment closely and make sure your work meets all of the listed requirements. If you are unsure of what is expected from you, ask your instructor.

76a

76a Academic Proposals

Formal academic proposals (sometimes called "research plans") are common requirements for major research projects and theses. While formal proposals often contain many of the same elements as do research plans meant for personal use (e.g., a researchable question, a realistic timeline, a working bibliography; see #74), they generally require a greater amount of preliminary research—enough to ensure your approach to the topic is novel and that what you are proposing is feasible. An academic proposal will usually include a detailed rationale that explains why the project is worth pursuing and, if applicable, how it relates to the course material. It also will likely include some form of literature or research review that summarizes what has already been said about your topic and how your project will build on the existing research to say something new. Sometimes a proposal will include an outline of the essay or thesis itself (see #2i). The elements included in an academic proposal as well as its depth and specificity can vary greatly and will depend on the discipline you are working in, so it is important to first check if an established format has already been set by your instructor, supervisor, or department.

76b Annotated Bibliographies

An annotated bibliography is similar to a working bibliography (#74b), except that in an annotated bibliography the descriptive and evaluative comments are generally developed in greater detail and presented in full sentences, the entries are set as a continuous list rather than separated into boxes, and the entries do not generally require a slug or label corresponding to a preliminary outline. Essentially, an annotated bibliography looks like a regular bibliography that you would find at the end of an essay or a book, only with a short paragraph of 150 or so words following each bibliographic entry. Preparing an annotated bibliography typically requires you to describe or summarize the source, identify the main argument(s) within the source, and comment on the overall value of the source in relation to your essay. It may also require you to comment on the author's credentials or qualifications, the intended audience, the reading level, the theoretical basis of the author's arguments, and any biases or weaknesses you can detect. Below is an example of an entry in an annotated bibliography; this entry has been adapted from the example given in #74b:

76b

Cole, Stewart. "Believing in Tigers: Anthropomorphism and Incredulity in Yann Martel's *Life of Pi.*" *Studies in Canadian Literature* 29.2 (2004): 22–36. *MLA International Bibliography.* Web. 12 Oct. 2011.

This 6000-word scholarly article, written by a doctoral candidate currently teaching literature studies at the University of Toronto, examines Yann Martel's treatment of belief and faith in *Life of Pi.* Focusing on Francis Adirubasamy's and the narrator's assertion that Pi's story "will make you believe in God," Stewart Cole investigates what it means, within the novel, to (1) believe in a story and (2) believe in God. Cole applies Samuel Taylor Coleridge's notion of "poetic faith," which requires a reader to temporarily suspend her or his disbelief, to Martel's novel, arguing that the novel conflates poetic faith and religious faith. Ultimately, Cole objects to this conflation, noting that it obliterates the distinction between subjective and objective truth, a distinction he feels is crucial to discussions of religion. Cole's observations on belief provide an interesting contrast to my own analysis of why "the story with the animals is the better story" (Martel 352).

Note that the writer has followed MLA style in presenting the bibliographic information and the parenthetical citation; in your own annotated bibliographies, make sure the bibliographic information appears in the style you plan to use for your final essay (see #80).

76c Critical Summaries

A **critical summary** is similar to the summary you would write for an entry in an annotated bibliography, but it requires a greater level of critical thought and analysis. In a critical summary, you must not only identify and summarize but also evaluate a work's main points and arguments. This evaluation requires you to be knowledgeable in the subject area, and it often requires you to have read other academic sources that examine the same or similar topics. In some cases, you may be asked to comment specifically on how well the ideas and arguments in the source you are examining hold up against counterarguments from other sources. Note, however, that you are not required to find fault with a source in a critical summary; being critical, in this context, simply means engaging in thoughtful analysis. The following list offers examples of questions you may want to address when writing a critical summary:

- Do the author's arguments make sense?
- Does the author support her or his claims with solid evidence?
- Does the author appeal to reason rather than prejudices or emotions? (See #3e.)
- Does the author acknowledge and build on the work of other respected academics in her or his field?
- Does the author acknowledge and adequately address opposing viewpoints or evidence that doesn't support her or his position? (See #3f.)
- Is the progression from idea to idea logical? Does the author make any errors in logic? (See #3g–h.)
- Is the author qualified to discuss the topic?
- Does the author approach the topic objectively? Is there any evidence of bias?
- Does the author use clear, straightforward language?
- Who is the intended reader?

Even if your instructor does not specifically ask you to prepare critical summaries as part of your research assignment, you should get into the habit of asking yourself these sorts of questions when you examine your sources. Critical analysis is an essential step in the research process.

77 Writing the Essay

When your research is complete and you have finished any required preliminary assignments, you are ready to begin writing the essay. If your note-taking has been efficient—that is, if you have kept quotation to a minimum, assimilating and interpreting and evaluating as much as possible as you went along, and if you have made detailed notes about your own ideas—then writing the first draft should be a fairly simple task; you will need do little more than arrange material logically and compose necessary transitions as you move from note to note and follow your outline. (Of course the usual steps of revising and proofreading must follow the writing of the first draft, as described in chapter I; see #2-l–n and appendix 3.)

As you write your first draft, proceeding from note to note, include in your text a brief parenthetical reference to the source of any material that is not your own. That is, at the end of each quotation, paraphrase, summary, or direct reference, enclose in parentheses the last name of the author, an abbreviated version of the work's title, the date the work was published or created, and the relevant page number or numbers. When you prepare your final draft, you can reformat these parenthetical notes to be consistent with the citation style you are using for your references (see #80).

RESEARCH TIP

Saving and Backing Up Your Work

As you compose your essay, remember to save files at frequent intervals, and when you rework material, always leave a backup file on the hard drive. For example, when you revise a first draft, make sure to retain a copy of the original draft, just in case you aren't happy with the way the revision turns out; then you can retrieve the original and try again. And you should also save backup copies of your files to an external storage device (e.g., a USB flash drive), in case of virus, power failure, or printer problems.

78

78 Quotation, Paraphrase, Summary, and Plagiarism

When you incorporate someone else's ideas into your own work, make sure you give credit to the original source. A **quotation** must be exact. A **paraphrase**, on the other hand, reproduces the content of the original, but in different words. Paraphrase is a useful technique because it enables writers to make use of source material while still using their own words and thus to avoid too much direct quotation. But a paraphrase, to be legitimate, should give clear credit *at its beginning* to the source and should not use significant words and phrases from the source without enclosing them in quotation marks. In other words, you should begin your paraphrase by identifying your source (e.g., "Biographer John English suggests . . ."

or "John English, Pierre Trudeau's biographer, argues . . ."). You must also provide the page number(s) for the material you have presented, as you would for a direct quotation. A paraphrase will usually be a little shorter than the original, but it need not be. A **summary**, however, is by definition a condensation, a boiled-down version in one's own words that expresses the principal points of an original source. It is often the best evidence of a writer's effective synthesis of secondary source material.

Some writers make the serious mistake of thinking that only direct quotations need to be documented; on the contrary, it is important to know and remember that paraphrase and summary must also be fully documented. Failure to document a paraphrase or summary is a breach of academic integrity known as **plagiarism**, a form of intellectual dishonesty for which there are serious academic penalties. To familiarize yourself with your institution's policies on academic integrity and on plagiarism, consult your institution's most recent academic calendar.

To illustrate the differences between legitimate and illegitimate use of source material, here is a paragraph, a direct quotation, from Rupert Brooke's *Letters from America*, followed by

a. legitimate paraphrase,
b. illegitimate paraphrase,
c. combination paraphrase and quotation,
d. summary, and
e. a comment on plagiarism.

> Such is Toronto. A brisk city of getting on for half a million inhabitants, the largest British city in Canada (in spite of the cheery Italian faces that pop up at you out of excavations in the street), liberally endowed with millionaires, not lacking its due share of destitution, misery, and slums. It is no mushroom city of the West, it has its history; but at the same time it has grown immensely of recent years. It is situated on the shores of a lovely lake; but you never see that, because the railways have occupied the entire lake front. So if, at evening, you try to find your way to the edge of the water, you are checked by a region of smoke, sheds, trucks, wharves, storehouses, "depôts," railway-lines, signals, and locomotives and trains that wander on the tracks up and down and across streets, pushing their way through the pedestrians, and tolling, as they go, in the American fashion, an immense melancholy bell, intent, apparently, on some private and incommunicable grief. Higher up are the business quarters, a few sky-scrapers in the American style without the modern American beauty, but one of which advertises itself as the highest in the British Empire; streets that seem less narrow than Montreal [sic], but not unrespectably wide; "the buildings are generally substantial and often handsome" (the too kindly

78

> Herr Baedeker). Beyond that the residential part, with quiet streets, gardens open to the road, shady verandahs, and homes, generally of wood, that are a deal more pleasant to see than the houses in a modern English town. (Brooke 80–81)

The parenthetical reference for this block quotation, which is given in MLA style (see #80a), begins one space after the final punctuation mark. It includes the author's surname and the page numbers on which the original appeared. The complete bibliographical entry for Brooke's work would appear in the works-cited list as follows:

> Brooke, Rupert. *Letters from America*. London: Sidgwick and Jackson, 1916. Print.

(For more information about handling quotations, see #54.)

78a Legitimate Paraphrase

> During his 1913 tour of the United States and Canada, Rupert Brooke sent back to England articles about his travels. In one of them, published in the 1916 book *Letters from America*, he describes Toronto as a large city, predominantly British, containing both wealth and poverty. He says that it is relatively old, compared to the upstart new cities farther west, but that nevertheless it has expanded a great deal in the last little while. He implies that its beautiful setting is spoiled for its citizens by the railways, which have taken over all the land near the lake, filling it with buildings and tracks and smell and noise. He also writes of the commercial part of the city, with its buildings which are tall (like American ones) but not very attractive (unlike American ones); one of them, he says, claims to be the tallest in the British Empire. (He pokes fun at Baedeker for being overgenerous with his comments about the city's downtown architecture.) The streets he finds wider than those of Montreal, but not too wide. Finally, he compares Toronto's attractive residential areas favourably with those of English towns (80–81).

78a

This is legitimate paraphrase. Even though it uses several individual words from the original (*British, railways, tracks, American, British Empire, streets, residential, English town[s]*), they are a small part of the whole; more important, they are common words that would be difficult to replace with reasonable substitutes without distorting the sense. And, even more important, they are used in a way that is natural to the paraphraser's own style and context. Had the writer said "in the American style" or "the entire lake shore," the style (and words) would have been too much Brooke's. Paraphrase does not consist in merely substituting one word for another, but rather in assimilating something and restating it in your own words and your own syntax.

Note that the parenthetical reference contains only the page numbers, since the author is named in the text. Though this reference comes at the end of a long paragraph, it is clear because the paragraph begins by identifying its overall subject and because the writer has carefully kept Brooke's point of view apparent throughout by including him in each independent clause (a technique that also establishes good coherence): *Rupert Brooke, he describes, He says, He implies, He also writes, he says, He pokes fun, he finds, he compares.*

78b Illegitimate Paraphrase
An illegitimate paraphrase of Brooke's paragraph might begin like this:

> Brooke describes Toronto as a <u>brisk</u> kind of city with nearly <u>half a million inhabitants</u>, with some <u>Italian faces popping up</u> among the British, and with both <u>millionaires and slums</u>. He deplores the fact that the <u>lake front</u> on which <u>it is situated</u> has been <u>entirely occupied by the railways</u>, which have turned it into a <u>region of smoke and storehouses</u> and the like, and <u>trains that wander back and forth, ringing their huge bells</u> (80–81).

The parenthetical reference at paragraph's end does *not* protect such a treatment from the charge of plagiarism, for too many of the words and phrases and too much of the syntax are Brooke's own. The underlined words and phrases are all illegitimate: a flavourful word like *brisk*; the intact phrase *half a million inhabitants*; the barely altered phrase *Italian faces popping up*; and so on. Changing *the railways have occupied the entire lakefront* to the passive *the lakefront . . . has been entirely occupied by the railways*, or *trains that wander . . . up and down* to *trains that wander back and forth*, or *tolling . . . an immense . . . bell* to *ringing their huge bells* does not make them the writer's: they still have the diction, syntax, and stylistic flavour of Brooke's original, and they therefore constitute plagiarism.

Had the writer put quotation marks around "brisk," "half a million inhabitants," "Italian faces . . . pop[ping] up," "millionaires," "slums," "lake front," "it is situated," "occupied," "a region of smoke," "trains that wander," and "bell[s]," the passage would no longer be plagiarism—but it would still be an illegitimate, or at least very poor, paraphrase, for the writer would have done little more than lightly "edit" the original.

78c Paraphrase and Quotation Mixed
A writer who felt that a pure paraphrase was too flat and abstract, who felt that some of Brooke's more striking words and phrases should be retained, might choose to mix some direct quotation into a paraphrase:

> In *Letters from America*, Rupert Brooke characterizes Toronto as a "brisk," largely British city having the usual urban mixture of wealth and poverty. Unlike the "mushroom" cities farther

78c

> west, he says, Toronto has a history, though he points out that much of its growth has been recent. He notes, somewhat cynically, that the people are cut off from the beauty of the lake by the railways and all their "smoke, sheds, trucks, wharves, storehouses, 'depôts,' railway lines, signals, and locomotives and trains" going ding-ding all over the place (80–81).

This time the context is very much the writer's own, but some of the flavour of Brooke's original has been retained through the direct quotation of a couple of judiciously chosen words and the cumulative list quoted at the end. The writer is clearly in control of the material, as the writer of the preceding example was not. Here again, Brooke's name is excluded from the parenthetical reference because Brooke is named in the attribution in the first sentence of the paragraph. (See also #78f below.)

78d Summary

The purpose of a summary is to substantially reduce the original, conveying its essential meaning in a sentence or two. A summary of Brooke's passage might go something like this:

> Rupert Brooke describes Toronto as large and mainly wealthy, aesthetically marred by the railway yards along the lake, with wide-enough streets and tall but (in spite of Baedeker's half-hearted approval) generally unprepossessing buildings, and a residential area more attractive than comparable English ones (80–81).

In general, try to refer to an author by name in your text—and the first time by full name—when you are summarizing, paraphrasing, or quoting. If for some reason you do not want to bring the author's name into your text (e.g., if you were surveying a variety of opinions about Toronto and did not want to clutter your text with all their authors' names), then you would still need to make the source clear, according to whichever citation style you are using (#80).

78e Maintaining Academic Integrity and Avoiding Plagiarism

Had one of the foregoing versions of the passage not mentioned Brooke, nor included quotation marks, nor ended with documentation, it would have been plagiarism. A student doing research is part of a community of scholars (professors, investigators, instructors, other students, and researchers), all of whom are governed by the codes of academic honesty that define effective research and identify plagiarism—whether intentional or accidental—as a serious offence against academic integrity. Your college or university calendar will no doubt include a detailed definition of plagiarism and a statement of policy on the academic discipline (failing marks, suspension, a note on one's academic transcript) arising from a finding of plagiarism. You should review this information and discuss any questions or concerns you have about your research practices with your instructors and academic advisers.

When you are working on a research project, keep in mind that you are ethically bound to give credit twice—*in the text* of the written document and *in the works-cited list*—to all sources of information you have used. All of the following kinds of material require acknowledgement:

- direct quotations—whether short or long;
- your summaries and paraphrases of sources;
- ideas, theories, and inspirations drawn from a source and expressed in your own words;
- statistical data compiled by institutions (e.g., think tanks and governmental or non-governmental organizations) and other researchers;
- original ideas and original findings drawn from course lectures and seminars; and
- graphic materials (diagrams, charts, photographs, illustrations, slides, film and television clips, and audio and video recordings).

Remember that giving credit for this kind of material does not diminish your own work: it enhances the credibility of your claims and demonstrates just how much genuine research you have done on your project. It shows you adding your voice and your views to those of the community of scholars and researchers of which you are a part.

One final note. It is possible to commit self-plagiarism. This happens when a writer submits the same work—in whole or in part—for two different courses or assignments. If you are working in the same subject or topic area for two different courses or assignments, it is essential to discuss the ethical issues involved with both instructors to whom the work will be submitted.

See *ack* and *doc* in appendix 2.

78f Integrating and Contextualizing Quotations

When you include quoted material within one of your own sentences, you may well have to alter it in one way or another to incorporate it smoothly. That is, you may have to change the grammar, syntax, or punctuation of a quotation to make it conform to the grammar and syntax of your own sentence. Note how the writers have altered the quoted material in the following examples. (See also #54i–j.)

The original quotation (from Mary Shelley's *Frankenstein; or, The Modern Prometheus*):

> I am by birth a Genevese; and my family is one of the most distinguished of that republic. My ancestors had been for many

78f

> years counsellors and syndics; and my father had filled several public situations with honour and reputation. He was respected by all who knew him for his integrity and indefatigable attention to public business. He passed his younger days perpetually occupied by the affairs of his country; a variety of circumstances had prevented his marrying early, nor was it until the decline of life that he became a husband and the father of a family.

(a)   altered for pronoun reference:

> Victor Frankenstein begins his story by stating that "[he is] by birth a Genevese; and [his] family is one of the most distinguished of that republic" (Shelley 31).

The first-person pronouns have been changed to third person in order to fit the third-person point of view in the sentence as a whole. The changed pronouns and the accompanying verb (*is* for *am*) appear in square brackets. (The opening *he is* could have been left outside the quotation, but the writer preferred to incorporate the parallelism within the quotation.)

(b)   altered for consistent verb tense:

> As we first encounter him in the description at the beginning of his son's narrative, Victor's father is a man "respected by all who [know] him for his integrity and indefatigable attention to public business" (Shelley 31).

The verb in square brackets has been changed from past to present tense to conform with the tense established by the *is* of the student's sentence.

(c)   altered for punctuation:

> The first words of Victor Frankenstein's narrative—"I am by birth a Genevese" (Shelley 31)—reveal a narrator preoccupied with himself, his birth, and his nationality.

The semicolon of the original has been dropped to avoid its clashing with the enclosing dashes of the student's own sentence.

(d)   selective quotation:

> The first paragraph of Victor's narrative focuses more on Victor's father than on any other member of the Frankenstein family. Victor takes pains to describe him as a man of "honour and reputation . . . respected by all who [know] him for his integrity and indefatigable attention to public business" and

"perpetually occupied by the affairs of his country" (Shelley 31).
A first-time reader of the novel might well assume that Victor's
narrative will be more a tribute to his father than an account of
his own creation of a monster.

Here, the student writer has selected key words and phrases from the
opening paragraph of Victor Frankenstein's narrative in order to make a
point about the novel's focus. The ellipsis indicates that material has been
omitted in the interests of the student's own sentence structure.

Exercise 78 Paraphrasing and Summarizing

Here are two more paragraphs from Rupert Brooke's *Letters from
America*. For each, write (a) a paraphrase, (b) a paraphrase with
some quotation mixed in, and (c) a summary. Include an effective
lead-in (attribution) for the material and a parenthetical reference in
MLA style for each piece you write.

(1) Ottawa came as a relief after Montreal. There is no such sense
of strain and tightness in the atmosphere. The British, if not
greatly in the majority, are in the ascendancy; also, the city
seems conscious of other than financial standards, and quietly,
with dignity, aware of her own purpose. The Canadians, like the
Americans, chose to have for their capital a city which did not
lead in population or in wealth. This is particularly fortunate in
Canada, an extremely individualistic country, whose inhabitants
are only just beginning to be faintly conscious of their
nationality. Here, at least, Canada is more than the Canadian.
A man desiring to praise Ottawa would begin to do so without
statistics of wealth and the growth of population; and this can
be said of no other city in Canada except Quebec. Not that
there are not immense lumber-mills and the rest in Ottawa.
But the Government farm, and the Parliament buildings, are
more important. Also, although the "spoils" system obtains a
good deal in this country, the nucleus of the Civil Service is
much the same as in England; so there is an atmosphere of
Civil Servants about Ottawa, an atmosphere of safeness and
honour and massive buildings and well-shaded walks. After all,
there is in the qualities of Civility and Service much beauty, of a
kind which would adorn Canada. (Brooke 54–55)

(2) Winnipeg is the West. It is important and obvious that in Canada
there are two or three (some say five) distinct Canadas. Even
if you lump the French and English together as one community
in the East, there remains the gulf of the Great Lakes. The
difference between East and West is possibly no greater than

78f

that between North and South England, or Bavaria and Prussia; but in this country, yet unconscious of itself, there is so much less to hold them together. The character of the land and the people differs; their interests, as it appears to them, are not the same. Winnipeg is a new city. In the archives at Ottawa is a picture of Winnipeg in 1870—Main street, with a few shacks, and the prairie either end. Now her population is a hundred thousand, and she has the biggest this, that, and the other west of Toronto. A new city; a little more American than the other Canadian cities, but not unpleasantly so. The streets are wider, and full of a bustle which keeps clear of hustle. The people have something of the free swing of Americans, without the bumptiousness; a tempered democracy, a mitigated independence of bearing. The manners of Winnipeg, of the West, impress the stranger as better than those of the East, more friendly, more hearty, more certain to achieve graciousness, if not grace. There is, even, in the architecture of Winnipeg, a sort of *gauche* pride visible. It is hideous, of course, even more hideous than Toronto or Montreal; but cheerily and windily so. There is no scheme in the city, and no beauty, but it is at least preferable to Birmingham, less dingy, less directly depressing. It has no real slums, even though there is poverty and destitution. (Brooke 102–03)

79 Acknowledging Sources

The purpose of documentation is fourfold:

1. It demonstrates that you, the writer, are a genuine researcher who has done the considerable work of investigating authorities and experts in the field(s) assumed in your researchable question.
2. It acknowledges your indebtedness to particular sources.
3. It lends weight to your statements and arguments by citing experts and authorities to support them, and by demonstrating the extent of your investigation of a topic.
4. It enables an interested reader to pursue the subject further by consulting cited sources, or possibly to evaluate a particular source or to check the accuracy of a reference or quotation, should it appear questionable.

To be effective, documentation must be complete, accurate, and clear. Completeness and accuracy depend on careful recording of necessary information as you do your research and take notes. Clarity depends on the way you present that information to your reader. You will be clear only if your audience can follow your method of documentation (see #80). Therefore, it is important that before you begin any research project, you investigate the method of documentation you need to use.

79a Common Knowledge

It is not necessary to provide documentation for facts, ideas, and quotations that are so widely known that they are considered to be **common knowledge**—such as the fact that Shakespeare wrote *Hamlet*, or that Hamlet said "To be or not to be," or that Sir Isaac Newton formulated the law of gravitation, or that the story of Adam and Eve appears in the book of Genesis in the Bible, or that the moon is not made of green cheese. But if you are at all uncertain whether or not something is "common knowledge," play it safe: it is far better to over-document and appear a little naive than to under-document and engage in the unethical practice of plagiarism.

In general, if a piece of information appears in the same form in multiple sources, it qualifies as "common knowledge" and need not be documented. For example, such facts as the elevation of Mt. Logan, the current population of the world, or the date of the execution of Louis Riel can be found in dozens of reference books. But it can be risky for a student, or any non-professional, to trust to such a guideline when dealing with other kinds of material. For example, there may be dozens of articles, websites, and books referring to or attempting to explain something like a neutrino, or red shift, or black holes, or discoveries at the Olduvai Gorge, or Jungian readings of fairy tales, or the importance of the Human Genome Project, or deep structure in linguistic theory, or warnings about bioterrorism, or Neoplatonic ideas in Renaissance poetry, or the nature and consequences of the great potato famine, or the origin of the name *Canada*; nevertheless, it is unlikely that a relatively non-expert writer will be sufficiently conversant with such material to recognize and accept it as "common knowledge." If something is new to you, and if you have not thoroughly explored the available literature on the subject, it is best to acknowledge a source. When in doubt, check with your instructor.

When the question of "common knowledge" arises, ask yourself: *common to whom?* Your readers will probably welcome the explicit documentation of something that they themselves do not realize is, to a few experts, "common knowledge." Besides, if at any point in your essay you give your readers cause to question your data, you will lose their confidence. So be scrupulous: document anything about which you have the least doubt.

80 Methods of Documentation

There are four main methods of documentation:

1. the *name–page method* recommended by the Modern Language Association (MLA), which is in wide use in the humanities (see #80a);

2. the *name–date method* recommended by the American Psychological Association (APA), which is used in some of the social and other sciences (see #80b);

3. the *note method* outlined in *The Chicago Manual of Style*, which is in use in various disciplines (see #80c); and

4. the *number method*, which is used in some of the sciences (see #80d).

Which method you choose will depend on what discipline you are writing in and on the wishes of the audience for whom you are writing.

Below, we cover the basics of the four main methods. As you read through the examples, note that in an actual paper, the lines of text would be double-spaced rather than single-spaced.

80a The Name–Page Method (MLA Style)

The name–page method is described in detail in the seventh edition of the *MLA Handbook for Writers of Research Papers* (2009). Using this method, you provide a short, usually parenthetical, in-text reference to each source as you use it in the body of your paper. Then, you provide complete bibliographical information about all sources you have used at the end of the essay, in a list titled "Works Cited."

The pages that follow provide examples of the most common patterns of MLA documentation. (See also the examples in #78a–d.) First we cover the basics of in-text citation; then we give examples to show how you should treat various types of publications in the works-cited list. Note that most examples presented in the section on in-text citations correspond to entries given as examples in the section on the list of works cited.

In-Text Citations

The in-text citation contains the information readers require to find the full source in the works-cited list. Generally, this information consists of the author's surname and the number of the page on which the quoted or paraphrased material appears. Parenthetical references are usually placed at the end of the sentence in which the citation occurs:

80a

> The reaction in China to the end of World War I has been described by one historian as "popular rejoicing"—particularly among young people, who had "an uncritical admiration for Western democracy, Western liberal ideals, and Western learning" (MacMillan 322).

If a sentence is long and complicated, a reference may be placed earlier, immediately after the quotation itself. If you include the author's name your text, you do not need to repeat it in the parenthetical reference:

> The reaction in China to the end of World War I has been described by historian Margaret MacMillan as "popular rejoicing"—particularly among young people, who had "an

uncritical admiration for Western democracy, Western liberal ideals, and Western learning" (322).

Note that most of the following conventions apply to print as well as electronic sources.

A Work by One, Two, or Three Authors
Include the surnames of all authors and the page reference, with no intervening punctuation:

> The reaction in China to the end of World War I has been described as "popular rejoicing" (MacMillan 322).

> Although the exact dates are a matter of debate among scholars, the Viking Age is often considered to have begun around the year 793 and to have ended around 1066 (Somerville and McDonald 2).

> In the introduction, the editors question how a region should be defined—by geographical location, by a common history, or by a shared culture (Perry, Jones, and Morton 1).

A Work by More Than Three Authors
Include the name of the author whose name appears first on the title page of the work, followed by the abbreviation *et al.* (for Latin *et alii*, "and others"):

> Messenger et al. advise students to become familiar with the resources available through their school's library before they receive their first research assignment (458).

80a

A Work by a Government Agency or a Corporate Author
If a work published by a government agency, a corporation, or another such collective body does not list an author, provide the organization's name in the in-text citation:

> A six-page report published in 2011 sets out the Canadian government's official recommendations on balanced nutrition (Health Canada).

Here, there is no page number because the reference is to the report as a whole.

A Work with No Identified Author
For an article with no identified author, include the title in place of the author's name. If the title is longer than a few words, you can use a shortened version:

> When governments fail to resolve public-sector strikes, "final offer arbitration may be the best option for all taxpayers" ("How to End" 5).

This article, entitled "How to End Needless Strikes? Start with Good Faith Offers," appeared in *Maclean's* magazine in April 2012.

A Multivolume Work

When you have used several volumes from a work of two or more volumes, include the volume number in the parenthetical reference, followed by a colon and a space, and then the page number:

> In an entry dated 3 August 1908, she described her second book as "not nearly so good as *Green Gables*" (Montgomery 1: 338).

To refer to the entire work, add a comma after the author's name and the abbreviation *vol.* before the volume number: "(Montgomery, vol. 1)." If you have used only one volume from a multivolume work, you do not need to include the volume number, as long as you indicate that number in the works-cited list.

A Well-Known Work of Literature Available in Many Editions

When citing a novel, a play, a poem, or some other work of literature that is well-known and available in many editions, include the page number for the edition you have consulted as well as the chapter number and/or any other divisional numbers that would help your reader locate the material in a different edition of the same work. Use a semicolon to separate the page number from the other number(s):

> Jane Austen presents readers of *Pride and Prejudice* with the heroine's father, the likable Mr. Bennet, an "odd . . . mixture of quick parts, sarcastic humour, reserve, and caprice" (32; vol. 1, ch. 1); only much later do we learn that these qualities in part contribute to his serious shortcomings as a father.

80a

If the work is divided into books, use the abbreviation *bk.*; if it is divided into sections, use *sec.*

A Play in Prose

When citing a prose play, include the page number for the publication you have consulted as well as the act number, separated with a semicolon:

> In Chekhov's *The Cherry Orchard*, Trofimov says to Anya, "All Russia is our orchard" (122; act 2).

If the play is divided into scenes instead of acts, provide the scene number in place of the act number: "(12; scene 1)." If the play is divided into scenes as well as acts, provide both numbers: "(67; act 2, scene 1)."

A Play in Verse

For a verse play, include the act, scene, and line numbers of the material you reference, separated with periods; you need not include a page number:

> In the final act of *As You Like It*, Silvius answers the question of what it means to love with these memorable words:
> It is to be all made of fantasy,
> All made of passion, and all made of wishes,
> All adoration, duty, and observance,
> All humbleness, all patience and impatience,
> All purity, all trial, all obedience[.] (5.2.89–94)

A Poem

When citing a poem, include the line number(s) in place of the page number:

> Milton's *Paradise Lost* begins by recalling the story "Of man's first disobedience, and the fruit / Of that forbidden tree, whose mortal taste / Brought death into the world, and all our woe" (lines 1–3).

The word *lines* tells readers that you are referring to lines instead of pages. Subsequent references to the same poem need not include the words *line* or *lines*; the number will be enough. Note the need for a space before and after the slash mark indicating a line break in the verse.

MLA STYLE

On the Treatment of Number Ranges

When you cite a range of numbers in MLA style, list all digits for numbers up to 99 (e.g., lines 5–88; pages 97–99). When you cite numbers above 99, include only the last two digits of the second number unless more are necessary to prevent confusion (e.g., lines 108–22 for a range from line 108 to line 122, but pages 385–485 for a range from page 385 to page 485.)

80a

A Work of Scripture

If you are citing a work of scripture, refer to the work's internal divisions (e.g., books, chapters, verses) rather than its pages. Also include a shortened title of the edition you are using the first time you reference the work:

> In the biblical account of the Flood, Noah is presented as a dutiful servant of God, "a just man and perfect in his generations" (*Holy Bible*, Gen. 6.9). In contrast, the earth is said to be "filled with violence" and "corrupt" (Gen. 6.11–12).

Note that while you do not italicize the general names of religious texts (for example, the Bible, the Talmud, the Qur'an), you do italicize the title of a specific edition of the text—in this case, *The Holy Bible*.

An Online Document with No Page Numbers

Most documents created for the Web do not consist of numbered pages; as a result, it is often not possible to provide a page number for material quoted from an online source. If the sections or paragraphs of an online document are numbered, you should include the paragraph or section number where you would normally include the page number, and add the abbreviation *par.* (for numbered paragraphs) or *sec.* (for numbered sections) before the number:

> Reflecting on the importance of the artistic process, poet Jon Sands has described art as "how you explain what it feels like to be alive in the 21st century" (sec. 1).

If the author's surname also appears in the parenthetical citation, add a comma between the name and the abbreviation—for example, "(Sands, sec. 1)." For documents that provide no numbered divisions, include only the author's name in the parenthetical citation:

> *Online presence* has been described by one world-famous writer as "everything you say online" as well as "everything anyone says about you: in newspapers or magazine reviews, if in digital for or accessible online; on blogs; on social media" (Atwood).

Generally, online documents are easily searchable, so the reader should have no problem locating the material you have quoted.

Quotation at Second Hand

Try as often as possible to quote from primary sources. If you decide that you need to quote from a secondary source—for example, if you want to include something spoken by one person but recorded by another, the author—be careful to identify the original source and to contextualize the words you quote:

> When US president Woodrow Wilson set out for the Paris Peace Conference in late 1918, he stated that he felt a "duty" to support American servicemen: "It is now my duty . . . to play my full part in making good what they gave their life's blood to obtain" (qtd. in MacMillan 3).

80a

Citing Two or More Works by the Same Author
If you cite multiple works by a single author in your paper, the in-text references to those works must include an abbreviated form of the title:

> The study of emotions requires consideration of "a wider range of phenomena and evidence than is usual in psychology" (Oatley, *Best* 1). Indeed, the fiction writer's approach to understanding emotion is to devote "time and effort into exploring particular emotional issues" and learning "how to externalize" the expression of emotion (Oatley, *Passionate* 187).

In this example, the student has referenced two books by Keith Oatley: *Best Laid Schemes* (1992) and *The Passionate Muse* (2011). Including an abbreviated form of each title in the in-text citations tells the reader which work the writer is referring to in each case.

Citing More Than One Work in the Same Sentence
If you include quotes from two different sources within a single sentence, place the parenthetical citations as close as possible to the material to which they correspond:

> World War I left Canadians "a deeply divided people who had inherited a staggering debt" (Morton 226), but it has also been said to have "mark[ed] the real birth of Canada" (Gwyn xxi).

If you cite more than one source in a single parenthetical reference, simply write each citation in the usual way and separate the entries with a semicolon:

> World War I caused Canadians great personal loss and suffering, but it also brought them closer together through a growing sense of national identity (Morton 226; Gwyn xix–xxi).

80a

In the list of works cited, include separate entries for Desmond Morton's article "First World War" (an article in the 2004 reference book *The Oxford Companion to Canadian History*, edited by Gerald Hallowell) and Sandra Gwyn's book *Tapestry of War* (1993).

Works-Cited References
The list of works cited appears at the end of your essay and includes the full publication information for all works that you have referenced. It should begin on a new page, with the title "Works Cited" centred at the top of the page. The first line of each entry begins at the left-hand margin, with second and subsequent lines indented. (You can achieve this format by selecting the entries and setting your word-processing program's paragraph orientation to "hanging indent.")

Entries in the list are alphabetized by surnames of authors (or editors; or by title, when no author or editor is named). Two or more works by the same author (or editor) are listed alphabetically according to the titles, and the author's (or editor's) name is replaced by three consecutive hyphens in all entries after the first:

> Oatley, Keith. *Best Laid Schemes: The Psychology of Emotions.* Cambridge: Cambridge UP, 1992. Print.
>
> ---. *The Passionate Muse: Exploration of Emotion in Stories.* New York: Oxford UP, 2011. Digital file.

When alphabetizing entries that begin with a title, ignore any introductory article (*A, An, The*), and treat any numerals as if they were spelled out (e.g., *two* rather than *2*):

> *Beowulf.* . . .
>
> *The Epic of Gilgamesh.* . . .
>
> *1001 Nights.* . . .
>
> "The Quest for the Holy Grail." . . .
>
> *Sir Gawain and the Green Knight.* . . .
>
> "The Six Swans." . . .

MLA STYLE

80a

On Capitalization

The seventh edition of the *MLA Handbook for Writers of Research Papers* sets out the following rules for capitalizing titles:

- Capitalize the first word and the last word of all titles and subtitles.
- Capitalize all nouns, pronouns, verbs, adjectives, adverbs, and subordinating conjunctions.
- Do not capitalize articles, prepositions, coordinating conjunctions, or the word *to* in infinitives (unless they are the first or last word in a title or a subtitle).

Note that this style is similar to the style we have used in previous chapters and recommended in #58m, except that in MLA style *all* subordinating conjunctions are capitalized and *all* prepositions and coordinating conjunctions are lowercased, regardless of length.

A Book by One Author

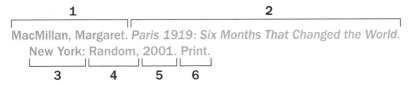

A standard works-cited reference for a book includes

1. the author's name (surname, followed by a comma, and full first name, followed by a period);
2. the full title of the book (italicized), followed by a period;
3. the city of publication, followed by a colon;
4. the name of the publisher (in shortened form), followed by a comma;
5. the year of publication, followed by a period; and
6. the medium of publication, followed by a period.

Note that the medium of publication for an e-book is the type of file you have accessed—for example, "PDF file" or "Kindle file" or, if you cannot identify the type of file, "Digital file."

MLA STYLE

On the Treatment of Publishers' Names

When using MLA style, shorten the name of a work's publisher as much as you can without making it difficult for your reader to identify the publisher. Omit articles (*A, An, The*), generic descriptive words (e.g., *Books, Company, House, Publishers*), and standard business abbreviations (e.g., *Co., Inc., Ltd.*). Use *UP* in place of *University Press* (e.g., *Oxford UP, U of Ottawa P*), and include standard abbreviations wherever you can (see the box on pages 499–500 for a list of abbreviations commonly used in MLA style). Finally, if the publisher's name contains one or more names of individuals, include only the first surname listed (e.g., *McClelland* instead of *McClelland and Stewart*; *Norton* instead of *W.W. Norton and Co.*).

80a

A Book by Two or Three Authors

When you have two or three authors in a works-cited entry, the names following the first name appear in first-name–last-name order:

> Somerville, Angus A., and R. Andrew McDonald. *The Vikings and Their Age*. Toronto: U of Toronto P, 2013. Print.

> Hoffman-Goetz, Laurie, Lorie Donelle, and Rukhsana Ahmed. *Health Literacy in Canada: A Primer for Students*. Toronto: Canadian Scholars', 2014. Print.

A Book by More Than Three Authors
When listing a book by more than three authors, include only the first author's name, followed by *et al.*:

> Messenger, William E., et al. *The Canadian Writer's Handbook*, 6th ed. Toronto: Oxford UP, 2015. Print.

Note the placement and abbreviated form of the edition number.

An Anthology or Other Collection with a General Editor
Treat an anthology or other collection compiled by a general editor as you would treat a book, but include the editor's name in place of the author's name, and add a comma followed by the abbreviation *ed.* after the editor's name:

> Loft, Steven, ed. *Coded Territories: Tracing Indigenous Pathways in New Media Art*. Calgary: U of Calgary Press, 2014. Print.

For two or more editors, use the abbreviation *eds.*:

> Forsyth, Janice, and Audrey R. Giles, eds. *Aboriginal Peoples and Sport in Canada: Historical Foundations and Contemporary Issues*. Vancouver: U of British Columbia P, 2013. Print.

> Perry, Adele, Esyllt Wynne Jones, and Leah Morton, eds. *Place and Replace: Essays on Western Canada*. Winnipeg: U of Manitoba P, 2013. Print.

> Vance, Jonathan F., et al., eds. *The Great War: From Memory to History*. Waterloo: Wilfrid Laurier UP, 2014. Print.

80a

A Book with an Author and an Editor
If a book has an author as well as an editor (e.g., a scholarly edition of a novel, a play, or a collection of short stories or poems), follow the title with the name(s) of the editor(s), preceded by the abbreviation *Ed.*:

> Scott, Walter. *Waverly*. 1814. Ed. Peter Garside and Claire Lamont. London: Penguin, 2011. Print.

In this case, the work was originally published in 1814, but the version edited by Garside and Lamont was published in 2011. Note that the original publication date is optional.

A Book in Translation
For a book that has been translated into English from another language, add *Trans.* followed by the name of the translator after the title:

> Charcot, Jean-Martin. *Charcot in Morocco*. Trans. Toby Gelfand. Ottawa: U of Ottawa P, 2012. Print.

A Work by a Government Agency or a Corporate Author
Begin an entry for a work credited to an organization rather than an author or authors with the name of the organization:

> Health Canada. *Eating Well with Canada's Food Guide*. Ottawa: Health Canada, 2011. Print.

If you access an online version of a government or corporate work that appeared in print, add the name of the website through which you accessed the work, change *Print* to *Web*, and end with the date you accessed the material:

> Health Canada. *Eating Well with Canada's Food Guide*. Ottawa: Health Canada, 2011. *Health Canada*. Web. 31 Mar. 2013.

If you access a government or corporate work that is available online but not in print, follow the conventions for a work available only online (see page 496).

A Work with No Identified Author
If you are citing a work that has no identified author, begin the entry with the work's title:

> "How to End Needless Strikes? Start with Good Faith Offers." *Maclean's* 2 Apr. 2012: 4–5. Print.

A Book Published in Print but Accessed Online
If you consult an online version of a book that has previously been published online, follow the standard guidelines for citing a book, and add the title of the database or website through which you accessed the book (italicized), the medium (Web), and the date you accessed the work:

> Grant, Jeannette. *Through Evangeline's Country*. Boston: Knight, 1894. *Early Canadiana Online*. Web. 31 Mar. 2012.

In this case, the book was originally published by J. Knight in Boston in 1894, and a digital scan of the entire book appears online on the website *Early Canadiana Online*. (See "A Book by One Author," above, for details on how to cite an e-book.)

A Multivolume Work
If you have used more than one volume of a multivolume work, include the number of volumes before the city of publication:

> Montgomery, Lucy Maud. *The Selected Journals of L.M. Montgomery*. Ed. Mary Rubio and Elizabeth Waterston. 5 vols. Toronto: Oxford UP, 1985–2004. Print.

The year "1985–2004" indicates that the first volume of the journals was produced in 1985 and the last volume in 2004.

If you have used only one volume of a multivolume work, include the volume number in place of the number of volumes:

> Montgomery, Lucy Maud. *The Selected Journals of L.M. Montgomery.* Ed. Mary Rubio and Elizabeth Waterston. Vol. 1. Toronto: Oxford UP, 1985. Print.

A Republished Work

Include the original publication date for a republished work:

> Austen, Jane. *Pride and Prejudice.* 1813. Oxford: Oxford UP, 1970. Print.

In this case, the year 1813 is the year of the work's first publication.

A Play

Published plays, whether written in prose or in verse, follow the same conventions that apply to books:

> Chekhov, Anton. *The Cherry Orchard.* Trans. Laurence Senelick. New York: Norton, 2010. Print.

> Shakespeare, William. *As You Like It.* Ed. Roma Gill. Oxford: Oxford UP, 2002. Print.

A Poem in a Collection

The poem's title appears in quotation marks, followed by the title of the book in which it appears, set in italics; after the year of publication, add the number(s) for the page(s) on which the poem appears:

> Lee, Dennis. "Tango." *Testament.* Toronto: Anansi, 2012. 103–04. Print.

A Long Poem with Divisions

Treat a long poem published as a complete work as you would treat a book:

> Milton, John. *Paradise Lost.* Ed. William Kerrigan, John Rumrich, and Stephen M. Fallon. New York: Random, 2007. Print.

A Work of Scripture

Begin an entry for a work of scripture with the title of the specific edition you have used. If the edition is based on a specific version of the text, include this information at the end of the entry:

> *The Holy Bible.* Nashville: Nelson, 1944. Print. King James Vers.

If the text lists a general editor, place his or her name after the title, preceded by *Ed.*

An Article in a Reference Book
If an article in a reference book is attributed to a specific author, begin with the author's name:

> Morton, Desmond. "First World War." *The Oxford Companion to Canadian History*. Ed. Gerald Hallowell. Toronto: Oxford UP, 2004. Print.

If the author's name is not listed, begin with the title, as you would for a work with no identified author (see above).

An Essay in an Edited Collection
For an entry referring to an essay in an edited collection, begin with the name(s) of the essay's author(s), followed by the title of the essay (in quotation marks), the title of the collection (in italics), and the name(s) of the editor(s) of the volume. Include the pages on which the essay appears before the medium of publication.

> Leach, Jim. "Beyond the National-Realist Text: Imagining the Impossible Nation in Contemporary Canadian Cinema." *Double-Takes: Intersections between Canadian Literature and Film*. Ed. David R. Jarraway. Ottawa: U of Ottawa P, 2013. 25–38. Print.

MLA STYLE

On "Missing" Publication Information

If a work you are citing does not include the place of publication, the publisher's name, or the date of publication, try searching online. If you find the missing information, include it in square brackets:

> Hall, Phil. "Becoming a Poet." *Killdeer*. [Toronto]: Bookthug, 2011. 17–32. Print.

If you can't find what you need, use the appropriate abbreviation in place of the missing element:

n.p.	no place of publication
n.p.	no publisher
n.d.	no date of publication

Note that you should capitalize the letter *n* if it appears after a period.

If the pages in a printed work are not numbered, you should use the abbreviation *n. pag.* ("no pagination") to explain to your reader why you have not referred to page numbers in your citations.

80a

An Article in a Journal

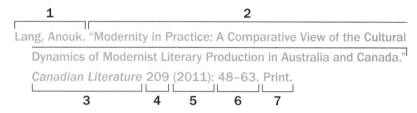

A standard works-cited entry for an article in a journal includes

1. the author's name, inverted and followed by a period;
2. the title of the article, followed by a period and enclosed in quotation marks;
3. the title of the journal, italicized;
4. the volume and/or issue number;
5. the year of publication, in parentheses and followed by a colon;
6. the pages on which the article appears, followed by a period; and
7. the medium of publication, followed by a period.

Note that the journal given in the example, *Canadian Literature*, uses only issue numbers. Were there a volume number as well, the issue number would follow it in the entry. For example, 19.2 would mean that the article appeared in the second issue of volume 19.

Treat an article from a journal that publishes exclusively online in the same manner, but replace *Print* with *Web* and add an access date:

> Martin, Mathew. "Pious Aeneas, False Aeneas: Marlowe's *Dido, Queen of Carthage* and the Gift of Death." *Early Modern Literary Studies* 16.1 (2012): n. pag. Web. 4 Aug. 2014.

In this case, the journal is not paginated, so *n. pag.* replaces the page range.

If you have accessed a journal article through an online database, add the title of the database (in italics), the medium (Web), and the date you accessed the article:

> Hathaway, Rosemary V. "Reading Art Spiegelman's *Maus* as Postmodern Ethnography." *Journal of Folklore Research* 48.3 (2011): 213–47. *Project Muse.* Web. 15 Feb. 2015.

A Newspaper or Magazine Article

Give the writer's name, the title of the article (in quotation marks), the name of the publication (in italics), the date of publication, the page number, and the medium:

> Rabin, Roni Caryn. "Will an Aspirin a Day Keep Cancer Away?" *Globe and Mail* 22 Mar. 2012: L5. Print.

Note that the page number is L5, as this article appeared on page 5 of section L ("Globe Life") within the newspaper. If an article is spread across multiple pages that are nonconsecutive, list the first page followed by a plus sign—for example, T1+.

If you have accessed the article online, include after the article's title the name of the website (in italics), the name of the site's publisher or sponsor, the date of publication, the medium (Web), and the date you accessed the site:

> Sorensen, Chris. "Forest Fighters." *Maclean's*. Rogers Publishing, 17 May 2013. Web. 8 July 2013.

An Editorial

Treat an editorial as you would treat any other article in a newspaper or magazine, but add the label *Editorial* after the title:

> Florida, Richard. "Urban Workers Need More Pay." Editorial. *Globe and Mail* 7 Feb. 2014: A13. Print.

If the writer is not identified, begin with the title:

> "A Victory Won with Dignity." Editorial. *Globe and Mail* 5 Nov. 2008: A20. Print.

For an online editorial, follow the format for an online newspaper or magazine article, and add *Editorial* after the article's title:

> "The Case for Early Police Retirement Is Unproven." Editorial. *Globe and Mail*. Globe and Mail, 22 Mar. 2012. Web. 30 Mar. 2012.

A Review

For a review of a book, a movie, or some other work, begin with the reviewer's name; if the review has a title, add that title (in quotation marks) after the reviewer's name. Next, for a work credited to an author or authors, add "Rev. of [*Title of Work*], by [Author(s)]," replacing the bracketed elements with the appropriate title and name(s). If the work is credited to an editor, a translator, a director, a performer, or some other creator, add the appropriate abbreviation (e.g., *ed.*, *trans.*, *dir.*, *perf.*) in place of *by*. Conclude with the relevant publication information:

> Macfarlane, Heather. "Memoir of Manitoba." Rev. of *Manitowapow: Aboriginal Writings from the Land of Water*, by Niigaanwewidam James Sinclair and Warren Cariou. *Canadian Literature* 217 (2013): 184–85. Print.

> Nestruck, J. Kelly. "A Contemporary Twist on Chekhov." Rev. of *The Seagull*, dir. Peter Hinton. *Globe and Mail* 11 Feb. 2014: L2. Print.

80a

For an online review, follow the format given above and modify it as necessary to indicate the source of the review—for example, an online newspaper, magazine, or journal, or an independently produced website.

An Interview
For published, broadcast, or recorded interviews, begin with the name of the person who was interviewed, followed by the title of the interview (if the interview has a title) or the label "Interview" (if the interview is untitled). Add the name of the interviewer if this information is relevant to your paper. Finally, add the publication or release information, and indicate the medium through which you encountered the interview: print, radio, television, Web, etc.

> Itani, Frances. "Hear, Overhear, Observe, Remember: A Dialogue with Frances Itani." *Canadian Literature* 183 (2004): 40–56. Print.

> Dryden, Ken. Interview by Peter Mansbridge. *Mansbridge One on One*. CBC. 1 Jan. 2012. Television.

For an interview you conducted yourself, begin with the name of the subject and note the format (e.g., *personal interview, telephone interview, email interview*) and the date of the interview:

> Atkinson, Joseph. Email interview. 12 June 2014.

A Website or a Work Available Only Online
Include as much information as you can find for a work published only on the Internet. Begin with the name of the author, editor, or creator, followed by the title of the work, the name of the website, the publisher of the website, the date of publication, the medium (Web), and the date you accessed the site:

> Sands, Jon. "So That If I Died It Mattered." *The Millions*. The Millions, 6 May 2013. Web. 27 Dec. 2013.

If the title of the work is the same as the name of the website, include this title only once, set in italics. For an article with no noted publisher, use *N.p.* (no publisher) in place of the publisher's name; for an article with no date of publication, use *n.d.* (no date) in place of the publication date. Note that you are not required to include the website's URL unless the citation information you provide would not be enough to lead readers directly to the source. In cases where you think that the URL is necessary, include it at the end of the entry, enclosed within angle brackets, and add a final period at the end:

> Atwood, Margaret. "Your Online Presence." *Margaret Atwood*. Margaret Atwood, n.d. Web. 31 Jan. 2014. <http://margaretatwood.ca/your-online-presence>.

If you need to break a URL at the end of a line, do so *after* a slash; do not add a hyphen.

A Dissertation or a Thesis

For a dissertation or a thesis retrieved from an online database, give the author's name, the title (in quotation marks), the abbreviation *Diss.* followed by the name of the institution and the year of publication, the name of the database you used to access the work, the medium (Web), and the retrieval date:

> Babiak, Peter. "Shakespeares on Film: Locating Adaptations within the Context of Their Production." Diss. York U, 2011. *Theses Canada.* Web. 5 Apr. 2013.

For a printed version of a published dissertation, cite it as you would a book, with the title in italics, but add the abbreviation *Diss.* followed by the name of the institution and the year of publication (as shown in the example above) before the standard publication information. Treat an unpublished print dissertation in the same way, but enclose the title in quotation marks and omit the publication information. For a master's thesis, replace *Diss.* with the appropriate designation (e.g., *MA thesis*, *MS thesis*).

A Lecture

List the speaker's name, the title of the lecture, the name of the event at which the lecture was given and/or the name of the organization that sponsored the event, the location of the lecture, the date the lecture was given, and the medium (lecture):

> Rennie, Bob. "Why Collect Art? Who Cares?" Vancouver Institute Lecture. Vancouver Institute. P.A. Woodward Instructional Resources Centre, University of British Columbia, Vancouver. 15 Feb. 2014. Lecture.

80a

A Television Program

Begin with the title of the episode, followed by the title of the series, the network, the date of initial broadcast, and the medium (television):

> "Mysteries of the Animal Mind." *The Nature of Things.* CBC. 16 Dec. 2013. Television.

A Motion Picture

In most cases, you will begin an entry for a motion picture with the title of the film (italicized), followed by the director, the distributor, the year of release, and the medium—*film* for a film you saw in a theatre, *Blu-ray* or *BD* for a Blu-ray Disc, *DVD* for a DVD, *videocassette* for a videocassette, and so on:

> *The Grand Seduction.* Dir. Don McKellar. Entertainment One, 2013. Film.

You may wish to include other information as well—whatever you think relevant. Begin with the element that is most significant to your use of the work:

> McKellar, Don, dir. *The Grand Seduction*. Perf. Taylor Kitsch and Brendan Gleeson. Entertainment One, 2013. Film.

> Baichwal, Jennifer, adapt. and dir. *Payback*. By Margaret Atwood. NFB, 2012. DVD.

An Audio Recording

References to audio recordings generally begin with the name of the writer, the composer, or the performer. The title of an entire work should be set in italics, while the title of a shorter work—such as an individual song—should appear in quotation marks. Also include the producer or manufacturer of the recording, the year, and the medium (usually *CD*, *audiocassette*, or *digital file*):

> Vaillant, John. *The Tiger: A True Story of Vengeance and Survival*. Random House Audio, 2010. CD.

> Ryder, Serena, perf. "Sisters of Mercy." By Leonard Cohen. *If Your Memory Serves You Well*. EMI, 2006. Digital file.

A Painting or Other Work of Visual Art

For a work of visual art, list the artist's name, the title of the work, the date the work was created, the medium (e.g., painting, sculpture, or photograph), and the institution and city in which you viewed the work:

> Hughes, E.J. *Trees, Savary Island*. 1953. Oil on canvas. Museum of Fine Arts, Montreal.

80a

If you are using a reproduction of the work—for example, a photograph that appears in a book about the artist—omit the original medium and add the necessary information to indicate the source:

> Hughes, E.J. *Trees, Savary Island*. 1953. Museum of Fine Arts, Montreal. *E.J. Hughes*. By Ian Thom. Vancouver: Douglas and Vancouver Art Gallery, 2002. 117. Print.

Using Notes as well as Parenthetical References

If circumstances demand, you may also use an occasional note along with the name–page method. For example, if you think that a reference requires some explanation, add an endnote rather than an obtrusive parenthetical comment or reference. But keep such notes to a minimum; if you cannot comfortably include such discursive comments in your text, it may be that they aren't relevant after all. Try to limit such notes to those commenting in some useful way on specific sources, such as a "See," "See for example," or "See also" note.

In the text, insert a superscript numeral where you want to signal the note (usually at the end of a sentence). Format the note itself as either a footnote (at the bottom of the page) or an endnote (on a separate page, titled "Notes," placed just before the list of works cited). The notes should be double-spaced.

MLA STYLE

Some Common Scholarly Abbreviations

In MLA style, the following abbreviations are commonly used in notes; many are also used in lists of works cited:

abbr.	abbreviation
abr.	abridgement, abridged by
adapt.	adaptation, adapted by
anon.	anonymous
arch.	archaic
attrib.	attributed to
bk.; bks.	book; books
c. (sometimes ca.)	(Latin *circa*) around, approximately (used with dates: e.g., c. 510)
cf.	(Latin *confer*) compare
ch.; chs.	chapter; chapters
col.; cols.	column; columns
comp.	compiler, compiled by
cond.	conductor, conducted by
dir.	director, directed by
diss.	dissertation
distr.	distributor, distributed by
ed.; eds.	edition, editor, edited by; editions, editors
e.g.	(Latin *exempli gratia*) for example
esp.	especially
et al.	(Latin *et alii*) and others
etc.	(Latin *et cetera*) and so forth
ex.	example
fig.; figs.	figure; figures
fwd.	foreword, foreword by
i.e.	(Latin *id est*) that is
illus.	illustration(s), illustrator, illustrated by

80a

MLA STYLE

introd.	introduction, introduced by
NB	(Latin *nota bene*) note well, take notice
n.d.	no date of publication given
no.; nos.	number; numbers
n.p.	no place of publication given, no publisher given
n. pag.	no pagination
n.s.	new series
obs.	obsolete
OED	*Oxford English Dictionary*
op.	opus, work
P	Press (as in UP)
par., pars.	paragraph, paragraphs
perf.	performer, performed by
pl.	plate
pref.	preface, preface by
prod.	producer, produced by
pub., publ.	publisher, published by
qtd.	quoted
rev.	revision, revised, revised by; review, reviewed by
rpt.	reprint, reprinted by
sec.	section
ser.	series
sic	(Latin) appears thus in the source (see #54j)
st.; sts.	stanza; stanzas
supp.; supps.	supplement; supplements
trans.	translation, translator, translated by
U	University
UP	University Press
usu.	usually
vers.	version
vol.; vols.	volume; volumes
vs. (v.)	versus (v. used in legal contexts)
writ.	writer, written by

80a

A Sample Research Paper in MLA Style

The following sample research paper illustrates the style and formatting set out in the seventh edition of the *MLA Handbook for Writers of Research Papers*. It is also a good example of a well-researched, well-written academic paper. Note the paper's logical organization, precise diction, consistent style, and lack of grammatical or spelling mistakes—all signs that the writer took her time to carefully plan, research, write, and proofread her work. When preparing your own essays, you should aim for the level of professionalism this writer has achieved.

Although the *MLA Handbook* does not recommend including a separate title page, many instructors will prefer that you use one. In such a case, the title page should include the title of the essay, your name, your instructor's name, the course code and section number, and the date of submission; the text should be double-spaced and centred on the page. If your instructor does not require you to include a title page, include the necessary information in the following order, aligned left, double-spaced, and on separate lines: your name, your instructor's name, the course code and section number of the class for which you are preparing the essay, and the date. Then, add your title, centred and in roman type. If your title contains the title of another work, set the title of the other work in italics or quotation marks, as appropriate (see #59). Similarly, if you use a quotation from another source, enclose it in quotation marks, as the student writer does in the sample essay below. Following your title, begin your first paragraph, indented.

Most instructors will allow you to use the standard margin settings of your word-processing program. If you are required to set your margins manually, the MLA recommends margins of 2.5 centimetres (or 1 inch) at the top, bottom, and both sides of the page. The lines of text should be double-spaced throughout, and the right margin should remain unjustified (i.e., ragged, uneven). Use only one text space between sentences. Additionally, number all pages in the top right-hand corner, and include your surname before each page number (you can do this using your word-processor's automatic page-numbering function).

80a

The list of works cited should begin on a new page at the end of your paper. Centre the title, "Works Cited," at the top of the page. Each entry should be set with a hanging indent, so that the first line begins at the left-hand margin and the second and subsequent lines are indented approximately 1.5 centimetres (or half an inch). Alphabetize entries by the first letters of the first author's surname or, for entries that have no author, the first letters of the title (ignoring an initial *A*, *An*, or *The*).

See also #56 for additional information on formatting an essay.

Badica 1

Gabby Badica

Professor Brown

English 390, Section 002

21 May 2012

"The Story with Animals Is the Better Story":
The Co-Existence of Human and Animal
Intelligences in Martel's *Life of Pi*

The co-existence of human and animal intelligences lies at the
heart of the survivor's narrative presented in Yann Martel's *Life of Pi*.
From its very first mention, the account of Pi's 227 days of endurance
is argued to be "a story that will make you believe in God" (Martel
ix). Martel himself has described his novel as one that will achieve this
task (Wood 1), insisting that this central claim "is not a throw-away
line" (qtd. in "Author Yann Martel"). However, this crucial point
becomes significantly more complicated when the text presents two
distinct narratives that explain Pi's survival in markedly different ways.
While the first account, characterized by meaningful interactions
between human and animal intelligences, presents a tale of endurance,
intelligence, perseverance, and controlled struggle, the second version,
devoid of any animal intelligences, is a dark account of cannibalism and
human nature at its most savage.

The stark contrast between the two explanations of Pi's survival
immediately makes those on the receiving end of the accounts question
not only which version they believe to be the truthful one, but also
which one they prefer. When faced with the question of which of
the accounts is "the better story" (Martel 352), even the novel's most
fact-driven and logically oriented characters identify the version with
animals as superior. However, is the first account better simply because
it is a feel-good story rather than a tale that illustrates how even the

80a

Badica 2

most religious and idealistic of men can be led to savagery in desperate and dire circumstances? This essay will explore the implications of the co-existence of human and animal intelligences in the first account of Pi's existence at sea; it will also explore the manner in which the connection that is formed between these two types of intelligences is crucial to religious belief and spirituality. While the second version of Pi's survival also holds significant value, especially when considered in conjunction with survivor-trauma theory, the first story is the one that allows for a holistic understanding of the role that religion plays in Pi's life, both during and after his shipwreck. Essentially, the story with animals is the better story because it offers the reader insight into the human identity-formation process and highlights the important connection between animality and divinity.

    The text highlights Pi's deep connection to animals and religion early in the narrative. As the son of "Mr. Santosh Patel, founder, owner, director" of the Pondicherry Zoo, Pi has "nothing but the fondest memories of growing up in a zoo" (15). He claims that he "lived the life of a prince," with an alarm clock of lions' roars and a breakfast that was "punctuated by the shrieks and cries of howler monkeys, hill mynahs and Moluccan cockatoos" (15). He anthropomorphizes the animals around him from an early age, recounting such daily routines as leaving for school "under the benevolent gaze not only of Mother but also of bright-eyed otters and burly American bison and stretching and yawning orang-utans" (15). Pi dismisses the frequent criticism that zoos strip animals of freedom through his claim that freedom in the wild, where "fear is high and the food low and where territory must constantly be defended and parasites forever endured" (17), is not something that would be in any way beneficial to animals. As James Mensch has highlighted, Pi describes zoos as an artificial Garden of Eden in which all animals are perfectly content (136).

80a

Zoos are immediately paralleled with religion in this defence, as
Pi states: "I know zoos are no longer in people's good graces. Religion
faces the same problem. Certain illusions about freedom plague them
both" (Martel 21). While Pi does not specifically state what the illusion
about freedom that plagues religion is, it is evident that he does not
feel constrained by religion at all. On the contrary, Pi has an inherent
curiosity for learning about different religions; he becomes a practising
Hindu, Christian, and Muslim all at once. Rather than choosing a single
religion, he clings to his freedom to "love God" however he wants
(74). Correspondingly, he asks his father both for a prayer rug and to be
baptized. For Pi, embracing religion is a liberating experience. Indeed,
along with his connection to animals, religion is one of the main pillars
of Pi's identity formation from the early days of his childhood.

Pi's connection to animals undoubtedly informs his initial account
of his time at sea. In the confined space of the lifeboat, the species
boundary he observed in his childhood crumbles, and he recognizes
a potent animality in himself. Previously a "puny, feeble, vegetarian
life form" (203), Pi must now kill in order to survive. Over time, he
"develop[s] an instinct, a feel, for what to do" (216). He asserts that he
"descended to a level of savagery [he] never imagined possible" (238). As
the days go by, his clothes rot away, and he is forced to live "stark naked
except for the whistle that dangle[s] from [his] neck by a string" (213).
Yet perhaps the most potent moment that crumbles the species boundary
is when Pi realizes, "with a pinching of the heart," that he had begun to
eat "like an animal, that the noisy, frantic unchewing, wolfing-down of
[his] was exactly the way Richard Parker ate" (250). This recognition of
his animality becomes crucial to Pi's perspective and his identity.

Nevertheless, although the species boundary is certainly blurred,
it is never fully crossed. One of the chief mechanisms that allow Pi to
maintain a semblance of his humanity is his devotion to religion. Each

Badica 4

day, he carefully says his prayers as part of the schedule that he creates for himself. Additionally, as Mensch highlights, although many of the differences between Richard Parker and Pi collapse over the period of their co-existence in the lifeboat, their reactions to lightning during a thunderstorm illustrate that the species boundary is preserved (138). While Pi is "dazed . . . but not afraid" and praises Allah, interpreting the storm as "an outbreak of divinity," Richard Parker trembles and hides in fear (Mensch 138). Thus, the crucial pillar that religion represents in Pi's identity never falters; as a result, it prevents the species boundary from completely collapsing. Ultimately, Pi's effort to understand Richard Parker, a feat that is necessary for his survival, leads Pi to gain a deeper understanding of his own identity. As Martel explains, it is in "understanding the other [that] you eventually understand yourself" (qtd. in Sielke 20).

The relationship between animality and divinity is explored in a different manner when it comes to considerations of which of Pi's accounts is "the better story" (Martel 352). As Stratton argues, the two conflicting stories highlight the novel's "philosophical debate about the modern world's privileging of reason over imagination, science over religion, materialism over idealism, fact over fiction" (6). The two sides of the debate are embodied in the characters of Mr. Okamoto and Mr. Chiba, who initially have very different responses to Pi's story. For Mr. Okamoto, the voice on the side of reason, the story with animals is "incredible" (Martel 328), "too hard to believe" (329), and "very unlikely" (332) at first. Mr. Chiba, who represents imaginative creativity and emotion (Stratton 7), immediately favours the animal version, exclaiming "What a story!" (Martel 345).

While Pi recognizes the importance of reason as a practical tool, asserting that "reason is excellent for getting food, clothing and shelter," and for "keeping the tigers away," he also cautions: "be excessively

80a

reasonable and you risk throwing out the universe with the bathwater"
(331). The debate comes to a climax when both Mr. Okamoto and Mr.
Chiba answer Pi's question about "the better story":

> [Pi Patel]: So tell me, . . . which story do you prefer? Which is the
> better story, the story with animals or the story without animals?
>
> Mr. Okamoto: "That's an interesting question. . . ."
>
> Mr. Chiba: "The story with animals."
>
> Mr. Okamoto: "Yes. The story with animals is the better story."
>
> Pi Patel: "Thank you. And so it goes with God." (352)

Mr. Okamoto's ultimate willingness to recognize the story with
animals as the better one demonstrates a change in his own identity,
one that Stratton identifies as a development of his imaginative capacity
(8). Martel himself has stated that the mechanism of faith uses both
imagination and reason (Sielke 25), the principal elements of the story
with animals. However, what is most crucial is the analogy that Pi
introduces after having deconstructed the reason–imagination binary.
The created link between the story with animals and religious belief
illustrates that God's existence occupies the same status in relation to
truth and reality as does Pi's experience of shipwreck. In this way,
"God's existence is a better story than the one told by those who doubt
or deny His being: atheists lack imagination and miss the better story"
(Martel 6).

Stewart Cole takes issue with the comparison between believing
in the story with animals and believing in God, arguing that it is
"problematic in failing to recognize the difference between believing
in a story—that is, acknowledging its aesthetic impact—and believing
in God" (23). Cole also points out that to conflate these two types of
belief is to obliterate the important epistemological distinction between
subjective and objective truth, a distinction that he identifies as crucial
to discussions of religion (24). However, what this view fails to take

80a

Badica 6

into account is that Martel's aim is to justify a belief in God's existence rather than to prove God's existence, and—as with the acceptance of the first of Pi's accounts as the better story—such faith might require a suspension of disbelief.

As Martel has argued, "religion operates in the same exact way a novel operates. . . . For a good novel to work, you have to suspend your disbelief. . . . Exactly the same thing happens with religion" (qtd. in Steinmetz 18). Martel also asserts that religion works the same way as a novel does in that it makes its recipients suspend their disbelief so that factual truth becomes irrelevant (Sielke 24). He cautions that this does not mean that facts are ignored, but rather that "it's more how you interpret the facts and how much you value facts that affect the totality of your sense experience"; therefore, "to say that the book will make you believe in fiction . . . isn't very far from saying it'll make you believe in God" (qtd. in Sielke 24). He also emphasizes that it is acceptable to say that God is a fiction if you understand that "this doesn't necessarily mean that this fiction doesn't exist. It just exists in a way that is only accessed through the imagination" (25).

While the story with animals is the one that presents the enriching facet of the empathetic imagination, the second account has its own value, particularly when considered alongside the implications of the first story being untrue. Several critics have interpreted Richard Parker as the outward manifestation of an internal split. As Robert Rogers notes, an individual suffering from internal conflict often grapples with contradictory impulses by "developing separate personality constellations" (109). Trauma theory explains that severe trauma explodes the cohesion of consciousness, and that "when a survivor creates a fully realized narrative that brings together the shattered knowledge of what happened and the emotions that were aroused by the meanings of the events, the survivor pieces back together the

80a

fragmentation of consciousness that trauma has caused" (Shay 188). Therefore, while Pi's inherent goodness is contrasted with the ferocity of Richard Parker throughout the first account, the consideration of Richard Parker as the evil portion of Pi's psyche results in Richard Parker's violence and guilt really being Pi's.

In a stark comparison to the first version, the story without animals portrays a view of life that is centred on greed, cruelty, corruption, and futility. God is notably left out of the picture, and human beings are completely alone and exiled from the comfort of religion. Thus, the second account demonstrates how even the most pacifist, devoted, and idealistic of men can be led to savagery in extenuating circumstances. While the story without animals contains its own intrinsic value, its lack of the co-existence of animal and human intelligences does not permit for either the fulfillment of the empathetic imagination or a connection between animality and divinity, two elements that remain crucial to Pi's identity.

While it is undeniable that, of Pi's two accounts, the story with animals is a feel-good tale of courage, endurance, and intelligence, and the story without animals is a horrifying description of human savagery and desperation, this difference appears only on the surface. The facet of the first account that is most significant and most illuminating is that the co-existence of human and animal intelligence is crucial to the process of identity formation and motivation for spiritual belief. Highlighting the link between animality and divinity, an empathetic imagination allows for the ignition of the "spark that brings to life a real story" (Martel vii), thereby representing the key to a holistic understanding not only of oneself, but of all subsequent social interactions that determine identity construction.

80a

Badica 8

Works Cited

"Author Yann Martel." *HotType*. CBC. 16 Dec. 2002. Television.

Cole, Stewart. "Believing in Tigers: Anthropomorphism and Incredulity in Yann Martel's *Life of Pi*." *Studies in Canadian Literature* 29.2 (2004): 22–36. *MLA International Bibliography*. Web. 12 Oct. 2011.

Martel, Yann. *Life of Pi*. Toronto: Random, 2001. Print.

Mensch, James. "The Intertwining of Incommensurables: Yann Martel's *Life of Pi*." *Phenomenology and the Non-Human Animal: At the Limits of Experience*. Ed. Corinne Painter and Christian Lotz. Dordrecht: Springer, 2007. 135–47. Print.

Rogers, Robert. *A Psychoanalytic Study of the Double in Literature*. Detroit: Wayne State UP, 1970. Print.

Shay, Jonathan. *Trauma and the Undoing of Character*. New York: Touchstone, 1994. Print.

Sielke, Sabine. "'The Empathetic Imagination': An Interview with Yann Martel." *Canadian Literature* 177 (2003): 12–32. *MLA International Bibliography*. Web. 17 Nov. 2011.

Steinmetz, Andrew. "Pi: Summing Up Meaning from the Irrational: An Interview with Yann Martel." *Books in Canada* 31.6 (2002): 18. *Academic Search Complete*. Web. 17 Nov. 2011.

Stratton, Florence. "'Hollow at the Core': Deconstructing Yann Martel's *Life of Pi*." *Studies in Canadian Literature* 29.2 (2004): 5–21. *MLA International Bibliography*. Web. 12 Oct. 2011.

Wood, James. "Credulity." Rev. of *Life of Pi*, by Yann Martel. *London Review of Books* 24.22 (2002): 1. Web. 17 Nov. 2011.

80a

80b The Name–Date Method (APA Style)

The name–date system is described in detail in the sixth edition of the *Publication Manual of the American Psychological Association* (2010). Using this system, you provide a short parenthetical reference in the text, and you list all sources in a reference list at the end of your paper.

Here are some examples of name–date in-text citations, followed by some examples of bibliographical entries set in APA style.

In-Text Citations

In-text citations consist of the author's last name followed by a comma, and the date the source was published. If the reference is to a general argument or evidence presented by the entire work, list only the author's name and the year of publication:

> National identity is deeply connected to a sense that there is a boundary between those who belong to a nation and those who do not (Winter, 2011).

But if you refer to a particular part of the source, or if you quote from it, supply the relevant page number or numbers, preceded by the abbreviation *p.* (or *pp.* for a page range):

> As Elke Winter (2011) notes, "a pluralist 'national we' is bounded by opposition to a real or imagined 'Others' with a capital O" (p. 5).

If you name the author in the text, don't repeat the name in the parenthetical reference.

A Work by One or Two Authors

For works by one or two authors, include the author's or authors' surname(s) each time you refer to the source:

> One study has found that discourses on climate change are "being narrated differently to English- and French-speaking audiences in Canada" (Young & Dugas, 2012, p. 48).

A Work by Three or More Authors

If the work has three, four, or five authors, list all of them the first time you cite the work, but only the first and *et al.* thereafter:

> Articles published in academic journals are the best sources for academic research because they are peer-reviewed and therefore highly credible (Messenger, de Bruyn, Brown, & Montagnes, 2015, p. 459). Whenever you incorporate someone else's words or ideas into your own work, you must credit the original source; failure to do so may constitute plagiarism (Messenger et al., 2015, pp. 473–477).

If the work has six or more authors, include only the surname of the first author and *et al.* each time you cite the work, including the first.

80b

APA STYLE

On the Treatment of Number Ranges

When you cite a range of numbers in APA style, list all numbers: 5–88, 108–122, 254–258, 385–485, 1033–1046.

A Work by a Government Agency or a Corporate Author

For a work that lists a collective body as its author, include the name of the group each time you cite the work:

> A six-page report sets out the Canadian government's official recommendations on balanced nutrition (Health Canada, 2011).

If a group with a long name is more commonly known by a shorter name (e.g., *UNESCO* for the *United Nations Educational, Scientific, and Cultural Organization*), use the shorter name.

A Work with No Identified Author

For an article that has no identified author, include the first few words of the work's title:

> When governments fail to resolve public-sector strikes, the most cost-effective solution may be "final offer arbitration" ("How to End," 2012).

A Work of Scripture

For a work of scripture, provide the name and number of the book and section, along with the standard name of the version or edition:

> In the biblical account of the Flood, Noah is described as "a just man and perfect in his generations" (Gen. 6:9, King James Version).

Note that you do not need to include an entry in the reference list if you've consulted a widely available version of a classical work, such as the King James Version of the Bible.

An Online Document with No Page Numbers

If you need to cite a specific portion of an online document that does not have page numbers, count the paragraphs following the title or a heading and assign a number to the relevant paragraph:

> Anne Kingston (2014) lists a number of familiar issues that many people worry about: "H5N1, vaccine fear, bioterrorism, your kid passing his finals, cyberterrorism, those grey hairs, the grid going dark, drivers who text, stock market collapse, job loss, gluten, debt, that guy eyeing your job, your RSP, *E. coli* in packaged salad" (Kingston, 2014, para. 1).

80b

If you begin counting after a heading, include the first few words of the heading:

> World Wildlife Fund Canada (2011) notes that its work in the Arctic involves "planning for an Arctic future that conserves wildlife while respecting the practices and traditions of local communities" ("Planning," para. 3).

In this case, the quotation comes from the third paragraph following the heading "Planning for a Healthy Arctic Future."

If you want to refer readers to an entire website, you can include the site's URL in the text:

> World Wildlife Fund Canada provides a number of recent news reports on its website (http://www.wwf.ca).

In such a case, you do not need to list the source in the reference list.

Quotation at Second Hand

If you must cite a quotation at second hand—for example, if you cannot find the original work that another author has cited—include the name of the original author and the title and date of publication for the original work (if known), and give a citation for the secondary source:

> As Edward Said has put it, in *Culture and Imperialism* (1994): "No one today is purely *one* thing" (as cited in Winter, 2011, p. 213).

Citing More Than One Work

If you cite more than one source in a single parenthetical reference, order the citations alphabetically and separate them with a semicolon:

> Several studies have looked at the ways in which the loss of sea ice in the Arctic is impacting Inuit peoples' lives and customs (Ford, Pearce, Gilligan, Smit, & Oakes, 2008; Pearce et al., 2010).

Here, the first reference is to a journal article written by five authors, and the second reference is to an article with six authors.

If you cite two or more works by the same author in a single parenthetical reference, list the dates chronologically and separate them with commas. For more than one work by the same author published in the same year, include lowercase letters to distinguish between the works:

> Sport can be a useful tool for international development, but it must be used with care to avoid reinforcing social and political biases within a community (Darnell, 2010a, 2010b).

The letters correspond to those assigned in the reference list (see below).

Reference List

The reference list appears at the end of your paper and includes the full publication information for all works that you have referenced. It should begin on a new page, with the title "References" centred at the top. Each entry should be formatted with a hanging indent, with the first line beginning flush left and the second and subsequent lines indented.

List entries in alphabetical order, according to the surnames of authors or editors (or titles, when no author or editor is named). List works by the same author(s) or editor(s) chronologically, with the earliest article listed first. Arrange works by the same author published in the same year alphabetically by title, and assign a letter to each entry, following the year:

> Darnell, S. (2010a). Power, politics and "sport for development and peace": Investigating the utility of sport for international development. *Sociology of Sport Journal, 27*(1), 54–75.

> Darnell, S. (2010b). Sport, race, and biopolitics: Encounters with difference in "sport for development and peace" internships. *Journal of Sport & Social Issues, 34*(4), 396–417.

Note that in titles of books and articles, only the first letter of the title, the first letter after a colon or a dash, and the first letter of a proper noun are capitalized. In titles of periodicals (and in all titles that appear in the body of the paper), lowercase articles, coordinating conjunctions, and prepositions with fewer than four letters; capitalize all other words.

APA STYLE

On the Treatment of Authors' Names

In an APA-style reference list, use initials in place of authors' full given names. Invert the name of each author, and use commas to separate the names. If a work has been written by seven or fewer authors, include the names of all of the authors in the entry. If the work has eight or more authors, include the first six names followed by three ellipsis points and the final author's name:

> Schwartz, S. J., Kim, S. Y., Whitbourne, S. K., Zamboanga, B. L., Weisskirch, R. S., Forthun, L. F., . . . Luyckx, K. (2013). Converging identities: Dimensions of acculturation and personal identity status among immigrant college students. *Culture Diversity and Ethnic Minority Psychology, 19*(2), 155–165.

A Print Book (Standard Reference)

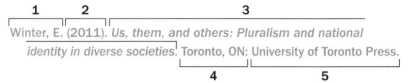

A standard reference entry for a book includes

1. the author's name (surname, followed by a comma, and initial or initials, followed by a period);
2. the year of publication, enclosed in parentheses and followed by a period (if the work does not list a date, write *n.d.*);
3. the title of the book (italicized), followed by a period;
4. the city and province (or state) of publication, separated by a comma and followed by a colon; and
5. the name of the publisher, followed by a period.

In the publisher's name, omit unnecessary words such as *Inc.*, *Ltd.*, *Co.*, and *Publishers*, but retain the words *Books* and *Press*. If the publisher is located outside of Canada or the United States, include the full name of the country in place of the province or state abbreviation. And if the name of the province or state is included within the publisher's name, you can omit the abbreviation. And if you need to include in your reference list an entire book that has an editor in place of an author, include the editor's last name and first initial, followed by *Ed.* enclosed in parentheses; use *Eds.* if there are multiple editors:

> Peters, E., & Andersen, C. (Eds.). (2014). *Indigenous in the city: Contemporary identities and cultural innovation*. Vancouver: University of British Columbia Press.

80b

An Electronic Book (Standard Reference)
If you have used an electronic version of a book that appears in print, replace the publication information with a description of the version (in square brackets), and add the necessary retrieval information or the DOI (digital object identifier) assigned to the book:

> Duncan, D. (2011). *Canadians at table: A culinary history of Canada* [Adobe DRM version]. Retrieved from http://www.kobobooks.com /ebook

> Woods, R. (2013). *Children's moral lives: An ethnographic and psychological approach* [Adobe PDF version]. doi:10.1002 /9781118326176

For a book that appears only online, include the retrieval information:

> Stevens, K. (n.d.). *The dreamer and the beast.* Retrieved from
> http://www.onlineoriginals.com/showitem.asp?itemID=321

In this case, the abbreviation *n.d.* signifies that no publication date was given for the book.

APA STYLE

On Citing Electronic Sources

When you cite an electronic source in the APA system, include the work's digital object identifier (DOI) or, if there is no DOI assigned to the work, the uniform resource locator (URL) of the page on which you found the work. For a journal article with no DOI, include the URL for the journal's homepage. If you need to break a DOI or URL across two or more lines, do so *before* a punctuation mark; do not add a hyphen. Note that you do not need to include the date you accessed the site.

A Work by a Government Agency or a Corporate Author

For a work created by an organization, include the full name of the organization in place of an author's name:

> Health Canada. (2011). *Eating well with Canada's food guide.*
> Ottawa, ON: Author.

In this case, the word *Author* indicates that the publisher is the author (in this case, Health Canada). If you accessed the document online, include the work's URL rather than its publication information:

> Health Canada. (2011). *Eating well with Canada's food guide.*
> Retrieved from http://www.hc-sc.gc.ca/fn-an/alt_formats
> /hpfb-dgpsa/pdf/food-guide-aliment/view_eatwell_vue
> _bienmang-eng.pdf

A Work with No Identified Author

If no person or group is identified as the author (or the editor), use the title of the work in place of the author's name:

> How to end needless strikes? Start with good faith offers. (2012,
> April 2). *Maclean's, 125*(12), 4–5.

80b

A Book in Translation

For a book that has been translated into English from another language, add the name of the translator and the abbreviation *Trans.* (enclosed in parentheses) after the title:

> Benjamin, W. (2006). *Berlin childhood around 1900* (H. Eiland, Trans.). London, England: Belknap Press.

An Edition Other Than the First

For a second or subsequent edition, include the edition number after the title:

> Newman, J., & White, L. A. (2012). *Women, politics, and public policy: The political struggles of Canadian women* (2nd ed.). Toronto, ON: Oxford University Press.

A Republished Work

For a republished work, include the original publication date at the end of the entry:

> Alder, A. (1998). *Understanding human nature: The psychology of personality* (C. Brett, Trans.). Center City, MN: Hazelden. (Original work published 1927)

A Multivolume Work

For a work published in multiple volumes, include the number(s) of the volume(s) you have referenced:

> Dutch, S. I. (Ed.). (2010). *Encyclopedia of global warming* (Vols. 1–3). Pasadena, CA: Salem Press.

80b

If the volumes were published in different years, use the date range as the year of publication—for example, *2011–2015*. If you have referenced only one volume and the volume number appears in the title, omit the parenthetical reference to the volume.

An Article in an Edited Book

Begin with the name of the article's author, followed by the year of publication, the title of the article, the name of the book's editors, the title of the book (in italics), the pages on which the article appears (enclosed in parentheses), and the publisher's location and name:

> Lund, K. (2010). The helping relationship: A context for learning. In A. Meier & M. Rovers (Eds.), *The helping relationship: Healing and change in community context* (pp. 138–152). Ottawa, ON: University of Ottawa Press.

An Article in a Journal

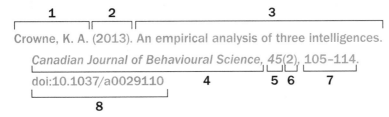

A standard reference entry for an article in a journal includes

1. the author's name (last name followed by one or more initials);
2. the year of publication, enclosed in parentheses and followed by a period;
3. the title of the article, with only first words and proper nouns capitalized, followed by a period;
4. the title of the journal, italicized, with all words other than articles, coordinating conjunctions, and prepositions with fewer than four letters capitalized, followed by a comma;
5. the volume number, italicized;
6. the issue number (if applicable), set in parentheses and followed by a comma;
7. the pages on which the article appears, followed by a period; and
8. the digital object identifier (DOI).

Note that there is no space following the volume number or following the colon that introduces the DOI. Also note that there is no period following the DOI.

If you have retrieved an article online but there is no DOI, include the URL for the journal's homepage:

> Young, N., & Dugas, E. (2012). Comparing climate change coverage in Canadian English- and French-language print media: Environmental values, media cultures, and the narration of global warming. *Canadian Journal of Sociology, 37*(1), 25–54. Retrieved from http://ejournals.library.ualberta.ca/index.php/CJS/index

If you have accessed an article online before it has been officially published, add "Advance online publication." before the DOI or "Retrieved from" statement. If you have referenced a printed article, provide the standard publication information:

> Karras, J., Van Deventer, M. C., & Braumgart-Rieker, J. M. (2003). Predicting shared parent–child book reading in infancy. *Journal of Family Psychology, 17,* 134–146.

For an abstract, add "[Abstract]" after the title, before the period.

80b

A Magazine Article

Treat an article from a magazine as you would treat an article from a journal, but note that magazines publication dates often include the day and month of publication. Here is an example of a reference to a magazine article in print:

> Geddes, J. (2012, February 27). A disposable workforce. *Maclean's, 125*(7), 22.

For a magazine article you accessed online, include the DOI; if no DOI has been assigned to the article, include the URL of the magazine's homepage:

> Kingston, A. (2014, February 5). The new worry epidemic. *Maclean's*. Retrieved from http://www2.macleans.ca

In this case, the title of the online magazine is the same as the title of the print version of the same magazine, but the online magazine does not use volume or issue numbers.

A Newspaper Article

Treat a print newspaper article as you would treat an article from a print journal or magazine, but add *p.* or *pp.* before the page number or numbers:

> Rabin, R. C. (2012, March 22). Will an aspirin a day keep cancer away? *The Globe and Mail*, p. L5.

For an online newspaper article, include the URL of the newspaper's homepage

> Macdougall, J. (2012, February 4). How we assess stress: It's the most common mental health issue, so why is it so hard to measure? *National Post*. Retrieved from http://www.nationalpost.com

80b

An Editorial

Treat an editorial as you would treat any other newspaper article, but add the label *Editorial* (enclosed in parentheses) after the title:

> Florida, R. (2014, February 7). Urban workers need more pay [Editorial]. *The Globe and Mail*, p. A13.

If the editorial is not attributed to a particular writer or editor, begin with the title:

> A victory won with dignity [Editorial]. (2012, March 22). *The Globe and Mail*, p. A20.

A Dissertation or a Thesis

For a dissertation, include the author's name, the date of publication, the title of the work, *Doctoral dissertation* (in parentheses), and the retrieval information. If you found the dissertation in a database, provide the name of the database and the retrieval number assigned to the work:

> White, M.A. (2012). Intimate archives, migrant negotiations: Affective governance and the recognition of "same-sex" family class migration in Canada (Doctoral dissertation). Retrieved from Theses Canada. (AMICUS No. 40589105)

If you found the dissertation on a website, replace the database information with the exact URL that directs to the dissertation. Treat a master's thesis in the same way, but replace *Doctoral dissertation* with *Master's thesis.*

A Music Recording
Include the name of the writer or composer, the copyright year, the title of the song (if you are referring to a specific song), the name of the performer (if different from the writer or composer), the name of the album, the medium (in brackets), the music label's location and name, and the year of recording (if different from the copyright year):

> Cohen, L. (1967). Sisters of mercy [Recorded by Serena Ryder]. On *If your memory serves you well* [CD]. Toronto, ON: EMI. (2006)

A Motion Picture
List the producer and director, the year of release, the title, the medium (in brackets), the country of origin, and the studio's name:

> Din, R. (Producer), & Baichwal, J. (Director). (2012). *Payback* [Motion picture]. Canada: National Film Board of Canada.

A Television Program
For an episode from a television series, include the name of the writer and/ or the director, the original date of broadcast, the title of the episode, a description of the medium (in brackets), the name of the series, and the location and name of the broadcasting network:

> Ravetch, A. (Director). (2012, April 8). Polar bears: A summer odyssey [Television series episode]. In *The Nature of Things.* Toronto, ON: Canadian Broadcasting Corporation.

A Podcast
List the name of the producer, the writer, or the host; the date of release; the title of the episode; the medium (in brackets); the name of the series; and the URL:

> Luksic, N. (Producer), & Kennedy, P. (Host). (2014, February 12). Top dog: The science of winning and losing [Audio podcast episode]. In *Ideas.* Retrieved from http://www.cbc.ca/ideas/

80b

Material from a Website

For web material that does not fit into any of the categories listed above, include the name of the author or creator, the date the material was created or last updated (often provided at the bottom of a web page), the title of the web page, a short description of the format, and the retrieval information:

> World Wildlife Fund Canada. (2011). What WWF is doing [Online statement]. Retrieved from http://www.wwf.ca/conservation /arctic/whatwwfisdoing

Be brief but specific when describing the format—for example, for a posting to an online forum or message board, write *Online forum comment*; for a blog post, write *Web log post*.

A Sample Research Paper in APA Style

The research paper presented below was written and formatted according to the guidelines set out in the sixth edition of the *Publication Manual of the American Psychological Association*. Note that it begins with a separate title page, which lists the title of the paper, the author's name, the instructor's name, the course code and title, and the date of submission.

If you are required to provide an abstract, do this on the first page following the title page. The heading "Abstract" should appear centred at the top of the page, and the abstract itself should provide a brief summary of your paper. In some cases, you may be required to add a list of key words following the main paragraph of the abstract. If you aren't sure what to include in the abstract, ask your instructor, or consult APA-style papers published in your discipline.

Repeat your title on the first page of the essay itself, immediately before your first paragraph. Make sure to double-space your paper, and indent the first line of all paragraphs, including the first. Your margins should be approximately 1.5 centimetres (or 1 inch) all around; in most cases, you can use the default settings of your word-processing program. Do not justify the right margin, and avoid breaking words at the end of a line. Finally, remember to number each page in the top right-hand corner, and include the title in the top left-hand corner of each page (you can do this using your word-processor's automatic headers).

Begin your reference list on a new page at the end of your paper. Centre the title, "References," at the top of the page, and list the entries in alphabetical order. Each entry should be set with a hanging indent, so that the first line begins at the left-hand margin and the second and subsequent lines are indented.

80b

THE POWER OF SOCIOLOGICAL KNOWLEDGE   1

The Power of Sociological Knowledge

Kasia Bulgarski

Professor P. Moore

SOC 290: Sociological Practice

10 December 2011

80b

The Power of Sociological Knowledge

Sociology offers valuable tools for deconstructing and analyzing the social constructs and ideologies embedded in our societal framework. The sociological perspective is useful in a variety of real-world contexts, as it seeks to interpret and understand human behaviour. It also has the potential to help restructure inequalities faced within society. Yet sociologists, particularly in their roles as makers and disseminators of sociological knowledge, must be careful to avoid losing their objectivity. This goal is crucial in the classroom, where students depend on instructors to put aside personal biases and create an environment that promotes critical engagement and independent thought. Sociological knowledge is most powerful when it is constructed and shared in open-minded, forward-thinking, socially aware manners.

People inevitably view the world through personal lenses. Often, these lenses are influenced by individual biases that can inhibit inclusive, solutions-oriented thinking. Such biases—whether they are overt or implicit—are particularly dangerous when they are revealed by educators within the classroom. Weber (1919/1946) argues that, while teachers will never entirely eliminate their personal opinions regarding a subject, imposing personal judgements on students is certainly not part of an educator's job (p. 146). Moreover, Weber continues, the potential for students to fully understand facts no longer exists when the teacher reveals bias while teaching. Indeed, the teacher's primary role should be to encourage students to be aware of facts that oppose their opinions (Weber, p. 147). Teachers should stimulate open discussion in the classroom rather than obstructing such discussion with their personal judgements. Therefore, the teacher is not a leader (Weber, p. 150) but an enthusiast within a conversation about society.

80b

THE POWER OF SOCIOLOGICAL KNOWLEDGE   3

Weber also examines religion as a force that fosters moral judgement regarding matters of society (p. 149). He argues that Christian moral fervor has blinded society for thousands of years and led to compromises and relative judgements. In a recent article on the debate over sharia law, Razack (2007) explores how academics might unknowingly reinforce the colour line and the secular–religious divide (p. 4). Discussing a presentation on honour killings that she attended in Europe, Razak recounts how the keynote speaker began by showing photographs taken at the funeral of a Kurdish woman who was killed by her father because he did not approve of her going to live with a non-Kurdish man. Razack was puzzled by the exploitation involved in showing the woman's dead body to an audience of over three hundred, mostly white, Western academics. Overall, the presentation misrepresented Muslims as barbaric and Westerners as civilized. As a result of the presenter's implicit bias, the audience became morally outraged instead of motivated to deconstruct the embedded social inequalities that had led to the woman's death in the first place.

Unfortunately, the prejudice that Razack experienced is not uncommon, and similar projections of bias can be found even in the field of sociology. Becker (2007) writes that sociologists frequently seek to understand the social structure by looking for problematic situations (p. 129). In doing so, they may take on the role of the storyteller, which traditionally involves taking sides by introducing a hero and a villain. Users of this knowledge become captivated by the maker's report; they imagine that what they are hearing or reading is based on systematically gathered materials from the "real world" and, as a result, they fail to tackle the underlying issues (Becker, 2007, p. 144).

Moral judgements are sometimes apparent in the words researchers choose when they describe social phenomenon. Becker (2007) discusses

80b

the "labeling theory" of deviance, noting that many critics oppose the relativism associated with the term "deviant" (p. 145). He uses the example of murder and questions whether or not such an act would be classified as "very deviant." Significantly, labels such as "deviant" are applied not only in relation to community standards, but also in connection with scientific standards (Becker, p. 145). Thus, it is important to deconstruct the terms used within the field of sociology, as they can signify underlying biases.

Researchers, as makers of knowledge, must also avoid biasing their reports through the misrepresentation or fictionalization of facts. As Becker (2007) observes, "makers incorporate reasons for users to accept what they present as true" (p. 111). Thus, users must rely on makers to be accurate in the presentation of information. Becker uses journalists as an example of knowledge-makers who at times provide the public with accounts that are distorted through the subtraction or addition of factual information (p. 130). In such instances, the individual bias of the makers becomes insidious, and readers are unknowingly affected through this process (Becker, p. 133). Such misrepresentation may also happen implicitly within scholarly sources. Thus, academics must retain the responsibility of providing the users of their knowledge with factual and accurate reports of the human condition.

Further, Becker (2007) notes that "representations are made in a world of cooperating users and makers" (p. 30). He writes that makers do most of the work, leaving users to interpret and theorize on the data. This relationship may be problematic: the freedom of interpretation allotted to users is somewhat of an illusion, as the makers have not left much room for interpretation (Becker, p. 30). Statistics, for example, have little value on their own; their significance must be *interpreted*. The researcher's method of coding data, finding variables, creating labels,

THE POWER OF SOCIOLOGICAL KNOWLEDGE   5

and so on effectively tells users how to interpret the data. Thus, in order
to give the user a full picture, researchers should provide users with
accurate explanations of how they choose their variables, why they feel
that the variables are important, and why they chose to leave out other
possible variables.

Similarly, teachers of sociological research have the responsibility
of forcing students to develop their critical-thinking skills. Vaughn
(2005) explains that teaching critical thinking helps transform students
from passive learners into active learners (p. xvii). The focus of critical
thinking is the basis of a belief, not the question of whether something
is worth believing. It is the systematic evaluation of statements, by
means of rational standards (Vaughn, 2005, pp. 3–4). Critical thinking
leads to understanding, knowledge, self-improvement, and, ultimately,
empowerment. For students and researchers, empowerment comes from
the ability to actively participate in the sociological examination of
societal inequalities and ideologies.

As Lemert (2004) notes, reflecting on Michel Foucault's theory
of knowledge as power, knowledge is empowering in that it breaks
down the binary opposition between the ruler and the ruled (p. 466).
In terms of the classroom experience, knowledge breaks down the
barrier between the teacher and the student. Ideally, students can attain
power by deliberating openly, from an informed perspective, amongst
themselves and with the teacher.

In a recent interview, Stuart Hall has described the learning
process as a journey (de Peuter, 2007). In the beginning, the teacher
is in an elevated position because he or she has been to a place that the
learner has not yet experienced; over time, as the learner searches for
and eventually finds the source of knowledge that the teacher possesses,
the relationship becomes more equal (de Peuter, 2007, p. 117). Yet

80b

the burden of achieving this goal does not rest solely on the student. Educators must not only disseminate the knowledge they possess, but also recognize the cultural framework of the student and work to overcome the existence of social hierarchies embedded in the learning process; ultimately, they can do this by progressively equalizing the dialogue throughout the relationship with the learner (de Peuter, 2007, p. 118).

Neave (2000) explains that universities, in particular, have always been required to preserve, develop, and provide individuals with knowledge (p. xiii). The more society expects from the institutions of higher learning, the more complex the responsibility of academics becomes. Neave suggests that academics should analyze whether or not their research has improved the understanding of social inequalities (p. 67). Furthermore, educators should assess whether the students have been able to grasp the message that was initially sent out regarding the importance of societal matters at hand (Neave, 2000, p. 67). Thus, just as academics must focus on the needs of their students, they must also focus on the needs of society as a whole and aim to devise real-world solutions to social impediments.

A fairly recent development, service learning within post-secondary institutions has helped broaden experiences of students by means of hands-on work within the community. In their report on a service-learning initiative that has taken place in Queensland, Australia, Carrington and Saggers (2008) argue that community-based service learning promotes inclusive, socially aware education. Such courses, which foster work within the academic setting as well as in the real world, provide students with the ability to address the civic responsibility all sociologists face. With teachers, students, and community workers working together, students gain practical

THE POWER OF SOCIOLOGICAL KNOWLEDGE   7

knowledge and experience; as a result, they are able to critically analyze their environment by working within it.

As researchers and educators, academics must use their interpretations and analyses to equip the world with sociological knowledge. Teachers have a duty to disseminate sociological knowledge both within and beyond their classrooms, and they must prepare their students to likewise disseminate this knowledge. In the absence of bias, sociology offers a way of looking at life as it is rather than as we wish it to be. It offers inquiring minds a deep, meaningful understanding of social structures, and it allows researchers to critically and productively engage with real-world social issues.

80b

THE POWER OF SOCIOLOGICAL KNOWLEDGE   8

References

Becker, H. S. (2007). *Telling about society.* Chicago, IL: University of
Chicago Press.

Carrington, S., & Saggers, B. (2008). Service-learning informing the
development of an inclusive ethical framework for beginning
teachers. *Teaching and Teacher Education, 24*(3), 795–806.
doi:10.1016/j.tate.2007.09.006

de Peuter, G. (2007). Universities, intellectuals, and multitudes:
An interview with Stuart Hall. In M. Coté, R. J. F. Day, &
G. de Peuter (Eds.), *Utopian pedagogy: Radical experiments against
neoliberal globalization* (pp. 108–128). Toronto, ON: University of
Toronto Press.

Lemert, C. (2004). *Social theory: The multicultural and classical readings*
(3rd ed.). Boulder, CO: Westview Press.

Neave, G. (2000). *The universities' responsibilities to society.* Paris, France:
International Association of Universities.

Razack, S. (2007). The "sharia law debate" in Ontario: The modernity/
premodernity distinction in legal efforts to protect women
from culture. *Feminist Legal Studies, 15,* 3–32. doi: 10.1007
/s10691-006-9050-x

Vaughn, L. (2005). *The power of critical thinking.* New York, NY: Oxford
University Press.

Weber, M. (1946). Science as a vocation. In H. H. Gerth & C. W.
Mills (Eds. & Trans.), *Max Weber: Essays in sociology* (pp. 129–156).
New York, NY: Oxford University Press. (Original work
published 1919)

80b

80c The Note Method (Chicago Style)

The note method, which uses either footnotes or endnotes and a bibliography, appears in different versions. If your instructor wishes you to use the note method of documentation, find out which version is required. The following guidelines are based on the version described in the sixteenth edition of *The Chicago Manual of Style*.

CHICAGO STYLE

On Chicago's Two Methods of Documentation

The sixteenth edition of *The Chicago Manual of Style* sets out two distinct methods of documentation—a note method (which we describe below) and an author–date method (which is similar to APA style). If your instructor asks you to use "Chicago style" in preparing your paper, make sure you understand which of the two methods you should use.

Footnotes and Endnotes

Whether you use footnotes or endnotes, you must number the notes consecutively throughout your paper, beginning with *1*. The in-text number should, whenever possible, appear at the end of a sentence, after the period. If you need to place the number earlier in the sentence—for example, if only part of the sentence relates to a particular source—insert it *before* a dash or *after* any other punctuation mark. If you are using endnotes, begin the notes on a new page, with the word *Notes* as the heading. The notes themselves—whether they are footnotes or endnotes—should be single-spaced and formatted with either a first-line indent or a hanging indent. Although the note numbers in the text are superscript, the note numbers preceding each endnote or footnote are not.

The details you include in the note itself depend on how detailed your bibliography is. If your instructor has asked you to provide a *select bibliography* (e.g., one that lists only the most relevant or up-to-date sources you have cited), you will need to provide *full notes*—with full publication information—for any sources that do not appear in your bibliography. If your instructor has asked you to provide a *full bibliography* (i.e., one that provides full citation information for all of the sources you cite in your paper), you can use *short notes*—notes that give only the surname(s) of the author(s), a shortened version of the title, and the page number(s) on which you found the relevant material. In either case, you can use short notes for second and subsequent references to the same source.

80c

CHICAGO STYLE

On the Treatment of Number Ranges

When you cite a range of numbers in Chicago style, list all numbers for ranges that begin with a number that is less than 100 (e.g., 22–29; 87–110), 100 (e.g., 100–112), or a multiple of 100 (e.g., 200–212; 300–301; 800–843). For ranges that begin with numbers between 101 and 109, 201 and 209, 301 and 309, and so on, include in the second half of the range only numbers that have changed (e.g., 105–9; 309–32; 702–801). For all other ranges, list the first number in full, the final two digits of the second half of the range, and any other numbers that are needed to show a change (e.g., 120–25; 245–59; 298–304; 1234–345).

The following examples illustrate how to treat various types of works in full notes and in short notes.

A Book by One, Two, or Three Authors (or Editors)

FULL NOTE

A full note for a book should contain the name(s) of the author(s) or editor(s), the title (in italics), the city of publication, the publisher's name, the year of publication, and the page or pages on which the material you are referencing appears:

> 1. Roberta M. Styran and Robert R. Taylor, *This Great National Object: Building the Nineteenth-Century Welland Canals* (Montreal: McGill-Queen's University Press, 2012), 77–79.

80c

If an editor or editors are listed in place of an author, follow the names with a comma and the abbreviation *ed.* (for one editor) or *eds.* (for two or more editors). If you downloaded an electronic version of the book, include a description of the file (for example, "PDF e-book." or "Kindle edition.") at the end.

SHORT NOTE

> 1. Styran and Taylor, *This Great National Object*, 77–79.

If the work is credited to an editor or editors, you do not need to include the abbreviation *ed.* or *eds.* in the short note.

A Book by More Than Three Authors (or Editors)

For works with more than three authors, give the last name of the first author, followed by *et al.*:

FULL NOTE

> 2. William E. Messenger et al., *The Canadian Writer's Handbook*, 6th ed. (Toronto: Oxford University Press, 2015), 204.

If the source is credited to one or more editors, add a comma and the abbreviation *ed.* (for one editor) or *eds.* (for two or more editors) after *et al.*

SHORT NOTE

> 2. Messenger et al., *Canadian Writer's Handbook*, 204.

Note that in short notes unlike in full notes, introductory articles (*A*, *An*, *The*) are omitted from titles.

A Book with a Translator or an Editor in Addition to an Author

FULL NOTE

Use the abbreviation *trans.* to denote a translator (or translators); use the abbreviation *ed.* to denote an editor (or editors):

> 3. Jean-Martin Charcot, *Charcot in Morocco*, trans. Toby Gelfand (Ottawa: University of Ottawa Press, 2012), 118.

SHORT NOTE

Do not include the translator's or editor's name in the short note:

> 3. Charcot, *Charcot in Morocco*, 118.

A Work by a Government Agency or a Corporate Author

FULL NOTE

> 4. Health Canada, *Eating Well with Canada's Food Guide* (Ottawa: Health Canada, 2011), 2.

SHORT NOTE

> 4. Health Canada, *Eating Well*, 2.

A Chapter or Article in an Edited Book

FULL NOTE

> 5. Kristine Lund, "The Helping Relationship: A Context for Learning," in *The Helping Relationship: Healing and Change in Community Context*, ed. Augustine Meier and Martin Rovers (Ottawa: University of Ottawa Press, 2010), 83.

SHORT NOTE

> 5. Lund, "Helping Relationship," 83.

A Journal Article (Print)

FULL NOTE

In a full note for a journal article, include the name(s) of the author(s), the title of the article (in quotation marks), the title of the journal (in italics), the volume and/or issue numbers, the year of publication, and the page number(s) for the material you have referenced:

> 6. Anouk Lang, "Modernity in Practice: A Comparative View of the Cultural Dynamics of Modernist Literary Production in Australia and Canada," *Canadian Literature* 209 (2011): 49.

SHORT NOTE

> 6. Lang, "Modernity in Practice," 49.

A Journal Article (Electronic)

FULL NOTES

In a full note for an electronic journal article, include everything you would include in a full note for a journal article available in print, as well as the digital object identifier (DOI) assigned to the work; if there is no DOI, include the full uniform resource locator (URL) that will direct the reader to the article:

> 7. Tim Stockwell et al., "Does Minimum Pricing Reduce Alcohol Consumption? The Experience of a Canadian Province," *Addiction* 107, no. 5 (2012): 913–14, doi:10.1111/j.1360-0443 .2011.03763.x.

> 8. Nathan Young and Eric Dugas, "Comparing Climate Change Coverage in Canadian English- and French-Language Print Media: Environmental Values, Media Cultures, and the Narration of Global Warming," *Canadian Journal of Sociology* 37, no. 1 (2012): 32, http://ejournals.library.ualberta.ca/index.php/CJS/index.

SHORT NOTES

> 7. Stockwell et al., "Minimum Pricing," 913–14.

> 8. Young and Dugas, "Comparing Climate Change Coverage," 32.

A Magazine Article

FULL NOTES

> 9. John Geddes, "A Disposable Workforce," *Maclean's*, February 27, 2012, 22.

80c

CHICAGO STYLE

On the Inclusion of DOIs and URLs

When you cite an electronic source, include a digital object identifier (DOI) whenever possible. If the material has not been assigned a DOI, include the URL for the page on which you found the material. The DOI or URL is generally placed at the end of the citation. If you need to break either of these elements across two or more lines, do so *after* a colon or a double slash, *before or after* an equal sign or an ampersand, or *before* any other punctuation mark. Never add a hyphen.

For an online magazine article, include the URL of the page where you accessed the article:

> 10. Chris Sorensen, "Forest Fighters," *Maclean's*, May 17, 2013, http://www2.macleans.ca/2013/05/17/forest-fighters.

SHORT NOTES

> 9. Geddes, "Disposable Workforce," 22.

> 10. Sorensen, "Forest Fighters."

A Newspaper Article

FULL NOTES

> 11. Roni Caryn Rabin, "Will an Aspirin a Day Keep Cancer Away?," *Globe and Mail*, March 22, 2012, L5.

For an online newspaper article, include the URL of the page where you accessed the article:

> 12. Lauran Neergaard, "Scientists Create Robotic Hand Wired with a Sense of Touch for Amputees," *Globe and Mail*, February 6, 2014, http://www.theglobeandmail.com/life/health-and-fitness/health/scientists-create-robotic-hand-wired-with-a-sense-of-touch-for-amputees/article16725333.

SHORT NOTES

> 11. Rabin, "Will an Aspirin," L5.

> 12. Neergaard, "Scientists Create Robotic Hand."

80c

Material on a Website

FULL NOTE

In a full note for material that is published on a website, provide as much information as you can: the author's name, the title of the web page you have consulted, the site's sponsor (if different from the author), the date on which the material was posted (or the date the material was last revised, preceded by *last modified*; or the date you accessed the site, preceded by *accessed*), and the page's URL:

> 13. Doctors without Borders, "South Africa: Stand Strong against Aggressive Pharma Campaign," January 21, 2014, http://www.doctorswithoutborders.org/article/south-africa -stand-strong-against-aggressive-pharma-campaign-1.

Note that while titles of web pages are set in roman and enclosed in quotation marks, titles of websites (for example, *Maclean's*) should be italicized.

SHORT NOTE

> 13. Doctors without Borders, "South Africa."

A Thesis or a Dissertation

FULL NOTE

> 14. Melissa Autumn White, "Intimate Archives, Migrant Negotiations: Affective Governance and the Recognition of 'Same-Sex' Family Class Migration in Canada" (doctoral dissertation, Carleton University, 2012), 3, Theses Canada (AMICUS No. 40589105).

80c

Note the inclusion of the database (Theses Canada) and the retrieval number following the page reference. If the work is a master's thesis, enter *master's thesis* in place of *doctoral dissertation*. If you retrieved the work from a website (other than that of a database), include the website's URL in place of the database name and retrieval number.

SHORT NOTE

> 14. White, "Intimate Archives," 3.

A Lecture

FULL NOTE

> 15. Bob Rennie, "Why Collect Art? Who Cares?" (lecture, Vancouver Institute, University of British Columbia, Vancouver, BC, February 15, 2014).

Short Note

15. Rennie, "Why Collect Art?"

Sound and Audiovisual Recordings

For sound and audiovisual recordings, begin with the name of the creator (e.g., the writer, the composer, the performer, or the director) who is most relevant to your discussion. If you want to list more than one creator, you may do so either before or after the title. The title of a full work, such as an album or a film, should be set in italics; the title of part of a work, such as a song on an album, should be enclosed in quotation marks.

Full Notes

In the full note for a musical recording, list the creator(s), the title of the song and/or the album, the name of the recording company or producer, the date of release, and the medium (e.g., compact disc, audiocassette, digital audio file):

16. Serena Ryder, "What I Wouldn't Do," on *Harmony*, EMI, 2012, compact disc.

If you are citing a film, treat the production information as you would treat the publication information for a book, and add the medium at the end:

17. Ken Scott and Michael Dowse, *The Grand Seduction*, directed by Don McKellar. (Toronto: Entertainment One, 2013), DVD.

For a work accessed online, insert a comma followed by the URL after the medium:

18. Nadia Myre, *As I Am* (Montreal: National Film Board of Canada, 2010), audiovisual file, http://www.nfb.ca/film /as_i_am.

Short Notes

16. Ryder, "What I Wouldn't Do."

17. Scott and Dowse, *Grand Seduction*.

18. Myre, *As I Am*.

More Than One Work Cited in a Single Note

Full Note

If you need to include more than one work in a single note, separate the entries with semicolons, and list them in the order in which they apply to the text:

19. Lea Berrang-Ford, James Ford, and Jaclyn Patterson, "Are We Adapting to Climate Change?," *Global Environmental Change* 21 (2011): 33; Ford et al., "Climate Change and Hazards Associated with Ice Use in Northern Canada," *Arctic, Antarctic and Alpine Research* 40, no. 4 (2008): 649.

SHORT NOTE

19. Berrang-Ford, Ford, and Patterson, "Are We Adapting," 33; Ford et al., "Climate Change and Hazards," 649.

Referring to a Source Given in the Previous Note

If you are referring to the exact same source as you referred to in the previous note, use the abbreviation *Ibid.* (from the Latin *ibidem*, "in the same place"), and provide the page number:

20. Ibid., 33.

To avoid any potential confusion, don't use *Ibid.* in a note until you are certain that your notes are in their final order.

Bibliography References

Unless you are instructed to do otherwise, list all of the sources you have used—including those you consulted but did not refer to directly—in a bibliography at the end of your paper. Bibliography entries contain the same information as full notes, except for page references, and they should be listed in alphabetical order, based on the authors' last names.

A Book by One, Two, or Three Authors (or Editors)

Styran, Roberta M., and Robert R. Taylor. *This Great National Object: Building the Nineteenth-Century Welland Canals.* Montreal: McGill-Queen's University Press, 2012.

If editors rather than authors are listed, follow the editors' names with a comma and the abbreviation *eds.* (or *ed.* if there is only one editor).

A Book by More Than Three Authors (or Editors)

For works with four to ten authors, list all names:

Messenger, William E., Jan de Bruyn, Judy Brown, and Ramona Montagnes. *The Canadian Writer's Handbook.* 6th ed. Toronto: Oxford University Press, 2015.

For works with eleven or more authors, list the names of the first seven, followed by *et al.* If the work is credited to more than three editors rather than authors, use the same format, but add a comma and *eds.* (or *ed.*, for one editor) after *et al.*

A Book with a Translator or an Editor in Addition to the Author
Instead of using an abbreviation, as you would in a note, spell out *Translated by* or *Edited by*:

> Charcot, Jean-Martin. *Charcot in Morocco.* Translated by Toby Gelfand. Ottawa: University of Ottawa Press, 2012.

A Work by a Government Agency or a Corporate Author

> Health Canada. *Eating Well with Canada's Food Guide.* Ottawa: Health Canada, 2011.

A Chapter or Article in an Edited Book

> Lund, Kristine. "The Helping Relationship: A Context for Learning." In *The Helping Relationship: Healing and Change in Community Context,* edited by Augustine Meier and Martin Rovers, 138–51. Ottawa: University of Ottawa Press, 2010.

Note that the number range following the names of the book's editors indicates the pages on which the entire chapter appears.

A Journal Article (Print)

> Lang, Anouk. "Modernity in Practice: A Comparative View of the Cultural Dynamics of Modernist Literary Production in Australia and Canada." *Canadian Literature* 209 (2011): 48–63.

Note that the number range at the end indicates the pages on which the entire article appears within the journal.

A Journal Article (Electronic, with a DOI)

> Stockwell, Tim, M. Christopher Auld, Jinhui Zhao, and Gina Martin. "Does Minimum Pricing Reduce Alcohol Consumption? The Experience of a Canadian Province." *Addiction* 107, no. 5 (2012): 912–20. doi:10.1111/j.1360-0443.2011.03763.x.

A Journal Article (Electronic, without a DOI)

> Young, Nathan, and Eric Dugas. "Comparing Climate Change Coverage in Canadian English- and French-Language Print Media: Environmental Values, Media Cultures, and the Narration of Global Warming." *Canadian Journal of Sociology*

37, no. 1 (2012): 25–54. http://ejournals.library.ualberta.ca
/index.php/CJS/index.

A Magazine Article

Geddes, John. "A Disposable Workforce." *Maclean's*, February
27, 2012.

Sorensen, Chris. "Forest Fighters." *Maclean's*, May 17, 2013.
http://www2.macleans.ca/2013/05/17/forest-fighters.

A Newspaper Article

Rabin, Roni Caryn. "Will an Aspirin a Day Keep Cancer Away?"
Globe and Mail, March 22, 2012.

Neergaard, Lauran. "Scientists Create Robotic Hand Wired with
a Sense of Touch for Amputees." *Globe and Mail*, February 6,
2014. http://www.theglobeandmail.com/life/health-and
-fitness/health/scientists-create-robotic-hand-wired-with-a
-sense-of-touch-for-amputees/article16725333.

Note that you do not need to include newspaper articles in your bibliography if you have already given the relevant citation information in the text or in a full note.

A Website

Doctors without Borders. "South Africa: Stand Strong against
Aggressive Pharma Campaign." January 21, 2014.
http://www.doctorswithoutborders.org/article/south-africa
-stand-strong-against-aggressive-pharma-campaign-1.

If the site's publisher differs from the author, you should include the name of the publisher (followed by a period) immediately before the date. If you cannot find the date on which the material was posted to the site, include the date the material was revised (preceded by *Last modified*) or the date you accessed the site (preceded by *Accessed*).

A Thesis or a Dissertation

White, Melissa Autumn. "Intimate Archives, Migrant
Negotiations: Affective Governance and the Recognition of
'Same-Sex' Family Class Migration in Canada." PhD diss.,
Carleton University, 2012. Theses Canada (AMICUS No.
40589105).

For a master's thesis, replace *PhD diss.* with *MA thesis.* If you found the work online (but not in a database), replace the database name and retrieval number with the appropriate URL.

A Lecture

> Rennie, Bob. "Why Collect Art? Who Cares?" Lecture presented through the Vancouver Institute, University of British Columbia, Vancouver, BC, February 15, 2014.

An Audio Recording

> Ryder, Serena. "What I Wouldn't Do." On *Harmony*. EMI, 2012, compact disc.

A Motion Picture

> Scott, Ken, and Michael Dowse. *The Grand Seduction*. Directed by Don McKellar. Toronto: Entertainment One, 2013. DVD.

> Myre, Nadia. *As I Am*. Montreal: National Film Board of Canada, 2010. Audiovisual file. http://www.nfb.ca/film/as_i_am.

80d The Number Method (CSE Style)

The number method is most often used in the natural, physical, life, and applied sciences. It involves inserting into the text numbers that correspond to numbered reference-list entries. The following guidelines are based on those set out in the eighth edition of *Scientific Style and Format: The CSE Manual for Authors, Editors, and Publishers* (2014), which also describes a name–date system similar to the one outlined in #80b. Note that there are many versions of the number method, so you should always find out what your audience or instructor prefers before you submit your paper.

80d

In-Text Citations

The citation numbers in the text most often appear as superscript numbers, directly following the information to which they correspond:

> Hawking discusses black holes in great detail.[3]

> The study found no link between sugar consumption and chronic heart disease,[7] but several recent studies have brought this conclusion into question.[4,7,18-21]

Note that when a citation number must be placed beside a punctuation mark, it appears *after* the punctuation mark. If the reference is to more than one source, as illustrated by the second example above, the items are listed in numerical order. Numbers that are not consecutive are separated by a comma, with no space following the comma; for a sequence of consecutive numbers—for example, 18, 19, 20, and 21—list the first and last number, separated by a hyphen.

A less common style, which is not recommended by the CSE, is to include the numbers in parentheses:

> Hawking (3) discusses black holes in great detail.

If you use the parenthetical style, be sure to distinguish other parenthetical numbers from citation numbers by providing a description or a unit:

> The distance the fluid travelled (27 mm) was shorter than the researchers had predicted (89).

CSE STYLE

On Keeping Track of Citations

If you are required to use the number method to cite your sources, leave the numbering until the end, after you have finished writing your final draft. During the writing and pre-writing stages, place a parenthetical name–date citation (see #80b) in the text where you want to cite a source; once your paper is finished and all you have left to do is proofread it for a final time, replace the name–date citations with the appropriate numbers. This approach will help you keep track of your sources while you are developing your paper.

80d

Reference List

The end references should begin on a new page, titled "References" or "Cited References." The works are listed either in the order in which they are first cited in the text or in alphabetical order. In either case, each source is listed only once and given only one number. (The one number assigned to a source in the reference list should appear in the text wherever the source is cited). In the reference list, the information for each entry is presented in the following order:

1. the note number, followed by a period;
2. the first author's last name, followed by his or her initial(s) and the inverted names of any additional authors;
3. the title of the work and, if applicable, the title of the larger volume (e.g., a journal or a reference book) in which the work appears;
4. for a book, the place of publication (city and province or state for Canadian and US publications; city and country for works published in other countries) and the name of the publisher;

CSE STYLE

On the Treatment of Titles

Set the title of all works in roman type, and capitalize only the first word of the title and any proper names appearing in the title. For the names of journals, omit articles, conjunctions, and prepositions; capitalize all significant words; and abbreviate the significant words according to the rules set out by the International Organization for Standardization (ISO). The International Standard Serial Number (ISSN) International Centre provides a list of ISO 4 abbreviations, called the "List of Title Word Abbreviations" (or "LTWA"), on its website (http://www.issn.org).

5. the date of publication (as well as any date of modification and the date you accessed the information, if the source is online);
6. for journal articles, volume, issue, and page information; and
7. for online sources, the uniform resource locator (URL) and, if applicable, the digital object identifier (DOI).

For works by up to ten authors, include the names of all authors; for works by more than ten authors, list the first ten, followed by *et al.* If no person or organization is listed as the author, begin the entry with the work's title.

The following are some examples of entries as they would appear in a reference list in CSE style.

A Book with an Author or Authors

> 1. Styran RM, Taylor RR. This great national object: building the nineteenth-century Welland Canals. Montreal (QC): McGill-Queen's University Press; 2012.

An Edition Other Than the First
Add the edition number following the title:

> 2. Pecorino L. Molecular biology of cancer. 3rd ed. Oxford (England): Oxford University Press; 2012.

A Book with an Editor in Place of an Author
Include the designation *editor* (for one editor) or *editors* (for two editors):

> 3. Baldwin A, Cameron L, Kobayashi A, editors. Rethinking the great white north: race, nature, and the historical geographies of whiteness in Canada. Vancouver (BC): University of British Columbia Press; 2011.

80d

A Book with a Translator or Editor in Addition to an Author

Add the name of the translator or the editor after the title, and add the designation *translator(s)* or *editor(s)*, as appropriate:

> 4. Benjamin W. Berlin childhood around 1900. Eiland H, translator. London (England): Belknap Press; 2006.

A Chapter or Article in an Edited Book

Begin with the name of the article's author, followed by the title of the chapter or article. Introduce the full publication with the word *In*, then give the full reference information for the book in which the article was published. Conclude with the pages on which the article appeared.

> 5. Lund K. The helping relationship: a context for learning. In: Meier A, Rovers M, editors. The helping relationship: healing and change in community context. Ottawa (ON): University of Ottawa Press; 2010. p. 138–151.

A Work by a Government Agency or a Corporate Author

If a work is credited to an organization rather than an author, list the name of the organization first:

> 6. Health Canada. Eating well with Canada's food guide. Ottawa (ON): Health Canada; 2011.

If the organization's name begins with *The*, omit the opening article.

An Article in a Journal (Print)

For a journal article, list the author(s), the title of the article, the name of the journal, the date of publication, the volume number, the issue number (if there is an issue number), and the pages on which the article appears:

> 7. Kawasaki K, Symons DTA. Paleomagnetic dating of magmatic phases at the Cantung tungsten deposit, Northwest Territories, Canada. Can J Earth Sci. 2014;51(1):31–42.

See the box on page 541 for more information on using ISO 4 abbreviations for journal titles.

An Article in a Journal (Internet)

Treat an article you accessed online—for example, through an online database—as you would treat a print article, but add the date you accessed the article, the relevant URL, and the DOI assigned to the article (if available).

80d

8. Stockwell T, Auld CM, Zhao J, Martin G. Does minimum pricing reduce alcohol consumption? Addict. 2012 [accessed 2013 Aug 24];107(5):913–914. http://onlinelibrary.wiley.com/doesminimumpricing/abstract. doi:10.1111/j.1360-0443.2011.03763.x.

CSE STYLE

On the Inclusion of URLs and DOIs

When you cite an online source, always include the URL for the page from which you retrieved the work. If the material has been assigned a DOI, include this information as well, beginning on a new line after the URL. If you must break a URL or a DOI across two lines, do so *after* a slash. Do not add a hyphen.

An Article in a Newspaper or a Magazine

Treat a newspaper or magazine article as you would treat a journal article, but do not abbreviate the title of a newspaper. Include the month and day of publication for newspapers and for magazines that do not use volume and issue numbers. For newspaper articles, also note the section (just before the page number) and the column in which the article appears.

9. Rabin RC. Will an aspirin a day keep cancer away? Globe and Mail. 2012 Mar 22;Sect. L:5 (col. 1).

10. Geddes J. A disposable workforce. Maclean's. 2012;125(7):22.

A Thesis or a Dissertation

11. White MA. Intimate archives, migrant negotiations: affective governance and the recognition of "same-sex" family class migration in Canada [dissertation]. Ottawa (ON): Carleton University; 2012.

For a master's thesis, replace *dissertation* with *master's thesis*.

Material Found on the Web

For material (other than journal articles) you have found online, include as much of the following information as you can: the name of the author(s), the title of the page or article, the location of the material's publisher, the publisher's name, and the date of publication. Also include, in square brackets, the date you accessed the page. Conclude the entry with the URL of the page on which you found the material.

80d

12. Doctors without Borders. Children with TB must not be neglected. New York (NY): Doctors without Borders; 2013 Dec 17 [accessed 2014 Apr 2]. http://www.doctorswithoutborders.org/article/children-tb-must-not-be-neglected

If the site does not display a publication date, you should supply the copyright date, preceded by the letter *c*, in place of the publication date—for example, "c2012." If the site provides a date on which the information was updated, include this date just before the access date—for example, "[updated 2014 Oct 31; accessed 2014 Nov 15]."

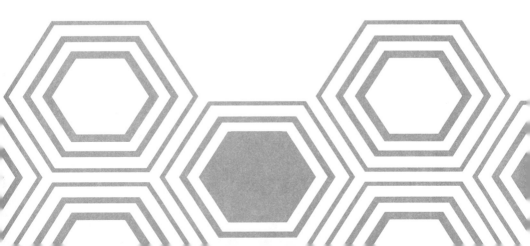

1

Appendix

Sample Student Essays with Comments and Grades

The student essays that follow vary in length, kind, and quality. The marginal and final comments focus on structure, content, and style following the criteria many instructors use in assessing a piece of writing. If you are unfamiliar with any of the marking symbols and abbreviations that appear in the following pages, consult appendix II and the list that appears inside the back cover. The final grades reflect the following system:

A	80%–100%	Excellent
B	68%–79%	Good to Very Good
C–D	50%–67%	Weak to Fair
F	0%–49%	Unsatisfactory (Fail)

Brief Introductions to the Essays that Follow

The first two essays address the topic of drugs; one student chose to define a related term while another set up an argument. The third and fourth essays are in need of significant revision. They have been included here to show you the types of weaknesses you should look for in your own writing. The fifth essay is from a student who has English as an additional language. Because this student is still in the beginning stages of writing at the university level, this essay has not been given a grade. The final two essays tackle the analysis of literature: the first explores a soliloquy from Shakespeare's *Hamlet*, while the second examines aspects of L.M. Montgomery's *Anne of Green Gables* from a modern perspective. Both of these essays are thoughtfully constructed and well organized, but as the comments reveal, they could still benefit from careful revision (and, in the case of the final essay, thorough proofreading).

Sample Essay 1

Addiction

A common definition of the word *addiction* may read: the compulsive need for and use of a harmful, habit-forming substance characterized by recognizable, clearly defined physiological reactions upon withdrawal of said substance. For most people, this definition of *addiction* is a familiar one that conjures up images of drug addicts portrayed in popular movies and television shows such as Trainspotting or Breaking Bad. The problem with this definition of *addiction* is its narrow focus on the biological and physiological symptoms of withdrawal from chemical substances, to the exclusion of psychological addiction and a variety of other addictive "substances."

[Marginal annotations: A1; source for this definition?; good allusion ✓; italicize these titles; clear thesis ✓]

This transition is too formal and stiff.

Considering almost everyone has had an experience with alcohol, I will use it to demonstrate both the physiological and the psychological symptoms of addiction. Alcohol is a chemical that is classified as a depressant because it slows down the functioning of the nervous system. When ingested, alcohol produces certain predictable physiological effects, including decreased reaction time, slurred speech, and loss of balance. In terms of addiction, alcoholism, and the associated physical withdrawal, symptoms include shivering and sweating, increased blood pressure, and a condition known as *delirium tremens*, a violent state of mental confusion accompanied by tremors.

Many people have experienced but may not consciously be aware of the psychological effects associated with the consumption of alcohol. Indeed, some individuals use alcohol as a kind of social anesthetic because it <u>helps them relax</u>, <u>relieves their anxiety</u>, and <u>erases their inhibitions</u>. However, psychological addiction to alcohol (and many other "substances") is not as widely recognized or understood, despite its importance and prevalence. Psychological withdrawal symptoms associated with alcohol include irritability, increased anxiety, agitation, nervousness, anger, uncontrollable urges, and a preoccupation with attaining alcohol to the exclusion of other things.

redundancy?

good attempt at a transition, but you still need to make a logical connection between alcohol and other substances

A1

By redefining addiction in terms of both psychological and physiological effects, we can now expand the list of "substances" that could be classified as addictive. Have you ever gone shopping and purchased an article of clothing that you really liked, leaving you feeling happy and confident? Individuals who are addicted to activities such as shopping, gambling, or eating are in fact addicted to this euphoric high and the reduction of anxiety they get when they indulge in these behaviours. Those who suffer from an addiction to non-chemical "substances" or behaviours also experience psychological withdrawal symptoms similar to those described in the example with alcohol: irritability, increased anxiety, agitation, nervousness, (etc.) and so on

good use of question

Do they ever experience any negative feelings as a result of these behaviours?

Can you think of a smoother, less mechanical way of ending the essay?

<u>In conclusion</u>, when you think of the word *addiction* you should keep in mind that there are a large number of substances and behaviours that may be harmful and habit-forming, and thus are classifiable as addictive. In addition, remember

?

that one of the critical features of addiction is the experience of withdrawal effects, either physiological or psychological, that occur when the substance is withdrawn or the behaviour is stopped.

B+ Melanie,
You have written a competent and well-organized definition of addiction. I like how you narrowed the focus to a specific addiction, alcoholism, and addressed the physical and psychological aspects of this addiction. Do you think you could have narrowed the topic down even further? Also, make your transitions a little smoother, especially the transition to your conclusion, which is stiff and mechanical. The conclusion itself summarizes the paper, but it is not necessary to summarize such a short paper—readers will remember what you have written. Perhaps you could end with a statement that focuses on the social implications of addiction or a prediction about what future studies on addiction might reveal?

Sample Essay 2

Handle With Care   *lower case*

Who? Can you be more specific?

Who?

Patent medicines and vitamins are bought in increasing quantities by people every day. They are placed on open shelves in stores to be bought without prescription by individuals who have little knowledge of what the chemical effects will be on their bodies. Many of the drugs are potentially harmful; they should be removed from the shelves, and their sales should be more strictly controlled. To be sure, many of the drugs that are so readily available to consumers are not harmful

Who? Some? Avoid generalizing.

if administered properly. But people have come to believe that many drugs on the shelves are not harmful at all. Certain medicines have become so commonly used that they are taken as panaceas and administered for any discomfort. Acetylsalicylic acid, universally known under the brand name "aspirin," is an obvious example.

Use examples of harmful drugs in the body of your essay.

Clear position, but is it placed in the best part of your introduction?

A1

Who?

Perhaps some parents? Qualify your point here.

People take one, or two, or several aspirin tablets for headaches, stomach pains, insomnia, nervous and emotional upsets—the whole range of disturbances—and many parents use aspirin to dose their children at the first sign of hyperactivity! These common cures are not safe when used in excess or when taken without being needed. Medicines are drugs; when used incorrectly, drugs can be poison.

Awk. How about "unnecessarily"?

P

Of course, one might say that the government cannot be expected to pass regulations protecting people from themselves. Individuals are expected to exercise

Is this a true premise? The government is expected to do this all the time.

their own intelligence when using drugs. However, this reasoning assumes that

good use of a simple emphatic statement

the public is given information that will help it to act wisely. <u>Unfortunately, that is</u> <u>not so.</u> Most of the information received by society today is transmitted through

popular media. What the public hears about patent medicines is conveyed via radio

and television in the form of advertising. Drug companies have launched extensive

Who?

campaigns designed to tell <u>people</u> how accessible drugs are and how little they

cost. The advertisements are little more than popularity contests between brands.

awk. sent. construction

<u>To the consumer, what is the value of</u> a film clip showing a famous actor loading a

shopping cart with fancy packages picked off a shelf in a drug store? It is all very

P

well to be told that in a conveniently located store, the prices are always "right," but

that says nothing about the drugs. The message is to buy.

syntax: on every package of medicine

Of course, some may say that instructions about dosage are <u>on the package</u> <u>of every medicine.</u> Moreover, individual drug companies often warn the public

about misuse of their products. But in an advertisement, the warning against

the detrimental effects of the drug is cleverly disguised. For example, there

are several medicines on sale that are too strong for children's use. When one

interesting interpretation

company says (boasts) that its product is "not even recommended for children,"

the message somehow gets mixed up. Adults are made to feel that they are part

good word choice

of an exclusive class of people who can, and therefore should, rush out and buy

the product. No one would rationally accept this line of reasoning, but <u>this same</u>

Your meanin is uncle Try rewordi

<u>principle, that kind of advertising appeals to the emotions, and people think what</u> <u>they are made to feel.</u>

good concession

Still, one must admit that many of these products are helpful in controlling

ailments or in maintaining proper health, and that more stringent control of sales

would cause prices to rise. This may be so, but after all, medicines are used by

many people who do not need them. If these drugs—as well as vitamins—were

less available or cost more, people would find alternative, more natural ways of

maintaining good health. For instance, exercise can cure many ailments as quickly

P

as aspirin, and regular exercise is a better preventive medicine than regular doses

of patent bottled cure-alls. Moreover, many people would soon discover that the

body functions very well on a well-balanced diet, even without vitamin supplements.

Humans "survived," but they were not all in good health. Also, "generations" is vague. Further development is needed.

Indeed, the body is designed to assimilate what it needs from good food. In this age of technology, people are beginning to forget that the human race survived for generations before nourishment was compressed into little capsules, and the entire ￢ daily requirement swallowed with a drink of water in one gulp.

I will concede that there are <u>individuals</u> who do need to use these drugs   *Be more specific.*

or vitamins regularly, and other people who need to use them occasionally. Nevertheless, there is no good reason for the excessive use of medicine found in today's society. People have mistakenly concluded that if a drug can make them "better" when they are sick, then by the same principle, that drug will improve their condition when they are not sick. What could possibly be "better" than good health? Overdosing oneself with medicine is not the way to find out. In fact,

begging the question?

<u>excessive drug use will surely cause more harm than good</u>. Drug companies have had ample time to warn the public about the need to take care when using their products. More stringent <u>methods</u> are obviously required.   *word choice: "controls"?*

B-   Alec,
This essay is a well-written and thought-provoking argument. Although your introductory paragraph needs to be more focused, your thesis is strong. The body paragraphs are well developed, especially those in which you concede points. But your conclusion should have a stronger call to action. What exactly do you want the reader to do? What are the specific recommendations you want to make? Your argument would also be stronger if you used more specific words, avoided vague generalizations, and gave more examples.

Sample Essay 3

<u>Living with Animals</u>   *Your title indicates a process essay - is it?*

A1

shift in person

<u>Human beings</u> have always depended on animals to meet <u>our</u> needs. Animals have been used as <u>food, labour, drug testing, and even entertainment</u>. All these   *list elements should be parallel*

Ⓤⓢⓔⓢ for animals are Ⓤⓢⓔⓕⓤⓛ, even vital for human needs, but management of animal

awk. repetition

Ⓤⓢⓔⓢ must be responsible.   *thesis: explain how*

Order? Food should be covered first.

Animals can be seen as the first slaves of man. Many pictures <u>can be formed</u>   *pas*

of oxen plowing fields, of horses pulling carts. I refered to animals as slaves but no   *and | sp.*

Can animals = way? Maybe "using animals is one way"?

one opposed it as no one should. <u>Animals</u> were the only <u>way</u> to get things done faster and more economically. There weren't any harmful effects as the animals were well kept, for they were more important as labourers than broken down "nags." But as labour techniques were developed, animal labour became obsolete and is now very insignificant.

Is this true? Where?

Animal entertainment is ever present in todays society as it was over a thousand years ago. Even as far back as Roman times, in events such as chariot racing and bear-baiting, animals have been a source of entertainment. Horse racing and the circus have substituted for entertainment of the past but the same enjoyment is there. Animal rights activists have spoken out against the poor treatment of animals in circuses. This is absurd. Why would the circus harm the things which make the circus thrive? It is, however, a reminder that we should not take advantage of the rights of animals as they are living beings as well.

Order? This should be your fourth point.

now substitute

=| p

p

You need to define "harm" to make this statement

vague ref
You need to define "rights" and which groups believe in these rights.

p | vague ref
?

order? After labour, animals are seen as food. Animals have provided mankind with food ever since we learned how to catch them. Some animals were hunted to extinction, which is sad as they will be lost forever but with better food management animals can be a food source forever. It's sometimes sad to think that some animals live their whole life producing food or becoming food, but then again what did I eat today: eggs, milk, beef, so I can't really complain.

gender bias
are being hunted?
example?
P

weak afterthought contradicts previous statement

Killing animals may save human lives. Using test animals gives researchers better understanding of diseases and can also be used to test potentially life saving drugs, all in search of a cure. It is true that hundreds of animals may die so that few humans live, but then the future will safer against disease and may result in a better world. The ends justify the means. *sweeping generalization*

Does the subject fit the verb?

=|
a

might | missing verb

A1

Humans use animals to meet human needs. I do not oppose this, but we must understand that animals are a limited resource, and careful management of animal uses must be practised so that the world will not feel the loss of another species.

You must be more specific. Which animals in particular are in danger? Are they being used for food, labour, or drug testing?

F William,
You clearly have some ideas and opinions you wish to express about this topic, and this essay seems like a first draft of those ideas. In revising the essay, you should consider the following:

1. Identify your purpose. What exactly do you want the paper to do? Do you want to persuade the audience to treat animals with more respect? Make sure your thesis and title reflect your purpose.

2. Develop a focused thesis, and use it to write your topic sentences and to determine the order of your paragraphs.

3. Proofread for sentence structure errors. Make sure your subjects and verbs "fit" together.

If you do the above, the essay will have a clear sense of direction and your writing will be more coherent.

Sample Essay 4

Contrasting Vancouver and Abbotsford

t: use present perfect

Unbelievably, I <u>lived</u> in almost 10 different places in Canada. When I first came to Canada, I lived in Lethbridge and then I moved to Calgary. After that my family moved to BC where I subsequently lived in Nanaimo, Langley, Aldergrove, Walnut

correct verb tense

Grove, Surrey, Abbotsford, and Vancouver. I have attended <u>about</u> 15 different

be specific

schools. Different places evoke a different atmosphere, due to the surrounding

sp: "surroundings"

and the people. I moved from Abbotsford to Vancouver just a year ago; they are

weak thesis: focus on specific points of comparison

the two most recent places that I've lived in. Abbotsford and Vancouver have many similarities and differences.

Abbotsford is a mixed rural-urban place where agriculture is a major part of the economy. Driving through the country, we can breathe in the fresh air and

unnecessary

look at the farm animals grazing <u>on the grass</u>. I love the fresh open land of green

art. (use "the" with a limiting phrase)

grass everywhere and large spaces between the houses. Fortunately, houses here are much cheaper than the houses in Vancouver; hence, there is a lower demand

A1

Should this be plural? "roads are"

for land in the country. The <u>road is</u> less crowded here because there are fewer

id: "On the sidewalks everywhere"

occupants, less likely to get into car accidents.

add a conjunction & a subject & a verb

Vancouver is an urban place where the land is more valuable. <u>Everywhere on the sidewalk</u> there <u>would be</u> people walking. I have made many friends here

use present tense – not conditional form

because there are more opportunities for me to encounter <u>them</u>. Sometimes I

people?

sp

feel that there is no fresh <u>are</u> here because of the busy traffic at every hour of the

tr

day, polluting the air. The houses here are very close together; in addition, there

are <u>no garages in the front of the house.</u>

Is this meant to describe all houses? Why is this significant?

lc

Can you use a more
natural transition?

In Conclusion, Vancouver and Abbotsford are unique in their own ways; therefore, I like both places. However, I wouldn't choose to live in Abbotsford for the rest of my life because there the shops and the mall are very far away. I would like to live in Vancouver and come back to Abbotsford every once in a while. Sometimes

Explai
why y
like t
be ne
shops.

Use a more
specific word.

we need to travel to different places to learn the things that each place brings.

ww: "has"
"offers"?

C- Amanda,

You certainly can speak from experience! You might, however, want to spend more time developing your thesis to take advantage of your experiences. Do you really want to focus on the urban vs. rural aspects of the two cities, or is there some personal element you would like to add? Your thesis mentions similarities, but you don't really cover them in your paper. Continue proofreading for the occasional article and verb tense error in your next essay.

Sample Essay 5 (ungraded practice exercise)

Special Days

Chinese Lunar New Year, also known as Spring Festival, is the most important traditional holiday in China. It usually falls in January and February, lasting for fifteen days. These fifteen days are special days for people to celebrate the new start of a new year, visit friends, and have fun. From big government-sponsored events to individual families, various activities are held to observe the occasion.

comp / fp
("small family
gatherings"?)

stronger topic
sentence needed

d: can you be
more specific?

Make
your
thesis
into an
opinion

Several days before the new year, people are busy preparing for the holiday. They buy new clothes, food, and other stuff. The houses are decorated with flashing lights, flowers, and typical pictures with the character fu, which means "fortune." On New Year's Eve, family members get together to enjoy a feast. After dinner, married adults will give kids red envelopes with lucky money inside. At night, most Chinese watch the gala show broadcast by China Central Television and count down the last minute to welcome the coming of a brand new year.

ital

d

A1

stronger topic
sentence needed

On the first day of the new year, parade take place in the street. Lion dancing is a routine program. In parks, there are some exhibitions with topics like calligraphy and Chinese painting. Businesses take advantage of the festival. Tons of people can be seen in big shopping malls and department stores. Firework show is also an annual event. The last day of the new year is the lantern festival. People will eat

tr

art/
agr:
subj/
verb

art.

tr / tr

ital   Yuanxian, which means "reunion." It is also considered as the Chinese Valentine's

Day because many young people came across their <u>beloveds</u> while appreciating the   *ww: "future partners"?*

beautiful lanterns in ancient China. After the last day of the Spring Festival, people

are supposed to <u>move back to their normal track of life</u>.   *id: "go back to their regular routines"*

art   Spring Festival has long history in China. It <u>gives</u> a break for people to enjoy   *ww: "provides"?*

themselves and spend more time with their family. It makes life more meaningful

sp   and colorful. The holiday should be <u>passed to the future generations</u>.   *id: "passed on to future generations"*

Nicole,
Your essay is full of many interesting details regarding the Chinese Lunar New Year.
The holiday sounds like a wonderful time. However, your thesis should be a little
more focused. This would lead to stronger topic sentences for your paragraphs. With
stronger topic sentences, your paragraphs will be more coherent, and you will have
an easier time making transitions between your ideas. You can start by using more
periodic sentences with transitional tags. (Too many of your sentences are loose,
giving your essay a choppy feel.) Also proofread your work more carefully.

Sample Essay 6

This essay was written in class, in response to an examination question that
asked students to analyze the following passage from *Hamlet* (I. v. 92–112):

> *Hamlet.* O all you host of heaven! O earth! What else?
> And shall I couple hell? Oh fie! Hold, hold my heart,
> And you, my sinews, grow not instant old,
> But bear me stiffly up. Remember thee!
> Ay, thou poor ghost, while memory holds a seat
> In this distracted globe. Remember thee!
> Yea, from the table of my memory
> I'll wipe away all trivial fond records,
> All saws of books, all forms, all pressures past
> That you and observation copied there,
> And thy commandment all alone shall live
> Within the book and volume of my brain,
> Unmixed with baser matter. Yes, by heaven!
> O most pernicious woman!
> O villain, villain, smiling damnèd villain!
> My tables—meet it is I set it down
> That one may smile, and smile, and be a villain.
> At least I am sure it may be so in Denmark. [*Writes.*]
> So, uncle, there you are. Now to my word:
> It is "Adieu, adieu, remember me." I have sworn't.

A1

Analysis of Hamlet's Remembrance Soliloquy

It is a good strategy to begin with a question, but can you make it more focused?

What is Shakespeare's *Hamlet*? It is a tragedy, a calamity, and a gigantic puzzle, to begin with. The play's central character is a young man with great gifts of intellect, and yet all of his talents cannot save him or the people around him when he decides to follow a commandment from a ghost <u>that haunts the night</u>. In this *necessary cliché?* soliloquy, Hamlet, more alone than ever, expresses his horror at the truth, his rage at those who have betrayed his father, and his determination to remember his oath of vengeance against his father's killer.

This thesis reflects character and motivation; but you also need to address the themes of the passage.

This soliloquy in blank verse comes near the end of the first act, immediately following Hamlet's terrifying meeting with a figure whom he accepts as the tormented spirit of his dead father. The soliloquy marks the first turning point in the play, for from this point on, Hamlet is never quite the same. Now, Hamlet has some evidence—or at least testimony—to back up his previous suspicions about the evil nature of the new king, Claudius. Before this speech, Hamlet has been brooding about a marriage he regards as deeply sinful, but he has pledged to hold his tongue about it; now, he is committed to taking action against a murderer and an illegitimate king. From this point on, Hamlet's life of scholarship and romance and friendship is all but dead; he is about to become a man obsessed and an actor playing the role of a madman all too well.

good short summary of the soliloquy

well said

Hamlet's character is complex: he is brilliant, sad, funny, brutal, kind—an incredible mixture of elements. He is a man caught in a struggle between his reason and his passions. In this speech, the passion emerges first. In two exclamations and two questions, he begins his speech with strong emotions of shock and horror. He prays to heaven, shouts at earth and wonders about hell as he does elsewhere in the play when his passions overcome his reason. He speaks of his own physical weaknesses and described his mind metaphorically as a "distracted globe." In the *signifi- cance?* first of many pledges, he promises to "wipe away all trivial fond records" and give up everything that has meant anything to him: his books, his sayings, his youthful interests. In a way, Hamlet becomes old and careworn before the audience's eyes as the ghost retreats with the rising of the sun.

v: use present tense

good observation

A1

This paragraph needs to be developed. Perhaps combine it with the following one?

The most emotional part of the soliloquy comes when Hamlet expresses his thoughts about his mother and his new stepfather. His mother is a "most pernicious woman," the word "pernicious" suggesting someone who is deeply evil. Claudius for his part is "a villain, a smiling villain," and Hamlet is having a hard time understanding how one so corrupt—so sinful—could appear to be so amiable, such a smiling, polished, perfect king.

repetitious? unnecessary definition?

Q: a "villain, [a] smiling . . . villain"

Just when Hamlet's passion seems about to boil over into an act of public violence against his "aunt-mother" and "uncle-father," his mind asserts itself and reason prevails in him for the time being. The physical action of Hamlet in this passage matches this physical change. When Hamlet picks up his diary to write about his experience, he shows himself trying to organize the experience with his student's mind. He makes notes about what he has seen; he writes an essay about it. Such an action is but the first example of Hamlet's many attempts to make order out of a disordered, disjointed, and rotten world.

Apart from revealing the complexities of Hamlet's character, this soliloquy presents the audience with several themes. It shows us Hamlet as a Dane deeply disgusted by his own country because it is a place where one may smile and prosper and be a villain. It shows us that the world for Hamlet has become, in just a few minutes on the battlements, a place in which the appearance of a man may not match at all the reality of his soul. In this passage, the word "memory" becomes a refrain, and the reader must wonder how Hamlet could ever forget what he has heard in the chill of the night. The last line, "I have sworn't," echoes other moments in the play in which characters swear oaths: the soldiers' pledge to keep the ghost secret; Ophelia's and Laertes's pledge to follow their father's advice; Gertrude's pledge to abandon Claudius's bed after Hamlet has "cleft [her] heart in twain" in the closet scene. Like the others, Hamlet has a dreadful time—a tragic time—living up to the pledge. In Denmark, it seems, pledges are made to be broken or at least forgotten.

A1

good emphasis

good observation

This soliloquy is important to the play, then, as a contributor to the plot, the characterization, and the theme. Without it, the audience would be deprived of a turning point in the plot; it would lose a glimpse at Hamlet's brilliant, embattled mind; it would lose an opportunity to understand the ironic gap between what is and what seems—even in the highest realms of government and power. [Without neces... the remembrance soliloquy, in short, *Hamlet* just wouldn't be *Hamlet*.]

A- Robin,
Your essay is a thoughtful analysis of the soliloquy. Your observations about the language and placement of the soliloquy are both well put and interesting. However, your introduction needs to be more focused and your thesis more clearly stated. In fact, your conclusion should be your introduction! In your next examination essay, you may want to write your introduction after drafting the body of the essay.

Sample Essay 7

The Value of Emotional Intelligence in the Town of Avonlea *an excellent title*

How an author of children's literature defines and distinguishes a child's intelligence from that of an adult's reveals much about the author's (and his or her era's) beliefs about children's education. Moreover, how an author approaches the

Can one story affect a child both ways at different points?

distinction between the minds of adults and the minds of children may very subtly affect the child reader so that one story may empower a child while another story makes him or her feel impotent. Lucy Maud Montgomery's *Anne of Green Gables* offers the child reader an empowering experience, as they observe the triumph of a *agr* girl who faces a life of obstacles with good humour, good nature, good will, and an

good balanced sentence

innate insight into human nature. Lucy Maud Montgomery depicts Anne as a funny, quirky, silly little girl who can't seem to stay out of trouble, but the author also manages to illuminate the young redhead's intelligence as distinct from and often

A1

Vary your sentence structure to avoid always starting with the author's name.

more competent than that of the adults in the novel. Montgomery defines Anne's intelligence in a way that would be described today as "emotional intelligence," while the adults in the story have an intelligence based on varying degrees of (and often limitations of) knowledge or wisdom acquired over time. Montgomery begins the novel conveying the flaws of the story's key adult characters and uses these adults as contrasting characters to Anne, illustrating the differences between the intelligence of a child and that of an adult. The author also contrasts Anne and

an ori... readin... of the value educa... intelli... in the novel

awk: "their" or "this pair's"

Gilbert with the other Avonlea children to demonstrate the value and potency of these two's dynamic young intelligence. ✓

clear thesis

For the purposes of this paper, the psychological term, "emotional intelligence" should be defined and linked to Montgomery's approach to the intelligence of the child and adult characters in her novel. This paper will define "emotional intelligence" by using the definitions of two psychologists: Daniel Goleman and Howard Gardner. Daniel Goleman defines emotional intelligence as, "abilities such as being able to motivate oneself and persist in the face of frustrations; to control impulse and delay gratification; to regulate one's moods and keep distress from swamping the ability to think; to empathize and to hope" (Goleman 34). Howard Gardner defines emotional intelligence in terms of "personal intelligences":

no p

no p

> *Interpersonal intelligence* denotes a person's capacity to understand the intentions, motivations, and desires of other people and, consequently, to work effectively with others. . . . *Intrapersonal intelligence* involves the capacity to understand oneself, to have an effective working model of oneself—including one's own desires, fears, and capacities—and to use such information effectively in regulating one's own life. (Gardner 43)

good to define the terms, but can you use paraphrases?

Given that she wrote the novel in the early 1900's, Montgomery was not exposed to any such precise definitions of or likely even the term "emotional intelligence"; however, in the late nineteenth and early twentieth centuries, the nature of children's intelligence was being examined and understood in new ways. Child psychology had emerged in the latter half of the nineteenth century, and "quasi-psychologists" such as John Locke and Jean-Jacques Rousseau had been analyzing children since the seventeenth and eighteenth centuries (Tucker 158–59). So, while Montgomery may not have understood "emotional intelligence" in the same way as today's child psychologists do, she would have had (and apparently did have) her own informed opinions* about the uniqueness and value of children's intelligence, and an understanding about the distinctions between the way adults and children think.

*Were these opinions informed by reading of quasi-psychologists or by her own experience?

A1

The first step Montgomery takes in her novel towards distinguishing the differences between adults' and children's intelligence is characterizing the important adult characters as being flawed. She begins the novel by giving the reader some initial insight into the minds of the leading adult characters: Rachel, Marilla, and Mathew. By exploring their intellect, views, and feelings, Montgomery conveys a message to the child reader: the wisdom and knowledge acquired by these adults <u>has not seemed</u> to have made them happier or <u>better</u> people.

sp [margin note]

v: "does not seem" [margin note]

What you m by "be Are t adult chara not g or vir anyw [margin note]

Montgomery begins the novel with introductions to Rachel Lynde and Marilla Cuthbert in the first chapter. Both women seem to experience life through the guidance of scripture, being ever mindful of what is deemed respectable behaviour. Rachel Lynde occupies the first line of the novel, and the narrator's description of her conveys a character with strict Victorian ideals who gives "due regard for decency and decorum. . .," while occupying most of her spare time observing the comings and goings of the townsfolk (Montgomery 7). Rachel's character is representative of the town of Avonlea, where everyone knows everybody else's business. Marilla comes across as a no-nonsense utilitarian woman who spends her time putting herself to good use: keeping her house and her yard spotless, and rarely taking the time to sit down and relax (Montgomery 10). Neither woman seems very happy, and both seem to lack the ability to seek out pleasure in life by appreciating the little things, such as the beauty of nature. Rachel believes "trees aren't much company. . ." (Montgomery 9) and Marilla is "always slightly distrustful of sunshine, which seem[s] to her too dancing and irresponsible a thing for a world which [is] meant to be taken seriously. . ." (Montgomery 10). <u>Neither</u> of these women <u>show</u> great Intrapersonal Intelligence.

well [margin note]

MLA: misuse of ellipses [margin note]

good choice [margin note]

MLA [margin note]

A1 *MLA | agr: "Neither . . . shows"* [margin note]

lc (x2 [margin note]

Also in this first chapter, Montgomery gives the reader some insight into both women's levels of interpersonal intelligence. Marilla's and Rachel's friendship seems somewhat cold and unaffectionate. On the day Mathew goes to fetch Anne, Rachel's main motivation for calling on Marilla is not to enjoy her friend's good company or to inquire if she's well, but to satisfy her own curiosity about where Mathew is going and why. In fact, Rachel must know or else won't have "a minute's peace of mind or conscience . . ." (Montgomery 9). Upon hearing their

effective transition [margin note]

"Maril" and Rachel [margin note]

sp [margin note]

news, Rachel, instead of trying to be a good friend by listening to Marilla's and

Mathew's reasons for taking in an orphan, immediately expresses her disapproval.

Rachel's offer of a "Job's comforting" to Marilla (Montgomery 13) is <u>due either to</u>

<u>the fact that</u> Rachel does not care enough about her friend to extend true comfort,

<u>or it is due to the fact that</u> Rachel does not have a sense of how to help people

during stressful times. This failure to read Marilla's needs is indicative of Rachel's

possession of a low level of interpersonal intelligence. This interaction between

Rachel and Marilla also sheds some light on the way Marilla's mind works. As she

complains about the lack of good labour in Avonlea, Marilla demonstrates a narrow,

discriminatory outlook by making negative comments about "stupid, half-grown

little French boys [. . . and] London street Arabs . . ." (Montgomery 12). Overall,

Marilla's and Rachel's discussion at Green Gables leaves both of them looking

unhappy, close-minded, and intolerant.

Throughout the novel, it is Mathew who comes across as the most forgiving

adult character. In the beginning of the story, he seems to be the most emotionally

intelligent adult, due to his natural shyness and apparent sensitivity. However,

Montgomery is quick to point out his <u>flaws</u>. When the narrator first gets inside

Mathew's head and discloses some of Mathew's feelings, the reader finds out about

Mathew's phobia of women: "he [has] an uncomfortable feeling that the mysterious

creatures [are] secretly laughing at him" (Montgomery 16). Mathew appears to be

an unreliable adult character because of his timidness, and it makes his meeting

with Anne humorous because they are such opposites. <u>It is</u> during Mathew's and

Anne's meeting at the train station and their drive to Green Gables that Montgomery

begins her contrasts of children's and adult's intelligences.

In her novel, Montgomery manages to distinguish between adult's and

children's intelligence, showing the value and uniqueness of children's intelligence,

without showing too much bias towards the child characters. However, respect for

the protagonist's intellect is important, and Montgomery begins her characterization

of Anne by establishing her level of emotional intelligence immediately, contrasting

her behaviour with Mathew's. Anne shows intrapersonal intelligence straight away

by using her self-knowledge to comfort herself in a situation that is undoubtedly

Margin notes:

awk: rewrite sentence removing "due to the fact that"

*Which is the more likely explanation?

too strong a word?

weak expletive

A1

*Would you say this is the case with other writers for children?

highly stressful for her. Having been dropped off at the train station, she waits for her new adoptive parents to pick her up, not knowing what to expect, and most likely expecting very little, considering her past experiences in orphanages and foster homes since her parents' deaths. Instead of worrying and brooding in the waiting room, she chooses to wait outside because "There [is] more scope for imagination" (Montgomery 17). Here Anne takes what could be a distressing experience and turns it into an opportunity to delve into her world of fantasy and daydreams, which (Montgomery implies in the novel) has helped her through traumatic experiences throughout her eleven years. Goleman would say that Anne exhibits self-awareness. He says that "typical thoughts bespeaking emotional self-awareness include 'I shouldn't feel this way,' 'I'm thinking good things to cheer up,' and . . . 'Don't think about it' in reaction to something highly upsetting" (Goleman 47). Anne recognizes situations that cause her distress and takes a proactive approach towards keeping herself in good spirits. Anne also uses her intrapersonal intelligence—the knowledge of her own "desires, fears, and capacities" (Gardner 43)—on her drive home with Mathew. Instead of mentally pushing against things that are strange to her, Anne begins renaming and romanticizing everything she sees in an effort to become enthusiastic about her new home.

good use of secondary source

Montgomery also uses the scene between Anne and Mathew to contrast Mathew's and Anne's interpersonal intelligence. While Mathew appears helpless and at a loss about what to do about the problem (receiving a girl orphan instead of a boy), Anne takes charge by rising and addressing Mathew first, instead of waiting for him to come to her. The narrator states that Anne "had been watching [Mathew]" throughout his upsetting conversation with the station master (Montgomery 18–19). It is entirely possible that Anne approaches Mathew first because she sees that he is uncomfortable and anxious. By reacting to the situation this way, Anne exhibits a high level of interpersonal intelligence. She plays the role of comforter to Mathew, the adult, in a situation that would usually (by) much more stressful on her, the child. Here Montgomery exhibits how extraordinary and valuable Anne's emotional intelligence is, and she foreshadows how skilled and reliable Anne will be in future times of crisis.

In a way, Matthew's profound uncertainty is a good thing—it allows Anne a foot in the door of Green Gables.

A1

sp

an interesting observation

Anne's emotional intelligence also comes through in her ability to learn from the adults in her life. While she teaches them, she is also grateful and heedful of what they have to teach her. Although the reader's initial view of Anne emphasizes her emotional intelligence, Montgomery is careful to portray her throughout the story as a <u>realistic</u>, imperfect character. She has a temper that flares up on occasion. Conveying the findings of psychologist Dolf Zillmann, Goleman points out that a universal trigger for anger is the sense of being endangered. Endangerment can be signaled not just by an outright physical threat but also, as is more often the case, by a symbolic threat to self-esteem or dignity: being treated unjustly or rudely, being insulted or demeaned, being frustrated in pursuing an important goal (60).

ambig: lifelike or pragmatic?

tr

This results in an energy surge that "lasts for minutes, during which it readies the body for a good fight or a quick flight, depending on how the emotional brain sizes up the opposition" (Goleman 60). It seems that in Anne's separate altercations with Rachel and Gilbert, she is ready for a good fight. In both situations, Anne faces from her antagonists a threat to her self-esteem because of their comparing the colour of her hair to carrots. It is clear to the reader that Anne overreacts in both cases, and it isn't until she learns from Marilla and Mathew to work on managing her anger, and from Marilla not to be so sensitive about her appearance, that she becomes truly emotionally intelligent (Montgomery 80–85). While emotional intelligence may seem something innate, Goleman argues that "there is ample evidence that emotional skills such as impulse control and accurately reading a social situation can be learned" (Goleman 83). If it weren't for Marilla's and Mathew's knowledge, life experience, role modelling, and wisdom, Anne would not have grown into the extraordinary young woman she becomes.

This transition implies a close connection to the previous paragraph. Perhaps you could restructure these paragraphs or change the topic sentence to avoid the vague "This."

Reference the primary text only when you are quoting from it.

A1

Another of Anne's role models, and the person who is closest to being Anne's equal in the novel, is Gilbert. In conveying the fact that Anne and Gilbert are connected in some way, Montgomery uses the other children of Avonlea to contrast their two characters. The novel portrays Gilbert as Anne's equal in terms of both emotional and academic intelligence. The other child characters: Diana, Ruby, Charlie, etc. are no match for Anne's and Gilbert's conventional intelligence (in terms of IQ), but neither are they any match for <u>these two's</u> emotional intelligence.

p: use dashes around this list

reword

avoid: "and so on"

Instead of emphasizing Anne's and Gilbert's IQ's, Montgomery emphasizes their

singular   emotional intelligence, one aspect of which is their <u>abilities</u> to hope. Goleman

argues that the ability to hope is one of the most important indicators of a student's

future success. He refers to C.R. Snyder's study of college students, where Snyder

agr   found that a <u>student's</u> hope about <u>their</u> academic performance or achievement

"was a better predictor of their first-semester grades than were their scores on the

SAT . . . . Emotional aptitudes make the critical difference [because . . .] 'students

with high hope set themselves higher goals and know how to work hard to attain

Where do the other children show themselves losing hope?   them'" (qtd. in Goleman 86). By characterizing Anne and Gilbert with higher

emotional intelligence than the other children, and by showing them to have higher

academic successes than the other children, Montgomery sends a message to the

child reader that hope, hard work, and determination are <u>more the ingredients</u> for   *awk*

success than is conventional intelligence.

Some of the most powerful evidence for Anne's emotional intelligence comes

through in the fact that she feels absolutely no shame about her lack of religious

education or spiritual connection to God. Daniel Goleman states that "there is

growing evidence that fundamental ethical stances in life stem from underlying

emotional capacities" (Goleman xii). Unlike the respectable citizens of Avonlea,

Anne is not guided by religious and culture-based rules of life. She trusts her own

instincts about the right ways to treat others and what is right for herself. She tells

Marilla that "if [she] really wanted to pray . . . [she'd] go out into a great big field

all alone or in the deep, deep woods, and . . . look up into the sky . . . and then . . .

good use of text   just feel a prayer" (Montgomery 58–59). Anne feels no shame about her lack of a

relationship with God because she steadfastly believes in her own innocence. Her

belief in her own innocence is remarkable because although Montgomery does

not show the citizens of Avonlea blatantly persecuting Anne for her scandalous

orphan status, her alienation by the townsfolk is implied by Rachel's assumptions

about the evil nature of all orphans ~~(Montgomery 13)~~ and Mrs. Barry's belief that

Anne intoxicated Diana with malicious intent ~~(Montgomery 144)~~. In those days

from other children or equally from children and adults?   it was generally thought that all orphans were criminals or just commonly bad or

evil. Furthermore, since Anne faces <u>humiliation</u> on account of her lack of "puffed

A1

sleeves," she must certainly face ostracism due to her lack of parents. So, although Montgomery doesn't show every act of cruelty, no matter how subtle, exacted on Anne by her schoolmates or the townspeople, the reader may infer that such occurrences are taking place. ✓

a skilfully argued point

Besides emphasizing the value of a child's intelligence as distinctive from that of an adult's intelligence, Montgomery succeeds in developing an important child-hero <u>whom</u> is of the most value to young girls. Anne's heroism is displayed through her ability to develop her own identity, sense of individualism, and intelligence. She works fiercely and steadily towards her ultimate goal of becoming a teacher, and she succeeds in life, no matter the obstacles. Obvious obstacles are her traumatic experiences from her past, which the reader <u>only</u> hears of briefly, and much of which the reader has to imagine: her parents' deaths, and the emotional and physical harm she experiences as an orphan and a foster child. But what the reader is most privy to are the less seedy, more ordinary obstacles that Anne shares with other girls of Avonlea, indeed <u>with all girls and women in Western society</u>.* She grows up in an age that still honours Victorian values. It is a world where men and women have separate domains: a man's place is in the public sphere, and a woman's place is in the private sphere. A man's intelligence is more highly valued than a woman's intelligence. Avonlea society's acknowledgment of a woman's value and place is reflected in the behaviour, expectations, and dreams of the other girls of Avonlea. Although Anne's desires for higher education are supported by Marilla—who, uncharacteristically for women of her time, believes a woman should always be able to support herself—it would likely have been perfectly acceptable for Anne to go the way of Diana: concentrating on becoming a competent housekeeper and maintaining her good looks in preparation for marriage. But Anne doesn't go that way, she chooses to put a value on her own intelligence equal to the value society puts on a man's intelligence. She chooses to take control of her own life and to strive towards becoming a better person, without becoming too distracted with conforming to the types of behaviour deemed by society as indicative of a "good woman." She is a good woman . . . as defined by Anne Shirley. ✓

"who" (subject of "is")

mm

in what time period?

*Be cautious about making sweeping statements.

to anyone but Anne!

A1

cs

excellent, strong conclusion

Works Cited

Gardner, Howard. *Intelligence Reframed: Multiple Intelligences for the 21st Century.* New York: Basic, 1999. Print.

Goleman, Daniel. *Emotional Intelligence.* 10th anniversary ed. New York: Bantam, 2005. Print.

Montgomery, L.M. *Anne of Green Gables.* 1908. Toronto: New Canadian, 2008. Print.

Tucker, Nicholas. "Good Friends, or Just Acquaintances? The Relationship between Child Psychology and Children's Literature." *Literature for Children: Contemporary Criticism.* Ed. Peter Hunt. London: Routledge, 1992. 156–173. Print.

B+ Tara,

I enjoyed reading your well-written and well-documented essay. Your strong opening and fresh approach to the text raise several thought-provoking issues and questions about the meaning of wisdom, including emotional wisdom, in literature for children. There are several potential future essays in this one essay! What you do need to work on for your next essay is proofreading. Be particularly careful with the spelling of characters' names, punctuation, agreement (subject-verb; noun-pronoun), and sentence structure.

A1

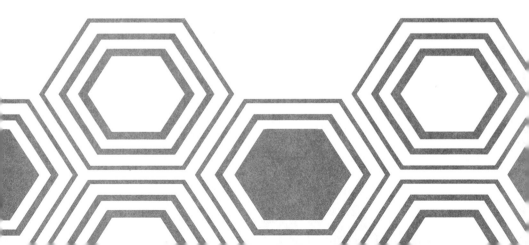

2

Appendix

Marking Symbols and
Abbreviations Explained

Instructors and others who routinely grade students' writing assignments generally use a number of conventional marking symbols and abbreviations, many of which you have encountered throughout this book. The following list briefly explains the meaning of the most commonly used *symbols*:

ℛ	Delete, omit.
¶; no ¶	Paragraph; no paragraph. See ***para***, below.
//	Faulty parallelism. See ***fp***, below.
✕	Obvious error (e.g., typographical).
⋀	Something omitted? Insert.
=/	Insert hyphen.
∽	Transpose.
◡	Close up space.
#	More space required; inconsistent spacing.
?	Something questionable or unclear: Is this what you mean?
✓	Something especially good.
!!	Something brilliant!

Some markers may use symbols that differ slightly from the ones given here, so you may need to consult your instructor if you are having trouble deciphering a symbol that appears on your paper.

The rest of this appendix provides an alphabetical list of the *abbreviations* most commonly used in marking students' essays. Most abbreviations are followed by brief explanations of their meaning and of the steps required to correct or revise particular errors or stylistic weaknesses, including one or more examples of each. We have also provided cross-references for abbreviations that have more than one form; some instructors, for example, will use ***fs*** (*fused sentence*) where others would use ***run-on*** (*run-on sentence*).

When you approach a marked draft of your work for the purpose of correction and revision, you will probably find it helpful to consult this chapter first. If the brief explanation you find here doesn't enable you to make a correction or revision, follow the cross-reference to the fuller discussion elsewhere in the book; only a few of the categories listed below are not discussed specifically elsewhere.

Reminder: The abbreviations that appear on the following pages are also listed inside the back cover.

A2

abbr **Undesirable or Incorrect Abbreviation**

Generally, avoid abbreviations in formal writing. Instead of *e.g., i.e., viz., etc.,* use the more formal expressions *for example, that is, namely, and so forth.* Some abbreviations are so common that they are frequently used as substitutes for the full terms to which they correspond. For example, we often speak or write of British Columbia as *B.C.* and of Prince Edward Island as *P.E.I.,* but never of Alberta as *Alta.* or of Ontario as *Ont.* Abbreviations like *B.C.* and *P.E.I.* are acceptable in writing (but the name should be spelled in full the first time it appears), whereas *Alta.* and *Ont.* are not. Whenever you aren't sure, avoid the abbreviation; the full word or words will not be inappropriate.

See #57 for more information about abbreviations.

ack **Acknowledgement of Sources**

Whenever you include in an essay information, statistics, ideas, diagrams and other graphic materials, or wording that you obtained from investigating any electronic or non-electronic source, you must acknowledge your indebtedness in accordance with the conventions of documentation; this is true even if you aren't writing a full-fledged research paper. Even specific information from lectures, interviews, online discussions, and conversations should be scrupulously acknowledged.

Failure to indicate fully the use of outside sources—whether you quote directly or paraphrase—is plagiarism. Instructors and institutions usually apply severe academic penalties for such unethical conduct.

See #78–80. See also ***doc*** (*documentation*).

ad **Adjectives and Adverbs Confused or Misused**

The most common kind of mistake in this category is the use of either an adjective or an adverb where the other should appear. For example:

ad: After eating three pepperoni pizzas, he didn't sleep very good.

Here the adjective *good* should be replaced by the adverb *well.* (See #20b.2 and **good, bad, badly, well** in #72.)

See #19 and #20.

A2

agr   ## Agreement

1. *Agreement between subject and verb*: A finite verb agrees with its subject in person and number.

    agr: This group of tourists are headed to Cape Breton.

    The singular *group*, not the plural *tourists*, is the subject; to agree in number, therefore, the verb should be *is*, not *are*.

    See #18.

2. *Agreement of pronouns with their antecedents*: A pronoun must agree in person and number with its antecedent, the word—usually preceding it—to which it refers.

    agr: When the lab assistant asked for volunteers, nobody in the lecture hall raised their hand.

    The indefinite pronoun *nobody* is singular; to agree with it in number, the pronoun referring to it should also be singular. But to avoid gender-biased language, you would not use the formerly common *his*, but rather *his or her*—or avoid the problem by rephrasing the sentence: "When the lab assistant asked for volunteers, not a single hand went up" (see #15d).

    See #15. For shifts in the person and number of pronouns, see *shift*, *pv* (*point of view*) and #39d–e.

al   ## Illogical or Incongruous Alignment of Elements

If you find this mark on an essay it means that there is an illogicality that you must remove. The illogicality may be a matter of faulty predication:

al, pred: The professions many undergraduates dream of pursuing are doctor and lawyer.

But *doctors* and *lawyers* are not professions; they are *professionals*. The sentence needs revising:

revised: The professions many undergraduates dream of pursuing are medicine and law.

revised: Many undergraduates dream of becoming doctors or lawyers.

A2

Other alignment errors result from trying to make words behave in ways that their meanings don't permit:

> **al**: The general believed that acts such as courage and initiative should be recognized.

But *courage* and *initiative* are not acts.

> **revised**: The general believed that acts of courage and initiative should be recognized.

See #38; see also **log** (*logic*) and **comp** (*incomplete comparison*).

ambig   ## Ambiguous

Ambiguity is a lack of clarity that permits a reader to understand a passage, sentence, or word in two different ways. Although ambiguity is sometimes intentional—for example in poetry, where it can enrich the meaning—it is generally unwelcome in expository prose, where it can obscure the meaning and confuse the reader.

> **ambig**: The prime minister was in favour of elimination of violent crime and gun control.

Here coordination appears to link eliminating violent crime and eliminating gun control—a highly unlikely political stance. The ambiguity can be removed by rearranging elements of the sentence or by changing the syntax:

> **clear**: The prime minister was in favour of gun control and elimination of violent crime.

> **clear**: The prime minister was in favour of maintaining gun control and eliminating violent crime.

In this second version, the parallel gerunds *maintaining* and *eliminating* help convey the intended meaning.

See also **cl** (*clarity*), **dm** (*dangling modifier*) and #36, **mm** (*misplaced modifier*) and #35, **fp** (*faulty parallelism*) and #40, **p** (*punctuation*) and chapter V, and **ref** (*faulty reference*) and #16b.

apos   ## Apostrophe Missing or Misused

1. An apostrophe indicates the possessive inflection of nouns. Here the necessary apostrophe is omitted:

    > *apos*: We noted the professors behaviour during the orientation for new students.

    Without an apostrophe, one can't tell whether the possessive *professors* is singular (*professor's*) or plural (*professors'*).

2. An apostrophe is not used for the possessive case of personal pronouns:

    > *incorrect*: her's, your's, their's

3. An apostrophe indicates the omission of letters in contractions; omitting the apostrophe in a contraction results in a misspelling. Some examples of correctly contracted forms:

he'll (*he will*)	shouldn't (*should not*)
hasn't (*has not*)	we're (*we are*)
it's (*it is*)	you're (*you are*)
they're (*they are*)	who's (*who is*)

4. Don't confuse a contraction with a possessive form:

    > *wrong*: Who's book is this? (*Whose*)

    > *wrong*: Is this where your going to sleep? (*you're*)

    > *wrong*: She put the dog in it's kennel. (*its*)

    See #62m.8 and #62o for complete information on the apostrophe.

PROOFREADING TIP

The Place of Contractions in Formal and Informal Writing

Contractions are usually out of place in formal writing. If you want a relatively informal tone, however, they are not only permissible but desirable. See #64b.

A2

art   ## Article Missing or Misused

> ***art***: We are looking for computer lab where our class is scheduled to meet.

Supply the missing *the* before *computer lab*, which is made specific by the subordinate clause following it.

> ***art***: My sister wants to write on an historical topic related to the city of Vancouver.

Change *an* to *a*.

> ***art***: It was at this point in the life that he decided to reform.

Remove *the* or change it to *his*.

See #19c; see also ***id*** (*idiom*) and #70.

awk   ## Awkwardness

Awk is the symbol some use when they know something is wrong with a sentence but can't put a finger on a particular error, or when the combination of several faults is unusually complicated. ***Awk*** could be translated as something like "Revise this sentence in a significant way to make it clearer." Awkwardness can result from several causes, among them the following:

- haste when you don't have time to edit or revise;
- overly elaborate or imprecise diction and wordiness (see ***w***—*wordiness*—and #71);
- overly elaborate sentence structure;
- ineffective use of the passive voice (see ***pas***—*weak passive voice*—and #17p);
- mistakes in punctuation (see chapter V);
- confused thinking and insufficient explanations.

Here are some examples of awkward sentences, each followed by an attempt to straighten the problem out:

> ***awk***: Caught up in this new way of life, I felt a closer existence to every thought of today.

> ***revised***: Caught up in this new way of life, I developed a greater interest in contemporary thought.

A2

awk: Now, as I began to get some feeling of confidence restored in me, I thought how silly my previous experience had been.

revised: Now, as I regained confidence, I realized how foolish my response to the earlier experience had been.

awk: I looked for a familiar face among that great sea of faces, but this was done in vain.

revised: I looked in vain for a friend in that great sea of faces.

awk: The essay is written in a way that he relates his beliefs to the reader, but does not force the reader to digest his beliefs.

revised: The writer explains his beliefs although he does not expect the reader to share them.

awk: The poem also gives a sense of lightness in the way it rhymes and in its metre.

revised: The poem's rhymes and metre contribute to its light tone.

awk: During the eighteenth century, chemistry became a real science instead of the previous alchemy.

revised: In the eighteenth century, chemistry became a true science, evolving out of and replacing the pseudoscience of alchemy.

awk: In the poem, "To an Athlete Dying Young," by A.E. Housman, the author poses an argument of why the athlete benefited from dying young.

revised: In A.E. Housman's poem "To an Athlete Dying Young," the speaker argues that it was fortunate for the athlete to die so young.

ca

The Case of the Pronoun Is Wrong

The case of a pronoun depends on its function in its own clause or phrase. A pronoun that is a subject or a complement must be in the subjective case:

ca: Hans and me dug the ditch ourselves. (*I*)

ca: He's the one whom I predicted would win the race. (*who*)

ca: That is her. (*she*)

A2

A pronoun that is an object of a verb or a preposition must be in the objective case:

> *ca*: They told Alberta and I to leave. (*me*)

> *ca*: It was up to Gillian and I to finish the job. (*me*)

> *ca*: It doesn't matter who you take with you. (*whom*)

See #14e. For information about the possessive case of nouns and pronouns, see #13a.2, #13b, #14a–d, #19a, #21h, and #62n.

cap

Capitalization Needed or Faulty

> *cap*: Great bear lake extends north of the arctic circle in the Northwest Territories.

> *corrected*: Great Bear Lake extends north of the Arctic Circle in the Northwest Territories.

See #58; see also *lc* (*lower case*).

cl

Lack of Clarity

Like awkwardness, a lack of clarity can result from a number of causes. The parts of a sentence may fail to go together in a meaningful way, or the words chosen to express an idea may not do so adequately, or the writer may have expressed only a vague idea needing further thought and development. Sometimes, writers lacking confidence will add unnecessary qualifications that muddy or, at the very least, water down the ideas they are trying to convey:

> *cl*: There is also a general sense of irony in the plot or story behind the play.

What is *a general sense* as opposed to *a sense*? What is *a sense of irony* as opposed to *irony*? Why the choice of *plot or story*? And how is it that the plot (or story) is *behind* the play? It is impossible to be sure what the writer meant, but here is a clear sentence that uses the major features of the original: "There are ironic elements in the plot of the play."

> *cl*: This blessing is intended to restore faith in God when things happen such as death which you don't understand and want to blame God for letting them happen.

This sentence could also have been marked *awk*, but the muddiness of the thought and its expression seem to be its principal problems. Sorting out the logical connections and the syntax produces a clearer and more succinct version:

revised: This blessing is intended to restore faith in God, which may be lost when incomprehensible events like death make one question God's justice.

But here is an example of an unclear sentence that remains impenetrable:

cl: Absurdist plays work on the situation in much greater detail than the dramatic level.

Here is another sentence that goes astray; one can only wonder what the intended meaning was:

cl: He compares the athlete's achievements and victories to that of death.

Sometimes punctuation or the lack of it is part of the trouble:

cl, p: Before I really had time to think they wanted me to report for work in the morning.

A comma after *think* makes it likely that a reader will understand the sentence on the first reading rather than on the second or third.

See also *ambig* (*ambiguous*), *awk* (*awkward*), #16, #31, and #35–42.

cliché   ## Cliché
See *trite* (*trite, worn-out, hackneyed expression*). See #71e.

coh   ## Not Coherent; Continuity Weak
Coherence is weak or faulty when there is insufficient transition between two sentences or two paragraphs. The first sentence of a paragraph, whether it is the topic sentence or not, should provide a connection to the preceding paragraph. Similarly, sentences within paragraphs should flow smoothly from one to another. Here, for example, are two sentences that are not smoothly connected:

coh: Rachel is invited both to dine at Willard's and to go out with Calla. Despite her desire to accept one of the invitations she declines both of them because she has promised to play cards with her mother.

Although the idea of the invitations is present in both, and although a reader can more or less work out the connection, a *But* to begin the second sentence or a *however* (between commas) after the word *invitations* would make the two sentences more coherent and the reader's task much easier.

See #1b and #7; see also **tr** (*transition weak or lacking*) and #31.

colloq   ## Colloquialism
See **inf** (*informal, colloquial*). See #64b.

comb   ## Combine Sentences
An instructor may write **coord** (*coordinate*) or **sub** (*subordinate*), or even **coord or sub** together, to indicate that some kind of improvement (e.g., economy, coherence, logic, or just a decrease in choppiness) could be gained by putting two (or more) sentences together. Sometimes, however, rather than specify **coord** or **sub**, an instructor may write **comb**, meaning simply "Combine these sentences into one in the way you think best." In the following, for example, which could as well have been marked **w** (*wordiness*), the improvement in the revision is apparent:

w, comb: The whiteness of the snow piled on their outstretched branches gave their green colour an extra richness. This added attractiveness seemed to enhance their beauty.

revised: The whiteness of the snow piled on their outstretched branches gave their green colour an extra richness, enhancing their beauty.

See **coord** (*coordination needed*), **sub** (*subordination needed*), #41, and exercises 11q, 23c (2), and 71a–h (2).

comp   ## Incomplete Comparison
Revise to correct incomplete or illogical comparisons.

comp: She is a better chef than any chef in the city.

revised: She is a better chef than any other chef in the city.

revised: She is the best chef in the city.

comp: Life in a small town is better than a big city.

revised: Life in a small town is better than (life) in a big city.

comp: I think cranberry juice is as good, if not better, than orange juice.

revised: I think cranberry juice is as good as, if not better than, orange juice.

revised: I think cranberry juice is as good as orange juice, if not better.

comp: Fresh vegetables have more vitamins.

revised: Fresh vegetables have more vitamins than canned or frozen ones.

comp: I like snowboarding more than Yan.

revised: I like snowboarding more than Yan does.

revised: I like snowboarding more than I like Yan.

Note that **ambig** (*ambiguous*), **cl** (*lack of clarity*), or **log** (*logic*) would be appropriate marks for some of these sentences.

See #38 and #42.

conc **Insufficient Concreteness**

Revise by increasing the concreteness of your diction. Replace abstract words and phrases with concrete ones, or expand upon general and abstract statements with specific and concrete details.

conc: Seymour was a very deep young man.

The word *deep* here is suggestive, but too abstract to be very meaningful. *Deep* could mean any one of several different things here (consult your dictionary); more information, especially in the form of concrete examples, would enable a reader to understand precisely what the writer meant to convey. Here are two sentences whose vague abstractness and illogical circularity (see #3h.5, *begging the question*) render them almost meaningless:

conc, log: The author makes the setting so good that it is very convincing.

conc, log: The characters are presented as fully described people.

Don't write empty sentences like those. Inject some specific, concrete content.

See #66.

coord   ## Coordination Needed; Combine Sentences

When two sentences are closely related—for example, when they express a contrast—it is often preferable to combine them, using either punctuation or a coordinating conjunction (see #23a) or both.

> *coord*: Life in a farming community can be very challenging. Life in a large city offers more variety.

> *revised*: Life in a farming community can be very challenging, but life in a large city offers more variety.

Depending on context and desired emphasis, such sentences could also be joined with a semicolon, or one or the other could be subordinated with *though* or *whereas*.

See also *sub* (*subordination needed*), *comb* (*combine sentences*), *cs* (*comma splice*), *coh* (*coherence*), and *fc* (*faulty coordination*), and #41.

cs   ## Comma Splice

A comma splice results from putting a comma between two independent clauses that are not joined with a coordinating conjunction; "splicing" the clauses together with only a comma is not enough.

> *cs*: The flight from Vancouver to Toronto takes only about four hours, it seems to last forever.

Here, a semicolon (or period) would be correct, but a poor solution because the two clauses obviously are closely related. The desired contrast would best be emphasized either by using an appropriate coordinating conjunction along with the comma:

> *revised*: The flight from Vancouver to Toronto takes about four hours, but it seems to last forever.

or by using a subordinating conjunction to change one of the clauses to a subordinate clause:

> *revised*: Although the flight from Vancouver to Toronto takes only about four hours, it seems to last forever.

Another example:

> *cs*: Contemporary poetry is, if nothing else, plentiful, it pours daily from a number of small presses.

A2

Here, since the second clause illustrates the idea expressed in the first, a coordinating conjunction would not be the most appropriate connector. Using *for* would work, but it would be better to emphasize the syntactic integrity of the second clause by simply changing the comma to a semicolon. Even a colon would work well (see #43c and #44h). The following is an instance where a colon would be the preferred mark to replace the comma:

> *cs:* Slavery took hold in the American South in part for economic reasons, large numbers of workers were needed to maintain white-owned plantations.

Comma splices, then, can be corrected by replacing the comma with an appropriate punctuation mark—usually a semicolon, sometimes a colon, or even a period if you decide to turn the clauses into two separate sentences—or by showing the relation between the two clauses with a precise coordinating or subordinating conjunction. One last solution is to reduce one of the clauses to a modifying phrase:

> *cs:* The poem gives us several clues to the speaker's attitude toward love, one of these is the imagery.

> *revised:* The poem gives us several clues to the speaker's attitude toward love, one of these being the imagery.

See #44e and g; for exceptions, see #44f. See also **comb** (*combine sentences*), **coord** (*coordination*), *fc* (*faulty coordination*), **sub** (*subordination*), and exercises 21 (3–4) and 22a–c (2).

d
Faulty Diction

Mistakes in diction are often marked with one or another specific symbol, such as **ww** (*wrong word*), **nsw** (*no such word*), **inf** (*informal or colloquial*), or **id** (*faulty idiom*). But sometimes a reader will simply use *d*, implying either that the error does not fall into one of the particular categories or that the writer is expected to find out just what the specific error is. In either event, the first thing the writer should do is consult a dictionary; *d* could be said to stand for *dictionary*.

> *d:* If we regard the poem in this way, the recurring images of the "unwatered," aimless, barren mind of modern man would be one of the musical themes, and the imagery of water <u>plus</u> its symbolism of replenishment would be another.

A2

In this otherwise well-crafted sentence, the word *plus* creates a stylistic disturbance. *Plus* is normally a mathematical term; it is not a conjunction, nor appropriate to this context. In an expository context the meaning of *plus* is usually conveyed by the conjunction *and*; the preposition *with* would also serve the meaning here.

Diction can also be poor by being weak or imprecise. In the following sentence, for example, the word *done* is inadequate for the job it is being asked to do:

> ***d*:**   The program should be <u>done</u> in such a way that learning can take place in the field as well as in the classroom.

A word like *designed, planned,* or *organized* would be better.

See chapter VII. See also **inf** (*informal, colloquial*), **conc** (*concreteness*), **id** (*faulty idiom*), **jarg** (*jargon*), **nsw** (*no such word*), and **ww** (*wrong word*).

dev   ## Development Needed

This mark indicates that an idea, a point, or a subject needs to be developed further, expanded upon. The weakness occurs most often in the form of an inadequately developed paragraph. Revise by supplying details, examples, or illustrations, by defining or explaining, or by some other method appropriate to the particular instance.

See #2d, #2g.2, #9b, and #66.

dm   ## Dangling Modifier

> ***dm*:**   Floating down the aisle to the strains of "Here Comes the Bride," the groom smiled nervously at his best man.

Correct a dangling modifier by changing it so that it no longer dangles:

> ***corrected*:**   As the bridal party floated down the aisle to the strains of "Here Comes the Bride," the groom smiled nervously at his best man.

> ***corrected*:**   Floating down the aisle to the strains of "Here Comes the Bride," the bridal party approached the groom, who was smiling nervously at his best man.

See #36.

doc **Documentation**
Use the correct forms for your notes (whether parenthetical, at the foot of the page, or collected at the end) and your works-cited list or bibliography. In chapter VIII you will find model notes and bibliographical entries.

See #80. See also ***ack*** (*acknowledgement of sources*) and #79.

emph **Emphasis Weak or Unclear**
Make a marked sentence or paragraph emphatic by rearranging or by otherwise clarifying the relationships among its parts.

> ***emph***: The older generation of our society, like the younger, is also continually confronted with both beneficial and harmful advertisements, which are effective on our society in some way or other.

This is a flabby sentence—and what strength it has is mostly dissipated by the final prepositional phrase; simply removing this phrase would sharpen the end of the sentence, which should be its most emphatic part. But further improvement can be gained by sorting out and rearranging its content and by cutting the repetition and deadwood:

> ***revised***: All of society—not just the young but the older generation as well—is bombarded by advertising, which can be beneficial as well as harmful.

This may not be the best possible version, but at least its emphasis is clear.

See #1c, #8, and #29; see also ***fc*** (*faulty coordination*) and #41.

euph **Euphemism**
Avoid unnecessary *euphemism* ("good sounding," though not necessarily good in fact). Often directness and precision are preferable to even well-intentioned delicacy and vagueness. Is someone lacking money to buy enough food really made to feel better by being described as "disadvantaged" rather than "poor"?

When you are tempted to use a euphemism to avoid an unpleasant reality (for example, describing a person as "inebriated" or "in a state of intoxication" rather than "drunk"), consider the possible benefits of being direct and succinct instead.

See #68.

A2

fc

Faulty Coordination

Faulty coordination occurs when unrelated clauses are presented as coordinate, or when related clauses are linked by punctuation or coordinating conjunctions that fail to indicate the relation correctly.

> *fc*: Lawren Harris was born in 1885, and he was an influential member of the Group of Seven.

The coordinating conjunction *and* is misleading: Harris's birth date and his role as an influential Canadian painter are not significantly related or equal in value. The significant comment is contained in the second clause; the opening clause contains a minor fact that should be subordinated to the main statement:

revised: Lawren Harris, who was born in 1885, was an influential member of the Group of Seven.

revised: Lawren Harris (1885–1970) was an influential member of the Group of Seven.

Here is another example in which the second of two clauses is more important; the first clause should be subordinated or even changed to a participial phrase:

> *fc*: We are working together to write an evaluation of websites focusing on contemporary poetry, and we are spending hours searching the Internet.

revised: Since we are working together to write an evaluation of websites focusing on contemporary poetry, we are spending hours searching the Internet.

revised: In working together to write an evaluation of websites focusing on contemporary poetry, we are spending hours searching the Internet.

See #41; see also **comb** (*combine sentences*), **coord** (*coordination*), and **sub** (*subordination*).

fig

Inappropriate or Confusing Figurative Language

This mark is used to signify that some wording needs to be revised to change or remove figurative language (similes, metaphors) that is inappropriate or mixed.

fig: The decline of the provincial economy is skyrocketing; tax reform is the path we need to follow to break through this wall of stagnation.

The image of a rocket hurtling through the sky clashes with the image of a decline or fall; the image of the path is inconsistent with both skyrocketing and decline, and it clashes with the image of the wall, which itself clashes with the idea of stagnation. The sentence can be recast using the single metaphor *remedy*:

revised: The provincial economy is declining rapidly; the remedy for this problem is tax reform.

Or, two or more metaphors (*propping, sagging*) can be used as long as they are complementary:

revised: Tax reform should help to prop up the sagging provincial economy.

Here is another example:

fig: Like a bolt from the blue the idea grabbed him, and it soon grew into one of his most prized pieces of mental furniture.

One of the troubles with clichés that are dead metaphors is that we can fail to visualize them; when used unthinkingly they can make writing absurd. The *bolt from the blue*, even if allowed, could scarcely *grab* anyone, nor could it grow (like a plant?) into a piece of furniture. The urge to be metaphorical here backfired on the writer.

See #65 and #71e.

fp, // Faulty Parallelism

Revise by making coordinated elements grammatically parallel.

fp: For me England brings back memories of pleasant walks in Cornwall on some windblown lea, looking out to sea dressed in warm woollen jerseys, and feeling a warmth brought about by being with my family in that place.

The three objects of the preposition *of* here are all nouns, but *looking* and *feeling*, unlike *walks*, are gerunds. Repeating *of* before each gerund would help, but it is better to make the three grammatically parallel (and the phrase "dressed in warm woollen jerseys" seems more appropriate to the windblown lea than to looking out to sea):

revised: For me England brings back pleasant memories of walking on some windblown lea in Cornwall dressed in warm woollen jerseys, looking out to sea, and feeling a warmth brought about by being with my family in that place.

There is also the kind of awkwardness that occurs when a parallel structure breaks down—or isn't sufficiently built up:

fp: During my trip I had the chance to learn some of the language and to help with the shopping and cooking—all of which helped make the experience enjoyable.

The sentence structure implies that we're going to be given more than two things—and the phrase "all of which" makes it sound as though we have been. Perhaps the writer subconsciously thought of "shopping" and "cooking" as separate items; but the parallelism is in the verbs *learn* and *help*. That is, the implied parallel series after *to* is not fulfilled.

revised: During my visit I had the chance to learn some of the language and to help with the shopping and the cooking; these activities helped make the experience enjoyable.

Alternatively, a third element could be supplied, or *cooking* could be governed by a third verb, such as *participate in*.

See #40.

frag
Unacceptable Fragment

A2

Word groups that are punctuated as sentences but don't fulfill the requirements of sentences are usually unacceptable. Apart from passages of dialogue, any word group that cannot stand by itself and communicate effectively is problematic.

frag: Vancouver was the site of the 2010 Winter Olympics. The city being the second one in Canada to be awarded the Winter Games.

The second part here has no verb (*being* is a participle), nor is it an acceptable minor sentence. It should be set off with a comma as part of the preceding sentence.

> *frag*: The convention was held at the Chelsea Hotel. Because it has a large banquet room which would accommodate us all.

The second part is a subordinate clause dependent on the predicate of the preceding sentence; as such it should be set off with a comma.

See #12a–b and #32.

fs   **Fused Sentence**
See *run-on*.

gen   **Inadequately Supported Generalization**
See #66b and *conc* (*insufficient concreteness*).

id   **Faulty Idiom, Unidiomatic Usage**
Idiom refers to the structures and forms of expression particular to a given language. Idioms are not necessarily logical or explicable in grammatical terms. In English, errors in idiom most often occur with prepositions, as in the following examples:

> *id*: The extent of television's influence toward our view of global issues is incalculable. (*on*)

> *id*: Our university has a reputation of innovative undergraduate programs. (*for*)

See #70; see also *art* (*articles*) and #19c.

inc   **Incomplete Comparison**
See *comp*.

inf   **Inappropriate Informal or Colloquial Diction**
Replace the inappropriate word or words with something more formal.

> *inf*: This is the goofiest plot I've read in some time. (*most improbable, most unlikely*)

See #64b.

ital   ### Italics Needed or Incorrect

Correct by italicizing or by removing unwanted italics. (In handwritten material, italics are represented by underlining.)

> *ital*:   A Night to Remember is a film about the sinking of the Titanic.

> *corrected*:   A Night to Remember is a film about the Titanic.

See #60; see also #59.

jarg   ### Jargon

Revise to avoid unnecessary jargon.

> *jarg*:   The research team utilized every methodological approach it could conceptualize to produce bottom-line outcomes.

> *revised*:   The research team used every method it could to produce results.

See #71h.

lc   ### Lower Case

Change incorrect capital letter(s) to lower case.

> *lc*:   Although there are many sparkling wines, authentic Champagne is produced in France. (*champagne*)

> *lc*:   My grandmother was one of the first women in her community to get a University education. (*university*)

See #58.

leg   ### Legibility, Illegible

You are most likely to find this mark on an in-class paper or examination when your handwriting or revisions are difficult or impossible to decipher. If you are doing a revision, redo the illegible passages in consideration of your readers. Keep in mind that word-processed documents can be illegible if prepared too hastily. Don't, for instance, use whiteout and pen or pencil to correct typographical errors. Instead, make the correction in the document and print a clean copy of the page you have revised.

lev ## Inappropriate Level of Diction
See #64.

log ## Logic: Illogical as Phrased; Logicality of Reasoning Questioned
Illogic underlies many different problems in writing and thinking. Nevertheless, *log* is frequently the mark used to indicate an error of logic arising out of the way something has been phrased. For example:

> *log*: Insecurity is a characteristic basic to Davies's nature, and it becomes a consistent weakness of his throughout the play.

If insecurity is a basic characteristic, it can't *become* consistent in the course of the play; and it can't *become* consistent *throughout* the play, since *throughout* logically contradicts the meaning of *become*. Here is another example:

> *log*: In giving a precise definition of what this mental science is, Asimov is very vague.

The illogicality is evident. At least three meanings are possible:

> *clear*: Asimov fails to provide a precise definition of this mental science.

> *clear*: Asimov's definition of this mental science is very vague.

> *clear*: Asimov deals only vaguely with this mental science and makes no attempt to define it.

See also #41, #42, *al* (*alignment*) and #38, and #3e–h.

mix ## Mixed Construction
This mark indicates a shift from one syntactical pattern to another within a single sentence:

> *mix*: The war was justified as a strike against terrorism was viewed skeptically by most Canadians.

In order to revise an error such as this, you must decide on one pattern or the other:

> *revised*: The war, which was justified as a strike against terrorism, was viewed skeptically by most Canadians.

A2

> ***revised:*** The war, <u>which was viewed skeptically by most Canadians</u>, was justified as a strike against terrorism.

See #37.

mm   ## Misplaced Modifier

Revise a misplaced modifier by moving the modifying word or phrase to the logical place in the sentence.

> ***mm:*** Sauron wished to be Dark Lord of Middle-earth, and he <u>almost</u> had enough power to succeed <u>twice</u>.

> ***revised:*** Sauron wished to be Dark Lord of Middle-earth, and <u>twice</u> he had <u>almost</u> enough power to succeed.

See #35; see also ***wo*** (*word order*).

ms   ## Improper Manuscript Form or Conventions

Conscientious writers are careful to follow certain conventions pertaining to the form and presentation of a manuscript. These include such things as indenting paragraphs clearly, double-spacing lines, leaving adequate margins, paginating correctly, and being consistent with punctuation marks.

See chapter VI.

nsw   ## No Such Word

Don't make up words (unless perhaps for humorous purposes or other special effects). If you can't think of a particular word you want, try consulting a thesaurus. And if you use a word that looks or sounds unusual, that doesn't quite ring true, consult a good dictionary to see if it's there. A little extra care will enable you to avoid using such concoctions as these:

ableness (use *ability*)

afraidness (use *fear*)

artistism (use *artistry*)

condensated (use *condensed*)

cowardism, cowardness (use *cowardice*)

deteriorized (use *deteriorated*)

disgustion (use *disgust*)

enrichen (use *enrich*)

fruitition (use *fruition*)

infidelous (use *unfaithful*)

irregardless (use *regardless, irrespective*)

nonchalantness (use *nonchalance*)

prejudism (use *prejudice*)

prophesize (use *prophesy*)

skepticalism (use *skepticism*)

superfluosity (use *superfluity, superfluousness*)

num ## Incorrect Use of Numerals
See #61 for the conventions governing the use of numerals.

org ## Organization Weak or Faulty
Repetition, choppiness, lack of proportion or emphasis, haphazard order—all these and more can be signs of ineffective organization. It may be necessary to rethink your outline.

See #2g–i, #3d, and #7a.

p ## Error in Punctuation
Punctuation marks are symbols that should be just as meaningful to readers as are the symbols of speech (words) with which they are associated in writing. In speech, "punctuation" takes the form of inflections of voice, pauses, and changes in pitch or intensity. In order to communicate clearly and effectively on paper, one must be as careful with punctuation as one is with words and syntax. When you find the letter *p* in the margin, refer to chapter V to find out not only *what* is wrong or weak, but also *why* it is so.

para, ¶ ## Paragraphing
See #5–10.

pas ## Weak Passive Voice
This mark means that the sentence in question would be more effective with a verb in the active voice than with one in the passive voice—some form of *be* followed by a past participle, making the subject of a clause the receiver of the action: *Jo brought the ice* is active; *The ice was brought by Jo* is passive.

> *pas:* This issue is being spotlighted by the leader of the opposition.

> *active:* The leader of the opposition is spotlighting this issue.

A2

pas: In this article, the styles of tennis stars Venus and Serena Williams <u>are compared</u> by the sports editor.

active: In this article, the sports editor <u>compares</u> the styles of tennis stars Venus and Serena Williams.

See #17p. See also #29f.

passim   **Error Throughout**

This mark, which is Latin for *throughout*, is used to indicate that an error, such as the misspelling of a name, needs to be corrected throughout an essay.

pred   **Faulty Predication**

See *al* (*alignment*) and #38.

pron   **Error in Use of Pronoun**

This abbreviation usually marks such errors and weaknesses as the use of an intensive pronoun as a casual substitute for a personal pronoun, or the overuse of vague demonstrative pronouns, or perhaps *which* to refer to a person.

See also *agr* (*agreement*), *ca* (*the case of the pronoun is wrong*), *ref* (*weak or faulty pronoun reference*), *shift* (*shift in perspective*), and #14–16.

pv   **Point of View Inconsistent**

See *shift* (*shift in perspective*).

Q   **Error in Handling Quoted Material or Quotation Marks**

Sometimes this correction symbol will refer to nothing more than the omission of quotation marks (usually at the end of a quotation). But it could also refer to incorrect punctuation with quoted material, ineffectively introduced quoted material, and so on. If the error marked is not an obvious one, you may have to consult the section on quotation, #54, to find out what is wrong. See also #78, on handling quotations in research writing.

red   **Redundancy**

Redundancy can mean simply wordiness, but it is often used to refer specifically to unnecessary repetition of the meaning of one word in another word. In the sentence "But he was not unfriendly though," *But* and *though* do the same job; one of them should go (omit *though*, since it is informal and also weakens the end of the sentence: see **although, though** in #72, and #29c).

A2

Here are two more examples:

> *red*: Throughout the entire story the tone is one of unrelieved gloom.

Since *throughout* means "all through, from beginning to end," the word *entire* merely repeats what has already been said.

> *revised*: Throughout the story the tone is one of unrelieved gloom.

But this is still redundant, for if the tone is *unrelieved*, it must be constant throughout the story. Hence further tightening is possible:

> *re-revised*: The story's tone is one of unrelieved gloom.

Again:

> *red*: Puck's playful pranks include tricks on housewives and village maids.

Here the writer's choice of the word *pranks* is accurate and effective, but since *pranks* are *frolicsome tricks*, the addition of the adjective *playful* is redundant and decreases the effectiveness. One might even want to get rid of the word *tricks*:

> *revised*: Puck plays pranks on housewives and village maids.

See #71c; see also *w* (*wordiness*).

ref
Weak or Faulty Pronoun Reference

Pronouns need to refer to their antecedents in a clear way. The following sentence, for example, is muddled because it isn't clear whom the pronouns refer to:

> *ref*: Because of all the attention Seymour and Buddy gave to Franny and Zooey when they were young children, they never allowed them to develop their own ideas of life.

One can, by careful reading, extract the sense of this sentence, but it is the writer's job to make the meaning clear, not the reader's to puzzle it out.

A2

revised: When Franny and Zooey were young, Seymour and
Buddy gave <u>them</u> so much attention that the children
were never able to develop <u>their</u> own ideas of life.

The revised sentence contains two clear pronouns instead of four
confusing ones (and the redundant *young children* has been broken
up as well). Here is another example:

ref: Merlin's power, quite naturally, is partially a result
of his Sight and what are thought to be his magical
powers. An example of <u>this</u> is given during the battle
between King Ambrosius and the Saxons.

Clearly one must also be careful with demonstrative pronouns:
here the reference of *this* is obscure. Probably in the writer's
mind *this* somehow referred to the entire idea expressed in the
first sentence. In other words, *this* has no precise antecedent, and
the reference is therefore loose at best. A clearer and more precise
version (clearing up the problem with parallelism and the passive
voice as well) is possible:

revised: Merlin's power derives from a combination of his
Sight and his reputed magic. The battle between King
Ambrosius and the Saxons provides an illustration of
this fact.

Changing the demonstrative pronoun to a demonstrative adjective usually makes things clearer. But the passage is still wordy.
Try again, combining the sentences:

revised: As the battle between King Ambrosius and the
Saxons illustrates, Merlin's power derives from a
combination of his Sight and his reputed magic.

See #16; see also #15.

A2

rep   ## Weak, Awkward, or Unnecessary Repetition
This mark indicates another kind of wordiness that requires
pruning. Although repetition is often useful for achieving emphasis and coherence, unnecessary repetition slows the
writer's momentum and bogs the reader down.

rep: The snow was falling heavily, but I didn't mind the
snow, for I have always enjoyed the things one can do
in the snow.

The repetition of *snow* at the end is all right, but the middle one must go; replace *the snow* with *it*, or—better yet—with nothing at all.

See #71b.

run-on ## Run-on or Fused Sentence

Failure to put any punctuation between two independent clauses not joined by a coordinating conjunction results in a run–on sentence. Since a run-on is often merely a slip caused by writing too fast and not proofreading, it should be relatively easy to prevent with strategies for close editing.

> ***run–on***: Vancouver is the most beautifully situated city in Canada it also has some serious drug problems in a number of its neighbourhoods.

Like the comma splice, a run-on can be corrected by inserting a semicolon, by inserting a comma and a coordinating conjunction, by subordinating one of the clauses and inserting a comma, or even by inserting a period.

See #34 and #44i; see also *cs* (*comma splice*).

shift, pv ## Shift in Perspective; Point of View Inconsistent or Unclear

Revise a passage marked ***shift*** or ***pv*** to remove the awkward or illogical shift in tense, mood, or voice of verbs, or person or number of pronouns.

> ***shift***: On winter hikes in the back country, one should never forget your snowshoes. (*one's*)

> ***shift***: It was four in the afternoon, beginning to get dark, and we are still only halfway down the mountain. (*were*)

See #39.

Perspective can also seem to shift because of a lack of parallelism:

> ***shift, fp***: Ralph said that it was raining and he preferred to stay home.

If "he preferred to stay home" is part of what Ralph said, then a second *that* is required after *and*; otherwise, "he preferred" could be taken as parallel to "Ralph said." That is, without the second *that*, "he preferred" would be from the writer's point of view rather than Ralph's.

See #40a.

sp ## Spelling

If you misspell a word, don't simply try to guess how it should be corrected, for you may get it wrong again. The spell-check feature of your word-processing software can help, but don't rely on it alone. Check the word in your dictionary, and take the opportunity to find out all the dictionary can tell you about the word—not only for the sake of learning something, but also because studying the word will help fix it and its correct spelling in your mind. Then check chapter VI to see if your error fits any of the categories discussed there; if it does, study the principles involved. And keep a list of the words you misspell so that you can review them as often as necessary to become thoroughly familiar with their correct spellings.

split ## Unnecessary Split Infinitive
See #21c.

squint ## Squinting Modifier

A squinting modifier is one that is ambiguous because it seems to look both ways, so that a reader can't be sure which of two elements it is supposed to modify. This kind of problem can usually be solved fairly simply by moving the modifier closer to the element you want it to apply to.

See #35b.

ss ## Sentence Structure or Sentence Sense

Sometimes an instructor will put *ss* (or just *s*) in the margin opposite a sentence to indicate that something is wrong with its sense or its structure, leaving it to the writer to discover what the problem is. It may, for example, be a grammatical error, or a faulty arrangement, or a lack of clarity. Or the sentence may be faulty in some way not covered by any of the more specific categories. If this mark appears often, you may need to review chapters II, III, and IV.

stet ## Let It Stand

This mark indicates that you were right the first time, that when you changed something, such as a punctuation mark or the spelling of a word, you should have left it the way it was. To correct, therefore, merely restore it to its original form. (Note that an instructor will be able to advise you this way only if you cancel a handwritten word or phrase with a single neat line through it; if you blot it out entirely, you may never find out that your first choice was correct.)

sub   ## Subordination Needed; Combine Sentences

> *sub*: Suzuki has also done a superb job in his use of examples. His examples are clear and precise.

> *revised*: Suzuki has also done a superb job in his use of examples, which are clear and precise.

As two sentences (or even as one sentence consisting of two independent clauses) this example is wordy. Even the revised version could be tightened:

> *revised*: Suzuki has also done a superb job of providing clear and precise examples.

Or even:

> *revised*: Suzuki's use of clear and precise examples is superb.

See also **coord** (*coordination*), **comb** (*combine sentences*), **fc** (*faulty coordination*) and #41, **coh** (*coherence*), #11n–p, #23c, and #29i.

t   ## Error in Tense

> *t*: I often think back to the day, five years ago, when I bought my first horse. To many people this wouldn't be very exciting, but I have wanted a horse for as long as I can remember.

Change the present perfect *have wanted* to the past perfect *had wanted*, and the present *can* to the past *could*.

See #17g–k.

title   ## Manuscript Conventions for Titles
See #59.

tr   ## Transition Weak or Lacking
This mark will appear where the transition between two sentences or two paragraphs is weak or non-existent. Revise by

providing some kind of transitional word or phrase, by improving upon an existing one, or by otherwise improving the transition at the place indicated.

See **coh** (*coherence*), #1b, and #7, especially #7a.1 and #7b.4.

trite,   ## Trite, Worn-out, Hackneyed Expression
cliché   As the following example illustrates, some clichés will simply be wordy and therefore wholly or partly expendable; others will have to be replaced with something fresher; and often the sentence will require other rewording as well:

> *trite*: It <u>goes without saying</u> that <u>over the years</u> <u>many and diverse</u> opinions have been held regarding the origin of the universe.

> *revised*: Ever since people began thinking about it, astronomers and others have held many different opinions about the origin of the universe.

Here the passive voice *have been held* also contributed to the sluggishness of the original sentence.

See #71e.

u   ## Unity of Sentence, Paragraph, or Essay Is Weak
See #1a, #6, and #41.

uc   ## Upper Case
Change to upper-case (capital) letter(s). See **cap** (*capitalization needed or faulty*) and #58.

us   ## Usage
A subcategory of diction, this refers specifically to the kinds of problems discussed in the usage checklist, #72.

var   ## Variety
Try to improve the variety of lengths, kinds, and patterns of your sentences (see #28) or your paragraphs (see #9c).

vb   ## Verb Form
This abbreviation will mark an error in the form of a verb, for example an incorrect inflection or an incorrect principal part of an irregular verb.

See #17b–g.

w   ## Wordiness

If you find this mark in the margins of your essays, you may have to take drastic measures. Try thinking of words as costing money, say a loonie apiece; perhaps that will make it easier to avoid a spendthrift style. Mere economy, of course, is not a virtue; don't sacrifice something necessary or useful just to reduce the number of words. But don't use several words where one will not only do the same job but do it better, and don't use words that do no real work at all. Here are some examples of squandered words:

> *w*:   In today's society, Canada has earned itself a name of respect with many in the world.

> *revised*:   Canada has earned widespread respect. ($11 saved)

> *w*:   His words have a romantic quality to them.

The phrase *to them* does no work. In fact, its effect is negative because it undermines the emphatic crispness of the meaningful part of the sentence. Cut it and save $2.

> *w*:   Hardy regarded poetry as his serious work; he wrote novels only in order to make enough money to live on.

> *revised*:   Hardy regarded poetry as his serious work; he wrote novels only to make a living. ($5 saved)

> *w*:   Othello's trust in Iago becomes evident during the first encounter that the reader observes between the two characters.

> *revised*:   Othello's trust in Iago becomes evident during their first encounter. ($8 saved)

> *w*:   The flash of lightning is representative of the god's power.

> *revised*:   The flash of lightning represents the god's power. ($2 saved)

See #71, especially #71a; see also *red* (*redundancy*) and #71c, and *rep* (*repetition*) and #71b.

A2

wo   ## Word Order

A misplaced modifier is one kind of faulty word order, but there are other kinds not so easily classified.

> *wo*:   She was naturally hurt by his indifference.

> *revised*:   Naturally she was hurt by his indifference.

The potential ambiguity could also have been removed by putting commas around *naturally*, but that would slow the sentence down (though it would also emphasize the word).

> *wo*: I will never forget the day July 17, 2009, when I began my first job.

> *revised*: I will never forget July 17, 2009, the day I began my first job.

> *wo*: The image created in the advertisement is what really makes us buy the product and not the product itself.

> *revised*: The image created in the advertisement, not the product itself, is what makes us buy it.

This is not the only possible revision, of course, but it is the simplest, and the sentence is now clearer and less awkward.

> *wo*: Only at the end was clearly revealed the broad scope of the poem and the intensity of the emotions involved.

There seems no reason for the distortion of normal sentence order.

> *revised*: Only at the end were the poem's broad scope and intensity of emotion revealed.

See **mm** (*misplaced modifier*) and #35, #11s–t, #19d–e, #20d, and #22b.

PROOFREADING TIP

Word Order in Comparisons Using *Similar To, Superior To,* or *Inferior To*

In a stated comparison using *similar to, superior to,* or *inferior to,* a noun modified by the adjective should precede, not follow, the comparative word (*similar, superior, inferior*):

> *wo*: The film has a similar plot to that of Shakespeare's *The Tempest*.

> *revised*: The film has a plot similar to that of Shakespeare's *The Tempest*.

ww   ## Wrong Word

This category of diction error covers those mistakes that result from confusion about meaning or usage. For example:

ww: Britain is a nation who has brought the past and the present together.

The pronoun *who* refers to persons, not things; usage demands *that* or *which* in this context (see #14d, and the proofreading tips at the end of #48a).

ww: He came to the meeting at the special bequest of the chairperson.

A glance at the dictionary confirms that *bequest* cannot be the right word here; the writer probably confused it with *request* and *behest*.

See #69; see also #62f–g.

A2

3

Appendix

*Checklists for Use
in Revising, Editing,
and Proofreading*

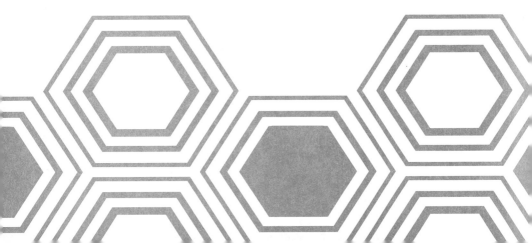

Omnibus Checklist for Planning and Revising

As you begin to prepare a piece of your writing for final submission to your reader(s), it is good strategy to ask yourself a series of questions designed to ensure that you have polished your work to the point where you can consider it a finished and appealing discourse. What we have listed here are the kinds of questions we ask ourselves in reading and evaluating students' writing. If you can ask and answer all of the questions we have listed here in the affirmative, your essay should be not just adequate, but very good.

1. **During and after planning the essay, ask yourself these questions:**

    Subject

    - ❏ Have I chosen a subject that sustains my interest? (#2a)
    - ❏ If I am doing research, have I formulated a researchable question? (#74)
    - ❏ Have I sufficiently *limited* my subject? (#2b)

    Audience and Purpose

    - ❏ Have I thought about audience and purpose? (#2c)
    - ❏ Have I written down a statement of purpose and a profile of my audience?

    Evidence

    - ❏ Have I collected or generated more than enough material/evidence to develop and support my topic well? (#2f)

    Organization and Plan

    - ❏ Does my *thesis* offer a focused, substantive, analytical claim about the subject (#2h)?
    - ❏ Is my *plan* or *outline* for the essay logical in its content and arrangement? (#2i)
    - ❏ Considering my plan or outline, do I have the right number of *main ideas*—neither too few nor too many—for the purpose of my essay?
    - ❏ Are my main ideas reasonably *parallel* in content and development?
    - ❏ Have I chosen the best *arrangement* for the main parts? Does it coincide with the arrangement of ideas in the thesis?

2. **During and after your revision of the essay, ask yourself these questions:**

    Title

    - ❏ Does the *title* of my essay clearly indicate the *subject* and *topic*?
    - ❏ Is the title original?
    - ❏ Does the title contain something to catch a reader's interest?

Structure

- ❏ Does my *beginning* engage a reader's curiosity or interest?
- ❏ Have I clearly stated my *subject* (and my *thesis*) somewhere near the beginning? (#2j.3)
- ❏ Have I kept the beginning reasonably short and to the point? (#2j.4)
- ❏ Does my *ending* bring the essay to a satisfying conclusion? (#1c, #4.9)
- ❏ Have I used the ending to do something other than re-hash ideas already well presented in the rest of the essay?
- ❏ Have I kept my ending short enough, without unnecessary repetition and summary?

Unity and Development

- ❏ Is my essay *unified*? Do all its parts contribute to the whole, and have I avoided digression? (#1a)
- ❏ Have I been sufficiently *particular* and *specific*, and not left any generalizations unsupported? (#66)

Emphasis

- ❏ Have I devoted an appropriate amount of space to each part? (#1c)

Paragraphs

- ❏ Does the *first sentence* of each paragraph (except perhaps the first and last) somehow mention the particular *subject* of the essay? (#1a, #7a.1)
- ❏ Do the early sentences of each body paragraph clearly state the topic, or part of the topic? Or, is the topic sentence, when it isn't among the first sentences, effective where it is placed? (#7a.1)
- ❏ Is each body paragraph long enough to develop its topic adequately? (#9b)
- ❏ Does each paragraph *end* adequately, but not too self-consciously? (#7a.3)

Coherence

- ❏ Do the sentences in each paragraph have sufficient coherence with each other? (#7)
- ❏ Does the beginning of each new paragraph provide a clear *transition* from the preceding paragraph? (#7a.1, #1b)
- ❏ Is the coherence between sentences and between paragraphs smooth? Have I removed all unnecessary or illogical transitional devices? (#7b)

Sentences

- ❏ Is each sentence (especially if it is compound, complex, or long) internally *coherent*? (#31)
- ❏ Is each sentence clear and sufficiently *emphatic* in making its point? (#29)

A3

❏ Have I used a variety of *kinds, lengths,* and *structures* of sentences? (#28)

❏ Have I avoided *the passive voice* except where it is clearly necessary or desirable? (#17p, #29f)

Diction (ch. VII)

❏ Have I used *words* whose meanings I am sure of or checked the *dictionary* for any whose meanings I am not sure of? (#63, #69)

❏ Is my diction sufficiently *concrete* and *specific?* (#66a)

❏ Have I avoided *unidiomatic* usages? (#70)

❏ Have I weeded out *unnecessary repetitions, ready-made phrases, clichés,* and other *wordiness*? (#71)

❏ Have I avoided unintentional *slang* and *informal diction,* as well as *overformal* diction? (#64)

❏ Have I avoided inappropriate or confusing *figurative language*? (#65)

❏ Have I avoided *gender-biased, sexist language*? (#15d, #72)

Grammar

❏ Are my sentences *grammatically* sound—that is, free of dangling modifiers, agreement errors, incorrect tenses, faulty verb forms, incorrect articles and prepositions, and the like? (chs. III and IV)

❏ Have I avoided *run-on sentences* and unacceptable *fragments* and *comma splices*? (#44i, #12b, #44e)

Punctuation (ch. V)

❏ Is the punctuation of each sentence *correct* and *effective*?

❏ Have I proofread sentences slowly with special attention to the punctuation?

Spelling (ch. VI)

❏ Have I checked all my words—reading backward if necessary—for possible spelling errors?

❏ Have I then used the spell-checker in my software package to check the essay?

Mechanics

❏ Have I carefully *proofread* my essay in hard copy and corrected all typographical errors? (#2n)

❏ Is my manuscript *neat* and *legible*? Does it conform to all *manuscript conventions* (esp. spacing, margins, font size, pagination, and headers)? (#56)

❏ Have I introduced and handled all *quotations* and *references* properly? (#54, #78)

❏ Have I checked all quotations for accuracy? (#78)

A3

Acknowledgement

☐ Have I acknowledged everything that requires acknowledgement according to the guidelines and rules of my university or college? (#78, #79)

☐ Have I double-checked my *documentation* for accuracy, consistency, and correct form? (#80)

The Last Step

☐ Have I *read my essay aloud*—preferably to a colleague—as a final check on how it sounds and made adjustments for *clarity* and *emphasis*?

See also the proofreading tip on checking for conciseness, which appears after #71h.

Specialized Checklist for Writers with English as an Additional Language

What follows is an additional checklist we hope will be of particular help to those of you who are bilingual or multilingual and working to achieve fluency in English as your second, third, or fourth language. The questions we have listed are meant to help you target your editing on those issues that are often problematic for a writer whose own first language differs significantly from English in its grammatical patterns. For example, English is a language with a complex set of tenses that inflect or change verbs to express actions and states of being. In contrast, other languages may express changes in time through adverbial expressions and not change or inflect verb forms at all.

When you take this targeted approach to checking a draft you have written, you need to re-read several times, checking each time for patterns with which you have had difficulty in previous writing. In each reading (ideally a slow check of a hard copy you read aloud), you should focus on one or two patterns in a sentence-by-sentence and paragraph-by-paragraph review. Your short-term objective is to polish the paper itself; your long-term objective is to become a self-sufficient proofreader who will not have to rely on others to edit your work.

Next to each of the questions that follow, you will find references to the sections of this book in which we have treated these various patterns. You will also see, in a number of cases, the abbreviation *OALD*, which stands for the *Oxford Advanced Learner's Dictionary*. This dictionary is an invaluable resource, and one we have used throughout our teaching careers in working with many students aiming to perfect their writing in their new language. The *OALD* can be of significant help to you in checking for verb forms, prepositional idioms, and accurate use of the indefinite articles *a* and *an*. You should take some time to read the introduction to the dictionary to learn how to use its specialized features.

Use the questions on this checklist and on the omnibus checklist preceding it *selectively*; that is, focus on the questions targeting problem areas you and your readers have identified in your recent writing. We hope that our cross-references here to particular sections of this book and to the *OALD* will help you to achieve mastery in your expression and confidence in your style.

Sentence Structure

❏ Have you checked your longer sentences for *mixed constructions*? (#37)

❏ Have you checked your sentences for *faulty predications*? (#38)

❏ Have you checked for *ineffective fragments*—especially at points where you are introducing examples and illustrations into your work? (#12b, #21e (proofreading tip), #32)

❏ Have you checked your compound sentences for *faulty coordination*? (#41)

❏ Have you checked your complex sentences for *excessive* or *faulty subordination*? (#27b, #55j)

❏ Have you checked your longer and balanced sentences for *faulty parallelism*? (#40)

❏ Have you checked your longer sentences for *comma splices* and *misused semicolons*? (#33, #44e, #55j)

Grammatical Patterns Within Sentences

❏ Have you checked nouns for *countability* and *uncountability*, and have you then checked as well for correct number form (singular or plural) for these nouns? (#13a and *OALD*)

❏ Have you checked that *singular countable nouns* in an indefinite context are preceded by an *indefinite article*? (#19c and *OALD*)

❏ Have you checked that *uncountable nouns* are in singular form and unaccompanied by *indefinite articles*? (#19c and *OALD*)

❏ Have you checked that nouns made specific by their context are modified by the *definite article*? (#19c)

❏ Have you checked that *verbs* appear in their correct *regular* or *irregular forms*? (#17b–f and *OALD*)

❏ Have you checked that you have used *gerund* and *infinitive verbals* correctly? (#21)

❏ Have you checked that *subjects* and *verbs* in your sentences *agree*? (#18)

❏ Have you checked that *noun antecedents* and *pronouns* referring to them *agree*? (#15)

❏ Have you checked that *verbs* used in *the passive voice* are *transitive*? (#17-o–p and *OALD*)

❏ Have you checked that the *tenses* of your verbs are correct? (#17g–h, #17k)

A3

❏ Have you checked for correct *sequence* of tenses in sentences where you have used more than one tense? (#17i)

❏ Have you checked that the *prepositions* you have used in combination with particular nouns or verbs are *idiomatic*? (*OALD*)

Diction

❏ Have you checked that the *level of your diction* fits your audience and purpose, and have you steered away from the kind of artificial diction created by overuse of a thesaurus? (#64)

❏ Have you checked that you are using words new to your vocabulary in their correct *parts of speech*? (ch. III and *OALD*)

Composing

❏ Have you checked that you have used *transitions* correctly and in moderation? (#7b.4)

❏ Have you checked that your paragraphs position their *core* or *topic sentences* effectively and strategically? (#7a.1)

Index

List of Exercises